BUSINESS RESEARCH

Text and Cases

BUSINESS RESEARCH

TEXT AND CASES

ERWIN ESSER NEMMERS

Professor of Business Administration

JOHN H. MYERS

Professor of Accounting

*Both of Graduate School of Business
Administration in the School of Business,
Northwestern University*

MCGRAW-HILL BOOK COMPANY
*New York   St. Louis   San Francisco
Toronto   London   Sydney*

BUSINESS RESEARCH *Text and Cases*

This book, designed for a first course in business and economics research, is a pioneering book. While a number of books adequately cover the theory of research methodology or the principles of scientific method (some are cited in Part 2), or deal with the use of advanced statistical techniques in research (some appear in the selected bibliography of Part 3), no book has been available which implements business research at the beginner's level. Somehow this has always been left either to the student on a sink-or-swim basis or to the graduate thesis director, who has the chore of wearily repeating the process with each succeeding student. In this process, a selected reading list is usually combined with individual discussion.

The authors believe that, as in the natural sciences, the study of business and economics ought to involve the use of data and the laboratory from the very beginning of study. The available books closest to our conception are *An Introduction to Scientific Research* by E. Bright Wilson, Jr., and *Research Methods in Economics and Business* by Robert Ferber and P. J. Verdoorn. Combined (some 948 pages) they would come closer to our idea than either does alone. But this combination lacks the consideration of business and economics data and their problems that forms Part 1 of this book. And though such information may be found in Oskar Morgenstern's revised edition of *On the Accuracy of Economic Observations* (322 pages), this would still leave us without the heart of this book, namely, the cases of published research carefully selected for their methodological values (Part 4).

Lastly, we have added in Part 5 a student effort presented in the chronological order in which the student proceeded. At this point we introduce the use of the computer. We have chosen multiple correlation as the specific use of the computer so that the widest possible variety of types of computer might be employed. Multiple correlation programs are readily available for all computers.

This book crystallizes the course in research that has since 1950 been part of the program for the degree of Master of Business Administration at Northwestern University. (The course might also be given in the senior year of the undergraduate programs in business and economics.)

v

This course was initiated by Professor Paul Morrison, now vice-president, General Finance Corporation. Shortly thereafter, Professor John H. Myers, presently chairman of the Accounting Department at Northwestern, took over and headed the course until 1957, when Professor Erwin E. Nemmers assumed responsibility.

The course on which this book is based can be paired with a second course in which the main thrust is the student's research on a much more independent basis.

The only specific assumption we have made regarding prior course work for those using this book is one elementary course in statistics.

Good illustrations for research purposes abound. We have selected illustrations on their merits and not by date of publication. These studies lend variety to the treatment of such areas as finance, marketing, transportation, industrial relations, and insurance. We are grateful to the copyright owners for permission to reproduce these studies, and we are indebted to the Literary Executor of Sir Ronald A. Fisher, F.R.S., Cambridge, to Dr. Frank Yates, F.R.S., Rothamsted, and to Messrs. Oliver & Boyd, Ltd., Edinburgh, for permission to reprint Table 4 from their book *Statistical Tables for Biological, Agricultural & Medical Research.*

For various assistance with the manuscript we express our thanks to Professors Robert Barr of Marquette University, Edwin Cox of Boston University, and Oscar R. Goodman of the University of Michigan.

We are grateful to the many faculty members of the School of Business at Northwestern University who have taught sections of the research course on which this book is based and whose experiences and judgment shaped the contents of this book. After fifteen years that list is a long one.

In particular, we express our thanks to Mr. Don Cooke and all former students at the Graduate School of Business Administration at Northwestern University for permission to use their work.

We are grateful for the typing assistance of Misses Lillian Mattsson-Boze, Donna Thompson, and Mary Ann Norton, and Mrs. Ann Crost.

All the text in this volume is the work of Professor Nemmers, while the cases and various readings were included by the decision of both authors.

Erwin Esser Nemmers
John H. Myers

CONTENTS

vii

Assignment Using United States Censuses, Alternate Assignment Using United States Censuses, Assignment Using Basic Statistical Sources Other Than United States Censuses, Alternate Assignment Using Basic Statistical Sources Other Than United States Censuses

2 RESEARCH AND SCIENTIFIC METHOD   87

Defects in the Crude Concept of Scientific Method

Scales and Measurements, Errors in Measurement, Lack of Experimental Design and Error, Lies and Error, The Observer and Error, Questionnaires and Error, Mass Observations and Error, Definition and Classification in Relation to Error, Instruments and Error, Time Factor and Error, Uniqueness and Error, Interdependence, Stability in Errors

Price Statistics

Mill's Five Canons, Controls, Experiment Design, Analysis of Variance, Replication and Interaction, Factorial Design, Randomizing, Analysis of Covariance, Sample Size

5 STUDENT RESEARCH PROJECT   481

BUSINESS RESEARCH

Text and Cases

DATA SOURCES AND PROBLEMS

INTRODUCTION

Research in the business and economic areas is governed by the same principles that apply to research in any of the natural sciences. Hence, it is true, the principles of scientific method, which will be examined in Part 2, are universal in their application. But before examining questions of methodology, we shall explore the matter of the raw materials for research, namely, the data.

Business and economic research relies heavily upon what we may call historical data, that is, data reporting events which have happened in the past, such as a time series reporting the quantities of a particular item sold in a particular period and in a particular market or area. At present as in the past, only a small part of business research involves the use of data generated from controlled experiments such as those resulting from the (at least partially) controlled[1] introduction of a new product in a particular area.

Hence, the materials of Part 1 are directed especially to exploring the sources of and the problems involved in dealing with historical data. The problems involved in dealing with data resulting from controlled experiments are more closely tied to research methodology and hence will be examined partially in Part 2.

Data Sources

The sources of historical data of interest in business research are developed, first, through a brief survey of the principal sources which immediately follows this Introduction and, second, through the assignments which appear at the end of Part 1.

Sources of business and economic data are easily classified in several ways. One classification separates government and nongovernment sources. Another recognizes the collection of data by topical areas such as financial data, labor data, or national-accounts data. As is inevitable, the data collected in the various sources duplicate and overlap each other. Although the brief summary of sources presented below serves

---

[1] *Although we use the term "controlled experiment" at this point, we must realize that the control exercisable in business experiments is more limited than that possible in the natural sciences.*

1

as a convenient beginning, there is no substitute for actual investigation of the sources themselves in order to develop a knowledge of what is available and where it is to be found. In general, we suggest that the neophyte in business and economic research is very likely to underestimate what is available. This underestimate occurs because the beginner does not exhaust all the possible sources. Too often when he fails to find the particular data in the particular source where (he thinks) they would be most appropriately reported, he is prepared to conclude that they have not yet been collected.

Data Problems

There is a tendency on the part of the beginning researcher to feel that if only he can find the right data, most of his difficulty will be at an end. Unfortunately, when the researcher has located the relevant data, his problems are only beginning.

The reprint of Chapters 2 and 3 from *Introduction to Economic Statistics* by Professors Crum, Patton, and Tebbutt has been included in Part 1 to furnish a discussion of economic variables and the problem of homogeneity together with the matter of primary and secondary sources. This work, which was published in 1938, is presented here more than a quarter of a century later to bring out the fact that the data problems that were acute in 1938 are still with us and that not much has been accomplished in reducing the seriousness of the problems. Indeed, it will require the expenditure of tremendous resources to make substantial progress in this area.[2]

The *Fortune* article by Prof. Oskar Morgenstern entitled "Qui Numerare Incipit Errare Incipit" (Whoever Begins Counting Starts Making Mistakes) goes into specific detail on the matter of the accuracy of economic data, a theme which Professor Morgenstern has developed more fully in the second (1963) edition of his book *On the Accuracy of Economic Observations*. Professor Morgenstern's devastating exposition of the imperfections and inaccuracies of published business and economic data has raised some controversy as to whether the picture he presents is proportioned and fair or whether it is distorted. For this reason, we follow his article with the communication by Raymond T. Bowman, Chief Statistician of the Bureau of the Budget, which appeared in the *American Statistician*. This communication examines the position of Professor Morgenstern in some detail and to some extent rehabilitates our confidence in existing data. In addition, Mr. Bowman has appended a valuable list of publications giving the current status of many economic series and critical evaluations of them.

[2] *This statement, which is supported by Professor Morgenstern in the references given in the next paragraph of the text, is in sharp contrast with the recent assertion by Prof. Paul H. Rigby in his* Conceptual Foundations of Business Research: *"There can be no argument with the professional manner with which traditional business research has collected facts. Great precision has been achieved to insure the accuracy of statistical surveys and computations"* (New York: John Wiley & Sons, Inc., 1965), p. 9.

The assignments at the end of Part 1 cover separately, first, the United States Census and, second, the other principal data sources. These assignments are intended to establish some familiarity with the sources of business and economic data and also to raise some questions about the data. We shall illustrate just one type of problem. In the first assignment involving sources other than the United States Census, item 8 calls for the amount of refined lead produced from domestic ores in 1957. The *Commodity Yearbook*, 1964, at page 195 shows the amount to be 347.7 thousand short tons for 1957. The source given by the *Commodity Yearbook* is the Bureau of Mines, a governmental agency. At page 198 of the same *Commodity Yearbook*, however, the amount is shown as 604.4 thousand short tons for 1957. At this point, the source is shown as the American Bureau of Metal Statistics, a private agency. The table on each of these pages of the *Commodity Yearbook* carries the identification of "refined lead produced from domestic ores." The reconciliation appears to be that the editors of the *Commodity Yearbook* took the figure of 604.4 from the wrong table in *Metal Statistics*, the yearbook of the America Bureau of Metal Statistics, namely, from the table on page 417 rather than from the tables on page 415 or page 422. The figure 604.4 covers "refined lead produced from all sources, including domestic and foreign ores and base bullion together with the output from some secondary material by primary refiners."[3] This error in the title of the table on page 198 of the *Commodity Yearbook* exists in many of the prior issues of that yearbook.

This short illustration demonstrates the need for care in using secondary sources and likewise the advisability, whenever possible, of cross-checking every figure in another reference before the figure is accepted. Just how and where such cross-checking should be done in any particular instances cannot be specified.

The principal sources of published business data are organized below as follows: (1) the United States censuses and related series,[4] (2) other Federal publications, (3) privately published sources, (4) business records, (5) selected indices to business references, (6) books on business sources, and (7) index of forecasts.

THE UNITED STATES CENSUSES AND RELATED SERIES

Census of Population; Current Population Reports

The Bureau of the Census in the Department of Commerce of the Federal government is the largest gatherer of statistical information in the

---

[3] *Private communication from N. J. Langer (ed.), Metal Statistics.*
[4] *Cf. Philip M. Hanser and William R. Leonard,* Government Statistics for Business Use, *2d ed. (New York: John Wiley & Sons, Inc., 1956). This work covers the procedure for locating a series and gives some guides for evaluating series. Also cf. Office of Statistical Standards, Bureau of the Budget,* A Federal Statistics Program for the 1960's, *A Study Prepared for the Subcommittee on Economic Statistics of the Joint Economic Committee, 87th Cong., 2d Sess., Oct. 15, 1962, particularly chap. IV, "Periodic Censuses."*

United States. Its most widely known publication is the *Census of Population*. The United States Constitution requires that the population of the country be determined every 10 years in order to apportion the representation of the states in the House of Representatives. The first such census was taken in 1790, and a census of population has been taken every 10 years since that date. Gradually, the *Census of Population* has been expanded beyond a mere count of people so that now data are collected on sex, age, marital status, education, racial characteristics, occupation, and many other demographic characteristics.

Although the *Census of Population* appears decennially, the interim period is handled on an annual basis in a series, *Current Population Reports*, issued by the Bureau. The current reports make effective use of the latest information on migration between states, birth and death rates, and similar determinants. Their accuracy is indicated by the errors of closure, which compare the last current report preceding the decennial census with the census itself. In addition, *Current Population Reports* includes projections of population that assume various birth rates.

Not all of the census is prepared by a complete count. The count of many characteristics is collected on a sample basis such as 20 per cent and then exploded to get an estimate of the total population. Not all of the possible classifications are published by the Bureau of the Census, but because the census information is on punched cards, researchers can have classifications run to their own specification upon paying the out-of-pocket costs of the machine runs.

Not many years after the first population census of the United States, the census law for 1810 required the collection of certain industrial statistics.

Census of Manufactures; Annual Survey of Manufactures; Current Industrial Facts; U.S. Industrial Outlook

In the years intervening between its activities with the decennial *Census of Population*, the Bureau of the Census performs many other census activities. One of these is the *Census of Manufactures*, which was taken most recently in 1963. This census was taken decennially from 1810 to 1900 except for 1830, quinquennially from 1900 to 1920, and then biennially from 1922 to 1940. After a lapse during World War II, the census has been taken quinquennially beginning with 1948.

The *Census of Manufactures* employs the Standard Industrial Classification code, which is discussed in a separate Bureau publication entitled *Standard Industrial Classification Manual*. This code does not coincide with the Standard International Trade Classification code. Its classes are changed from time to time to keep them abreast of the shifts in industrial organizations that occur as products appear and disappear. Basically, the first four digits of the code describe the industry, and the last three digits the product.

The *Census of Manufactures* includes such information as the specialization ratio (the percentage of the output of those firms classified as in an industry that is confined to one product area), the concentration ratio (the percentage of the total output of a product supplied by those firms whose principal activity is making that product), and the coverage ratio (the percentage of the total output of a product supplied by those firms classified as in the industry producing the bulk of that product). In addition, such data as sales and value added by an industry, plant location, and classification of producers by number of employees are gathered.

Supplementing the *Census of Manufactures* on an interim basis is the *Annual Survey of Manufactures,* which has been conducted annually since 1943 except for the census years 1954 and 1958. On a quarterly basis, data are published for some industries in a series entitled *Current Industrial Facts* (formerly *Facts for Industry*). Another supplement to the *Census of Manufactures* is the *U.S. Industrial Outlook,* which updates the latest census.

Census of Business

The *Census of Business* was taken in 1929, 1933, 1935, 1939, 1948, 1954, 1958, and 1963, and is authorized on a quinquennial basis. It covers the retail, wholesale, and service trades and gathers data such as number of establishments, employment and payroll, and receipts. Such data are classified in various ways. The *Census of Business* does not cover the professions such as medicine, law, and education. Neither does it cover insurance, real estate, and recreation.

Census of Housing

The *Census of Housing* was taken in 1940, 1950, and 1960 in conjunction with the *Census of Population* and covers structural characteristics, building condition, occupancy, facilities, and financial aspects classified by states, counties, standard metropolitan statistical areas, rural areas, and similar subdivisions. New housing starts on an interim basis were gathered by the Bureau of Labor Statistics for nonfarm units and by the Department of Agriculture for farm housing units, but this topic has now been transferred to the Bureau of the Census. Housing statistics are difficult to reconcile because of conversions, demolition, new starts, temporary units, trailers, and similar problems.[5]

Census of Construction

In 1929, 1935, and 1939, censuses of construction were taken as part of the *Census of Business.* In 1949, the Bureau of Labor Statistics made a survey of the residential-construction industry. Since then no such census has been made.

[5] *Cf. Charles Roos,* Dynamics of Economic Growth (*New York: Econometric Institute, 1957*), pp. 201ff.

Census of Agriculture; Agricultural Statistics; Commodity Yearbook

The *Census of Agriculture,* conducted by the Bureau of the Census, was taken decennially from 1840 to 1920 and quinquennially after 1920; it is now authorized quinquennially beginning with 1954. This census covers number of farms, types, acreage, land-use practices, facilities, employment, expenditures, value of products, and similar data. Various parts of the census are based on samples, and the sampling-error estimate is reported. In 1959, the census covered all farms of more than 1,000 acres with sales of at least $100,000 and sampled 20 per cent of all other farms. The sample was stratified by size of farm. The definition of "farm" has changed from one census to another. In 1959, places of less than 10 acres were counted as farms if they had sales of $250 in agricultural products for the year, whereas in 1950 and 1954, places of 3 acres with sales of $150 in agricultural products for the year were counted as farms.

This census is supplemented by the annual volumes *Agricultural Statistics* (prior to 1936 the *Yearbook of Agriculture* and ultimately extending back to 1867) and the *Commodity Yearbook,* published by the Department of Agriculture. These contain estimates, but the sampling error of 15 per cent will be reduced to 1.6 per cent through using trained enumerators rather than mailing questionnaires. In addition, the Department of Agriculture issues a number of bulletins, often including specific data not otherwise published. These bulletins are grouped into series such as Agricultural Estimates, Agricultural Economics Research, Agricultural Marketing Service, and Agricultural Research, which recently were reorganized to form the Economic Research Service and the Statistical Reporting Service. Estimates of world production for many commodities are made by the Office of Foreign Agricultural Relations.

Census of Mineral Industries; Minerals Yearbook

The *Census of Mineral Industries,* conducted by the Bureau of the Census, gathers information about the mineral industries in a manner parallel to the *Census of Manufactures.* This census was conducted in 1850, 1860, 1870, 1880, 1889, 1902, 1909, 1919, 1929, 1935, 1939, 1954, 1958 and 1963 but is now authorized on a quinquennial basis starting with 1963. On an interim basis, it is supplemented by the *Minerals Yearbook,* published by the Bureau of Mines of the Department of the Interior. This yearbook contains considerable information in addition to statistical tables. The data in the *Census of Mineral Industries* differ somewhat (by as much as 28 per cent for sand and gravel in 1954, for example) from the data in the *Minerals Yearbook* in common years. These differences arise from a number of causes. The census figures follow an industrial classification, whereas the Bureau of Mines data are classified by product. Any mining undertaken by industrial companies is not included in the census. The point at which measurements are taken and the cutoff point for the exclusion of small operations are different. The *Minerals Yearbook* also includes some data on foreign production and on United States imports and exports of minerals.

Census of Governments; Municipal Yearbook

The census publication gathers data on state and local governments such as employment, revenue, and debt. The *Municipal Yearbook,* published by International City Managers' Association in Chicago, gives current data on population, areas, and finance.

Census of Transportation

Legislation authorized a *Census of Transportation* to be made for the first time in 1963. This census has three segments: (1) a survey of the distribution of commodities by all classes of transportation, (2) a survey of passenger travel, and (3) a truck and bus inventory. It does not duplicate statistics collected by other Federal agencies or by any other source.

OTHER FEDERAL PUBLICATIONS

Statistical Abstract of the United States

This publication is prepared by the Bureau of the Census annually and reproduces more than 1,000 tables from sources published elsewhere. It covers economic, social, industrial, price-index, demographic, mineral, financial, and other data. In each instance, the original source is indicated so that the researcher can pursue the data further.

The *Cities Supplement* to the *Statistical Abstract* gives data for cities over 25,000 in population. This also appears under the title *County and City Data Book.*

Economic Almanac; Handbook of Economic Statistics

This volume, which is privately published by the National Industrial Conference Board, is included here for pairing with the *Statistical Abstract.* Although data from Federal agencies dominate the *Statistical Abstract,* many data from private sources, particularly trade associations, are included. There is considerable overlapping with data in the *Economic Almanac,* but the latter gives greater emphasis to data from private sources and complements the *Statistical Abstract.* A third book in this area is the *Handbook of Economic Statistics,* published by the Economic Statistics Bureau.

Historical Statistics of the United States from Colonial Times to 1957

This publication by the Bureau of the Census supplements the *Statistical Abstract.* Whereas the *Statistical Abstract* gives data of the most recent years annually and decennially or quinquennially for several decades, *Historical Statistics* runs some 3,000 series annually (or to the extent possible) back to the earliest year available. In addition, it revises series to adjust them for changes in definitions and classifications which have occurred through the years. In this way, data are made more comparable and consistent. Originally *Historical Statistics of the United States,*

1789–1945 was published as a smaller volume covering data to 1945, and then a *Continuation to 1952 of Historical Statistics of the United States, 1789–1945* brought the data to 1952.

Economic Report of the President

This publication is issued annually by the Council of Economic Advisers. Beginning with 1947 the President of the United States has issued an economic report to Congress early each year. The back part of the report contains statistical tables from data collected elsewhere.

Federal Reserve Bulletin; Banking and Monetary Statistics

The *Federal Reserve Bulletin* is issued monthly by the Board of Governors of the Federal Reserve System. In the statistical section of this publication appear detailed data on the American banking and monetary picture, the index of industrial production, the index of department store sales, rates of foreign exchange, and banking data for many foreign countries.

In 1943, the Board of Governors published *Banking and Monetary Statistics,* which systematizes financial data back to 1914 and, in some cases, further.

Survey of Current Business; Business Statistics

The *Survey of Current Business,* issued monthly by the Office of Business Economics in the Department of Commerce, contains the basic national-income accounts, studies, charts, and business statistics in great detail. Each issue gives monthly data of the preceding 12 months and annual data prior to that time. The June issue contains the *National Income Supplement* for each year. The *Survey* collects data not only from Federal agencies outside the Department of Commerce but from private sources. A weekly supplement contains some important series on a weekly basis. Biennially a supplement to the *Survey* is published under the title *Business Statistics;* beginning with 1947 it cumulates all series.

The *1954 National Income Supplement* to the *Survey* gives detailed explanation as to how national-income accounting is carried out. Revisions can be found in the *Survey: 1958 U.S. Income and Output* and *1965 National Income and Product Accounts Revised.*[6] The margin of error in national-income accounting has been estimated at ±20 per cent.[7]

---

[6] *The national-income data are evaluated in National Bureau of Economic Research,* A Critique of the United States Income and Product Accounts, vol. 22, Studies in Income and Wealth (*Princeton, N.J.: Princeton University Press, 1958*). *For the national income of other countries, see Paul Studenski,* The Income of Nations, Theory, Measurement and Analysis: Past and Present (*New York: New York University Press, 1958*).

[7] *Oskar Morgenstern,* On the Accuracy of Economic Observations, 2d ed. (*Princeton, N.J.: Princeton University Press, 1963*), *pp. 254–257.*

The *Survey* also includes the quarterly and annual surveys of planned business investment, prepared jointly by the Department of Commerce and the Securities and Exchange Commission. Additional business investment surveys by McGraw-Hill appear in *Business Week*, and by the National Industrial Conference Board in *Newsweek*.

Monthly Labor Review; Monthly Report on Labor Force; Handbook of Labor Statistics; Manpower Report of the President

These publications of the Bureau of Labor Statistics in the Department of Labor contain studies as well as statistics on employment, labor turnover, earnings and hours, consumer and wholesale prices, and work stoppages. The *Monthly Report on Labor Force*, which was begun in 1959, comes from four sources: the Bureau of the Census, the Bureau of Labor Statistics, the Bureau of Employment Statistics, and the Department of Agriculture. It contains employment and unemployment figures based on a geographically stratified random sample of 35,000 households in 330 areas plus 20,000 farm establishments. Government unemployment figures go back to 1940. Prior to that date, from 1929 to 1940, nine different series were kept by private sources; of these five are complete as to years.[8]

In 1963, the first annual *Manpower Report of the President* appeared. As the title indicates, it covers statistics of various aspects of the labor force.

Economic Indicators; Business Cycle Developments

Economic Indicators is published monthly for the Joint Economic Committee by the Council of Economic Advisers. This publication prepares tables and charts from other sources as to national-income accounts; it does not include indicators of current business activity as the term "indicators" is understood today.

Business Cycle Developments is a monthly publication of the Bureau of the Census, begun in October, 1961, and covering some 70 economic indicators with their many components and the sources from which these are drawn.

Construction Review

This publication of the Business and Defense Services Administration of the Department of Commerce gives statistics on housing starts, con-

[8] *These series are available in W. S. Woytinsky and Associates, Employment and Wages in the United States (New York: The Twentieth Century Fund, 1953), p. 716. For the period prior to 1929 there are three series from 1900 in S. Lebergott, "Annual Estimates of Unemployment in the United States, 1900–1954," in National Bureau of Economic Research, The Measurement and Behavior of Unemployment (Princeton, N.J.: Princeton University Press, 1957), p. 218.*

tracts awarded and construction put in place, prices, costs, building permits, and employment. Some of this information comes from the F. W. Dodge Corporation, a private organization.

Quarterly Summary of Foreign Commerce; FT (Foreign Trade) Reports

The *Quarterly Summary*, which was published by the Department of Commerce, reported quarterly data on imports and exports on a cumulative basis. It was discontinued with the January–June, 1961, issue. The *FT (Foreign Trade) Reports* are published monthly and cumulated annually, using different classifications from those of the former *Quarterly Summary*.[9] FT110 (now merged with FT120 in FT125) covers imports and FT420 exports. The FT series uses the Standard International Trade Classification system.

Statistics of Income

This annual publication of the Internal Revenue Service of the United States Treasury Department is prepared from Federal income tax returns of corporations and individuals.

PRIVATELY PUBLISHED SOURCES

Directory of National Trade Associations; Fact Books

The *Directory* is published by the Department of Commerce and lists more than 2,000 trade associations in the United States. Many of these associations publish annual fact books under varying titles. These annual handbooks usually include government data from many sources of interest to the industry concerned and sometimes present data gathered by the association itself as a primary source. Outstanding fact books are issued by the American Iron and Steel Institute, the Edison Electric Institute, the American Gas Association, the Association of American Railroads, the National Timber Manufacturers Association, the United States Savings and Loan League, the Institute of Life Insurance, the National Canners' Association, the National Frozen Food Association, and the Air Transport Association.

Sometimes a fact book is issued commercially by a publisher other than the trade association. Examples of this practice are the *Insurance Year Book* and *Brown's Directory of American Gas Companies*.

[9] *A good discussion of foreign-trade statistics appears in R. G. D. Allen and J. E. Ely,* International Trade *Statistics (New York: John Wiley & Sons, Inc., 1953). On balance-of-payments statistics, see* The Balance of Payments Statistics of the United States; Report of the Subcommittee on Economic Statistics, *89th Cong., 1st Sess., July 26, 1965;* The Balance of Payments Statistics, Hearing before the Subcommittee on Economic Statistics, *89th Cong., 1st Sess., part I, May 11, 1965; part II, June 8, 1965; part III, June 9, 1965.*

Moody's Manuals

These manuals—*Industrials, Municipals and Governments, Transportation, Public Utilities,* and *Banks and Finance*—show financial data of individual companies and of governmental bodies, including stock and bond issues publicly held. Balance sheets, income statements, dividend and interest records, and market prices are included. Similar manuals are published by Standard and Poor.

Monthly Economic Letter of the First National City Bank of New York

The April issue each year contains a table "Net Income of Leading Corporations" for the most recent two years. This table covers the 3,800 largest publicly owned corporations in the United States and shows by industrial groups their sales, reported net income after taxes, book net assets, and percentage earned on sales and book net assets. It has been issued each year since 1920 and is the source most promptly available after the end of each year. The number and composition of companies change each year but are the same for each two-year comparison.

Standard and Poor's Trade and Securities Statistics

This publication collates data from many sources and particularly stock market statistics which are of interest to investors. While *Moody's Manuals* gather data about individual security issues and issuers, this publication gathers nonduplicating data such as statistics on an industry basis.

United Nations Statistical Yearbook

The *Statistical Yearbook* contains statistics on a wide range of domestic activities in many foreign countries, including population, agriculture, forestry, mining, manufacturing, energy, consumption, transportation, communications, exports, balance of payments, wages, national income, finance and public financing, housing, and education. The reliability of data gathered in foreign countries is lower than that of those gathered in the United States. Additional breakdowns are available in separate volumes.

The Fortune Directory: The 500 Largest U.S. Industrial Corporations, the 50 Largest Banks, Merchandising, Transportation, Life-insurance and Utility Companies, and the 200 Largest Foreign Industrial Companies

This directory, which was begun in 1954, is issued in August of each year. It ranks companies by sales but also gives assets, profits, invested capital, employees, and percentage returns on sales and invested capital. A companion volume, *Fortune Plant and Product Directory,* gives all plants of the 1,000 largest United States manufacturing companies, products produced, and number of employees. These plants cover 70 per cent of the United States production.

United Nations Yearbook of International Trade Statistics

This annual contains import and export data for most foreign countries classified by the Standard International Trade Classification code.[10] In addition, the data are arranged by regions.

Sales Management

This magazine prepares an annual estimate of buying power for each county and many cities of the United States.

BUSINESS RECORDS

Annual Reports

Annual reports are published by all corporations whose securities are publicly held. These reports vary considerably as to the data they contain, but many publish much information beyond what is summarized in such financial sources as *Moody's Manuals*.

Prospectuses

At the time of public offering of the securities of a corporation, a formal prospectus is required for all issues exceeding $300,000. This prospectus is reviewed by the Securities and Exchange Commission before issuance by the underwriters. Frequently, it contains information not otherwise available. This is particularly true of breakdowns of product lines in diversified companies. All prospectuses are available at three offices of the Securities and Exchange Commission, in Washington, D.C., New York, and Chicago; and the local offices of brokers have copies of many of the prospectuses of the last year or two.

SELECTED INDICES TO BUSINESS REFERENCES

Monthly Catalog of U.S. Government Publications

This publication lists all the publications of Federal departments and agencies.

---

[10] Standard International Trade Classifications, Revised, *United Nations Statistical Papers, ser. M, no. 38, New York, 1963.*

Business Periodical Index

This publication by the H. W. Wilson Company lists all articles appearing in certain important business periodicals.

Index of Economic Journals, 1886–1959

This publication[11] lists all articles appearing in 89 economic journals.

Wall Street Journal Index

This publication by Dow Jones and Co., the publishers of the *Wall Street Journal,* indexes stories in the *Journal,* beginning with 1957.

New York Times Index

This publication indexes stories in the *New York Times,* including the material in the extensive financial section of that newspaper.

Other Indices

In addition, there are many specialized indices such as the *Accountant's Index* (irregularly), *Agricultural Index* (from 1916), *Engineering Index* (from 1884), *Index of Publications of Bureaus of Business and Economic Research, Industrial Arts Index* (from 1913), *International Index to Periodicals, Public Affairs Information Service* (from 1915), and *Reader's Guide to Periodical Literature* (from 1920).

BOOKS ON BUSINESS SOURCES

R. D. G. Allen and J. E. Ely: *International Trade Statistics* (New York: John Wiley & Sons, Inc., 1953).

Arthur H. Cole: *Measures of Business Change* (Homewood, Ill.: Richard D. Irwin, Inc., 1952).

Edwin T. Coman, Jr., *Sources of Business Information* (Englewood Cliffs, N.J.: Prentice-Hall, Inc., 1949); (Berkeley, Calif.: University of California Press, 1964).

Philip M. Hanser and William R. Leonard: *Government Statistics for Business Use,* 2d ed. (New York: John Wiley & Sons, Inc., 1956).

H. Webster Johnson and Stuart W. McFarland: *How To Use the Business Library with Sources of Business Information,* 3d ed. (Cincinnati: South-Western Publishing Company, 1964).

Marian C. Manley: *Business Information: How to Find and Use It* (New York: Harper & Row, Publishers, Incorporated, 1955).

Richard M. Snyder: *Measuring Business Changes* (New York: John Wiley & Sons, Inc., 1955).

[11] (*Homewood, Ill.: Richard D. Irwin, Inc., 1961–1962*), 5 *vols.*

What's the Answer? A Brief Guide to Sources of Business Statistics (Washington, D.C.: Chamber of Commerce of the United States of America, Committee on Business Statistics, 1953).

INDEX OF FORECASTS

Predicasts

This publication by Economic Index and Surveys, Inc., Cleveland, Ohio, began in 1960 and appears quarterly. *Predicasts* shows industry forecasts by four- and five-digit numbers of the Standard Industrial Classification code and forecasts of other economic series. Forecasts go as far forward as 1980. These forecasts are drawn from a wide variety of sources, and all sources are stated. The same publisher now issues *Worldcasts*, a parallel index for foreign-trade forecasts.

VARIABLES AND
HOMOGENEITY*

ECONOMIC VARIABLES

Statistical science, as applied in economics or any other field of inquiry, is almost without exception concerned with comparisons. As already noted, in certain rare and exceptionally simple instances the only numerical fact required as evidence may be a single isolated statistical item. But such instances are so unusual that they may be ignored in making the general assertion that statistical analysis treats of bodies of statistical data and their comparison and summarization. Statistical series, rather than isolated statistical items, form the factual basis of statistical analysis. Comparison of the items of a series, or of several series, is a central objective of statistical study.

In even the simplest study in economic statistics, therefore, we are concerned with an economic magnitude capable of taking on several different sizes—the various sizes being reflected in the various items of some appropriate statistical series. Such a magnitude, capable of taking on different sizes, is called a *variable;* and each of the several particular sizes is called a *variate.*

Variation in Time and Otherwise

The term *variable* unfortunately tends to convey to our minds the notion of change over time—we unconsciously infer that the different sizes which the variable is capable of taking on occur at different times. It is true, of course, that some variation does occur over time. In such a case, the several variates are recorded in a statistical *time series.* But we must get rid of the notion that the words *variable* and *variation* necessarily imply change from time to time. They also refer to mere *differences* at a given time—differences between place and place, differences among persons, differences among objects, or differences among any other entities properly defined or described. Variation of this sort, from which the time element is absent, is represented in its simplest form by a *categorical series.*

The *frequency series* is a special case of representation of statistical variation from which the time element is ordinarily absent. The peculiar feature of the frequency series is that the variate appears in the rule of classification—generally the stubs of the table—rather than in the nu-

* This and the following reading reprinted from Introduction to Economic Statistics, by William L. Crum, Alson C. Patton, and Arthur R. Tebbutt, pp. 18–49. Copyright © 1938. McGraw-Hill Book Company. Used by permission.

merical item itself. In the time series or the categorical series, on the contrary, the variate is the numerical item itself. In the frequency series, the numerical item states merely the number of times—frequency—of occurrence of a variate of particular size (or within a specified size interval). Thus, in Table 1, the first item—2,104—is a variate, a particular size of the variable; and likewise in Table 2, the first item—195—is a

Table 1. Exports of heavy iron and steel products from the United States in 1935*

Scrap	2,104.0
Tin plate, terne plate, etc.	134.5
Ingots, blooms, billets, sheet bars, and skelp	104.2
Black steel sheets	100.5
Galvanized sheets	75.0
Iron and steel bars	53.5
Steel rails	51.7
All other products	440.3
Total	3,063.7

* Unit: thousand long tons (of 2,240 lb.). Source: "Statistical Abstract of the United States, 1936," Washington, U.S. Department of Commerce, 1936, p. 706. (Classes with under 50 thousand tons have been combined.)

Table 2. Treasury deposits with federal reserve banks at end of each month in 1937*

January 31	195	July 31	233
February 27	194	August 31	139
March 31	311	September 30	141
April 30	88	October 30	114
May 31	73	November 30	121
June 30	93	December 31	142

* Unit: million dollars. Source: *Federal Reserve Bulletin*, March, 1938, p. 198.

variate; but in Table 3, the first item—2—merely states that there are two variates between 2.00 and 2.49. To repeat: in a *time* or *categorical series*, the *variable is represented by the numerical items* themselves; in a *frequency series*, the *variable is represented by the rule of classification*—the succession of size classes.

As already indicated, the time element is ordinarily absent from a frequency series. The variable—represented by the size classes—customarily refers to differences among persons, objects, or other observed cases, at one particular time. Occasionally, however, frequency series are studied for which the variable—represented by the size classes—refers to changes over time.

For example, if we had a record of monthly steel ingot output, analogous to that of Table 4 but extending over the 144 months from 1926 to 1937 inclusive, we could classify those 144 variates according to size

Table 3. *Number of United States Class 1 railroads employing stated depreciated percentage rates upon freight-train cars in 1936*°

Rate (%)	Number of roads	Rate (%)	Number of roads
2.00–2.49	2	5.00–5.49	2
2.50–2.99	18	5.50–5.99	2
3.00–3.49	41	6.00–6.49	1
3.50–3.99	42	6.50–6.99	4
4.00–4.49	14	7.00–7.99	
4.50–4.99	5	8.00–8.99	1

* Source: "Statistics of Railways in the United States, 1936," Washington, Interstate Commerce Commission, 1937, p. S–80.

Table 4. *Steel ingot production in the United States, monthly, 1937*°

January	4,725	July	4,556
February	4,414	August	4,876
March	5,216	September	4,298
April	5,070	October	3,393
May	5,150	November	2,154
June	4,184	December	1,472

* Unit: thousand long tons. Source: *Survey of Current Business*, February, 1938, p. 48.

and thus obtain a frequency series. Table 5 shows the *time series* for the 144 months, with each variate recorded as a separate statistical item; and Table 6 shows the corresponding frequency series, with the number of instances (months) in which variates occur within particular size intervals recorded in the corresponding statistical item.

And here appears an important fact about a frequency series: *the identity of a particular variate is lost in the frequency series.* This is true whether the frequency series classifies a variable representing changes in time (as in Table 6) or mere differences without any time element

Table 5. Steel ingot production in the United States, monthly totals*

	Jan.	Feb.	Mar.	Apr.	May	June	July
1926	4,132	3,785	4,469	4,106	3,928	3,734	3,635
1927	3,823	3,845	4,575	4,163	4,083	3,526	3,232
1928	4,028	4,081	4,549	4,345	4,246	3,778	3,841
1929	4,500	4,329	5,068	4,950	5,286	4,903	4,851
1930	3,778	4,035	4,254	4,109	3,983	3,419	2,922
1931	2,512	2,547	3,054	2,767	2,552	2,128	1,888
1932	1,485	1,481	1,433	1,260	1,125	913	807
1933	1,017	1,073	898	1,345	1,976	2,564	3,168
1934	1,997	2,212	2,798	2,936	3,399	3,059	1,489
1935	2,870	2,774	2,865	2,641	2,634	2,259	2,268
1936	3,046	2,964	3,343	3,942	4,046	3,985	3,923
1937	4,725	4,414	5,216	5,070	5,150	4,184	4,556

* Unit: thousand gross tons. Source: for 1926–1935, Standard Statistics Company's *Basic Statistics*, Sec. G, June 5, 1936, p. G9; for 1936, *Survey of Current Business*, February, 1937, p. 48; for 1937, *ibid.*, February, 1938, p. 48.

Table 6. Frequency distribution of the 144 months, 1926–1937, according to size of steel ingot output*

Lower limit of size class[a]	Number of months
500	6
1,000	16
1,500	11
2,000	9
2,500	20
3,000	18
3,500	19
4,000	26
4,500	14
5,000	5
Total	144

* Compiled from Table 5.
[a] Unit: thousand tons.

Aug.	Sept.	Oct.	Nov.	Dec.
3,987	3,913	4,074	3,706	3,467
3,529	3,298	3,345	3,155	3,203
4,217	4,186	4,693	4,306	4,055
4,939	4,528	4,534	3,521	2,903
3,061	2,840	2,693	2,212	2,080
1,717	1,545	1,591	1,592	1,301
847	992	1,087	1,032	861
2,864	2,283	2,085	1,521	1,799
1,381	1,269	1,482	1,611	1,964
2,916	2,825	3,143	3,150	3,073
4,195	4,161	4,545	4,337	4,432
4,876	4,298	3,393	2,154	1,472

(as in Tables 3 and 7). *In a time series or categorical series,* on the other hand, *the identity of each variate is preserved*—it is recorded in a separate statistical item. Thus in Table 5 the variate for October, 1930, is definitely stated as 2,693 thousand tons; whereas in Table 6 this variate is buried among the twenty cases falling in the interval between 2,500 and 3,000 thousand tons. Of course, for those classes in a frequency series—there is no such class in Table 6—for which the frequency is 1, the particular variate remains alone and is not mingled with others; but even here we should not know from the frequency table the date of that variate—its identity is lost.

The frequency series, then, in placing its entire emphasis upon size, cuts loose from the descriptive classification in terms of time or category. As already stated, most frequency series, unlike that of Table 6, are based upon variables which reflect not changes over time but rather differences at some particular time. The theory of frequency series, as we shall see, is developed in terms of this commoner type of frequency series, that in which the variates reflect mere differences at a given time; and certain special adaptations of the theory are needed for the less common type of frequency series, that in which the variates reflect changes over time.

Complexity of Variables

The variables which are encountered in economic statistics are, in the great majority of practical problems, not simple and elementary but more

Table 7. *Number of consolidated corporation tax returns in United States in 1933 having stated
numbers of subsidiaries**

Number of subsidiaries	Number of returns	Number of subsidiaries	Number of returns
1	3,638	11	53
2	1,199	12	51
3	608	13	36
4	360	14	39
5	260	15	28
6	154	16	26
7	128	17	26
8	93	18	20
9	80	19	12
10	50	20 or more	218

* Source: "Statistics of Income, 1933," Washington, U.S.
Treasury, 1935, p. 35. (Twenty-two returns, with number
of subsidiaries not reported, are excluded. Classes above
19 have been combined.)

or less complicated composites. By industrious search we can, of course,
find some instances of simple or elementary variables; but the very difficulty of finding such instances emphasizes their rarity, and most
instances which at first glance appear to be of this sort are found upon
examination to have in fact a composite nature.

For example, a categorical list showing the number of bushels of
wheat, of a specified grade, sold on specified terms of sale in each separate transaction at the Chicago Board of Trade during a specified trading
day appears to be a series having an elementary rather than a composite
nature. Likewise, a time series recording the number of tons of anthracite, of a specified size and quality, raised at a single shaft of a single
mine on each working day for some specified period of time appears
to be elementary. Also, a frequency series showing the number of cattle,
of specified quality, according to classified weights, delivered to a railroad shipping point by a specified cattle raiser in a single specified shipment reflects an elementary variable.

But these cases, which were discovered only by considerable effort,
pertain to situations which are so narrowly defined and so specialized
that they are of little use for studying any significant economic problems.
They do in fact assist in numerically describing particular elements in
the economic system. Only a moderate relaxation of the narrow specialization of the above cases is needed to yield variables which are not
elementary. Thus, the number of bushels of wheat, of the specified grade,
sold on the specified terms of sale at the Chicago Board of Trade during
the stated day by each of several traders—assuming that he does or

may participate in several transactions—is not an elementary variable. For each trader, the total sales is a composite of his sales in separate transactions, which may be in various amounts, at various prices, and to various purchasers. Likewise, the daily tonnage output of anthracite by a company which operates several mines, or even several shafts at a single mine, is a composite variable. And the frequency series of weights of cattle shipped by a group of producers does not have the elementary character of the series for the single producer.

Economic science is concerned mainly with the study of situations and conditions which are not narrowly particular and specialized. Economics is chiefly concerned with simple and complex commodities in the mass, with commodities which are complex because of fabrication and services which are compounded of numerous functions, with processes which often involve numerous and intricate operations, with factors of production and agencies of consumption which are made up of more or less distinguishable parts, with complicated institutions and systems which carry on the work of production and distribution, and with the ramifying interrelations of all these elements. In the nature of economic problems, therefore, lies the reason for the inevitably composite character of most economic variables. Although the student may, by diligent search, find a moderate number of simple or elementary economic variables, and although careful study of the more common composite variables often requires an attempted expression in terms of elementary variables, the great bulk of the variables actually encountered and studied in economic problems must be regarded as composite. The following paragraphs describe briefly some types of composite economic variables.

Aggregates

Many economic variables are mere aggregates—each is the sum or total of elementary economic variables of the same nature. Thus, steel ingot production (Table 5) is an aggregate of the production by various steel companies in their various plants and in the various furnaces of the several plants. Moreover, the monthly figure may be regarded as the total of daily figures, or even—if we wished to push the time recording that far—of hourly figures. Perhaps we should agree that the elementary variables, many of which when combined yield the composite variable reported in Table 5, are the outputs each day of each particular steel furnace. Several of the other variables illustrated in the foregoing tables are aggregates—in Table 8 each increase in loans is an aggregate of constituents for different banks in the group of banks specified by the stub and of different specific loans for each bank; each export item of Table 1 is an aggregate of numerous specific shipments; and each item of Table 2 is an aggregate of the specific Treasury deposits at the several reserve banks.

Instances of variables which are aggregates are very numerous and appear in cases in which the economic concept involved seems at first

*Table 8. Increase in commercial, industrial, and
agricultural loans at member banks of the
Federal Reserve System during 1937°*

Central reserve city banks in New York	285
Other reserve city banks (including Chicago)	400
Country banks	265
Total, all member banks	950

* Unit: million dollars. Source: *Federal Reserve Bulletin*,
March, 1938, p. 184.

glance fairly simple. Thus, the cost of production—whether of a simple
commodity like a bushel of corn or an elaborate commodity like a loco-
motive—is an aggregate of more or less numerous specific costs (subject
to the adequacy of accounting techniques) for materials of various sorts,
for the use of land, for the use of equipment of various sorts, and for
various sorts of labor and superintendence. Likewise, the value of a particular piece of real estate is a sum of various constituents—value of
the land in one or more parcels, value of the building stated perhaps
in terms of the specific values of various parts or features of the building.
The weekly pay roll of a cotton-spinning factory is an aggregate of the
wages paid to workers in each particular occupation and, more fundamentally, of the wages paid to each individual worker. The consumption
expenditures of a specified family in a specified week are an aggregate
of amounts spent for numerous items of food, clothing, fuel, shelter,
amusement, and other types of consumption. The freight tonnage moved
by a particular railroad in a particular month is an aggregate of various
specific commodities, of different sizes and weights, hauled different distances, paying different rates, and involving different costs of transportation. The list can be extended indefinitely with ease, but enough cases
have been cited to show how common the aggregate is as a type of
composite economic variable.

Rates and Ratios

Another important type of economic variable appears as a rate, or ratio.
This is obviously a composite in that the given variable is the quotient
of two other variables, the numerator and the denominator. For example,
the *operating ratio* of a railroad is the quotient of its operating expenses,
in a given interval such as a specified month, divided by the operating
revenues. Here variation in the ratio—for example, from month to
month—is manifestly the composite, or resultant, of variations in both
numerator (expenses) and denominator (revenues). Likewise, the *rate
of turnover* of inventory in a retail store in a specified year is the quotient
of the sales during the year by the value of the stock of goods (expressed
as an average, because the stock varies during the year) held for sale

during the year. Here variation in the rate—for example, from store to store—is the composite, or resultant, of variations in both numerator (sales) and denominator (value of stocks).

The same is true of a long list of economic variables which, though they may not include in their titles the word *ratio* or *rate*, are in fact mere quotients. Thus, important examples include: (1) *reserve ratio* of a bank, (2) *traffic density* of a railroad, (3) *net worth ratio* of a corporation, (4) *velocity of circulation* of money, (5) *rate of turnover* of labor, (6) *yield* of a bond, (7) *markup* of retail merchandise, (8) *yield per acre* of a crop, (9) *factor of safety* of a bond, (10) *current ratio* of a business firm, (11) *earnings ratio* of a corporation, (12) *productivity* of labor, (13) *unit cost* of output of a commodity, (14) *load factor* of a power plant, and (15) *turnover rate* of receivables.[1]

Certain economic variables are in fact rates, or ratios, though we do not customarily think of them as quotients of a numerator by a denominator. Thus, *price* is strictly a ratio: the quotient of the money paid divided by the amount of the commodity received. Likewise, the *rate of interest* is the quotient of the amount of the interest divided by the amount of the principal. A *wage rate* is the ratio of the amount of wages to the time worked. An *exchange rate* is the ratio of the amount of one currency to that of another for which it is exchanged. A *depreciation rate* is the quotient of the loss of value—usually estimated in physical terms, with respect to "useful life"—of a machine (or other capital instrument) during a year divided by its value at the beginning of the year, or more generally at the beginning of its use. A *freight rate* is the ratio of the charge for transportation between two points to the volume, or weight, hauled. A *tariff rate*, of the ad valorem sort, is the ratio of the duty paid to the value of the imported article. A *tax rate* is the amount of tax levied, divided by the tax base—usually the value, but sometimes the quantity, of the thing taxed. A *commission rate* is the ratio of the charge for selling to the value sold. This is part of a long list of economic variables which are in fact ratios but which are customarily treated as if they were elementary—rather than composite—variables. Such treatment is the consequence partly of legal arrangements which express business and economic relations in terms of these ratio concepts, and partly of mere custom in the conduct of economic affairs.

For these rates, as for the more obvious type of rates (like types 1 to 15 above), the variation of the ratio is a composite, or resultant, of possible variations in both numerator and denominator. In this second class—which includes rates such as price, wage rate, tax rate—we find it less easy to think of numerator and denominator varying independently of each other, than for the first class—which includes such rates as reserve ratio or velocity of circulation or earnings ratio. In the second class, we are in the habit of thinking of the rate as *given*, and the "numerator"

[1] *The definitions of some of these concepts are obvious, but the concepts are defined and explained in textbooks dealing with banking, railway operations, corporation finance, etc.*

thus appears merely as the "denominator" multiplied by the rate. But a moment's thought will show that, if the rate is not fixed, both numerator and denominator can vary separately.

In studying ratios of all sorts, in fact, we have to consider that both numerator and denominator can vary, though recognizing that the degree of independence of the variations of the two elements differs from case to case. In a case where the rate is legally fixed, as for a tax rate of a particular kind at a particular time, dependence of numerator upon denominator is practically complete. Near the other extreme is the case of the *current ratio*—the ratio of current assets of a firm to current liabilities—for which a variation in the numerator is to a very important degree, though not wholly, independent of a variation in the denominator.

A special class of rates arises in connection with all sorts of per capita figures. In all such cases, some aggregate (numerator) is divided by the corresponding number of people (denominator). Examples are: per capita income, per capita expenditures on amusements, per capita output of soap.

The per capita rates suggest an important general point. A per capita figure is obviously an average: per capita income is the average income per person. In general, for any rate or ratio, the average idea is implied: thus, *acre yield* of corn on a farm is the average number of bushels per acre. The theoretical importance of this point is very great. . . . The significance of a statistical average depends largely upon its typicalness; and the same is accordingly true also of a rate or ratio. The full implications of this assertion cannot, however, be brought out until we have explored the theoretical foundations of averages.

Variables as Products

Just as an economic variable may be a ratio of a variable numerator to a variable denominator, a type of composite variable exists which implies multiplication of two or more elementary variables. For example, the variable representing performance of railroad transportation is the number of *ton-miles*—obtained in multiplying the weight hauled by the distance covered. A variable measuring performance of equipment in a factory is the number of *machine-hours*—obtained in multiplying the number of machines in operation by the time operated. A similar measure for labor performance is stated in *man-hours*.

Similarly, other composite variables may result from combining pairs of groups of variables by other more or less elaborate arithmetical formulas. The arithmetical operation of dividing merely happens to be the most common and that of multiplying the next most common. And, of course, several arithmetical operations may be used in making one composite variable. For example, traffic density (defined as ton-miles per mile of road) is a ratio in which the numerator also involves a multiplication. Also, rate of turnover of inventory (defined as the quotient of the sales during the year divided by the value of the stock of goods expressed as an average) is a ratio in which the denominator may be the result of the statistical process of averaging.

Derived Statistical Variables

Another important type of composite economic variable takes the form of a calculated statistical number. Examples are: all sorts of statistical averages, measures of variability, index numbers, correlation coefficients. These concepts are too intricate to admit of brief explanation at this point, and will be discussed in latter chapters. They are mentioned here, however, to emphasize the important fact that even an elaborately calculated statistical summary figure, derived from economic data, becomes at once an economic variable, capable of changes from time to time or of differences between places or cases. And always in the study of such an economic variable, as for any composite variable, we must bear in mind that its variation is the resultant of variations in its constituents.

HOMOGENEITY

We have seen above that many economic variables are composites, and an obvious implication of this complexity of a particular variable is that the study of such a variable—of statistics pertaining to that variable—must be in the light of the capacity of its constituents to vary, and of such constituent variations to be more or less independent of each other.

The statistician seeks not only to *describe* a variable by the use of statistics but also—though often less successfully—to *explain* the variation. Ultimately, such explanation aims at discovering causes or possible causes of variation, but this phase of explanation so clearly involves theoretical considerations that the work of the statistician generally stops short of assigning causes. What he generally does, rather, is to explain—perhaps only partially and tentatively—the variations of one variable in terms of those of other variables. Clearly, for those cases in which a given variable is a composite of other variables this kind of explanation first aims at relating statistics of the changes or differences in the given variable to those of its constituent variables. This method is one of *analysis,* in its literal sense: the breaking up of a whole into its parts in the expectation that knowledge of the parts will afford knowledge of the whole. The complexity of the typical economic variable thus suggests a useful approach for studying statistics reflecting economic variation.

But this complexity has another practical implication: it increases the danger that a statistical series, reflecting an economic variable, will not be homogeneous. The term *homogeneity,* as pertaining to an economic series, does not readily admit of definition; and an understanding of the term will perhaps best be secured by studying the circumstances or conditions which impair or destroy homogeneity. The difficulty of definition is enhanced, as will be observed in the following paragraphs, by the fact that the same statistical series may be tolerably homogeneous for one purpose and very far from homogeneous for another. In particular, the homogeneity here under examination has not the specialized connotations of that term as used in the theory of sampling.

A tentative definition can be stated in this form: A statistical series is strictly homogeneous, for a given purpose of study, if its various items accurately record the variations—over the interval of time or range of cases studied—of a single variable having a rigid and unchanging definition. This suggests that impairment of homogeneity may result from the facts that: (1) the statistics are not accurate, (2) they do not pertain to a single variable, (3) the variable does not have a rigid and unchanging definition. As indicated above, the homogeneity concept will be clarified by studying ways in which homogeneity may be impaired. In the cases cited below, frequent mention will be made of the extent to which the purpose for which statistics are used affects the question of homogeneity.

Changes in Definition over Time

The definition of a variable, represented by a statistical time series, sometimes changes with passing time. Such changes are not always—perhaps not often—evident in the statistical record as presented in a table; and an initial task of the statistician is to test by every available means the homogeneity of his time series, from this point of view of the definition of the variable.

As a first example, consider the series in Table 9. It is a mistake to suppose, merely because the statistical item is described by a fixed phrase in the title of the table, that the variable had an unchanging definition over these fourteen years. By consulting the source we find a long list of notes (pages 112–119) concerning comparability of the figures from individual income tax returns. Some of these notes pertain to the definition of net income; among the most important of these are changes in the law and regulations as to treatment of capital gains and capital losses and as to the carrying forward of a net loss incurred in one year to later years. By examining these notes, the statistician at once learns that the variable reflected in Table 9 is not rigidly defined and that the series is therefore not homogeneous.

Similarly, a series recording the number of individual income tax returns filed would be discovered to be lacking in homogeneity. Reference to the same source cited for Table 9 would show that various changes in the law, chiefly with reference to the minimum income for which a return must be filed, destroy all semblance of rigidity in definition of the variable "number of returns."

As another example, consider the annual average price of lead at New York in cents per pound during the period 1930–1937. Recalling that, until early in 1933, the currency of the United States had for many years been redeemable in gold at a fixed ratio, that during part of 1933 and early 1934 the relation between the currency dollar and gold was subjected to official manipulation, and that the Gold Standard Act of early 1934 and subsequent official proclamations "fixed" a new relation but not redeemability between currency and gold, we observe that the series for price of lead cannot be regarded as homogeneous. "Price" of lead—or of any other commodity having a price stated in dollars—is not rigidly

Table 9. Aggregate net income
reported on individual
income tax returns in
the United States*

1921	19,577	1928	25,226
1922	21,336	1929	24,801
1923	24,777	1930	18,119
1924	25,656	1931	13,605
1925	21,895	1932	11,656
1926	21,959	1933	11,009
1927	22,545	1934	12,797

* Unit: million dollars. Source: "Statistics of Income, 1934, Part 1," Washington, U.S. Treasury, 1936, p. 22.

Table 10. Average number of
employees of the United
States Steel Corpora-
tion and subsidiaries,
annually*

1919	252	1928	222
1920	267	1929	225
1921	192	1930	211
1922	215	1931	204
1923	261	1932	158
1924	247	1933	173
1925	250	1934	190
1926	253	1935	195
1927	232	1936	222

* Unit: thousand employees. Source: *Annual Reports* of the U.S. Steel Corporation, 18th (1919) to 35th (1936).

defined during that interval. To be sure, if we are definitely interested in price in terms of United States *currency*, such a series may be treated as homogeneous; but as soon as we even by implication think of price in terms of gold or of foreign currencies, homogeneity disappears.

Table 10 shows average number of employees of United States Steel Corporation and subsidiaries in each year since the war. This series is not, despite its appearance, homogeneous. Recalling that, shortly after the war, agitation for replacing the standard 12-hour shift then common in many branches of the steel industry by an 8-hour shift was successful, we examine the source cited in the table for evidence. The 1923 issue of the source shows (page 29) that the change went into partial operation in August, 1923, and into full operation in February, 1924; part of the effect of the change was felt in 1923 and 1924 and the full effect in 1925. The fact of this change does not render the series nonhomogeneous for the purpose of recording changes in the size of the labor force of the corporation; but, as a measure of the amount of labor going into production or as an indicator of activity of the corporation, and for numerous other collateral purposes, the series is not homogeneous. Again, we find in the 1930 issue of the source (page 10) reference to the "stag-

Table 11. Freight revenues of the
         New York Central
         Railroad Company,
         annually*

1927	234	1932	193
1928	235	1933	194
1929	242	1934	204
1930	307	1935	218
1931	246	1936	258

* Unit: million dollars. Source: "Statistics of Railways in the United States," Washington, Interstate Commerce Commission, issues for 1927 to 1936.

gering" of employment during depression, and subsequent issues give further textual and tabular evidence enabling us to study part-time employment by the corporation. This change in policy in 1930, and the developments of the new policy thereafter, must also be noted as an impairment of homogeneity. The acquisition of important new subsidiaries by the corporation during the period covered by the table must also be examined, along with other possible causes of nonhomogeneity not here mentioned, before the extent of the defects in the homogeneity of the series can be known.

As an example of the effects of acquisition of new property upon homogeneity, consider Table 11. The series of freight revenues is not homogeneous because on February 1, 1930 (see source, 1930 issue, page 24) the New York Central Railroad Company leased certain lines it had controlled by stock ownership, including the Michigan Central, Big Four, and certain smaller lines, and the operating revenues of the lessee thereafter included figures for the leased lines. Detailed examination of back issues of the source would enable us, by combining figures, largely—but not wholly—to restore homogeneity to the series.

Suppose a series of annual averages, since 1919, of the price of steel bars, quoted for delivery at Chicago is given. Recalling the long controversy concerning "Pittsburgh plus" in the steel industry, we examine collateral records and find: that for many years prior to 1922, various steel products, wherever manufactured, had generally but not invariably been quoted in each market on the basis of the Pittsburgh price plus freight charges from Pittsburgh to that market; that in January, 1922, this practice was abandoned for some products, including bars; and that a further partial abandonment occurred in July, 1924. Later, under the N.R.A. [National Recovery Administration], a modified form of the basing-point system of quoting prices was put into effect.[2] These changes in the manner of quoting steel prices affect the homogeneity of the series: it remains homogeneous as a mere record of the cost of steel bars to Chicago consumers, but it is not homogeneous for the purpose of analyzing price conditions in the steel industry.

Changes in Definition, in Categorical Series

Several illustrations, given herewith, will indicate the danger that a variable reflected by a categorical series, though it may appear superficially to be rigidly defined, can have serious defects in homogeneity. The series in Table 12, for example, is defective in homogeneity because the word *cotton* does not imply precisely the same commodity, from the point of view of quality and therefore of technical and commercial usefulness, in the various countries. The chief element in the quality of cotton is the length of staple; and staple length varies somewhat for cotton produced within each country, but differences between the countries as to average length are important. On the average, Egyptian staple is long, generally ranging from $1\frac{3}{16}$ to $1\frac{3}{4}$ inches; Indian and Chinese staples are short, mainly of $\frac{7}{8}$ inch or shorter; whereas the bulk of American cotton has staple between $\frac{7}{8}$ and 1 inch. Direct comparisons of the items in Table 12, without reference to these facts, are misleading.

A series giving the assessed valuation of real estate in each city of the United States is not homogeneous for the purpose of studying differences in physical wealth, although it is tolerably homogeneous for comparing differences in the "tax base"—the value against which a tax is levied—among cities. The essential point is that differences in law or in administrative practice result in differences, among cities, in the degree to which assessed valuation reflects "true" value. No satisfactory data exist, telling the percentage relation of assessed value to true value, in various cities, largely because the very definition and determination of "true" value are difficult or impossible. But experience teaches that such percentages, if they did exist, would vary widely from city to city; and we are warned therefore against treating the assessment data as homogeneous.

[2] Arthur R. Burns, "The Decline of Competition," McGraw-Hill Book Company, Inc., New York, 1936, pp. 299–317.

*Table 12. Production of commercial cotton in leading
countries, in 1936–1937 crop year**

United States	12,375	Egypt	1,863
India	5,661	Brazil	1,708
China	3,256	Other countries	2,587
Russia	3,250	Total	30,700

* Units: thousand running bales, for the United States; thousand equivalent bales of 478 lb. net weight, for foreign countries. Source: "Cotton Year Book of the New York Cotton Exchange, 1937," New York, p. 11.

A series showing the principal property account—value of lands, buildings, and equipment—of several companies, as taken from their balance sheets, may not be homogeneous. Examination of the sources (balance sheets and related documents) may disclose that some of the companies report their property values at original cost whereas other companies give net figures after a deduction for depreciation.

Again, a series giving the physical property values, as stated in balance sheets, for several retail establishments may be defective in homogeneity for the purpose of studying differences in the amount of real estate and equipment used in the several businesses. Some firms may own all or practically all of the property used, whereas others rent a large share of the necessary plant and equipment. In the first case, the property would appear in the balance sheet; in the second, it would not. Careful study of the sources of data, and collateral evidence, will generally—though not necessarily—bring out these facts, and the user of such a statistical series must not fail to make this study.

Similarly, a series of balance-sheet figures on inventory, for a list of companies, may not be homogeneous, because some companies value their inventories at cost while others report cost or market value, whichever is lower. Particularly in a period when market prices are declining rapidly, the effect of disparity between cost and market values upon balance-sheet valuations may be very important. Here also, unless the facts are specifically recorded in the table giving the series, the user of the data has no choice but to discover the facts before he interprets or analyzes the statistics.

The series giving volume of passenger traffic in Table 13 is not homogeneous for many purposes. Examination of the source—as well as general information—shows that the typical passenger is hauled much farther on some lines, like the Burlington or the Atchison, than on others, like the New Haven or the Lackawanna. Moreover, the passenger business of some lines, like the Long Island or the Jersey Central, consists very largely of commuters; whereas commutation traffic is negligible on other lines, such as the Southern or the Union Pacific. These facts impair the homogeneity of the series for many studies, including those of rates, costs, need for equipment, maintenance of equipment and plant, operating employment and pay roll, stability of revenues, and the like.

A series giving, for a particular time, the number of manufacturing companies in Belgium, England, France, Germany, Italy, and the United States would not be homogeneous. Differences between countries—as to laws, customs, and public policy—control in an important degree the extent to which an industry is organized in the company form, and the very meaning of the term *company*. Moreover, for any one country, a mere count of the number of companies ignores the great range in size among particular companies. Though each item of the supposed series wears the same name as the others, it manifestly has a meaning peculiar to itself; and no careful statistician treats such a series as homogeneous.

A series purporting to record, for a given year, the national income of each of several countries is not homogeneous. Comparability of such data is impaired by numerous basic factors which affect the size, structure, and significance of the national income—factors such as the size, racial, age, and other characteristics of the population; by the degree

Table 13. Revenue passenger-miles in 1935 for
            selected Class I railways of the United
            States*

Boston and Maine	318
New York, New Haven, and Hartford	1,036
Delaware, Lackawanna and Western	424
New York Central	2,246
Baltimore and Ohio	460
Long Island	1,277
Pennsylvania	2,217
Central of New Jersey	333
Atlantic Coast Line	301
Louisville and Nashville	349
Illinois Central	482
Southern	484
Chicago and Northwestern	554
Chicago, Milwaukee, St. Paul, and Pacific	350
Atchison, Topeka and Santa Fe	748
Chicago, Burlington and Quincy	425
Chicago, Rock Island, and Pacific	360
Southern Pacific	1,138
Union Pacific	367

* Unit: million passengers one mile. Source: "Statistics of Railways in the United States, 1935," Washington, Interstate Commerce Commission, 1937, Section A, pp. 16–125.

of urbanization, the extent of organization and mechanization of industry, the forms of property ownership, and other economic and social characteristics of each country. But, waiving these factors which impair homogeneity of the national income data, we find those data lacking in homogeneity merely on the basis of definition. An intricate concept such as national income is defined only with difficulty; and the estimates for various countries, despite some effort by estimators to use equivalent definitions, rest upon widely various definitions. This fact alone detracts from the homogeneity of this series.

Indexes of the cost of living, for each of several localities in the United States, do not constitute a homogeneous series for most purposes for which they are likely to be used. Even if each index has been computed in the same way, according to a definition and formula fixed for all localities, the comparability is merely superficial. The essential fact is that the concept *cost of living* means different things with reference to different localities—because of differences in climate, structure of population, and numerous physical and social factors.

Other Defects in Homogeneity

The foregoing illustrations, of time series and categorical series which are not homogeneous, have emphasized lack of uniformity or fixity in definition of the variable. This is a very common cause of nonhomogeneity, and frequently the easiest cause to discover. The student will, as he acquires experience and skill, become acquainted with other and more subtle causes of nonhomogeneity and develop some understanding of where and how to look for them. As already noted, no rigid definition of the term *homogeneity* can be given; and no positive criterion can be set up by which, in a particular case, the homogeneity of a series can be tested once for all. The process of testing consists rather in a ramifying, but not therefore unsystematic, search for causes which *might* impair homogeneity.

Moreover, we have seen that homogeneity is a relative term: for some purposes a series may be tolerably homogeneous while for others it is not. The process of testing is therefore influenced by the use to be made of the statistics. The particular use will often suggest the possible causes of nonhomogeneity; and, in fact, scientific interpretation of a statistical series—by making comparisons or by other sorts of analysis—often uncovers causes which limit its homogeneity.

In the discussion of lack of rigidity of definition, we have made no mention of fixity of the unit in which the variable is measured. This seems to be an obvious requirement, and yet the sober fact is that some so-called statistical series do state the different items in different units. No excuse exists, of course, for failing to insist upon a uniform unit—or at least upon full knowledge as to any differences in the unit.

Likewise, the foregoing illustrations—except possibly in the property assessment and national income cases—have not stressed the *accuracy* of the statistics as a source of nonhomogeneity. Any evidence that particular items of a series are imperfect numerical observations of the variable, especially if the imperfection varies from item to item, must be weighed as bearing upon homogeneity.

One of the requirements stated above for a homogeneous series is that the items pertain to a single variable. Actual cases in which all the various items of a series do not pertain to the same variable are fortunately infrequent where good tabulation techniques are used, and can generally be recognized at sight. A more elusive difficulty arises, however, in any case involving a composite variable; and this difficulty has to do with interpretation rather than with the intrinsic quality of the series. Frequently, in studying a composite variable, we are prone to regard its values as indicative not only of changes in the variable itself but also of changes in one or more of its constituent variables. Strictly, this does not have any bearing upon the homogeneity of the series itself; but, as the purpose for which a series is used governs somewhat its homogeneity, this point is mentioned in the present connection.

A wide range of cases in which series are not homogeneous, which the foregoing illustrations do not emphasize, arises because of lack of rigidity of definition of the *object* observed rather than of the variable itself. The individual net income case is of this sort in one respect: changes in the requirement for filing returns (related to changes in the exemption) result in a different coverage in different years. The number of people liable to file returns changes from year to year—the *object* observed, the total body of people filing tax returns, is not rigidly defined.

Another example of this sort is a series of annual steel output by Germany from 1910 to 1936: changes in the national boundaries and political domain of Germany—particularly with reference to the Ruhr area—imply changes in the "object" under observation. In a sense, this is still a question of "definition of the variable," but cases in which the "coverage" is not rigidly fixed occur so commonly that some advantage flows from regarding such cases separately.

Homogeneity in Frequency Series

As a frequency series merely organizes the several values of the variable—variates—in a special arrangement according to size, any of the causes which can impair the homogeneity of a time or categorical series can also limit the homogeneity of a frequency series. The fact that a frequency series conceals the identity of the variate, however, obstructs testing of homogeneity by the procedure indicated above. This does not mean that such procedure is futile and should not be attempted, but it does mean that causes of nonhomogeneity, which are suspected for a particular frequency series, can sometimes not be directly examined. And the very form in which a frequency series appears removes somewhat our disposition to suspect such causes, gives us rather an insidious prejudice in favor of homogeneity.

Fortunately, on the other hand, certain characteristics of the form of distribution of frequencies according to size of variate afford presumptive evidence as to the homogeneity or lack thereof. We shall see that lack of homogeneity in a frequency series often arises from the inclusion, among the cases tabulated, of different groups of objects for which the variate in question has naturally different average sizes. But the whole question of homogeneity is peculiarly involved for frequency series; and, beyond emphasizing at this point that the student must use every known means for testing the homogeneity of such series, we postpone further comment until the methods of analyzing frequency distributions are discussed.

Homogeneity and Comparability

The great importance of homogeneity, as a characteristic of a statistical series, is that it is essential for comparability. Except in the rare instances in which isolated statistical items are used merely to give numerical reality to an economic concept, the use of statistics in economic analysis—and in other branches of science—involves and aims at comparisons among items. In making scientific comparisons a fundamental rule is that we must compare similar things.

Comparison among the items of a statistical series which is not homogeneous obviously defies this rule. Of course, the things compared are not exactly similar in all respects, else they would be exactly alike even as to size of the variable under observation, and there would then be nothing to compare. Unless the items differ in magnitude—unless they reflect a variable—there is nothing to be compared. What we really have in mind, in stating the fundamental rule, is that the cases or objects must be similar *except* as to the size of the variable under study. A series which is homogeneous meets this requirement: comparisons among the items of such a series really tell us something about the variable in question, instead of giving us a confused picture of the joint effect of several variables.

This manner of stating the case explains why homogeneity is so difficult to define and so difficult to determine in practice; why it depends upon the purpose for which the data are used, on the sort and significance of the comparisons to be made; and why it is so seldom fully realized in economic data. Economic data, because of the composite character of most economic variables and because of the complex nature of most economic objects—such as families, commodities, companies, nations, industries, machines, plants, and even individual men and women—are inherently of the sort not amenable to description in terms of a single and truly elementary variable. Comparisons among such data are accordingly liable to reflect the effects not of a single and truly simple type of variation but of a multiplicity of variable causes.

In view of this circumstance, much of the method of statistics is directed to furnishing a means of analyzing *complex* variation, of breaking such variation into its parts, and of revealing if possible the separate elements in such variation. To be sure, elementary comparisons, which merely state which of the items of a series are larger than others and how much larger, have some use in economic analysis by the aid of statistics. But this rudimentary process of comparison is sufficient in relatively few cases, and chiefly only in those cases for which the statistical series are highly homogeneous. More elaborate analytical methods are, of course, of value even for analyzing such highly homogeneous series; and we shall find it helpful to begin and carry forward the study of such methods with reference to tolerably homogeneous series. But an important purpose of analytical methods is to provide some means, however imperfect, for understanding variation which is not homogeneous. All this is said without any intent to minimize the desirability, amounting almost to absolute necessity, of ensuring that every statistical series is made as nearly homogeneous as possible. The best raw material we can possibly obtain, for statistical analysis, will be none too good; and, before undertaking analysis, the student should exhaust every means of rendering his data homogeneous.

SOURCES AND
THEIR USE

PRIMARY AND SECONDARY DATA

The great bulk of statistical analyses in economic investigations rest upon statistical material copied from published sources and therefore not originated for the immediate purpose of the investigation in hand. Such statistics are called *secondary data*. Because secondary data are the chief materials of statistical work in economics, problems connected with their use are the main subject of this chapter.

On the other hand, statistical material which the investigator originates for the purpose of the investigation in hand are called *primary data*. The process of assembling primary data is called *collection* of statistics. The student may be tempted to apply the term *collection* to the process of compiling statistics (secondary statistics) from various published sources, but he should note that the term is used strictly in the narrow sense defined above. Collection means the assembling, for the purpose of a particular investigation, of entirely new data, presumably not already available in published sources.

As noted above, most statistical analyses rest upon secondary data, and the statistical investigator in economics will therefore ordinarily make little use of primary data. He takes his numerical materials mainly from existing compilations, and frequently he makes no use of primary data. One reason why he relies so largely upon secondary data is that, particularly in recent times, the amount and diversity of published statistics are so great that he finds more or less ready to hand the main materials needed for studying numerous economic problems. A second reason is that because of the great complexity of many economic questions and the resultant necessity of securing data on a grand scale the mere burden of labor and expense stands in the way of extensive collection of primary data by the individual investigator.

The economic statistician needs, however, to have some familiarity with the problems of collecting primary data. He may, in a particular investigation, discover that secondary data do not afford an adequate basis for his analysis and that he *must* secure some of his material by collecting primary data. To conduct this operation wisely, he needs to understand at least the principal difficulties likely to be encountered in such collection. He needs to know how to plan and conduct a survey directed to collecting primary data along lines which will effectively yield the desired information. Moreover, he may in the course of his professional work be attached to an organization or participate in an undertaking which has as one of its main objectives the collection of primary data. The purpose of an investigation, in the work of certain organizations, is precisely the collection and publication of primary data. Such is, in a broad sense, the case with the Bureau of the Census and various other governmental agencies, and, to a less degree, with certain agencies outside the government. The statistician who is to take part in such an enterprise needs sound understanding of the problems of collection and of the methods which have proved most effective in collection.

But there is a deeper reason why even the statistician who seldom or never uses any but secondary statistics should understand the collection process. Ultimately all secondary data which he uses rest upon a collection operation: somebody, sometime, must have brought those data into existence by a process of collection. Hence, true insight into the significance and limitations of secondary data requires knowledge in detail of the methods used in their collection by the person or agency which originally collected them as primary data. Without such knowledge, the user of secondary data remains in uncertainty as to many factors, some of which may be highly important for his purpose, affecting the quality and adequacy and other characteristics of the raw materials for his investigations. . . .

PRIMARY AND SECONDARY SOURCES

In taking secondary data from a source, the initial question to be answered is whether the source originated the data—collected them as new—or merely quoted them from still another source. If the source which publishes the data collected them—if the statistics are primary data from the point of view of that source—that source is called a *primary source*, or sometimes an *original source*. If the source merely quotes the data from some other publisher—if the statistics are secondary data from the point of view of the source—the source is called a *secondary source*. The first and general rule in compiling secondary data is to use the primary source. Assuming that we are not using primary data in an investigation, we seek secondary data in one or more sources. If we discover them in some particular source, we then inquire whether that source is primary for those data. If we discover that it is not the primary source, the rule requires us to go back of it until we finally locate the data in their primary source. This is the general rule; we shall note some exceptions and qualifications, but they are so slight that the student should almost invariably apply this general rule rigidly.

The rule is not essentially different, in its purport or its justification, from the same rule which applies to the use of all evidence whether statistical or other. It is the rule of insisting upon first-hand evidence, of excluding so far as possible the second-hand and hearsay elements. It applies in every branch of scientific inquiry, and should require no special emphasis with respect to statistical inquiry. Perhaps the disposition to ignore or violate it is peculiarly present in statistics because of the attractive accessibility of data in numerous secondary sources. But, whatever the temptation to accept data from a secondary source, the student does well to insist obstinately upon primary sources. By so doing he will protect himself from many errors and imperfections in the raw material of his analyses.

Chief Advantages of Primary Source

The main reasons for insisting upon the rule are two. A primary source is more likely to describe carefully the process of collection than a secondary source. The user of a primary source therefore has the advantage of information concerning the collection process, emphasized above, and can appraise its adequacy and reliability for the purpose of his study. To be sure, a secondary source sometimes discusses and criticizes helpfully the collection process used by the primary source from which it quotes; and such a practice, whenever it is encountered, is of great aid to the user. But the practice is not common, and the user should not count upon finding it. Even when he does find it in a secondary source, he is all the more impelled to consult the primary source and form his own opinion as to the validity of the criticism.

The second main reason for the rule is that a secondary source cannot be relied upon to give an accurate and complete quotation of statistical data from a primary source. Mere numerical errors in transcription may, and frequently do, impair accuracy in the secondary source. Here also a qualification is necessary: sometimes a secondary source discovers and corrects an error in the primary source, but these instances are not sufficiently frequent to warrant setting aside the rule on their account. Defects in completeness of quotation are far more serious than mere numerical errors. The secondary source often fails to reproduce all of the pertinent data from the primary source—perhaps merely in the interest of economy, but perhaps because the secondary source has a purpose in reproducing the data which leads it to omit or suppress some of them. Moreover, the secondary source often fails to reproduce significant footnotes, or textual comments, by which the primary source had qualified the data or their definition or the units.

Sometimes a secondary source gives data in a different form from that of the primary source; for example, the secondary source may give the data in the form of percentages of some total or base figure, whereas the primary source gives the actual figures without any arithmetical conversion. Or, a secondary source may present merely a chart of the data, whereas they appear in tabular form in the primary source. In all such cases, danger that the process of conversion may have introduced errors, or otherwise damaged the accuracy or completeness of the data, is an argument for insisting upon the primary source.

Revised Figures

Systematic use of the primary source is more likely to reveal revisions in the data previously published. This practice of revising previous data most commonly arises, of course, in connection with time series, and particularly in cases in which successive periodical issues of a primary source publish the current data of a time series and republish, with revisions where necessary, earlier data. For example, Table 1 is an abstract of series from the *Federal Reserve Bulletin,* which is the primary source for these production indexes. The items marked *r* have been revised from earlier issues of the periodical; in the February, 1938, issue (page 152) they were reported as 89 and 100, respectively. Obviously, quoting data for these production indexes from some secondary source which, for one reason or another, had not "caught" the revisions would result in errors in the data used by the investigator.

Revisions of data in a primary source are not always so plainly marked as in the source quoted in Table 1; the *r* symbols in that case are quoted directly from the source. For example, the *Commercial and Financial Chronicle,* which is a primary source for data on security flotations, gives in its issue of March 5, 1938 (page 1457), "municipal" new capital issues for February, 1937, as $33,504,423. By consulting the issue of March 6, 1937 (page 1501), we find the figure then currently given as $34,345,523. Obviously, unless there is a mere misprint or erroneous transcription in the more recent issue, there has been a revision of the February, 1937, figure during the year. Quotation of the February, 1937, figure from a secondary source which had not "caught" this revision

Table 1. *Indexes of industrial production in the United States, monthly from January, 1937°*

Month	Total	Manufactures	Minerals
1937			
January	114	115	110
February	116	116	115
March	118	117	128
April	118	118	115
May	118	118	116
June	114	114	114
July	114	114	112
August	117	118	112
September	111	110	115
October	102	101^r	113
November	88^r	85	109
December	84	79	114
1938			
January	81^p	76^p	108^p

* Unit: per cent of 1923–1925 average. Adjusted for seasonal variation. Source: *Federal Reserve Bulletin,* March, 1938, p. 222.

^{r} revised; ^{p} preliminary.

would supply the investigator with an erroneous item. Study of this primary source reveals frequent revisions of this sort: the monthly figures published currently are revised one year later, when they are published alongside the new data then current. A careful secondary source may include these revisions, but it is only by using the primary source that we can be sure of catching them.

Finally, cases occur in which the primary source makes revisions in previous data without any systematic republication of the old table with the newly revised items. In such instances we discover evidence that revisions have been made only by examining the textual material or supplementary notes not necessarily attached to any table, in later periodical issues of the primary source. For example, *Statistics of Income* for 1931[1] carries on pages 32 and 33 text notices of revisions of particular items in tables of issues of the same report for earlier years. Most of these revisions pertain to items in *Statistics of Income* tables which were not subsequently republished in tabular form even in issues of the primary source. Only by careful examination of the *text* in the successive issues of the primary source can we be sure of catching the revisions. A good secondary source *may* have caught these revisions, if it was not published before the revisions appeared in the primary source, but the chance is too slim to be relied upon.

Referring again to Table 1, we note that January, 1938, items are marked "preliminary." Many sources, even primary sources, do not systematically label preliminary items. But, where such a notation is encountered, it serves two main purposes. It notifies the user of the data that those particular figures are estimates, and not strictly comparable with the final figures for earlier dates. It also warns him that revisions are to be expected and prepares him to look for them in subsequent issues. . . .

Recognition of a Source as Primary

It is evidently necessary that the compiler of secondary data be able to discover which source is primary for any particular series. It is not always easy to answer this question, and not infrequently a single source is primary for certain series or tabulations and secondary for others. In the case of the economic treatise or textbook containing statistical material, little difficulty is likely to be encountered: ordinarily the author clearly states the sources of his secondary data and discusses in full the collection of such primary data as he presents. Likewise in the case of an economic or statistical memoir appearing in the journal of a learned society, the data presented are usually marked or described so clearly that they can be classified readily as primary or secondary. Similar remarks apply to the statistical publications of government agencies: these documents generally contain data assembled by the several publishing offices; and where secondary material is presented the original source is ordinarily stated.

[1] *Washington, U.S. Treasury, 1933.*

The problem is somewhat more perplexing when the other prominent sources of economic data are considered. The official publications of trade associations and other journals devoted to the interests of particular industries give, with few exceptions, some data which are primary and some which are secondary; and in many instances the distinction between the two groups is not clear, or, if such distinction is made, reference to the original source of secondary figures is missing or inadequate. There are many nonspecialized periodicals, including the great weekly newspapers disseminating general financial, industrial, and commercial information, which present extensive tables of secondary data with relatively few indications of the original sources; but it will be found, although with difficulty in some cases, that several of these journals publish some series which are strictly primary. Numerous banks, large manufacturers, and public utility corporations now publish occasional or periodical statistical bulletins giving a review and prospect of business conditions, and here also the distinction between primary and secondary data is seldom clear. The practice of the more careful business forecasters is somewhat more satisfactory: in many of their publications adequate statement of the origin of data appears, and most of the data which they use are secondary.

If every secondary source systematically followed the rule of citing the reference to the primary source for each series of secondary data published, the difficulties of the user of the secondary source would largely disappear. He would assume that the source was primary for all its tabulations which did not bear such a reference citation. Although the practice of thus citing references is commendably general for all careful secondary sources, it is very far from universal. The investigator is therefore in frequent danger of finding, in some particular source, a series of data bearing no reference to another source, and of being in doubt whether the source in hand is truly primary for such series or has merely neglected to give reference citation.

He can sometimes dispel his uncertainty by careful examination of the source in hand. In the most favorable cases, the tabulation bears an unmistakable notation that the data are primary for the source. Even where no such notation appears, examination of the accompanying text may show beyond doubt that the source was in fact the original collecting agency. Sometimes, in the case of a periodical source, such textual evidence may be found more or less hidden in some earlier issue of the publication. Occasionally the investigator has no recourse except to communicate with the publisher and inquire specifically whether the data in question are primary for that source. If all these devices fail, the investigator remains in doubt, and the only safe assumption to make is that the source is secondary for those data and that the primary source is "unknown."

As the statistician develops experience in the use of sources of economic data, he will come to have a broad acquaintance with them and to know which sources are primary for particular types of data. At the same time he will acquire skill in discovering the sorts of evidence which determine whether a source is primary or secondary. And he will build an increasing respect for those careful publications which always supply him with unambiguous information as to how they secured the data which they publish.

QUALITY OF SOURCES

In much of his statistical work the investigator will find it necessary to make a choice among available sources for any particular series of data. Even with respect to primary sources such a choice is frequently necessary, for often more than one source collects original data for a particular economic variable. For example: various agencies, official and otherwise, collect and publish data on unemployment in the United States; various financial newspapers give data, presumably original with them in each case, upon market interest rates; different trade journals in a particular industry give data, presumably originated by them, on prices and other aspects of the industry.

Where a choice must be made among primary sources, tests of reliability discussed below would normally be applied. But an additional test is usually helpful in selecting primary sources: the investigator should study the process of collection used by each such source and seek to determine which set of data more probably gives a true record of the economic variable under study. Where there is only one primary source the general rule obtains: unless there is very strong reason to the contrary, that primary source is preferred to all secondary sources.

In cases where secondary sources are used, the necessity of a choice among sources is much more common. Usually there are various secondary sources which publish the data of any particular series. Granting that the investigator has for good reason decided to use a secondary rather than a primary source, he is forced to choose an available secondary source. Unless he steadfastly resists the temptation, he is in danger of making this decision on the mere ground of ease. He will be tempted to "choose" the secondary source which comes first and most readily to hand, or to take that source which arranges the data most nearly in the form desired for his own use and thus saves him the job of reorganizing them, or to take that source which includes all or most rather than just a fragment of the statistical information he needs.

Without denying the importance of making wise economies in all statistical work, we insist that the easy grabbing of data in the most convenient source is seldom a wise saving of labor. The statistician who desires to safeguard his analysis and results from imperfections entering at the very start—in his statistical raw materials—should rest his choice among sources upon a test of reliability rather than upon accessibility and convenience. Instead of being content with the first source he discovers, the statistician should discover several—perhaps all—of the existing sources and examine and compare them as to their quality. He may expect often to find that one source is preferable for part of his data and some other source for another part. Moreover, he may discover that the quality of a particular source changes over time: earlier issues of a publication may not be of the same quality as later issues, because of changes in control of the publication or for other reasons.

Evidences of Quality

No exhaustive list of the tests to be applied in determining the quality of a source can here be given. Some of the chief tests are mentioned briefly. The statistician, as he develops experience, will acquire a special skill in discovering evidences of quality. He should begin early in his statistical career to pause in his study of data and try to form a judgment of the quality of the source presenting those data, and this practice should become a settled habit in all his subsequent work. In dealing with sources the statistician needs to know as much as possible about their character, because the validity of his own work depends upon the reliability of the work done by his sources.

The major tests of the quality of a source have already been indicated or implied on previous pages. A secondary source which fails to give any citation of the primary source from which it quotes data is manifestly defective. A source which is found upon examination—not necessarily in connection with the series or tabulation immediately under study—to have made imperfect reproductions from a primary source is not entitled to confidence in the immediate case. Such imperfections may consist in actual errors in transcription, in faulty quotation of labels or units, in omission of significant footnotes, or in failure to reproduce all the essential data. A source which presents data in poorly arranged and improperly organized tabulations, or otherwise uses slovenly methods, is to be suspected; but the use of workmanlike arrangements is not a sufficient test of quality. A source which contains internal evidence of conflict among data, whether in a single issue or in various issues (if it is a periodical source), is suspect: tables and groups of tables which are not consistent are evidence of poor quality in the source.

Purpose of Publication

General facts about the source, apart from facts related to the tabulations, sometimes aid in forming judgments as to its quality. The purpose of publication of a source often suggests questions as to the reliability of its data, though knowledge of the purpose is seldom a sufficient basis for condemning a source. Sources published to promote sales, to advance the interests of an industrial or commercial or other group, to present the case of a political party, or to carry on any sort of propaganda, are suspect. Data published anonymously, or by an organization which is on the defensive, or under conditions which suggest a controversy, or in a form which reveals a strained attempt at "frankness," or to controvert inferences from other data, are generally suspect. To say that sources or data are suspect is not, of course, equivalent to condemnation;

but the statistician has to protect himself by avoiding so far as possible use of data which are even likely to be unreliable.

A source which publishes data as a main or the chief function of its publication operation has ordinarily none of the foregoing counts, as to purpose, against it. If the publication of data is itself the purpose of the source, business reasons favor the maintenance of high quality. This is especially true if the source has been established over a long time and has an enviable reputation the maintenance of which is a business asset. Data compiled in a scientific inquiry, which bears the usual marks of careful scientific work, are usually of high quality, and so is the primary source presenting them. Data submitted under oath, or otherwise under conditions subjecting the issuer to a penalty, are generally of high quality. A source which is established and maintained by individuals requiring certain data, as a cooperative agency for collecting such data, is generally of high quality.

The daily newspaper, whether the nonspecialized paper which gives incidental attention to the presentation of statistical data or the financial or trade daily which regularly exhibits much of its news in numerical form, is on the whole the least satisfactory of sources. There are numerous and notable exceptions to this statement, and the energy and persistence of certain newspapers have been chief contributors to the development of that broad foundation of economic and business data which now enables us to conduct empirical studies of economic phenomena. Nevertheless, one of the essential characteristics of competitive news publishing operates to minimize the efforts made to safeguard the accuracy of data printed in dailies. Speed is most important in the operation of a newspaper enterprise; and statistical material, like other "stories," must be issued while it is yet news. Moreover, once issued, it is in many cases beyond correction or revision: the interest in later and more accurate figures is frequently not considered sufficient to warrant expenditure of further time and space. In consequence, the student must have a discerning appreciation of the difficulties of the publisher if he would safely use newspaper data. Even after he has noted the wide differences in reliability as between different publishers, and also the considerable differences in reliability among the several groups or series of data in any one publication, he will need to be alert to detect the occasional serious slips in newspapers selected as most reliable.

COMPILATION FROM SEVERAL SOURCES

A practical problem of considerable difficulty and importance in the compilation of many series or bodies of data is the selection for joint use of a group of several sources. The inability to find in a single source all the data essential to a particular statistical investigation is perhaps the rule rather than the exception. Where primary sources are available for separate portions of the material, no problem ordinarily arises. When, however, some or all of the sources must be secondary, a decision is necessary as to which secondary sources should be used. The obvious plan is to choose the best, but in practice there are often too few which have the best qualifications or too many which appear equally good without being entirely satisfactory. It is very important that sufficient material be obtained, even at the expense of accepting some figures which are not quite so reliable as the best. Insufficient data sometimes preclude the finding of any worth-while results, whereas imperfect data often yield conclusions upon which one can generally rely within tolerable limits. This point is not, however, warrant for "solving" economic problems by using data which are seriously or generally defective. The investigator will ordinarily select the one best source for data of a particular sort; but he will frequently need to set aside this rule, either because no one source gives a complete series of figures or because the best source is so unreliable that it must be checked by comparison with other sources on the chance that comparison even of poor sources may disclose errors.

Actual experience in the compilation of sections of the statistical material of a problem from various sources will arise frequently in the work of the statistician, and examples are therefore not given here. To illustrate the intricacy of piecing together sources, however, reference is made to a portion of a recent study of national income in the United States.[2] On pages 170 to 175 of the reference cited, descriptive comments indicate the sources used in compiling each of eight tables in the text of the document. Although many instances of joint use of several sources involve no such intricate compilations as those in the case cited, this example is by no means a rare exception.

Too great care can scarcely be given to the preliminary study leading to a selection of sources of data. A vigorous initial search to enlarge the field of choice and a painstaking examination of each possibility will give assurance that the data finally used are indeed the best available and will furnish the student with a knowledge of their imperfections and the consequent limitations upon the results of their analysis. Failure to make a thorough initial survey may result in the compilation of faulty data which must be abandoned later when better sources are discovered. Frequently the waste occasioned by such a blunder is very great, for it includes not only the labor of securing the improper data but also the work incident to such analyses as may be applied to those data before they are finally discarded.

[2] "National Income, 1929–1932," Senate Document 124, 73rd Congress, 2nd session, Washington, 1934.

"QUI NUMERARE
INCIPIT ERRARE
INCIPIT"*

It is no news that imperfections exist in the statistics used in discussions of business, economics, and politics. But it is not generally recognized how significant the imperfections may be. That is what this article is about. Greater awareness of these flaws may lead to a more cautious use of certain statistics and force government agencies and other producers of statistical material toward explicit calculation of the error margins involved in their figures.

The following article is a condensation by Oskar Morgenstern of his book. On the Accuracy of Economic Observations, *which in turn is a complete revision of an earlier work with the same title. . . .*

Dr. *Morgenstern believes that an increasingly sophisticated handling of statistics will yield important insights into economic behavior. While the statistics now in use obviously cannot be abandoned, further progress in economics must start from scholarly recognition that the figures aren't as precise as they seem. For as some Roman once put it: "He who begins to count begins to err."*

Although the natural sciences—sometimes called the "exact" sciences—have been concerned with the accuracy of measurements and observations from their earliest beginnings, they nevertheless suffered a great crisis when it became clear that absolute precision and certainty of important kinds of observations were impossible to achieve in principle. At least all sources of error that occur in the natural sciences also occur in the social sciences: or, in other words, the statistical problems of the social sciences cannot possibly be less serious than those of the natural sciences. But the social sciences pay far less attention to errors than the physical. This is undoubtedly one of the reasons why the social sciences have had a rather uncertain development.

In the physical sciences, when an error is not mentioned explicitly, it is because it can generally be assumed to be well known, or because the values have already entered into physical theories that determine an admissible error level, and their limitations are then those of the respective theory. To give an illustration, it may not be necessary to state every time the error in the measurement of the velocity of light because this value is indissolubly tied up with the theory of relativity. But when new measurements are made the error margin must always be stated.

* By Oskar Morgenstern. Reprinted from the October, 1963, issue of Fortune Magazine, pp. 142–144, 173, 174, 178, 180, by Special Permission; © 1963 Time Inc.

Thus exaggeration of the significance of the new results is avoided, and they assume their proper place in physical theory.

It ought to be clear a priori that most economic statistics should not be stated in the manner in which they are so often reported, pretending an accuracy that may be completely out of reach. Changes in consumers' total spending power down to the last billion or less (i.e., variations of less than one-half of 1 per cent) are reported and taken seriously. Price indexes for wholesale and retail prices are shown to second decimals, even though there have been so many computing steps that the rounding-off errors alone may preclude such a degree of precision. Unemployment figures of several millions are given down to the last 1,000's (i.e., one-hundredths of 1 per cent "accuracy"), when certainly the 100,000's or in some cases perhaps even the millions are in doubt It will be seen later that national income and consumers' spending power probably cannot be shown now in part without an error of plus or minus 10 to plus or minus 15 per cent.

Business must be deeply concerned about these matters; its decisions are dependent upon statistical information. For example, wage agreements involving millions of workers are sometimes based on price indexes that record alleged changes of price levels up to one-tenth of 1 per cent! Common price and cost-of-living indexes are reported in this form. They are splashed across the front pages of newspapers together with the most important political news of the day. These price changes are then interpreted as a measure of the success or failure of government policy and the existence or absence of inflation. In fact, these minute changes show nothing at all. The public in general and Congress in particular must be made to understand that there cannot be absolute accuracy, that there must be error, and that the important thing to do is to try to uncover, remove, or at least limit the error.

DO ERRORS CANCEL OUT?

People gathering statistics all too often face a deliberate attempt to hide information. In other words, economic and social statistics are frequently based on evasive answers and even deliberate lies. Lies arise principally from fear of tax authorities, from dislike of government interference, or from the desire to mislead competitors. Nothing of this sort stands in the path of the physical scientists. Nature may hold back information, is always difficult to understand, but it is believed that she does not lie deliberately. Einstein has aptly expressed this fact by saying: *"Raffiniert ist der Herr Gott, aber boshaft ist er nicht."* ("The Lord God is sophisticated, but not malicious.")

In addition to deliberate lies and evasions there are many other sources of error in the data from which economic observations are made. Anyone familiar with the actual handling of statistical data at the primary level is aware of the great number of possible errors and mistakes and of the frequency with which they occur. The increasing use of machines in handling economic data does not eliminate the main sources of error. These are so deeply rooted that it is impossible, on purely theoretical-probabilistic grounds, to eliminate all of them all of the time. The problem is to appraise them and to reduce them to the minimum.

It is possible that the influence of one error that drives a number in one direction is exactly offset by the influence of another error doing the opposite. In that case, by coincidence, the errors could cancel out—if their "extent" or "strength" balance—and we obtain a "true" figure for our observation. But we have not *made* a true observation. The notion that errors do cancel out is widespread, and when not explicitly stated, it appears as the almost inevitable argument of investigators when they are pressed to say why their statistics should be acceptable. Yet any statement that errors cancel one another has to be proved. The world would, indeed, be even more of a miracle than it is if the influence of one set of errors offset that of another set of errors so conveniently that we need not bother much with the whole matter.

It is also widely believed that more recent statistics are more accurate and trustworthy than earlier ones. This is probably sound, in a vague, general way, but only when sufficiently large intervals of time are taken. There are, however, many instances where statistics produced today are probably no better—and are indeed worse—than statistics produced decades ago. It is obviously more difficult, for example, to describe statistically an economy in a state of vigorous development, signified by the introduction of many new products, changes in quality of existing products, and a rapidly advancing technology.

In particular, modern statistics of the value of foreign trade—an enormously important field—are virtually worthless where countries practicing discriminatory exchange rates are concerned; many nations do so right now and did not in earlier years. Domestic statistics do not necessarily improve either. Sometimes governments change rapidly and bring forth the deliberate falsifications associated with Nazi and Communist practices. Or "strategic" considerations play havoc with reliability.

HOW OLD IS THE RIVER?

There is a tendency toward specious accuracy, a pretense that things have been counted more precisely than they can be—e.g., the U.S. Army published *enemy* casualties for the Korean war to 1/1,000 of 1 per cent, at a time when our own losses were not well known even to the thousands of men! An even better example is given by the official publication of the Austrian Finance Administration, which states that the population of Salzburg Province in 1951 was 327,232 people—*4.719303 per cent* of the entire population of Austria. The classical case is, of course, that of the story in which a man, asked about the age of a river, states that it is 3,000,021 years old. Asked how he could give such accurate information, the answer was that twenty-one years ago the river's age was given as three million years. There is a fair amount of this in economic (and other social) statistics.[1] Economic series, reported in billions, are often aggregated with others, reported in millions or thousands, by simple addition. The result is a new series which gives the impression that the aggregate has been measured, counted, or determined to far more digits than is actually the case.

Another kind of specious accuracy is perhaps even more dangerous. It is functional speciousness. Here data are given that, even when they have only a very small margin of error, are nevertheless useless. This is the case, for example, when the exchange rate of a country with exchange control is given at the official rate (quite accurately to any desired number of decimals), although the vast majority of transactions take place at different rates that are not disclosed or cannot be determined.

The success or failure of a government's economic policy is often measured by the number of the nation's involuntary unemployed. "Full employment" is a national goal in most advanced nations. But as soon as one tries to discover when that desired condition has been reached, considerable difficulties are encountered. They are conceptual as well as statistical.

First, it is known that there is always some "unemployment" which may not be truly involuntary, because labor shifts from one place to another, young people enter the labor force, others more or less gradually slip from it because of age, ill health, emigration. These transitions take time for purely technological reasons, such as slow transmission and dissemination of knowledge, time needed to move to other places of employment, etc. This is then the so-called "frictional" unemployment, which is at some level unrelated to the state of the economy. There is also possibly a great deal of "hidden unemployment," e.g., when persons becoming unemployed in industry go back to farms for varying periods of time. There is a shift in occupations, for example, when skilled workers are displaced by machines and then have to find employment at lesser skills.

Second, because of the high political significance of unemployment figures, this area is charged with emotions, insinuations, assertions, etc. This applies in particular to times of great stress, of political upheavals and changes in the form of government. Some countries, such as the Soviet Union, flatly assert that they never have unemployment, this allegedly being impossible because of their political system. Others, such as Nazi Germany, "reduced" unemployment by drafting men into the army and thereby changed the statistics to their liking.

In the U.S. two distinct series of unemployment statistics are produced by the Bureau of Employment Statistics and the Census. The discrepancies between these series are enormous; the BES series has averaged lower than that of the Census in every year but 1946. It is not uncom-

[1] Years ago an example made the rounds: in order to determine the precise height of the Emperor of China, whom none of his subjects has ever seen, it suffices to ask each of 300 million Chinese what he thinks the height is and average their opinions. This will necessarily give a very precise figure.

mon, indeed it is frequent, to find the government making strong statements about developments in unemployment over periods as short as *one* month. The nation's largest or most important newspapers play up a "drop" in the unemployment rate, say from 5.8 to 5.5 per cent, as a highly significant event and the Secretary of Labor will not hesitate to make speeches on that occasion. All this is done on the basis of "seasonal correction" and dealing with figures given to four "significant" digits. It is clear, of course, that statements of this kind are completely devoid of the meaning attributed to them.

In the notion of a "national income," most difficulties of economics culminate. Neither the conceptual nor the statistical problems in this field have been resolved to anyone's satisfaction, though a great deal of progress has been made in both respects. The two areas are interdependent, since nothing can be measured for which there exist no good concepts, and concepts, no matter how precise, are of little practical value if the corresponding measurements cannot be performed.

National income is a total of composites that differ in reliability from sector to sector and year to year, and hence the error of the composite is, as economist Simon Kuznets has said, a "complex amalgam of errors in the parts whose magnitude is not easily determined." The National Income Division of the Department of Commerce provides no measure of the possible error, taking the position that "meaningful mathematical measures of reliability cannot be calculated for national income statistics; only a frank evaluation of the sources and methods underlying them can provide the understanding which is needed for their effective use in economic analysis." Any quantitative estimate is left to the user of the statistics, who must base his estimate on his knowledge of the sources and methods as provided by the U.S. Income and Output and 1954 National Income supplements. It is impossible for the user to determine with what confidence he may employ the data. The fact that little or nothing is said about accuracy is more dangerous than if the margins of error were frankly stated to be very high.

To throw the burden of estimating the errors and the reliability upon the user, though exceedingly convenient for the maker, is a totally inadmissible procedure. How can the individual user be expected to accomplish something where the government with its vast resources for compiling statistics fails?

Kuznet's study on margins of error in national-income estimates is the most important one that has been make so far. He considered the aggregate national income as composed of 520 cells (forty industries, thirteen income and employment categories). Then he and two of his co-workers attempted to classify each of these entries according to its margin of error. The possible margins of error were grouped into four categories:

I 5–10% with average of 7.5%
II 11–20% with average of 15%
III 21–40% with average of 30%
IV 41–80% with average of 60%

And for each cell each of these three investigators made independent classifications. An average was taken of the investigators' judgments and the deviation between them was noted. As a result, a measure was obtained of the general magnitude of errors in each of the component estimates of national income as well as of the aggregate itself. From this classification, Kuznets distinguished three groups of industries according to the relative margins of error judged to be present in their estimates. First, those with a margin of error well below 15 per cent (in categories I and II above) were the basic manufacturing industries and public utilities—electric light and power, railroads, street railways, telephone, telegraph; second, with margins of error of about 15 per cent but well below 30 per cent, were agriculture, mining, manufactured gas, pipelines, trade, banking, insurance, and government—industries for which information is extensive but not complete; and third were industries with an error margin of about 30 per cent and higher—construction, water transportation, real estate, direct service industries, and the miscellaneous division.

Textbooks on national income and macroeconomics and trade journals accept the statistics at face value and do not seem to be conscious of their severe limitations. But let us see what even a 5 per cent difference in national income means. Assuming a gross national product of about $550 billion, a 5 per cent error equals plus or minus $30 billion. This is far more than the total annual production of the entire electronics industry in the U.S. Yet a 10 per cent error in national income is even more reasonable to assume than a 5 per cent error. But 10 per cent amounts to a plus or minus variation of about three times the total exports of the U.S. The possible differences are, of course, not concentrated in the manner of these illustrations; instead they are scattered in an unknown way throughout all activities producing the national income. On the other hand, the reader, like everyone else, has probably become conditioned to accept economic data as being so highly accurate that even an alleged mere 1 to 2 per cent variation of national income is considered significant enough for making statements about "true" variations in the state of the economy.

COMPARING ONE NATION WITH ANOTHER

There are two principal questions involved: the first is one referring to the comparability and applicability of concepts, and the second is one referring to the quality of the component data. Conceptually different situations arise for each class or category of countries. For example, home-consumed agricultural produce, which is an enormous part of the total in underdeveloped agricultural countries, is practically irrelevant in the U.S. Clearly, this is much more difficult to measure in the former than in the latter. Yet agricultural statistics in the U.S. are far from satisfactory. How, then, could the agricultural income of, say, Ceylon, the Congo, China, Bolivia, or Tibet be known at least as accurately? How can they be made comparable—e.g., on a per capita basis—when even the number of inhabitants in these countries is in far greater doubt than that in the U.S.?

International comparisons, however, are constantly being made. No doubt some information can be had from existing figures, and whether they are useful depends, as we shall not tire of repeating, on the purposes of the comparisons. To ascertain in a rather general manner the gross differences in the income of different nations, to show that they differ by large factors,[2] and to see whether these differences have changed over the years, etc., is one thing, but to believe that we can state this and much more reliably to two, three, or even four "significant" digits is an entirely different matter.

DEFECT OF SOVIET STATISTICS

A special problem is offered by the Soviet Union. The statistics of that country are exceedingly difficult to assess, but it is generally known that they are seldom what they purport to be. There has been a great deal of deliberate doctoring of statistics at many levels, in order, for example, to make production results appear better than they are or to receive assignments of raw materials that would not otherwise be allocated. Even Khrushchev has repeatedly referred to falsified accounts of various activities, especially in farming, and there is no reason to assume that statistical practices were better in Stalin's time. A particular trouble in measuring aggregates is (as in all other countries) the double counting, or rather the multiple counting. Double counting has apparently been a most serious defect of Soviet statistics, with the necessary result that accounts of national income have been exaggerated, and increasingly so in more recent times. This is the gist of criticism by S. G. Strumilin, a well-known Soviet economist. For example, in 1945 industrial output was, according to him, more than 30 per cent below 1940, rather than only 8 per cent, as the official statistics show. Again according to Strumilin, industrial production rose from 1945 to 1956 only threefold, rather than fourfold, as officially asserted. (Strumilin's own figure may, of course, still be an exaggeration.) Though industrial production is not identical with national income, it is a substantial component; its difficulties are illustrative for the larger aggregate and show how limited the value is of any "growth factor" based on such data.

Figures giving international comparisons of national incomes are among the most uncertain and unreliable statistics with which the public is confronted. The area is full of complicated and unsolved problems, despite great efforts to overcome them. This is a field where politics reigns supreme and where lack of critical economic appraisal is particularly detrimental.

[2] *But probably not by as large factors as is suggested by the official statistics. As Kuznets has observed, if the frequently stated low figures were correct the inhabitants of the poorest countries would all have starved a long time ago.*

THE ACCURACY OF GROWTH RATES

In recent years there has been much concern about the rate of economic growth of the U.S. and other countries. In addition to the goals of maintaining a high level of employment and providing for general stability in the price level, a third goal, that of maintaining a satisfactory rate of economic growth, has been added to the responsibilities of fiscal and monetary authorities.

The value of a growth rate depends on the accuracy both of the figures for gross national product and of the prices going into the construction of the deflator indexes. The former are subject to considerable uncertainties; the latter depend on the precision with which actual prices, as distinguished from posted prices, list prices, etc., can be determined and applied to the correct sectors of gross national product.

A reliable growth rate of two significant digits is impossible to establish. Even the first digit is in grave doubt, as will be shown below. Yet the emphasis of the public discussion is on the second digit, usually the first decimal, and it is carried on in all seriousness as if a distinction between say, 3.2 and 3.3 per cent were really possible, and as if the transition, within a short time, from the former to the latter constituted an advance by the country. But a growth rate simply cannot be computed with the stated or demanded degree of refinement and reliability. This applies to the existing national income data of any country in the world.

We know that countries have grown and that, at periods, some have grown faster than others. But such observations and statements can be made with confidence only qualitatively and for longer periods. They are impossible to make for one year (or less), when a nation's growth is as imperceptible as the growth of a person's teeth in a month.

The table below shows growth rates as commonly computed, but for 1, 3, and 5 per cent plus or minus variations of the underlying figures. We recall that the assumption of a plus or minus 5 per cent accuracy of the non-deflated gross national product is conservative. The results of this simple computation should shake the confidence of anyone who thinks that the difference between, say, 3.2 and 3.3 per cent is significant.

The computation is for a (hypothetical) change in U.S. gross national product from \$550 billion in Period I to \$560 billion in Period II. The first column lists the values of gross national product assuming the reported figure for Period I—i.e., \$550 billion—to be subjected to the above-mentioned error of plus or minus 1 per cent, 3 per cent, and 5 per cent. The top row carries the same assumption through for the Period II figures. The body of the table contains the growth rates obtained for all combinations of the assumed possible errors. When there is no error assumed or when an error of a given magnitude is exactly compensated by an error of the same magnitude and with the same sign, the growth rate is 1.8 per cent. This rate would, according to current practices, be reported (and analyzed) as *the* rate. It is, of course, im-

Apparent rate of growth for ±1, ±3, ±5, percent errors

A. Assuming reported gross national product figures 550 and 560 in two successive periods

Period II GNP 560 ± error		532.0	543.2	554.4	569.0	565.6	576.8	588.0
Period I GNP 550 ± error	% error	−5	−3	−1	0	+1	+3	+5
522.5	−5	1.8	4.0	6.1	7.2	8.2	10.4	12.5
533.5	−3	− .3	1.8	3.9	5.0	6.0	8.1	10.2
544.5	−1	−2.3	− .2	1.8	2.9	3.9	5.9	8.0
550.0	0	−3.3	−1.2	.8	1.8	2.9	4.9	7.0
555.5	+1	−4.2	−2.2	− .2	.8	1.8	3.8	5.9
566.5	+3	−6.1	−4.1	−2.1	−1.2	− .2	1.8	3.8
577.5	+5	−7.9	−5.9	−4.0	−3.0	−2.1	− .1	1.8

Computed rate of growth assuming the reported figures to be correct is $\frac{560-550}{550}$

$= 1.8\%$.

B. Assuming reported gross national product figures 550 and 566.5 in two successive periods

Period II GNP 566.5 ± error		538.2	549.5	560.8	566.5	572.2	583.5	594.8
Period I GNP 550 ± error	% error	−5	−3	−1	0	+1	+3	+5
522.5	−5	3.0	5.2	7.3	8.4	9.5	11.7	13.8
533.5	−3	.9	3.0	5.1	6.2	7.3	9.4	11.5
544.5	−1	−1.2	.9	3.0	4.1	5.1	7.2	9.2
550.0	0	−2.2	− .1	2.0	3.0	4.1	6.1	8.2
555.5	+1	−3.1	−1.1	1.0	2.0	3.0	5.0	7.1
566.5	+3	−5.0	−3.0	−1.0	0.0	1.0	3.0	5.0
577.5	+5	−6.8	−4.8	−2.9	−1.9	− .9	1.0	3.0

Computed rate of growth assuming the reported figures to be correct is $\frac{566.5-550}{550}$

$= 3.0\%$.

possible that there be no errors at all, and most improbable that they always exactly compensate for each other. The table now shows clearly what happens when even the modest 1 per cent or 3 per cent errors are introduced. Magnitudes and even signs are affected. If we assume that the reported figure of 550 for Period I is 5 per cent too high and the figure for Period II 5 per cent too low, we arrive, instead of at 1.8 per cent, at 12.5 per cent as the growth rate. If we reverse the signs, the growth rate is —7.9 per cent. Suppose gross national product for the second year is only plus 1 per cent off and gross national product for the preceding one is minus 1 per cent off (a total error of only 2 per cent), then the growth rate is 3.9 per cent. But if the signs of the errors are reversed, the growth rate is —0.2 per cent! It is in the essence of an error estimate that the occurrence of a positive and negative deviation has to be admitted. Surely, the assumption of only a 1 per cent error for each period is a very mild one. The reader should contemplate what this trifling difference in our assumption entails. If our basic figures of 550 and 560 are more than 1.8 per cent apart, say 3 per cent, the results of a corresponding table are necessarily worse. For example, a minus 1 per cent error in the first period and a plus 1 per cent error in the second then give a growth rate of 5.1 per cent, and if the signs are reversed a growth rate of 1 per cent. With plus or minus 3 per cent the corresponding figures are 9.4 per cent and —3 per cent.

The computations obviously apply to *any* situation where rates of change are involved and where the data are subject to error. In other words, *they apply to all economic data.* And it cannot be assumed without further proof that the errors remain constant over time, that they change uniformly over time, and that the signs of the errors never reverse themselves.

This simple arithmetical exercise combined with the indisputable fact that our final gross national product or national income data cannot possibly be free of error raises the question whether the computation of growth rates has any value whatsoever.

PICK YOUR TIME

The usefulness of growth rates becomes even more dubious when revisions are considered. If the rate for the change from 1947 to 1948 was determined in February, 1949, when the first figures became available, it was 10.8 per cent. In July, 1950, using officially corrected figures, it became 12.5 per cent; in July, 1956, it fell to 11.8 per cent—a full percentage point. All this for the growth from 1947 to 1948! Similar observations apply to the other years for which this computation has been made. There is no consistency in the changes. In stating what the growth rate of the country is, much depends, therefore, on the moment of time when a growth rate is computed. Though not surprising in the light of our previous investigations, this result is nevertheless noteworthy. And all this applies to figures where we have *abstracted* from the fact that they are necessarily afflicted with errors which, when low, must be at least 5 per cent.

In addition to all these difficulties, there is the ambiguity in choosing the base year. The need for a base year arises from the desire to compare long periods by means of the compound rate. Such periods will often comprise a whole series of business cycles and therefore several decades. If a year with a high (or low) gross national product is chosen as base year, this will depress (or raise) the growth rate of subsequent years. Since there is no such thing as a "normal" year, the investigator has a great amount of freedom in determining a base year. An unscrupulous or politically oriented writer will choose that base year which produces the sequence of (alleged) growth rates best suited to his aims and programs. An advocate of government spending and inflation will pick a year with a high gross national product as base year in order to show a low rate of growth and thereby strengthen his argument in favor of inflation, government deficits, and the like. An opponent of such policies will choose a relatively poor gross national product as base year, thus obtaining a series of growth rates carrying the comforting message that the development of the country is progressing well. These are, of course, standard tricks, used undoubtedly, ever since index numbers were invented.

Suppose a 3.5 per cent growth is considered desirable: then the goal has been reached only when 1949 is chosen as a base year.

It is clear, furthermore, that in view of the high degree of unreliability of its basic national-income data, the growth rates for the U.S. are at best very shaky. From their relatively better quality we have to go over to the lesser and lesser quality of the national-income statistics of other countries. The computation, and hence the comparison, of international growth rates under these conditions is a most dubious undertaking.

It will always be necessary to supplement the rates by qualitative information. We emphasize again that there can be no doubt that countries develop at different speeds and that this fact is noticeable over longer periods of time, particularly when the initial level of economic activity is low and the state of technology is primitive. When big gaps exist, a comparison of change can be made with some confidence provided a sufficiently long time interval is admitted. When countries are very dissimilar in their structure, such comparisons become immeasurably more difficult and unreliable.

If there is any value at all in the notion that countries grow in characteristic patterns, depending on their history, technological age, geographic position, size, etc., then it is unlikely that a single simple number can state adequately (or at least not in a misleading sense) how they evolve relatively to each other. In this respect, the problems of finding a proper solution for describing the gross national product of the national income are compounded many times.

SWIMMING POOLS OR POWER PLANTS

There is also a conceptual problem that has to be taken care of even if the statistics are in good shape. Let us say country A expands by adding to its output of automobiles, refrigerators, swimming pools, etc., while country B increases its output of machine tools, power plants, mines, etc. B is laying the foundation for further output increase while A is not. Similar considerations apply when weapons and other tools for war are involved. The ordinary growth rate, computed for the big gross-national-product aggregate, covers up these profoundly different developments and would easily give entirely erroneous and misleading information about the relative development of these countries. Yet this is the figure commonly used to assess past progress and future tendencies. The answer would be to compute instead "power indexes" (of growth), which would have to be based on the information given by special aggregates made up of better related components.

To summarize: precise uses of "growth rates" are entirely inadmissible, whether for comparing different countries or short periods of the same country. Their computation is largely arbitrary. The concept itself is vague and unreliable.

An argument often heard is: "True, the statistics are not as good as we would want them to be, but what would we do without them?" This is, indeed, a dilemma. The answers, of course, are manifold. The primary consideration is to make the data better (admittedly easier said than done and involving costs and time delays, both of which may not be permissible; many statistics are needed precisely because decisions have to be made at the moment when the first estimates become available). The next point is to distinguish in what sense the data are unsatisfactory: Is it due to deliberate obstruction, lies, falsifications? Or is it due to inherent difficulties of measurement and observation, which otherwise have been carried out scrupulously?

In the first case there is but one answer: discard the data if the element of lying affects a significant part of the information or is suspected of doing so.

In the second case, where the data are unsatisfactory because of incomplete information or inherent difficulties of measurement, the only answer must be to say: modify the theory into which the poor data are to be fitted. Here the truth is that much of economic theory merely appears to be highly accurate and precise. It can maintain this appearance, like any theory, by virtue of being an abstraction. The problems arise therefore in the act of application; it is here that the difficulties have to be faced.

ABANDON OLD VIEWS

Economics is not nearly so much of a science as the free use of allegedly accurate figures would seem to indicate. On the other hand, there is no reason to conclude that there cannot be or is no theory at all. The belief that we have to get more and more data, make more and more descriptions before we can formulate valid theories is entirely mistaken. A theory means a commitment, and in scientific life that is exactly what is wanted. When new facts come to light and new interpretations are needed, a new situation can arise. This may then call for abandoning the old views and for making a new decision.

There is, however, one definite action that is possible, though it will take time before desirable results will become visible. That is to stop important government agencies, such as the President's Council of

Economic Advisers, the various government departments, the Federal Reserve Board, and other agencies, public and private, from presenting to the public economic statistics as if these were free from fault.

Perhaps the greatest step forward that can be taken, even at short notice, is to insist that economic statistics should not be released without an accompanying estimate of their error. Even if only roughly estimated, this would produce a wholesome and perhaps a profound effect. Makers and users of economic statistics both might refrain from making claims and demands that cannot be supported scientifically if the publication of error estimates became a general practice.

Eventually a new generation of economists will have learned to live with data of widely differing quality. In that they will emulate the physicists, who have created a magnificent and terrifying theory though their data range in accuracy from better than 1/100,000,000 per cent to only 50 per cent—that is, when they can measure at all. In appreciating the true condition of the data, economists cannot fail to develop economic theory in conformity with the high scientific standards set in the physical sciences.

COMMENTS ON "QUI NUMERARE INCIPIT ERRARE INCIPIT" BY OSKAR MORGENSTERN*

Executive Office of the President[1]

Bureau of the Budget
Washington, D.C. 20503

February 5, 1964

Honorable Thomas B. Curtis
House of Representatives
Washington, D.C. 20515

Dear Mr. Curtis:

I greatly appreciate your note to me requesting my comments on the article by Professor Oskar Morgenstern which appeared in the October 1963 issue of *Fortune* magazine. I have delayed replying until I could give this important matter my personal attention.

As you know, I have for many years been particularly interested and concerned, both personally and in official capacities, with promoting and developing economic and social statistics better designed to aid analysis. I had been familiar with the first edition of Professor Morgenstern's book *On the Accuracy of Economic Observations* published in 1950, which presented much the same points of view he has recently elaborated. The *Fortune* article, as you know, was based on the second edition of this book, which was published in 1963.

Error in measurement, as well as conceptual problems in the economic and social sphere, have been and are receiving extensive and intensive attention throughout the Government's statistics program. I agree that much still remains to be done. It must also be recognized that this type of problem will never be completely solved. It is my hope that your comments in the *Congressional Record,* together with Professor Morgenstern's *Fortune* article, will be helpful in extending the efforts to improve Federal statistics by calling special attention to measurement problems.

It is also my hope that, while recognizing and emphasizing the need for attention to error, this emphasis will not lead to an uncritical dis-

* By Raymond T. Bowman. Reprinted from The American Statistician, Vol. 18, No. 3 (June, 1964) pp. 10–20. Used by permission.

[1] Raymond T. Bowman's letter appeared in the Congressional Record, Vol. 110, No. 35, Feb. 27, 1964—88th Congress, 2nd Session.

crediting of economic and social statistics. Simon Kuznets clearly recognized this danger in his review[2] of the 1950 edition of Morgenstern's book. I quote a passage from that review which is particularly pertinent:

> Because errors in the economic data are essentially complex historical phenomena, the fundamental difficulty is bound to remain. Methods of freeing data from their historical conditions are exceedingly limited; and reducing the difficulty by means of an empirically founded theory that would yield constants (like those in the natural sciences) is not likely in the face of rapidly changing historical reality. We must therefore, be prepared for a situation in which economic and social statistics will continue to be affected by large errors; and in which quantification of such errors will remain a difficult, and often impossible, job of laborious *ad hoc* detection.
>
> Nothing in these comments detracts from the force of Professor Morgenstern's emphasis on need for greater attention to the problem. But they should serve to indicate a dissent from Professor Morgenstern's tendency in his discussion to set up the natural sciences as a feasible ideal; to understate the institutionally changing elements in economic statistics; to dwell primarily upon errors in single items or series, thus overlooking the variety of practices used in dealing with the data, either in scientific research or in policy formulation. The reader might too easily conclude from Professor Morgenstern's discussion that the trouble lies largely in the lack of attention paid by economists and statisticians to the problem; and that increased attention would go far towards solving the problem, as it has been solved in the natural sciences. To such a conclusion the reviewer, and most likely also the author, would enter a strong objection.

Before commenting specifically on points raised by Professor Morgenstern let me begin with certain general observations. I have no disagreement with the basic concern which Morgenstern sets forth, that economic statistics should be used with a fuller understanding of their errors and their relevance. As to *Qui Numerare Incipit Errare Incipit* few would disagree but almost everyone would also agree, and I feel certain Morgenstern would be among them, that not to measure would be to err even more. Moreover, it must be clear to all users of our official statistics that we do not present them as though they were 100 per cent correct.

It is axiomatic that measurement of social and economic phenomena (in fact measurement in all fields) is subject to "error." The users of statistics should bear this in mind and the producers and publishers of statistics should present the limitations associated with the data. I know of virtually no social analyst who would not agree to these principles, recognizing, of course, that the significance of the error depends upon the particular analytical uses to which the statistics are put. Some current uses in aggregate mathematical models or for micro-analysis require more   refined   and   conceptually   explicit   economic   and   social

[2] Journal of the American Statistical Association, *Vol. 45, No. 252, December, 1950,* pp. 578–579.

measurements than were needed heretofore. In fact Professor Morgenstern's early interest was closely related with the problems of constructing and using input-output tables.

It is generally accepted that the errors in economic measurements, if known in some meaningful sense, should be stated. In recognition of this principle, particularly during the last two decades, major stress has been placed on probability sampling. When probability sampling is used, the sampling error can be determined and published in explicit terms. Furthermore, it is generally possible, within limits of available resources, to tailor the sample size and design to meet predetermined levels of accuracy so far as sampling errors are concerned. In addition, sampling has other advantages since it facilitates the taking of more effective actions with respect to other types of error by concentrating efforts on a sample rather than the universe generally. This permits, without too severe a strain on financial and personal resources, better training of enumerators, more careful inspection and analysis of primary sources and more attention to conceptual problems.

Sampling error could receive this special attention for several reasons. First, remarkable advances in statistical theory had taken place which made possible precise meaning for such measures which are clearly useful for guiding analysis. In other words, we are able to isolate one kind of error, to estimate it, and to state its significance in probability terms. Second, sampling error as measured in statistical surveys includes those components of observational error that are ordinarily reported in the physical sciences so that parallel efforts across the fields of science are thus possible. Other types of error, on the other hand, such as bias of the observer, bias of the measuring instrument, bias of the thing being observed, while increasingly dealt with in the social sciences cannot be handled with the same facility as in the physical sciences because experimental controls are not generally feasible. Under experimental controls bias errors can often be eliminated or standard error coefficients developed in relationship to such conditions as change in temperature, acceleration, etc. In the social sciences much of our observation is historic and generally cannot be repeated or reversed under experimentally controlled conditions. While we are beginning to measure and reduce response variability, we must still face the fact that it may be customary to misrepresent one's age, one's income, or one's occupation at one time but not at another; to give one answer to the census taker and another to the doctor; or that a firm may not respond the same way to a regulatory agency as to the Census Bureau under provisions of confidentiality. Professor Morgenstern is certainly aware of these features of economic observations.

In the social sciences, for the reasons mentioned, errors due to misunderstanding, ignorance, falsehood, the lack of records based on standard procedures, the difficulty of developing and utilizing standard classifications, all these and many more, make it difficult and often impossible to define such error so as to measure it, particularly as a specific ± magnitude with concise and useful meaning.

Nevertheless, even in the light of all the difficulties let me repeat what I said on another occasion.[3]

The stress now being placed on sampling errors in official statistics is entirely appropriate. I am not so sure, however, that the people who use and interpret the data understand the sense in which sampling errors are useful as contrasted with other types of errors in the data. I believe, therefore, that we should give more attention to errors other than those of sampling. Errors arising from biases induced by falsehood or ignorance, or by the enumeration process, are important and real and warrant the research efforts of statisticians concerned with methodology to find ways to eliminate them.

Thus far, I have restricted my comments to error in measurement specifically—what was the wage bill? how large was GNP? how many people are employed? But often the discussion of error takes on a broader context, sometimes, as with Morgenstern, without recognizing the broadening. For example, the United Nations, as you know, has developed a System of National Accounts commonly referred to as SNA. The hope is that if the various countries use this system the results will be comparable. In my opinion this development is an excellent one. Yet, even if the figures for each country were precisely accurate in a strict measurement sense, certain types of comparisons might not be valid. First, even if two countries with similar economic, social and political institutions and at the same level of economic development like the United Kingdom and the United States are to be compared, special difficulties other than the accuracy of their GNP measures must be taken into account. In this instance economists agree that conversion of the money value figures to a common currency by the use of exchange rates is generally not appropriate. Because of the difference in price structures a precise comparison requires special adjustments for this purpose. But economists recognize that no completely precise comparison is possible because of what is commonly referred to as "the index number problem." Briefly, one comparison can be made by valuing the British output in U.S. prices. But another one can be made by valuing the U.S. output in British prices. Generally these will not be the same. One interpretation of the correct answer, under U.K. and U.S. circumstances, is that it lies somewhere between the two answers.

It is obvious that the wider the institutional and economic development differences among the countries to be compared the more difficult it becomes to make precise valid comparisons and the more subject to qualifications such comparisons must be. A comparison of India and the U.S., or of Kenya or Albania and the U.S., cannot reasonably assume similar economic, social and political institutions or levels of economic development. Therefore, even the basic measurable quantities are not comparable. One economy may produce and consume much of its output

[3] Raymond T. Bowman, "The American Statistical Association and Federal Statistics," Presidential Address at the Annual Meeting of the American Statistical Association, Cleveland, Ohio, Sept. 5, 1963.

within households. Under these conditions the output is not valued in markets. If such output is actually discoverable it is difficult to value in the same way as it would be valued in free markets. It may not even be quantified because it does not get recorded in any systematic way. The difficulties of different price structures are of course still present but are often insignificant relative to the other problems just mentioned.

It should be noted, however, that some of these difficulties, particularly the conversion problem, affect level comparisons among countries more than within countries. But comparisons over time in any one country are subject to similar difficulties. The longer the period the more likely it is that the things being compared are so different as to require special cautions—e.g., the horse and carriage age in the U.S. with the modern automobile age. Current value series must be adjusted by the use of a price index but price changes are inextricably interwoven with quality and quantity changes. With the rise of new commodities and the disappearance of old ones how can we develop a comprehensive measure of the prices of a constant content of commodities or services (the price index problem) or of a varying content of commodities and services at constant prices (the production index problem)? But some comparisons must be made to gain any perspective whatsoever.

Because of these problems most analysts recognize that GNP in real terms would go up more if adjustments for price changes took better account of quality changes. This would be true assuming historic quality improvements because price indexes would rise less or fall more if such quality changes were fully accounted for. If this type of problem is to be included in a discussion of error in economic and social statistics then it must have a special context. It cannot be dealt with by some ± quantity.

Please forgive this long introduction to the more specific comments which follow. These issues, however, are important basic considerations in any evaluation of current-day economic statistics. Finding fault with the statistics we have so as to promote improvements is my mission in life. But it would be incorrect not to note that Federal statistics as currently produced are not only useful but indispensable for many policy and analytical purposes. Their basic accuracy, the care with which they are compiled and the cautions provided to users have undergone and are undergoing major improvements. That we can and should do even better to meet the analytical needs of tomorrow is equally true and any criticism that can be turned to this end is welcome.

Notwithstanding my basic agreement with Professor Morgenstern's desire to have a wider understanding of inaccuracies in economic observations, I wish to point out several aspects of his article which may not promote such understanding. Let me be specific about certain criticisms he makes of Federal statistics.

Criticisms of Federal economic statistics in Professor Morgenstern's article are focused chiefly on the statistics of national income and product. Among other data, the unemployment series also receive particular notice. It is in connection with these areas of statistics that most of the key issues of the article are raised and to which I wish to direct special attention.

There is no disagreement with Professor Morgenstern's view that virtually all of the problems of error in economic time series must be dealt with in national income and product estimates. These include errors in the collection of the primary data, in their tabulation and classification, in record-keeping, in the concepts used in the national accounts, in estimation and in analysis—all these activities are inextricably part of the construction of the national accounts. How does Professor Morgenstern deal with the significance of these errors? He takes three approaches, as follows:

1. A reference to the Kuznets study of national income in order to indicate the size of uncertainties in national income estimation and the feasibility of quantifying the amount of error.[4]
2. A hypothetical tabulation, or "arithmetical exercise" as it is called in the article, to show the wide disparity in growth rates between two successive periods arising from assumed errors in data for each period.
3. A statement about the magnitude and frequency of revisions to further indicate the uncertainty in the accounts data.

In what follows, I point out that Morgenstern (1) misinterprets the Kuznets study; (2) seriously exaggerates the extent of error by highlighting the worst possible—often least likely—interpretation of error in time series; and (3) overstates the uncertainties arising from the magnitude and frequency of the revisions mentioned.

On the Kuznets study, which pertains to the Kuznets estimates and not the official data, the *Fortune* article implies that the values of errors assigned to various categories were *average* errors, when in fact they were *maximum* errors. Kuznets says:

> Our classification was based upon maximum errors, not minimum or average errors; i.e., we were concerned with how large the error could be. An error of 5 per cent meant that this was the maximum error to which the estimate was likely to be subject. The minimum error is zero and the average error too indefinite to estimate.[5]

Professor Morgenstern suggests that the margins of error are either plus or minus. For example, the paragraph directly following the discussion of the Kuznets study says:

> Assuming a gross national product of about $550 billion, a 5 per cent error equals plus or minus $30 billion.

[4] *Simon Kuznets*, National Income and Its Composition, 1919–1938, *Vol. 2, Chapter 12, National Bureau of Economic Research, 1941.*
[5] Ibid., *p. 503.*

But Kuznets seriously questions whether errors, if quantified, can be considered as indicating a plus or minus. He says:

As a matter of fact the maximum errors are in one direction for a majority of the estimates.[6]

Professor Morgenstern suggests that errors in the level of a series can also be applied directly to calculate errors in the measurement of change and that errors in change are likely to be far greater than the error in level. Kuznets makes clear that the estimates of maximum error in his study pertain to levels in a given period, not to changes. No quantitative estimate was made of error in changes over time. He does, however, suggest that the errors in change are probably not more and frequently less than the errors in level. Kuznets says:

Since most estimates are derived by applying interpolation and extrapolation indexes to some basic, comprehensive value, there is a natural tendency for the error implicit in the basic quantities to persist through the period covered. This makes for a positive correlation of the signs of errors for adjacent time units when the error margins in the totals are at all substantial.[7]

In other words, if the errors in level retain their sign and approximate size, the effect on changes over time will be small. For example, the Decennial Censuses counted the population to be 151,326,000 in April 1950, and 179,323,000 in April 1960, an increase of approximately 28,000,000 or about 19 per cent. Special evaluation studies, however, estimated that each of these levels was below the "true" population by 2 to 2½ per cent. Here we have an illustration in which the sign of the error in level remains positive and the change in the size of the error remains small. "Corrections" in level would therefore have only a small effect on the change.

Between censuses, with the previous census as a benchmark base, the Census Bureau estimates the population of the U.S. each month using data on births, deaths, and net immigration. It is interesting to note that the change in level from 1950 to 1960 estimated in this way differed by only 277,000 or 0.16 per cent from the count made by the Decennial Census.

True enough, Kuznets does warn that the error in the change could sometimes be very sizeable relative to the change shown. This is likely to occur when the change shown is a very small proportion of the level. In this case a small "correction" in the level can have a great effect on the "correction" of the change. For example, in the most recent revision of the payroll employment series to 1962 benchmarks, the revised estimate of level for the stone, clay, and glass group differed by 3.3 per cent from the earlier estimate obtained by carrying the old bench-

[6] Ibid., *p. 504.*
[7] Ibid., *p. 531.*

mark forward on the basis of current sample reports. On the basis of new benchmark data employment in this industry was 554,000 in 1961 and 564,700 in 1962 indicating an increase of 10,700 or about 2 per cent. Before the benchmark revisions the estimates had indicated an increase of 4,400 employees. It may be said that the more comprehensive data showed 140 per cent more increase than the current reports. On either basis the rise was very small—2 per cent on the revised basis and about 1 per cent on the preliminary basis. Care must always be used in interpreting percentages figured on small bases.

For many purposes the error level just described is insignificant. Comparisons of this sort over short periods, as Morgenstern suggests, should be carefully appraised to see if the benchmark revisions have been frequent and are reliable.

Over longer periods of sizeable change the nature of the estimating procedures and the character of basic estimates from which the change is derived would more likely produce a smaller error in the change than in the level. Yet the *Fortune* article implies that the errors in change are likely to be far greater than in level.

This implication is brought out in a table of hypothetical figures consisting of a 7×7 matrix formed by pairing the rows which show the assumed errors for the first period with the columns which show the assumed errors for the second period. The assumed errors in each period are zero, and plus and minus 1, 3, and 5 per cent. The exercise is hypothetical but is intended, so it seems, to indicate possible orders of magnitude of errors in the GNP data. In introducing the hypothetical exercise, Professor Morgenstern says:

> We recall that the assumption of a plus or minus 5 per cent accuracy of the nondeflated gross national product is conservative.

By means of this exercise Professor Morgenstern seeks to demonstrate that a reported change of 1.8 per cent might just as well be +12.5 per cent or −7.9 per cent. As a consequence he states:

> This simple arithmetical exercise combined with the indisputable fact that our final gross national product or national income data cannot possibly be free of error raises the question whether the computation of growth rates has any value whatsoever.

Let me approach this quite positively. Take the following statement on growth from *U.S. Income and Output* [1958 supplement to *Survey of Current Business*], p. 2: "Thus, total real output has quadrupled over the last 50 years. This rise represents an average annual growth of about 3 per cent—a rate which held approximately both in the 1909–29 period and in the subsequent 3-decade period." Is such a statement without any value whatsoever? I think not. Too much evidence of every description supports it. In the national accounts we have this evidence organized in ways that reduce the chance of significant error in any one segment.

The indicated rate might have been a little more or less perhaps; but not much more or less. In fact even if the level estimate in 1909 had been 5 per cent higher and the 1929 estimate 5 per cent lower, the calculated growth rate would have been about 0.5 per cent lower. Over the 48-year period, the difference in growth rates would have been about 0.2 of a percentage point lower.

The table below, which is organized in a similar fashion to that of Professor Morgenstern, illustrates this point, using reported figures of $104.1 billion for 1909 and $407.0 billion for 1957.

Annual rate of growth in GNP, 1909 to 1957, with assumed errors of ±5%

Year 1909 Reported figure: $104.1 Bill.	Year 1957 Reported figure: $407.0 Bill.		
Arbitrarily *assumed error of:*	*Arbitrarily* *assumed error of:* −5% 0 +5%		
	Implied growth *rates per year*		
−5%	2.9	3.0	3.1
0	2.8	2.9	3.0
+5%	2.7	2.8	2.9

The table illustrates that when a long time period is considered the effect of errors in the levels of the terminal years on the growth rate is small. Professor Morgenstern is apparently aware of this point in his book but failed to note its importance in the *Fortune* article. Nothing in this demonstration should be taken to mean that I agree with the propriety of assigning ±5 per cent errors to the terminal years. The differences in growth rates shown in the table are, of course, sizeable but they are very much smaller than the huge magnitudes highlighted by Professor Morgenstern.

Nevertheless, much of the criticism against the use or rather misuse of growth rates is deserved. Over a short period the selection of terminal years can determine the rate, and even if all intervening years in the short period are considered in calculating growth, the rate can be unduly affected by the level of a single year. More important perhaps is the need to recognize that there is little meaning to growth rates unless account is taken of the cycle. With proper care the term growth or trend if properly explained can be used for intercycle movements or even phases of cycles, but growth rates are more commonly calculated for periods that are long in relation to the length of a cycle.

Controversy over measurement of growth usually centers on the problems of measuring real product, that is, either physical quantities or value of output corrected for changes in prices. There is clearly a basis for a belief, as stated earlier, that a major source of error in our efforts to measure real product is our inability to measure adequately the output of new products and the changing quality of existing products. Our measures of growth then are understatements if qualities improve generally over time—and while errors may be in either direction in many periods, such random components of error are likely to be small compared to those errors (generally of understatement in the case of real product measures) which are in the same direction.

The *Fortune* article makes much of the uncertainties resulting from frequent revisions in the national income estimates. This subject has been discussed in greater detail elsewhere and only brief amplification seems desirable here.[8]

The principal revisions in the national income series appear in the July issue of the *Survey of Current Business*. The most recent three calendar years of data are usually subject to revision each July. The three-year revision permits the incorporation of trailing benchmarks provided by the Internal Revenue Service "Statistics of Income" and other annual data. From time to time major revisions such as those in the 1954 supplement (*National Income*) and the 1958 supplement (*U.S. Income and Output*) are made over much longer periods in order to incorporate basic data provided by the censuses (manufactures, trade and service, population, government, etc.). Revisions appearing in issues of the *Survey* other than the July issue are usually limited in number and result from special considerations.

A few years ago, we compared the quarter-to-quarter changes in the first estimates of several national income series published during the period 1947–1958 with the revised estimates in use at the end of 1958.[9] We found that the movements of the initial and final estimates of total GNP showed similar cycle-trend changes. For some series, e.g., gross private investment (including inventory changes) the revisions were much more marked.

There is attached a chart showing how year-to-year movements in national income have remained essentially the same over the period from 1947 to 1961 notwithstanding a number of revisions in data. The main point of the chart is to show that uncertainties in measuring changes caused by revisions in total national income can be overstated. Revisions have not appreciably altered the important shifts in total national income. Not all series would, of course, show the same consistency. For

[8] See, e.g., (a) The National Economic Accounts of the United States: Review, Appraisal and Recommendations, *Joint Economic Committee Reprint, 1957, pp. 220–222;* (b) George Jaszi, "The Statistical Foundations of the Gross National Product," Review of Economics and Statistics, *May, 1956.*
[9] Revisions of First Estimates of Quarter-to-quarter Movement in Selected National Income Series, 1947–1958 (Seasonally Adjusted Data), *Statistical Evaluation Reports, No. 2, Office of Statistical Standards, Bureau of the Budget, February, 1960.*

National income—successive July revisions, 1951–1961
SOURCE: United States national-income revisons, generally
in July supplements to Survey of Current Business, United
States Department of Commerce.

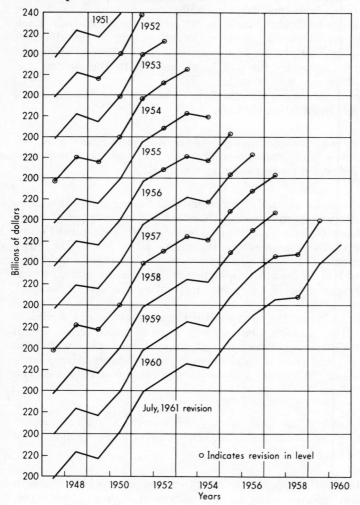

example, the series on entrepreneurial income was altered appreciably
by various revisions. Also the quarterly revisions referred to earlier would
be somewhat larger. Thus the chart is not necessarily a demonstration
of reliability of the estimates nor is it intended to minimize the need
for efforts to cut down on error.

Revisions in data reflect the needs for timeliness, frequency of reporting and accuracy. Timeliness can be obtained only at the price of using

partial information. Frequency—needed so that we can detect the onset of important changes—also can be obtained only with incomplete information. More complete information necessarily comes later, and it comes at different times, from different sources, for different items. In the accounts, checks are make quarterly, annually, quinquennially and over longer periods from trade data, surveys, tax returns, and censuses. Each of these sources contributes to revisions at different times for different items of income or expenditure. Hence a number of revisions are made over time in the aggregates for any given period. In the process the accuracy of the estimates is increased.

Data on unemployment are also singled out in Professor Morgenstern's treatment of errors in statistics. He says:

> In the United States two distinct series of unemployment statistics are produced by the Bureau of Employment Statistics [sic] and the Census. The discrepancies between these two series are enormous. . . .

This is an instance in which differences in data arising from differences in coverage and concepts are used in the article as an example of error, and the impression is given that the two series measure identical things. One series covers unemployment in the entire labor force. The other series is not intended to cover all unemployment, but reports only that insured by State and Federal unemployment insurance programs, which affect about 80 per cent of all wage and salary workers outside of agriculture.[10]

The President's Committee to Appraise Employment and Unemployment Statistics (the "Gordon Committee") went to considerable length to analyze the differences between estimates of unemployment from household surveys and from insured unemployment reports. After allowing for a number of differences, a close reconciliation was obtained. The Committee stated:

> In conclusion, the validity and accuracy of both series is largely confirmed by their similarity, on an adjusted basis, in level, trend, and cyclical behavior during the postwar period.[11]

In view of the Gordon Committee's findings, the statement in the article on "enormous" discrepancies in unemployment figures is quite surprising when it is realized that Professor Morgenstern mentions the Committee report in his book, from which the article was drawn. In his book, he says:

[10] See 1962 Supplement to Economic Indicators, *Historical and Descriptive Background Prepared for the Joint Economic Committee*, 87th Congress, 2nd Session, pp. 33, 37.

[11] Measuring Employment and Unemployment, *President's Committee to Appraise Employment and Unemployment Statistics*, 1962, p. 109, Chart No. 4.3; p. 110.

The Committee s report forms a very valuable addition to the material available on employment statistics and is a fine example of the sort of appraisal that needs to be made if users of economic statistics are to be sufficiently informed to make worthwhile use of statistics.[12]

Errors exist in data on unemployment—errors of response, of definition, and of seasonal adjustment, for example. The Morgenstern book discusses these. In the article, as in the book, however, the unfortunate impression is given that the "discrepancies" between the two sources of unemployment data constitute an indication of a major error in unemployment statistics.

The Gordon Committee summarized its investigation of the technical adequacy of the series as follows:

> On the basis of a careful examination supplemented by specially prepared studies, the Committee is convinced that the technical procedures utilized to provide employment and unemployment statistics are reasonably appropriate, given the practical circumstances under which the data are produced. It seems to the Committee that the general reliability of the estimates has been substantiated by close examination of the techniques and methods utilized and by the degree of agreement which the different series were found to exhibit during the course of the business cycle.[13]

Professor Morgenstern makes brief mention of data on prices and foreign trade. In the case of foreign trade his article appears to focus mainly on data from other countries, which in the present context are not our main concern. So far as United States data are concerned, the problem of error has been the object of sustained, organized study and planning under the coordination and leadership of my Office, and this effort is continuing. Hundreds of thousands of dollars have been devoted to projects designed specifically to improve the level of accuracy in these data, for which an unusually high standard is already imposed as a consequence of the amount of detail in which the data are made available. Moreover, the adequacy of our foreign trade data as a major component of the balance of payments is currently under study by the Review Committee for Balance of Payments Statistics—a panel of nongovernmental experts appointed for this purpose by the Director of the Bureau of the Budget.

The chief criticism of price data in the *Fortune* article is that the indexes of wholesale and retail prices are reported to two decimal places. The indexes are in fact reported to only one decimal place—but in any case this is hardly a major issue. I have some sympathy with Professor Morgenstern's view on the matter of rounding of figures generally, but I must point out that in fact rounding is common practice. How often

---

[12] Oskar Morgenstern, On the Accuracy of Economic Observations, 1963. *See Chapter 13, "Employment and Unemployment Statistics."*
[13] Measuring Employment and Unemployment, *pp. 16–17.*

have we seen the familiar footnote to a statistical table that "details do not add to totals because of rounding"?

It should also be added that there are reasons for as well as against showing figures beyond what Professor Morgenstern might consider an acceptable level of detail. While some gains may be obtained by avoiding the impression of spurious accuracy, some loss to the analyst may result from excessive rounding. One aspect relates to detail needed in a tabulation in any given period of time. A detailed composition of a total, by sector, subsector, geographic area, and other breaks is simply a cleaner job—and more useful for analysts—if parts are shown with more digits than the accuracy of the overall total warrants. Balance sheets sometimes require a similar use of "extra digits."

The second consideration relates to changes over time. Excessive rounding tends to result in very discrete movements which may distort changes over time. Also, sustained movement in a given direction for a series subject to very small changes, say an upward movement in consumer prices, is revealed much more clearly and correctly if shown to one decimal than if further rounded.

Apart from presentation of detailed tabulations, and of extended time series, it is probably true that some rounding would avoid unnecessary public attention given to a small change in a particular series.

Aside from the recommendations implicit in his discussion of the topics dealt with up to this point, there are essentially two recommendations explicit or implicit in Professor Morgenstern's article. One is philosophical, which seems to set up the natural sciences as the ultimate standard by which the achievements of the social sciences should be judged. The other is more concrete: namely, to assign quantitative measures to errors in Federal statistics. The article also recommends that agencies such as the Council of Economic Advisers, the Federal Reserve Board, and others, including private agencies "stop presenting economic data to the public as though they were free from fault."

As implied in the Kuznets quotation at the outset of this letter, Professor Morgenstern probably does not seriously expect the social sciences ever to achieve conditions of "controlled experiment" in the gathering of its main observations. (I am not referring here to what some might consider "controlled experiments" in simulation studies, but only to the gathering of data.) It has often been emphasized that the gathering of data in the social sciences (particularly the main bodies of economic data) will always involve an essential lack of control by the collection and tabulating agency, by those who construct the large systems of data, and by final analysts.[14] At each such stage, from the respondent to the final analyst, data are "collected" for a variety of purposes and are adapted rather than controlled for the inferences that are to be made.

Changes over time in economic and social processes also imply that our time series stretching over many years are measuring different phe-

[14] Simon Kuznets, "Conditions of Statistical Research," Journal of the American Statistical Association, March, 1950. See also Raymond T. Bowman, op cit.

nomena. The uniqueness of economic events is also an important feature of economic analysis. No two business cycles are exactly alike, and changes in growth over the years reflect complex changes in the economy.

Although Professor Morgenstern is well aware of the special problem in the social sciences, he nevertheless, in some vague way, wants to use the natural sciences as an ideal. He says:

> In appreciating the true condition of the data, economists cannot fail to develop economic theory in conformity with the high scientific standards set in the physical sciences.

In line with this quotation the *Fortune* article recommends that economic statistics should not be released without an accompanying estimate of their error. This is Professor Morgenstern's major recommendation.

How this is to be done for the major data systems such as GNP is not made clear except for the implication that subjective evaluations by the data producers would be helpful. These subjective valuations have a doubtful reliability particularly when applied to changes over time. A principal reason for having comprehensive data on total economic activity is to measure such changes.

The British Central Statistical Office has attempted to grade the reliability of levels in components of their accounts.[15] But similar grading for changes over time was generally not considered feasible except to indicate that errors in levels tended to be larger than in changes.

For the official U.S. estimates, while such quantitative grading has not been done, the major supplements to the *Survey of Current Business* do describe the different orders of reliability of components. Take two extreme examples: On the one hand,

> The annual estimates of total wages and salaries for the period since 1939 are extremely reliable. Over 90 per cent of the total consists of reported payroll information taken from accounting records of business and government. The lag between preliminary and final estimates is short, and the largest revision that has been required in recent years by the accession of later data has been less than 1 per cent of the total.[16]

On the other hand, with regard to income of unincorporated enterprises:

> Revisions were quite sizeable . . . and serve to point up the extreme difficulty of estimating entrepreneurial income well, particularly on an industry basis.[17]

[15] *Great Britain, Central Statistical Office*, National Income Statistics, Sources and Methods, *1956. See especially pp. 33–36.*
[16] National Income, *1954 Edition, p. 68. See also pp. 62–67.*
[17] U.S. Income and Output [*1958 supplement to Survey of Current Business*], p. 90.

Morgenstern's emphasis on the need for indicating errors in data to the public has some justification. This matter may not be a technical or statistical problem, however, so much as one of educating the public as to the basic nature of the data. It may involve the need for more consistency of tone between the reporting of increases and of decreases in activity. Some simpler explanatory material in statistical publications (for example a chart showing the movement of preliminary figures on retail sales in relation to final figures) might provide some gain for the general user of economic statistics.

Generally speaking, cautions on errors are rather technical statements. When they accompany regular reports (as in the case of the "Explanatory Notes" to the *Monthly Report on the Labor Force*)[18] they often constitute the most difficult part of the publication. This probably means they are not often read. They are, however, readily available to all analysts.

While agreeing with Morgenstern that more emphasis on error in statistics would be justified, I do not wish to leave the impression that little has been done. Indeed, the amount of effort devoted to problems of error in statistics by Federal Government agencies seems to me quite impressive, and the record of what has been accomplished is open to anyone who cares to read it. The record is too voluminous even to summarize here, but for the guidance of anyone wishing to pursue it, I have listed in an annex to this letter some of the kinds of materials that are readily available dealing with problems of error in economic and social statistics that have received attention of Government statisticians both in official publications and in professional journals. It is significant, I think, and I am sure it will not escape your attention, that the list includes valuable contributions to the literature in this field sponsored by the Joint Economic Committee.

A summary view of the appended list of publications indicates that we have done a great deal with quantifying and controlling errors in primary data. But understandably, we have done less with errors in large systems of data such as the economic accounts and industrial production.

It seems clear that these major data systems are faced with the most difficult problems of measurement of error in economic statistics. In these frameworks, quantitative measures of error, other than those based upon subjective judgments, have so far not been feasible. We have not adequately solved the problem of combining the overall effects of sampling error, response error, errors of estimation and concept and to evaluate their changing effects as a whole over time.

---

[18] *Each issue of the* Monthly Report on the Labor Force *carries estimates of the average standard error of major employment status categories from the household survey, showing the variations that might occur by chance because only a sample of the population is surveyed. The reader is referred to* Employment and Earnings *for a more complete statement, including estimates of errors of change as well as of level. For the employer survey, the* Monthly Report on the Labor Force *carries an indication of the effects of the most recent benchmark revision, comparing the sample estimates with the benchmark figures.*

This situation seems to suggest a dilemma. On the one hand we say that measurement of accuracy of such data has not been feasible. On the other hand we seek the continued improvement in accuracy of such data. How can we know whether accuracy is being improved if it has not been measured?

In point of fact we do try to "measure" or control accuracy, as the appended list of publications suggests, albeit not in the overly simplified sense implied in Professor Morgenstern's article.

Starting with the primary data, the essential ingredients for the accounts, we are exploring the sources and beginning to measure the extent of response error. These attempts include systematic audits of tax returns, recheck of responses furnished by households in the Current Population Survey, and examination of institutional records for checking individual reports of savings and debt. The subject of response error is a difficult one but we are making important beginnings.

Increasingly, information on the original schedule is transmitted direct to the computer, thus eliminating card punching errors. This procedure is not foolproof and is being improved.

Probability sampling procedures, as noted earlier, are followed where feasible to minimize bias due to sampling and to provide a basis for estimating sampling error. Samples also include a portion of identical respondents over periods of time to cut down on errors in measuring changes stemming from sampling error.

Estimates based on partial information are periodically adjusted to benchmarks for major economic series, as is well known. Benchmark adjustments constitute a principal basis for analysis of error in the major systems of data such as the economic accounts and industrial production.

Classification errors are being studied and reduced as classification systems are revised and made more detailed and as matching studies permit translation from one classification system to another. The company-establishment matching program at the Census Bureau is an example of this latter type of work.

In seasonal adjustment, assigning magnitudes to the "irregular" component of economic time series has permitted some evaluation of errors in seasonal factors. More broadly this has permitted the assessment of current changes in a time series in relation to its past behavior.

With improvements in basic data, the accuracy of our major data systems is improved. While most of the primary data are not collected specifically for use in the major data systems, we are increasingly adapting the various programs of primary data collection for such needs.[19]

It should be recognized that while the major frameworks inherit all the sources of error in primary data and introduce others besides, they do not compound these errors. They, in fact, tend to reduce or reconcile them. In part at least, errors do tend to offset one another. Also, the bringing together of primary data into the frameworks of our major data

[19] See A Federal Statistics Program for the 1960's, A Study Prepared for the Subcommittee on Economic Statistics of the Joint Economic Committee, 87th Congress, 2nd Session, Oct. 15, 1962, pp. 2, 10, 11.

systems—the national accounts, industrial production, flow-of-funds— serves in important ways to check relations between income and product, spending and savings, input and output, output and its financing and distribution, and the prices of transactions at these various levels of activity. These checks, often involving detailed comparisons among series, reflect the constraints involved in accounting and other economic relationships. The discrepancies revealed in the process are often disheartening but such disclosures lead to improvement.

Finally, in our analysis of economic changes, our judgments of changes are verified by the use of many series in combination.

On all levels, therefore, from collection of data to final analysis work is being done to try to insure and improve accuracy.

From all the foregoing it is evident that while we can work to describe errors as specifically as possible, we can never hope to eliminate them. We can hope to control them within manageable bounds.

Professor Morgenstern is an eminent mathematical economist who has done a service in calling the attention of less alert users to errors in economic statistics. But I am disappointed that his book and article have contributed little to proposing the framework or the practical procedures which might advance the work now going forward on the reduction of statistical errors. I know that I speak for my colleagues in other parts of the Federal statistical service as well when I say that we will welcome all suggestions for solving the difficult problems of error in economic data. In the meantime, work will continue to go forward on the many problems of identifying, measuring, controlling and reducing errors and informing the public of the statistical pitfalls facing the users.

Sincerely yours,

Raymond T. Bowman
Assistant Director for
Statistical Standards

PUBLICATIONS AND AVAILABLE MATERIAL
DEALING WITH ERROR IN
ECONOMIC AND SOCIAL STATISTICS

Census Bureau

POPULATION AND HOUSING

Evaluation and Research Program of the U.S. Censuses of Population and Housing 1960: Background, Procedures and Forms, Series ER 60, No. 1, 1963.
Infant Enumeration Study, 1950, 1953, 64 p.
The 1950 Censuses—How They Were Taken, 1955, 222 p.
The Post-enumeration Survey: 1950, Technical Paper No. 4, 1960.
Procedural Report on the 1960 Census of Population and Housing, Working Paper No. 16, 1963.

Taeuber, Conrad, and Morris H. Hansen, "A Preliminary Evaluation of the 1960 Census of Population," American Statistical Association, *Proceedings of the Social Statistics Section*, p. 56–73, 1963.

U.S. *Census of Population: 1950, Characteristics of the Population*, Vol. II, Part I, United States Summary, p. 1–71, 1953. U.S. *Census of Population: 1960, General Social and Economic Characteristics*, Final Report PC(1)-1c, United States Summary, p. XL–XLV, p. 1-342–1-344, 1962.

CURRENT POPULATION SURVEY

The Current Population Survey—A Report on Methodology, Technical Paper No. 7, 1963.

The Current Population Survey Reinterview Program: Some Notes and Discussion, Technical Paper No. 6, 1963.

Hansen, M. H., and W. N. Hurwitz, H. Nisselson, and J. Steinberg, "The Redesign of the Census Current Population Survey," *Journal of the American Statistical Association*, Vol. 50, No. 271, p. 701–719, September, 1955.

Hansen, Morris H., and Joseph Steinberg, "Control of Errors in Surveys," *Biometrics*, p. 462–474, December, 1956.

CENSUS OF AGRICULTURE

Check Enumeration, 1945 Census of Agriculture, Survey Report, June 20, 1947. (Not published.)

Hurley, R., and T. Jabine and D. Larsen, "Evaluation Studies of the 1959 Census of Agriculture," American Statistical Association, *Proceedings of the Social Statistics Section*, p. 91–103, September, 1962.

Jabine, Thomas B., "Checking the Accuracy of Area Statistics Obtained in the United States Census of Agriculture," Statistical Research Division, June 22, 1962.

Jabine, Thomas B., and Ray Hurley and William N. Hurwitz, "Sample Design and Estimation Procedure for the 1960 Sample Survey of Agriculture in the U.S.A.," Revised and expanded version of paper appearing in *Review of International Statistics*, Vol. 29, No. 3, January, 1963.

ECONOMIC CENSUSES

"Completeness of Coverage," *Census of Manufactures: 1958, Summary Statistics*, Vol. 1 (also see earlier volumes), p. 9, 1961. *Enterprise Statistics: 1958, Part 1—General Report, and Part 2—Central Administrative Offices and Auxiliaries*, 1963.

North, Max, and Ralph Woodruff, *Problems in Reconciling the 1958 Census of Retail Trade with the Monthly Retail Trade Report*, Draft, May 8, 1963.

"Problems of Measurement" and "Effects of Weight Year on Index Results," *Census of Manufactures: 1954, Indexes of Production*, Vol. IV, Chapters 3 and 4, 1958.

OTHER CENSUS BUREAU MATERIALS

The Accuracy of Census Statistics with and without Sampling, Technical Paper No. 2, 1960.

"Business Cycle Indicators: The Known and the Unknown," *Business Cycle Developments*, Series ES 1, No. 63-9, Appendix H, p. 69–79, Appendix C (in each issue), p. 63, and Bibliography, p. 79, September, 1963.

Eckler, A. Ross, and William N. Hurwitz, "Response Variance and Biases in Censuses and Surveys," *Bulletin of the International Statistical Institute*, Vol. 36, Part 2, 1958.

Hansen, M., and W. N. Hurwitz and Max A. Bershad, *Measurement Errors in Censuses and Surveys*, presented at the Annual Meeting of the International Statistical Institute, 32nd Session, May 30–June 9, 1960, Tokyo, February 8, 1960.

Neter, John, and Joseph Waksberg, "Effect of Length of Recall Period on Reporting of Expenditures in a Survey of Home-owners' Expenditures for Alterations and Repairs," American Statistical Association, *Proceedings of the Business and Economic Statistics Section*, p. 210–216, 1962.

Neter, John, and Joseph Waksberg, "Measurement of Non-sampling Errors in a Survey of Home-owners' Expenditures for Alterations and Repairs," American Statistical Association, *Proceedings of the Social Statistics Section*, p. 201–210, 1961.

Bureau of Labor Statistics

"The BLS Employment-series and Manufacturing Reporting Practices," *Monthly Labor Review*, Vol. 80, No. 11, p. 1367–1375, November, 1957.

"Explanatory Notes," *Monthly Report on the Labor Force*, p. 29–31, October, 1963.

Evans, W. Duane, "The Control of Non-sampling Errors in Social and Economic Surveys," *Bulletin of the International Statistical Institute*, Vol. 36, Part 2, p. 36–43, Stockholm, 1958.

Evans, W. Duane, "The Effect of Structural Matrix Errors on Inter-industry Relations Estimates," *Econometrica*, Vol. 22, No. 4, p. 461–480, October, 1954.

Kaitz, H., "The Irregular Component in Seasonal Adjustment," American Statistical Association, *Proceedings of the Business and Economic Statistics Section*, p. 200–209, September, 1962.

Pearl, Robert B., "Gross Changes in the Labor Force: A Problem in Statistical Measurement," *Employment and Earnings*, Vol. 9, No. 10, p. IV–X, April, 1963.

Raff, Morton S., and Robert L. Stein, "New Seasonal Adjustment Factors for Labor Force Components" and "BLS Seasonal Factor Method, 1963 Revision," *Monthly Labor Review*, Vol. 83, No. 8, August, 1960.

"Technical Note" and "New Benchmark Levels for BLS Establishment Employment Estimates," *Employment and Earnings, Annual Supplement Issue*, Vol. 10, No. 3, p. 1-E–11-E, p. IV–IX, September, 1963.

Bureau of Employment Security

"Insured Unemployment and Wage Statistics: Their Source, Nature and Limitations," *The Labor Market and Employment Security*, March, 1960.

Office of Business Economics

"Considerations of Reliability," *U.S. Income and Output: A Supplement to the Survey of Current Business*, p. 75–76, November, 1958.

Jaszi, G., *The Quarterly National Income and Product Account of the United States, 1942–62*, A paper written for 1963 meetings of International Association for Research in Income and Wealth, Corfu, Greece, 1963.

Jaszi, G., "The Statistical Foundations of the Gross National Product," *The Review of Economics and Statistics*, May, 1956. "Reliability of the Estimates," *National Income: A Supplement to the Survey of Current Business*, p. 62 et seq., 1954.

Internal Revenue Service

The Audit Control Program: A Summary of Preliminary Results, May, 1951.

Deming, W., *Review of the Sampling Procedures Used by the Internal Revenue Service to Produce Statistics of Income from Individual Tax Returns, with Special Emphasis on Achievement of Quality*, June 16, 1963.

"Description of the Sample and Limitations of the Data," *Statistics of Income, 1960–61, U.S. Business Tax Returns*, No. 438, p. 11 et seq., June, 1963.

Farioletti, Marius, "1948 Audit Control Program for Federal Income Tax Returns," *National Tax Journal*, June, 1949.

Farioletti, Marius, "Some Results from the First Year's Audit Control Program of the Bureau of Internal Revenue," *National Tax Journal*, March, 1952.

Agricultural Marketing Service

"Limitations," *Agriculture Handbook*, Vol. 7, No. 118, Chapter 1, December 4, 1957. (Also see other relevant sections of volumes 1–10 of this handbook.)

Joint Economic Committee

Reports of Federal Reserve Consultant Committees on Economic Statistics, Hearings before the Subcommittee on Economic Statistics of the Joint Committee on the Economic Report, 84th Congress, 1st Session, July 19 and 26, October 4 and 5, 1955 ("Statistics on Business Plant and Equipment Expenditure Expectations," Report of the Consultant Committee on Business Plant and Equipment Expenditure Expectations, p. 3–42; "Statistics of Saving," Report of the Consultant Committee on Savings Statistics, p. 65–226; "Consumer Survey Statistics," Report of the Consultant Committee on Consumer Survey Statistics, p. 251–372; "Statistics of Business Inventories," Report of the Consultant Committee on Inventory Statistics, p. 401–480; "An Appraisal of Data and Research on Businessmen's Expectations about Outlook and Operating Variables," Report of the Consultant Committee on General Business Expectations, p. 493–700).

Employment and Unemployment Statistics, Hearings before the Subcommittee on Economic Statistics, 84th Congress, 1st Session, p. 312, December 18–20, 1961.

Employment and Unemployment Statistics, Hearings before the Subcommittee on Economic Statistics, 84th Congress, 1st Session, p. 2–43, p. 162–167, November 7 and 8, 1955.

Measuring Employment and Unemployment, Hearings before the Subcommittee on Economic Statistics, 88th Congress, 1st Session, p. 47–53, June 6 and 7, 1963.

A *Federal Statistics Program for the 1960's,* A Study Prepared for the Subcommittee on Economic Statistics of the Joint Economic Committee by the Office of Statistical Standards, Bureau of the Budget, 87th Congress, 2nd Session, October 15, 1962.

Government Price Statistics, Part 1, Hearings before the Subcommittee on Economic Statistics of the Joint Economic Committee, 87th Congress, 1st Session, January 24, 1961.

Government Price Statistics, Part 2, Hearings before the Subcommittee on Economic Statistics of the Joint Economic Committee, 87th Congress, 1st Session, May 1–5, 1961.

Office of Statistical Standards

Nassimbene, Raymond, and Benjamin T. Teeter, *An Appraisal of OBE-SEC Estimates of Plant and Equipment Expenditures, 1947–58,* Statistical Evaluation Reports, Report No. 1, October, 1959.

Nassimbene, Raymond, and Benjamin T. Teeter, *Revisions of First Estimates of Quarter-to-quarter Movement in Selected National Income Series 1947–1958 (Seasonally Adjusted Data),* Statistical Evaluation Reports, Report No. 2, February, 1960.

Palmer, Gladys L., *The Reliability of Response in Labor Market Inquiries,* Technical Paper No. 22, July, 1942.

"Presentation of the Data," *Statistical Services of the United States Government,* Rev. Ed., p. 24–26, 1963.

Standards for the Publication of Statistical Data, A Guide Circular, Office of Statistical Standards, June 16, 1947.

NOTE: *This is not intended to be a complete bibliography of publications on the subject of error in economic and social statistics. It does, however, give an indication of the extent of materials available on the subject originating in U.S. Government sources.*

Bureau of the Budget
Office of Statistical Standards
February, 1964

ASSIGNMENTS FOR USE OF UNITED STATES CENSUSES AND ELEVEN OTHER LEADING SOURCES OF BUSINESS DATA

There are several purposes in the following two sets of assignments, one of which uses the United States Census and the other noncensus sources.

The first objective is to acquire a general knowledge of each reference in order to become ready to use the reference for research or to evaluate the research studies of others. This knowledge should include definitions, methods, and classifications. For example, the United States Census ordinarily gives great detail, but as a matter of policy it does not publish the data when there are only one or two items in a class. Otherwise, a specific manufacturer's information would be revealed if he were the only one in a class, and each of two manufacturers could determine the figure of the other by subtracting his own figure from the class total if there were only two in a class.

For each figure you are asked to determine, be sure of the unit used and preserve the exact reference, namely, the source, year of publication, volume, table, and page. You should examine the title of the table carefully, watch column and row tabs, inspect footnotes, and determine the source of the data as primary with the particular reference or secondary (reprinted from another source). This point is important because the particular sources you are consulting are often used as indices to other sources.

You should learn to use each source efficiently in order to get the most recent revision of figures. Usually, it is most efficient to start with the most recent compilation and work backward.

Observe the date of the most recent data contained in the current issue of each of the sources and the frequency of publication.

For each particular statistic you are seeking, be conscious of its complexity; that is, ascertain whether a count of the universe or a sample is the basis, whether the figure was derived by manipulation beyond a mere count, and whether the figure is an aggregate involving the combination of classifications.

Assignment Using United States Censuses

1. *Census of Population*
   How many women private-household laundresses were there in your home state in 1950?

2. *Census of Population*
   What was the median contract monthly rent paid in 1950 for dwelling units in the tract of your present residence?

3. *Census of Population*
   How many college presidents, professors, and instructors were there in your home state in 1950? How many earned $7,000 or more in 1949? What percentage earned $7,000 or more in 1949?

4. *Census of Housing*
   In what type of structure do you now reside? How many one- and two-dwelling units, semidetached, were there in the largest urban place of your home state in 1950?

5. *Census of Agriculture*
   How many farms in Illinois in 1954 reported that they grew cut flowers, potted plants, etc., under glass?

6. *Census of Manufactures*
   What was the (1) quantity and (2) value of product, Code 2031011, shipped by all manufacturing establishments for the United States in 1954? (You will need to use the *Standard Industrial Classification Manual.*)

7. How many drug and proprietary stores were there in Cedar Rapids, Iowa, and in the Cedar Rapids metropolitan area in 1954? How many drug stores with payroll? Reconcile the figures.

8. *Census of Business*
   How many retail trade establishments were there in Illinois and in your home state in 1954? In 1948? How many gasoline service stations were there in your home county in 1954?

9. *Census of Agriculture*
   What was the value of threshed or combined winter wheat produced on reporting farms in Tennessee in 1954? What state had the largest acreage in threshed or combined winter wheat, and how much was produced?

10. *Census of Manufactures*
    What was the value added by manufacture for all industries in the United States in 1954? In 1947? For cigarettes in 1954? In 1947?

11. *Census of Manufactures*
    How many man-hours were worked in the steel-springs industry in 1954? What was the average hourly wage?

Alternate Assignment Using United States Censuses

1. *Census of Business*
   How many automotive dealers were there in 1958 in Montgomery County, Texas? How many had paid employees?

2. *Census of Manufactures*
   What was the value of shipments and other receipts of the cellulosic–man-made–fibers industry in 1958? Of this amount how much was accounted for by the shipment of secondary products? How is a primary product defined?

3. *Census of Agriculture*
   How many farms were there in Minnesota in 1959? In 1935? In 1850? What is the definition of "farm" in these instances? What is the sampling error for items emunerated for only sample farms? What is the definition of "farm" in these instances?

4. *Census of Housing*
How many owner-occupied units valued at $25,000 or more were there in 1960 in the Kalamazoo, Michigan, Standard Metropolitan Statistical Area? Was this a sample or an actual count? What is an owner-occupied unit? How large a sample was used in the Kalamazoo area?

5. *Census of Governments*
How many local-government employees were there in Kentucky in October, 1962? How many full-time equivalent employees for fire protection?

6. *Census of Population*
How many foreign-born females under one year of age were there in the United States in 1960? Of these, how many were nonwhite? How many employed female rural-farm fishermen and oystermen were there in the United States in 1960?

7. *Censuses of Population and Housing; Census Tracts*
In the Haynes Heights area of Nashville, Tennessee, how many workers went to work in private automobiles in 1960? How many walked to work?

8. *Census of Mineral Industries*
What was the value added for the oil and gas field contract services industries in 1954?

Assignment Using Basic Statistical Sources Other Than United States Censuses

1. *Statistical Abstract of the United States*
What were the sources and uses of funds for research and development in this country in 1950 and 1957? What change is most noticeable between these two years?

2. *Survey of Current Business* (including biennial, weekly, and national-income supplements)
What was the index of industrial production for electrical machinery and wool textiles in 1956?

3. *Monthly Labor Review*
Find the number of new dwelling units started in nonmetropolitan places in the fourth quarter of 1953 and the first quarter of 1958.

4. *Federal Reserve Bulletin; Banking and Monetary Statistics*
What were the adjusted loans of all weekly-reporting member banks outside New York City on the dates nearest May 15, 1924, and November 15, 1957?

5. *Minerals Yearbook*
By what method has most of bituminous coal and lignite been shipped from mines in the United States? Find the average for the percentage of these shipments for the years 1953 to 1957.

6. *Economic Almanac*
What were annual shipments of wire rods in 1948 and 1956? What percentage of annual shipments of steel products did these shipments of wire rods represent in 1956? What was the percentage of disposable income received by the top 5 per cent of the population in 1939 and 1946? What were personal savings of individuals as a percentage of the personal income in 1929 and 1956? Find the rate of change in personal savings between 1929 and 1956 in undeflated and deflated values.

7. *Agricultural Statistics*
What were the exports of United States oranges to Mexico in 1954 and 1955?

8. *Commodity Yearbook*
What was the total production of refined lead from domestic ores in 1957?

9. *Quarterly Summary of Foreign Commerce*
What was the number of lawn-tennis balls imported into the United States in the third quarter of 1957?

10. *Standard and Poor's Trade and Securities Statistics*
What was the gross debt of the Federal government in 1917, 1918, 1939, 1942, 1945, and 1957? Express the 1917 and 1957 figures on a per capita basis. What were the receipts of the Federal government in March, 1954, and how does this figure compare with the average monthly receipts? In which month are these receipts generally lowest?

11. Using the *Year Book of the American Bureau of Metal Statistics, Minerals Yearbook,* and *Statistical Abstract,* determine the United States apparent consumption of aluminum in 1954 and 1960.

Alternate Assignment Using Basic Statistical Sources Other Than United States Censuses

1. *Statistical Abstract of the United States*
What percentage of the total number of spending units in the United States owned automobiles in 1952? What percentage of automobiles owned were seven years old or older?

2. *Survey of Current Business* (including biennial, weekly, and national-income supplements)
What was the number of short tons of primary aluminum production in the United States in February, 1957, February, 1953, and February, 1941?

3. *Historical Statistics of the United States from Colonial Times to 1957; Statistical Abstract*
What was the total mileage of public roads built by and under the control of state highway departments in 1929, 1947, and 1954?

4. *Monthly Labor Review*

What were the average weekly earnings of production workers or nonsupervisory employees in the total paper and allied products industry in June of each of the years from 1954 to 1957, inclusive?

5. *Federal Reserve Bulletin; Banking and Monetary Statistics*

What were adjusted loans of all weekly-reporting member banks in New York City on the dates nearest February 15, 1957, and February 15, 1922?

6. *Minerals Yearbook*

What was the number of active sand and gravel pits in Cook County, Illinois, in 1953? How much fluorspar was shipped from mines in Illinois in the year of greatest shipments? What was the average value per ton in Illinois that year?

7. *Economic Almanac*

What was the value of the residential building construction contracts awarded in 37 Eastern states in 1946? What were the 11 states not covered? (Use of another source is suggested.) What was realized national income per capita adjusted by cost of living in 1839, 1941, and 1957? What was the personal saving of individuals as a percentage of personal income in 1929 and 1956?

8. *Commodity Yearbook*

What was the stock of wheat on hand in the continental United States on July 1, 1955, and July 1, 1956? Account for the change if you can.

9. *Agricultural Statistics*

In question 8 your reconciliation required the figure for production. Does this production figure tie in with what you can find in *Agricultural Statistics*?

10. *Standard and Poor's Trade and Securities Statistics*

What was the consumption of scoured apparel-class wool in May, 1938, May, 1953, and May, 1957?

11. *Quarterly Summary of Foreign Commerce*

What was the number of lawn-tennis balls imported into the United States in the third quarter of 1957?

RESEARCH AND SCIENTIFIC METHOD

LOGIC AND TERMINOLOGY

Many books have been written about scientific method and, in fact, about various subdivisions of this topic. Hence this treatment, while seeking to be comprehensive, will not be extensive. For more extensive development of each aspect of scientific method, the reader is referred to the Selected Bibliography at the end of this part.

Our approach to the subject is to break scientific method into a series of specific problems or aspects and to consider each in turn. We shall not be as deeply concerned with the specific techniques as with the method of organizing the total research effort.

Logic is an important element in research, but mere logic can be sterile. Another important element is evidence, but evidence requires interpretation. Particularly when one piece of evidence is paired with another, conclusions can differ depending on what pieces of evidence we pair.

Before we go further, it is wise to specify the terms we shall be using. Logic can be defined as the laws governing thinking. We may outline thinking as involving (1) ideas which are the objects of thought and are stated in units called terms, (2) judgments which express the mutual relations of ideas or terms in the form of propositions, and (3) arguments which employ syllogisms.

The syllogism is the form of reasoning to which all others can be reduced. It consists of three propositions so related to one another that given two of them, the third necessarily follows. These three propositions are identified as the major premise, the minor premise, and the conclusion. In a syllogism there must be only three terms: the major term, the minor term, and the middle term. The following example makes this clear:

	Middle term:	Major term:
Major premise:	All jewels are mineral substances.	
	Minor term:	Middle term:
Minor premise:	All diamonds are (some of) jewels.	
	Minor term:	Major term:
Conclusion:	Therefore, all diamonds are mineral substances.	

Although this use of the syllogism leads to identifying the reasoning as deductive, namely, reasoning from a universal proposition to a particular, it should be noted that reasoning from particulars to a universal, a process called inductive or experimental reasoning, must also employ the syllogism. Later in this part, extended consideration will be given to the contrasting of deductive and inductive reasoning.

The general rules governing the syllogism are as follows:

1. There must be three terms and only three.
2. No term can have greater extension in the conclusion than it has in the premises.
3. The middle term must not appear in the conclusion.
4. The middle term must be distributed; that is, it must appear in one premise (the major premise) with the word "all" before it (at least impliedly) and in the other premise (the minor premise) with the word "some" before it (at least impliedly).
5. No conclusion can be drawn from two negative premises.
6. A negative conclusion cannot be drawn from two affirmative premises.
7. No conclusion can be drawn from two particular premises. (A particular premise is one which in effect has "some" before the first term.)
8. The conclusion must follow the weaker premise; that is, it must be particular if either premise is particular and must be negative if either premise is negative.

We may agree with the proposition in a conclusion but object to the logical process by which it is established. An example is the saying "You are right but for the wrong reason."

There are three terms which are commonly used interchangeably: conclusion, inference, and generalization. Strictly speaking, however, the term "inference" describes the outcome of inductive reasoning, and the term "conclusion" the end result of deductive reasoning. Usually "generalization" involves a more modest identification of a conclusion or an inference, one that because of inaccuracies in measurements or some other source of doubt does not seem to be securely established.[1]

It goes without saying that these definitions and the short treatment of the syllogism are far from covering the subject of logic.

Evidence consists of facts, that is, observations and measurements, which are cited to support a proposition. In terms of the syllogism, the proposition which involves the use of evidence is usually the minor premise since the major premise is most often assumed as true for purposes of the particular research project. Evidence also includes those computations and tests based on the observations and measurements. Thus, for example, statistics generated by computations from the observed data are evidence.

[1] *"Generalization" is also used loosely in a way that does not have meaning in a discussion of scientific method.*

We shall not invade the realm of philosophy, and hence we shall not wrestle with the problem of what it means to prove a conclusion. We shall maintain the skeptical attitude that we are merely seeking to determine whether an extensive network of evidence is *consistent* with a particular conclusion, inference, or generalization. Many times in the history of science, a researcher has become convinced that he has *proved* this or that proposition, but later researchers have discovered evidence which cannot be incorporated into his theory and is not consistent with his conclusion.

SUMMARY STATEMENT OF SCIENTIFIC METHOD

As a prelude to our explanation of scientific method, we can frame our concern as follows:

1. What is the problem or purpose being pursued?
2. How can the problem be solved or the purpose attained?

As we shall see, the answer to the first question may involve serious difficulties, but it is the second question that more immediately involves scientific method. In a rough way, we can state that the answer to the second question is to establish a working hypothesis, that is, a proposed explanation or answer. This hypothesis is then tested by observations and measurements. It is more than likely that the evidence so gathered will not jibe with the working hypothesis. Hence the hypothesis will be stated in a revised form which is consistent, or at least more nearly consistent, with the evidence. Then further testing is undertaken. This process may be repeated many times. There is no guarantee, of course, that the end result will be labeled successful, but at least we shall accumulate much negative knowledge; that is, we shall learn that the exact activities we have undertaken in the research do not support the hypothesis. This type of knowledge may be particularly useful in business, where our purpose often is not only to find projects with which we want to become involved but also to identify an area to be avoided because our research has demonstrated that *we* cannot be successful in such an area other than coincidentally (at least not without further research).

In the process just described, the critical question is: Where does one find a working *hypothesis?* This is a matter of creative insight. The likelihood of achieving a creative insight may be increased by having a comprehensive knowledge of the general area in which the research will be undertaken. Thus a knowledge of many established propositions collateral to the research area will likely direct the researcher's thinking. This appears to be so because each researcher builds upon the work of previous researchers. On the other hand, knowledge of the general area may handicap us by making it more difficult to challenge propositions that seem well established, whereas a researcher who is new to the area may balk more readily at accepting such propositions.

Once the problem or purpose being pursued has been established and a working hypothesis selected, we are immediately confronted with the matter of definitions. In fact we are confronted with definitions both in setting our problem and in proposing a working hypothesis. How things will be defined will depend upon the problem and the working hypothesis. As will be developed later, we are thinking of definitions in a sense other than that in which definitions are given in a dictionary, where the thing being defined is related to other concepts already known to the reader. Rather we are using "definition" in the sense of the so-called operational definition. Thus in the dictionary "wood" may be defined as the structural part of a tree, but this definition assumes we know what a tree is. An operational definition, in contrast, involves describing all the characteristics that might be used to distinguish wood from other materials. Thus, combustibility under given test conditions, electrical conductivity under given test conditions, and the exact status of wood with reference to many such attributes would be used until we identified a category which included only wood and everything in the category was wood.

The matter of definitions is related not only to the problem being pursued and to the working hypothesis but also to the measurements and testing to be undertaken. For example, once terms have been defined, measurements will be made and these will involve errors in measurement. It is clear that some alteration of a definition may reduce the errors of measurement without impairing the definition's usefulness in pursuing the problem and testing the working hypothesis.

In conducting tests of a working hypothesis, the use of a control group is indicated. Such a group consists of items which will proceed side by side with the test items. The members of the control group will not, however, be subject to the same treatment as the test group, so that we can infer that any difference in results between the control and test groups is associated with the difference in treatment. This inference will finally be compared with the results of other relevant research to determine whether or not there is consistency.

Defects in the Crude Concept of Scientific Method

At this point, the popular concept of scientific method can be presented simply; indeed it is oversimplified.[2]

---

[2] *A popularly written attack on the popular concept of scientific method appears in James B. Conant,* Science and Common Sense, *rev. ed. (New Haven, Conn.: Yale University Press, 1960). In chap. 3, "Concerning the Alleged Scientific Method" (pp. 42–62), the former president of Harvard dissents from the classical statement by Karl Pearson in* The Grammar of Science *(New York: E. P. Dutton & Co., Inc., 1937). Conant summarizes his criticism of Pearson's position very well at p. 44: "To attempt to formulate in one set of logical rules the way in which mathematicians, historians, archaeologists, philologists, biologists and physical scientists have made progress would be to ignore all the vitality in these varied undertakings. Even within the narrow field of the development of concepts and conceptual schemes*

In this conception, we proceed through the following steps:

1. Observations
2. Measurements
3. Hypotheses
4. Theories (a set of hypotheses)

At each of the three "higher" levels, there is a reversion to the preceding levels for testing. Thus measurements are related to observations for a first-level generalization. Likewise, hypotheses are tested by measurements and observations. Finally, theories are tested with hypotheses, measurements, and observations.

The difficulty with this bald statement of scientific method can be illustrated as follows: We may *observe* that a man prefers situation X to situation Y and *conclude* the man prefers X to Y. We may *observe* that man prefer situation Y to situation Z and *conclude* the man prefers Y to Z. If there is transitivity[3] among X, Y, and Z, then X will be preferred to Z. This can be tested by *observing* whether X is preferred to Z. We can give a concrete example: A man may prefer an orange to a boat ride and prefer a boat ride to owning a picture, and yet it is quite possible for him not to prefer the orange to owning the picture.

Similarly, we can test the hypothesis that there is a significant difference in, say, honesty between two groups. Note, however, that a number of different conclusions are possible:

1. Accepting or rejecting the hypothesis
2. Rejecting the measurements
3. Rejecting the observations

The summary of the popular conception of scientific method as observations, measurements, hypotheses, and theories sounds plausible, but there are errors of omission and commission. The distinctions between observation, measurement, hypothesis, and theory are not easy to make, and the question whether a particular statement is a statement of fact

---

from experiments (experimental science), it is all too easy to be fascinated by oversimplified accounts of the methods used by the pioneers. . . . There is no such thing as the scientific method" [emphasis in original]. Pearson had written: "The scientific method is marked by the following features: (a) careful and accurate classification of facts and observations of their correlation and sequence; (b) the discovery of scientific laws by the aid of the creative imagination; (c) self-criticism and the final touchstone of equal validity for all normally constituted minds." Conant crystallizes the three elements of modern science as "(1) speculative general ideas, (2) deductive reasoning, and (3) experimentation [to test hypotheses]."

[3] *Transitivity exists when we are considering only one dimension. When we are comparing X and Y in one dimension (such as weight) and Y and Z in another dimension (such as length), it is possible to prefer X to Y because X is lighter than Y and to prefer Y to Z because Y is shorter than Z, but to prefer Z to X because Z is sweeter.*

or a statement of theory is not easily answered. Fortunately, that question need not be finally decided en route to the more important question whether a particular statement should be accepted, rejected, or declared meaningless.

It is quite legitimate to inquire whether the measurement language is unambiguous. It is also legitimate to reject the measurement as inadequate, and this rejection may rest on intuitive grounds. With reference to our previous example, if a man is indifferent in choosing between an orange and a boat ride and between a boat ride and owning a picture, we might conclude that these give him equal utilities *or* we might conclude that this is evidence that the man is confused rather than that he rates the utilities of the goods as equal.

Similarly hypotheses may be held to be meaningless when there is an absence of rigorous statement, as often occurs with the crude statement of scientific method. Thus the proposition that "four out of five people endorse cigarette smoking" is most likely not accompanied by a rigorous definition of "people" or of "cigarette smoking." Without such definitions the statement is meaningless, that is, lacking in precision, and hence it has no legitimate usefulness. We grant that there might be "usefulness" to the person who claims a fee for doing the survey that leads to the statement. We deny that the one who bought the results could make *legitimate* use of the statement although he might employ the statement in his advertising in order to increase cigarette sales.

The key difficulty with the whole popular conception of scientific method lies at the very base, namely, in the thought that observations are facts, that these facts are somehow more secure than measurements, that measurements are more secure than hypotheses, and that these in turn are more secure than theories. Ultimately, the acceptance of facts or observations must rest on sense experience. The need to rely on sense experience is the reason why scientists check and recheck observations. Whether a fact or an observation is accepted or included depends on one's *theory*. Conant recognizes this point when he describes experimental science in this way: "(1) A problem is recognized and an objective formulated; (2) all the relevant information is collected (*many a hidden pitfall lies in the word 'relevant'!*); (3) a working hypothesis is formulated; (4) deductions from the hypothesis are drawn; (5) the deductions are tested by actual trial; (6) depending on the outcome, the working hypothesis is accepted, modified, or discarded."[4]

Thus even such a seemingly direct observation as cash on hand for a business involves problems of observation. Aside from observation, the certified public accountant draws on considerable accounting theory before he forms an opinion on a statement he is examining. For example, what is the appropriate definition? Are checks drawn but not yet cashed to be deducted from the bank balance or is the bank balance to be shown as it is and the outstanding checks shown as a liability?

---

[4] *Conant, op. cit., p. 50. The italics are supplied and bring out the need for theory even at the inception of research.*

The reason why an observation involves a theory is that observation implies selection. We must have a subuniverse that is small enough to observe, and it is difficult to be sure that each time we make an observation we have the same subuniverse.[5]

FORMULATING THE PROBLEM

It is axiomatic that research cannot proceed in a vacuum. A researcher who denies he has a specific purpose is simply refusing to state it explicitly even to himself, for the purpose is there at least implicitly. One of the penalties for not being explicit is that bias can filter in. The purpose of the research is usually stated in the very first paragraph of the research project and indicated in the title of the report.

From experience we find that the initial research project of a student in the social sciences often leads him to feel that if he can only find the appropriate data, all the remaining difficulties will be largely self-liquidating. This stage in the experience of a researcher in business is quite understandable. There are two reasons for such a feeling.

First, research in the social sciences often involves a situation different from that in the physical and biological sciences. The data of the typical researcher in the physical or biological sciences are generated by his own activities. At the present stage of the social sciences this is seldom true, although the likelihood of such self-generated data is greater in the fields of business and economics than in some of the other social sciences such as sociology and, certainly, history.[6] As a result of the necessity for relying on data gathered by others, the researcher in the social sciences must be quite conscious of his dependence on such data.

Second, and by the same token, since the researcher in the social sciences is not generating his own data, he is likely to forget the problems of data. Such data are certainly subject to all the errors which afflict data in the physical and biological sciences. Unfortunately, many of the gatherers of data in the social sciences do not furnish a complete report of the circumstances surrounding the collection of the data, such as the method of drawing a sample or the choice of an interviewer to take down responses as opposed to a questionnaire to be answered with no one else present. In fact, there may not be any report on the circumstances, and either the gatherer of the data or the present researcher may be unaware of the importance of data problems.

Thus the data of the social sciences are snarled in difficulties which tempt the researcher to focus primarily on the data area and in many cases to exhaust himself in the pursuit of these problems. If one's stamina is great enough, this is a blessing in disguise because the closer the researcher is to his data, the more effective he can be in research.

[5] *Cf. E. Bright Wilson, Jr.,* An Introduction to Scientific Research *(New York: McGraw-Hill Book Company, 1952), p. 24.*
[6] *Cf. Oskar Morgenstern,* On the Accuracy of Economic Observations, *2d ed. (Princeton, N.J.: Princeton University Press, 1963), pp. 14ff.*

It might seem that we have placed the cart before the horse by raising data problems before formulating the research problem. In the case of a simple research problem, we may be able to formulate the problem before raising data questions. The problem may be self-evident. We know what we are seeking. Thus, for example, we may seek the determinants of demand in the toy industry. In many cases, however, research enters more difficult areas. Thus all we may know is that what had been a working and effective organization of men, machines, and materials has more or less suddenly lost efficiency and deteriorated. In a broad sense, this *is* the problem. But to come to grips with the situation the area of investigation must be narrowed if the likelihood of finding answers is to be raised very far above the level of chance probability of success.

The approach we have just indicated places research in the area of decision making. As such, the problem of defining or formulating the research problem is susceptible to the same techniques that are applied to all decision making.[7] The elements of such decision-making problems are:

1. The decision maker
2. His objectives
3. Possible courses of action
4. The environment, which consists of
   a. States of nature
   b. Conduct of other decision makers and hence reactions and counteractions.

The initial difficulty centers in the environment, which has currently been described as a "system." In this usage, a system may be defined as a set of desires and activities connected by a flow of information which ultimately yields actions intended to satisfy desires.

Having framed the problem of formulating the problem for research in this way, we have identified the areas for study. The dominant desires must be identified: conflicting or incompatible desires may have developed. The information channels must be identified, and their efficiency assessed. For example, information channels have capacity limits. The points at which this information flow is analyzed, sorted, or combined with other flows are important. Ultimately, this information arrives in the hands of decision makers, who act so as to produce changes in present activities or operations which in turn have efficiencies. For example, these operations have capacities.

Thus, the broad area of research might be work stoppages at an economy-wide, industry-wide, company-wide, or plant level. Instead of striking out on a strictly hunch basis to investigate one factor after another in a somewhat unorganized manner, we may conduct a systems analysis

[7] Cf. Russell L. Ackoff, S. K. Gupta, and J. Sayre Minas, *Scientific Method: Optimizing Applied Research Decisions* (*New York: John Wiley & Sons, Inc., 1962*), *chap. 3, pp. 67–107.*

in an effort to narrow the number of alternatives for investigation. In one sense we are narrowing the areas we shall pursue, and yet we are making more certain that we do not miss presumptively likely areas.

We have indicated how analysis of the environment is relevant to the problem of formulating the research problem. But we mentioned three other elements: the decision maker, his objectives, and possible courses of action. It may seem gratuitous to list the decision maker. In many cases the researcher determines all questions, but in numerous others a foundation, the Federal government, a business, or a trade association may be sponsoring the research and defining the investigation. Just who is making the decisions for the sponsoring group?

Similarly, the statement of the decision maker's objectives may seem to present no problems. Platitudes are often stated and are of no help at this point. There may be problems of suboptimization[8] hidden in the platitudes.

As soon as we have stated an objective, we are necessarily involved with problems of measuring the degree of achievement of that objective.[9] Perhaps the most frequently stated objective of business research is to increase profits. We can define profits as the difference between income and costs. This would seem simple enough, but is our objective to maximize profits in the current period or over the long range? How far into the future is our horizon? The further we look into the future, the greater the degree of uncertainty. And since a dollar received sometime in the future is presently worth less than a dollar received today, we are necessarily confronted with the determination of a discount rate. Further, a dollar of profit received as the result of one alternative action cannot be directly compared with a dollar of profit received from another action unless the risk in each alternative is the same.

The possible courses of action in research depend heavily on the variables which affect the problem. Which of these can be controlled? Variables may be essentially quantitative or qualitative in nature. To establish which variables are significant for the problem may require preliminary regression analysis or designed experiments.

TENTATIVE MODEL

The concept for which the physical sciences employ the term "working hypothesis," the social sciences describe by the term "model." We have now come far enough to realize that a model precedes observations.

[8] *Suboptimization arises when there are conflicting objectives. Thus to state that we want the best solution to a business problem may be interpreted to mean that we want to maximize immediate profits or that we want to achieve a maximum share of the market. If these two objectives are in conflict in a particular case, one will be given preference over the other. The subordinated objective will then be maximized after the prime objective has been maximized and will be subject to the constraint that the maximization of the prime objective be not disturbed.*
[9] *Cf. C. West Churchman,* Prediction and Optimal Decision: Philosophical Issues of a Science of Values *(Englewood Cliffs, N.J.: Prentice-Hall, Inc., 1961), pp. 50–69.*

There are several characteristics of all models. First, the model is simpler than reality, and the model is teleological, that is, directed to representing what is considered (for our purposes) as relevant to reality. Thus in mechanical models of the solar system, the balls used to represent planets do not need to have the same temperatures as the planets they represent. A model is also easier to manipulate than reality because it does not include as many variables. Likewise, the relationship used in the model, for example, a linear relationship, may be only an approximation of a far more complicated relationship in reality.[10]

The model, if it is a successful representation of reality, will not only explain the present and past reality but will have predictive properties which in turn establish a basis for control over the future. These added properties are premised on (1) the continuation of (stability in) the same set of independent variables as dominant and (2) the continuation of the relationship between the independent variables and dependent variables.

We can classify models as iconic, analogue, and mathematical (or symbolic). An iconic model is one that differs from reality only in scale, such as a model of a dam. One prime concern is that the reduction or enlargement of the scale of *all* aspects of the iconic model be proportionate.

In an analogue model, one property of the model is used to represent another property in reality. The slide rule is an analogue in which quantities are represented by distances in proportion to the logarithms of the quantities. Hydraulic systems are sometimes represented by electrical systems, the flow of the liquid being represented by the flow of electricity. Thus a legend is always used in an analogue model.

Mathematical models use symbols to represent quantities. Equations constitute a symbolic model showing the relationship of variables.

As representations of reality these models vary from the iconic, which is closest to reality, to the symbolic or mathematical, which is more abstract. On the other hand, the ease in manipulation of the models increases as we depart from reality, the order of ease being the mathematical model, the analogue, and the iconic model.

The iconic and analogue models have considerable pedagogical value since they are easier to understand,[11] and often they are used as preludes to setting up a mathematical model.

Mathematical models employ equations (using an $=$ sign) and inequations (using greater than $>$, less than $<$, equal to or greater than $\geq$, and equal to or less than $\leq$) with the dependent variable on the

[10] Cf. E. F. Beach, Economic Models (*New York: John Wiley & Sons, Inc., 1957*).
[11] *The large hydraulic machine invented at the London School of Economics by A. W. Phillips is an analogue of income flows in the British economy as a result of monetary policies of the government. The machine, dubbed the Moniac, is described in W. T. Newlyn, "The Phillips-Newlyn Hydraulic Model,"* Yorkshire Bulletin of Economic and Social Research, *vol. 2, no. 2, pp. 111–127, July, 1950; and by A. W. Phillips, "Mechanical Models in Economic Dynamics,"* Economica, N.S., *vol. 17, no. 67, pp. 283–305, August, 1950.*

left-hand side and the independent variables on the right-hand side. In its most general form, the model states that the dependent variable is a function of (that is, varies with) the independent variables in a stable relationship. This is simply stated in symbols as

$$D = f(I_1, I_2)$$

where D is the dependent variable and I_1 and I_2 are the independent variables with f (function of) describing the relationship (linear, for example).

It is clear that all variables not expressly stated in the equation are assumed to be constant, or self-canceling with regard to other nonstated variables, or, lastly, so minute in their effect that they can be ignored. Thus the key problem in constructing a model is to attain a balance between (1) accurate representation of reality, which would require recognition of a very large number of variables and their introduction into the equation or system of equations, and (2) practical considerations of ease in manipulating the model mathematically.[12]

The model may be quite simple; for example, one variable may change linearly with another. In a simple form, the model may be called a working hypothesis, but even a more complicated model can be called a working hypothesis.

DEFINITIONS

To proceed to test the model, each of the variables, each of the constants, and the relationship must be defined. The model or hypothesis is no more than a skeleton until its terms have been defined. Unfortunately, it is frequently the case that all too much effort is expended on the model and little or no attention given to explicit definitions. Without careful definitions, the questions of the relevance of observational data cannot be pursued effectively.

[12] *Models may be further classified into two categories. The first is a model of the behavior of phenomena. Into this category fall scientific laws and generalizations. The second category involves a model in which the values of some of the independent variables (called "input variables" and reflecting the alternatives open to the one using the model) are subject to constraints or determinations by the one employing the model but in which other independent variables (also called input variables but further described as "parameters") cannot be so controlled. This is called a decision model. In this type of model, the dependent variable (or "output variable") is some measure of the value of alternative choices available to the one using the model. It is in the case of the decision model that the employment of inequations is most frequently made to reflect constraints. Thus the dependent variable may be limited to a given amount of resource. In such a case, the inequation can be stated as $D \leq I_1, I_2$. A series of such constraints would result in a system of inequations to be solved simultaneously. The area of decision models falls within a field called operations research. Cf. D. W. Miller and M. K. Starr, Executive Decisions and Operations Research (Englewood Cliffs, N.J.: Prentice-Hall, Inc., 1960).*

Defining seems a simple enough matter. We are all familiar with the dictionary. This type of definition is called conceptual because the procedure is to relate the term being defined to one or more other concepts. Since the important work of Bridgman[13] in 1927 in the theory of defining, however, another category of definitions has been established, namely, the operational definition, which for purposes of definition refers any concept to the concrete operations by which we gain knowledge of the thing being defined. In brief, we can gain knowledge of a thing (beyond very skeletal information from "looking at" or "hearing" it) only by trying to burn it and reporting what happens, or by subjecting it to low temperatures, and so on. The difficulty is that we do not yet have a workable theory of operational defining.

Perhaps the matter of defining can best be developed by an example. Suppose that we are studying the demand for room-type air conditioners. Such a demand should have some relation to the number of rooms in the country. Unfortunately, there are no statistics available as to the number of rooms in the country. But even if there were, how should a "room" be defined? As a space with four walls, a floor, and a ceiling? Does the size (cubic space) of the room make any difference? A closet fits the definition thus far. Is an auditorium a room? It is clear that the definition we want is related to the purpose at hand. Likewise how precise a definition we want depends on what margin of error we are willing to accept in the results of the research.

If we are able to formulate a definition in terms of the operations of the thing defined, we have established a link with the problem of measurement. Much remains to be done in the field of operational definitions, and in the meantime use is made of an older approach which we shall outline.

As we have already indicated, the model for research will employ variables and constants and their relationship. The most common characteristics of these variables and constants will be (1) the number or count and (2) the amount of some property of the variable. The most common types of variables and constants to be defined are classified as objects, events, or properties of either objects or events. In defining an object or an event, we are in turn forced to make the definition in terms of properties.

While there are many ways in which properties can be classified, the most important distinction for research purposes is made between structural and functional properties. We can best bring out the difference between the two by identifying a structural property as one that is deterministic and a functional property as probabilistic. A structural property normally exists in physical terms, whereas a functional property involves a cause-and-effect or producer-product relationship.

In defining a structural property, we seek to define (identify) the class of objects to be observed, the conditions for observation, the operations

[13] P. W. Bridgman, The Logic of Modern Physics (New York: The Macmillan Company, 1927).

(if any) to be performed, the instrument or standards used, and the observations to be made. In the case of a functional property, we are concerned with the probability that a result will occur, such as an individual's choosing a path or a course of action's producing an outcome.

MEASUREMENT AND ERRORS

The purpose of measurement[14] is to make the events or objects being analyzed amenable to mathematical description and analysis. We have established that a definition should tell us the conditions or circumstances under which we should make observations. Measurement is the way we get symbols to represent the properties of objects or events. In a restricted sense, it involves the use of a constant unit of measurement.

The use of classification as a device straddles the problems of definition and of measurement. Classification enables us to isolate that part of the universe which is being studied. Classification also enables us to establish classes or categories within the part of the universe being studied. At least to the extent of classification, all knowledge of all types of subjects is capable of being quantified. And once we have counts, numerical analysis is possible. For example, in studying work stoppages in the field of labor relations, the record of stoppages can be classified by the time when the stoppage occurred, by length of stoppage, by whether the stoppage occurred in a union or a nonunion situation and the type of union in the union case, by whether preceding relations had been consistently good or bad or mixed, by whether the stoppage arose from questions of wages, work conditions, grievances, or some other factor, and so on.

Scales and Measurement

The simplest type of classification employs a nominal scale in which names are assigned to categories. All that is necessary to use a nominal scale is that the categories be mutually exclusive so that any one item cannot fit into two categories. If we can go further than this and rank the categories as to any one property, we can use an ordinal scale.

Various techniques are available for analyzing rankings. For example, rank correlation may be used to get a measure of the degree of association between the variables.

In addition to the nominal and ordinal scales, we have two scales available for measurement in the strict sense, namely, the interval and ratio scales. The interval scale involves a determination of the equality of intervals or distances, as is the case of temperature (Fahrenheit or Celsius) or calendar time. The ratio scale involves the determination of equality of ratios such as temperature (Rankine or Kelvin) or loudness measured in sones.

---

[14] *In general, see C. West Churchman and P. Ratoosh (eds.),* Measurement: Definitions and Theories (*New York: John Wiley & Sons, Inc., 1959*).

Stevens[15] has summarized some statistical measures appropriate to each scale as follows:

Scale	Measures of location	Dispersion	Association or correlation	Significance tests
Nominal	Mode	. . .	Contingency correlation	Chi-square test
Ordinal	Median	Percentiles	Rank-order correlation	Sign test, run test
Interval	Arithmetic mean	Standard deviation	Correlation ratio	t test, F test
		Average deviation	Product-moment correlation	
Ratio	Geometric mean	Percentage variation	. . .	. . .
	Harmonic mean			

Additional scales can be developed.[16]

In measurement, there are four critical properties of relations between variables: reflexivity, symmetry, transitivity, and connectivity. A relationship is reflexive if it holds between a thing and itself, for example, if we can use the = sign in the case of real numbers, if we can state as to human beings that A resembles B, or if we can say "is similar to" regarding geometric elements such as planes. A relationship is symmetric if, in relating one thing to another, it similarly relates the second to the first, as is true of "is married to" in a monogamous society. A relationship is transitive if, when it holds between the first thing and a second and between the second and a third, it also holds between the first and the third. A relationship is connected if it applies to every pair of elements whether taken in one order or another order.[17] Unless we are careful, we shall make unwarranted assumptions as to the status of the variables in our research with respect to these four critical properties.

Measurements, whether nominal, ordinal, interval, or ratio, are of little significance unless there is some knowledge of the accuracy of the measurement. With such knowledge it is possible to employ controls to keep the margin of error within predetermined limits. The range of uses for a measurement increases with the exactness of the measurement. This is best illustrated by a homely example. If we want to determine whether a piano in a downtown store will go through the door of a prospective buyer's home, we can employ measurements. How accurate the measurements must be depends on the situation. If the measurements are per-

[15] S. Stevens, "Measurement, Psychophysics, and Utility," in C. W. Churchman and P. Ratoosh, op. cit., p. 27.

[16] Cf. C. H. Coombs, H. Raiffa, and R. M. Thrall, "Some Views on Mathematical Models and Measurement Theory," in R. M. Thrall, C. H. Coombs, and R. L. Davis (eds.), Decision Processes (New York: John Wiley & Sons, Inc., 1954).

[17] For more precise definitions, see Russell L. Ackoff, S. K. Gupta, and J. Sayre Minas, op. cit., pp. 184–187.

fectly accurate, we can answer our question not only for this door but for all other possible doors.

In addition, when we make measurements, we may not know all the possible uses for which the measurements will later be employed. If we make the measurements as accurate as possible, we reduce the likelihood of a future remeasurement process.

Errors in Measurement

The sources of error in measurement may be classified[18] in different ways. Thus errors can be classified as originating (1) with the observer,

[18] *The most important references on errors of measurement in the areas of economics and business are Oskar Morgenstern, op. cit.; and Geoffrey Moore, "Accuracy of Government Statistics," Harvard Business Review, vol. 25, pp. 306–317, Spring, 1947. The classification of errors we use follows Morgenstern.*

Although Morgenstern has been largely a voice crying in the wilderness of economists, the naivete of much economic research has drawn this comment from mathematician Norbert Wiener:[*]

The success of mathematical physics led the social scientists to be jealous of its power without quite understanding the intellectual attitudes that had contributed to this power. The use of mathematical formulae had accompanied the development of the natural sciences and become the mode in the social sciences . . . so the economists have developed the habit of dressing up their rather imprecise ideas in the language of the infinitesimal calculus. . . .

The mathematics that the social scientists employ and the mathematical physics that they use as their model are the mathematics and the mathematical physics of 1850. An econometrician will develop an elaborate and ingenious theory of demand and supply, inventories and unemployment and the like with a relative or total indifference to the methods by which these elusive quantities are observed or measured. Their quantitative theories are treated with the unquestioning respect with which the physicists of a less sophisticated age treated the concepts of the Newtonian physics. Very few econometricians are aware that if they are to imitate the procedure of modern physics and not its mere appearances, a mathematical economics must begin with a critical account of these quantitative notions and the means adopted for collecting and measuring them.

Difficult as it is to collect good physical data, it is far more difficult to collect long runs of economic or social data so that the whole of the runs shall have a uniform significance. . . .

Under the circumstances, it is hopeless to give too precise a measurement to the quantities occurring in it. To assign what purports to be precise values to such essentially vague quantities is neither useful nor honest and any pretense of applying precise formulae to these loosely defined quantities is a sham and a waste of time.

[*] *Norbert Wiener, God and Golem, Inc. (Cambridge, Mass.: Massachusetts Institute of Technology Press, 1964), at pp. 89ff.*

The confession of economist Paul Samuelson illustrates the provincialism of many economists in the area of scientific method: "To help my understanding of these issues [of scientific method], [philosophy] Professor Massey kindly provided me with minimal references to related writings that should be of interest to economists. . . ." Paul Samuelson, "Professor Samuelson on Theory and Realism: Reply," American Economic Review, vol. 55 (December, 1965), pp. 1164–1172 at p. 1166, n. 3.

(2) with the instruments employed, (3) with the environment, and (4) with the object observed.[19] Another classification groups errors arising (1) from a lack of designed experiments, (2) from hiding information (lies), (3) from the level of training of observers, (4) from questionnaires, (5) from mass observations, (6) from lack of definition, (7) from instruments, (8) from the factor of time, (9) from the fact that the phenomena are unique, and (10) from interdependence. We shall pursue the latter classification because it establishes categories more useful to considering questions of economics and business. It should be noted, however, that neither classification includes the error of sampling which is expressed as the probable error or sampling error.

Before illustrating some of these classes of error, we should first point out that the data of economics and business are at a great disadvantage in comparison with those of other sciences. As has already been indicated, in economics and business the researcher usually uses data observed by others whereas in other sciences the researcher is most often the observer. Very seldom do published data in economics or business contain any indication of error problems. Even when one gets in direct touch with the source of the data, such as a government agency, little can be gained on error questions. Usually, the observer gave no attention at all to these questions.

Second, it is frequently possible to sort out the various origins of errors and to measure an error quantitatively. If the items being measured are destroyed in the process of measurement, it may seem that we cannot separate out, for example, the error arising from the observer. Since the items have been destroyed, we cannot repeat the measurement on the same items. We can, however, make an estimate of the error originating with the observer. If we divide the items to be measured into two equal groups and allocate groups to observers at random, the differences in the distribution of observations reported by each observer will include errors due to the observer and differences actually present in the groups. The probabilities which are connected with the differences due to forming each group can usually be determined and can be decreased by increasing the size of each group. These differences when subtracted from the total error leave the error due to the observer.[20] In a similar manner, we can estimate the error arising from instruments by using the same observer but different instruments.

Lack of experimental design and error. Seldom are economic or business statistics the product of designed experiments such as are employed in other sciences. In fact, these statistics are typically by-products of business activities and are collected to satisfy legal definitions rather than definitions which the business researcher desires. This is true of tax information, for example.

---

[19] *As is done in Russell L. Ackoff, S. K. Gupta, and J. Sayre Minas, op. cit., pp. 206–214.*

[20] *R. H. Hanson and E. S. Marks, "Influence of the Interviewer on the Accuracy of Survey Results," Journal of the American Statistical Association, vol. 53, no. 283, pp. 635–655, September, 1958.*

It is not an answer to our problem for the observer to list many foot-notes giving all manner of information about the data but furnishing no numerial estimate of the errors. Only in the case of sampling has it become somewhat common to indicate an estimate of the sampling error, but here we are still left with errors of other kinds.

Lies and error. The fact that economic and business statistics are by-products of activities of government and business introduces peculiar problems. Situations for hiding data arise not only in the field of taxes, where the taxpayer has an incentive to misrepresent, and in the case of national security, in which governments have need to hide information about military expenditures, but in many other instances, ranging from keeping information from competitors to a woman's unwillingness to give her true age.

The observer and error. The lack of training of observers is a particular plague of economic and business statistics. In addition, the opportunities for bias are under no controls. Double counting and enumeration errors increase as more and more numerous observers handle the data en route to the final table.

Questionnaires and error. Most economic and business statistics are derived from questionnaires. Poor design of a questionnaire results in ambiguous questions which do not have unique answers. Even if a ques-tion calls for a unique answer, it may exceed the intelligence of the respondent or it may be emotionally loaded and provoke reacting re-sponses which could be avoided. The questionnaire may go to people who are indifferent and respond capriciously, or only those adversely concerned in the subject under survey may respond. It is a cardinal rule of published research that the complete questionnaire be reproduced. Recent development of statistical techniques[21] gives some help in identi-fying "outliers," or extreme values which come from another universe and are erroneously mixed with other data.

Mass observations and error. The fact that most economic and business statistics involve large masses of observations is a particular source of error. In the case of the *Census of Population,* for example, millions of observations are involved. The reader may be surprised to learn that in the 1950 *U.S. Census of Population* some 5 million persons were omitted.[22] When we consider that the 1950 population was reported as 151 million, however, we have an error of only 3 per cent. We may contrast this with the fact that a probable error of 2 or 3 per cent in measuring the stability of planetary motions is acceptable in astronomy.[23]

[21] *Cf. T. S. Ferguson, "Rules for Rejection of Outliers,"* Revue de l'Institut Interna-tional de Statistique, *vol. 29, pp. 29–42, 1961.*

[22] *A. J. Coale and M. Zelnik,* New Estimates of Fertility and Population in the United States: A Study of Annual White Births from 1855 to 1960 and of Com-pleteness of Enumeration from 1880 to 1960 (*Princeton, N.J.: Princeton University Press, 1963*).

[23] *Oskar Morgenstern, op. cit., p. 9, note 3, citing G. M. Clemence, "Relativity Effects in Planetary Motion,"* Proceedings of the American Philosophical Society, *vol. 93, no. 7, pp. 532–534, 1949.*

Definition and classification in relation to error. One of the most difficult problems for economics and business is that classifications and definitions used in gathering data are ambiguous. First is the problem that over a period of time products and processes change, causing categories to shift and making a time series of comparable data difficult to establish. Mergers add to this problem. Because of diversification such a company as General Motors defies classification. Profits and other data of the company are not published by categories. Tools such as the Standard Industrial Classification code of the Department of Commerce[24] are improvements that will continue to make advances.

Instruments and error. Human beings are the instruments used in questioning, recording, interpreting, and classifying economic and business data. While the role of computing, data-processing, and other machines is increasing, the human factor still survives. Many of the errors in the *U.S. Census of Population* of 1950 originated in mispunched machine cards (wrong column, wrong row, etc.).[25] In most cases, the only way to make a beginning in locating errors is to have the same data collected independently by more than one agency. The totals and subtotals of the data of one source seldom agree with those of the other.

Time factor and error. Time as a factor in economic observations causes its own difficulties. Classifications and definitions are changed over time to follow product changes, but the significance of the changes is frequently not noted by the respondent, who may still find the old definitions more appropriate. Time is required for counts, and despite elaborate controls to deal with the fact that the items being counted are in motion during counts, error creeps in. One classic case is the testimony in 1949 before the Joint Congressional Committee on Atomic Energy[26] that the gold in Fort Knox could not be weighed with an error of less than ±$20 million. The gold in Fort Knox on December 31, 1948, was reported as $24,399 million. Hence only four digits are significant. The error, of course, is less than one-tenth of 1 per cent. Economics cannot, however, make effective use of data accurate to more than four digits.

Uniqueness and error. Another problem common to economic data is the matter of uniqueness, which is closely associated with the time dimension. Since economic data are part of an historical process, the situation giving rise to the data will never repeat itself. (It may also be true, but in a different degree, that in the physical sciences any situation can never be repeated.)

Morgenstern points out[27] that successive errors occur as economic sta-

---

[24] *Technical Committee on Industrial Classification,* Standard Industrial Classification Manual (*Washington, D.C.: Government Printing Office, 1959*).

[25] A. J. Coale and F. F. Stephan, *"The Case of the Indians and Teen-age Widows,"* Journal of the American Statistical Association, *vol. 57, no. 298, pp. 338–347, June, 1962.*

[26] Investigation into the U.S. Atomic Energy Project, *81st Cong., 1st Sess., June 16, 1949, p. 412.*

[27] *Oskar Morgenstern, op. cit., p. 51.*

tistics are processed so as to become (1) more inclusive through summation and aggregation, (2) more complex as computations are performed (e.g., in establishing indices), and (3) more refined as computations are performed (e.g., as in time series analysis).

Interdependence. Interdependence of errors exists, as is illustrated when a company's production department (which may be subject to faulty classification and the desire to hide information) passes data on to the accounting department, where the preparation of tax returns (subject to the error of lies) compounds the error. One hopeful path through the rat's nest, as indicated by Morgenstern, lies in cross-checks not only between two independent sources gathering the same data but between theory or theoretical constructs and data. In short, we can use theory to test data as well as data to test theory, particularly when we feel quite certain of our ground because of the rigid technological relations which exist in the modern world.

Stability in errors. Lastly, we have the problem of stability in the errors of measurement in economic statistics. We cannot simply say that as time goes by, statistics improve. The change in the United States economy since the end of World War II has been so rapid and extensive that the question arises whether any improvements in the error situation that have occurred with the passage of time are not more than offset by errors originating from the accelerated rate of change. We even have the question whether as statistics cover more numerous areas and close in more tightly, there is not an increased incentive to hide information, to lie, and to evade.

One mitigating fact is that there may be "autocorrelation of errors," by which we mean a stability in the pattern of errors over time. If such autocorrelation exists, then those analyses which are based on changes from one period to the next (rather than on the absolute values) will be benefited.

Price Statistics

Price statistics are notoriously misleading to the uninitiated researcher. Listed prices are often highly artificial. The question is at what price business is actually being done, not what prices buyers or sellers are quoting for publication.

Table 2–1[28] shows in column 4 the annual average published price for Frasch sulfur. This price is compared with the average price (column 3) computed from total tonnage (column 1) and value of shipments (column 2), as reported to the Bureau of Mines in its annual survey purporting to cover all producers of sulfur.

[28] *Prepared by Richard P. Kiep, M.B.A. (Northwestern). It is to be noted that the value of shipments in column 2 has apparently been rounded in many years, especially from 1920 to 1951. As a result, the accuracy of the digits beginning with the fourth digit of the average price in column 3 is certainly in doubt during this period, and the accuracy of the third digit in all probability is to be doubted.*

Table 2–1. Posted and computed prices per ton of American sulfur, 1905–1962

	Long tons	Shipments Value f.o.b. mine (In thousands)	Average price per ton f.o.b. mine	Average posted prices per ton f.o.b. mine
	(1)	(2)	(3)	(4)
1905	162	$ 3,305	$20.40	$22.00
1906	185	3,207	17.34	22.00
1907	272	4,771	17.54	22.00
1908	206	3,727	18.09	22.00
1909	258	4,782	18.53	22.00
1910	251	4,522	18.02	22.00
1911	254	4,573	18.00	22.00
1912	305	5,289	17.34	22.00
1913	319	5,617	17.61	22.00
1914	342	6,214	18.17	22.00
1915	294	4,959	16.87	22.00
1916	767	12,246	15.97	31.33
1917	1,120	23,987	21.42	43.33
1918	1,267	27,868	22.00	32.29
1919	687	10,252	14.92	28.00
1920	1,518	30,000	19.76	23.85
1921	954	17,000	17.82	15.91
1922	1,344	22,000	16.37	14.08
1923	1,619	26,000	16.06	14.00
1924	1,537	25,000	16.27	14.10
1925	1,858	29,000	15.61	14.67
1926	2,073	37,300	18.00	18.21
1927	2,072	38,300	18.48	18.00
1928	2,083	37,500	18.00	18.00
1929	2,437	43,800	17.97	18.00
1930	1,989	35,800	18.00	18.00
1931	1,377	24,800	18.01	18.00
1932	1,109	20,000	18.03	18.00
1933	1,637	29,500	18.02	18.00
1934	1,614	28,900	17.91	18.00
1935	1,635	29,300	17.92	18.00
1936	1,969	35,400	17.97	18.00
1937	2,467	44,300	17.96	18.00
1938	1,629	27,300	16.76	17.51
1939	2,234	35,500	15.89	16.00
1940	2,599	40,900	15.74	16.00
1941	3,401	54,400	16.00	16.00
1942	3,129	50,100	16.01	16.00
1943	2,954	47,300	16.01	16.00
1944	3,519	56,300	16.00	16.00
1945	3,833	61,300	15.99	16.00
1946	4,128	66,100	16.01	16.00
1947	4,828	85,200	17.65	16.50
1948	4,979	89,600	18.00	18.00

Table 2–1. Continued

	Long tons	Shipments Value f.o.b. mine (In thousands)	Average price per ton f.o.b. mine	Average posted prices per ton f.o.b. mine
	(1)	(2)	(3)	(4)
1949	4,789	$ 86,200	$18.00	$18.00
1950	5,505	104,000	18.89	18.90
1951	4,988	107,300	21.51	21.00
1952	5,141	110,925	21.58	21.00
1953	5,224	141,054	27.00	24.38
1954	5,328	142,014	26.65	26.50
1955	5,839	163,156	27.94	26.50
1956	5,676	150,356	26.49	26.50
1957	5,035	122,915	24.41	25.50
1958	4,644	109,272	23.53	25.50 ·
1959	5,222	121,777	23.32	23.50
1960	5,003	115,494	23.08	23.50
1961	5,083	117,884	23.19	23.50
1962	4,917	107,069	21.78	23.50

SOURCE: Columns 1, 2, and 4, 1907–1924 from United States Geological Survey, *Mineral Resources of the U.S.* (Washington, D.C.: Government Printing Office, annually); 1925–1931 from U.S. Bureau of Mines, *Mineral Resources of the U.S.* (Washington, D.C.: Government Printing Office, annually); 1932–1962 from U.S. Bureau of Mines, *Minerals Yearbook* (Washington, D.C.: Government Printing Office, annually). Column 3 is column 2 divided by column 1.

This is not to say that even the computed price is without error. Although it is more accurate than the listed price, it does not reflect special services to large buyers, which are buried in costs. Such services are in effect price cuts. The figures of recent years are for Frasch-processed sulfur. (The Frasch process uses hot-water mining.) Older figures are for sulfurs of a different grade than the 99 per cent pure Frasch.

HYPOTHESIS TESTING, CONTROLS, AND EXPERIMENT DESIGN

In testing hypotheses, we may become involved in the problem of cause and effect. The presence of one event every time another event happens is no assurance that there is a causal relationship between the two and still less an assurance of which way the causation flows. Both events may very easily be the effect of a third factor which is the cause. Thus, it is usually felt that to establish causation one must be able to suppress one of the events and find that the other event does not occur. For some purposes, our understanding of the existing causation may not be an important factor. This may be true if a lead-lag relation exists between the two variables and our primary concern is to establish a forecast but not to effect a control.

Wilson has succinctly stated, "The difficulty of testing hypotheses in the social sciences has led to an abbreviation of the scientific method in which this step is simply omitted."[29] Unfortunately, this statement has considerable truth. The omission frequently occurs because experiments are usually not available to the student of economics or business in order to test hypotheses. The difference between an experiment and an observation is hard to establish. Perhaps the best that can be done by way of distinction is to point out that the experiment involves an interference by the researcher with nature in order to hold other variables at predetermined values while the values of the key variables are changed and observations made.

Laboratory-type controls are usually not available to the student of economics and business, but he is free to employ observations. One widely used method of testing an hypothesis in economics and business is to search for a similar circumstance in history separated either in time or in geography or in both from the situation whose analysis gave rise to the hypothesis. Then the hypothesis may be verifiable in the new situation. Another method involves checking the results of a time series analysis (such as the regression coefficients and correlation coefficients) against the results of a cross-sectional analysis. For example, if income has been found by analysis of a time series to be an important determinant of quantity demanded of a particular good, then a cross-sectional analysis (on a regional, state, or other geographical basis or in a study of family budgets of different income levels) ought to verify the hypothesis. It goes without saying that, in each of the verifying tests, factors other than those involved in the hypothesis as variable must be verified to stand in the same relationship in the test situation as in the situation which generated the hypothesis.

Still another method of testing is to make a deduction from the hypothesis and then to test the deduction. We must be careful to distinguish between a condition which is necessary for the truth of a statement and one which is sufficient. The terms "necessary" and "sufficient" are words of art, and their meaning is illustrated by the following examples. That a number end in 0 is a condition sufficient to prove that it is divisible by 5, but it is not a necessary condition. Although it is necessary that a number be even to be divisible by 6, it is not sufficient. But it is both necessary and sufficient that a number be even for its square to be even. Most deductions designed as tests for hypotheses are necessary results of the hypotheses but not sufficient proof of the truth of the hypotheses.

Mill's Five Canons

The fundamental reason why a model (hypothesis) may fail to work is either that it contains irrelevant factors or that it does not contain

[29] E. Bright Wilson, Jr., op. cit., p. 26.

one or more relevant factors. More than a century ago, J. S. Mill[30] laid down the first set of principles to be used in scientific analysis to determine relevant and irrelevant factors. In 1843, he set down his five canons of induction: the method of agreement, the method of difference, the joint method, the method of residues, and the method of concomitant variation.

The method of agreement states that if in one case stated factors are present and a result occurs but in the next case all these factors but one are present and the result does not occur, then we can conclude that the one factor present in one case but not in the other is the cause of the result. But we cannot say the factor is established as a sufficient condition. The reason is that another factor not stated in either case may be a cause, or to state the problem in another way, we can never be sure that the one factor which we identified is the only one not common to both situations. Another difficulty is that two apparently similar results may have different causes and then the method of agreement will fail. Here the problem is one of diagnosis. In addition, a negating factor (contamination) may creep into the situation when the putative "causal" factor is removed. The failure of the result to develop may be due to the contaminant present in the second test but not in the first. Thus even if we *assume* we have *all the possible factors*, in order to establish sufficiency it is necessary to conduct experiments in which the putative causal factor is severally tested with all the possible combinations of absence and presence of every other factor and the result occurs in each test. Then finally we remove the putative causal factor, and the result does not occur. In addition, we must assume that all the factors have only two values (present or absent), since the tests we have specified are not adequate when any of the factors can vary quantitatively.

The method of difference states that when two situations differ in only one factor and the result occurs when that factor is present but not when it is absent, then that factor is the cause of the event. The primary difficulty with this method is that we can never be sure the two situations are identical in all respects except the one putative factor. The test apparently is designed to determine whether the one factor is a necessary condition for the result. Essentially, the same objections apply to this method as apply to the method of agreement. This time it would be necessary that the absence of the putative causal factor be tested with all other possible combinations of the presence and the absence of each other factor with no result occurring. Then the presence of the putative causal factor with the result occurring would establish the necessity of the putative causal factor. To use a very simple business illustration, suppose that we have a company with a successful record during the period when A is present as president but with an unsuccessful record when he is absent. Before we can say that the difference between the

[30] J. S. *Mill*, A System of Logic (*New York: Longmans, Green & Co., Inc., 1930; original ed., 1843). While we shall criticize Mill's canons as defective, they are included because the ideas involved are still encountered today.*

two situations is due to the president's presence or absence, we must offer evidence that no other factors changed during the two periods.

The joint method combines the first two methods so that the putative causal factor together with all the other factors present produces the result and the presence of the putative causal factor without any of the other factors produces the result but the absence of the putative causal factor when all the other factors are present produces no result. This test is designed to establish the putative causal factor as a necessary and sufficient condition for the result. The criticisms of this joint method are the same as our criticisms of the first two methods.

The fourth method is the principle of residues that if from any situation those factors whose effects are known are removed, the remainder of the situation is due to the remaining factors. This method is a variation of the method of agreement, since the removed factors whose effects are known are irrelevant. Without these factors we proceed as in the first method. One putative causal factor plus other factors produces a result. Removal of the putative causal factor is followed by no result. Hence, the criticisms of the first method are applicable.

The fifth method is the principle of concomitant variation, which states that if a variation of the intensity of one factor results in a parallel variation in the result, then this factor is the cause. This is a variation of the joint method and is subject to the same criticisms. In addition, Mill's rule is completely qualitative (it uses two-valued variables). The ability to handle variables each of which may have many values is one of the advances of modern science. Thus, the modern use of regression analysis for variables which vary quantitatively stems from Karl Pearson's handling of this problem.

Instead of the deterministic methods of Mill which allow for only two-valued variables, modern science uses statistically designed experiments employing, for example, the principles of probability and sampling.[31] Some of these tools will be dealt with in the following sections.

While modern science has tools to deal with complicated situations, it is somewhat paradoxical that it is basic for the modern scientist to cast the problem for analysis in its simplest form and where possible to break it down into parts.

Controls

Controls are a very important part of modern scientific method. A good illustration is the familiar medical example of treating one-half of a random group of people with a drug, say, in pill form, and the other half with a placebo (a pill identical in all apparent respects but not containing the drug). The members of the group receiving the drug are called subjects, and those not receiving it are called controls. We would not

[31] *The crystallization of the modern concept rests with R. A. Fisher*, Statistical Methods of Research Workers (*London: Oliver & Boyd Ltd., 1948*); The Design of Experiments, 5th ed. (*London: Oliver & Boyd Ltd., 1949*).

need controls if we could hold all *relevant* variables in our study constant. Too often controls are dispensed with on the ground that all relevant variables are constant. This *assumption* can never be accepted.

One example should suffice to establish the need for controls, although many others are available. In testing the effect of additional vitamin C for cold prevention,[32] 363 students at the University of Minnesota unusually susceptible to colds were divided on a random basis into 208 subjects who received the additional vitamin C and 155 controls who received a placebo. The 208 subjects reported a 65.5 per cent decrease in colds compared with prior experience, but the controls reported a 62.7 per cent decrease! Without the controls an erroneous conclusion is clearly indicated.

Not only are controls needed, but proper handling of the experiment is vital so that subtle bias does not creep in. Some techniques in proper handling are random choice and withholding from all those involved in the experiment the identification of which items are controls and which are subjects.

Additional benefits are gained if the controls are standards so that the results of one experiment can be directly compared with those of another. Standards involve the use of standard units. To illustrate this matter, Wilson[33] cites the case of standard samples of benzoic acid uniformly prepared by the U.S. Bureau of Standards for use in comparing calorimetric measurements of the heat of combustion of organic compounds. Other researchers can make comparisons when such a standard has been employed.

Matched pairs are sometimes employed as controls, but this technique raises some problems. Such pairs involve the selection of two (one subject and one control) as nearly identical as possible in all respects. But if we selected matched pairs from the telephone book in the 1930s, when a smaller (wealthier) percentage of the population had telephones, and studied them in some experiment, we would have a serious problem of bias if wealth were a relevant factor in the subject of our study.

Controls are not limited to laboratory-type situations. For example, in economics and business, the total economy other than the segment under study may be considered a control or a quasi control. Thus, if we were studying the question whether banks discriminate against small business in their loan policy during times of tight money, we might compare the experience of small business on loan applications with that of all other business on loan applications.[34] Another illustration would be a comparison of a part of the economy with the whole economy which includes this part. Thus, we may compare the performance of General

[32] D. W. Cowan, H. S. Diehl, and A. B. Baker, "Vitamins for the Prevention of Colds," Journal of the American Medical Association, vol. 120, no. 16, pp. 1268–1271, December, 1942.

[33] E. Bright Wilson, Jr., op. cit., p. 41.

[34] The details of such a study appear in G. L. Bach and C. J. Huizenga, "The Differential Effects of Tight Money," American Economic Review, vol. 51, no. 1, pp. 52–80, March, 1961. This study is reprinted in this book at pp. 381–409.

Electric stock against the Dow-Jones industrial average. In these cases it is desirable to exclude the part being analyzed from the whole.

Experiment Design

Mill's canons fail us as efficient rules for the following reasons:

1. They are designed for qualitative variables, i.e., two-valued, namely, present or absent.
2. They assume there is no interaction between the variables.
3. They are inefficient in that they limit us to the study of one causative (or associated) variable at a time.
4. They take no account of statistical (random) variation in tests.

Modern techniques include analysis of variance, replication and interaction, factorial design, randomizing, the analysis of covariance, regression analysis and correlation, and simulation. We shall treat these briefly.[35]

Analysis of Variance

Let us assume we have two controlled variables A and B, whose effect on O, the outcome, we wish to examine. Variable A might be water per acre, variable B chemical fertilizer per acre, and output O bushels per acre in yield of corn. We might take three values of each factor A and B and proceed to plant nine comparable fields, using all the possible combinations of factors A and B.[36] We then cultivate and harvest

[35] *Regression and correlation analysis are dealt with below at pp. 145–159. Many refinements such as the Latin square, fractional replication, and confounding which have been found to be useful infrequently in economic and business research will not be covered. All of these techniques are the subjects of many books. A few outstanding works are Russell L. Ackoff, S. K. Gupta, and J. Sayre Minas, op. cit.; W. G. Cochran and G. M. Cox, Experimental Designs, 2d ed. (New York: John Wiley & Sons, Inc., 1957); Mordecai J. B. Ezekiel and Karl A. Fox, Methods of Correlation and Regression Analysis, 3d ed. (New York: John Wiley & Sons, Inc., 1959); Robert Ferber and P. J. Verdoorn, Research Methods in Economics and Business (New York: The Macmillan Company, 1962); R. A. Fisher, op. cit.; Charles R. Hicks, Fundamental Concepts in the Design of Experiments (New York: Holt, Rinehart and Winston, Inc., 1964); Oscar Kempthorne, The Design and Analysis of Experiments (New York: John Wiley & Sons, Inc., 1952); William S. Ray, An Introduction to Experimental Design (New York: The Macmillan Company, 1960); B. J. Winer, Statistical Principles in Experimental Design (New York: McGraw-Hill Book Company, 1962); E. Bright Wilson, Jr., op. cit.*
[36] *We have used an agricultural example rather than an economic or a business illustration because it is easier to concede that the uncontrolled factors do not affect the nine fields (cells) differently. What we are saying is that the typical economic or business problem will involve more than two factors and involve problems of nonnormal distributions.*

the crops. Using A1 for the first value of A, A2 for the second, and so on for the other variables, we can arrange the results as follows:

		Quantity of factor B			
		B1	*B2*	*B3*	
	A1	01 field output	04 field output	07 field output	*Row 1 mean*
Quantity of factor A	A2	02 field output	05 field output	08 field output	*Row 2 mean*
	A3	03 field output	06 field output	09 field output	*Row 3 mean*
		Column 1 mean	*Column 2 mean*	*Column 3 mean*	

We can compute the mean of each row of outputs and of each column of outputs. The differences of column averages are due to the differences in column values *provided*[37] (1) the observations come from normal populations with the same variance; (2) any observation can be considered as the sum of (a) a constant component not affected by A or B, (b) a component due to A, (c) a component due to B, and (d) a component due to residual variables; and (3) the residual outputs are independent, are normally distributed with zero mean, and have the same variance for all observations.

Then, if we let σ_c^2 be the variance of the column averages, σ_r^2 the variance of the row averages, and σ_t^2 the total variance between the nine outputs, we can state that $\sigma_t^2 = \sigma_r^2 + \sigma_c^2 + \sigma_u^2$ if these two variables are the only ones contributing to total variance and uncontrolled factors are contributing a variance σ_u^2 which equals $\sigma_t^2 - (\sigma_r^2 + \sigma_c^2)$. Hence, if $\sigma_u^2 > \sigma_r^2$, the row factor is not significant to the output, but if $\sigma_u^2 < \sigma_r^2$, the row factor is significant. Similarly, if $\sigma_u^2 > \sigma_c^2$, the column factor is not significant to the output, but if $\sigma_u^2 < \sigma_c^2$, the column factor is significant.

We cannot observe the variances just discussed, but we can estimate them from a sample of observations in each cell and employ the F table[38] to determine the level of significance for the size of our sample.

Replication and Interaction

If in the preceding example we have two or more observations for each cell, we have a replication (repetition). How many replications are desirable depends on the precision of our observations, the uniformity in

[37] *The following conditions are not so restrictive as they might seem. Cf. W. G. Cochran, "Some Consequences When the Assumptions for the Analysis of Variance Are Not Satisfied," Biometrics, vol. 3, pp. 22–38, March, 1947; Churchill Eisenhart, "The Assumptions Underlying the Analysis of Variance," Biometrics, vol. 3, pp. 1–21, March, 1947.*

[38] *The F test is explained in Part 3 at pp. 162–163.*

what is being studied, and the magnitudes of differences that we consider worth pursuing.

Once we have replications, we have several readings in each cell and we can compute a within-the-cell variance which can be called σ_w^2. Then $\sigma_t^2 \geq \sigma_c^2 + \sigma_r^2 + \sigma_w^2 + \sigma_u^2$. Any variance now unexplained must be due to the interaction of the row and column factors. Such an interaction exists in the example we are using. As the amount of water increases, the amount of water-soluble chemical fertilizer available to the crop increases. In short, the amount of fertilizer that can become available to crops depends on the water available.

Thus, the variance which was attributed to uncontrolled factors (σ_u^2) in the case of one observation per cell (in the prior example) may contain the interaction variance we have just described. To separate σ_u^2 into these two components (σ_w^2 and the remaining residual variance) would require that the variance due to uncontrolled variables be computable from within-the-cell variance, but this cannot be done from only one value per cell. Herein lies the value of replication.

Much more analysis, such as the establishment of first-order and second-order interaction, has been done in the theory of interaction.

Factorial Design

The two examples we have just given involve factorial design. It is clear that the essence of factorial design lies in observations of each possible combination of the factors. Factorial design gives an overview of the effects of the factors rather than, for example, the maximum or optimum combination. The optimum would result from multiple regression analysis, which often is combined with factorial design as a second and subsequent step. Thus the use of factorial design and the analysis of variance may establish whether the putative variable has a relationship to the outcome. If the putative variable is shown to have such a relationship, then we can determine what that relationship is through simple or multiple correlation analysis.

If the factors are independent of each other, factorial design can reduce the amount of experimental material used by comparison with pursuing individual factors separately.[39] On the other hand, as the number of factor combinations increases, the standard error increases in comparison with the situation in a single factor analysis. The factorial design tends to be used more frequently in the physical and biological sciences, whereas the technique of multiple correlation tends to be used more frequently in the social sciences because of the reasons we have just suggested: the nonindependence of the factors and the greater variances in the social sciences.

An assumed set of data in a business situation may be helpful. Suppose we use two types of truck tires and have a large fleet of vehicles. Likewise we have two different uses; intercity and intracity hauls. To keep

[39] Cf. W. G. Cochran and G. M. Cox, op. cit., p. 150.

the problem simple, we assume the price of each type of tire is the same and the probability of intercity and intracity use is equal. Further, the cost of specializing the trucks by use is prohibitive.

The following experience, showing the average number of miles (in thousands) achieved by type of tire in each use, is available:

	Type A	Type B
Intracity use	28	34
Intercity use	38	40

The average value for the superiority of type B is:

$$\tfrac{1}{2}[(40 - 38) + (34 - 28)] = 4$$

This value of 4 is a more representative figure of the advantage of type B tire than either 2 (which is $40 - 38$) or 6 (which is $34 - 28$) because it covers a wider range of situations and this range actually occurs.

By the use of the factorial design we also get other information, such as the average effect of the kind of haul, namely,

$$\tfrac{1}{2}[(38 - 28) + (40 - 34)] = 8$$

which is the average advantage of intercity driving.

If we assume no factors other than these two (type of tire and type of haul) cause the mileage variation, then we can also conclude that the advantage of type B is greater in intracity hauls by the amount $(34 - 28) - (40 - 38) = 4$, or what comes to the same thing, the increase in mileage of intercity use is greater for type A than for type B: $(38 - 28) - (40 - 34) = 4$. The last two computations are the same except for the order of the numbers and show the interaction between tire type and type of haul. Of course, as was previously explained, the last result may involve only error if there is no interaction.

These results can be shown in another form:

$$\begin{matrix} Data \\ \begin{pmatrix} 28 & 34 \\ 38 & 40 \end{pmatrix} \end{matrix} = \begin{matrix} Average \\ \begin{pmatrix} 35 & 35 \\ 35 & 35 \end{pmatrix} \end{matrix} + \begin{matrix} \text{Effect of} \\ \text{type} \\ \begin{pmatrix} -2 & 2 \\ -2 & 2 \end{pmatrix} \end{matrix} + \begin{matrix} \text{Effect of} \\ \text{haul} \\ \begin{pmatrix} -4 & -4 \\ 4 & 4 \end{pmatrix} \end{matrix} + \begin{matrix} \text{Effect of error} \\ \text{or interaction} \\ \begin{pmatrix} -1 & 1 \\ 1 & -1 \end{pmatrix} \end{matrix}$$

A word of explanation of this table is in order. The overall average mileage of the four cells in the table shown above is 35, namely, $(28 + 34 + 38 + 40)/4$. Using the cell figure of 28 (for the upper-left cell), we see that this average is made up of the general average of 35 adjusted by a deduction of 2 for the effect of type A tire and further reduced by -4 for the effect of type of haul and by -1 for the effect of interaction or error.

The older view was that the experimental design should carry out the comparisons for, say, type of tire with all variables except type of tire held constant. Here that would mean examining the two tire types in the same use, such as intercity; then the replication would also be made on intercity runs. This view is subject to two objections: (1) it is inefficient, and (2) the desired information is not obtained. If the hauls were only intercity, that would be a different case, but in the present situation the fleet owner wants to know what difference type of tire and type of haul make and what the interaction of these factors is.

Randomizing

It has been indicated several times that randomizing such as occurs with the use of a table of random numbers is vital to scientific work. The purpose of randomizing is clear. Besides the variables formally recognized in an experiment, many unknown variables and some variables with unknown effects are at work. Randomization converts the effects of the randomized variables into unbiased error. With unbiased error, tests of significance[40] and mathematical methods of estimating error can be applied.

The following example cited by Wilson[41] illustrates the need for randomization. In an industrial laboratory, experiments were performed to determine the effect of the length of time under pressure in a mold on the strength of a plastic part. Hot plastic was injected and pressed for 10 seconds and then removed. The next batch was kept under pressure for 20 seconds, and so on, increasing the pressure period by 10 seconds for each batch. The results are plotted in Figure 2–1. It appears that strength increases with the duration of pressure up to a limit.

The director of research criticized the experiment as not being randomized and directed that the test be repeated with randomized determination of which batches stayed in the mold for 10, 20, 30, 40, 50, and 60 seconds. The results are shown in Figure 2–2, with the order of the batches as marked. It now appears that length of pressure was not important but that the order of batches determined the increase in

[40] Tests of significance are discussed later in this book at pp. 160–166.
[41] E. Bright Wilson, Jr., op. cit., p. 55.

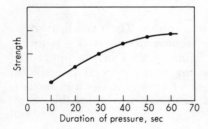

Figure 2–1. Plot of strength against duration of pressure with points plotted from left to right in the order of mold use

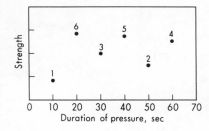

Figure 2–2. Plot of strength against duration of pressure with order of mold as indicated

strength. The reason is simple enough: the mold was getting warmer the longer it was in operation and reached its limit in heat in about 200 seconds.

Analysis of Covariance

The analysis of covariance is an important extension of the analysis of variance. The analysis of variance requires that we be able to control the factors in an experiment in connection with our design. The analysis of covariance can deal with the situation in which one of the factors in the experiment may affect the outcome and although this factor cannot be controlled during the experiment (or what is the same thing in economics, cannot be determined in advance), the method of analysis enables us to establish whether this variable is related to the outcome.

Thus A may be thought to have an effect on O and can be controlled, but B may also be thought to have an effect but cannot be controlled although readings can be taken for B at the same time as for O. By the analysis of covariance we can adjust the O readings for the effect of B. For example, we may be studying the effect of three different quantities $A1$, $A2$, and $A3$ of lubrication (in order of increasing amounts) for the key part on a given type of machine. We know when the machines have been lubricated. The machines are all run for different periods of time (factor B). On a random basis, we select from a large number of machines four that received each quantity of oil, transcribe the number of hours run, have the machines knocked down, and determine the amount of wear O on the key part. The amount of wear is measured on a scale showing increasing wear as a numerical scale increases. We gather the data in Table 2–2.

In Figure 2–3 all values of B and O are plotted with the means of B and O as coordinates.

Figure 2–4 shows the plot of the set of B and O values for each A value separately, using the mean of B values and of O values for each A value as coordinates.

Then if we superimpose the three parts of Figure 2–4 on each other to make the three means coincide, we have Figure 2–5.

If the dispersion about the regression line in Figure 2–5 is significantly less than in Figure 2–3, this process of making the means of the sub-

Table 2–2 Hypothetical data of amount of wear O associated with values of two variable factors A and B

| | A1 | | A2 | | A3 | |
	B	O	B	O	B	O
	3	9	5	11	1	7
	2	8	4	12	3	6
	1	8	2	7	5	9
	2	11	5	14	3	6
Totals	8	36	16	44	12	28
Means	2	9	4	11	3	7
Total, all B readings		36				
Total, all O readings		108				
Mean of B		3				
Mean of O		9				

Figure 2–3. Plot of wear O values against factor B values, using means of O and B values as coordinates SOURCE: *Table 2–2.*

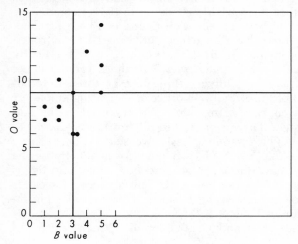

groups coincide has had a significant effect. As a result, we can infer that the means of each set for the three values of A are significantly different and that A has an effect on O.

We can then proceed to apply the analysis of variance to the adjusted B values and the adjusted O values to establish the relationship of B and O.

*Figure 2–4. Plot of wear O values against factor B values for
each A value separately, using means of O and B values of each
A value as coordinates* SOURCE: *Table 2–2*

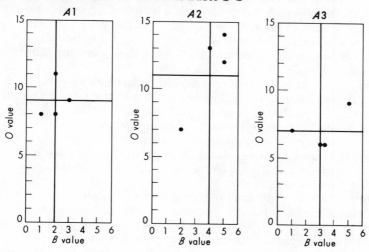

*Figure 2–5. Superimposition of three parts of Figure 2–4 to
make the means of the three parts coincide* SOURCE: *Table
2–2.*

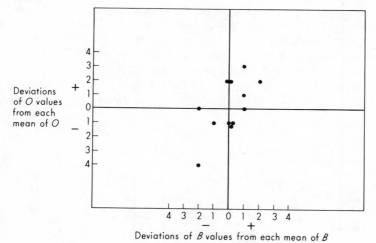

Sample Size

In general, the sampling error varies inversely with the square root of
the number of items drawn from a universe. In other words, to cut the
sampling error in half, we increase the size of the sample fourfold, and
to cut the sampling error to one-third, we increase the sample size
ninefold.

Without accurate prior knowledge of the sizes of the mean or means and the standard deviation or deviations that will be obtained, however, there is no statistical method for determining the size of sample to use. If we know the means and standard deviations to be expected and set the level of confidence to be met, we can establish the size of the sample N, which would then be the only unknown in the t-test formula[42] for the difference of two means, for example. We can then solve the problem for the unknown, the size of the sample.

We should not forget that the sample should be large enough to permit analysis of subsamples in the smallest breakdown of data. As a rule of thumb, this smallest number of items in a cell should be 30.

There is a tendency to overemphasize the importance of sample size. The precision, accuracy of measurement (including exclusion of definitional error), and usefulness of a sample depend more heavily on the procedure of stratification, the choice of sampling unit, and the formula for estimating than on sample size.[43]

Nonetheless, the following example may suffice to show that care is required in considering sample size. Suppose we are testing the effectiveness of a drug and select 5 subjects and 5 controls, who are matched in pairs by tossing a coin for randomization. Placebos are used, and all possible precautions are taken. Suppose 4 of the subjects recover from their illness more quickly than their controls but in the fifth case the control recovers more quickly. Is this good evidence of the beneficial effect of the drug?

Because of randomization, we can work from the probability of 5 coin tosses, there being only 2 alternatives (effective or not) available in this drug experiment. How likely is the combination of 4 and 1? There are 32 possible combinations, namely 2^5, ranging from 1 possibility of 5 consecutive heads to 5 possibilities of 4 heads and 1 tail (starting with 1 tail, then 4 heads, and proceeding to 1 head, 1 tail, then 3 heads, etc.), and so on. We can summarize these as follows:

Result of coin tosses	Possible ways
5 heads	1
4 heads, 1 tail	5
3 heads, 2 tails	10
2 heads, 3 tails	10
1 head, 4 tails	5
5 tails	1
Total combinations	32

Thus on a purely chance basis in 6 of 32 runs duplicating this experiment we would get 5 cases of 4 drug recoveries in 5 instances and 1 instance in the 32 of all 5 drug recoveries. Chance explains $\frac{6}{32}$, or 18.8 per cent, of the total. If we admit the possibility that the nurse

[42] This matter is developed in Part 3 of this book at pp. 163–166.
[43] Cf. W. Edwards Deming, Sample Design in Business Research (New York: John Wiley & Sons, Inc., 1960), pp. 28, 387; also chap. 5.

confused the doses containing the drug and the placebo, chance can explain 37.6 per cent of the instances in which we get 4 recoveries out of 5 using the drug when actually the drug has no effect.

Suppose we increase the size of the test group from 5 to 20 but get the same proportion of recoveries, namely, 16 in 20, as with the 4 in 5 originally. Then the risk of chance has been reduced from 37.6 to 1.2 per cent. This is computed as follows: the possible combinations are 2^{20}, of which 12,392 would show 16 to 20 positive or negative, and $12,392(2^{-20}) = 0.012$.

HYPOTHESIS TESTING: TYPE I AND TYPE II ERRORS

Sometimes the results of an experiment are clear-cut and obvious, but usually this is not the case. Actually, there is no method of drawing conclusions from experimental data with zero risk of error. Hence statistical techniques are used, since they operate on principles of logic and probability and should produce correct answers more often than mere guessing does. These statistical techniques each carry an estimate of the error involved.

When we are testing any hypothesis that a variable has a negligible effect on the outcome, the level of significance gives the maximum risk that we shall take of rejecting the hypothesis as irrelevant when it actually is relevant. The error of such a rejection is called a Type I error. The risk of such an error is called α. The researcher sets the level for the risk he is willing to take with regard to that type of error, namely, Type I error.

As the researcher reduces the risk of error of the first kind, i.e., Type I (rejecting hypotheses that are true), the risk of accepting hypotheses that are false becomes larger. This is the error of the second kind, or Type II, and the risk of that type of error is called β. Both risks can be reduced simultaneously only by increasing the number of replications (or the size of N).

Thus, in experiment design, four elements are involved: (1) the size of effect by variables which we desire to detect, (2) the variability expected, (3) the level of significance desired, and hence (4) the number of replications needed to produce these results.

After an experiment has been finished, we can use the results not only to test the null hypothesis (that the results are due to the chance effects of uncontrolled variables) but also to test an alternative hypothesis. Thus if the experiment is designed to test whether the standard has been met and we should err in stopping a machine, we can use the same results to test whether the machine should be stopped because the number of rejects in a sample is exceeding the standard we guarantee.

One example should suffice to make the matter clear. Suppose that we have determined that a machine should be stopped when it is turning out more than 30 per cent defective pieces. (This rule might be established on the basis of the cost to rework the defective parts, the cost of scrap, and other factors.) Suppose we take a sample of 100 and find

40 defectives. If we stop the machine, we expose ourselves to one type of error because the machine may be performing up to standard. Similarly, we expose ourselves to an error if we fail to stop the machine because it may not be performing up to standard. In this case, which error shall be called Type I and which Type II? By convention, we establish a preference for one and call it Type I error if we reject it. Let us identify our preference that the machine is working satisfactorily. Then if we stop it when we should not, it is a Type I error. If we allow the rule to be that we shall stop the machine only when 40 or more of 100 in a sample are defective, it is possible that the risk of making a Type II error (it is defective, and we are letting it run) is high if there are less than 40 defectives in a sample of 100 and we do not stop the machine.

To compute the risk of a Type I error we first determine the standard deviation of the sample proportion for samples of 100 from a universe with the proportion of defectives at 0.30 (the level of defectives that we decided above should be the point of stopping the machine). This is $\sigma_p = \sqrt{[p(1-p)]/N}$, where p is the percentage of defectives in the hypothesized universe. Solving this, the standard deviation of the sample's proportion is

$$\hat{\sigma}_p = \sqrt{\frac{0.3(1-0.3)}{100}} = 0.045$$

The sample proportion deviates by $0.4 - 0.3 = 0.1$ from the hypothesized universe proportion, or $0.1/0.045 = 2.2$ standard units (a value which we designate as Z for later use). Consulting the area table for the normal curve, we find that the risk of making a Type I error when $Z = 2.2$ is only 1.4 per cent. We shall take only a 1.4 per cent risk of stopping the machine when we should not have done so. This is shown in Figure 2–6. On the other hand, the risk of Type II error may be large, but we cannot say how large since we do not know what the true failure rate is.

Figure 2–6. Frequency distribution of defectives on the assumption that 30 per cent or less are defectives with α the risk that 40 per cent or more are defectives

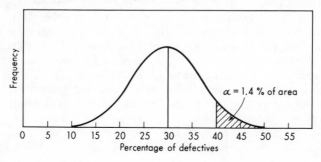

Figure 2–7. Frequency distribution of defectives when defectives are truly 34.5 per cent or less with β the risk that 40 per cent or less are defectives

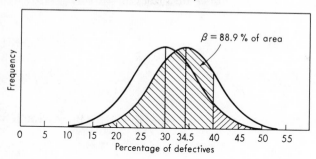

Suppose that the hypothesized 30 per cent failure rate of the machine is not true, and as a specific example suppose that the machine's true failure rate is 34.5 per cent. Then 34.5 per cent becomes the mean of the sample means with the standard deviation equal to 0.048, which is $\sqrt{0.345(1 - 0.345)/100}$. Thus in Figure 2–7 the left-hand curve is the same curve as in Figure 2–6 with the shaded area of 1.4 per cent risk of Type I error when the hypothesized failure rate is 30 per cent. The right-hand curve represents the case as we now know it: the true failure rate of 34.5 per cent. By stopping the machine at a 40 per cent failure in a sample, we should have a risk of a Type II error of 88.9 per cent.

This is computed as $Z = (0.40 - 0.345)/0.048 = 1.22$, which corresponds to 38.9 per cent for the area under the right half of the right-hand normal curve. When added to the half of the curve's area under 34.5 per cent, this totals 88.9 per cent of the samples in which failures would be under 40 per cent when the true failure rate is 34.5 per cent.[44]

We can determine what percentage of failures in a sample to use as a cutoff point and the size of sample to use once we have set the risks of Type I and Type II errors that we are willing to accept. Thus in our present example suppose that we decide to take only a 1 per cent chance of stopping the machine if the machine is actually producing 30 per cent defectives or less (Type I error) and that we decide to take only a 10 per cent chance of letting the machine run when it is actually producing more than 35 per cent defectives (Type II error). We convert 0.01 probability to a Z of 2.33 (from the table of areas of the normal curve) and 0.10 probability to a Z of 1.29. To determine the probability of a given sample outcome, the value of Z is the difference between the sample rate of failures and the hypothesized true rate divided by the standard deviation of the sample rate of failures (the standard deviation of a sample of failures is the square root of the difference between the hypothesized true rate and the square of that

[44] *For a more complete discussion of Type I and Type II errors, see* W. J. Dixon *and* F. J. Massey, Jr., Introduction to Statistical Analysis, 2d ed. (*New York:* McGraw-Hill Book Company, 1957), chap. 7, pp. 88–101.

rate divided by N, namely, $\sqrt{(\hat{p} - \hat{p}^2)/N}$, which is the same as $\sqrt{[p(1-p)]/N}$, which we used earlier).

Then we establish the equations for N and the critical value of $\hat{p}$:

$$2.33 = \hat{p} - 0.30 \Big/ \sqrt{\frac{0.30 - 0.30^2}{N}} \qquad (Type\ I\ risk)$$

$$1.29 = 0.35 - \hat{p} \Big/ \sqrt{\frac{0.35 - 0.35^2}{N}} \qquad (Type\ II\ risk)$$

This gives us two equations with two unknowns which can be rearranged as

$$\frac{1}{\sqrt{N}} = \frac{\hat{p} - 0.30}{2.33 \sqrt{0.30 - 0.30^2}}$$

$$\frac{1}{\sqrt{N}} = \frac{0.35 - \hat{p}}{1.29 \sqrt{0.35 - 0.35^2}}$$

and the right-hand sides of these equations can be set equal to each other and solved for $\hat{p}$, which is 0.33. In turn, we get $N = 1,275$.

For each fixed N and α, we can compute the β involved for various assumed values of the parameter (i.e., values other than the universe value assumed when α was fixed). This leads to power curves, a subject beyond the scope of this book.

We summarize the preceding ideas with regard to Type I and Type II errors in Table 2–3.[45]

Table 2–3. Summary of concepts with regard to Type I error and Type II error

The actual situation as to the null hypothesis	Decision as to the null hypothesis	Probability
If it is true, and we	Accept it (correct decision)	$1 - \alpha$
	Reject it (Type I error)	α = level of significance
If it is false, and we	Accept it (Type II error)	β
	Reject it (correct decision)	$1 - \beta$ = power of test

[45] *After Howard W. Alexander,* Elements of Mathematical Statistics (*New York: John Wiley & Sons, Inc., 1961*), p. 179.

Up to this point, we have not used the term "null hypothesis" although we have identified its content. The null hypothesis states that the supposed condition does *not* exist (hence the word "null"), but as we indicated in the machine illustration, the researcher decides what condition shall be supposed. On the other hand, in cases such as examining dice to find out if they are loaded, we know the true performance of unloaded dice from the laws of probability. In this type of case, the null hypothesis, by convention, is that the dice are not loaded.

CORRELATION AND REGRESSION ANALYSIS

These techniques are discussed in Part 3 of this book. The techniques we have just considered might easily have been combined with Part 3 but are included here because of their value in considering scientific method and its development.

SIMULATION AND SOLUTIONS FROM MODELS

Simulation is a method of research and of testing hypotheses that has gained in use in recent years. It involves the manipulation of a model (we recall that models can be iconic, analogue, or symbolic). The purposes of the manipulation can be grouped into four categories. The first purpose is to optimize controlled variables as in queuing theory, i.e., waiting-line processes (there are cases in which the required mathematical integration cannot be performed and hence the problem cannot be

Table 2–4. Experience record of failures of parts A and B

Day of failure	Frequency of failures	Probability of failures	Range of Monte Carlo numbers assigned
(1)	(2)	(3)	(4)
Part A			
1	2	$\frac{2}{20} = 0.10$	00–09
2	9	$\frac{9}{20} = 0.45$	10–54
3	7	$\frac{7}{20} = 0.35$	55–89
4	2	$\frac{2}{20} = 0.10$	90–99
Total	20	$20 = 1.00$	00–99
Part B			
1	1	$\frac{2}{40} = 0.05$	00–04
2	3	$\frac{2}{40} = 0.05$	05–09
3	7	$\frac{6}{40} = 0.15$	10–24
4	10	$\frac{10}{40} = 0.25$	25–49
5	18	$\frac{18}{40} = 0.45$	50–94
6	1	$\frac{2}{40} = 0.05$	95–99
Total	40	$40 = 1.00$	00–99

solved mathematically and must be solved by simulation). A second purpose is to explore transitions where the model may simply yield the final
result or the situation of stable operation but the process by which this
result or situation is attained is the subject being studied. A third purpose
is to estimate the values of the unknown when the outcomes of the model
are known and some of the variables are controlled, and hence the search
is for those possible values of the missing parameters which are consistent with the outcomes and the known values of the controlled variables. A fourth purpose is gaming, which involves placing a decision
maker in a set of circumstances (rules of the game) to examine his behavior and the effect of other variables on the outcome.

The currently popular management games are an illustration of simulation. Although a computer is a frequent tool of simulation, not all simulation is sufficiently elaborate to need a computer.

One of the earlier types of simulation involves the Monte Carlo technique. We shall set out an example not only to illustrate simulation by

Table 2–5. Simulated experience of failures

Part A		Part B		Parts A and B
Random number from column 1 of Table 2–8	Day of failure from Table 2–4, columns 4 and 1	Random number from column 2 of Table 2–8	Day of failure from Table 2–4, columns 4 and 1	Day of failure of the sooner of Part A or Part B from columns 2 and 4 of this table
(1)	(2)	(3)	(4)	(5)
68	3	92	5	3
50	2	27	4	2
88	3	67	5	3
59	3	28	4	3
06	1	64	5	1
72	3	83	5	3
44	2	68	5	2
63	3	94	5	3
83	3	10	3	3
93	4	80	5	4
83	3	80	5	3
08	1	48	4	1
13	2	23	3	2
48	2	27	4	2
71	3	02	1	1
16	2	30	4	2
34	2	39	4	2
98	4	27	4	4
12	2	84	5	2
92	4	42	4	4

Table 2–6. Summary of simulation results in Table 2–5 and probability density function

Day of failure	Frequency of failure from column 5 of Table 2–5	Probability of failure of product (combined parts)
1	3	$3/20 = 0.15$
2	7	$7/20 = 0.35$
3	7	$7/20 = 0.35$
4	3	$3/20 = 0.15$
5	0	$0 = 0.00$
6	0	$0 = 0.00$
Total	20	$20 = 1.00$

Table 2–7. Summary of simulation results in Table 2–5 and probability density functions using different sets of random numbers

Day of failure	Probability using columns 1 and 2 of random numbers in Table 2–8	Probability using columns 3 and 4 of random numbers in Table 2–8	Probability using columns 5 and 6 of random numbers in Table 2–8
1	0.15	0.15	0.20
2	0.35	0.55	0.50
3	0.35	0.30	0.25
4	0.15	0.00	0.00
5	0.00	0.00	0.05
6	0.00	0.00	0.00

the Monte Carlo method but also to show the employment of a table of random numbers for randomization.

In the example we have chosen, we shall seek to predict the probabilities of outcomes from combining two factors whose separate probabilities are known from experience. Suppose that we have a record of the failures of two parts, A and B, which are combined to make a product. We shall *assume* that when the parts are combined, we introduce no new element subject to failure. In fact, it may be that the new element (such as dropping by the assembler) has such a low rate of failure that we are prepared to ignore its effect. We start with the data shown in Table 2–4.

If we assign a range of Monte Carlo or random numbers as shown in column 4 of Table 2–4 to the probability shown in column 3, using the range of random numbers indicated by the probability density of column 3, we can employ the random numbers in Table 2–8 (columns 1 and 2) to simulate the failure record for as large a sample as we wish (remembering that the frequency of column 2 is also involved with a sampling error). In this way we can develop Table 2–5.

The last column of Table 2–5 can then be collated to establish the frequency distribution of failures of the product (combined parts A and B). This frequency in turn is converted into a probability density function, as appears in Table 2–6.

If we repeat this simulation process, using columns 3 and 4 and then columns 5 and 6 of the random numbers in Table 2–8, we get the results shown in Table 2–7.

Table 2–8. Random numbers

68	92	60	92	93	99
50	27	64	21	54	68
88	67	51	24	48	99
59	28	42	84	10	43
06	64	74	03	70	13
72	83	81	75	91	00
44	68	78	92	03	22
63	94	17	76	26	69
83	10	20	95	86	16
93	80	70	03	04	85
83	80	60	37	06	94
08	48	44	55	48	57
13	23	05	13	41	10
48	27	29	41	17	95
71	02	65	07	52	86
16	30	44	81	11	43
34	39	36	78	89	97
98	27	84	87	61	24
12	84	43	95	48	31
92	42	47	21	57	79

INFERENCE: DEDUCTIVE AND INDUCTIVE REASONING*

HYPOTHESIS AND SCIENTIFIC METHOD

Those who refuse to go beyond fact rarely get as far as fact. . . . Almost every great step [in the history of science] has been made by the 'anticipation of nature,' that is, by the invention of hypotheses which, though verifiable, often had very little foundation to start with.—T. H. Huxley.

How odd it is that anyone should not see that all observation must be for or against some view, if it is to be of any service.—Charles Darwin.

1. The Occasion and the Function of Inquiry

In the second book of his fascinating *History*, Herodotus recounts the sights that met him on his travels to Egypt. The river Nile aroused his attention:

> Now the Nile, when it overflows, floods not only the Delta, but also the tracts of country on both sides the stream which are thought to belong to Libya and Arabia, in some places reaching to the extent of two days' journey from its banks, in some even exceeding that distance, but in others falling short of it.
>
> Concerning the nature of the river, I was not able to gain any information either from the priests or from others. I was particularly anxious to learn from them why the Nile, at the commencement of the summer solstice, begins to rise, and continues to increase for a hundred days— and why, as soon as that number is past, it forthwith retires and contracts its stream, continuing low during the whole of the winter until the summer solstice comes around again. On none of these points could I obtain any explanation from the inhabitants, though I made every inquiry, wishing to know what was commonly reported—they could neither tell me what special virtue the Nile has which makes it so opposite in its nature to all other streams, nor why, unlike every other river, it gives forth no breezes from its surface.

* *Reprinted from Chapters 11 and 14 by Morris Cohen and Ernest Nagel,* Introduction to Logic and Scientific Method, *pp. 197–206, 273–279. Copyright 1934 by Harcourt, Brace & World, Inc.; renewed 1962 by Ernest Nagel and Leonora Cohen Rosenfield. Reprinted by permission of the publishers.*

Some of the Greeks, however, wishing to get a reputation for cleverness, have offered explanations of the phenomena of the river, for which they have accounted in three different ways. Two of these I do not think it worth while to speak of, further than simply to mention what they are. One pretends that the Etesian winds [the northwest winds blowing from the Mediterranean] cause the rise of the river by preventing the Nile-water from running off into the sea. But in the first place it has often happened, when the Etesian winds did not blow, that the Nile has risen according to its usual wont; and further, if the Etesian winds produced the effect, the other rivers which flow in a direction opposite to those winds ought to present the same phenomena as the Nile, and the more so as they are all smaller streams, and have a weaker current. But these rivers, of which there are many both in Syria and in Libya, are entirely unlike the Nile in this respect.

The second opinion is even more unscientific than the one just mentioned, and also, if I may so say, more marvellous. It is that the Nile acts so strangely because it flows from the ocean, and that the ocean flows all round the earth.

The third explanation, which is very much more plausible than either of the others, is positively the furthest from the truth; for there is really nothing in what it says, any more than in the other theories. It is, that the inundation of the Nile is caused by the melting of snows. Now, as the Nile flows out of Libya [Central Africa], through Ethiopia, into Egypt, how is it possible that it can be formed of melted snow, running, as it does, from the hottest regions of the world into cooler countries? Many are the proofs whereby anyone capable of reasoning on the subject may be convinced that it is most unlikely this should be the case. The first and strongest argument is furnished by the winds, which always blow hot from these regions. The second is, that rain and frost are unknown there. Now, whenever snow falls, it must of necessity rain within five days; so that, if there were snow, there must be rain also in those parts. Thirdly, it is certain that the natives of the country are black with the heat, that the kites and the swallows remain there the whole year, and that the cranes, when they fly from the rigors of a Scythian winter, flock thither to pass the cold season. If then, in the country whence the Nile has its source, or in that through which it flows, there fell ever so little snow, it is absolutely impossible that any of these circumstances could take place.

As for the writer who attributes the phenomenon to the ocean, his account is involved in such obscurity, that it is impossible to disprove it by argument. For my part I know of no river called Ocean, and I think that Homer, or one of the earlier poets, invented the name and introduced it into his poetry.[1]

Herodotus then goes on to state his own explanation of the behavior of the Nile.

Has the reader ever been guilty of believing or saying that the way to find out what the truth is, is to "study the facts" or to "let the facts

[1] *George Rawlinson* (tr.), The History of Herodotus (*New York: D. Appleton & Company, Inc., 1859–1860*), vol. II, pp. 24–29.

speak for themselves"? Then let him examine this quotation for the light it may throw on the nature of the circumstances under which contributions to knowledge are made. We have suggested in the introductory chapter of the present Book that unless habitual beliefs are shaken into doubt by alterations in our familiar environment or by our curiosity, we either do no thinking at all, or our thinking, such as it is, has a routine character. We wish now to reinforce this suggestion and indicate its importance in understanding the nature of reflective or scientific method.

This excerpt from Herodotus illustrates clearly the Greek zest for scientific knowledge and speculation. But it also illustrates the great difference between the habit of simple acceptance of apparently stray, disconnected information, and the attitude that searches for some order in facts which are only superficially isolated. The observable inundation of the Nile was to many a brute fact, unconnected with other familiar but isolated facts. For Herodotus, however, the behavior of the Nile was not simply a brute fact. It presented a *problem* that could be resolved only by finding some general *connection* between the periodic inundation of the Nile and *other* facts.

It is an utterly superficial view, therefore, that the truth is to be found by "studying the facts." It is superficial because no inquiry can even get under way until and unless *some difficulty is felt* in a practical or theoretical situation. It is the difficulty, or problem, which guides our search for some *order among the facts*, in terms of which the difficulty is to be removed. We could not possibly discover the *reasons* for the inundation of the Nile unless we first recognized in the inundation a *problem* demanding solution.

If some problem is the occasion for inquiry, the *solution* of the problem is the goal and function of the inquiry. What constitutes a satisfactory solution of a problem and in particular of the problem: Why does the Nile overflow its banks? The sort of answer for which Herodotus was looking was the discovery of a connection between the fact of the Nile's behavior and *other* facts; in virtue of that connection, apparently isolated facts would be seen to be *ordered* facts. And in general, scientific investigations must begin with some problem, and aim at an order connecting what at first sight may seem unrelated facts. But the ability to perceive in some brute experience the occasion for a problem, and especially a problem *whose solution has a bearing on the solution of other problems*, is not a common talent among men. For no rule can be given by means of which men can learn to ask significant questions. It is a mark of scientific genius to be sensitive to difficulties where less gifted people pass by untroubled with doubt.

2. The Formulation of Relevant Hypothesis

How does such a search for an order among facts proceed? The reader must note in the first place that a problem cannot even be *stated* unless we are somewhat familiar with the subject matter in which we discover the problem. The Greeks found a problem in the behavior of the Nile because, among other reasons, they were acquainted with the behavior of other rivers, and because the behavior of these other rivers was known to them to be connected with such things as wind, snowfall, and evaporation.

In order to state some obscurely felt difficulty in the form of a determinate problem, we must be able to *pick out,* on the basis of *previous knowledge,* certain elements in the subject matter as *significant.* Thus Herodotus noted the *distance covered* by the overflowing waters, the *time* at which the inundation *begins,* the *time* at which the overflow reaches its *maximum,* and the absence of *breezes* at the river's surface. It was in terms of such distinguishable and repeatable elements in the total situation known as "the inundation of the Nile" that Herodotus stated his difficulty. But his attention was drawn to these elements, rather than to others, because he was familiar with certain *theories* dealing with the behavior of rivers. It was his familiarity with such theories which made him look to facts like the winds, snowfall, or evaporation rather than to other facts in order to find a connection between them and the Nile's behavior.

We cannot take a single step forward in any inquiry unless we begin with a *suggested* explanation or solution of the difficulty which originated it. Such tentative explanations are suggested to us by something in the subject matter and by our previous knowledge. When they are formulated as propositions, they are called *hypotheses.*

The function of a hypothesis is to *direct* our search for the order among facts. The suggestions formulated in the hypothesis *may* be solutions to the problem. *Whether* they are, is the task of the inquiry. No one of the suggestions need necessarily lead to our goal. And frequently some of the suggestions are incompatible with one another, so that they cannot all be solutions to the same problem.

We shall discuss below the formal conditions a satisfactory hypothesis must fulfill. The reader should note at this point that Herodotus examined three hypotheses (besides his own) for solving the problem of the Nile's periodic inundation. He accepted his own, after rejecting the other three. As a matter of fact, all four explanations are false. Nevertheless, the procedure he followed in rejecting some hypotheses and accepting others is still a model of scientific method.

How important hypotheses are in directing inquiry will be seen clearly if we reflect once more on the frequent advice: "Let the facts speak for themselves." For what *are* the facts, and *which* facts should we study? Herodotus could have observed the rise and retreat of the Nile until the end of time without finding in that particular repeated fact the sort of connections he was looking for—the relations of the inundation to the rainfall in Central Africa, for example. His problem could receive a solution only with the discovery of an invariable connection between the overflow of the Nile and some other fact. But *what* other fact? The number of other facts is endless, and an undirected observation of the Nile may never reveal either the other facts or their mode of connection. Facts must be *selected* for study on the basis of a hypothesis.

In directing an inquiry, a hypothesis must of necessity regard some facts as *significant* and others as not. It would have been humanly impossible for Herodotus to examine the relations of the Nile to *every other* class of events. Such a task, however, would have been regarded by him as preposterous. For most of these other facts, such as the number of prayers offered by the Egyptians every day, or the number of travelers visiting Naucratis each season, were judged by him to be *irrelevant*.

What is meant by saying that some hypotheses express "relevant" connection of facts, and others do not? The melting of snows is a relevant fact for understanding the Nile's behavior, Herodotus might have explained, because *on the basis of previous knowledge* melting snow can be regarded as related more or less constantly and in some determinate manner with the volume of rivers. But the number of visitors in Naucratis each season is not relevant to the Nile's behavior, because no such relation is known to exist between changes in the visiting population of a city and variations in the volume of rivers. A hypothesis is believed to be relevant to a problem if it expresses determinate modes of connections between a set of facts, including the fact investigated; it is irrelevant otherwise.

No rules can be stated for "hitting upon" relevant hypotheses. A hypothesis may often be believed to be relevant which subsequent inquiry shows to be not so. Or we may believe that certain facts are irrelevant to a problem although subsequent inquiry may reveal the contrary. *In the absence of knowledge concerning a subject matter, we can make no well-founded judgments of relevance.*

It follows that the valuable suggestions for solving a problem can be made only by those who are familiar with the kinds of connections which the subject matter under investigation is capable of exhibiting. Thus the explanation of the Nile's periodic overflow as due to heavy rainfall would not be very likely to occur to anyone not already familiar with the relation between rain and swollen rivers. The hypotheses which occur to an investigator are therefore a function, in part at least, of his previous knowledge.

3. *The Deductive Development of Hypotheses*

Let us now reëxamine the procedure of Herodotus in terms of the distinctions already familiar.

The search for an explanation of the Nile's behavior was a search for a *general rule* which asserts a *universal* connection between facts of that kind and other facts of different kind. The task of Herodotus was to show that the general rule which was suggested to him in the form of a hypothesis *did truly and in fact* apply to the specific problem at hand. How did he perform it?

The argument which Herodotus employed to reject the first theory may be stated as follows: The defender of the theory offers the following argument:

If the Etesian winds blow, the Nile rises (*general rule*).
The Nile rises for one hundred days beginning with the summer solstice (*observed fact*).
∴ The Etesian winds blow, beginning with the summer solstice (*inferred event*).

The inference is, of course, invalid as a conclusive proof. But its proponent may claim that the reasoning is a *presumptive probable inference,* so that the conclusion is probable on the evidence. Herodotus shows that this is not the case. He points out that we can find an occasion when the Nile rises (*observed case*) and the Etesian winds do not blow. Such a case is obviously not explained by our general rule. He therefore concludes that the hypothesis of the winds will not *always* account for the inundation of the river. But he is not content with this, for the defender of the theory may perhaps be satisfied with an explanation of the overflow which is not invariable. Herodotus showed further that the logical consequences of the Etesian wind theory were *contrary* to the known facts. In order to do this, he had therefore to point out some of the other consequences of that theory by discovering what it *implied.*

His argument continues:

If the blowing of the Etesian winds produced inundations, other rivers should behave as the Nile does (*elaborated rule*).
These other rivers do not overflow their banks (*observed fact*).
∴ The blowing of the Etesian winds does not invariably produce inundations.

This inference is a valid mixed hypothetical syllogism. Herodotus has therefore shown that the Etesian-wind theory cannot be regarded as a satisfactory explanation of the problem.

In this rejection of the first theory, Herodotus was compelled to elaborate it deductively. The importance of this step can be seen even more clearly by considering his rejection of the third theory. This may be stated as follows: If there are periodic melting snows in the interior of Africa, then the Nile will inundate periodically. Herodotus rejects this explanation not because he can *actually observe* the absence of snow in Central Africa, but because he can observe what he believes to be the consequences of Central Africa's being a warm country. And since he rejects the possibility of snowfall in warm places, he also rejects the theory of melting snows as the cause of the Nile's behavior. Let us restate part of his argument:

If hot winds blow from a region, then that region itself is hot (*general rule*).

Hot winds blow from the interior of Africa (*observed fact*).

∴ The interior of Africa is hot (*inferred fact*).

If snow falls in a region, then that region cannot have a hot climate (*rule*).

The interior of Africa *is* hot (*inferred fact from the previous inference*).

∴ Snow does not fall in the interior of Africa (*inferred fact*).

From this analysis we may conclude that the deductive elaboration of a hypothesis must follow its formulation. For we can discover the full meaning of a hypothesis, whether it is relevant and whether it offers a satisfactory solution of the problem, only by discovering what it *implies*. It is worth noting that Herodotus rejected the second theory simply on the ground that it was obscurely stated, so that it was impossible to find out what it did imply.

We are therefore already in the position to appreciate how important the technique of deduction is for scientific method. In the chapter on mathematics we have seen how a complex set of assumptions may be explored for their implications. The techniques we have discussed there are relevant for the deductive elaboration of any theory. Without writing a textbook on some special science one cannot illustrate the full scope of those methods in a particular subject matter. But by attending to a few more relatively simple examples the reader can appreciate the indispensability for scientific procedure of developing a hypothesis deductively.

Galileo's study on falling bodies is one of the most far-reaching in modern times. He had shown that if we neglect the resistance of air, the velocity with which bodies fall to the ground does not depend on their weight. It was known that bodies pick up speed as they approach the ground. But it was not known what the relation is between the velocity, the space traveled, and the time required for the fall. Of what general law could the fall of a body be regarded as an instance?

Galileo considered two hypotheses. According to the first, the increase in the velocity of a freely falling body is proportional to the *space* traversed. But Galileo argued (mistakenly, as we now know) that one consequence of this assumption is that a body should travel *instantaneously* through a portion of its path. He believed this was impossible, and therefore rejected the proposed law of the increase in velocity.

Galileo next considered the hypothesis that the change in velocity of a freely falling body during an interval of time is proportional to that interval. This assumption may be expressed in modern notation as: $v = at$, where v represents the velocity, a the velocity acquired in one second, and t the number of seconds the body has fallen. It may also be expressed by saying that the acceleration of a falling body (defined as the change in velocity during any unit interval of time) is constant.

But the assumption that the acceleration is constant could not be put to the test *directly*. Galileo was compelled to strengthen his argument by *deducing other consequences* from the acceleration hypothesis, and showing that these consequences were capable of direct verification. The argument was strengthened because these consequences had not previously been known to be true. For example, he deduced from the hypothesis $v = at$, the proposition: The distances freely falling bodies traverse are proportional to the square of the time of their fall.

Instances of this rule can be established experimentally. Thus a body which falls for two seconds travels four times as far as a body which falls only one second; and a body falling three seconds travels nine times as far as a body falling one second. This, therefore, strengthens the evidence for the hypothesis that bodies fall so that their acceleration is constant.

In a similar fashion, Galileo deduced other propositions from the acceleration hypothesis, all of which he could verify with much precision. In this way the evidence for that hypothesis was increased. *But it was possible to increase it only after exploring its directly verifiable implications.*

Nevertheless, the evidence for the acceleration hypothesis always remains only *probable*. The hypothesis is only probable on the evidence because it is always logically possible to find some other hypothesis from which all the verified propositions are consequences. Nevertheless, it shows itself the best available so long as it enables us to infer and discover an ever greater variety of true propositions. A comprehensive theory is established as true with a high probability by showing that various *samplings* from its logical consequences are empirically true.

Let us now summarize the general features of Galileo's procedure. We find that he *selected* some *portion* of his experiences for study. His experiments from the Tower of Pisa resolved some of his doubts. But the resolution of these doubts only raised others. If the behavior of freely falling bodies did not depend upon their weight, upon what did it depend? The ancients, as well as his own contemporaries, had already isolated some properties of bodies as *irrelevant* to their behavior in falling. The temperature, the smell, the color, the shapes of the bodies, were tacitly assumed to be irrelevant qualities. The ancients also regarded the distance and the duration of fall as unimportant. But this assumption Galileo refused to make. And he ventured to formulate hypotheses in which these properties of bodies were the determining factors of their behavior.

This selection of the relevant factors was in part based on his previous knowledge. Galileo, like the ancients, neglected the color and smell of bodies because general experience seemed to indicate that their color or smell could vary without corresponding changes in their behavior when falling. In part, however, the selection was based on a tentative guess that properties heretofore regarded as unimportant were in fact relevant. Galileo had already made successful researches in physics, in which the quantitative relations exclusively studied by the mathematics of his day played a fundamental rôle. He was also well read in ancient philosophy, and had an unbounded confidence that the "Book of Nature" was written in geometric characters. It was not, therefore, with an *unbiased* mind, it was not with a mind empty of strong convictions and interesting suggestions, that Galileo tried to solve for himself the problems of motion. It was a conviction with him that the only relevant factors in the study of motion were velocity, time, distance, and certain constant proportions.

We may thus distinguish two sets of ideas which Galileo employed in studying the motions of bodies. One set, by far the larger, consisted of his mathematical, physical, and philosophical convictions, which determined his choice of subjects and their relevant properties. The other set consisted of the *special* hypotheses he devised for discovering the relations between the relevant factors. The first set was a relatively stable collection of beliefs and prejudices. It is very likely Galileo would have held on to these, even if neither of his two hypotheses on falling bodies had been confirmed by experiment. The second set, especially at the stage of scientific development in Galileo's time, was a more unsettled collection of suggestions and beliefs. Thus Galileo might easily have sacrificed his very simple equations between velocity, time, distance, and acceleration for somewhat more complex ones if his experiments had demanded the latter.

It is these special assumptions which become formulated consciously as hypotheses or theories. And it is to a more careful study of the conditions which such hypotheses must meet that we now turn. . . .

PROBABILITY AND INDUCTION

1. What Is Inductive Reasoning?

Modern science is often contrasted with the science of antiquity as being "inductive," while the latter was "deductive." According to this view, deductive and inductive reasoning are antithetical modes of inference. Deductive logic is then believed to be concerned with the conditions under which particular or instantial propositions are inferable from universal premises. Inductive logic, on the other hand, is conceived as dealing with those inferences which enable us to derive universal conclusions from particular or instantial premises.

Part of this characterization, as we have already seen, is certainly wrong. The essence of deduction is not the derivation of particular conclusions from universal propositions, but the derivation of conclusions which are *necessarily* involved in the premises. For no conclusion of a deductive inference can be instantial unless at least one of the premises is instantial. The theory of gas engines, a set of universal propositions, can give us no information about the automobile we actually possess unless the instantial proposition is added to the premises that this actual automobile has a gas engine.

But how about induction? Is there a distinct type of inference which proceeds from instantial to universal propositions? Some distinctions should be noted before a determinate answer is given.

1. One of the senses in which Aristotle employed "induction" was to denote the mental process through which a universal character or relation is discriminated and identified in an actual case or event. Our earliest experiences are vague and our attention is directed to certain pervasive qualities in which differences are not recognized. To the infant the world is very likely a "buzzing, blooming confusion," just as to the untrained eye all the trees in a forest are just trees, or to the untrained ear a symphony is just sound. We pay attention to certain abstract or universal features, like "trees" or "sound," but very little order or structure is recognized within the qualitative whole to which we react. Nevertheless, by examining several cases of qualitative wholes we learn to apprehend a formal pattern in them. Let us imagine Boyle studying the behavior of a gas at a constant temperature. He may write the numerical measures of its volume at different pressures in a parallel column, as follows:

Pressure	Volume
1	12
2	6
3	4
4	3

An examination of these few numbers may enable him to recognize in these instances the law that the product of pressure and volume is constant.

Aristotle describes this process of discovering a general rule in a special case of it in a famous passage:

Though sense-perception is innate in all animals, in some the sense-impression comes to persist, in others it does not. So animals in which this persistence does not come to be have either no knowledge at all outside the act of perceiving, or no knowledge of objects of which no impression persists; animals in which it does come into being have perception and can continue to retain the sense-impression in the soul: and when such persistence is frequently repeated a further distinction at once arises between those which out of the persistence of such sense-impressions develop a power of systematizing them and those which do not. So out of sense-perception comes to be what we call memory, and out of frequently repeated memories of the same thing develops experience; for a number of memories constitute a single experience. From experience again—i.e., from the universal now stabilized in its entirety within the soul, the one beside the many which is a single identity within them all—originate the skill of the craftsman and the knowledge of the man of science. . . .

RESEARCH AND SCIENTIFIC METHOD   139

We conclude that these states of knowledge are neither innate in a determinate form, nor developed from other higher states of knowledge, but from sense-perception. It is like a rout in battle stopped by first one man making a stand and then another, until the original formation has been restored. . . . Thus it is clear that we must get to know the primary premises by induction; for the method by which even sense-perception implants the universal is inductive.[2]

This process is an important stage in our getting knowledge. Induction, so understood, has been called by W. E. Johnson *intuitive induction*. Nevertheless, this process cannot be called an *inference* by any stretch of the term. It is not a *type of argument* analyzable into a premise and a conclusion. It is a perception of relations and not subject to any rules of validity, and represents the gropings and tentative guessings of a mind aiming at knowledge. Intuitive induction is therefore not antithetical to deduction, because it is not a type of inference at all; and the discovery of the implications of a set of premises requires very much the same sort of guessing and groping. *There can be no logic or method of intuitive induction.*

2. Aristotle, and others after him, have employed "induction" in another sense. Suppose we wish to establish that *All Presidents of the United States have been Protestants*. We may offer as evidence the propositions *Washington, Adams, Jefferson, and so on were Protestants* and *Washington, Adams, Jefferson, and so on were Presidents of the United States*. The evidence is not conclusive unless we know that the converse of the second proposition is also true: unless we know, that is, that *All the Presidents of the United States are Washington, Adams, Jefferson, and so on*. In that case, the argument may be presented as follows: *Washington, and so on, were Protestants; all the Presidents of the United States are Washington, and so on; therefore all the Presidents of the United States have been Protestants.*

Induction, in this sense, means establishing a universal proposition by an exhaustive enumeration of *all* the instances which are subsumable under it. It has been called *perfect* or *complete induction*. Perfect induction is not antithetical to deduction. As we have just seen, *perfect induction is an example of a deductive argument*. The conclusion has been established by strict syllogistic reasoning.

It is evident that a perfect induction is possible only when all the instances of the universal proposition are already known to conform to it. But if general propositions could be employed only if they were the conclusions of a perfect induction, they would be utterly worthless for inferring anything about *unexamined instances*. They could serve simply as mnemonic devices to remind us of the host of examined instances which they summarize. Moreover, the *legitimate* application of such universal propositions would always

[2] *William D. Ross (tr.) , "Posterior Analytics of Aristotle," Works (Oxford: Clarendon Press, 1928), vol. 1, p. 99B.*

require a circular argument. Thus, suppose we concluded that *Woodrow Wilson was a Protestant* because *All Presidents of the United States have been Protestants* and *Woodrow Wilson was a President of the United States.* The argument is valid. If, however, we examine the evidence for the premise *All Presidents of the United States have been Protestants,* and if this proposition is established by perfect induction, we find that *Wilson was a Protestant* is one of the premises for the proposition in question. Consequently, a proposition must be included among the premises of the argument which serves to establish that very proposition.

3. We are rarely in the position to establish a general proposition by perfect induction, since the number of instances subsumable under it is either too large or inaccessible in space and time. There are classes with an indefinite number of possible members. The real problem in science, and so it has been conceived by logicians from Aristotle down, is to discover the basis for a generalization when the instances *examined* are not *all* the possible instances. Is there any opposition between induction and deduction when induction is understood in this way?

Suppose that we suspect a connection between the color of people's hair and bad temper, perhaps as a result of an unfortunate encounter with a red-haired professor. We find that A, B, C, D, who are red-haired, are ill-tempered. We conclude that all red-haired individuals have bad tempers. Here seems to be an inductive inference which establishes a universal proposition on the basis of an examination of some only of its instances. But is this conclusion adequately established? Obviously not, unless we know the truth of the additional proposition, that *Whatever is true of A, B, C, D, is true of all red-haired people.* In that case, however, we may state the argument in a *deductive* form. The reasoning is in fact syllogistic:

1. Whatever is true of A, B, C, D, is true of all red-haired people.
2. Ill tempers characterize A, B, C, D.
3. ∴ Bad tempers characterize all red-haired people.

When, therefore, we state all the premises of such an inductive argument, we find that not only is there no opposition between induction and deduction, but also that the argument is an example of necessary reasoning. Therefore in none of the senses in which "induction" may be understood is induction a mode of reasoning antithetical to deduction.

Here the reader may object that the foregoing account misses the essence of induction, which is concerned with establishing the *material truth* of universal propositions. Do we really help to establish the truth of our conclusion by introducing a major premise, in our instance proposition 1, which is not known to be true?

This objection is based upon a sound perception. What most interests men in what is popularly called induction is really the process of generalization, the passage from a statement true of some observed instances to a statement true of all possible instances of a certain class. But the question of logic, we must insist, is one of the weight of evidence for such a generalization. We are concerned here not with the undoubted human need for generalization, but with the question what evidence is conclusive, that is, will prove the universal proposition to be true. Obviously many of our generalizations are not true. And the fact that a number of red-headed people have bad tempers is certainly not sufficient evidence for the proposition that all have.

The syllogistic form calls our attention to the real condition which distinguishes valid from invalid generalizations, and that is the homogeneity of the class of which members have been examined. In the actual state of human knowledge such homogeneity cannot be established except with more or less probability. The human need for generalization is so great that we are often impatient with those who point out the logical inadequacy of our ordinary evidence for our generalizations. If we are not to venture beyond what we already know, how shall we ever learn from experience? This is perfectly sound. Nevertheless, mankind also suffers from hasty generalization, of which race prejudice is a notable instance. In any case, scientific procedure requires that even those generalizations which cannot be conclusively proved should have the highest attainable degree of probability.

How can we assure this? That obviously depends upon our knowledge of the given field in which the generalization occurs. Logic can only supply us with a negative precept. We must eliminate the fallacy of selection, that is, the mistake of supposing that that which characterizes observed instances of a class (such as red-headed men) is necessarily true of all possible members of that class. For the red-haired men we have observed may in fact possess peculiar characters, such as being tired, overworked, poor, and so on, which they do not share with the other members of the red-headed group; and their irritability may be due to these peculiar characters. We shall discuss later the rules to help us overcome the fallacy of selection. Here it is sufficient to indicate that our putting the inductive argument in syllogistic form serves to call attention to the real conditions under which valid generalizations can be obtained.

Consequently, whether we know the *truth* of propositions of the form of proposition 1 above or not, the conclusion of the argument *logically depends* upon such propositions. Inductive inferences in so far as they are *demonstrative* must conform to the canons of all valid inference. We must also note that we do not even always know *which* are the premises required as conclusive evidence for the conclusion. But this, once more, does not alter the fact that the conclusion does depend logically upon such unknown premises. In this respect, however, there is no difference in the histories of the mathematical sciences, which are thoroughly deductive, and the natural sciences, which are regarded as inductive. For example, it is a mistake to suppose that the science of plane geometry developed in time by starting with axioms and then demonstrating the theorems. We know, on the contrary, that some of the theorems were known to Thales, who lived in the sixth century B.C. The great contribution of Euclid did not consist in adding new theorems to those already known, but in systematizing the subject by discovering the propositions upon which it depends (the axioms). Similarly, the *systematic basis* for the discoveries of Galileo concerning falling bodies was laid *after* his work was formulated by him. *The order of nature, and the order of logical dependence, are not the same as the order of our discoveries.*

But to return to the reader's objections. In general, not all the premises required logically in an inductive argument are known to be true. For we do not know that the examined instances in which a general proposition is verified are representative or fair samples of the entire class to which they belong. The specific problem of induction is to determine to what extent the samples are fair. Consequently, while induction and deduction are not opposed as forms of *inference*, nevertheless deduction is not concerned with the truth or falsity of its premises, while the characteristic nature of induction is to be concerned with just that. Induction may therefore be viewed as the method by means of which the *material truth* of the premises is established. The proper contrast is not between deductive and inductive inference, but between inferences that are necessary and inferences that are probable. For the evidence for universal propositions which deal with matters of fact can never be more than probable. . . .

RECONCILING ONE'S RESEARCH RESULTS WITH THE RESULTS OF OTHERS

It is necessary to have some knowledge of the area in which one proposes to conduct research. Hence, it may seem that the present material on the research results of others should have appeared at the start of this part rather than at the end, but the danger of omission at the end appears greater.

Often there has been previous research in the area currently being explored. Reconciliation of one's research with the results reported by others may reveal agreement or disagreement. Particularly in the case of disagreement, the researcher must attempt to isolate, if possible, the area of disagreement. If he does so, further work may be indicated in an effort to resolve the conflict.

SELECTED BIBLIOGRAPHY

SCIENTIFIC METHOD IN GENERAL

Russell L. Ackoff, S. K. Gupta, and J. Sayre Minas: *Scientific Method: Optimizing Applied Research Decisions* (New York: John Wiley & Sons, Inc., 1962), chaps. 1, 3–10.

R. B. Braithwaite: *Scientific Explanation* (New York: Cambridge University Press, 1955).

Morris Cohen and E. O. Nagel: *Introduction to Logic and Scientific Method* (New York: Harcourt, Brace & World, Inc., 1934).

James B. Conant: *Science and Common Sense,* rev. ed. (New Haven, Conn.: Yale University Press, 1960), chap. 3.

Karl Pearson: *The Grammar of Science* (New York: E. P. Dutton & Co., Inc., 1937).

Paul H. Rigby: *Conceptual Foundations of Business Research* (New York: John Wiley & Sons, Inc., 1965).

E. Bright Wilson, Jr.: *An Introduction to Scientific Research* (New York: McGraw-Hill Book Company, 1952), chaps. 1–4.

MODELS

E. F. Beach: *Economic Models* (New York: John Wiley & Sons, Inc., 1957).

D. W. Miller and M. K. Starr: *Executive Decisions and Operations Research* (Englewood Cliffs, N.J.: Prentice-Hall, Inc., 1960).

DEFINITIONS AND MEASUREMENT

Russell L. Ackoff, S. K. Gupta, and J. Sayre Minas: *Scientific Method: Optimizing Applied Research Decisions* (New York: John Wiley & Sons, Inc., 1962), chaps. 5 and 6.

P. W. Bridgman: *The Logic of Modern Physics* (New York: The Macmillan Company, 1927).

C. West Churchman and P. Ratoosh (eds.): *Measurement: Definitions and Theories* (New York: John Wiley & Sons, Inc., 1959).

C. H. Coombs, H. Raiffa, and R. M. Thrall: "Some Views on Mathematical Models and Measurement Theory," in R. M. Thrall, C. H. Coombs, and R. L. Davis (eds.), *Decision Processes* (New York: John Wiley & Sons, Inc., 1954).

Geoffrey Moore: "Accuracy of Government Statistics," *Harvard Business Review,* vol. 25, pp. 306–317, Spring, 1947.

Oskar Morgenstern: *On the Accuracy of Economic Observations,* 2d ed. (Princeton, N.J.: Princeton University Press, 1963).

E. Bright Wilson, Jr.: *An Introduction to Scientific Research* (New York: McGraw-Hill Book Company, 1952), chaps. 7 and 9.

TESTING OF HYPOTHESES AND DESIGN OF EXPERIMENTS

Russell L. Ackoff, S. K. Gupta, and J. Sayre Minas: *Scientific Method: Optimizing Applied Research Decisions* (New York: John Wiley & Sons, Inc., 1962), chaps. 9–13.

W. G. Cochran and G. M. Cox: *Experimental Designs,* 2d ed. (New York: John Wiley & Sons, Inc., 1957).

Robert Ferber and P. J. Verdoorn: *Research Methods in Economics and Business* (New York: The Macmillan Company, 1962).

R. A. Fisher: *The Design of Experiments,* 5th ed. (London: Oliver & Boyd Ltd., 1949).

Charles R. Hicks: *Fundamental Concepts in the Design of Experiments* (New York: Holt, Rinehart and Winston, Inc., 1964).

Oscar Kempthorne: *The Design and Analysis of Experiments* (New York: John Wiley & Sons, Inc., 1952).

William S. Ray: *An Introduction to Experimental Design* (New York: The Macmillan Company, 1960).

E. Bright Wilson, Jr.: *An Introduction to Scientific Research* (New York: McGraw-Hill Book Company, 1952).

B. J. Winer: *Statistical Principles in Experimental Design* (New York: McGraw-Hill Book Company, 1962).

SAMPLING

W. Edwards Deming: *Sample Design in Business Research* (New York: John Wiley & Sons, Inc., 1960).

F. Yates, *Sampling Methods for Censuses and Surveys* (London: Charles Griffin & Company, Ltd., 1949).

3 BASIC STATISTICAL TECHNIQUES BEYOND THE FIRST COURSE IN STATISTICS

MULTIPLE CORRELATION

Multiple correlation is a subject well developed in available statistics texts,[1] and this note is intended for those who are relatively unsophisticated in the statistical area. This material thus is a crutch which may enable some use to be made of the technique of multiple correlation when computer programs are available to perform the computations and to give the resulting regression equation and other statistics. Hence, the material is directed at interpreting and understanding the results of the computer operation.

For our purpose, a graphical development will facilitate understanding multiple correlation. A linear multiple regression equation takes the general form $Y = a + bX + cZ + \cdots + mR$, where Y is the dependent variable, X the first independent variable, and so on. This equation is in what is called the "additive" form, so named because of the plus signs between the terms. There are other forms of multiple regression equations, one of which, the multiplicative, will be indicated later.

We shall assume the data in Table 3–1 for illustration. We are exploring the association between unit sales of a product and per capita income and temperature. The hypothesis is that the sales of the product are associated with[2] the level of income and the relative temperature.

---

[1] See, for example, Mordecai J. B. Ezekiel and Karl A. Fox, Methods of Correlation and Regression Analysis, 3d ed. (New York: John Wiley & Sons, Inc., 1959).

[2] The term "associated with' is used to distinguish the matter of causation. Correlation analysis does not establish causation but merely measures the degree of association between two or more variables. The decision by the researcher that the analysis of association leads him to make inferences about causation is a separate judgment. To illustrate this point, we can cite an agricultural example. Whenever it rains, the temperature most often falls. Additional rain tends to produce larger crops. These are facts, but if we were ignorant of these relationships, we might examine the relationship of temperature and crop production and find a negative correlation! We know the fact to be, however, that if we can control the supply of water, greater crop production will occur in warm weather than in cool. The

This example happens to involve a time series, but we might have used a cross-sectional analysis of the variation at one point in time among the 50 states as to sales, income, and temperature. Or we might be analyzing data generated by controlled experiments. We have selected a time series example because two problems peculiar to time series, namely, autocorrelation and multicollinearity, will be considered later.

We can start with a scatter diagram of Y against X such as appears in Figure 3–1. The first point plotted is the arithmetic mean of the Y series against the arithmetic mean of the X series. This point is marked with an X. All the other points are then plotted, and each is identified as to year.

Table 3–1. Hypothetical data

	Unit sales (In thousands) Y	Per capita income (In hundreds of constant dollars) X	Temperature index (year 8 = 100) Z
Year 1	139	144	149
Year 2	93	88	50
Year 3	112	98	122
Year 4	111	83	120
Year 5	122	83	175
Year 6	133	133	138
Year 7	128	111	126
Year 8	104	86	100
Year 9	121	107	130
Year 10	120	136	75
Total	1,183	1,069	1,176
Arithmetic mean	118.3	106.9	117.6

SOURCE: Hypothetical.

Through the arithmetic means marked by X we then pass a straight line such that the number of points over and under it are about equal all along the line, paying attention to the fact that points farther from the line carry greater weight since we are attempting to approximate a line of least squares.[3] Points farther from the line carry greater weight because in a correlation computation the deviations of points from the line are squared and we are seeking to approximate such a computation by a graphic technique.

statistical relation of temperature and crop production, which is strictly one of association, can lead to a wrong conclusion when we infer that low temperature increases crop production. Cf. B. E. Goetz, Quantitative Methods: A Survey and Guide for Managers (New York: McGraw-Hill Book Company, 1965), p. 263.
[3] Any elementary statistics book includes an explanation of a line-of-least-squares fit.

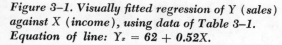

*Figure 3–1. Visually fitted regression of Y (sales)
against X (income), using data of Table 3–1.
Equation of line:* $Y_x = 62 + 0.52X.$

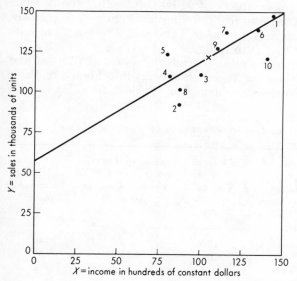

We can easily write the equation of this line. Since the line is straight, the general form of its equation is $Y = a + bX$, where a is the Y intercept (value of Y when the value of X is 0) and b is the slope of the line (the change in Y associated with a change of 1 unit in X).

At this point, we have two important observations: First, the line indicates the average relationship of Y to X without regard to Z. Second, we have visually fitted a line of least squares which minimizes the sum of the squared deviations (*measured vertically*) of Y values from the line. There is another line which minimizes the sum of the squared deviations (*measured horizontally*) of the Y values from this second line (which will also pass through the arithmetic mean of Figure 3–1). In correlation, the coefficient of correlation r is the geometric average of the slopes of these two lines, namely, the line minimizing the sum of the squares of the vertical deviations and the line minimizing the sum of the squares of the horizontal deviations. Hence, when the degree of correlation is low, the graphic method we are developing will not provide a good approximation of the regression equation that results from the standard methods of computing correlation. This is so because when the degree of correlation is high, the slopes of the two lines (one minimizing the sum of the squared vertical deviations and the other minimizing the sum of the squares of the horizontal deviations) are close to each other numerically and by visually fitting the line minimizing the sum of the squared vertical deviations, we get a good approximation of the average relation of the two variables.

We are now in a position to adjust Y sales for the effect (association) of X and then to proceed to establish the relationship of Z of that part of the Y values not explained by X, the first independent variable. We adjust Y for the effect (association) of X by substituting the X value of each year in the equation for the line in Figure 3–1, namely, $Y_x = 62 + 0.52X$. These results appear in Table 3–2. We use Y_x to indicate the relationship of Y to X at this stage.

We are now in a position to make a scatter diagram of (1) the part of the Y values not explained by X (which appears in column 3 of Table 3–2) against (2) the Z values (column 4 of Table 3–2). This is done

Table 3–2. Adjustment of $\mathbf{Y}$ *(sales) for effect of* $\mathbf{X}$ *(per capita income)*

	Actual Y = sales (1)	Y adjusted for X from Y = 62 + 0.52X (2)	Difference in Y not explained by X (column 1 minus column 2) (3)	Temperature index Z (4)
Year 1	139	137	2	140
Year 2	93	108	−15	50
Year 3	112	113	−1	122
Year 4	111	105	6	120
Year 5	122	105	17	175
Year 6	133	131	2	138
Year 7	128	120	8	126
Tear 8	104	107	−3	100
Year 9	121	118	3	130
Year 10	120	133	−13	75
Arithmetic mean			0.6	117.6

in Figure 3–2, and again an X identifies the arithmetic mean of each of these two series. Again a line is run through this arithmetic mean with about the same number of points over and under it, giving due regard to the fact that points farther away from the line carry greater weight. Note that the arithmetic mean of the part of the Y values not explained by X is taken to be 0 (which it should be[4]) rather than the mean of 0.6 resulting from our approximation of a line of least squares. This difference of our mean from 0 is an error arising from the fact that our visually fitted line is an approximation of the actual line of least squares.

Again we can determine the equation of this line as $Y_z = -30 + 0.26Z$ from the Y intercept and the slope of the line. Note that this time the

[4] *The algebraic sum of the deviations of points from a line of least squares is 0. This follows from two properties of the arithmetic mean: (1) the algebraic sum of deviations from the arithmetic mean is 0, and (2) the sum of the squares of the deviations from the arithmetic mean is a minimum.*

Figure 3–2. *Visually fitted regression of unexplained deviations of Y (from Table 3–2) against Z (temperature index)   Equation of line:* $Y_z = -30 + 0.26Z.$

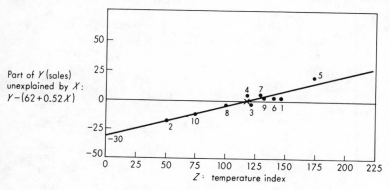

Part of Y (sales) unexplained by X:
$Y - (62 + 0.52X)$

Z: temperature index

Figure 3–3. *Visually fitted regression of Y (sales) adjusted for association of Z (temperature) against X (per capita income)   Equation of line:* $Y_x = 70 + 0.44X.$

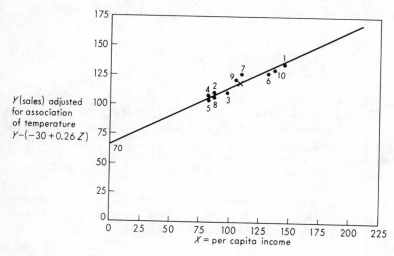

Y (sales) adjusted for association of temperature
$Y - (-30 + 0.26Z)$

X = per capita income

equation shows the relationship of Y to Z with Y adjusted for the effect (association) of X. In the case of the first line (Figure 3–1), Y was not adjusted for the effect (association) of Z.

We are now in a position to redo Figure 3–1, using Y after adjustment for the effect (association) of Z which we have just established in Figure 3–2 against X. This is done in Figure 3–3 from the data Table 3–3, by deducting from each original Y value the effect (association) of its associated Z value as indicated by the equation resulting from Figure 3–2.

150   BUSINESS RESEARCH

*Table 3–3. Adjustment of Y (sales) for effect of Z
(temperature)*

	Actual Y sales	Y adjusted for Z, namely, Y − (−30 + 0.26Z)	X per capita income
Year 1	139	132.6	144
Year 2	93	110.0	88
Year 3	112	110.3	98
Year 4	111	109.8	83
Year 5	122	106.5	83
Year 6	133	127.1	133
Year 7	128	125.2	111
Year 8	104	108.0	86
Year 9	121	117.2	107
Year 10	120	130.5	136
Arithmetic mean	118.3	118.0	107

Again we can establish the equation of the line $Y_x = 70 + 0.44X$.

We now have two equations (equations 1 and 2) that can be combined (equation 3) to show the effect (association) of X and Z on Y:

$$Y_x = 70 + 0.44X \text{ (from Figure 3–3)} \tag{1}$$
$$Y_z = -30 + 0.26Z \text{ (from Figure 3–2)} \tag{2}$$
$$Y = 40 + 0.44X + 0.26Z \tag{3}$$

Note that when we combine equations 1 and 2, we do not get 2Y because we are combining Y adjusted for X with Y adjusted for Z.

The final combined equation 3 approximates the regression equation resulting from a multiple correlation computation. The equation resulting from a least-squares solution on an IBM-650 computer is $Y = 43.9 + 0.42X + 0.25Z$, in contrast to the visual fit we have made as an approximation of this least-squares fit.

It is clear that the regression coefficient of X is the slope of a regression line of Y against X when Y has been adjusted for the effect (association) of the other independent variable, and similarly for the regression coefficient of Z.

We could continue our graphic process with any number of independent variables. For a third independent variable we could take the unexplained deviations of Y from the line in Figure 3–3 and plot these against the third independent variable on a scatter diagram, as was done in Figure 3–2.

In multiple correlation, R^2 is the ratio of the explained variation to the total variation. Total variation is always taken around the arithmetic mean and is the sum of the squares of the deviations of all points from the arithmetic mean of those points. Explained variation is the sum of the squared differences of (1) Y values computed from the regression equation from (2) the arithmetic means of Y. This is computed in column 4 of Table 3–4. The total variation of Y is taken around the arithmetic mean of actual Y values and is computed in column 8 of Table 3–4.

Graphically, the total variation is measured from the actual Y values to a horizontal line through the arithmetic mean of the Y values. Explained variation is measured from the Y value of the regression line for each point to the horizontal line of the mean of actual Y values.

The unexplained variation is the sum of the squared differences of (1) Y values computed from the regression equation from (2) the actual Y values. This is computed in column 6 of Table 3–4. The explained variation plus the unexplained variation equals total variation. Hence, we can always get either the explained variation or the unexplained variation by subtracting the opposite one from total variation.

Whether we are concerned with a multiple regression or with the amount of variation explained *by any line of least squares fitted to data* (a parabola, an hyperbola, etc), R^2 is used as the measure of explanation: the ratio of explained variation (total of squares of distance of points on the line to the mean of the actual values) to total variation (total of squares of distance from the actual values to the mean of the actual values).

It is not correct to say that R^2 is the percentage of *association* explained by the regression equation although such a statement is sometimes made. The reason this statement is incorrect is that the variation in R^2 is curvilinear and not linear when a plot is made of R^2 against the reduction in error.[5] The percentage reduction in error in estimating the dependent variable by the use of given independent variables is $(\sigma - \sigma_u)/\sigma$, where σ is the standard deviation of the dependent variable and σ_u is the standard deviation of the unexplained residuals. In our example this is computed in Table 3–4 as 81 per cent. We can transform R^2 to get this percentage by the following adjustment: percentage reduction in error in estimating dependent variable by independent variables $= 1 - \sqrt{1 - R^2}$. In our example this is $1 - \sqrt{1 - 0.96} = 0.81$.

The Concept of Degrees of Freedom

When the number of values of the dependent variable available for analysis is small (and this is frequently the case with business data), the matter of degrees of freedom is important. Serious error results if we do not adjust for degrees of freedom when N is small and the number of constants in the multiple regression is large relative to the size of N.

Perhaps the easiest way to see this is to consider the following: *any* 2 points can be fitted perfectly by a straight line. Here N is 2, and the number of constants in the fitted equation is 2 (since the equation of a straight line is $Y = a + bX$ and a and b are constants).

[5] *Cf. Frederick A. Ekeblad,* The Statistical Method in Business *(New York: John Wiley & Sons, Inc., 1962), pp. 503–519.*

Table 3–4. Computation of total variation, unexplained variation, and explained variation, using equation X = 43.9 + 0.42X + 0.25Z for values set out in Table 3–1°

(Y_a = actual Y value; $\bar{Y}$ = mean of actual Y values; Y_c = Y value computed from equation)

Year	Y_a (1)	Y_c (2)	$Y_c - \bar{Y}$ (3)	Explained variation $(Y_c - \bar{Y})^2$ (4)	$Y_a - Y_c$ (5)
1	139	139.38	21.08	444.3664	−0.38
2	93	93.36	−24.94	622.0036	−0.36
3	112	115.56	−2.74	7.5076	−3.56
4	111	108.76	−9.54	91.0116	2.24
5	122	122.51	4.21	17.7241	−0.51
6	133	134.26	15.96	254.7216	−1.26
7	128	122.02	3.72	13.8384	5.98
8	104	105.02	−13.28	176.3584	−1.02
9	121	121.34	3.04	9.2416	−0.34
10	120	119.77	1.47	2.1609	0.23
Total	1,183		−1.02	1,638.9342	+1.02
Mean	118.3				

* Columns 3 and 5 should total 0 but do not because of rounding involved in each term of the equation $Y = 43.9 + 0.42X + 0.25Z$. Despite the rounding error, however, the totals of columns 3 and 5 must be equal but with opposite signs. Standard deviation of $Y_a = \sqrt{1700.10/(10 - 1)} = \pm13.7$. Standard deviation of unexplained residuals $= \sqrt{56.7822/(10 - 1)} = \pm2.5$. Percentage reduction in forecasting error is $(13.7 - 2.5)/13.7 = 81$ per cent. R^2 = explained variation/ total variation = $1,639/1,700 = 0.96$. This value of R^2 is unadjusted for degrees of freedom (a concept to be presently explained) and happens to equal the value computed in the text when adjusted for degrees of freedom because the explained variation given above plus unexplained variation does not exactly equal total variation, as it should. This lack of equality arises from the fact that the estimating equation given above is not quite the line of least squares, having been established graphically and rounded to two decimal places and hence being slightly in error.

Similarly, *any* 3 points can be fitted perfectly by a parabola. Here N is 3, and the number of constants in the fitted equation is 3 (since the equation of a parabola is $Y = a + bX + cX^2$ and a, b, and c are constants).

Thus if N is 10 and the multiple regression employs 9 independent variables, R^2 must be 1 *regardless of the values of any of the variables.* We can generalize this to state that with a sample of size N and with k the number of constants, the degrees of freedom are $N - k$. Thus, if we are asked to give the arithmetic mean on the basis of the value of 1 item, we must answer that there is 1 degree of freedom and our best estimate of the arithmetic mean is the value of the 1 item. In the

Unexplained variation $(Y_a - Y_c)^2$ (6)	$Y_a - \bar{Y}$ (7)	Total variation $(Y_a - \bar{Y})^2$ (8)
0.1444	20.7	428.89
0.1296	−25.3	640.09
12.6736	−6.3	39.69
5.0176	−7.3	53.29
0.2601	3.7	13.69
1.5876	14.7	216.09
35.7604	9.7	94.09
1.0404	−14.3	204.49
0.1156	2.7	7.29
0.0529	1.7	2.89
56.7822	0	1,700.10

case of the standard deviation we need at least 2 items in order to make an estimate or $N - 1$ degrees of freedom since 1 degree of freedom is used in determining the arithmetic mean, which in turn is used in computing the standard deviation.

Adjustment to R^2 for Degrees of Freedom

When the number of items being analyzed is less than, say, 60 (which is a conventional cutoff point), an adjustment is made for the fact that degrees of freedom have been reduced by the number of terms in the form of equation fitted. Without this adjustment, reducing the degrees of freedom increases artificially the explained variation. The adjustment to compensate for this is made to the ratio of the unexplained variation to the total variation by multiplying by the fraction $(N-1)/(N-M)$, where N is the number of items and M the number of constants in the equation.

In our example, $N = 10$ and $M = 3$ so that R^2 is adjusted as follows [remembering that the sum of the ratio of explained variation to total variation plus the ratio of unexplained variation to total variation equals 1 and hence $R^2 = 1 - $ (unexplained variation/total variation)]:

$R^2 = 1 - 0.03 \left(\dfrac{10-1}{10-3}\right) = 0.96$, the percentage of variation explained after adjustment for the degrees of freedom. In words, the percentage of explained variation (R^2) equals 1 (total variation divided by total variation) less the ratio of unexplained variation to total variation $(0.03/1)$ adjusted for degrees of freedom $\left(\dfrac{10-1}{10-3}\right)$.

Graphic Fitting of Transformations

We have examined the graphic fitting of a multiple regression in what may be called the additive form: $Y = a + bX + cZ$. We can also fit graphically a multiple regression[6] in what may be called the multiplicative form, $Y = aX^b Z^c$, which can be restated as

$$\log Y = \log a + b \log X + c \log Z$$

and graphically fitted as a straight line on double log paper or, what is the same thing, as a straight line fitted to the logarithms of the numbers plotted on arithmetic paper.

One of the prime reasons for fitting a multiplicative equation is that the exponent of each independent variable is the elasticity of that variable when the equation carries a multiplication sign between the terms of the right-hand side of the equation. Thus, if we fit $Y = aP^b$, where Y is quantity of a good consumed and P is price, then b is the price elasticity of demand. Thus, if $b = -1.5$, a 1 per cent change in price is associated with a 1.5 per cent change (in the opposite direction) in quantity consumed.

STANDARD ERROR OF ESTIMATE

The standard error of estimate of a regression equation is the square root of the mean of the squares of the unexplained deviations (adjusted

[6] *The detail of graphic fitting of these logarithmic equations to the exact numbers used in our example appears in Erwin E. Nemmers*, Managerial Economics: Text and Cases, *rev. printing (New York: John Wiley & Sons, Inc., 1964), pp. 27–33. We can also graphically fit a multiple regression equation of the form* $Y = aX^b + cZ^d$ *or* $Y = a + bX + cX^2$, *as appears in the same reference.*

for degrees of freedom). The computation of the standard error of estimate for the hypothetical data of Table 3–1, using the regression equation $Y = 43.9 + 0.42X + 0.25Z$, is shown in Table 3–5.

It must be emphasized that the use of the standard error of estimate assumes that the unexplained residuals are normally distributed.

The standard error of estimate carries a 2 out of 3 probability that the error will fall within the range of plus or minus the standard error and a 95 per cent probability that the actual item will fall within the range of double the standard error on either side of the estimate.

Table 3–5. *Computation of standard error of estimate for regression equation* Y = 43.9 + 0.42X + 0.25Z *fitted to data in Table 3–1*

	Actual Y (1)	Computed Y (2)	Square of unexplained deviations ([column 2 minus column 1] squared) (3)
Year 1	139	139.76	-0.76^2
Year 2	93	91.72	$+1.28^2$
Year 3	112	114.84	-2.84^2
Year 4	111	107.72	$+3.28^2$
Year 5	122	122.02	-0.02^2
Year 6	133	134.40	-1.40^2
Year 7	128	121.60	$+6.40^2$
Year 8	104	103.84	$+0.16^2$
Year 9	121	120.88	$+0.12^2$
Year 10	120	119.34	$+0.66^2$
Total unexplained variation			64.436

Standard error of estimate = $\sqrt{64.436/(10-3)}$ = ± 3.03.

SOURCE: Table 3–4.

The standard error of estimate also requires an adjustment for degrees of freedom, which is made in a way analogous to the adjustment to R^2 by multiplying the arithmetic mean of the unexplained variation (the square of the standard error of estimate) by the fraction $(N-1)/(N-M)$, as has been explained. This is

$$\sqrt{\left(\frac{\Sigma \text{ deviations}^2}{N-1}\right)\left(\frac{N-1}{N-M}\right)}$$

with the term $(N-1)$ canceling out to give in our example $\sqrt{64.4360/(10-3)} = \pm 3.03$. This adjustment corrects for the fact that we lost 3 degrees of freedom when we computed the standard error of estimate. We lost 1 degree of freedom in computing the arithmetic mean for subsequent use in the computation of the standard deviation.

Then in using the regression line to compute deviations another 2 degrees of freedom were lost.

SO-CALLED STANDARD ERROR OF FORECAST

The standard error of forecast is actually the standard error of estimate for a sample. The standard error of estimate is sometimes said, as to a sample, to be applicable to estimates of values of the dependent variable made within the range of values of the independent variables used in establishing the estimating equation. Further, unless we are willing to make the assumption of homoscedasticity,[7] even within this range the standard error of estimate is an average value, since the errors of estimate near the mean are lower than the standard error of estimate and the errors of estimate far from the mean are higher than the standard error of estimate.

This approach also leads to the statement that when an estimate is made with an estimating equation for values of the independent variables outside the range of the values used to establish that equation, the error of estimate increases the farther we move outside the range of the original values.[8] In this view, the error is called the standard error of forecast to distinguish it from the standard error of estimate.

The statements just presented are not technically accurate, and an examination of what is referred to as the standard error of forecast will confirm this. The usual formula for the standard error of estimate assumes that the arithmetic mean is certainly determined and the slope of the line of least squares is also certainly determined. But the standard error of forecast recognizes that each of these statistics (the mean and the slope) may be in error in the case of a sample. There is an additional reason why extrapolation beyond the known range involves an increase in error; namely, the assumed straight-line fit may not be the true relation, which may be curvilinear. This aspect is *not* included in the computation of the standard error of forecast, which recognizes only three factors, namely, (1) the dispersion or variance in the value of the variable Y, (2) the fact that the arithmetic mean of the values which is used may itself be subject to error, and (3) the fact that the slope of the regression line may also be subject to error. The last two factors become more serious the farther we extrapolate from the arithmetic mean. This is made clear in Figure 3–4 for the two-variable case.

[7] *A distribution is said to be homoscedastic when the standard error is a constant throughout the range of the distribution. That is, the dispersion in a distribution of one variable is the same at all levels of the values of the other variable.*
[8] *The process of estimating from values of the independent variables outside the range of values used in establishing the predicting equation is called extrapolation in contrast to the process of estimating values within that range, which is called interpolation.*

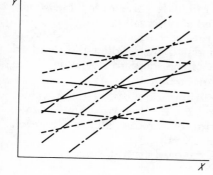

Figure 3–4. Illustration of effect of error in arithmetic mean and of error of slope of regression equation upon the standard error of estimate

The circle is the arithmetic mean computed from the values of Y and X. The dots indicate a range within which the true arithmetic mean will fall with a given level of confidence (say, 3 sigmas or 99 per cent of the time). The standard error of the arithmetic mean is the standard deviation of the items divided by the square root of N, where N is the number of values of Y.

The solid line through the circle is the line of least squares fitted to the values of X and Y. The dotted lines parallel to the solid line through the circle are the limits of the line of least squares that might result for an arithmetic mean different from the circle.

The dot-dash lines are the lines that might result if the slope of the line of least squares (solid line) is in error (up or down). Instead of running through the circled arithmetic mean, such dot-dash lines might actually be running through either dot arithmetic mean if that is the true one. In any event, it is clear that the farther the value of X used in a forecast is removed from the range of X values used in fitting the least-squares line, the greater the possible error in extrapolating the least-squares line.

Hence, we can argue that the standard error of forecast is not truly such but actually involves only a correction of the usual standard error of estimate for the fact that the standard error of estimate in the case of a sample should be adjusted for a sampling error. Thus, we might call the standard error of forecast the standard error of estimate for a sample. In this sense, there is no method for computing a true standard error of forecast.

The specific formula for any standard error of forecast based on a linear estimating equation with only one explanatory (independent) variable is

$$\sigma_f = \sqrt{\sigma_y{}^2 + \sigma_u{}^2 + (\sigma_b x)^2}$$

where σ_f = standard error of forecast.

σ_y = standard error of the arithmetic mean of the dependent variable Y. (This is $\sigma/\sqrt{n}$, where σ is the standard deviation of the Y values.)

σ_u = standard deviation of the residuals (also called the standard error of estimate) in the period of observation.

σ_b = standard error of the regression coefficient (i.e., slope of the regression line). This is computed by dividing the standard error of estimate by the product of the standard deviation of the independent variable times the square root of $N - 1$.

x = difference between (1) the arithmetic mean of the X values and (2) the X value being used for the forecast of a Y value. Hence, a different standard error of forecast attaches to each forecasted Y which uses a different X value.

The general formula[9] for the average standard error of forecast is

$$\sigma_f = \sigma_y \sqrt{1 + 1/N + x/\Sigma x^2}$$

where σ_y = standard error of estimate.

N = number of observations.

x = deviation of the value of X (used in the forecast) from the mean of X.

Σx^2 = sum of the squares of such deviations for all values of X.

One additional term is added under the radical for each additional independent variable, thus $z/\Sigma z^2$; but double the product of such terms is also added.

Using the following data as an example, we determine the standard error of forecast for 1960, 1965, and 1970.

Year	Sales in millions	Trend value*
1950	100	101.97
1951	106	104.51
1952	110	107.05
1953	108	109.59
1954	107	112.13
1955	115	114.67
1956	120	117.21
1957	126	119.75
1958	120	122.29
1959	126	124.83

* Taken from the line of least squares fitted to sales: $Y = 101.97 + 2.54X$ with X in years and origin at 1950.

1. Arithmetic mean of X values = $\Sigma X/N = 45/10 = 4.5$.
   Arithmetic mean of Y values = $\Sigma Y/N = 1,134/10 = 113.4$.
2. Standard deviation
   of Y values = $\sqrt{\Sigma(\bar{Y} - Y)^2/(N - 1)} = \sqrt{638.4/9} = \pm 8.4$ computed as follows:

[9] See Mordecai J. B. Ezekiel and Karl A. Fox, Methods of Correlation and Regression Analysis, 3d ed. (New York: Wiley & Sons, Inc., 1959), p. 320.

Year	Mean of Y	Y	Y deviation squared
1950	113.4 − 100 =		$13.4^2 = 179.56$
1951	113.4 − 106 =		$7.4^2 = 54.76$
1952	113.4 − 110 =		$3.4^2 = 11.56$
1953	113.4 − 108 =		$5.4^2 = 29.16$
1954	113.4 − 107 =		$6.4^2 = 40.96$
1955	113.4 − 115 =		$-1.6^2 = 2.56$
1956	113.4 − 120 =		$-6.6^2 = 43.56$
1957	113.4 − 126 =		$-12.6^2 = 158.76$
1958	113.4 − 120 =		$-6.6^2 = 43.56$
1959	113.4 − 122 =		$-8.6^2 = 73.96$
Total			638.40

3. Standard error of arithmetic mean
   of $Y = \sigma/\sqrt{10} = 8.4/\sqrt{10} = \pm 2.7$

4. Standard deviation of the residuals of Y (the standard error of estimate) $= \sqrt{\Sigma(Y - Y_c)^2/(N - M)} = \sqrt{103.857/8} = \pm 3.603$.

Year	Residual	Square
1950	−1.97	3.8809
1951	1.49	2.2201
1952	2.95	8.7025
1953	−1.59	2.5281
1954	−5.13	26.3169
1955	0.33	0.1089
1956	2.79	7.7841
1957	6.25	39.0625
1958	−2.29	5.2441
1959	−2.83	8.0089
Total		103.8570

5. Standard error of the regression coefficient = standard error of estimate$/\sigma_x\sqrt{N - 1} = 3.603/3.03\sqrt{9} = \pm 0.4$. Here σ_x is the standard deviation of X.

6. X for $1960 - X = 10 - 4.5 = 5.5$.
   X for $1965 - \bar{X} = 15 - 4.5 = 10.5$.
   X for $1970 - \bar{X} = 20 - 4.5 = 15.5$.

7. 1960 standard error of forecast $= \sqrt{2.7^2 + 3.6^2 + \overline{(0.4 \cdot 5.5)^2}}$
   $= \sqrt{25.09} = \pm 5.0$

   1965 standard error of forecast $= \sqrt{2.7^2 + 3.6^2 + \overline{(0.4 \cdot 10.5)^2}}$
   $= \sqrt{37.89} = \pm 6.1$

   1970 standard error of forecast $= \sqrt{2.7^2 + 3.6^2 + \overline{(0.4 \cdot 15.5)^2}}$
   $= \sqrt{58.69} = \pm 7.7$

**TESTING THE SIGNIFICANCE OF THE DIFFERENCE BETWEEN MEANS
AND PROPORTIONS**

One of the questions that frequently arises in business research is
whether the difference between the means of two samples is significant.
Means of different samples taken from a normally distributed universe
will vary merely because a sample is involved. The larger the sample,
the smaller the variation in the means which arises from sampling.

When we speak of a statistical test to determine whether differences
are significant, we are (1) setting up an hypothesis that the difference
is due to chance and then (2) arriving at a conclusion as to the probability that the observed event occurred on the basis of pure chance or
sampling error. If chance could easily be an explanation, we conclude
that the proposed explanation is not conclusive or not significant. If there
is only a slight probability that chance could account for the event, we
say the event (such as a difference in means) is significant. What
standard we apply to distinguish the probability that chance entered
(and hence the difference is not significant) from the probability that
chance did not enter (and hence the difference is significant) is sometimes said to depend on convention or the researcher's preference. We
can be more specific, however, and say that the standard should depend
on the utility (economic advantage) of right and wrong answers. Thus
the researcher may decide to apply the standard that if chance would
account for the result in less than 5 per cent of the cases, he will conclude the result is significant. Or he may apply the standard that if
chance would account for the result in less than 1 per cent of the cases,
the result is significant.

It is important to observe that we have been using the term "chance"
to include the effects from all causes or influences. Thus, if we are examining whether the difference in employment performance by married
and nonmarried employees is significant, we shall attribute to chance
all the difference arising from causes other than marital status.

We seek to assign to the specific source (here marital status) all the
variation exceeding an aggregate from which some average or standard
measure of chance results will be computed. This *variation* is defined
as the sum of squared deviations from a base of measurement. In the
case of means, the mean of these squared deviations from the mean
is called the *variance*. The square root of the variance is a standard
measure. In the case of the universe, this standard measure (square root
of the mean of the squared deviations from the mean of the universe)
is called a *standard deviation*, and in the case of a sample this standard
measure is the *standard error* (square root of the mean of the squared
deviations from the mean of the sample).

We can proceed at two different levels. We may investigate absolute
differences in comparison with the standard error, or we may investigate
squared differences in comparison with the squared standard error. The
former procedure is called the t test, and the latter the F test or the
analysis of variance.

If we test the same data with the same hypothesis and the same definition of chance, we shall arrive at the same probability conclusion by both levels of investigation.

The t Test

The hypothesis we employ is that the two samples come from the same universe and that the most probable difference to be expected between the two means is 0. This hypothesis is usually called the null hypothesis.

Let us assume the following data:

	Sample A	Sample B
N (number in sample)	30	30
M (arithmetic mean of items)	75	79.2
σ (standard error of sample)	± 6	± 6.2
Σx^2 (sum of squared deviations of items from mean of sample) $= N\sigma^2 =$	1,080	1,153.2
σ_M (standard error of the mean of the sample) $= \sigma/\sqrt{N-1} =$	± 1.114	± 1.151

The means of a sample like A should vary with $\sigma_M = \pm 1.114$ (remembering that 1σ includes 67 per cent of the cases), and the means of a sample like B with $\sigma_M = \pm 1.151$.

If there is no evidence from which to prefer sample A over sample B or vice versa, then the most reasonable estimate of the universe from which these samples come, if they come from the same universe, is obtained by combining all the information we have of both samples. Thus, the variance of the combined samples will be the sum of the two individual variances when the samples are of the same size. If the samples are of unequal size, we would weight each sample by its size to get a weighted combination, as will shortly be explained. Meanwhile, we proceed with two equal-sized samples.

The combined variance of the two means is $1.114^2 + 1.151^2 = 2.5658$, and the standard error of the difference between the two means is the square root of 2.5658 or $\sigma_{M_A - M_B} = \pm 1.60$.

Since we are examining the significance of the difference between two means, we shall employ the variance of the distribution of means in each sample. The difference of the two means in our example is 4.2 (i.e., $79.2 - 75$). This is just one of the values in a normal distribution whose expected mean is 0 and whose standard error is ± 1.60 (the above-mentioned standard error of the difference between two means). Thus, if we divide the difference of the two means, namely, 4.2, by the standard error of the difference of the two means, namely, ± 1.60, we get the deviation of the two means expressed in standard units, namely, 2.625 standard units. The area table of the normal distribution associates a probability of 0.4957 with 2.625 standard units, or reckoning both tails, there would be only 9 chances in 1,000 in which the magnitude of the difference of the means of these two samples would be exceeded.

But the use of a normal table misstates the case slightly for samples of 58. If we use the t table for 2.60 (instead of 2.625σ because the table does not show 2.625) and samples of 60 (instead of 58), the 9 chances in 1,000 decrease to 6.

The same result can be reached with different arithmetic which helps to show the relationship of the t and F tests. The total variation consists of 1,080 (for sample A) and 1,153.2 (for sample B). Each sample involves 29 degrees of freedom. Thus, we can combine these two values with weights of 1/30 for each sample:

$$\sigma_{M_A-M_B}^2 = (1/30 \cdot 1,080/29) + (1/30 \cdot 1,153.2/29)$$
$$= 2,233.2/870 = 2.566$$

$$\sigma_{M_A-M_B} = \sqrt{2.566} = \pm 1.60$$

Thus, the measurement for chance based directly on 2,233.2 units of variation can be taken as independent of the difference between sample A and sample B.

The preceding computation applies to samples of the same size. When the samples differ in size, the computation employs the following formula, which weights the contribution to variation of each sample in proportion to the size of the sample:

$$\sigma_{M_A-M_B}^2 = \frac{\Sigma x_A^2 + \Sigma x_B^2}{(N_A - 1) + (N_B - 1)} \cdot (1/N_A + 1/N_B)$$

The F Test: Analysis of Variance

Chance is again defined as all variation known to be independent of the difference between sample A and sample B, namely, in our example, 1,080 + 1,153.2, or a total of 2,233.2. The degrees of freedom are 29 for each sample. The mean squared error or variance is 2,233.2/58 = 38.5. We use this unit to measure chance.

The weighted mean of the two samples, which is the best estimate possible, is 77.1. This differs from the mean of each sample by 2.1. The squared difference is $2.1^2 = 4.41$, which would apply to each of the 60 observations for a total of 264.6. But there is only 1 degree of freedom in comparing these two means since the theoretical mean has been computed from the actual means. The mean squared deviation or variance due to the difference between the two means is 264.6/1 = 264.6. If we compare this measurement with our standard of 38.5, we get 264.6/38.5 = 6.88. This is an F value, and referring to an F table we find that for 1 degree of freedom for the observed difference and 60 degrees of freedom (since 58 is not in most tables) for chance, the 1 per cent probability point is 7.08; that is, the variation of the samples would have been exceeded by chance in only 1 per cent of the cases.

Notice that this is the same approximate answer as was obtained from the t test. We can summarize the F-test computations (where x is a deviation from the mean) as follows:

	x^2	Degree of freedom	Variance
Variation within samples	2,233.2	58	38.5
Variation between means $(30 \cdot 2.1^2) + (30 \cdot 2.1^2)$	264.6	1	264.6
Total	2,497.8	59	42.3

$$\text{Test} = \frac{\text{variance between means}}{\text{variance within}} = \frac{264.6}{38.5} = 6.88 = F$$

Thus, if the variance is estimated on the basis of the differences between the classes, it is 6.88 times as large as it would be if it were estimated on the basis of pure chance since the data for within samples represent chance.

To use the F test with samples of different size, it is apparent that all that must be done is to compute the above-mentioned variation between means by using the size of each sample as a weight. Thus, for samples of 30 and 40 we would have $(30 \cdot 2.1^2) + (40 \cdot 2.1^2)$.

Relation of t and F Tests to Each Other

The analysis used in both the t test and the F test revolves around the fact that there are 2,233.2 units of variation. In the t test, this variation was divided by 870, but in the F test (the analysis of variance) it was divided by 58. One test (t test) proceeds in terms of absolute measurements, and the other (F test) in terms of squares.

The t Test for Proportions

Sometimes the data to be tested appear as percentages and proportions rather than as averages and standard deviations. Suppose that two samples of employees of a large corporation have been classified, respectively, as successful and unsuccessful and the question is whether marital status is significantly associated with the success or lack of success. To avoid one problem suppose that we accept the classifications of married and unmarried as mutually exclusive and that we are willing to abstract from the problem the length of the married or unmarried status. Then we assume the following data:

	Successful	Unsuccessful
Employees	$N_1 = 100$	$N_2 = 100$
Proportion married	$P_1 = 0.85$	$P_2 = 0.75$

$$\sigma_{P_1}^2 = \frac{P_1(1 - P_1)}{N_1} \qquad \sigma_{P_2}^2 = \frac{P_2(1 - P_2)}{N_2}$$
$$= \frac{(0.85)(0.15)}{100} \qquad = \frac{(0.75)(0.25)}{100}$$
$$= 0.001275 \qquad = 0.001875$$

Then the standard error of the difference between the proportions is

$$\sigma_D = \sqrt{\sigma_{P_1}{}^2 + \sigma_{P_2}{}^2} = \sqrt{0.001275 + 0.001875} = \pm 0.056$$

The t test is

$$\frac{\text{difference in proportions}}{\text{standard error of the difference between the proportions}}$$

or $\dfrac{0.85 - 0.75}{0.056} = 1.79$

Checking the value $t = 1.79$ against the t table when $N = 198$ [namely, $(100 - 1) + (100 - 1)$], we find that at the 10 per cent level $t = 1.65$ and at the 5 per cent level $t = 1.97$. Hence, at the 5 per cent level the difference in the marital status is chance and not significant, but at the 10 per cent level the difference is significant.

Analysis of Variance, Three or More Means

When we come to the case of three or more classes or groups of data for each of which we have the number of items, the arithmetic mean, and the standard deviation, we can no longer use the methods for testing two means in order to test the probability that the three or more groups come from the same universe. It is true we can take any two of these means and test whether they come from the same universe, but we cannot then proceed to the three-mean problem because the three-mean situation can be properly dealt with only if we employ *all* the information available and use *all* this information in the same test.

An extension of the method of analysis of variance (F test) used in the two-mean case is the way to proceed. First, we determine the *total* variation of all three groups. This is easily done by totaling the variation $(N\sigma^2)$ of each of the three classes or groups. Then we determine the variation between the classes. This is done by first determining the mean of the total of the three classes. If each class has the same number of items, this is the total of the three means divided by 3. If each class has a different number of items, the mean of each class is weighted by the number of items in that class to get the weighted mean of the means of the three classes. Then the difference of the mean of each class from the total mean of three groups is determined. This difference is squared and multiplied by the number of items in that class to get the chance variation of that class. The total of the three variations so determined is called "between-classes" variation.

Since it can be shown that the between-classes variation plus the within-classes variation equals total variation, we can obtain the within-classes variation by subtracting the between-classes variation from the total variation. The between-classes variation and the within-classes variation are then divided by their respective degrees of freedom.

The ratio of the between-classes variation so adjusted to the within-classes variation so adjusted yields the F ratio. Consulting a table of F values, we can then determine the probability that the difference of the three means is due to chance. In consulting the F table, we note that the N value of the numerator is the degrees of freedom for between classes, and the N value of the denominator the degrees of freedom for within classes. In F tables, the N value of the numerator is shown in the row of the horizontal-column headings, and the N value of the denominator in the vertical column of row headings.

The procedure just outlined for testing whether the means of three groups come from the same universe is readily extended to testing means of any number of groups.

The steps set out above are now applied to an example, taken from the article "Rate Variations among Suppliers of Automobile Insurance," appearing in Part 4 of this book. In that article, the means of the rates quoted by three classes of insurers, namely, large, medium, and small companies, are set forth. We shall test whether the size of the insurer is significantly associated with the difference of the means of rates.

We are given:

	Large companies	Medium companies	Small companies
N	10	10	10
Mean	$174.25	$169.57	$181.19
σ	13.39	11.61	18.69

We then proceed to compute $N\sigma^2$, or the total variation for each group:

$N\sigma^2$	1,792.921	1,347.921	3,493.161

The total variation (sum of these three) is 6,634.003.

The mean of the combined classes is the mean of the three class means, or 175.00.

The difference of the mean of each class from the total mean is

-0.75	-5.43	6.19

This deviation squared and multiplied by the N of each class is

5.625	294.843	384.061

The total of these three variations, namely, 684.529, is the between-classes variation. Deducting this total from the total variation of 6,634.003 gives the within-class variation of 5,949.474.

The degrees of freedom between classes are 2, or $N-1$.

The degrees of freedom within classes are 27, or 3 $(N-1)$.

Adjusting the between-classes and within-classes variations for degrees of freedom yields:

Between classes:	684.529/2	= 342.264
Within classes:	5,949.474/27	= 220.351
F ratio:	342.264/220.351	= 1.55

Using $N = 2$ for the numerator and $N = 28$ for the denominator[10] (since the table does not show $N = 27$), we find:

At 5 per cent probability, F = 3.354.
At 10 per cent probability, F = 2.511.
At 25 per cent probability, F = 1.46.

Hence, there is 1 chance in about 5 (by interpolation) that the difference of these three means would be exceeded by chance.

CHI SQUARE AND THE TEST FOR GOODNESS OF FIT

The chi-square test is a method of determining the goodness of fit of a theoretical distribution (a universe) and an actual distribution (a sample) so as to form a judgment as to the probability that the theoretical distribution is applicable.

Suppose that of 200 consumers in a random sample, 56 prefer Zilch coffee. The question arises whether the true market share is 30 per cent or the 28 per cent indicated by the sample.

To apply the chi-square test requires that the total sample frequencies be equal to the total hypothesized frequencies. This is a restriction on the freedom of the hypothesized frequencies to vary because when we hypothesize that 30 per cent prefer Zilch coffee, we necessarily have stated that 70 per cent do not. From this condition, we infer that the data have only 1 degree of freedom.

We can set up the following table for the example:

Actual frequency (1)	Hypothesized frequency (2)	Difference (column 1 minus column 2) (3)	Difference (column 3) squared (4)	χ^2 (column 4 divided by column 2) (5)
28	30	−2	4	0.133
72	70	2	4	0.057
Σ 100	100	0	8	0.190

The algebraic sum of the differences of the hypothesized frequency from the actual will always total 0.

The sum of the division of the squared differences (column 4) by the hypothesized frequencies (column 2) gives the χ^2 value, which is an abstract coefficient that can be compared with a basic table.

[10] *Most statistics books show the F ratio at the 1 per cent and 5 per cent levels. The F ratio at the 10 per cent and 25 per cent levels as well as the 1 per cent and 5 per cent levels can be found in Charles R. Hicks,* Fundamental Concepts in the Design of Experiments *(New York: Holt, Rinehart and Winston, Inc., 1964), pp. 270–275. This table is reproduced below at pp. 590–599. In business research the need is greater than in the physical sciences for a table with a broader range than is usually found in statistics books. In the physical sciences, the F ratio is frequently set at 0.01 for the results to be acceptable.*

The χ^2 test assumes that the distribution of the differences between the actual and the hypothesized frequencies is normal.

From a χ^2 table we find that the probability of a χ^2 of 0.190 or larger with 1 degree of freedom is 0.66. The probability of a proportion of 28 per cent or less is 0.33 ($\frac{1}{2}$ of 0.66). Cutting in half is necessary because it is apparent that a χ^2 of 0.190 would also result from a sample with 32 per cent Zilch (as well as from our case of 28 per cent).

A More Complicated Example

Suppose we have 4 dice (6-faced) and toss them 216 times with the following results:

	Actual frequencies (1)	Theoretical frequencies (2)	Difference (column 1 minus column 2) (3)	Difference squared (4)	χ^2 (column 4 divided by column 2) (5)
4 of a kind	0	1	−1	1	1.00
3 of a kind, 1 odd	25	20	+5	25	1.25
2 pairs	11	15	−4	16	1.06
1 pair, 2 odd	125	120	+5	25	0.21
4 all different	55	60	−5	25	0.42
Total	216	216	0	92	3.94

The theoretical frequencies are established by the combination formulas of probabilities. Are the differences of column 3 so large that it is unreasonable to suppose the universe from which this sample comes is not like column 2?

The first problem is to determine the number of observations that are free to vary at random: this is the number of degrees of freedom. While there are 5 different events or observations, it is not the actual number of observations that is critical but the number of observations which are free to vary at random. This is always less than the total number of observations in a controlled problem. In this case, once the number of observations of 4 of a kind, 3 of a kind with 1 odd, 2 pairs, and 1 pair with 2 odd has been established, the last number, for 4 all different, is *determined*. Hence, 1 degree of freedom has been forfeited, and the number of degrees of freedom for this problem is 4.

Referring to the χ^2 table,[11] we find that the value 3.94 (or larger) with 4 degrees of freedom will occur in about 42 per cent of the cases, and we would conclude that the fit is good.

MULTICOLLINEARITY

Multicollinearity is the situation in which some or all of the independent variables in an analysis have a significant relationship to each other as well as to the dependent variable. When multicollinearity exists between

[11] See below, p. 588f.

the independent variables themselves as well as between the independent variables and the dependent variable, a multiple regression equation correctly predicts (shows the relationship to) the dependent variable. We are assuming that the combined effect (association) of all the independent variables (as measured by the t or F value applicable to the entire equation) is significant. We have difficulty, however, in separating the influences (associations) of each of those independent variables *which are interrelated* on the dependent variable. If only *some* of the independent variables are closely related to each other but other independent variables are not so related, then the association with the dependent variable of those independent variables that are not related to each other is validly stated separately. It is only the individual relation to the dependent variable of each of these independent variables that are interrelated that cannot be separately stated.

An example will illustrate the problem of multicollinearity. Suppose the hypothesis is that Y, the consumption of a particular good, depends upon X, the gross national product, and upon Z, the amount of savings. There may well be a relation between Y and X and between Y and Z, but there is also a relation between X and Z.

If we seek to fit a multiplicative equation of the form $Y = aX^bZ^c$ in an effort to develop b the elasticity of X with respect to Y or c the elasticity of Z with respect to Y, we cannot separately state these elasticities if there is multicollinearity. But if there were a third independent variable S, such as temperature, which would not be related to X or to Z, then the elasticity d of S developed by the equation $Y = aX^bZ^cS^d$ would be valid.

Testing for Multicollinearity

We can determine the existence of multicollinearity by a graphic test. The deviations of the observed Y values from the X trend line (fitting the Y values plotted against the X values) are plotted on one axis of four quadrants against the deviations of the observed Y values from the Z trend line (fitting the Y values against the Z values). In performing this plot of deviations, we use each year as a point. Table 3–6 gives the illustrative data, which are charted in Figure 3–5.

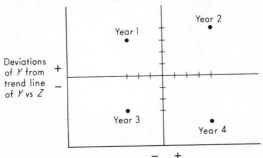

Figure 3–5. Plot of deviations of Y from trend line of Y versus X against deviations of Y from trend line of Y versus Z to test for multicollinearity

Table 3–6. *Illustrative data to be tested
for multicollinearity*

	Deviations of Y values from trend line fitted for Y against X	Deviations of Y values from trend line fitted for Y against Z
Year 1	−3	3
Year 2	4	4
Year 3	−3	−3
Year 4	4	−4

If a linear pattern appears on the graph, there is multicollinearity, and the clearer the pattern, the greater the multicollinearity. The precise degree of correlation between the two sets of deviations can be determined by the usual correlation technique.

Another but casual way of determining multicollinearity involves examining what happens to the regression coefficient of each independent variable as other independent variables are eliminated from the analysis. When multiple correlation is performed on a computer and advantage is taken of the rerun-and-delete possibilities to vary the independent variable that is eliminated, the stage is set for the use of this technique.

To use an illustration, suppose a case with Y as the dependent variable and X and Z as independent variables. Suppose that Y is related to each of X and Z and further that X and Z are related to each other. A moment's reflection will make it clear that if X and Z are related to each other, much more variation will appear in each of X and Z when considered simultaneously than when either one is taken separately and without the other in the problem.

Thus, suppose that Z has an effect on both Y and X. When Z increases, there is a twofold effect on X. Hence, when we consider the case of Y in relation to X and Z simultaneously, the variation in X will be greater than when we consider the relation of Y to X only.

Accordingly, when a rerun deleting an independent variable is made, we would expect the net regression coefficient of each of the remaining independent variables which has a relation to the omitted independent variable to change sharply.

Methods of Dealing with Multicollinearity

When multicollinearity exists, the present state of statistics offers little help in dealing with the problems. Partial correlation may be proposed. With this technique the effect (association) of X on Y is analyzed by simple correlation while the effect (association) of Z is held constant at its average value. But partial correlation is not effective when multicollinearity is extreme since Z's average relationship cannot be identified and hence cannot be held constant. We can say, however, that if the residuals of the correlation of Y and Z (the variation in Y unexplained by the regression equation) are independent of (not related in a systematic manner to) the independent variable Z, then the estimate of the coefficient of that independent variable is the best possible one and is unbiased.

One method of dealing with the problem of multicollinearity is the use of the simultaneous equation technique, which involves a system of equations with each equation stating a particular relationship of the variables. The solution of the system (which involves as many equations as there are unknowns) gives a result which takes account of both the interrelation between the independent and dependent variables and that between the independent variables themselves. The system of equations can be solved either by the method of determinants or by the addition-subtraction method, which takes the equations two at a time and eliminates one variable and proceeds with the resulting equation to the elimination of another variable in the same manner.[12]

AUTOCORRELATION

Autocorrelation may be defined as the situation in which one value of a variable in a time series is related to (not independent of) another value of the same variable at an earlier (or later) point in time. Thus, the sales of a company in one month are correlated to the sales of that company in a following month, or the price today of a commodity may be correlated to the price tomorrow. The presence of seasonality in data for periods of less than a year will involve autocorrelation, as will the presence of a cyclical aspect even for annual data.

One of the great advantages of cross-sectional analysis, which is defined as examining observations taken *at one point* in time but broken down by geographical areas, income classes, or other characteristics, is that the problem of autocorrelation is avoided. Autocorrelation is a vice of time series from the point of view of regression analysis, but it may be an aid in forecasting.

The vice of autocorrelation is that it makes difficult the isolation of the true effect (association) of independent variables on the dependent variable. Further, the presence of autocorrelation affects the use of the tests of significance such as the t and F tests, both of which assume a normal distribution of residuals.

On the other hand, the existence of strong autocorrelation can be a blessing for forecasting. When the forecasted (dependent) variable has autocorrelation, that the variable lagged one or more periods as an "inde-

---

[12] *The use of the simultaneous equation technique involves the assumption that the system of equations is just determined and not overdetermined or underdetermined. In short, the assumption is that there is an unique solution of the system of equations. Cf. Erwin E. Nemmers, "The Identification Problem," Managerial Economics: Text and Cases, rev. printing (New York: John Wiley & Sons, Inc., 1964), pp. 123–129.*

pendent" variable may facilitate short-range forecasting. Thus, if Y is the dependent variable, the forecasting equation may be in the form $Y = a + bY_{t-1} + cZ$, where Y_{t-1} is the value of the forecasted variable in a preceding period.[13]

Tests for Autocorrelation

The determination whether autocorrelation exists involves the use of probability. Thus, the existence of autocorrelation is usually detected by examining the residuals (from curve fitting) or the first differences between successive values. The fact that there is a secular trend over time in an economic series introduces autocorrelation into the series. Similarly, a regular seasonal pattern involves autocorrelation when we are dealing with monthly data.

Graphically, we can test for autocorrelation by plotting the residuals (from curve fitting) of one year on one axis against the residuals of the succeeding year on the other axis. If autocorrelation exists, a linear or curvilinear pattern will develop.[14] This is an inexact test.

For a precise test[15] (in the sense of making numerical comparisons between situations) we can employ the von Neumann ratio to establish a statistic K which is defined as the ratio m^2/s^2, where s^2 is the mean of the sum of the squared residuals (of the fitted variable) and m^2 is the sum of the squares of the successive differences of the residuals (of the fitted variable) divided by the number of observations of the variable less 1.

As N (the number of items) increases, the statistic K will approach 2 if there is no autocorrelation. K will start from above 0 and rise as N increases if there is perfect positive autocorrelation and conversely start above 4 and fall as N increases if there is perfect negative autocorrelation. The table (see below, p. 601) for testing K is set up on the assumption that the residuals in the universe are uncorrelated and normally distributed, and it gives the values of K that could occur by chance in finite random samples if K were actually approaching 2 in the universe.

We can illustrate the computation of the von Neumann ratio as applied to the residuals shown in Table 3–7.

[13] *In this case, the use of the von Neumann ratio or similar tests for autocorrelation (to be presently discussed) is inapplicable. Cf. Franklin M. Fisher's review (Ameri*can Economic Review, *vol. 54, no. 6, pp. 1132–1135, December, 1964) of J. Johnston,* Econometric Methods (*New York: McGraw-Hill Book Company, 1963), and of Arthur S. Goldberger,* Econometric Theory (*New York: John Wiley & Sons, Inc., 1964), in which he criticizes both authors for failure to point out the inapplicability of such tests in this situation.*

[14] *For an example, see Frederick A. Ekeblad,* The Statistical Method in Business (*New York: John Wiley & Sons, Inc., 1962), p. 655.*

[15] *This test is set out by B. I. Hart, "Significance Levels of the Ratio of the Mean Square Successive Differences to the Variance,"* Annals of Mathematical Statistics, *vol. 13, pp. 445ff., 1942.*

Table 3–7. Residuals from multiple correlation of annual expenditures on chemical fertilizers (dependent variable) and cash income of farmers in current and preceding years and percentage of prior year's cash income remaining after paying production expenses (independent variables)

1911	1	1921	−70	1931	11	1941	18
1912	−5	1922	11	1932	−3	1942	6
1913	0	1923	13	1933	0	1943	−2
1914	26	1924	−12	1934	−5	1944	−46
1915	2	1925	−6	1935	−19	1945	−27
1916	2	1926	−9	1936	−2	1946	−33
1917	−42	1927	−29	1937	25	1947 ˋ	−46
1918	−32	1928	20	1938	0	1948	7
1919	4	1929	6	1939	24	1949	64
1920	16	1930	22	1940	11	1950	163

SOURCE: Erwin E. Nemmers, *Managerial Economics: Text and Cases*, rev. printing (New York: John Wiley & Sons, Inc., 1964), Table 1, p. 155.

The computation of the K value is done in Table 3–8.

We compare this value of K (with the associated N size of sample) with the table (p. 601) setting limits for different levels of confidence. Values of K falling outside these limits establish autocorrelation with a given level of confidence. In the present example, the limits of K at the 5 per cent level are below 1.5304 for positive autocorrelation and above 2.5722 for negative autocorrelation.[16]

One Application of the Test for Autocorrelation

One of the uses of a test for autocorrelation is to examine the residuals of the dependent variable after a correlation has been performed. These residuals (differences between the actual values and the computed values of the dependent variable) may be random. In other words, if the test of the residuals of the dependent variable for autocorrelation shows no autocorrelation, we have *some* (but far from conclusive) evidence that we have exhausted the possibilities of using independent variables to explain the dependent variable. If autocorrelation remains, this is a sign that we *may* still be able to improve upon the proposed independent variables by using the dependent variable as an "independent" variable.

[16] *Other tests for autocorrelation are set out in R. L. Anderson, "Distribution of the Serial Correlation Coefficient," Annals of Mathematical Statistics, vol. 13, no. 1, pp. 1–13, 1942. See also J. Durbin and G. S. Watson, "Testing for Serial Correlation in Least Squares Regression I," Biometrika, vol. 37, pp. 409–421, 1950; Part II, vol. 38, pp. 159–178, 1951. The Durbin-Watson coefficient is $(N-1)/N$ times the von Neumann ratio, and the Durbin-Watson table is interpreted in the same way as the von Neumann ratio table.*

Table 3–8. Computation of von Neumann ratio for residuals in Table 3–7

Year	Residuals at T_i point in time	Successive differences $T_{i+1} - T_i$	Square of residuals T_i^2	Square of successive differences $(T_{i+1} - T_i)^2$
1911	1	−6	1	. . .
1912	−5	5	25	36
1913	0	26	0	25
1914	26	−24	676	676
1915	2	0	4	576
1916	2	−44	4	0
1917	−42	10	1,764	1,936
1918	−32	36	1,024	100
1919	4	12	16	1,296
1920	16	−86	256	144
1921	−70	81	4,900	7,396
1922	11	2	121	6,561
1923	13	−25	169	4
1924	−12	6	144	625
1925	−6	−3	36	36
1926	−9	−20	81	9
1927	−29	49	841	400
1928	20	−14	400	2,401
1929	6	16	36	196
1930	22	−11	484	256
1931	11	−14	121	121
1932	−3	3	9	196
1933	0	−5	0	9
1934	−5	−14	25	25
1935	−19	17	361	196
1936	−2	27	4	289
1937	25	−25	625	729
1938	0	24	0	625
1939	24	−13	576	576
1940	11	7	121	169
1941	18	−12	324	49
1942	6	−8	36	144
1943	−2	−44	4	64
1944	−46	19	2,116	1,936
1945	−27	−6	729	361
1946	−33	−13	1,089	36
1947	−46	53	2,116	169
1948	7	57	49	2,809
1949	64	99	4,096	3,249
1950	163	37	26,569	9,801
Total			49,952	44,225

$$K = m^2/s^2 = \frac{\Sigma(T_{i+1} - T_i)^2}{N - 1} \bigg/ \frac{\Sigma T_i^2}{N} = \frac{44,225}{39} \bigg/ \frac{49,952}{40} = 0.908*$$

* For sample size 40, the critical value of the von Neumann ratio from the Hart table (see below, p. 601) is 1.3266 at the 1 per cent level and 1.5304 at the 5 per cent level. Since the computed K is less than these critical values, positive autocorrelation is present at each level of confidence.

Methods of Dealing with Autocorrelation

Once we have determined whether autocorrelation exists, the next problem (if it is present) is how to eliminate its effects, since autocorrelation seriously affects the tests of significance such as the t and F tests.

The most common way to eliminate the effects of autocorrelation from any economic time series is to eliminate the trend from the series and then to proceed with the differences between the observed values and the trend values. These differences may then be analyzed, for example, by the methods of multiple correlation. Trend is only one possible source of autocorrelation, however, and hence autocorrelation may survive this operation.

As an alternative method, we can proceed by introducing "time" into the regression equation as an explicit term, for example, $Y = a + bX + cZ + dT$, with T having a defined origin and being measured in appropriate time units from that origin.

A third way of dealing with autocorrelation is the method of first differences, namely, using the differences between successive values of a series (at two successive points in time) and analyzing the differences against the corresponding differences of another economic series. Thus, the dependent variable is analyzed in terms of the change in consumption of a product between points 1 and 2 in time against the change in income (the independent variable) between the same two points in time.

It is advisable to test the series of these first differences of any variable for autocorrelation since there are situations in which first differences are autocorrelated.

THE USE OF A DUMMY VARIABLE

Changes in the Regression Relationship over Time

One of the problems that frequently arises in correlation studies of time series data is whether the relationship involved is stable throughout the period being examined or whether there has been a shift or shifts in the relationship of the variables. For example, we may suspect that the pre-World War II relationship of the variables is different from the post-World War II relationship or that the price elasticity of the demand for coal for space heating is different in the periods before and after the introduction of oil and gas for space heating.

One way to test this question is to split the data into two groups, one for the earlier years or period and the other for the later. Then substantially the same regression equation is expected for both "halves" if there has been no change in the relationship between the periods. Even if the same relationship among the variables exists for both halves, however, we would expect the two regression equations to differ from each other within certain limits on a random basis.

Another approach is to test for any suspected changes in the "true" relationship by the use of a dummy or discontinuity variable. Thus, we add a dummy variable to our independent variables and give it a value of 0 for all periods prior to a given date and a value of 1 for all subsequent periods. It is clear that this variable will have both an arithmetic mean and a standard deviation between 0 and 1. Likewise, the usual tests of significance (such as the t and F tests) can be applied to the net regression coefficient of the dummy variable if we make the usual assumptions as to the normal characteristics of the distribution. If this regression coefficient is found to be significant when it is tested, we can infer that there has been a significant change in the relationship between one half of the periods and the other half, namely, that the data of the two segments (before and after the given date) represent drawings from two different universes. In this event, we would fit two separate regression equations to the data before the given date and after that date.[17]

Use of Dummy Variable for Nonquantitative Variable with More Than Two Values

Another use of the dummy variable technique is the situation of nonquantitative variables. Suppose that we are investigating the association of the interest rate of municipal bonds (as the dependent variable) and a bond rating such as AAA, AA, etc. (as an independent variable).[18] The interest rate of municipal bonds is a quantitative variable in that it has a dimension and in that distances between readings of the variable are directly comparable and proportionate. On the other hand, the bond rating may, in a sense, be said to have dimension, but differences between ratings cannot be said to be equal. If we could assume the differences between ratings were equal, we could use a dummy variable for the bond rating and assign values such as the following: AAA rating = 1, AA rating = 2, A rating = 3, etc. Then regression analysis would determine whether this variable was significantly associated. If the differences between bond ratings were not equal and we used the step just indicated, however, we would be implying a scale of the bond-rating variable that does not exist.

To overcome this difficulty, we might proceed as follows: each *value* of the bond-rating variable can be treated as a separate variable with only two values, present or absent, designated by 0 or 1. We can summarize this in the following matrix:

	Entry on card for variable		
	AAA	*AA*	*A*
Card for bond rating AAA	1	0	0
Card for bond rating AA	0	1	0
Card for bond rating A	0	0	1

[17] For further development of dummy variables at an elementary level, see J. Johnston, Econometric Methods (New York: McGraw-Hill Book Company, 1963), pp. 221–228.

[18] For an illustration using these variables and the dummy technique, see A. James Heins, Constitutional Restrictions against State Debt (Madison, Wis.: The University of Wisconsin Press, 1963), pp. 60–68.

In addition, we would set the regression coefficient of one of the bond ratings (say AAA) equal to 0 to prevent perfect correlation. The variation that would have been reported by this regression coefficient would then be reported elsewhere, for example, in the constant term a or in other regression coefficients or in the unexplained variation.

Use of Dummy Variable to Avoid Assumption of Linearity

Even though the independent variable has discrete values and a uniform scale (such as dollars of sales), we may wish to avoid assuming arithmetic linearity (as in the additive form of equation[19]) or logarithmic linearity (as in the multiplicative form of equation[20]) in determining whether there is a significant relation between the dependent variable and the independent variables. Thus there are mutual savings banks in only 17 of the 50 states. If we are analyzing a problem in volume of bank deposits as the dependent variable, we can use a dummy variable for whether a state has mutual savings banks or not (the independent variable) rather than enter the actual deposits for such banks in 17 states and zero deposits for such banks for the other 33 states.[21]

SELECTED BIBLIOGRAPHY

GENERAL

W. J. Dixon and F. J. Massey, Jr.: *Introduction to Statistical Analysis,* 2d ed. (New York: McGraw-Hill Book Company, 1957).

Frederick A. Ekeblad: *The Statistical Method in Business* (New York: John Wiley & Sons, Inc., 1962).

R. A. Fisher: *Statistical Methods for Research Workers* (London: Oliver & Boyd, Ltd., 1948).

CORRELATION AND REGRESSION ANALYSIS

Mordecai J. B. Ezekiel and Karl A. Fox: *Methods of Correlation and Regression Analysis,* 3d ed. (New York: John Wiley & Sons, Inc., 1959).

PROBABILITY

William Fellner: *An Introduction to Probability Theory and Its Applications* (New York: John Wiley & Sons, Inc., 1950).

Robert Schlaifer: *Probability and Statistics for Business Decisions* (New York: McGraw-Hill Book Company, 1959).

[19] *Discussed above at pp. 145–154.*

[20] *Discussed above at p. 154.*

[21] *Cf. Edgar L. Feige,* The Demand for Liquid Assets: A Temporal Cross-Section Analysis *(Englewood Cliffs, N.J.: Prentice-Hall, Inc., 1964).*

SAMPLE RESEARCH FOR CRITICAL EVALUATION

INTRODUCTION

In this part we have included 18 articles and studies covering a wide range of subject matter. These are the "cases" which support our use of that word in the title of this book.

These cases provide an opportunity to test the principles and ideas developed in the first three parts of the book. They cover a wide range of journals, fields of business, and questions of methodology and of research problems. As is appropriate to the case method, no clues are given as to what issues each article raises. Sometimes the issues are fairly obvious, and sometimes they are quite subtle.

Not only are specific problems raised by each article, but the reader is invited to form a judgment as to whether the work as a whole should be classified as good or poor.

To facilitate the development of skill in critical evaluation, several instances involve a pair of articles on the same subject. Thus, the first two articles are concerned with the reading materials of a sample of businessmen. In this instance, the second article reveals several of the weaknesses of the first article and adopts methods of dealing with them. In the case of other pairs of articles dealing with the same subject, a comparison of the two studies will help in establishing an evaluation.

This group of studies includes two items issued by the business research departments of the United States Steel Corporation and the Standard Oil Company (Indiana). We are concerned less with whether some persons might argue that these items are improperly labeled as research than we are interested in them as examples of work undertaken by departments within a corporation and as cases suited to various research techniques.

As a crutch which may facilitate the reader's analysis of each of these studies, we propose the following check list, which is not to be considered complete. Determining which items of this list are dominant in each study may help start the reader's analysis of the research stature of any particular study.

1. Is there evidence of conscious or unconscious bias?
2. Is the research objective carefully and unambiguously set out?
3. Are there data problems and appropriate solutions of such problems?
4. Are there problems of definition and of classification?
5. Are control groups appropriate?
6. Does the author recognize problems of the level of confidence when statistics are computed?
7. Are hypotheses unambiguously stated?
8. Are inferences adequately supported by evidence?
9. What research methods (such as historical, case, statistical, etc.) are appropriate?
10. If a model is employed, is the model adequate and are the methods appropriate?
11. If interviewing is the technique for generating data, are the survey methods and the questionnaire sound?
12. If sampling is used, does the author deal with sampling errors and other problems inherent in the sampling technique?
13. Does the work reflect careful planning and the use of imagination in anticipating difficulties?
14. Is the presentation of the research activities and results unambiguous, free from distortion, and effective?
15. Is the research process free from logical fallacies and deficiencies?
16. Does the author consider relevant research work of others in the same area and deal with problems of reconciling his activities and results with those of other researchers?

There is a natural tendency at this stage of events to become hypercritical. Perhaps we can best characterize the attitude to be avoided as mere carping. One way of guarding against this attitude is to insist that every alleged defect from a research point of view in turn be met by the critic with a constructive recommendation for solution.

In the present book we have not devoted particular attention to the matter of adequate and effective presentation of research activities and results. It is clear that a researcher may perform a creditable piece of work but that the presentation of the fruits of his labor may be quite deficient. A number of well-known manuals deal with these problems.

Lastly, it will become apparent in the perusal of these studies that the depth of criticism possible for any one individual as to each article or study is partially dependent on the reader's previous knowledge of or training in the particular subject matter. On the other hand, the reader will find that some skill in scientific method and research techniques will enable him to form evaluations of work in areas where he has little background. In particular he will become aware of the universality of research problems and of the application of scientific method.

READING HABITS
OF BUSINESS
EXECUTIVES*

How much use do business executives really make of all the literature that is theirs for the asking and paying, or in some cases comes to them unsolicited and uninvoiced? Does this reading matter really do the job it allegedly is designed for—help them in the conduct of their business? The purpose of this article is to try to throw some light on such questions by analyzing the reading habits of business executives and deriving some conclusions about their attitude toward what they read.

The volume of business literature available is indeed tremendous. Standard Rate & Data Service lists over 1,600 business papers currently being published in the United States. The Special Libraries Association counted 577 commercial and financial digests, news letters, and information service in 1944. Business and economic books are produced at the rate of about 500 annually. There are thousands of "informational" press releases and "giveaways" that cross the executive's desk—or at least get as far as his secretary's wastepaper basket. And the libraries open to businessmen are crammed with a selection of all this material.

How can a busy man drink of the flood without being drowned in it? How can those who wish to influence the business executive by means of the literature he reads get through to him, make sure that he gives attention to their particular messages? The crux of the problem lies in executives' reading habits. What do they read? How do they read? Why do they read? Unfortunately, however, little is really known about this subject that is of a broad and comprehensive nature, and the dearth of knowledge cannot be rectified without extensive research. Indeed, the present article is frankly exploratory; it should be a beginning rather than an end of study.

Perhaps one of the greatest needs is for more knowledge of the reading habits of a particular group of executives—those who are in top, decision-making positions. If, in addition, they are also men who can be influenced by what they read—judged by their interest in the kind of literature which requires the characteristics of intellectual curiosity, receptivity to new ideas, willingness to look at both sides of a question, and thorough-going analysis—they will represent an even higher potential for communication via the printed page. Men of this caliber, in short, would be the effective agency by which *ideas* actually affect the economy.

* By Edward C. Bursk and Donald T. Clark. Reprinted from Harvard Business Review, May, 1949, pp. 330–345. Used by permission.

In this connection the observations to follow should be of especial significance, since the type of executives covered are concentrated in the decision-making, thoughtful category. Our statistical findings are based on the more than 20,000 subscribers to the *Harvard Business Review*. The "heavy" nature of the *Review's* editorial contents (side by side with evidence of more-than-average careful reading) automatically serves to screen out the less-thoughtful type of executives. In addition, the subscription list, while correlating closely with the normal geographical distribution and industrial classification of business, shows an unusually high level of company positions held (see Exhibit I).

A four-page questionnaire was sent to over 9,000 *Review* subscribers in the summer and fall of 1948 (see Exhibit II). For statistical purposes, however, main reliance has been placed on returns from a random sample of 1,600 subscribers (every fifteenth stencil in the address list), which was carefully tested for validity in comparison with known characteristics of the total *Review* circulation. The response from this typical cross section of subscribers was 37%. Another special sample of 600, where the individuals queried were all top, policy-making officers of the largest corporations, was selected for purposes of possible contrast; the basis of the selection was the companies whose annual statements are most frequently requested at the Harvard Business School library. Altogether 84% in this sample were presidents, vice presidents, and chairmen and members of the board of directors; and the assets of the 189 corporations which they represented came to over $81 billion. The response from this selected group was 28%. The returns from the balance of the 9,000 subscribers to whom questionnaires were sent have been used for statistical confirmation of doubtful points and for additional background information. Over 90% of all returns were signed, and over half carried voluntary comments—attesting to the sincerity and care with which the data were provided.

The statistical analysis has been supplemented by interviews with company presidents and other business leaders; intensive study of a few selected companies; conversations with librarians of business firms and librarians of business branches of public libraries; correspondence with officers of the Special Libraries Association; and of course the general experience of the authors as editor and librarian serving the interests of businessmen.

If there is one major conclusion that emerges from our investigation, it is that the kind of executive we are discussing does a great deal of reading related to his business interests. He is likely to take a business newspaper such as the *Wall Street Journal*. More often than not he reads a trade publication specifically devoted to his own field, like *Iron Age* or *Women's Wear Daily*. On the average he subscribes to four magazines of general business interest, like *Business Week, Fortune,* or *Time*. Almost invariably he buys books that he thinks will help him in business. He makes heavy use of digests and reports. And he often falls back on the reference service of libraries for help on special topics.

Exhibit I. Position analysis of subscribers to Harvard Business Review

---

Company officers and directors
    Board chairmen and directors   1 %
    Owners   6
    Partners   6
    Presidents   19
    Vice presidents   11
    Assistants to president   1
    General managers   6
    Treasurers   6
    Controllers   3
    Other officers   2
    Company subscriptions   6
Total   67 %

Department heads and division managers
    Sales, market research, advertising   4 %
    Plant superintendents & chief engineers   1
    Directors of industrial relations   1
    Other department heads   6
Total   12 %

Personal consultants to business
    Lawyers, C.P.A.'s, other consultants   4 %
Total officers, department heads and personal consultants   83 %*

Government
    Federal   2 %
    State, local and foreign   1
Total   3 %

Other company subscribers
    Sales representatives, accountants, engineers & other company positions   6 %

Libraries, educators, and miscellaneous
    Libraries   4 %
    Educators   1
    Students, retired, others   3
Total   8 %
Grand Total   100 %

---

* 83 % of subscribers are top management in that they are directly concerned with major company policies and long-range planning.

Exhibit II. Excerpts from questionnaire sent to Harvard Business Review subscribers

---

1. Do you read business books on subjects
   Specifically in your field   . . . . .
   Or on business matters generally   . . . . .
   Or both   . . . . .

2. Do you read nonbusiness books
   For entertainment   . . . . .
   For general information   . . . . .
   For study in some other field or fields   . . . . .

3. If you care to list one or more books on business subjects, which you found of interest the last six months, it will be helpful.   . . . .

4. In some instances top-management executives have a digest of pertinent current business information specially prepared for them. Do you have such assistance?
   YES. . . . . NO. . . . .
   If you do have such an assistant, will you ask him to list the primary sources from which he gathers this information.   . . . .

   . . . .

5. To what magazines in the following list do you subscribe?
   Barron's   . . .   Business Week   . . .
   Fortune   . . .   Newsweek   . . .
   Harvard Business Review   . . .   Time   . . .
   Wall Street Journal   . . .   U.S. News   . . .
   Nation's Business   . . .   Journal of Commerce   . . .
   Please list other trade magazines specifically written to your field of endeavor which you *read* . . . .

   . . . .

6. In what order would you place them (1, 2, 3, etc.) as of assistance to you in decisions on business policy?
   Barron's   . . .   Nation's Business   . . .
   Business Week   . . .   Newsweek   . . .
   Fortune   . . .   Time   . . .
   Harvard Business Review   . . .   U.S. News   . . .
   Wall Street Journal   . . .   Journal of Commerce   . . .
   Other trade magazines in your own field   . . .

7. To what nonbusiness magazines do you subscribe for your own reading? Name a few that you prefer.

   . . . .

   . . . .

8. In what manner do you read the magazines you have checked above?

	Read in full	Read in part	Read at office	Read outside office	In one sitting	In two or more sittings	Approx. time to each issue	Read and keep for reference
Barron's								
Business Week								
Fortune								
Journal								
Journal of Commerce								
Trade magazines written specifically to your field								

BUSINESS NEWSPAPERS

Information was secured on three representative business newspapers. The following tabulation of returns from the cross-section sample shows the percentage who subscribe to the individual newspapers and the extent of duplication:

46% subscribe to *Wall Street Journal*.
24% subscribe to *Journal of Commerce*.
19% subscribe to *Barron's*.
63% subscribe to at least one of the three.
34% subscribe to at least two of the three.
 6% subscribe to all three.

As to the way these newspapers are read: the average subscriber reads his copies in his office, in one "sitting," spending about one-half hour in the process. About 25% say they read each issue in full, and some 60% file their copies for future reference.

One surprising finding is that, although these newspapers are apparently read mostly for the sake of general information and news of recent developments, they are considered of relatively great assistance in making "business decisions." This was the basis on which the questionnaire asked for a comparative ranking (1, 2, 3, etc.) of the respondent's business newspapers, general magazines, and trade publications. Two kinds of information resulted: (1) the number of subscribers of a given paper or magazine who ranked that publication, expressed here as a percentage of the total number of its subscribers giving usable answers, and (2) the specific ranks assigned, expressed here as a median of the total rankings assigned to a particular publication. Of those subscribing to one or more of the three business newspapers listed, 84% assigned explicit rankings to a business newspaper. The *Wall Street Journal* by itself actually had a median rank of 1—that is, over half of those subscribing to it placed it at the top of their list—with the *Journal of Commerce* and *Barron's* being just enough less favorable to put the median rank for all three over the line into the 2 range.

Apparently there is a reflection here of the relation in executives' minds between up-to-the-minute information and ability to make business decisions wisely—the latter being an area in which executives expect little direct help. This feeling, demonstrated by many of the comments written in on the questionnaire, will be discussed at more length later.

Supplementary to the data on regular business newspapers are some figures on newspapers of the nonbusiness type, secured by a special post-card questionnaire. Virtually every executive reads at least one large metropolitan newspaper of the nonbusiness type. Only the *New York Times* and the *New York Herald Tribune* appear to have much more than a local circulation among business executives; these two, however, have a very wide distribution. As a matter of fact, 35% of all respondents subscribe to or read regularly the *Times* (but not the *Herald Tribune*), 7% make similar use of the *Herald Tribune* (but not the *Times*), and an additional 10% read both—a total of 52% as compared with only about 20% having physical location in the New York area. No other metropolitan newspaper is mentioned by as many as 10% of the executives covered.

How are these metropolitan newspapers regarded? The *New York Times*, with a strong emphasis on business and financial news, is ranked on practically equal terms with the *Wall Street Journal* as being of assistance in making business decisions, and the same amount of time is spent in reading each copy (30 minutes); the *New York Herald Tribune* is apparently in somewhat the same category but has a lower ranking. The other papers taken together—though of course there is variation—are given definitely less attention; the average reading time is 15 to 20 minutes, with quite a few returns specifying as low as 5 minutes per copy. In general, too, the nonbusiness newspapers are read in the office by only a small proportion of executives; the specific figures for reading outside the office are 58% in the case of the *New York Times* (again most nearly approaching the business newspapers) and 75% in the case of the balance.

Cities like Cleveland, Detroit, St. Louis, and Minneapolis on the whole show up better than most of the still larger metropolitan centers in the way their local newspapers are regarded. The situation in Chicago is mixed: the *Tribune* is ranked fairly high sometimes but more often quite low—one comment says, "I read its advice, then do the opposite"—while the *Daily News*, with fewer mentions, hovers in between. (It should be noted that the *Chicago Journal of Commerce*, not to be confused with the New York paper of similar name, is regarded highly.) In Philadelphia the *Inquirer* is at the top of the local papers but still sharply below the *New York Times*. In Boston the *Herald* is mentioned most often but, again, with marked lack of enthusiasm; the *Christian Science Monitor*, incidentally, gets a few very favorable mentions, all from other cities. And in New York the local papers run far behind the *Times* and *Herald Tribune*.

Returning to the business newspapers, one of the interesting findings is that, the more successful the executive is (judged by position and size of company), the more he apparently subscribes to such papers. For example, 76% of the special sample of "big" executives take at least one business newspaper, compared with only 63% of the general cross-section sample; and the number of the former taking several such papers is almost twice as large as the latter. Furthermore, the average reading time per copy is almost identical between the two samples, which means more actual time spent on business newspapers in the case of those making up the special sample.

TRADE PUBLICATIONS

It is impractical, and unnecessary, to list all the different trade publications mentioned on the returns. The titles are as varied as the interests of the executives concerned. Attention can be called, however, to several significant patterns which show up.

Some 75% of the executives making up the general sample take one or more trade publications. As a matter of fact, the average executive subscribes to $2\frac{1}{2}$ such magazines. It is clear, however, that there is a marked variation in the way in which trade publications are used and valued. Despite the multiple possibilities, only 44% of all executives gave any ranking at all to any trade publication, but those who did so usually assigned a high one—a median rank of 1, to be specific. The implication is that the quality or usefulness of trade magazines is uneven—or at least is unevenly appreciated—so that either they are taken (perhaps as a matter of "duty") without being read much at all, or else they are read with extreme care and with what their readers judge to be highly useful results. This implication is supported by the relatively low percentage of answers to the other questions asked in relation to total trade publication subscriptions—but the relatively favorable nature of the answers which were given.

In any event, the remaining observations should be considered as applying primarily to that portion of trade publications which are held in better-than-average esteem. Average reading time is $1\frac{3}{4}$ hours per copy. Some 35% say they read copies in full, 60% devoting more than one "sitting" to each copy; and 91% file copies for future reference. As high as 77% do their reading of trade magazines in the office, a very high figure, attesting to the close tie-in with immediate business interests.

As might be expected, the readership of this type of publication is less among executives at the top of the ladder—under $1\frac{1}{2}$ subscriptions per executive in the special sample, as compared with $2\frac{1}{2}$ in the general sample; and about $1\frac{1}{4}$ hours of reading time per copy, as compared with $1\frac{3}{4}$ hours. Presumably these men are less concerned with the technical, specialized problems of their own industries and more concerned with the general problems of administration and the whole economic environment.

BUSINESS AND NEWS MAGAZINES

Questions were asked about six representative business magazines of a general nature and news magazines with a large content of news of business interest, along with the *Review* itself. For all these magazines together, in competition with the business newspaper and trade publication groups, 68% of subscribers assigned rankings, and the median rank was 3. The fact that here again, as with trade publications, there is a great deal of variation among individual magazines will be noted in more detail when the individual magazines are discussed.

The average executive reads his general business magazines away from his office—in sharp contrast to his reading practice with business newspapers and trade publications. What are the implications of this fact? Of course, part of the reason is that some of the magazines, such as *Time,* are read by others in the family, and so a larger proportion of subscriptions are entered with home addresses. But the same reading practice is followed with *Business Week* and the *Review,* which would have little appeal—the latter in particular!—to wives and children. It would seem therefore that the business executive wants the relative quiet of evening hours in the home and the freedom from business pressures and distractions (including those constant interruptions by telephone) in which to absorb the more thoughtful content of the magazines in question.

Another, and perhaps complementary rather than different, interpretation is that every executive feels there just is not enough time to read all he wants to, and so he *must* read at home the material which is of less direct application to immediate problems. The wonder is not that the more specific literature is chosen for office reading, but that the more general material is considered of enough interest and value to be read so fully at home.

The regard in which executives hold their business and news magazines—not uniformly, to be sure, but all the more markedly in the case of the individual magazines which are most favored—is confirmed by comments written in on the questionnaires or otherwise available. A typical statement (in this case referring to the *Review*) is: "I keep my copy on my bedside table so as to be sure to get it read"—with no intimation, let us hope, that it is a sure cure for executive insomnia. Another confirming phenomenon is that—at least for the *Review* and, one would suppose, also for magazines like *Business Week* and *Fortune*—home reading is the rule even though a large proportion of copies are mailed to business addresses. What is more, copies are apparently taken back to the office for associates to read; to use *Review* experience for illustration again, two-thirds of subscribers say that they mark articles for other's reading, and the average subscriber shares his copies with 1.6 associates.

The other characteristics of the reading of general business and news magazines shown by our survey make a consistent pattern to the same effect: that businessmen do put a premium on reading their copies. The average subscriber to a general business or news magazine spends about two hours on each copy; 39% of such subscribers say they read their copies in full; 63% devote more than one sitting to reading each copy; and 93% keep their copies for future reference—in each case the figure being higher than the "score" of the trade publications by a narrow but definite margin. (See Exhibit III, where some of the significant cross-section data on the three types of publications discussed are drawn together for purposes of comparison.)

Exhibit III. Comparative data on executive readership of business news-papers, trade publications, and general business and news magazines

	Business newspapers	Trade publications	General business and news magazines
Percentage of total sample subscribing to one or more	63%	75%	100%
Average number of publications taken	1.5	2.5	3.5
Percentage of subscribers assigning rankings to publications*	84%	44%	68%
Median rank assigned*	2	1	3
Average reading time per copy†	½ hr.	1¾ hrs.	2 hrs.
Percentage of subscribers reading copies in full†	25%	35%	39%
Percentage reading copies away from their offices	36%	23%	85%
Percentage devoting more than one sitting to each copy	14%	60%	63%
Percentage filing copies for future reference	62%	91%	93%

* Subscribers were asked to rank publications read according to their provision of "assistance . . . in decisions on business policy."
† Probably overstated, judging by experience in other research projects of similar nature, but significant for comparative purposes.
NOTE: On the basis of cross-section sample of *Harvard Business Review* subscribers.

The inference is reasonable that businessmen as they near the "top of the ladder" have increasingly strong interest in literature bearing on increasingly broader problems. If this is so, it should show up further in the differences between the results of the two samples. Reference has already been made to the fact that the executives in the special sample subscribe to fewer trade publications and more business newspapers. In line with this is the fact that they also step up their subscriptions to general business and news magazines—4½ subscriptions per executive as against 3½ for the cross-section sample. No doubt reflecting the greater competition for their time of a greater bulk of literature—presumably at home too there is a limit beyond which time cannot be stretched—the "big" executives spend on the average about one-half hour less on each copy than do those in the cross section.

Comparison of Individual Magazines

Perhaps bearing on the same point, but in any event interesting in its own right, is the degree of variation among individual publications in the general business and news group. One cannot deny that business executives do discriminate, whether rightly or wrongly, among the magazines of this type to which they subscribe. In this connection, mention should be made of the comments which complained about having to rank magazines against each other when some were particularly useful for "long-range" policy decisions and some for "immediate-action" decisions. (The comparative data are presented in Exhibit IV.)

Some figures on the duplication or overlap of subscriptions to the various magazines drawn from the cross-section sample may be interesting. Not counting *Harvard Business Review* subscriptions, the largest single

Exhibit IV. Comparison of seven individual magazines in the general business and news group

	Harvard Business Review	Business Week	Fortune
Percentage of total sample subscribing to this magazine	100%	59%	46%
*Percentage of subscribers to this magazine ranking it**	76%	75%	64%
As among business newspapers, trade publications, and seven general business and news magazines: median rank	2	2	3
As among seven general news and business magazines only:			
Percentage of rankings in 1st place	30%	52%	11%
Percentage of rankings in 2nd place	33	17	30
Percentage of rankings in 3rd place	22	16	24
Percentage of rankings in 4th place	13	10	23
Percentage of rankings in first four places	98%	95%	88%
Average reading time per copy†	3 hrs.	1¼ hrs.	2½ hrs.
Percentage of subscribers reading copies in full†	35%	39%	33%
Percentage reading copies away from office	89%	58%	93%
Percentage devoting more than one "sitting" to each copy	92%	45%	88%
Percentage filing copies for future reference	98%	82%	93%

* Subscribers were asked to rank publications read according to their provision of "assistance . . . in decisions on business policy."
† Probably overstated, judging by experience in other research projects of similar nature, but significant for comparative purposes. Reported times in excess of five hours have all been tabulated as six hours; 11% of *Review* and 7% of *Fortune* answers are in this category, whereas no other publication has more than ½ of 1%.
NOTE: On the basis of a cross-section sample of *Harvard Business Review* subscribers.

group of executives taking *both* of two magazines is 35% (*Time* and *Business Week*); the next group on this basis comes to 33% (*Time* and *Fortune*); and the rest are all below 30%. The largest single group taking *all* of three magazines is 21% (*Time, Business Week,* and *Fortune*), with no other similar groups clos·. No group taking *all* of four or *all* of five magazines amounts to more than 10%. Finally—a surprisingly high figure—4% take *all* of the six magazines (indeed, *all* of the seven, when the *Review* is included).

There is another and perhaps more significant way of looking at the figures—from the standpoint of coverage rather than of duplication. How many executives can be reached by what combinations of magazines (again not counting the *Review*)?

1. The largest percentage that is reached by one magazine is of course 63% (*Time*), with the closest contender at 59% (*Business Week*).

2. The largest percentage that is reached by two magazines—i.e., the largest percentage subscribing to either or both of two

Time	U.S. News	Nation's Business	Newsweek
63%	32%	35%	28%
63%	66%	54%	61%
3	3	4	4
14%	36%	14%	18%
36	30	20	22
20	12	24	20
23	12	21	15
93%	90%	79%	75%
1¾ hrs.	1 hr.	¾ hr.	1¼ hrs.
64%	37%	12%	37%
97%	64%	46%	86%
51%	39%	45%	40%
50%	65%	74%	61%

magazines—is 86% (*Time* and *Business Week*), followed by a close series of combinations at 77% (*Time* and *Nation's Business*), 76% (*Business Week* and *Fortune*), 75% (*Time* and *Newsweek*), 71% (*Business Week* and *U.S. News*).

3. The largest percentage that is reached by three magazines—i.e., the largest percentage subscribing to any one, any two, or all three of three magazines—is 90% (*Time, Business Week,* and *Fortune; Time, Business Week,* and *U.S. News;* and *Time, Business Week,* and *Newsweek*—with only fractional differences separating those combinations).

4. The largest percentage that is reached by four magazines is 94% (*Time, Business Week, Fortune,* and *U.S. News*); with several combinations at 93% (*Time, Business Week, Fortune,* and *Nation's Business;* and *Time, Business Week, Fortune,* and *Newsweek*).

5. No combination of five magazines reaches more than 95% of the total.

6. All six magazines reach 96% of the total.

In other words, using the optimum combinations, one magazine reaches 63% of all the executives; the addition of a second magazine secures coverage of another 23%; the addition of a third reaches another 4%; the addition of a fourth increases the coverage by a further 4%; and a fifth and sixth each add only 1% more.

By way of addendum: Executives report that they subscribe to the following nonbusiness magazines for their own reading, in order of decreasing frequency: *Life* and *Saturday Evening Post* (tied for first place with 11% of the total respondents mentioning them), *Reader's Digest* (8%), *National Geographic Magazine* (5%), *Colliers* and *Atlantic Monthly* (4% each), *New Yorker* (3%), *Harper's Magazine* (2%), and some 50 others, ranging from the *New Republic* to *Field and Stream* (1% or less each). Since the instruction accompanying the question was phrased, "Name a few that you prefer," it is likely that the number of actual subscriptions is greater than the mentions; but the results would seem to be valid for comparative purposes and perhaps are all the more significant because they reflect preferences and therefore presumably actual reading.

BOOKS

One of the major purposes of our questions about books was to find out more about the role books play in the information and background-gathering efforts of business leaders. Here are some of the generalizations that can be made on the answers received.

Executives do read books; by their own report 91% read business books on a fairly broad basis. And only 11% of these men restrict their reading to business books written for their own field of endeavor. Perhaps the general feeling about books was best revealed by the many comments which can be summarized in the one statement, "There just isn't time to read one-tenth of all I would like to read." At the same time, there was an undercurrent of disappointment in the quality of business writing today. For example, quite a few gratuitous comments echoed this thought: "With the exception of books on technical subjects, we find that most of the books follow the same old pattern. There is nothing very new."

Less than 7% of the men submitting returns said that they did not read nonbusiness books. Entertainment and desire for general background information seem to be the leading reasons for reading books. The tabulation of purposes follows:

Entertainment	19%
General information	22
Study	3
Entertainment and general information	33
General information and study	5
Entertainment and study	1
All three	15

No effort was made to learn what kinds of nonbusiness books businessmen read, although the comments that were written in point to the high position held by reading about one's hobby. On the contrary, we were searching for some indication of the specific kinds of material businessmen are most likely to read in book form for business purposes. Even though the question on this point was phrased in a very permissive sort of fashion, the return was high. In answer to our statement, "If you care to list one or more books on business subjects which you found of interest in the last six months, it will be helpful," some 40% of the men listed one or more titles.

There were general replies such as: "Books relating to the handling of people interest me to the greatest extent because that seems to be the top problem today." Other respondents mentioned series of books without specific listing of titles: "numerous Brookings Institution books," "publications of the National Bureau of Economic Research," "reports of the National Industrial Conference Board," "Executive Book Club selections," "American Management Association reports."

Others indicated the nature of their reading merely by a general statement about the field of interest: "The list is a long one. They are subjects largely dealing with specific methods of management used to increase the stability and productivity of workers on the job." "Aside from strictly business books, I am most interested in the international picture." "Most of the books I have read lately have to do with business management and psychology in business." "Labor relations subjects." "Tax methods."

Of course, even business executives are human enough to exaggerate their claims to being well read. One respondent commented that he had resisted the temptation to list a few books which he had bought but not read; and certainly many of the mentions mean little more than turning the pages. But the weight of the evidence is not to be denied. Executives of the type covered by our study feel that they need business books.

Not only do the general comments create the impression that businessmen are seeking books of real practical value, but the titles indicate the preponderance of reading in this area as contrasted to theoretical or philosophical studies of business administration. There follows a list of the most popular titles, arranged in decreasing order of number of times mentioned:

16 MENTIONS

Edward R. Dewey and E. F. Dakin, *Cycles; the Science of Prediction* (New York, Henry Holt & Co., Inc., 1947).

14 MENTIONS

David R. Anderson, *Practical Controllership* (Chicago, Richard D. Irwin, Inc., 1947).

Wilson E. Wright, *Forecasting for Profit* (New York, John Wiley & Sons, Inc., 1947).

11 MENTIONS

J. Frederic Dewhurst and Associates, *America's Needs and Resources* (New York; The Twentieth Century Fund, Inc., 1947).

10 MENTIONS

Melvin T. Copeland and A. R. Towl, *Board of Directors and Business Mangement* (Boston, Division of Research, Harvard Business School, 1947).

7 MENTIONS

Henry Hazlitt, *Economics in One Lesson* (New York, Harper & Brothers, 1946).

Elton Mayo, *Human Problems of an Industrial Civilization* (Second edition, Boston, Division of Research, Harvard Business School, 1946).

5 MENTIONS

Rudolf Flesch, *The Art of Plain Talk* (New York, Harper & Brothers, 1946).

Paul E. Holden and others, *Top-Management Organization and Control* (Stanford, Stanford University Press, 1941).

Paul Pigors and Charles A. Myers, *Personnel Administration* (New York, McGraw-Hill Book Company, Inc., 1947).

F. J. Roethlisberger and William J. Dickson, *Management and the Worker* (Cambridge, Harvard University Press, 1939).

Mayo A. Shattuck, *An Estate Planners Handbook* (Boston, Little, Brown & Company, 1948).

Sumner H. Slichter, *Challenge of Industrial Relations* (Ithaca, Cornell University Press, 1947).

4 MENTIONS

Chester I. Barnard, *Organization and Management* (Cambridge, Harvard University Press, 1948).

Alvin Brown, *Organization of Industry* (New York, Prentice-Hall, Inc., 1947).

Norman S. Buchanan and Friedrich A. Lutz, *Rebuilding the World Economy* (New York, The Twentieth Century Fund, Inc., 1947).

Peter F. Drucker, *Concept of the Corporation* (New York, The John Day Company, 1946).

John Jewkes, *Ordeal by Planning* (New York, The Macmillan Company, 1948).

3 MENTIONS

Chester I. Barnard, *Functions of the Executive* (Cambridge, Harvard University Press, 1938).

Eric Berne, *Mind in Action* (New York, Simon & Schuster, Inc., 1947).

Victor Z. Brink, *Internal Auditing* (New York, The Ronald Press Company, 1941).

Taylor Hampton, *The Nickel Plate Road* (Cleveland, World Publishing Co., 1947).

Willford I. King, *Keys to Prosperity* (New York, Constitution & Free Enterprise Foundation Inc., 1948).

Coleman L. Maze, *Office Management; a Handbook* (New York, The Ronald Press Company, 1947).

Joseph Mindell, *The Stock Market; Basic Guide for Investors* (New York, B. C. Forbes Publishing Company, 1948).

F. J. Roethlisberger, *Management and Morale* (Cambridge, Harvard University Press, 1941).

Harold J. Rudolph, *Attention and Interest Factors in Advertising* (New York, Funk & Wagnalls Company, 1947).

Harry Scherman, *The Promises Men Live By* (New York, Random House, Inc., 1938).

Benjamin M. Selekman, *Labor Relations and Human Relations* (New York, McGraw-Hill Book Company, Inc., 1947).

George W. Stocking and Myron W. Watkins, *Cartels or Competition* (New York, The Twentieth Century Fund, Inc., 1948).

In all, 237 specific titles were mentioned. By general categories they break down as follows:

Industrial and personnel management	32
Principles of economics and economic theory	25
Marketing	19
Management principles—business policy	18
Money, banking, and finance	18
Accounting	16
Economic history, business history, and business biographies	16
Labor	11
Production and manufacturing	11
Real estate and land economics	9
Executive self-development	8
Taxation	8
Business and government	6
Statistics	5
Business law	4
Business cycle analysis	3
Insurance	3
Public utilities and transportation	3
Miscellaneous	22
Total	237

Do any significant patterns show up? For one thing, because most of the returns, as mentioned, bear signatures and also titles of positions held, it was possible to relate reading tastes to work interests, and, as one would expect, these two factors match to a high degree, particularly in the case of men "on the way up." For another thing, the special sample again shows a significant difference from the cross-section sample, confirming the points made previously to the effect that the nearer to the top executives are, the broader their reading interests are—in this instance, a smaller proportion of books of the know-how type and a larger proportion of books relating to management principles and executive action; with an indication that the total number of books read is only slightly less. Finally, there is evidence of the effect of mass distribution of books on the reading habits of executives: 22 of the 30 most popular titles were either selections or recommendations of the Executive Book Club (now Executive Books, Inc.).

DIGESTS AND INFORMATION SERVICES

Commercial digest and information services, as mentioned by respondents, fall roughly into four categories: (1) the letter type—*Kiplinger Washington Letter, Whaley-Eaton American Letter,* National City Bank *Monthly Letter, Public Relations News, Report for the Business Executive, Guaranty Survey,* and similar weekly or monthly letters; (2) loose leaf services—Commerce Clearing House, Research Institute of America, etc.; financial services such as Standard & Poor's and Moody's; *Daily Report for Executives; Crandall's Business Index;* (3) trade association bulletins such as those issued by the National Retail Dry Goods Association, Transportation Association of America, Machinery and Allied Products Institute, The Tanners' Council, and so forth; and (4) commercial services particularly addressed to one industry, such as *American Aviation Daily, Platt's Oilgram News,* and Russell Prudden's *Digest of Investment and Banking Opinions.*

Unfortunately, the extent to which executives use such services cannot be measured from the results of our survey. That the role they play must be an important one, however, can be gauged from the fact that executives insisted on mentioning them despite the fact that there were no specific questions asking them to do so. Our guess—and admittedly a guess—is that at least 20% of the type of executives covered subscribe to some such service. One company president wrote: "I should say that perhaps 90% of my background information on general business comes from reading such sources as the *Kiplinger* letter and the *Whaley-Eaton* service, and not more than 10% comes from books and magazines."

The growing use of commercial digests is, of course, an indication of the fact that many executives feel strongly a need for some "boiling down" of the great amount of published material. The same feeling is expressed in complaints about having to wade through so many pages to get needed facts or ideas, side by side with remarks that to get reliable information it is necessary to read all the publications and balance them against each other. Another manifestation is the use of internally staff-prepared digests.

Interviews with certain top executives suggested, initially, that these "home-made" company digests were highly valued. In order to find out how general this practice was, information about it was asked for on the questionnaire. Some 15% of subscribers said that they made use of such digests, but the supplementary data given suggest in quite a few cases that the question was not understood, and the percentage of actual users probably is less. The fact remains that many executives place reliance on such devices to keep themselves informed. One firm with quite a few branch offices over the country keeps references both to published articles and to company-prepared memoranda on IBM cards in each office. Several firms follow the practice of digesting the commercial digests! Out of all the comments entered under this heading, only one was adverse—and the respondent added, "I don't like predigested food either."

These indications of the fact that business executives often are overwhelmed by the volume of literature which they feel they ought to tap should be no occasion for surprise. The amazing thing is that executives are so persistent about doing all the reading that they do, and apparently with such care. Moreover, they seldom complain about editorial heaviness or length as such—indeed, they apparently welcome such treatment *if* it is also thorough or, as they often say, "meaty"—but rather are conscious, and sometimes resentful, of what they get *in proportion* to what they have to read to get it.

One of the interesting facts of our findings—and indeed a paradox—is what businessmen say when they are asked, person to person, whether they place much value on what they read. They say, "No." Some admit the value of reading as a means of procuring particular information but belittle it as a device for aiding in determining business policy. Again and again the first reaction of business executives whom we interviewed was to minimize the value of their own reading. They count reading as just one of many avenues for the gathering of information useful for the conduct of business. Their indicated reason is that an intimate knowledge of the sources of information is needed to judge its soundness and that this intimacy comes more readily through individual personal relationships, which of course are usually lost in print. Feeling that much published material is repetitive and inadequate for their purposes, they attach greater value to what they learn through lunch-table conversations, conventions, professional and trade association conferences, the quizzing of visitors, and the handy telephone call to some friend in the same or a similar line of endeavor. Indeed, an executive of a company large enough to have its own library often makes such a telephone call—say, to learn about pension plans from a friend who knows somebody who has been working on a plan—rather than calling upon the services of his own librarian. Yet he may well have in his own company library the published results of the experiences of not just one organization but 50 or 100. (How much of this practice is due to the inadequacy of internal library service or to the lack of understanding of the skills of a trained special librarian is a question that needs much further investigation.)

The fact remains that in our field survey we were surprised time and time again by the evidences of wide reading on the part of many executives. We can only conclude, then, that these same executives are actually gaining more from their reading than they admit or are even aware of. No doubt they have developed, without realizing it, an ability to scan effectively and to adapt readily to their own uses the ideas of others.

USE OF LIBRARIES

That business executives' frequent and growing demands for shortcuts to being kept informed and abreast of developments result primarily not from the incompetence of published material but from its sheer magnitude is attested to by their increasing use of library reference services. Indeed, the more such services are available, or their availability becomes known, the more they are sought after. The recent book by Edwin Coman, *Sources of Business Information* (Prentice-Hall, January 1949) should accelerate this trend—and incidentally alleviate some of the tasks and troubles of reference librarians harassed by confused inquiries.

Perhaps the work of the outstanding business branches of public libraries today will spread further and further. The publications of the business branch of the Newark Public Library and the Business Information Bureau of the Cleveland Public Library are already fairly well known to business. Each for years has published bulletins designed to aid businessmen in finding literature to solve particular problems. Other bulletins have been issued to make known with some degree of currency the important volumes that relate to business.

One new program that may well set the pattern for many libraries throughout the country deserves special comment. In January 1947, the John Crerar Library, a privately endowed free public library of science, technology, and medicine in Chicago, announced a new program of expanded services under the name of Research Information Service, with these objectives:

1. Making the vast store of accumulated knowledge at the library more readily available to technological, engineering, and scientific interests, the professions, industry and business, and the public generally, and

2. Facilitating the distribution and use of the unprecedented volume of information on current developments in these fields.

Under this program there has been no change in the access to the library's collections, catalogues, bibliographical equipment, special guidance, and assistance in the use of these facilities. Herman H. Henkle, in the *Library Journal* of January 15, 1949, described the new venture as follows:

The Research Information Service is intended primarily for those individuals and companies which prefer to have their library research performed for them. In addition it is designed to make available certain special facilities which were not contemplated by the original endowment, and have not been a normal part of the library's service program. These include dictaphones, typewriters, and specially assigned desks. These are further supplemented by a newly established photoduplication service.

The services offered on a reimbursable basis include special literature searches, continuing reports on or abstracts of new scientific and technical publications, detailed technical reports on the state of knowledge relating to certain research and development programs and a translation service. . . . Languages in the special qualifications of the R.I.S. and reference staffs are German, French, Italian, Spanish, Czech, Russian, and Scandinavian.

The method used for determining the reimbursement for the extra services of the library is that commonly used by non-profit research insitutes, namely, hourly or monthly rates, which include the salaries paid the participating staff members, plus a percentage of overhead to cover such factors as non-productive time, general administrative costs, and special service loads imposed upon the other departments of the library as a result of the special service.

The Detroit Public Library is currently sponsoring a somewhat similar plan. Also in Detroit a group of librarians has recently incorporated as "Information Service" to meet the research needs of smaller business and industrial corporations—organizations not yet large enough to have a full-time librarian. Their fees are set on an hourly or retainer basis.

Some idea of the potentialities of libraries for serving business executives' needs and of the obstacles to their realization can be gained from the example of Baker Library of the Harvard Business School. (Quite naturally in our field interviews the discussion turned more often than not to our own library.) The resources of Baker Library are great, but most "outsiders" are not aware that the library is open to the use of any legitimate businessman, nor are its resources yet organized to be utilized to the extent they should be.

Baker Library is an outstanding research library. It contains over 250,000 volumes and pamphlets and a large collection of documents both printed and manuscript relating particularly to individual business enterprises. Its collecting activities are wide. It currently obtains somewhat more than 1,000 different periodicals and also receives state and Federal Government reports, financial services, trade directories, business newspapers, and a large mass of current data on the financial aspects of individual businesses.

Its roots are deep. Two specialized groups of historical material are assembled in the Aldrich Room of Finance and the Kress Library of Business and Economics. The former contains chiefly the books and pamphlets on banking, finance, and the tariff, brought together by the late Senator Nelson W. Aldrich of Rhode Island. Purchases of noteworthy publications in these fields help to keep the collection current. The Kress Library contains one of the world's outstanding collections of material dealing with the historical aspects of business and economics concerned mainly with the period before 1848. This collection is a splendid complement to the material of a more recent date which is to be found on the stack shelves of Baker Library.

The fields covered by the interests of the library are continually increasing with the changes taking place in the American economy. The library is currently expanding its collection of material on the business aspects of the aviation industry, industrial relations, and public relations and responsibilities of business, to mention only a few of the newer areas.

Here is a rich source of the kind of information which business executives seem to want. Ways and means of making it more generally useful are now under discussion at the school. There is the question of proper methods. There is also the question of costs and of other demands on the library's facilities. Business executives, at least, show that they would welcome the decision, on the part of this and many another library, to extend the daily process of selecting and screening business literature by adding the manpower and skills to issue, say in digest form, some critical judgments about the material which appears to be most significant and most useful for developing a broad background of the social, political, and economic issues of the day.

CONCLUDING NOTE

One fact is clear beyond dispute as a result of our investigation. Business executives demonstrate—by their reading practices if not by their protestations—that they are avid for information and help through the medium of published material; and the nearer to the top they are, the more avid. They read a lot despite difficulties and time pressures—newspapers, trade publications, magazines, books, digests and information services, library material. The recurring complaints about quantity relative to quality, the discrimination shown among individual publications, the interest in screening of reading matter, all are part of the same picture; after all impatience usually expresses eagerness.

But that is no reason for self-satisfaction either on the side of the readers or on the side of those who provide them with what they read. The significance of the role of business literature would suggest the need for an increased degree of selectivity—not less time but more effective use of time—in business executives' own reading; for a still sharper focus by writers, editors, publishers, and librarians on business executives' needs; and, not altogether incidentally, for more judicious allocation of advertising budgets among media in the case of campaigns to reach business executives.

There is no point in saying more. We have told the executive who reads this article just about all we can tell him on the basis of our investigation—and we had better be true to the finding that time is precious to him. As noted at the outset, this has been an exploratory venture— helpful, we hope, but certainly not definitive—and anything additional awaits further study.

NEW DIMENSIONS
IN TOP EXECUTIVE
READING*

That executives feel they must keep up with a heavy volume of periodical literature has been amply evidenced by any number of published
studies, not to mention a wealth of unsolicited personal testimony. However, both from the standpoint of the executives themselves and of those
who wish to communicate with them—whether advertisers, public relations people, or individuals with ideas to share—there is need for more
information on specific questions:

> What differences do position, size of company, industry, and age make
> in the reading load of top executives?
> Why do top executives read so much—that is, for what different purposes
> do they use different publications?
> How do top executives with different work interests or job needs focus
> their reading on different kinds of publications; and what lessons can one
> executive learn from the experience of his colleagues?
> What bearing, if any, do these factors have on publishing, advertising,
> and communications strategy directed at top executives?

To answer such questions it is necessary to have a clear focus on top
executives—a focus which (a) will comprehend all or most of them,
yet (b) will not be blurred or weakened by others who do not belong
in the picture. On both counts, it is inadequate to look simply at executives who happen to be the subscribers of some particular publication
or who are grouped according to some other special circumstance, such
as industry, location, or membership in an organization. It is necessary
to cut across all such lines. In fact, one of the important objectives is
to identify those factors that differentiate between kinds of publications
and between kinds of top executives.

A study designed to meet these specifications has been conducted
under the direction of the HARVARD BUSINESS REVIEW as a part of a continuing program of research. Like all magazines, HBR needs to know
the characteristics of the audience it is seeking to serve.

* By Edward C. Bursk. Reprinted from Harvard Business Review, September, 1957,
pp. 93–112. Used by permission. Author's note: I should like to acknowledge the
assistance of the following graduate students in marketing research at the Harvard
Business School: Howard L. Brody, John F. Mellor, Constantine S. Nicandros,
Rollie Tillman, Charles A. Ullens, and J. Sylvain Wibaux; and of Mrs. Rose W.
Kneznek, Director of the Bureau of Business Research, Harvard Business School,
who supervised the machine tabulation of returns.

The specific findings about HBR readership are just about what should have been expected as a reflection of editorial policy. At the same time, the over-all picture of executive reading that emerges will come as a surprise to many, for it upsets accepted conceptions about the effect of position and size of company. It also adds new sharpness of difference to the relative coverage of the top executive group by the various publications; the effects of concentration and duplication have never, as far as I know, been explored so fully—and so revealingly.

Of special significance is the evidence that the growing "professional approach" to business is having a profound impact on the intellectual interests as well as on the reading habits of the men now running American industry—and, even more particularly, of the men now moving up to leadership.

COMPREHENSIVE PICTURE

In view of the possibly controversial nature of some of the material uncovered, it is important to establish the fact that the resulting picture is comprehensive and can be considered truly representative of the top executives of American industry.

Top Stature

Of prime importance in such research as this is the sample. The one used here employs *Poor's Directory of Officers and Directors* (1956 edition), consisting of some 70,000 names of leading executives of 23,000 companies. This is generally considered the most definitive and objective list available. Its comprehensiveness for the purposes of this survey becomes apparent in light of the following facts:

> In all United States industry, only 12,900 companies account for 80% of total corporate assets ($576 billion out of $722 billion), and 57% of total corporate receipts ($299 billion out of $525 billion).[1] The Poor's list covers almost twice as many companies, with an average of over 3 executives for each company.
>
> In the heavier industries, i.e., manufacturing, construction, transportation, and public utilities, only 4,200 companies account for 83% of total corporate assets ($222 billion out of $268 billion), and 70% of total corporate receipts ($217 billion out of $312 billion).[2] The sample from Poor's covers from two to three times as many companies in these industries—40,000 executives at an average of 4 to 5 per company.
>
> These industries, which will be referred to hereafter as *manufacturing, construction, etc.*, account for 71% of all expenditures for new plant and equipment ($20 billion out of $29 billion).[3]

[1] U.S. Department of Commerce, Statistical Abstract of the United States: 1956 (Washington, Government Printing Office, 1956), p. 493.
[2] Ibid.
[3] Ibid., p. 498.

In the United States there are only 3,200 firms employing more than 1,000 employees in all industries.[4] The Poor's sample covers 30,000 top executives in such companies (almost 10 for each such company in existence), of whom 16,000 are presidents and vice presidents (5 per company).

Likewise, there are only 2,400 firms employing more than 1,000 in manufacturing, construction, etc.[5] The Poor's sample covers 20,000 top executives in such companies (almost 10 per company), of whom 11,000 are presidents and vice presidents (5 per company).

Clearly, the 70,000 names on the Poor's list, compiled on the basis of size (over 50 employees) and scope (more than local activity), can be considered as representing the *bulk* of American industrial activity. Extrapolation of the Department of Commerce figures used above indicates that all together the companies in the Poor's list, screened as they have been, must account for more than 85% of total resources and 63% of total sales in all industries; and all together the companies in manufacturing, construction, etc., must account for more than 89% of total resources and 82% of total sales.

Furthermore, it appears that virtually *all* of the important executives in these companies are included. For, taking the range around the averages, there must be from 1 or 2 executives per company at the lower end of the size scale to 15, 20, or more per company at the upper end of the scale.

Representativeness

A few details of methodology will clarify the representativeness of the findings:

A four-page questionnaire was mailed to 10,000 executives in the alphabetical section of the Poor's Directory. Page 1 is reproduced in Exhibit I. Page 2 contains questions about the purposes for which executives use the various publications they read; page 3 investigates their reasons for *not* reading more of the publications; and page 4 calls for classification data about the executives' industry, position, size of company, age, etc.

So that the selection of names would be random, the list was turned over to an independent mailing house with instructions to send a questionnaire to every seventh individual. To avoid influencing the respondents in favor of HBR, the mailing envelopes and the introductory letter bore a hypothetical name, "Business Reading Research Institute"; and the return envelopes were also addressed to that name, at the street and number of the mailing house.

[4] *U.S. Department of Commerce,* Survey of Current Business, *May 1954, p. 23. Of the total 4,067,000 firms of all kinds, 3,040,000 have less than 4 employees; 3,990,000, less than 50 employees.*
[5] *Ibid. Of the total 881,000 firms in manufacturing, construction, etc., 541,000 have less than 4 employees; 832,000, less than 50 employees.*

Exhibit I. Sample of first page of questionnaire

QUESTIONNAIRE ON READING HABITS OF BUSINESS EXECUTIVES

1. Do you regularly read any business magazines or business newspapers? Yes......
   ...... No.........

2a. Which of the following publications do you regularly read for business purposes?
    Please check in "Read" column in the list below.

2b. What are the sources of the magazines or papers you regularly read? Please check
    in appropriate "Source" column.

		Read (1)	*Source*				
			Individual subscription (2)	*Company subscription* (3)	*Newsstand* (4)	*Gift* (5)	*Someone else's copies* (6)
Magazines							
Business Week	1						
Forbes	2						
Fortune	3						
Harvard Business Review	4						
Nation's Business	5						
Dun's Review and Modern Industry	6						
Newsweek	7						
Scientific American	8						
Magazine of Wall Street	9						
Time	10						
U.S. News and World Report	11						
Others	12						
Newspapers							
Barron's	13						
Journal of Commerce	14						
N.Y. Times	15						
Wall Street Journal	16						
Others	17						
Services and newsletters							
Kiplinger	18						
National City Bank	19						
Whaley-Eaton	20						
Others	21						

3. What trade magazines specifically written in your field of endeavor do you regularly read?
   ....
   ....

A total of 1,484 questionnaires were filled out and returned. On the basis of number of returns, by standard statistical formula we can be 99.7% confident that the resulting total readership figures for each publication are right within ±4%. However, we must be sure that respondents and non-respondents are similar. As a check on this, telephone calls were made to a random sample of 100 nonrespondents. Nonbiasing reasons for failure to respond were found in 44% of the cases (death, retirement, vacation, etc.), and there was a comfortable degree of agreement with the original respondents on the balance, both as to readership and important executive characteristics. On the proportion of presidents and vice presidents, for instance, there was a 2% difference, which compares with a standard deviation of 7%; and the variation in number of magazines read was 0.1.

To make sure that there was no serious overstatement of readership, particularly in the case of our own magazine, all those who had specified HBR readership were matched against the HBR subscription list. Altogether 93% of them were identified as having access to or receiving copies of the magazine—87% either through their own personal subscriptions or through the other sources they indicated (see Exhibit II). The actual degree of agreement must be even higher, for in any such searching of geographical files there are always names that cannot be located because of subsequent address change or residence in towns some distance from the individual's place of business.

Finally, Crossley, S–D Surveys, Inc., interviewed a random sample of subscriber-respondents for actual readership of contents. Some 90% had in fact read five or more articles in the latest or preceding issue of HBR, and the average reading time per copy was 2.4 hours. The percentage readership of other publications was also in line with the results from our mail questionnaire. No distortion traceable to the use of a mail questionnaire, or the particular listing of publications, could be found; on the proportion of Business Week and of Wall Street Journal readers, for instance, differences of 2% and 3% showed up between the mail questionnaire and the interview method, compared with a standard deviation of 5%.

In sum, the returns are such, both in number and in quality, to more than warrant analyzing the figures by various breakdowns (in each case with regard for statistical confidence limits), projecting the findings to the total Poor's list of 70,000, and considering the results representative of the total top executive group (which is the way the Poor's list is referred to hereafter).

EXTENT OF READING

This study strongly confirms the great amount of reading that executives do. The pattern of extensive reading cuts across position, size of company, industry, and age lines. All top executives, in all situations, do a tremendous amount of reading.

The average top executive reads 8½ publications for business purposes—3½ magazines, 1½ newspapers, 1 news service, and 2½ trade journals.

Exhibit II. Readership and source of copies, total top executive group

Publication	Read (per cent of total top executive group)	Source Individual subscription	Source Company paid subscription*	Source Gift subscription	Source Single copies bought	Source Someone else's copies
		(per cent reading the particular publication)				
Magazines						
Business Week	46%	32%	49%	4%	5%	4%
Forbes	20	50	27	14	2	4
Fortune	38	51	23	13	2	8
Harvard Business Review	24	38	54	3	. . .	4
Nation's Business	22	13	76	1	1	3
Dun's Review and Modern Industry	24	7	79	6	. . .	2
Newsweek	31	51	18	7	10	5
Scientific American	6	58	27	10	2	1
Magazine of Wall Street	3	31	29	2	13	20
Time	53	76	5	5	7	3
U.S. News & World Report	44	50	26	5	8	4
Others	19	40	45	5	2	2
Newspapers						
Barron's	11	46	40	1	2	5
Journal of Commerce	10	11	77	. . .	2	6
New York Times	33	53	11	. . .	30	1
Wall Street Journal	75	26	58	7	6	4
Others	23	54	24	1	15	3
Services and newsletters						
Kiplinger	48	14	73	1	. . .	6
National City Bank	30	29	35	22	. . .	2
Whaley-Eaton	10	6	78	1	. . .	3
Others	28	29	56	5	. . .	2

* Includes a large proportion of subscriptions entered by and addressed to individuals, but paid by company check.

However, within this general pattern some pronounced differences show up for the various segments of the top executive group. This further, more specific information should be directly useful to those wishing to reach particular kinds of executives, as well as of interest to the executives themselves.

Position, Size, Industry

There are four distinct and independent influences that serve to increase top executives' reading. Three of these show up unmistakably in the over-all figures (see Exhibit III):

1. *Higher position.* The average president, vice president, or assistant to the president reads one more publication than does the average top executive in other positions.

2. *Larger company.* The average top executive in companies with more than 1,000 employees reads 1½ more publications than does the average top executive in companies with less than 1,000 employees.

3. *Heavier industry.* The average top executive in manufacturing, construction, etc., reads 1½ more publications than does the average top executive in finance, trade, service.

That these influences are independent and do not simply reflect each other (e.g., manufacturing companies being also larger companies) is shown by the further breakdown in Exhibit IV. Note that when the effect of different position is neutralized by analyzing each position category separately, the company-size influence still makes a difference of 1 to 1½ publications; and again, when the effect of different company size is neutralized by analyzing each size category separately, the industry factor still makes a difference of 1 to 1½ publications.

Because these three influences are independent and also work in the same direction, they are cumulative in their effect. Thus, the average president or vice president of a company employing more than 1,000 in a manufacturing industry reads 10½ publications, while the average secretary or treasurer of a company employing less that 1,000 in a financial or trade industry reads 7 publications—a difference of 3½ publications.

The significance of this fact to advertisers and other communicators of ideas should be obvious. The top executives who make the crucial decisions, in the companies which make the large purchases, and in the industries which consume the bulk of supplies and equipment, are the very ones for whose reading time and attention the competition is strongest.

For individual executives, the significance is equally great. The more complex and responsible a top executive's job is, the greater are his reading requirements—and the more judicious he must therefore be in making the most of his reading time.

Contrary Age

The age factor also is strong, but it has a contrary influence. Older executives tend to read *less*. The effect of this factor does not show up in

Exhibit III. *Average number of publications read by top executives*

Publication	Total top executive group	By position		By company size	
		Presidents and vice presidents	*Other posi- tions*	*Over 1,000 employees*	*Under 1,000 employees*
Magazines	3½	3½	3½	4	3
Newspapers	1½	1½	1½	1½	1½
Services and newsletters	1	1½	1	1½	1
Trade journals	2½	2½	2	2½	2½
Total	8½	9	8	9½	8

the over-all figures (Exhibit III, referred to previously) precisely because it works in the opposite direction, and so is offset by the other
factors. Of course, executives in higher positions and more complex companies *as a whole* are older than executives who have not yet climbed
to such responsible positions. However, there also is an age spread within
each position and company-size segment, and the younger executives
tend to read more than do the older executives *in the same segments.*
Otherwise there would be no offset to the position and size influences,
and the total figures for over 50 and under 50 would not come out even
as they do.

Exhibit IV. *Average number of publications read in segments of the total top
executive group*

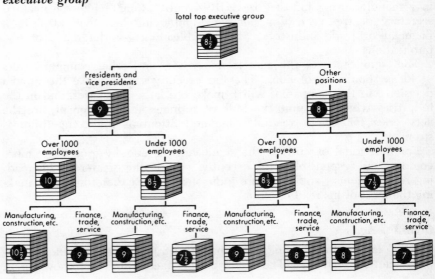

By industry		By age	
Manufacturing, construction, etc.	Finance, trade, service	Over 50 years	Under 50 years
4	3	$3\frac{1}{2}$	3
$1\frac{1}{2}$	$1\frac{1}{2}$	$1\frac{1}{2}$	$1\frac{1}{2}$
1	1	1	$1\frac{1}{2}$
3	$2\frac{1}{2}$	$2\frac{1}{2}$	$2\frac{1}{2}$
$9\frac{1}{2}$	8	$8\frac{1}{2}$	$8\frac{1}{2}$

The independence and strength of the age factor show up in further breakdowns where executives in the same segment are analyzed by age, and the effect of the other factors is thus neutralized. Even in such a high-reading position-and-size segment as presidents and vice presidents in companies employing more than 1,000, age makes some difference: those over 50 read 10 publications on the average, and those under 50 read $10\frac{1}{2}$. Perhaps even more revealing is the fact that for those of this same age-and-size group *in manufacturing, construction, etc.*, where reading requirements are the highest of all and therefore leave the least leeway, age makes only a negligible difference; whereas *in finance, trade, service*, where reading requirements are lower, those over 50 read 8 publications on the average and those under 50 read $9\frac{1}{2}$—a difference of $1\frac{1}{2}$.

Here the significance for advertisers and other communicators of ideas may be less obvious, but it is just as real. Everything else being equal, the younger an executive is, the more worthwhile it is to influence him—that is, the longer is the period in which to reap the benefit. With today's widespread policy of retirement at around 65 years, executives in their late 50's and early 60's are already training others to make the decisions.

And we are looking, it is to be noted, not at younger men in middle management but at younger men in top management, including presidents and vice presidents of the larger companies. The fact that these younger men represent the new, growing "professional approach" to management adds further significance, as we shall see shortly.

As for individual executives, the significance is brutally apparent. Younger executives may find reading easier or more clearly in line with their career development, but the responsibility of one's job is more important than one's age. Hence, again, the need for judicious use of the diminishing time and energy one has available as one climbs the ladder.

In particular, those trained in business administration as a profession may wonder what the effect will be when they *combine* that approach with the requirements of more responsible jobs—but we shall look at that in a subsequent section.

Job Requirements

That more responsible jobs do require more reading is just about inevitable under today's conditions:

> Business is becoming more and more complex. Today's management is aware of interlocking responsibilities to employees, stockholders, and the public; these interests cannot be handled summarily but require painstaking understanding and considered action.
>
> Increasing mechanization and other long-term investments of capital and effort put the focus on planning ahead; this calls both for knowledge of planning techniques and for awareness of the factors which are likely to change the shape of things in the future.
>
> The bigger the company, the more it influences the rest of the economy and the whole society, and the more it is affected in turn; the scope of reading must be broad enough to take in all sorts of trends and developments on a national or even international scale.
>
> Above all, the higher a man's position, the more he needs administrative ability to knit together the specialized skills of others into an effective organization; he must be concerned with management development, control and communication procedures, and a whole gamut of new ways of thinking about his organization.

No wonder top executives must do a lot of reading. There is more and more to keep up with, more and more to learn. But the older a man is, the farther away he is from learning habits, particularly if his earlier training for business was experience rather than a modern school of business administration.

Furthermore, the typical executive can hardly be blamed if the stress and strain of added responsibility leave him less energy for serious reading at the end of a hard day. Unfortunately, most top executives do not have the time or the freedom from interruptions at the office that such a pursuit demands, and therefore many of them take their magazines home to read (often in bed) or put them in their brief cases for a business trip.

Indeed, if there is anything surprising about top executives' burden of reading, it is that *even with the availability of personnel to screen and abstract reading material for them* they still feel they must do a lot of reading firsthand. I know of one large company where the top executives divide among themselves the responsibility for reading the various magazines, identifying important articles for their colleagues to read or reporting important ideas to them. Their feeling is that no one but a top executive can know what an article will or should mean to men in positions similar to his own.

Why, then, should this fact of heavier reading requirements of more responsible executives have failed to come to light like this before? There are three main reasons:

1. Most previous surveys have failed to make a distinction between top executives who make the crucial operating decisions in an organization (presidents and vice presidents) and executives who have simply advisory or ownership positions (silent directors, inactive chairmen of the board, proprietors of small shops, etc.). Our survey shows that the latter do in fact read less and thus bring down the average when lumped in with the more important operating executives.
2. Most previous surveys have not been made of top-stature men. The facts set forth in connection with the description of the sample are often overlooked. But they do mean that any grouping of executives—magazine subscription list or any other—which is much in excess of the 70,000 executives on the Poor's list must be well diluted with middle-rank or very-small-company executives; and any group of executives that exceeds the 45,000 executives in our president–vice president segment or the 30,000 executives in our over-1,000-employees segment cannot claim to represent important decision-making executives.
3. When analysis is not refined by position, size, and industry, particularly in the case of a group which has a high admixture of men in less than top responsible jobs and so is less responsive to the position and size influences, the age factor hides any differences in reading requirements caused by those influences and holds down the average of the group. And the discrepancy between the resulting picture and the true picture becomes more serious each year as the professional approach to business administration grows stronger.

RISE OF PROFESSIONALISM

Certainly, as of 1956–1957, the effects of the rise of professionalism on the reading of top executives—and hence on advertising and communications policy—seem unmistakable.

The extent of reading is itself an indication. The professional approach is more intellectual, perhaps even more theoretical (in the best sense of the word, implying application of principles and reasoning rather than guesswork, intuition, or just the lessons of hard knocks); and this requires more reading.

Other surveys show the same upward trend, but here for comparison is what has happened to the average number of publications read by HBR subscribers over the last decade (drawing on a previous survey of HBR readers[6]). A gain of 2 publications per executive may not seem

[6] See Edward C. Bursk and Donald T. Clark, "Reading Habits of Business Executives," HBR, May 1949, p. 330 (original data reworked), and footnote to Exhibit X.

like much—but it is when it comes on top of an already heavy reading load. Thus:

	Then		Now	
	Presidents and vice presidents	Other positions	Presidents and vice presidents	Other positions
Magazines	4½	3	5	4½
Newspapers	2	1½	2	1½
Services and newsletters	1	1	1	1
Trade journals	1½	2	3	2½
Total	9	7½	11	9½

The fact that younger executives read more than older executives is part of the picture, too. Not only is it probably easier for ambitious young men to fit reading in with their career demands, but an increasing number of them are already more prone to intellectual exercise by virtue of professional training, in either graduate schools or advanced management programs. Some of these men are already in top jobs. More are on their way up to positions where they will have to read still more to feel that they are doing justice to their responsibilities.

One manifestation of this is the way the figures cited above show HBR top executives with such high reading figures, 11 and 9½, compared with 9 and 8 for the total top executive group. Apparently, as we shall see, HBR has a well-defined appeal for those who have or feel the need for adopting the professional approach; and this means that, in contrast to the general run of publications, its share of the total top executive group has an unusually strong proportion of executives who hold high positions in large companies *at a definitely lower-than-average age*—40% under 50 years, against 28% for the total top executive group. (Of the other publications, Fortune, with 37% below 50 years, is the only one even close enough to be within shooting distance.)

So HBR readers provide an example of what happens when the age factor works with rather than against the position and size factors—the combined effect of the professional approach and the requirements of more responsible jobs.

Reading Attitudes

That executives in more responsible jobs feel the need of the professional approach and the intellectual exercise that goes with it, no matter what their age, their busy schedules, or their lack of formal training, is shown by their attitudes toward reading.

Their reasons for *not* adding other publications to those that they do read, when taken as indications of the relative strength of the opposite

Exhibit V. Profiles of readership, attitudes toward reading, and coverage in segments of total top executive group. NOTE: *Attitude profiles are based on reactions to all the magazines in the survey.*

Profile	Presidents and vice presidents		Other positions		Age
	Over 1000 employees	Under 1000 employees	Over 1000 employees	Under 1000 employees	Under 50 years
Average number of publications read					
Willing to make time for reading					
Not afraid of heaviness					
Want more meat					
Want broad scope					
Want original ideas					
Use for techniques of administration					
Coverage by magazines	Other magazines HBR				

positive attitudes and analyzed by position, company size, and age, make a sharp and consistent pattern. Again, the position, size, and age factors show a marked disposition toward intellectual exercise. The top executives in the higher positions, larger companies, and younger age brackets exhibit these positive attitudes to a much greater degree: "willing to make time for reading," "not afraid of heaviness," "want more meat," "want broad scope," and "want original ideas." The pattern is presented graphically, in the form of profiles, in Exhibit V.

The method used in converting negative reasons to positive attitudes and scoring them for the profiles is as follows:

The effect of nonreadership of individual publications through unfamiliarity with them, rather than through deliberate decision, has first been eliminated. Then, for each position, size, and age segment, the individual complaints about "not enough time," "too heavy," "not enough meat," "doesn't apply to my business," and "duplicates other reading" have been totaled and computed as percentages of the total number of reasons mentioned by the top executives in that segment.

The resulting figures have then been interpreted in terms of strength in the positive attitudes cited above. Thus, when 51% of the presidents and vice presidents in companies with over 1,000 employees complain about "not enough time," compared with 60% in companies employing less than 1,000, it is taken as an indication that the larger company men are *more* willing to make time for reading than their smaller company counterparts, and the 51% is considered a stronger score than the 60%. In the case of "not enough meat," on the other hand, a higher percentage is a stronger indicator of "want more meat."

For each item, the strongest percentage score is given the highest decile ranking (1), the weakest percentage score is given the lowest ranking (10), and the other scores are spaced proportionately between, as shown in the profiles.

For purposes of comparison, the number of publications read is translated into similar decile ratings and profiled at the top of the exhibit. Two further profiles of decile ratings, *use for techniques of administration* and *coverage by magazines,* which will be discussed shortly, are also included to round out the picture. Note how similar the shapes of the profiles are.

There are some very interesting matters for executives, advertisers, and publishers to ponder here, and they all center around the question: How far can one trust the expressed desire for streamlining and condensing? Certainly, nobody wants to waste time or read something just for the sake of heaviness; but most executives recognize that nothing valuable comes easily, and apparently the more responsible the job and the more professional the man, the more willing he is to pay the necessary price.

In other research which Crossley, S–D Surveys has done for HBR, one executive will criticize article *x* for being too long or too heavy and article *y* for not having enough details or enough substantiation, yet another executive will completely reverse these criticisms of the same two articles; and on further questioning it turns out that article *y* is in the first man's field of primary interest and article *x* pretty far removed, while article *x* is close to the second man's heart and article *y* only peripheral. Neither man would get what he wanted if both articles were streamlined!

This is not to say that successful advertising, successful publishing, or successful individual reading must be built on such a basis, but only that more responsible executives in larger companies do have a special focus of their own in the reading they do; that it is along the line of the professional approach; and that, perhaps just because it must be worked at in the face of time pressure, it represents a very purposeful kind of activity—and so should provide a valuable setting for communication on subjects of concern to such top executives.

Purposeful Use

With this picture as background, we are in a good position to examine the purposes for which top executives do their reading.

Of course, purposeful use does not necessarily mean that executives have consciously selected different publications for different purposes. But whatever publications they end up reading as a result of the pull and tug of circulation promotion and inertia, tiredness, or time pressure; of subscribing and renewing or not renewing; of trying out different

Exhibit VI. *Percentages of each publication's readers in total top executive group indicating they read it for information and assistance in various areas of usage*

Publication	Long-range policy	Day-to-day operations	Competitors' activities	Techniques of administration	General business conditions	New technical developments
Magazines						
Business Week	37%	25%	9%	14%	77%	21%
Forbes	35	16	6	7	56	4
Fortune	52	7	10	35	47	20
Harvard Business Review	56	6	1	65	12	14
Nation's Business	28	14	3	18	51	4
Dun's Review and Modern Industry	34	17	7	32	45	15
Newsweek	21	31	4	3	60	5
Scientific American	23	2	2	. . .	. . .	64
Magazine of Wall Street	47	36	4	7	73	11
Time	24	34	4	3	56	10
U.S. News & World Report	44	31	3	4	64	5
Others	26	24	22	16	28	28
Newspapers						
Barron's	37	36	5	4	63	9
Journal of Commerce	21	65	22	2	46	17
New York Times	26	63	14	5	54	11
Wall Street Journal	30	68	15	4	64	14
Others	20	45	17	6	33	13
Services and newsletters						
Kiplinger	49	35	2	3	62	4
National City Bank	47	15	2	2	63	1
Whaley-Eaton	48	32	1	3	58	3
Others	38	29	8	7	41	8

kinds of publications in a sort of "survival of the fittest" process—whatever the circumstances, executives do have definite ideas of the areas in which the publications they read are useful and continue to use them accordingly.

Thus, when given a choice of "long-range policy," "day-to-day operations," "competitors' activities," "techniques of administration," "general business conditions," and "new technical developments," executives' uses of the various publications are as shown in Exhibit VI (expressed as percentages of the readers of each publication). On the further question of which *one* publication is *most* helpful in the different areas, the results are as shown in Exhibit VII (also expressed as per-

Exhibit VII. Percentages of each publication's readers in total top executive group indicating they consider it the "one publication most helpful" in various areas of usage

Publication	Long-range policy	Day-to-day operations	Competitors' activities	Techniques of administration	General business conditions	New technical developments
Magazines						
Business Week	10%	5%	3%	6%	19%	12%
Forbes	2	1	...	1	...	...
Fortune	14	...	3	17	3	6
Harvard Business Review	12	...	...	28	...	3
Nation's Business	2	...	...	7	2	1
Dun's Review and Modern Industry	1	...	2	10	1	1
Newsweek	1	1	2	2	3	1
Scientific American	...	...	...	...	...	4
Magazine of Wall Street	...	...	...	...	...	...
Time	2	4	2	2	6	4
U.S. News & World Report	14	5	2	...	10	2
Others	2	1	7	4	1	6
Newspapers						
Barron's	1	1	...	...	1	...
Journal of Commerce	1	3	1	...	1	1
New York Times	3	12	5	1	5	3
Wall Street Journal	14	45	16	2	29	9
Others	1	2	4	2	1	2
Services and newsletters						
Kiplinger	10	3	...	1	7	1
National City Bank	2	...	...	...	5	...
Whaley-Eaton	1	...	...	...	1	2
Others	4	2	2	3	2	2
Trade magazines	5	14	53	14	2	41

centages of the readers of each publication); note how closely these figures follow the pattern set by the general mentions.

As should be expected in line with the previous analysis, several of the indicated areas stand out well above the others when the general mentions for all the magazines are totaled and analyzed by position, size of company, and age, as shown in Exhibit VIII. The fact that "general business conditions" and "long-range policy" show up as the two principal uses is consistent with the responsibilities of top executives under today's conditions as pictured.

But perhaps it is even more to the point that the one *positive* indication of specialized usage which reflects the position, size, and age influences is in the area of techniques of administration. The pattern is almost exactly the same as for number of publications read and reading attitudes; see the profile in Exhibit V, referred to previously. Thus:

1. The younger executives show a much greater interest in techniques of administration, primarily at the expense of day-to-day operations and general business conditions.

2. There is also a tendency for both higher position and larger company size to increase interest in techniques of administration, primarily at the expense of long-range policy and general business conditions.

3. With older men usually holding the more responsible jobs, the recurring pattern of the position and size influences offsetting the age influence (particularly strong here) is remarkable.

4. It is also significant that on this matter of techniques of administration (as indeed in the case of the number of publications read and reading attitudes generally) size shows more influence on the presidents and vice presidents than on the top executives in other positions.

Apparently, techniques of administration represent the central concern of operating executives with the problems and responsibilities of building an organization and seeing that it performs cooperatively and effectively—problems that increase in scope and complexity the higher an executive is and the larger his company; responsibilities that peculiarly belong to him and cannot be delegated to subordinates or staff specialists. Other problems and responsibilities may weigh heavier in total, but these seem to be more crucial; here is where the leverage can be found to handle the rest. It is hardly surprising, then, that techniques of administration also show up as the very essence of the professional approach on the part of men who are preparing themselves to meet such problems and take on such responsibilities, now or in the future.

FOCUS & CONCENTRATION

The pattern of purposeful use, as it works out in the actual reading of executives, not only substantiates this analysis of business reading requirements in general; but it also has a number of implications in terms of the individual publications.

Exhibit VIII. Purposes for which top executives read
business magazines

	Total top executive group	Presidents and vice presidents	
		In companies employing over 1,000	In companies employing less than 1,000
Long-range policy	25%	23%	25%
Day-to-day operations	15	15	15
Competitors' activities	3	4	3
Techniques of administration	11	14	10
General business conditions	37	36	39
New technical developments	9	8	8

It can be seen from Exhibit VI that the various publications have distinctive patterns of their own and that some of them contain elements of special strength in one or two particular areas of use. Presumably these patterns represent the editorial policies of their publishers, explicit or otherwise, ranging from a general appeal aimed at a wide or diffuse audience to a specific appeal with a compact, cohesive base of interest.

Primarily this is not a matter of *quality* but of *kind* of service. Quality is involved only when two or more publications appear to be competing for identical uses; otherwise competition for executives' reading is more a matter of having different mixes, or patterns, of use—or at least that is the way it works out.

The point is that to the extent publications have acquired different elements of strength in their patterns, executives tend to focus their reading where they find the uses that are most appropriate to their needs and interests. The result is that different kinds of publications have different degrees of concentration of readership in different segments of the total top executive group; see Exhibit IX.

Over-all Use

Let us look first at the extent to which greater percentage of use in the various areas results in a publication's having a larger proportion of its circulation in the total top executive group. Thus, lumping some roughly comparable publications together, we see that:

Dun's Review and Modern Industry and Business Week show higher ratios of top executive readership to circulation than do Forbes and Nation's Business—16% and 11% against 6% and 2%.

HBR shows a higher ratio than Fortune—34% against 9%.

U.S. News & World Report shows a higher ratio than Newsweek and Time—4% as against 2% and 2%.

The Wall Street Journal shows a higher ratio than does the New York Times—12% against 4%.

Other positions		Age	
In companies employing over 1,000	In companies employing less than 1,000	Over 50	Under 50
22%	24%	25%	24%
14	14	16	13
4	3	3	4
12	11	10	15
38	39	38	35
10	9	8	9

It should be emphasized that this kind of comparison is not a test of publishing success or editorial merit or anything like that. It only indicates that if publications do provide editorial service in areas of use which are of particular need and interest to smaller, more homogeneous groups, then they will have more limited total circulation but more concentrated readership in such groups.

This observation, obvious as it may seem, does have a much more significant application to publishers, advertisers, and other communicators of ideas than is generally recognized, as should be clear shortly. For present purposes the important conclusion is that the particular areas of use specified in this survey, whether or not they are precisely defined and labeled, do succeed in sharply differentiating publications in terms of executives' interests and needs and therefore are to be considered as representing valid factors in real life.

Individual Patterns

The differentiating effect of the magazines' individual patterns of use is even clearer when we look at particular segments within the total top executive group. Thus, comparing the usage figures in Exhibit VI with the concentration figures in Exhibit IX (the Column B ratios):

Distinctly greater use for long-range policy is a characterstic of U.S. News & World Report as compared with Time and Newsweek. It is matched with three times as much concentration in the president–vice president segment, and also has an edge in the over-1,000-employees and manufacturing segments (where the other magazines are actually below 1%).

Distinctly greater use for techniques of administration is a characteristic of Dun's Review and Modern Industry as compared with Business Week, Forbes, and Nation's Business. It is matched with half again as much concentration as Business Week, three times as much as Forbes, and twelve times as much as Nation's Business in the president–vice president segment, and has almost that much edge in the manufacturing segment.

Exhibit IX. Concentration of readership in top executive group

Publication	Circula-tion*	Readership in total top executive group (70,000)	Ratio of this readership to circulation
Magazines			
Business Week	289,010	32,200	11%
Forbes	216,376	14,000	6
Fortune	287,186	26,600	9
Harvard Business Review	51,478	16,800	34
Nation's Business	779,902	15,400	2
Dun's Review and Modern Industry	107,738	16,800	16
Newsweek	1,091,674	21,700	2
Scientific American	156,604	4,200	†
Magazine of Wall Street	20,135	2,100	†
Time	2,059,536	37,100	2
U.S. News & World Report	867,672	30,800	4
Newspapers			
Barron's	73,706	7,700	†
Journal of Commerce	38,894	7,000	†
New York Times	557,244	23,100	4
Wall Street Journal	420,761	52,500	12

* Publishers' statements as of 12/31/56, except *Journal of Commerce, New York Times*, and *Wall Street Journal*, as of 9/30/56.
† Numbers involved so small that percentage breakdown is misleading in comparison with other publications.

Distinctly greater use for techniques of administration is a characteristic of HBR as compared with Fortune. It is matched by over four times as much concentration in the position segment, five times as much in the size segment, and four times as much in the manufacturing segment. HBR's distinctiveness in this respect is emphasized by the fact that among executives who read both Fortune and HBR, 66% cite HBR as the *one* publication most useful for techniques of administration, and 8% cite Fortune.

Business Week, with outstandingly strong use for general business conditions, has much greater concentration than Forbes and Nation's Business, and is much closer to Dun's Review and Modern Industry, specifically in the over-1,000-employees segment. Apparently, use for general business con-

Proportion of this readership in particular segment (A), and ratio of number of readers there to circulation (B)

Presidents and vice presidents in all companies (45,000)		All executives in companies employing over 1,000 (30,000)		All executives in manufacturing, construction, etc. (34,000)		All executives under 50 years (20,000)	
A	B	A	B	A	B	A	B
69%	8%	35%	4%	53%	6%	31%	3%
63	4	40	2	54	3	25	2
70	6	37	3	54	5	37	3
74	25	49	17	58	20	40	14
69	1	36	1	53	1	27	1
73	12	30	5	71	11	34	5
64	1	32	1	46	1	26	1
†	†	†	†	†	†	†	†
†	†	†	†	†	†	†	†
68	1	34	1	46	1	32	1
65	3	30	1	48	2	24	1
†	†	†	†	†	†	†	†
†	†	†	†	†	†	†	†
62	2	35	1	40	2	30	1
63	8	34	4	49	6	29	3

ditions, which as pointed out earlier should be of particular concern to large companies, has a stronger concentrating effect in the size segment than in the position segment. On the other hand, use for techniques of administration has a strong enough effect in both segments to be only partially offset by Business Week's truly exceptional edge in general business conditions.

Note also the effect of use for techniques of administration in the younger age segment. Here the relative degrees of concentration of all the magazines almost exactly parallel their ranking for use of techniques of administration. The only notable exception is that Business Week shows the same concentration as Fortune though it has only half as much use for techniques of administration; apparently, again in this segment, its outstanding use for general business conditions wins additional readership.

Dynamic Trend

The significance of the strong interest of top executives in techniques of administration calls for further use of HBR readers to bring out some important points. Not that interest in this area of use is confined to HBR readers. It shows up just as strongly in many non-HBR readers; only they are spread more thinly over a number of magazines, and so there is not the same concentrating effect or the same opportunity to observe it in action.

Here, even more clearly than in the case of number of publications read, HBR demonstrates the effect of the interrelationship between the professional approach, represented specifically by use for techniques of administration, and the needs and interests of (a) more responsible top executives and simultaneously (b) younger top executives:

1. HBR top executive readers do 65% of all their reading for techniques of administration, as against 57% in the total top executive group and 44% for non-HBR readers in the total top group; see Exhibit X.

Exhibit X. Comparison of readers of Harvard Business Review and top executive group

	Total top executive group (70,000)	Non-HBR readers in top group (53,200)	HBR readers in top group (16,800)	Balance of HBR sub- scribers* (34,200)	Total HBR sub- scribers* (51,000)
Proportion in top positions Presidents, vice presidents	65%	62%	74%	11%	29%
Proportion in heavy industry Manufacturing, construction, etc.	48%	45%	58%	58%	58%
Proportion in large companies Over 1,000 employees	32%	26%	49%	51%	50%
Over 10,000 employees	6%	4%	13%	17%	16%
Proportion in younger age bracket Under 50 years	28%	25%	40%	80%	69%
Average number of publications read	8½	8	11	9	9½
Proportion using for techniques of administration	57%	44%	65%	78%	74%

* Based on material from another part of survey, made at same time and in same way as that of total top group.

2. Reflecting this concentrated appeal to those following the professional approach, HBR's coverage of the selective segments has almost exactly the same shape as the profile of use for techniques of administration *by readers of all the magazines* (portrayed earlier, along with the profiles of number of publications read and reading attitudes, in Exhibit V). That is, it has the biggest peaks in the segment of presidents and vice presidents in companies employing more than 1,000 *and* the under-50-years segment, and a lesser peak in the segment of other positions in companies employing more than 1,000.

In contrast, the profile of average coverage for the other publications shows a completely opposite shape—and, despite higher average coverage of the total top group, actually runs below HBR's peaks.

That executives should so sharply reflect the new and developing requirements of their jobs in their reading is important, not because of what it means for a single magazine or its subscribers, but because it indicates the strength of the basic forces, of which this is just one effect. In this connection, note that:

From 1947 to 1957, the number of men entering business from graduate schools of business has increased by approximately 250%.[7]

From 1948 to 1957, the number of men attending advanced management programs at universities has increased by about 295%.[8]

Also, over the last 10 years, the number of in-company executive development programs is estimated to have increased by 340%.[9]

In effect, we have a picture here of a rapidly growing number of men with the professional approach, whether trained in it and employed as they become available or as part of a corresponding effort for those not so trained to take advantage of it in other ways.

The fact that HBR's circulation has shown a parallel rise during the last ten years—260%—is what should be expected if executives are also increasingly seeking the professional approach in their reading. The significance is not in the size of the figures—either for the numbers of trained men or for the growth of HBR—but in the fact that editorial policy specifically designed to serve and stimulate executives with the professional approach could find them so fully responsive to the requirements of that approach.

The same professional executives, typified by HBR readers, have been sharpening their focus of readership throughout the whole range of pub-

[7] *Estimated from data in Delta Sigma Pi,* Surveys of Universities Offering Organized Courses in Commerce and Business Administration (*Chicago, biennial*).
[8] *Estimated on the basis of data in National Industrial Conference Board,* Executive Development Courses in Universities, *Studies in Personnel Policy, No. 160* (*New York, NICB, 1957*), and The Controller, *March 1953.*
[9] *Estimated on the basis of data in American Management Association,* Current Practice in Development of Management Personnel (*New York, AMA, 1955*).

lications.[10] Over the past decade they also have shifted some of their interest in the larger and more general publications toward other publications which they apparently feel serve their professional needs more closely:

	Then	Now
Business Week	59%	54%
Fortune	46	70
Nation's Business	35	19
Newsweek	28	23
Time	63	53
U.S. News & World Report	32	32
Barron's	19	10
Journal of Commerce	24	11
New York Times	45	35
Wall Street Journal	46	74

Moreover, taking HBR (with its readership for techniques of administration) as the prime expression of the professional approach, we see that the underlying forces will continue to have increasing effect. This follows, not only from HBR's greater concentration among the younger executives in the total top group, but from two further facts which develop from a comparison with HBR readers not in the total top group (likewise shown in Exhibit X):

1. The executives who make up the balance of HBR readers include a still greater proportion of younger men than their counterparts in the top group—80% under 50 as against 40%—and of course not as many of them are yet so advanced in position. However, the two HBR groups show almost exactly the same strong proportions in the size and industry categories. That is, they are alike in these basic respects, as against the general run of the total top executive group. The only difference between HBR readers in the total top executive group and their younger HBR colleagues is one of time—time for the latter to grow older, and time for them to rise to the more responsible positions that the top group represents.

2. Also, these other HBR readers show an even higher figure for techniques of administration—78% as against 65% for HBR readers in the total top group. As they move into more responsible positions and become subject to the additional pressures now felt by the same kind of older and more advanced executives, they can be expected to step up still further the high interest in techniques of administration that they already show. In short, the trend to the professional approach at the top should be accelerating.

So the picture is a dynamic one for all the publications with their different patterns of use appealing to different kinds of executives. Nothing is going to stop today's younger executives from moving on up the

[10] See Edward C. Bursk and Donald T. Clark, op. cit., and footnote to Exhibit X.

ladder, so we had better prepare for the fact that the focus of readership and the degree of concentration are going to become more and more accentuated in the future.

POLICY IMPLICATIONS

That different kinds of editorial policy, designed for different areas of use, can bring concentration in different audiences or markets is hardly a new or startling finding, but the magnitude of the concentrating effects, the identity of the particular factors (i.e., uses) which cause them, and the way this all works out in the selective segments of the total top executive group can provide new light for publishers who wish to increase their relationship in crucial spots—or for executives who wish to better fit their reading to their needs in the light of what other executives have found useful.

Selective Coverage

For advertisers and other communicators of ideas there may be even more practical implications. To the extent that they wish to direct their "messages" *primarily* to the total top executive group (which in a very real sense also is selective, compared with the usual loose grouping of so-called "top executives") or the even more selective segments within that group; or to the extent that they wish to reinforce their general coverage with *added* coverage on a selective basis—to such an extent, they now have more precise information to guide them.

As Exhibit XI shows, greater concentration of readership in the selective segments results in a corresponding increase of coverage. Moreover, the fact that advertising rates are usually based on total circulation makes the cost of such selective coverage considerably more economical.

This does not mean that it is necessarily more efficient to reach such segments through publications with concentrated readership (though the following section will indicate that this is more likely to be so than usually realized). It is of course possible, and often desirable, to cover selective segments as a part of a larger and more general coverage. But if any advertiser has special interest in one or more selective segments (because executives there are likely to be bigger or better customers) or in one or more concentrated publications (because the particular purposes for which executives read them are likely to give his message a quicker or better reception), then he may well consider the relative value of buying such selective coverage for its own sake.

Duplication of Readership

Concentration of readership has another effect which likewise may be of value to advertisers and other communicators of ideas. This stems from the fact that executives read so many publications and hence there

Exhibit XI. Coverage of segments of the total top executive group by selected publications

(*Percentage of group or segment covered by the particular publication's*

	Page rate*	Total top executive group (70,000)		Presidents and vice presidents in all companies (45,000)	
		%	Cost	%	Cost
Business Week	$ 2,885	46%	$ 90	49%	$131
Forbes	2,100	20	150	20	233
Fortune	3,890	38	146	40	216
Harvard Business Review	730	24	43	28	58
Nation's Business	3,750	22	244	24	347
Dun's Review and Modern Industry	1,375	24	82	27	113
Newsweek	5,540	31	255	31	397
Time	10,500	53	283	56	417
U.S. News & World Report	4,430	44	144	44	224

* For black-and-white page, single insertion, including announced increases, from Standard Rate & Data Service, Inc., February 1957.

are any number of possible combinations of publications which will cover them, as indicated by the four-page table in Exhibit XII (complete for combinations of Business Week, Fortune, HBR, Newsweek, Time, and U.S. News & World Report).

Note that in the total top executive group, and even more so in the two selective segments shown, the magazines with concentrated readership form parts of combinations with absolute (unduplicated) coverage equal to that of magazines of larger circulation. Thus, to cite one of the most striking examples:

Fortune, Newsweek, and Time, whose circulations add up to 3,438,396 and whose page rates add up to $19,930, together cover 77% of the total top executive group and 80% and 82% of the two selective segments.

But Business Week, HBR, and U.S. News & World Report, whose circulations add up to 1,208,160 (less than half as much) and whose page rates add up to $8,045 (less than half as much), also cover 76% of the total top executive group and even more in the selective segments—83% and 90%.

readership, and cost per thousand executives so covered)

All executives in companies employing over 1,000 (30,000)		All executives in manufacturing, construction, etc. (34,000)		Presidents and vice presidents in companies employing over 1,000 (16,000)		Presidents and vice presidents in companies employing, over 1,000 in manufacturing, construction, etc. (10,000)	
%	Cost	%	Cost	%	Cost	%	Cost
38%	$253	50%	$170	56%	$ 322	61%	$ 473
19	368	22	281	25	525	27	778
33	393	42	272	48	507	53	734
27	90	29	74	41	111	48	152
18	694	24	460	37	633	38	987
17	270	35	116	25	344	34	404
23	803	29	562	30	1,154	32	1,731
42	833	50	618	58	1,131	62	1,694
31	476	43	303	43	644	48	923

Such material can be useful in two ways. Advertisers desiring a given amount of coverage can see how to obtain it for the least money, as in the example just cited. Or, if they have a given amount of money to spend, they can see how to get the most coverage for it, like this:

Take an advertiser now spending $10,500 for Time, which gives him 53%, 58%, and 62% coverage of the total top group and the two selective segments, respectively.

Or take an advertiser now spending $9,430 for Fortune and Newsweek, which give him 57%, 64%, and 68% coverage of the total top group and the two selective segments.

The same advertiser could get 80%, 85%, and 92% coverage for approximately the same sum of money, $9,420, by using Business Week, HBR, Dun's Review and Modern Industry, and U.S. News & World Report.

This does not mean, again, that it is necessarily better to use combinations of smaller, more concentrated magazines just because they happen to be more economical or more effective in their own fields of strength.

Exhibit XII. Net coverage of top executive group by combinations of magazines

(Percentage of group or segment covered by the particular publica-

Total top executive group
(70,000)

Magazines	Combined page rates*	Per cent cover- age	Cost/M
Magazine of Wall Street	$ 500	3%	$238
Scientific American	1,800	7	367
Barron's	984	11	128
Forbes	2,100	20	150
Nation's Business	3,750	22	244
Harvard Business Review	730	24	43
Dun's Review and Modern Industry	1,375	24	82
Newsweek	5,540	31	255
Fortune	3,890	38	146
HBR, Dun's	2,105	40	75
US News & World Report	4,430	44	144
Business Week	2,885	46	90
Fort, HBR	4,620	48	138
HBR, NW	6,270	48	187
Time	10,500	53	283
BW, HBR	3,615	57	91
HBR, US	5,160	57	129
Fort, NW	9,430	57	236
NW, US	9,970	58	246
BW, NW	8,425	60	201
HBR, Time	11,230	62	259
BW, Fort	6,775	63	154
BW, HBR, Dun's	4,990	64	111
Fort, US	8,320	64	186
Fort, HBR, NW	10,160	66	220
Fort, Time	14,390	67	307
NW, Time	16,040	68	337
BW, Fort, HBR	7,505	69	155
BW, US	7,315	70	149
BW, HBR, NW	9,155	70	187
HBR, NW, US	10,700	71	215
Fort, HBR, US	9,050	72	180
BW, Fort, NW	12,315	73	241
BW, Time	13,385	73	262
Fort, HBR, Time	15,120	73	296
BW, Fort, HBR, Dun's	8,880	74	171
Fort, NW, US	13,860	74	268
Time, US	14,930	74	288

tion's readership, and cost per thousand executives so covered)

Presidents and vice presidents in companies employing more than 1,000 employees (16,000)			Presidents and vice presidents in companies employing more than 1,000 in manufacturing, construction, etc. (10,000)		
Magazines	Per cent coverage	Cost/M	Magazines	Per cent coverage	Cost/M
MWS	2%	$1,563	MWS	2%	$2,500
Barron's	9	683	Barron's	10	984
SA	10	1,125	SA	13	1,385
Dun's	25	344	Forbes	27	778
Forbes	25	525	NW	32	1,731
NW	30	1,154	Dun's	34	404
NB	37	633	NB	38	987
HBR	41	111	HBR	48	152
US	43	644	US	48	923
Fortune	48	507	Fortune	53	734
HBR, Dun's	53	248	NW, US	60	1,662
BW	56	322	BW	61	473
NW, US	56	1,113	Time	62	1,694
Time	58	1,131	HBR, Dun's	63	334
HBR, NW	60	653	HBR, NW	65	965
Fort, HBR	63	458	BW, NW	68	1,239
Fort, NW	64	921	Fort, NW	68	1,387
HBR, US	65	496	Fort, HBR	70	660
BW, NW	65	810	HBR, US	71	727
Fort, US	67	776	Fort, US	72	1,156
NW, Time	70	1,432	NW, Time	72	2,228
BW, HBR	71	318	Fort, Time	78	1,845
Fort, Time	73	1,232	BW, HBR	79	458
HBR, NW, US	74	904	HBR, NW, US	79	1,354
BW, US	75	610	Fort, NW, US	80	1,733
HBR, Time	75	936	Time, US	80	1,866
BW, NW, US	75	1,071	BW, US	81	903
Fort, HBR, US	76	744	Fort, HBR, NW	81	1,254
Fort, HBR, NW	76	836	HBR, Time	81	1,386
Fort, NW, US	76	1,140	Fort, NW, Time	82	2,430
Time, US	76	1,228	Fort, HBR, US	83	1,090
BW, Fort	77	550	BW, HBR, NW	83	1,103
BW, HBR, NW	78	734	BW, NW, US	83	1,549
Fort, NW, Time	80	1,557	BW, HBR, Dun's	84	594
BW, HBR, Dun's	81	385	BW, Fort	85	797
BW, Time	81	1,033	BW, Time	86	1,556
Fort, HBR, Time	81	1,167	HBR, NW, Time	86	1,950
BW, Fort, HBR	83	565	NW, Time, US	86	2,380

Exhibit XII. Continued

Total top executive group
(70,000)

Magazines	Combined page rates*	Per cent coverage	Cost/M
HBR, NW, Time	$16,770	75%	$319
BW, HBR, US	8,045	76	151
BW, Fort, HBR, NW	13,045	76	245
BW, NW, US	12,855	77	238
BW, HBR, Time	14,115	77	262
Fort, NW, Time	19,930	77	370
BW, Fort, US	11,205	79	203
Fort, HBR, NW, US	14,590	79	264
HBR, Time, US	15,660	79	283
BW, Fort, Time	17,275	79	312
BW, HBR, Dun's, US	9,420	80	168
BW, NW, Time	18,925	80	338
Fort, HBR, NW, Time	20,660	80	369
BW, HBR, NW, US	13,585	81	240
BW, Fort, HBR, Time	18,005	81	318
NW, Time, US	20,470	81	361
BW, Fort, HBR, US	11,935	82	208
Fort, Time, US	18,820	82	328
Fort, HBR, Time, US	19,550	84	332
BW, HBR, NW, Time	19,655	84	334
BW, Fort, NW, US	16,745	85	281
HBR, NW, Time, US	21,200	85	356
BW, Fort, NW, Time	22,815	85	383
BW, Time, US	17,815	86	296
BW, Fort, HBR, NW, US	17,475	87	287
BW Fort, HBR, NW, Time	23,545	87	387
BW, HBR, Time, US	18,545	88	301
Fort, NW, Time, US	24,360	88	395
BW, Fort, Time, US	21,705	89	348
Fort, HBR, NW, Time, US	25,090	89	403
BW, Fort, HBR, Time, US	22,435	90	356
BW, NW, Time, US	23,355	90	371
BW, HBR, NW, Time, US	24,085	92	374
BW, Fort, NW, Time, US	27,245	92	423
BW, Fort, HBR, NW, Time, US	27,975	93	430

* Based on black-and-white page rate, single insertion, including announced increases, from Standard Rate & Data Service, Inc., February 1957.

Presidents and vice presidents in companies employing more than 1,000 employees (16,000)			Presidents and vice presidents in companies employing more than 1,000 in manufacturing, construction, etc. (10,000)		
Magazines	Per cent coverage	Cost/M	Magazines	Per cent coverage	Cost/M
BW, HBR, US	83%	$ 606	BW, Fort, NW	87%	$1,416
BW, Fort, NW	83	927	Fort, HBR, Time	87	1,738
NW, Time, US	83	1,541	Fort, HBR, MW, US	89	1,639
Fort, HBR, NW, US	84	1,086	Fort, Time, US	89	2,115
HBR, NW, Time	84	1,248	BW, NW, Time	89	2,126
Fort, Time, US	84	1,400	BW, HBR, US	90	894
BW, Fort, HBR, Dun's	85	653	BW, HBR, NW, US	90	1,509
BW, HBR, Dun's, US	85	693	Fort, HBR, NW, Time	90	2,296
BW, Fort, Time	85	1,270	BW, Fort, HBR	91	825
BW, Fort, US	86	814	HBR, Time, US	91	1,721
BW, HBR, NW, US	86	987	BW, Fort. Time	91	1,898
HBR, Time, US	86	1,138	BW, HBR, Dun's, US	92	1,024
BW, NW, Time	86	1,375	BW, Fort, US	92	1,218
BW, Fort, HBR, NW	88	926	Fort, NW, Time, US	92	2,648
BW, HBR, Time	88	1,002	BW, Fort, HBR, Dun's	93	955
BW, Time, US	89	1,251	BW, Fort, HBR, NW	93	1,403
Fort, HBR, Time, US	89	1,373	BW, Fort, NW, US	93	1,801
BW, Fort, HBR, US	90	829	BW, Time, US	93	1,916
BW, Fort, NW, US	90	1,163	BW, Fort, NW, Time	93	2,453
BW, Fort, HBR, Time	90	1,250	BW, HBR, Time	94	1,502
Fort, HBR, NW, Time	90	1,435	Fort, HBR, Time, US	94	2,080
HBR, NW, Time, US	90	1,472	HBR, NW, Time, US	94	2,255
BW, Fort, NW, Time	90	1,584	BW, HBR, NW, Time	95	2,069
Fort, NW, Time, US	90	1,692	BW, NW, Time, US	95	2,458
BW, HBR, NW, Time	92	1,335	BW, Fort, HBR, US	96	1,243
BW, Fort, Time, US	92	1,475	BW, Fort, HBR, NW, US	96	1,820
BW, NW, Time, US	92	1,587	BW, Fort, HBR, Time	96	1,876
BW, Fort, HBR, NW, US	93	1,174	BW, Fort, Time, US	96	2,261
BW, HBR, Time, US	93	1,246	Fort, HBR, NW, Time, US	96	2,614
BW, Fort, HBR, NW, Time	93	1,582	BW, HBR, Time, US	97	1,912
Fort, HBR, NW, Time, US	93	1,686	BW, Fort, HBR, NW, Time	97	2,427
BW, Fort, HBR, Time, US	94	1,492	BW, Fort, NW, Time, US	97	2,809
BW, HBR, NW, Time, US	95	1,585	BW, Fort, HBR, Time, US	98	2,289
BW, Fort, NW, Time, US	95	1,792	BW, HBR, NW, Time, US	98	2,458
BW, Fort, HBR, NW, Time, US	96	1,821	BW, Fort, HBR, NW, Time, US	99	2,826

The advertiser must look at the whole picture, which may well indicate the desirability of coverage beyond the top executive group—or at other objectives beyond coverage, such as impressiveness—which the larger, less concentrated magazines can better provide. But it does mean that, in the light of all the possible combinations, advertisers have more flexibility, more opportunity to focus their coverage where they want it at minimum cost—and that perhaps they may have been wrong to assume they need to range so far afield.

There is nothing inherently wrong with duplication; it is not necessarily wasteful, as sometimes is implied. In fact, if it can be applied with full knowledge of how much there will be and where it will be, it can be used purposefully to secure desired results such as extra impact in strategic spots. It all depends on the advertising (and over-all marketing) objectives whether duplication should be avoided or intentionally sought.

The figures on concentration and the related figures on duplication simply make it possible to plan on the most economical way to carry out whichever is judged to be the most effective strategy—whether, for example, to hire a large sales force first, and *then* add some special salesmen for the trouble spots or the tough assignments; or whether to start with a core of crack salesmen for the big buyers, and *then* hire as many other salesmen as can pay their way calling on the rest of the prospects.

There is a lot to be said for getting away from gross statistics and for thinking of advertising in terms of the sales management analogy—employing magazines as salesmen and sending them out to call on individuals—particularly when such information as provided here is available. In any event, if receptivity to advertising messages has any relation to the readership of the publications containing them, the import here is like this:

Top executives have many salesmen (magazines) calling on them.
The higher their positions and the bigger their companies, the more salesmen they feel they must see even though they have less time to do so. . . .
Also, the more demanding they are that the salesmen really have something solid and substantial to offer. . . .
And, finally, the more willing they are to admit and listen to a salesman from whom they can get something to put to purposeful use in their jobs.

Of course, if this kind of approach is taken, some rethinking in areas beyond media selection may be in order. Thus, a move toward more selective coverage may raise the possibility that it is now worthwhile to write special copy for individual publications; this would be only logical in view of the fact that concentration is closely related to the particular purposes for which executives read various publications. In turn, all parties concerned may want to examine existing advertiser–advertising agency arrangements; in the circumstances, compensation to the agency as a standard percentage of media costs might be inconsistent with the kind of effort that is called for, and that the agency wants to provide.

Considering the importance of advertising to company sales and company costs, such analysis could well pay off—not just through specific decisions on points like those just mentioned but, even more, through soul-searching on the whole question of strategy *as the result of a new viewpoint*. And here is where this survey can be most useful. If there is one over-all finding to take and ponder, and then put to work, it is the pattern of purposeful use that makes top executives read as they do to meet their job requirements, particularly along the lines of the serious, intellectual, professional approach which is so strong today and is continually becoming stronger.

CONCLUSION

Executives complain a lot about their burden of reading. But this does not mean that they do not feel they should read extensively. On the contrary, it is a reflection of the fact that they very well recognize that the proper discharge of their administrative responsibilities requires them to do so—in the face of difficulties like time pressure and, for some older executives, lack of training or intellectual habituation.

The real need is for solid material that they can put to purposeful use, and the protest is they must read so much to get it. The fact that the professional approach is on the rise means that tomorrow they will need to get even more from their reading, and either (a) do even more reading to get it or (b) focus their reading even more sharply on the publications which best serve what are to them the most important users.

One obvious conclusion is that executives should be provided more time to do the firsthand reading their jobs require. But perhaps this is wishful thinking; unfortunately, reading seems to be the kind of activity that can be tucked into odd moments—and so it usually gets pushed out of office hours. The alternative is that individual executives themselves, or someone in management looking out for them, should see to it that they are more discriminating in their reading—that they should, for example:

1. Decide what range of ideas and developments must be kept up with on a broad and less intensive basis. There are many areas where an executive needs awareness more than grasp or detailed understanding.
2. Decide what areas of use are so important to the job requirements that they must, and can only, be explored thoughtfully and in depth. Subjects in these areas may demand that readers be able to follow the steps in the writer's reasoning, so they can agree with him or disagree with him but at least know why they do so and on what points. Otherwise they cannot translate ideas into terms of their own jobs or their own companies.
3 Decide what combinations of publications will serve these two needs with a minimum of wasted time and effort. This clearly leaves plenty of room for different magazines with different patterns of use.

Significantly, the executives covered in this survey, when asked whether they felt there was need for a new, different kind of magazine in the business field, very wholeheartedly said *no* (90%). Only a small number had any suggestions (255, or 17%); and, out of a scatter of very diffuse proposals, some 50 yearned for a good digest of important articles in existing magazines or, even better, a guide to what they should read in existing magazines. A number of them took the occasion to ask for less froth and more substance in their present magazines.

There is a moral here for publishers too—both a need and an opportunity. Top executives do not want streamlined or syncopated reading where the reading is easy because the intellectual guts have been removed along with the long words and the subtle phrases. At the same time, they do not want any more difficulty than they have to put up with, of course—and any publisher who does not try to do what he can for them on this score would seem to be missing a bet—but they would any day just as soon have twice as much hard reading if it would provide them three times as much useful "meat."

As for advertisers and other communicators of ideas, they will have to scrutinize publications more carefully and imaginatively. If the focus of readership and the consequent concentration in individual publications grow stronger—as seems likely since this is only the continuation of a present strong trend—they also will have a need and opportunity: to think more in terms of purposeful use than of quantitative coverage, as the basis for shaping their total programs to best fulfill their over-all marketing objectives.

CASHIERS'
ERRORS*

I. POLICIES AND PRACTICES

This is the first of a series of two articles dealing with the receipt of cash and the making of change for cash sales. The specific emphasis will be on the errors made in these processes. This part will describe the policies and practices instituted and followed by certain industrial firms in these cash-handling procedures. The second article in the series will attempt to present the quantitative measurements of the sizes of the errors, the patterns which they tend to maintain, and their variations with changes in certain influencing conditions. The second part of the study will also attempt to interpret these results and to explain something of their significances for industrial firms.

Stores Included

Only chain stores and other business enterprises whose cash-receiving characteristics place them in a similar category have been included in the study. In this group fall drug, grocery, and variety stores, and, in addition, certain department stores which "approximate many stores of a chain all under one roof."

The study has been limited to chain stores for five reasons:

1. The receiving of cash and the making of change in chain stores tend to become specialized and highly standardized functions among the business processes. This characteristic automatically rules out many other variables which might enter to effect the quantitative measurements.
2. The volume of cash received and handled by any given cashier or group of like cashiers is of sufficient magnitude that the characteristics revealed become statistically significant.
3. The concentrated volumes of cash received permit the limiting of the time factor to the point where the likelihood of policy change within any given segment is minimized. In other words, sufficient data are available to make it possible to study their characteristics in the short run.
4. The homogeneity in the personnel group filling the cash-receiving positions in the chain stores as well as the similarity of the policies

* By Lucile Derrick. Reprinted from Journal of Business of the University of Chicago, January, 1947, pp. 9–13, by permission of the University of Chicago Press. © 1947 The University of Chicago Press.

governing the practices of this same group permits certain classifications which greater heterogeneity would have precluded.

5. To chain-store management, which depends on small profit margins on large volumes of sales to produce the total profits, a small effect on the profit margin becomes very important. To some chain stores, for instance, shortages of .25 of 1 per cent of sales represent approximately one-fourth of the profits these chains make.

Cash Sales Receipts Records and Checks

The chains under study have followed fairly uniform practices with regard to the recording and checking of cash received for sales. The records can generally be classified into one of two groups: The first involves the daily recording and a comparison of the amount of cash which is in or has been in the cash drawer (minus the "bank") with the cash-register record which shows the amount rung. If the cash taken is less than the register reading, it is recorded as a shortage and if greater, as an overage. In the second group, slips or tickets are made out to cover each sale, and the total amounts of these slips are balanced against the amounts of cash received, and the error, if any, is similarly calculated. The cash may be deposited in a cash register or merely in a cash drawer.

In the first type the customer may or may not be given a receipt for his purchase; while in the second type the receipt is a duplicate of the sales slip. The cash-register receipt issued is merely a tape showing the items rung on the register with their total. If the customer questions an amount, he is required to call it to the attention of the cashier before he leaves the store. This requirement does not necessarily carry over to the second type since the names of the items purchased along with their prices are recorded.

In the first case the report is usually made daily to the auditing or other managerial department, where excessive shortages or overages are noted and proper steps are taken to examine their causes, along with remedial steps for their prevention. In the second case the same procedure may be followed, but exact records of each shortage and/or overage are sometimes difficult to ascertain because the delay in receipt of the proper records at the sales audit or other examining office permits offsets to cover the initial errors.

Cash-handling Techniques

The steps involved in receiving the cash, cash-ringing the sales, and making change have been standardized to a fairly high degree by all the major chains. The dependence on habit patterns in these processes, if greatest efficiency is to be achieved both with regard to speed and accuracy, has been recognized. In the normal procedure, girls who are prospective cashiers are put through a training period to drill them in these cash-handling habits. Because of the labor shortages during the war period, many deviations from the conventional practices had to be made, and, consequently, errors in cash-handling often increased greatly.

Cash-handling techniques vary somewhat, depending on the type of items handled, but most of the methods are similar. If an error is consciously made in ringing the register, a record usually is made to which the store manager or other official is a witness; then this discrepancy is taken account of in the day's figures. In every case the cashier is trained to place the customer's money—particularly if a large bill is received—in the cash drawer after change is verbally counted out to the customer, at which time the amount received by the employee is repeated. In stores where the price per item is small, the store manager or his assistants may handle all bills over one dollar.

In case the sales person passes the sales slip and money received over to a second person to make change, a double check is created: the cashier issuing the change to the sales person and the sales person, in turn, to the customer.

Although there are differences of opinion as to the degree which experience adds to the reduction of errors in cash-handling, there is general agreement that the experienced person is to be preferred. It may well be that the improvement of the habit patterns does follow a curve, but one of the modified exponential type which in the earlier stages of experience rather rapidly approaches its upper limit and then levels off, changing very gradually beyond a certain point. Many cash-handlers who have had experience are put through the training program to check their established habits and to be retrained if necessary.

The belief has been expressed rather uniformly that there is little correlation between the age of the cash-handler and the sizes or frequencies of errors made in the handling.

There are quite diversified opinions among executives, however, on the question of whether there are specific characteristics of some individuals which training or experience cannot surmount in making of those persons "good" cashiers. The opinions take such extremes as "anyone with average intelligence can be taught to handle cash with a minimum of error" to "regardless of the amount of training, some persons could never become efficient cash-handlers."

Some of these differences of opinion may spring from the fact that some persons who receive the cash for sales have only that specialized function to perform while others are, in addition, sales persons. With the second type the cash-handling function is often merely a part of the sales procedure. In the latter case, persons are chosen for their selling rather than their cash-handling abilities. But, because they do perform the second function, their errors are checked, and they are placed in the cash-handling category and rated with others in that group.

Types of Errors

It is believed that every discrepancy in cash-handling falls in one of two groups. One of these is what will be termed the "human error." These errors are unconsciously made and are involuntary mistakes on the part of the cash-handler. These errors are made in all good faith. The second type comprises those which are voluntarily and consciously planned and are dishonestly made. It is felt, however, that, while the total amount represented by the second type may at times be considerable, the number of cashiers whose errors fall in this group forms a relatively small percentage of the total number. It is also recognized that there is always the possibility that a cashier whose errors fall under the first type may under certain pressures be tempted by the presence of the cash to the point where her errors become those of the second type. While control measures necessary for the two types vary, they do have in common the fact that a discrepancy in cash is the revealing symptom. It is with the predominating first group, however, that the quantitative measurements in this study will principally deal.

Error Controls

Since the successful handling of cash from cash sales is so predominantly a matter of the formation of the correct habits, the general approach to error elimination of the "human error" type is through a checking or rechecking of the habits used. In cases where suggestions or retraining do not have sufficient effect, transfer or dismissal follows. The sizes of the errors as well as their frequencies of occurrence are major considerations in the practice determination. Again, the sizes and frequencies calling for certain actions have varied as between individuals and among stores, and have been conditioned by relative supplies of labor available.

There have been times when employees have been charged with their shortages. This practice was based on the theory that many errors were due to carelessness and that if cashiers had to pay for their shortages, they would practice greater care. So far as overcharging was concerned, it was felt that the customer would take care of himself. Different methods have been used to collect shortages. One type consisted of setting a limit beyond which the cashier was held accountable for the shortage. This amount was usually collected at the regular pay day. In another type the auditing office passed the information on to the field person in charge, and, if in the opinion of the supervisors the error was avoidable, the person was charged with the shortage.

This policy of charging shortages to employees has been abandoned by all the major chains. The philosophy has shifted to one of an accent on accuracy where a shortage is looked upon as an error in the same way as an overage. It is now recognized that customer good-will as well as efficient operation is dependent upon elimination, in so far as possible, of all types of errors. In most instances where the employee payment of shortages has been discontinued the change in policy has taken place during or immediately following the war period. Some states have placed on their statute-books regulations prohibiting the lowering of the amount stipulated to be paid any given employee unless the worker consents (usually in writing) to the deduction.

The competitive spirit is also resorted to in order to encourage employees to eliminate errors. The errors of a given store, as a percentage of sales of that store in the chain, are published periodically in the house organ. In that way a spirit of rivalry is developed, and all the employees of a given store act as a pressure on persons who tend to be careless.

Certain operating conditions behave in such a way as to preclude the exact assignment of errors to any given cashier. This has been the case where two or more cashiers have been using the same cash drawer. Usually, in situations of this kind, the shortages have been evenly allocated to each of the persons using the drawer. This has often been a source of dissension, however, since one employee may resent her assumption of what she considered others' carelessness. This same feeling has also been common when the cashier has been charged with errors which she felt were made while she was away from the register or while training an unskilled person. Some chains have avoided these objections, where sufficient equipment has been available, by assigning to any one person the exclusive use of a given cash drawer. When that is done, errors can definitely be pinned to the person responsible.

Oftentimes errors are made through the making of change between or among registers or cash drawers. These errors are deleted sometimes by balancing the cash containers in error. While this practice can be justified from one viewpoint, it tends to defeat the central purpose of exact measurement of errors regardless of by whom they are made.

During the war period stores have been more frequent prey to those who wantonly absconded with cash. This has been due in part to the fact that less careful selective processes were automatically imposed due to the decreasing supply of eligible persons and to the augmented demand. The control measures whereby these errors are detected were not always sufficient to catch the person who found it possible to rob registers. The conventional control measure for this type of error has consisted of the use of professional shoppers—persons who buy in a manner to facilitate the customary short-ringing of sales while the shopper carefully but inconspicuously notes the recordings. A second control measure has been to check the registers' readings against the cash drawer at frequent and unexpected intervals. A third method has been the periodic checking of inventories against sales. When by this method the dollar sales show a wide discrepancy from the "book sales," the need for further checking is obvious.

Some errors which cashiers make can be attributed to the conscious maneuvering on the part of customers. These wily individuals are usually known as "short-change artists." Since most of the methods used by this group of individuals are known, the cashier is warned against them. The chief method is a dependence upon the rapid creation of a situation sufficiently complex to confuse the person making change.

Summary

The preceding section has attempted to define the scope of the study and to describe the policies and practices followed by chain stores in their receipts of cash and in the making of change for cash sales. The specific reference has been to the type of records made and to receipts issued, the techniques applied, the types of errors encountered, and the methods used to control these errors. The second section of the study will deal with the error measurement and distribution.

II. ERROR MEASUREMENT AND DISTRIBUTION[*]

This is the second in a series of two articles dealing with the receipt of cash and the making of change for cash sales in chain stores. The

Table 1. Daily errors falling in
stated shortage or
overage classes

(Based on a total of 1,270 errors)

Error (amount and type)	Per cent of total shortages and overages	
	Shortages	Overages
$0.00–$0.24	15.6	17.0
0.25– 0.49	9.4	10.0
0.50– 0.74	5.0	6.9
0.75– 0.99	3.5	3.9
1.00– 1.24	2.8	3.2
1.25– 1.49	2.2	2.1
1.50– 1.74	1.7	1.9
1.75– 1.99	1.1	1.3
2.00– 2.24	1.0	1.3
2.25– 2.49	0.5	1.1
2.50– 2.74	0.8	0.8
2.75– 2.99	0	0.7
3.00– 3.24	0.2	0.6
3.25– 3.49	0.3	0.6
3.50– 3.74	0.5	0.2
3.75– 3.99	0.5	0.2
4.00– 4.24	0.4	0.5
4.25– 4.49	0.3	0.2
4.50– 4.74	0.3	0.6
4.75– 4.99	0.4	0.5

policies and practices instituted and followed by these stores in their handling and control of such errors have been discussed previously.

This article will attempt to analyze the character of these errors by determining the nature of their distributions, the patterns which they tend to maintain, and their relationships to certain selected factors. Some at-

[*] By Lucile Derrick. Reprinted from Journal of Business of the University of Chicago, April, 1948, pp. 74–79, by permission of the University of Chicago Press, © 1948 The University of Chicago Press.

tempt will also be made to interpret the significance of the results. In so far as possible, error limits will be chosen which will conform to the "human error" range. This will be done by including only those deviations which it is felt are randomly rather than systematically produced.

Data Employed

Daily records of the errors made by six hundred cashiers working at cash registers were studied over a period of time. Data were obtained from chain-store records, and these were supplemented by interviews with chain-store executives and cashiers. Stores in which cashiers were employed were located in all sections of the United States and ranged from small to large in sales volume. Overages and shortages in cash were treated alike as errors. It is recognized that, with daily readings, compensating overages and shortages could offset each other between times of recording. Therefore, the errors may be conservatively stated. However, owing to the fact that mistakes are frequently recorded when consciously made by the cashier, the differences may be relatively minor.

Error Distribution

Table I represents the pattern of daily errors made by all six hundred cashiers. Errors equal to or exceeding $5.00[1] have been eliminated from this distribution on the basis that they represent discrepancies in "banks" or systematic types of deviations which it is desired to eliminate from the present consideration. In the majority of cases an error equal to or exceeding $5.00, which appeared as a shortage, reappeared as an overage in some other register or even in the same register at some later date. Of the errors studied, approximately 93 per cent were under $5.00.

It can be noted from the preceding distribution that over one-half of all "human errors" made at the cash register are less than fifty cents in size, that almost three-fourths fall below one dollar, and that almost nine-tenths are less than two dollars in size. These relationships are even more vividly portrayed when charted (see Chart I). Shortages, which may be interpreted as negative overage, have been plotted in descending order of size to the left and overages in ascending order to the right on the horizontal axis. Smoothing has been employed at the extremes in order to eliminate the effects of sampling fluctuations. The curve of daily errors appears to be a unimodal one which is approximately symmetrical.

Effect of Sales Volume on Errors

The question arises concerning the effect of combining errors made in small stores with slow-moving and light traffic with those made in stores with heavy sales volumes, where the pressures on the cashiers are greatly increased. Cashiers differ in their opinions concerning the effect of pres-

[1] An element of subjectivity is present in the setting of this $5.00 limit. This amount was chosen after observing the character of the error distribution.

Chart I. Frequency of occurrence of daily errors of stated amounts and types

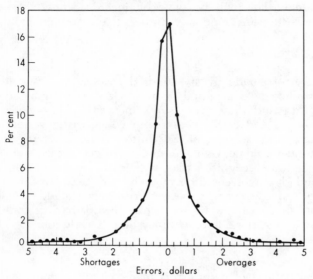

sures to increase their errors. One group believes that errors are most likely to occur when the cash-handler is rushed. Another group, however, contends that errors are more likely to be made when business is slack and concentration on the task is wavering.

In an attempt to answer this question, the errors have been subclassified by sales volumes on which they arose. Two classes—small and large sales volumes—have been employed for this purpose. It is recognized that a pattern of other factors, if consistently occurring, might explain any differences noted between the errors made while handling a large volume of sales and those connected with a small volume. In order to present a direct visual comparison, the data were grouped into two frequency polygons and these in turn superimposed upon each other. The results appear in Chart II.

On the whole, the curve of errors for large sales volumes tended to be above that of the curve of errors for small sales volumes in the extreme or large error ranges but to drop below it in the middle or small error range. The curves crossed at approximately fifty cents. In other words, for errors ranging from zero to fifty cents in size, stores with larger sales volume per cashier did the better job of cash-handling but failed to maintain their superiority when larger errors were involved.

Effects of Other Factors on Errors

Among the other factors considered which might affect the error sizes and frequencies of occurrence were age, education, and experience of

Chart II. Frequency of occurrence of daily errors made on small and large volumes of sales

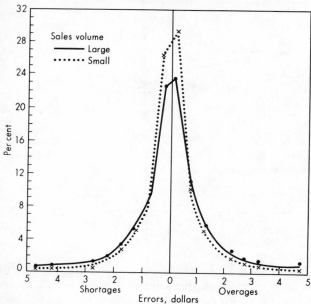

the cashiers. In order to eliminate the effects of sales volume, the errors were converted to a per one-hundred-dollar sales-volume basis. Table 2 and Chart III present the algebraic and geometric relationships between ages of the cashiers and the mistakes made in cash-handling.

If sampling fluctuations and discrepancies in age measurement were

Table 2. Average errors made by cashiers falling in various age groups

Age of cashier (In years)	Average error (per $100 sales volume)	Age of cashier (In years)	Average error (per $100 sales volume)
Under 20	$0.728	50–54	$0.414
20–24	.599	55–59	.419
25–29	.557	60 and over	.541
30–34	.580		
35–39	.736	Average for all cashiers	$0.622
40–44	.557		
45–49	.698		

Chart III. Relationship between age of cashiers and errors made

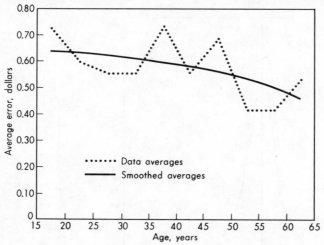

eliminated, there seems to be a slight tendency for younger cashiers to have higher errors on the average than those of more mature years. However, this is probably due to a third factor, experience, which the younger cashiers have not had time to acquire. As will be noted later, experience shows a definite correlation with error size.[2]

The effects of the second factor studied, that of formal education, upon error sizes are shown in Table 3 and Chart IV. There appears to be a

Table 3. Average errors made by cashiers having completed stated amounts of formal education

Formal education (In years)	Average error (per $100 sales volume)	Formal education (In years)	Average error (per $100 sales volume)
6 or 7	$0.629	12	$0.710
8	.563	13	.617
9	.549	14	.479
10	.552	15	.762
11	.591	16	.618

[2] *By a process of cross-classification or partial correlation, the factor experience might be held constant in order to study the net relationship existing between age and error size.*

Chart IV. Relationship between formal education and errors of cashiers

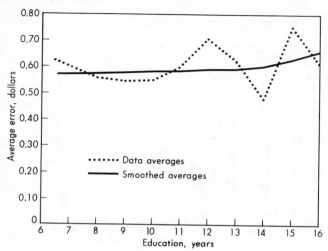

slight positive correlation between formal education of cashiers and the sizes of the errors which they make. In other words, the training given in the high schools and in institutions of higher learning has little effect on a cashier's ability to eliminate errors in her work. The slight tendency to have errors increase as the length of formal training period increases may be attributable to the fact that cashiers with more formal education usually have had less time in which to gain experience behind cash registers.

Experience was the third factor whose effects on errors was studied. The relationships derived are shown in Table 4 and on Chart V. Average errors tended to decrease as experience increased. This decrease seems

Table 4. Average errors made by cashiers with various amounts of experience

Experience	Average error (per $100 sales volume)	Experience	Average error (per $100 sales volume)
Less than 1 month	$1.095	3 to 4 years	$0.511
1 to 6 months	0.758	4 to 5 years	.540
6 to 12 months	0.573	5 to 10 years	.495
1 to 2 years	0.585	10 to 15 years	.474
2 to 3 years	0.714	15 years and over	.368

Chart V. Relationship between experience of and errors made by cashiers

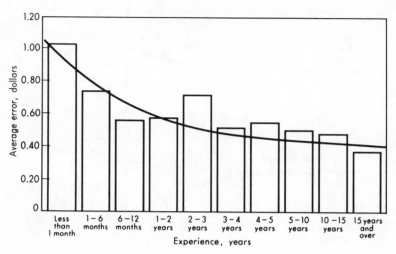

to be most rapid with approximately the first three years of experience. Beyond that point error decrease was achieved at a much slower rate. The curve of relationship appears to be one of the second degree.[3] The fact that in the "15 years and over" class are included persons with over twenty years' experience means that the full character of the curve is probably determined. The rapid decrease in errors during the first two years may be due to the fact that most training in service is concentrated in that period as well as to the fact that cashiers with increasing experience may tend to be on the whole less careful. Or it may be possible that additional training gained through experience brings relatively smaller returns as the time is increased.

Summary and Conclusions

Cashiers' daily shortages and overages seem to maintain a pattern of definite concentration around small errors. Over one-half are less than $0.50, almost three-fourths fall below $1.00, and almost nine-tenths are less than $2.00 in size. Beyond this point an error is very unusual. The cashier, then, has an even chance that a mistake which she will make will be less than $0.50 and only approximately ten chances in one hundred that it will be larger than $2.00.

The size of the sales volumes handled seems to have some effect upon the degree of concentration of the errors within certain ranges but does

---

[3] *Over the longer periods of experience there seems to be approximately a constant percentage decrease in error size. However, the drop in average error during the first two years is too rapid to be described by a straight line on semilogarithmic paper.*

not alter the general character of the distribution. The frequency of occurrence of less than $0.50 errors is slightly less on large sales volumes. Errors exceeding $0.50, however, occur with slightly greater frequency on the higher sales volumes. These results are in keeping with the relative frequency of occurrence of differing magnitudes of the volumes of sales.

The age of the cashier probably has little net effect upon the errors produced. However, the gross relationship does tend to show a slightly negative correlation. This is probably due to the concurrent existence of experience along with age.

It would seem at first that the slight positive correlation between formal education and errors would indicate that the more formal training a cashier had, the more subject to errors her sales would be. The fact that the years spent in high school or college consumed the time on other subjects not directly related to cash-handling probably explains this phenomenon. Many chain-store managers expressed preferences for cashiers having more formal education. In so far, however, as this furnished an indirect measure of intelligence, the manager was probably expressing a preference for cashiers who could learn quickly and take directions easily.

The experience of a cashier definitely has an effect on the errors made. The most pronounced effect seems to occur during the first two or three years. Beyond that point the rate of improvement in error elimination with added experience decreases. On the whole, in-service training applied during the first two years of employment of an inexperienced cashier should bring maximum results. It may be, however, that the character of the experience-versus-error curve could be changed if policies were adopted to apply training efforts after the first two or three years of experience had been acquired.

The fact that the cashier, on the average, either shortchanges or overchanges the customer six cents on every ten dollars handled means that additional training or emphasis on accuracy should be applied. It is recognized that if a recent period of time which might reflect more normal conditions had been available for study, the six cents might have been reduced.

It is suggested that chain stores study their own unique needs and situations in order to set up objective standards which might point the way toward elimination of errors at least beyond the $0.50 limit. At the present time a great deal of subjectivity is present in the handling of this problem. While it is recognized that the subjective element cannot be entirely eliminated, it can effectively be supplemented with some objective standards which in the long run will make for far greater efficiency and accuracy in cash-handling.

THE RAILROAD
LAND GRANT LEGEND
IN AMERICAN
HISTORY TEXTS*

In 1850, the United States government had a public domain of approximately 1,400,000,000 acres, vacant, unoccupied, and, for lack of transportation, largely unusable and unsalable.[1] Between that year and the end of 1871, the government undertook to use a portion of this land to encourage and assist the building of railroads in vacant or sparsely settled sections, in the same way in which previously it had aided the building of wagon roads and canals. The resulting series of transactions came to be known as the Federal railroad land grants, a subject frequently mentioned in high school and college texts which are the first, last, and only works on the history of their country read by many, if not most, Americans. This paper is the result of an examination of the treatment of the Federal land grant transactions in thirty-seven representative texts.

Since the treatment of a subject of this sort in such works must be brief, and even, in a sense, incidental, accuracy both as to the essential facts themselves and as to their place and proportion in the whole setting becomes all the more important. This inquiry is directed, therefore, to these facts and the manner of their treatment. It is limited to the Federal land grants because those are the grants which, for the most part, are discussed in the works examined, and are the grants about which the most complete information has been compiled, published, and made available.

A balanced story of the Federal land grant transactions requires reasonably correct answers to these questions, at the very least:

How much land was granted to railroads, and what proportion was this of the whole public domain?

* By Robert S. Henry. Reprinted from The Mississippi Valley Historical Review, September, 1945, pp. 171–194. Used by permission.
NOTE: Mr. Henry wishes to acknowledge the assistance given him in preparing this article by Carlton J. Corliss and L. I. McDougle.
[1] On June 30, 1852, the public domain remaining unsold or not used for public purposes amounted to 1,387,534,000 acres. From the opening of the land office in 1812 up to that time, the government had sold only 102,113,861 acres. Grants to wagon roads and canals had amounted to 10,007,677 acres. J. D. B. DeBow, Superintendent of the U.S. Census, Statistical View of the United States . . . Being a Compendium of the Seventh Census (Washington, 1854), 191.

What proportion of the railroad mileage of the country received land
grants from the government?

What was this land worth?

What were the terms and conditions of the grants? Were they gifts,
or did the government get as well as give?

HOW MUCH LAND?

The first of these questions, purely a matter of recorded fact, deals with
the amount of land granted to railroads by the United States government.
In the standard general work on the subject, Donaldson's *Public Domain*,
published by the government in 1884, the total amount of land that
would be necessary to fulfill all the acts granting lands to railroads was
estimated at 155,504,994 acres.[2] The amount of land actually patented
to railroads, however, fell substantially short of this acreage, for a variety
of reasons—noncompletion of the grants, or lack of sufficient acreage
within the designated limits to fulfill the terms of the grants. The acreage
to which the railroads actually received title appears in the annual reports of the Commissioner of the General Land Office, the latest such
report showing a total of 131,350,534 acres.[3]

Of the thirty-seven American history textbooks examined, twenty-four
make specific reference to the area granted to railroads by the Federal
government. Of these twenty-four, one gives clear and approximately
correct figures as to the whole area granted, while one other comes
within 10 per cent of the correct figure.[4] Two others which do not state

[2] *Thomas Donaldson,* The Public Domain (*Washington, 1884), 753.*
[3] *U.S. General Land Office,* Annual Report of the Commissioner, *June 30, 1943,
Table 76. Corresponding figures, with slight variations from year to year, appear
in this entire series of reports. The report cited is for the latest year available.
In addition to Federal land grants, it is estimated that railroads received from the
states grants totaling 48,883,372 acres. U.S. Federal Coordinator of Transportation,
Public Aids to Transportation, 1938, Vol. II, 32, and Table 13, p. 115, based on
Federal or state records to June 30, 1933. The state land grants are not dealt
with in this discussion. For a detailed and careful study of the state grants of
Texas, which were by far the most significant, see S. G. Reed, A History of the
Texas Railroads (Houston, 1941), Chap. XXIV. Right-of-way grants, by which the
Federal government granted to pioneer railroads running through the public domain
strips of land from 80 to 400 feet wide (the most common grants being 200 feet
wide) for right-of-way purposes, are mentioned in some of the works examined
but are not dealt with in this study. While in the aggregate they amounted to
a considerable acreage, the grants were of so little value without railroads, and
they were relatively such a minor part of the whole picture, that no separate discussion of them seems necessary. Donaldson, 286–7, 769–71, 940–3, 1262–3, Public
Aids to Transportation, II, 48–51.*
[4] *Ralph Volney Harlow,* The Growth of the United States (*2 vols., New York, 1943),
II, 15, gives 132,500,000 acres. George M. Stephenson, American History to 1865
(New York, 1940), 407, compares the grants with states having a total area of
144,224,000 acres.*

248   BUSINESS RESEARCH

the area as a whole, give correct partial figures.[5] In seven works, a substantially correct statement at one place is contradicted elsewhere, either by another larger figure or by a graphic presentation which greatly exaggerates the area granted.[6] Eight others show the area granted, either graphically or in text, or both, as anywhere from nearly one-fifth more than it was, up to about four times the correct area.[7] Five give partial figures only, which either are incorrect or are so presented as to give a misleading impression.[8] Others make neither arithmetical nor graphic presentation of the area granted, but rely entirely on adjectives. In most of the books, in fact, such adjectives as "huge," "vast," "enormous," "staggering," and "breath-taking" are parts of the treatment of the subject of area.

[5] *Carl Russell Fish and Howard E. Wilson,* History of the United States (*New York, 1936*), 545; *John D. Hicks,* The Federal Union: A History of the United States to 1865 (*Boston, 1937*), 552.
[6] *Charles H. Coleman and Edgar B. Wesley,* America's Road to Now (*Boston, 1942*), 401, 502; *Harold U. Faulkner, Tyler Kepner, and Hall Bartlett,* The American Way of Life (*New York, 1941*), 296–7; *Harold U. Faulkner and Tyler Kepner,* America, Its History and People (*New York, 1942*), 388, 455; *Willis Mason West and Ruth West,* The American People (*Boston, 1937*), *map underline facing p. 474, 554–5. Melville Freeman and Eston V. Tubbs,* The Story of Our Republic (*Philadelphia, 1943*), Part II, 47, 68; *Charles A. and Mary R. Beard,* The Making of American Civilization (*New York, 1942*), 552; *Edward C. Kirkland,* A History of American Economic Life (*New York, 1941*), 379.
[7] *Asa Earl Martin,* History of the United States (*2 vols., Boston, 1938*), II, 122; *Charles A. Beard and William C. Bagley,* The History of the American People (*New York, 1943*), 501; *Rolla M. Tryon, Charles R. Lingley, and Frances Morehouse,* The American Nation Yesterday and Today (*Boston, 1942*), 439; *Louis M. Hacker and Benjamin B. Kendrick,* The United States Since 1865 (*New York, 1943*), 160; *William A. Hamm,* The American People (*Boston, 1939*), 517–8; *David Saville Muzzey,* The United States of America (*2 vols., Boston, 1937*), II, 27; *Samuel Eliot Morison and Henry Steele Commager,* The Growth of the American Republic (*2 vols., New York, 1937*), II, 112, *and map facing p. 112; George Earl Freeland and James Truslow Adams,* America's Progress in Civilization (*New York, 1942*), *map facing p. 324.*
[8] *John T. Greenan and Albert B. Meredith,* Everyday Problems of American Democracy (*Boston, 943*), 451; *Arthur Meier Schlesinger,* Political and Social Growth of the American People 1865–1940 (*New York, 1943*), 47; *Gertrude Van Duyn Southworth and John Van Duyn Southworth,* American History, from the Discovery of America to the Present Day (*Syracuse, 1940*), 226. *In the three works above, the areas granted to the original Pacific railroads are shown as 100 million acres, as against actual grants to these routes of less than three-fourths that amount. Dwight Lowell Dumond,* A History of the United States (*New York, 1942*), 535, *states the grants to the first Pacific railroad as 33 million acres, as against an actual grant of slightly more than 18 million acres. Jacob Lewis Stockton,* A Topical Survey of American History (*New York, 1944*), 148, *takes as an example the grants to the railroad which received almost one-third of all the lands granted by the government to railroads, raises the amount of this grant from its actual figure of 36 million to 47 million acres, and then declares that "other roads were granted proportionate amounts."*

LAND GRANT MAPS, RIGHT AND WRONG

The most potent source of this exaggerated impression of the size of land grants, and the prevailing confusion of thought and inaccuracies of statement in their measurement, seems to be uncritical acceptance of land grant maps which are incorrectly understood and described by the text writers.

To understand the official land grant maps, it is necessary to bear in mind the "checkerboard pattern" in which land was granted to the railroads. First, there were original, or primary, limits within which the grantees were to receive alternate sections, non-mineral in character, or a total of one-half the area within a strip of land of a given width lying on both sides of the track, provided these sections had not previously been granted or otherwise disposed of, or reserved from grant for other public purposes, such as school grants, forest, and other reservations. In lieu of the land which had been previously disposed of or was reserved, the grantee was to be allowed to select a like amount of land from a contiguous zone—the so-called indemnity limits.[9] (It is necessary to bear in mind, also, the fact that the official maps include not only grants to railroads, but also grants for wagon roads, canals, and river improvements.) The four principal patterns followed, with variations, in the several different land grant acts were:

1. Grants of alternate sections of land in primary strips embracing the area within *six* miles on either side of the proposed railroad, with indemnity limits outside thereof extending fifteen or twenty miles from the railroad.
2. Grants of alternate sections of land in primary strips embracing the area within *ten* miles on either side of the proposed railroad, some without indemnity limits, others with indemnity limits outside thereof extending twenty or thirty miles from the railroad.
3. Grants of alternate sections of land in primary strips embracing the area within *twenty* miles on either side of the proposed railroad, some without indemnity limits, others with indemnity limits outside thereof extending twenty-five, thirty, or fifty miles from the railroad.
4. Grants of alternate sections of land in primary strips embracing the area within *forty* miles on either side of the proposed railroad, with indemnity limits outside thereof extending fifty, and in some cases sixty, miles from the railroad. This pattern applied to territories only.

Under Pattern 1, for instance, the railroad received the equivalent of six sections of land (three on either side of the railroad) within the primary strips if available; otherwise within the indemnity limits. In no case did the railroad receive more than six sections per mile of road. Thus, where the primary and indemnity limits embraced an area forty

[9] *Donaldson, 261–2, 274–9, 756–63.*

miles in width, the railroad actually received a maximum of only slightly less than one-seventh of that area, or the equivalent of a solid strip six miles in width.

Under Pattern 3, the railroad was granted the equivalent of twenty sections of land (ten on either side of the railroad) within the primary strips if available; otherwise within the indemnity limits. Where the indemnity limits extended fifty miles from the railroad, the maximum area that the railroad could receive was one-fifth of the total area embraced by the primary and indemnity strips.

The earliest of the general land grant maps, apparently, was published by the government in 1878, in connection with a report on arid lands. Revised and brought up to date, it was again published by the government in 1883, and is included in Donaldson's well-known and widely available *Public Domain*. Again brought up to date, the map was republished in 1913 by the United States Department of Commerce and Labor in its report on *The Lumber Industry*.[10]

Each of these maps showed the limits of both the primary and indemnity zones, while the latest of the maps, that of 1913, showed also, by a special hatching, the grants which had been forfeited for noncompletion of the roads within the terms of the acts making the grant and under which, therefore, no railroad had received lands. The whole was covered, on this map, by the correctly descriptive caption: "Map of the United States showing the limits within which land grants were made by the Federal Government to aid in the construction of railroads and wagon roads." The map also carried a legend explaining that "the maximum amount of land obtainable was one-half that within the primary limits, the lands granted being in the alternate survey sections. The maximum was often not obtained."

The last sentence refers to the fact that in many of the grants, especially in the older and more settled land grant states, it was not possible to locate the maximum acreage allowed even within the indemnity limits. The situation is thus outlined on page 222 of the 1913 report referred to:

> In this connection the caution is repeated against assuming that the entire area within the limits shown on the map was granted to the railroads. The first set of heavy lines on each side of a road indicates the "primary limits" of the grant . . . within which limits it was to receive each alternate section (or part thereof) not already disposed of or reserved. The possible maximum of a grant, therefore, was half of the land within the primary limits. The second set of heavy lines, seen farther out on each side of the road in many grants, indicates the "indemnity limits" referred to above within which

[10] *The original government map and its two revisions and republications are as follows: (1) accompanying an historical article by Willis Drummond on "Land Grants in Aid of Internal Improvements," published in connection with the report of Major J. W. Powell on the "Lands of the Arid Region of the United States," House Executive Document No. 73, 45 Cong., 2 Sess., 1878; (2) Donaldson, facing p. 949; and (3) U.S. Department of Commerce and Labor, Bureau of Corporations, The Lumber Industry: Part I—Standing Timber (Washington, 1913), 222 and facing.*

the railroad could select vacant alternate sections (or parts thereof) to make up for lands within the primary limits that had been previously disposed of or reserved. Often so much land had been disposed of or reserved both in the primary and the indemnity limits that a road received considerably less than its possible maximum. In Iowa so much land had already been disposed of at private sale, under warrants and to settlers, that although the State appears practically covered by grants, only a little more than one-eighth its area was received by the railroads. But in regions where there was less of prior purchase and settlement the railroads secured a higher proportion; in some cases the whole of the possible maximum.[11]

The several government publications of the map became the basis of two privately published maps, that of Professors Hart and Bolton in their series of American history maps published in 1919,[12] and that in Paullin's *Atlas of the Historical Geography of the United States*,[13] published in 1932, both of which are careful to give like information, either on the map itself or in accompanying explanatory material.

Even with the most scrupulous explanation, however, it is difficult not to get an exaggerated impression of size from maps which show a shaded area twice as great as the actual grants, as in the case of the Hart map, and approximately four times as great, as in the case of the government publications and the Paullin map. Without such understanding and explanation, the maps become downright wrong. And, unfortunately for popular understanding of the facts of history, it is in this misleading form and with incorrect captions that almost all land grant maps have been circulated.

The first such use of the map, apparently, was in the presidential year of 1884, when the Democratic party issued a campaign poster featuring what purported to be a map of lands granted to railroads, but was actually a map of the extreme limits of the widest zones within which some lands might have been granted not only to railroads but also to wagon roads and river improvements, under the caption: "How the Public Domain Has Been Squandered—Map showing the 139,403,026 acres of the people's land . . . worth at $2 an acre $278,806,052 given by Republican Congresses to Railroad Corporations. . . ."[14]

[11] *One publication (not included in the present study) which printed the usual land grant map did so with the caption: "The black bands on the map show the land that the government granted to the railroads. Notice that almost the entire State of Iowa was given to them"—an interesting example of the error against which particular warning is given in the explanation quoted. Building America: Railroads (New York, 1940), V, No. 6, p. 174.*

[12] *Albert Bushnell Hart, assisted by David Maydole Matteson and Herbert Eugene Bolton, A Teacher's Manual Accompanying the Hart-Bolton American History Maps (Chicago, 1919), 87–8, and Map A–18: "Western Statehood and Land Grants to Railroads."*

[13] *Charles O. Paullin, Atlas of the Historical Geography of the United States (Washington, 1932), 39–40, and plate 56–D.*

[14] *Democratic Party Platform, 1884, How the Public Domain Has Been Squandered, broadside, with land grant map.*

Apparently those who compiled the poster overlooked the fact that the shaded area on the featured map represented about four times the number of acres stated in the accompanying text. The figures given in the text, however, are completely overshadowed by the pictorial impression of the map itself—an interesting example of the validity of the Chinese proverb as to the comparative force and effectiveness of words and pictures.

This effective pictorial exaggeration is perpetuated in the maps subsequently appearing in history texts. Nine of the works examined in this study present maps which include wagon road and river improvement grants as well as those for railroads, and which show the full area of the indemnity limits of both completed and noncompleted grants, without explanation or distinction as between primary and indemnity zones, and with captions which, in all but two cases, unqualifiedly describe the shaded strips as showing lands granted to railroads.[15]

One work, indeed, enlarges upon its erroneous caption by declaring that "the nation gave the railroad builders a kingdom in land. No such lavish generosity was ever dreamed of before. The map on page 68 tells better than words what vast areas were presented to the railroad companies."[16]

The two books which qualify the statement that the shaded areas of the map show lands granted to railroads point out that they were to receive only alternate sections, or one-half the area shown, but show on their maps not the primary limits but the much more extensive indemnity limits.

Accompanying this article are two maps identified by number. Map No. 1 is typical of the sort published in many of the textbooks examined. In contrast, Map No. 2 is drawn so as to show the approximate location of the grants which were actually completed. The widths of lines are proportioned to show the equivalent of the areas actually certified and patented to the railroads. In many instances, the acreage certified and patented was considerably less than the acreage granted, due to forfeitures, previous transfers, Federal reservations, and other causes. The startling contrast between the two maps indicates the extent of the vivid misinformation about railroad land grants which has become all but staple in history texts.

Besides the works which reproduce the erroneous land grant map (No. 1) itself, others seem to have used it uncritically as the source of information for textual comparisons of area which, of course, reflect the map's own exaggerations and inaccuracies. Thus, according to one work, "more than half of the northern tier of states lying against Canada from Lake

[15] The seven works which show the whole of the shaded portions of the map as representing lands granted to railroads are Faulkner and Kepner, 455; Faulkner, Kepner, and Bartlett, 296; Morison and Commager, II facing p. 112; Hamm, 518; Muzzey, II, 27; Freeman and Tubbs, Part II, 68; Freeland and Adams, facing p. 324. The two works which state that the railroads received only half the area shown are Coleman and Wesley, 401; West and West, map underline facing p. 474.

[16] Freeman and Tubbs, Part II, 47.

Map No. 1. *This map, originally drawn to show the extreme outer limits of areas within which some land might be granted to railroads, is frequently reproduced in American History texts with captions describing it as showing land actually granted—thereby exaggerating by approximately four times the area received by railroads.*

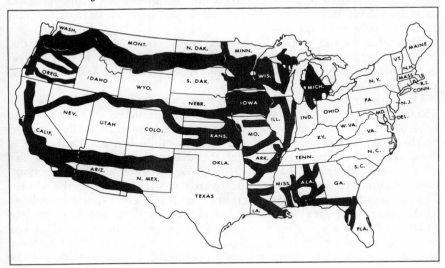

Map No. 2. *The Federal Government granted lands to railroads in alternate sections, retaining the sections between. It is impossible to present this "checkerboard" pattern on so small a map, but the solid black areas show the approximate locations of the land grants, and are in proportion to the amounts actually received by railroads.*

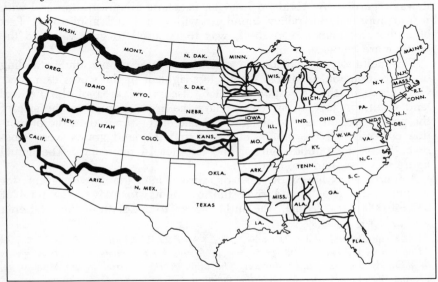

Michigan to the Pacific" and "about half of New Mexico, Arizona and California," were included in Federal land grants.[17] That would be approximately 272,000,000 acres in only eight states, and yet the same work gives the total area of all the Federal railroad grants in twenty-six states as only 155,000,000 acres—which itself is one-sixth more than the railroads actually received.

The table in the Appendix to this paper shows, by states, the discrepancy between the approximate acreage of land grants as they appear on Map No. 1 and the actual acreage received by the railroads as reported by the General Land Office.

Of course, the total Federal grants, whether the figure be the 155,000,000 acres which it was originally contemplated might be turned over to the railroads, or the 131,351,000 acres which were finally patented to them, when looked at by themselves, are indeed a great quantity of land. That objection was made in the debate on the bill for the first of the railroad grants, back in 1850. "We are met by the objection," said Senator William R. King, afterwards vice president of the United States, "that this is an immense grant—that it is a great quantity of land. Well, sir, it is a great quantity; but it will be there for five hundred years; and unless some mode of the kind proposed be adopted, it will never command ten cents." The Senator was looking at the land involved not as an absolute quantity but as a portion of a domain which, as he said, "can never be of any value . . . unless some direct communication by railroad, or some other way, is made."[18]

That was the way the land grant transaction was looked upon by the men who urged its adoption in the beginning—the Whigs, Henry Clay and William H. Seward among them, and the Democrats, Stephen A. Douglas, Thomas H. Benton, and Lewis Cass. It was the way in which it was regarded by Abraham Lincoln, in whose administration and with whose approval the policy found its widest use and application. Part of a domain, immense in itself, was to be used to give value to the vastly more immense whole.

This point of comparison, so essential to any proper understanding of the transaction, is almost wholly lost sight of in the works examined. Only three of the twenty-four which discuss the area of the Federal land grants, in fact, in any way relate the areas granted to the size of the public domain as a whole, and but one of the three gives the proportion correctly. Of the others, one says that the land grants were "one-seventh" of the public domain, and another 14 per cent.[19] The actual figure was less than one-tenth.

A fourth work lumps the area of railroad land grants with grants for wagon roads, canals, and river improvements, to arrive at a total of 337,740,000 acres, "equal," the author says, "to one-sixth of the total area

[17] *Beard and Beard,* 552.

[18] The Congressional Globe, 31 Cong., 1 Sess., April 29, 1850, pp. 845–6.

[19] *Coleman and Wesley, 502, gives correct figures for the areas of the land grants to railroads and the public domain. The other works referred to are Muzzey, II, 27; and West and West, map underline facing p. 474.*

of the United States and three times that of France."[20] The acreage given checks with no official report on the subject, but the Federal grants to railroads—on which the whole attention of the passage is focused—are much less than half the area mentioned.

HOW MUCH RAILROAD WAS BUILT WITH THE AID OF LAND GRANTS?

The second, and equally simple, question deals with the extent of railroad mileage, the construction of which was aided by the government's land grants. Such grants were made in aid of a total of 18,738 miles of railroad line[21]—less than 8 per cent of the total mileage of railroads built in the United States. The fact that more than 92 per cent of all the railroad mileage in the United States was built without the aid of an acre of Federal land grants is nowhere brought out in the texts examined—an omission which tends to throw the land grant transaction out of all proportion as a factor in the development of the national network of railroads.

The same tendency to exaggerate the government's financial part in railroad building appears in the treatment of the bond aid extended to six of the companies chartered to build the pioneer "Pacific" railroads. The government made a loan of its bonds to these railroads, in the total amount of $64,623,512. The roads were to pay 6 per cent interest on the bonds and to pay them off. During the long period of development and light traffic they were not always able to meet these charges, but in the final settlement in 1898 and 1899 the government collected $63,023,512 of principal plus $104,722,978 in interest—a total repayment of $167,746,490 on an initial loan of $64,623,512.[22] Professor Hugo R. Meyer of Harvard was well justified in saying that "for the government the whole outcome has been financially not less than brilliant"[23]—but none of this appears in the treatment of the transaction in the texts. Thirty-four of the thirty-seven texts examined mention the bond aid to

[20] *Beard and Bagley, 501. In a number of the books examined, areas are compared not with the areas of such states as those in which the lands were located, but with foreign countries, as in this case, or with thickly settled eastern states, a favorite selection for that purpose being the six New England states, New York, and Pennsylvania combined. While such comparisons might be arithmetically accurate, they do not present so true a picture as would comparisons with western acreage, such as used in two works: Coleman and Wesley, 401; Schlesinger, 47.*

[21] *U.S. General Land Office, Notice of Releases of Land Grant Claims by Railroad Carriers, May 17, 1941. Similar figures appear in earlier statements and reports of the General Land Office and other governmental departments and agencies concerned. In Lewis Henry Haney, A Congressional History of Railways in the United States (2 vols., Madison, Wisc., 1910), II, 14, the total mileage is given as 17,724 miles. The total route mileage of railroads on December 31, 1943, in the United States was 227,999 miles. Interstate Commerce Commission, Statistics of Railways in the United States (Annual).*

[22] *Public Aids to Transportation, II, 59, and table 19, p. 138.*

[23] *Hugo R. Meyer, "The Settlements with the Pacific Railways," Quarterly Journal of Economics, XIII (July, 1899), 443–4.*

these Pacific roads. In one-third of the works, it is not made clear whether the financial assistance referred to was a loan or a gift. Three describe the aid definitely as gifts—which they were not.[24] Twenty-one refer to the transactions as loans, but only four[25] mention the fact that the loans were repaid, while three[26] make the positively erroneous statement that the loans were never repaid.[27]

WHAT WERE THE LAND GRANTS WORTH?

One measure of the value of the lands granted—though no one would contend that it is the correct one—would be the cost to the government of acquiring them, which, according to Donaldson, was an average of 23.3 cents an acre.[28] On that basis, the 131,351,000 acres which the railroads received could be said to be worth less than $31,000,000.

Another possible measure is the standard "minimum" price at which the government offered the public domain for sale in the land grant period. This price was $1.25 an acre, though the government was never able to realize even this figure as an average selling price. But if the new railroad companies had bought from the government the 131,350,534 acres actually received, and had paid the full established price, the lands would have cost them $164,188,167.

Still another measure of the value of the lands during the period of the grants is to be found in the Graduation Act, under which the price of lands long on the market and unsold was graduated downward, starting with a price of $1 an acre after ten years, and ending with a price

[24] Howard C. Hill, The Life and Work of the Citizen (Boston, 1942), 392; Jeremiah S. Young and Edwin M. Barton, Growing in Citizenship (New York, 1941), 521; Sister of St. Joseph, American History (St. Augustine, Fla., 1932), Book II, 116.

[25] Repayment is mentioned in Hacker and Kendrick, 161; George M. Stephenson, American History Since 1865 (New York, 1939), 84; Kirkland, 380; Morison and Commager, II, 113.

[26] West and West, 464; Bruce Winton Knight, Economic Principles in Practice (New York, 1942), 262; W. E. Woodward, A New American History (Garden City, N.Y., 1938), 618.

[27] The same sort of disregard of repayment may be observed in the treatment of the government loans made to the railroads at the close of World War I, in connection with the difficult transition from government to private operation at that time. These loans, which totaled $1,080,575,000, are mentioned in three of the books examined. All of this huge sum except $28,698,000 has been repaid, with a total of $220,891,000 in interest (Annual Report of the Secretary of the Treasury . . . for fiscal year ended June 30, 1944, p. 173), but the fact is mentioned in none of the texts. The more recent depression loans made by the Reconstruction Finance Corporation and other Federal agencies receive the same type of treatment. Twenty books mention the fact that these loans were made. More than three-fourths of the loans made have been repaid or sold to the public, with a profit to the government in interest. Mention of repayment of any sort is made in only two of the books: Kirkland, 743; Hicks, II, 671.

[28] Donaldson, 21 and 524. This figure for cost of acquisition covers not only purchase price and payments to Indian tribes, but also costs of surveying and disposition.

of 12½ cents an acre for lands unsold after thirty years. Total sales in the years 1854–1862, during which the Act was in effect, even under such price arrangements as these, were only 25,696,420 acres.[29]

A more correct measure of value is the one applied in all ordinary transfers between buyer and seller—the worth of the land granted and received at the time of sale. During the period in which the land grants were being made to the railroads, the average sale price of government lands in the land grant states was less than $1 an acre.[30] Applying that price to the lands granted to the railroads gives a value as of the time of the grants, of less than $130,000,000.

It is sometimes contended that the measure of value in this case should be the amount finally realized by the railroads on their lands, after the roads had been built and after years of colonizing, advertising, sales effort, and development costs had been put upon them.[31] There is no more basis for setting up such a measure of value than there would be for putting it at the 23 cents an acre which it cost the government to acquire the lands in the first place, but because the point is raised in some of the works examined, it may be noted that the average realizations of the railroads from their Federal land grants, plus the estimated value of the lands remaining unsold, was put at $3.38 an acre according to one government study,[32] while in another report, including both state and Federal grants, the average is $2.81 an acre.[33]

Few of the works examined deal in detail with the question of value.

[29] Donaldson, 205–6, 291; Public Aids to Transportation, II, 35.

[30] The latest and most complete calculation of proceeds of Federal land sales during the period 1850–1871, when the land grants were made, shows an average sale price of 97.2 cents per acre. This calculation, however, is not restricted to the sale of lands in the land grant states, but covers also lands sold during this period in the older and more settled states. Eliminating these sales, the average per acre from sales of Federal public lands in railroad land grant states during this period was 94 cents per acre. From report of Federal Coordinator of Transportation, Public Aids to Transportation, II, 36.

[31] The extent of the effort and expense to which railroads went in marketing and settling their granted lands is indicated in the studies of Paul W. Gates, The Illinois Central Railroad and Its Colonization Work (Cambridge, 1934); James B. Hedges, "The Colonization Work of the Northern Pacific Railroad," Mississippi Valley Historical Review, XIII (December, 1926), 311–42, and "Promotion of Immigration to the Pacific Northwest by the Railroads," ibid., XV (September, 1928), 183–203; Richard C. Overton, Burlington West: A Colonization History of the Burlington Railroad (Cambridge, 1941). The somewhat similar situation in Canada is treated in James B. Hedges, Building the Canadian West: The Land and Colonization Work of the Canadian Pacific Railway (New York, 1939).

[32] U.S. Board of Investigation and Research, Report and Comments on H. R. 4184 . . . to the Committee on Interstate and Foreign Commerce of the House of Representatives, March 9, 1944, p. 28, shows net proceeds of sales of both Federal and state land grant lands to December 31, 1941, of $434,806,671, plus an estimated value of the unsold grant lands of $60,684,032. Of this total of $495,490,703, the sum of $55,090,652 is attributed to state land grants and $440,400,051 to Federal land grants.

[33] The report of the Federal Coordinator of Transportation, Public Aids to Transportation, II, 52, estimated the "aid received from all such grants," that is, state as well

An impression of richness is built up with such adjectives as "lavish," "munificent," and "princely," but figures are scarce. One suggests a value of two dollars an acre, which is the same figure used in the Democratic campaign document of 1884.[34] Others undertake to measure value by what the railroads realized from the lands when sold. One work states this as an "average price of $4.76 an acre."[35] Another quotes a "careful investigator" to the effect that it "has been under rather than over ten dollars an acre," out of which there had to come the costs of selling, from all of which the author concludes that "the actual financial assistance to the railroads from the land grants has probably been overestimated."[36]

The real contribution of the Federal land grants to the spread of the rails in the West and the newer South was not the cash realized upon them, but the fact that they furnished a basis of credit which got the job started and made it possible to get it done. The land grant acreage could be certified, patented, and sold only as the railroad itself was completed, in sections, and then could be sold mostly on long time credit. The selling price had to be low to get it sold at all, and the expense of sale was necessarily high. The net realizations from the sales, particularly during the period of construction, were but a tiny fraction of the cost of building the railroads. Thus, the Auditor of Railroad Accounts of the Department of the Interior reported that up to 1880 the several companies going to make up the five pioneer "Pacific" routes had sold only $36,383,795 worth of land. "The lands have been sold in small tracts, some for cash, but most of them on time," the Auditor wrote in describing the sales of one of the several companies concerned. The cost up to that time of building the several Pacific routes is shown in the same report as having been $465,584,029. This, the Auditor thought and so reported, was excessive, or at least much more than similar roads could have been built for when the report was made. Even the lesser figure of $168,045,000, which he estimated as enough to reproduce the roads, however, was considerably more than four times the realizations from land sales up to that date. Looking to the future, the Auditor estimated that the value of the railroad lands unsold in 1880 was $78,889,940, making a total estimated value for all lands sold and to be sold of $115,273,735, as against a total estimated cost of the several "Pacific" railroads, to completion, of $634,165,613. The Auditor thought that similar railroads could be built for $286,819,300, but even this figure is more than double the estimated total realizations from the lands granted to the "Pacific's."[37]

---

as Federal, at $516,144,749. This includes both proceeds of sales under Federal and state land and right-of-way grants, and also the estimated net value of lands still held by the railroads on December 31, 1927.

[34] Hacker and Kendrick, 161.

[35] Harlow, II, 15.

[36] Kirkland, 381.

[37] Department of Interior, Office of Auditor of Railroad Accounts, Report on the

The estimated worth of all lands which these and all other land grant railroads had received, or were to receive, from the Federal government was estimated by the Interior Department's Auditor as of November 1, 1880, at $391,804,610.[38] By way of comparison, the total investment in railroads in the United States in that year was $4,653,609,000.[39]

THE NATURE OF THE LAND GRANT TRANSACTION

The questions dealt with so far—that is, the amount of land granted and its relationship to the whole, the extent of the railroads thus aided and their relationship to the whole, and the value of the aid so extended—are, after all, matters of detail. While these details are more important than the treatment accorded them in so many of the works examined would indicate, they are not of the essence of the land grant transaction. The main question is, what was the nature of that transaction? Were the Federal land grants gifts? Or were they trades by which the government got, as well as gave, direct consideration?

No reference is made here to the immense indirect benefits arising from the early building of the railroads so aided, but only to the direct monetary return which the government of the United States received for the lands which it granted.[40]

Almost without exception, the works examined treat the transactions as "gifts," or "donations," or, as some put it, "free" or "outright" gifts, without in any way referring to the fact that the railroads which received these "gifts" or "donations" were required to haul mail and government freight and passengers at less than their regular charges.[41]

While the conditions of the several grants vary, in the overwhelming majority of cases the Acts of Congress making grants to railroads adopted the phraseology of the earlier canal and wagon road grants in requiring

---

Quantity and Value of Public Lands Granted by Congress to Aid in the Construction of the Pacific Railroad (*Washington, January 26, 1881*); Donaldson, 912–33 (*figures on 932*).

[38] Ibid., 753.

[39] *Interstate Commerce Commission, Bureau of Statistics*, Railway Statistics Before 1890, *Statement No. 32151* (*Washington, December 1932*), 4.

[40] *These indirect returns to the government are suggestively outlined in U.S. General Land Office*, Transportation: Information Concerning Land Grants for Roads, Canals, River Improvement and Railroads, *Information Bulletin, 1939 Series, No. 5* (*Washington, 1940*), 1–2. *While no figures are available, and the point is developed in none of the reports and studies examined, it is obvious that transfer of lands from Federal to private ownership had a substantial effect upon the taxable resources of the states, territories, and local governments. Only in recent years, with the increasing tendency in the other direction, with property passing from private to government ownership, has the importance of this fact begun to be appreciated.*

[41] *This is true of twenty-six of the texts examined. Only two, Stephenson,* American History to 1865, *407, and Robert I. Adriance,* Using the Wealth of the World (*Boston, 1943*), *268, make reference to deductions from railroad rates because of land grants.*

that the railroad to be built should "be and remain a public highway for the use of the government of the United States, free from toll or other charge upon the transportation of any property or troops of the United States." The effect of this clause, as finally determined by the Supreme Court, was that the government was entitled to the use of the roadbed without toll, by analogy to the free right of passage for its vehicles or boats over grant-aided wagon roads and canals, but that this did not extend so far as to require the railroad company to provide and operate without charge the engines, cars, and other equipment needed for transportation over the railroads.[42]

Under a formula subsequently worked out by the United States Court of Claims, the deduction from ordinary charges on account of this provision of the land grant acts was established at 50 per cent.[43] Still later, by a series of Acts of Congress, the same percentage of deduction from commercial rates was made applicable to the limited number of land grant roads whose grants did not contain the "toll-free" provision in this form,[44] while even railroads which received no land grant whatever from the government have long since entered into "equalization agreements" by which they also undertake to handle government traffic at the same rates applying by law on the land grant lines.[45] Compensation for handling mail on land grant lines was fixed by Act of Congress in 1876 at 80 per cent of the rates applying on other railroads.[46]

In the Transportation Act of 1940, the Congress eliminated these provisions in so far as they applied to mail pay and to rates on the government's civilian passenger and freight traffic. Deductions of 50 per cent were continued, however, on the charges for transportation of military and naval personnel and property moving for military and naval and not for civil uses.[47]

The resulting situation is thus described by a Committee of the House of Representatives in the most recent statement on the subject:

Certain of our railroads, because of lands granted by the Government many years ago to aid in the construction of lines of road now owned by them, are under statutory obligation to transport certain specified classes of Government traffic over such land-grant lines at 50 per cent of their established tariff charges for such transportation. While that statutory require-

[42] *Lake Superior and Mississippi Railroad* vs. *United States*, 93 U.S. Reports, 442, *October term, 1876. Decided January 15, 1877.*
[43] *Atchison, Topeka & Santa Fe Railway* vs. *United States*, 15 Court of Claims, *126, December term, 1879.*
[44] *The first of these Acts of Congress was adopted July 16, 1892.* 27 Statutes at Large, *174, 180.*
[45] *Since 1914 this agreement has been between the government and the railroads collectively.*
[46] *19* Statutes at Large, *78–82.*
[47] *Transportation Act of 1940, Part II, Section 321 (a),* 54 Statutes at Large, *Vol. I, 954.*

ment applies to only 14,411 miles of railroad, the reduced charges for which it provides have been extended to many times that mileage as the result of so-called equalization agreements entered into with the Government by other railroads to enable them to handle Government traffic.[48]

Thus it is that although less than 10 per cent of railroad mileage received grants of land, either Federal or state, the whole railroad system of the nation has paid for them a direct monetary return far exceeding the value of the lands granted.

"It is probable," said the Congressional Committee report already referred to, "that the railroads have contributed over $900,000,000 in payment of the lands which were transferred to them under the Land Grant Acts. This is double the amount received for the lands sold by the railroads plus the estimated value of such lands still under railroad ownership. Former Commissioner Eastman estimated that the total value of the lands at the time they were granted . . . was not more than $126,000,000."[49]

The total of deductions was not so large when the texts examined were written, of course, but even the fact that deductions are made is completely ignored in all but two of the books examined.

THE MAJOR FACT

The net result of the treatment of the land grant transaction as a whole is to present to the student a picture of a wastrel Uncle Sam scattering his substance with reckless extravagance, instead of the much more nearly correct picture of a canny landowner using part of his holdings to increase immeasurably the value of the rest, not as a gift but on terms which constituted a bargain shrewder than he realized. As far back as 1859, indeed, Charles Russell Lowell wrote that with the continued movement of troops and military supplies into the West "it may be found that even with the most liberal construction of the grant, the government has not been so 'munificent' as sharp." The same observer noted, about the same time, "that he who buildeth a railroad west of the Mississippi must also find a population and build up business."[50]

The "best and highest interests of the people of the United States in regard to this domain," said William H. Seward in the Senate debate on the passage of the first land grant bill, "is not to derive from it the highest amount of current revenue" from the sales of lands, "[b]ut it is to bring them into cultivation and settlement in the shortest space of time and under the most favorable auspices."[51]

[48] *Committee on Interstate and Foreign Commerce,* House of Representatives, Report No. 393, 79 Cong., 1 Sess., March 26, 1945, pp. 1–2.
[49] *The several authorities for the details of this statement as to the amount of the direct return to the government from the land grant acts are given in detail in* ibid., 4.
[50] *Overton,* 156, 159.
[51] Cong. Globe, 31 Cong., 1 Sess., April 29, 1850, p. 851.

To that end, the land grant device was adopted. Its adoption was sought not only by the people of the West and the newer parts of the South, but also by the people of the manufacturing East.[52] In its administration there were errors and abuses, both on the part of government authorities and on the part of railroads, as revealed, for example, in connection with the movement for forfeiture of land grants which reached its height in the 1880's. But the essential thing is that through the use of land grants, the result sought was accomplished. It may not have been the wisest way to achieve these results, though no one even yet has suggested a better way by which a nation long on land and short on cash and credit could have enlisted the driving forces, which, in the short space of less than a generation, laced the West with rails. It may not have been the wisest way, but it worked. The job was done.

While the existing monographs on the actual working out of specific grants confirm this fact,[53] few of the texts examined take note of it. Two books note the need of some such device for getting railroads built ahead of settlement.[54] Four refer to the value added to the lands retained by the government.[55] Another, although treating the grants as the bestowal of "great gifts of land," recognized that "the transcontinental railroads opened the way for settlers."[56] Two others, while questioning the wisdom of the "gifts" to the railroads, nevertheless recognized the part which the grants played in the earlier development of the country.[57] Although joining in the almost universal description of the land grants as gifts, one book declared that the railroads "earned" what they got, and that it was a "wise use of the public domain."[58]

But for the most part, this essential element in the transaction—its very heart, indeed—is ignored or glossed over in the history texts which form the foundation of the American citizen's idea of the history of his own nation and the forces which have shaped and builded it. From most of these texts, no one could learn that here was a transaction by which lands constituting less than one-tenth of the nation's public domain were granted to railroads constituting less than 8 per cent of the United States mileage, not as gifts but under terms and conditions by which the government received a direct monetary return far greater than the value of the lands granted.

This direct monetary return, however, is by far the smallest part of

[52] *This may be substantiated by sectional analysis of the vote in Congress on the land grant acts. See, for example, the 1856 vote on four grants in Iowa. Overton, 73–86.*

[53] *See works cited in footnote 31, above.*

[54] *Coleman and Wesley, 401; Dumond, 535.*

[55] *Kirkland, 378, 380; Stephenson,* American History to 1865, *407; Fish and Wilson, 355; Richard J. Purcell,* The American Nation *(Boston, 1937), 529.*

[56] *Roy F. and Jeanette P. Nichols,* A Short History of American Democracy *(New York, 1943), 270, 272.*

[57] *Eugene C. Barker, William E. Dodd, and Henry Steele Commager,* Our Nation's Development *(Evanston, Ill., 1937), 387; Kirkland, 381.*

[58] *Purcell, 532.*

the gain to the government and the people of the United States from the working out of the land grant transaction. When the policy was first adopted, nearly two and one-half centuries after the beginnings of permanent settlement on the Atlantic seaboard, the frontier of the United States was but a little way beyond the Mississippi River—still not half way across the continent. And then, within less than a generation, the frontier almost literally leaped across the Great Plains, the mountains, and the vast areas which the old maps showed as the "Great American Desert." Such a difference in the rate of settlement was not due to any one thing, of course, but obviously the most effective cause was the fact of the transportation service of the railroads.

The land grants did not build these railroads, but they furnished a basis of credit which made it possible for them to be built. So doing, they did what never had been done before—provided transportation ahead of settlement. The result is almost beyond measurement. It was to be found in a startling reduction in the cost of transportation, as is abundantly shown in the reports of the Quartermaster General of the Army during that period.[59] And a result "beyond any estimate the Quar-

---

[59] *From letter from Quartermaster-General M. C. Meigs to Secretary of War William W. Belknap, January 28, 1873, in H.R. Ex. Doc. No. 169, 42 Cong., 3 Sess., Vol. 9, relating to savings to the War Department in transportation costs from July 1, 1866, to January 28, 1873, as a result of the building of the Union Pacific Railroad:*

The average rates per mile for troops are, on through business, 5²⁄₁₀ cents; on local business, 8 cents, being an average of 6⅗ cents per man per mile. The average rates per mile for troops by the Overland Stage Company were, on through business, 12½ cents; on local business, 15 cents, being an average of 13¾ cents per mile per man.

Assuming that all of these troops would have traveled by stage, in the absence of the railroad (which is by no means probable), the total estimated cost by stage is shown by the following, based on the averaged rates above stated:

Average rate per man per mile: rail	*6⅗ cents*
Average rate per man per mile: stage	*13¾ cents*
Actual cost for troops at railroad rates	*$1,446,262.25*
Estimated cost at stage rates	*$3,013,046.35*

The average rates per 100 pounds per 100 miles charged for freight by the railroad during the period required are, on through business, 19 cents; on local business, 62 cents, being an average of 40½ cents per 100 pounds per 100 miles by railroad. . . .

The estimated cost of the transportation of the freight moved by the Union Pacific Railroad, including express charges as shown above, . . . would be as follows:

Rates per 100 pounds per 100 miles: railroad rates	*40½ cents*
Rates per 100 pounds per 100 miles: wagon rates	*$1.46*
Actual cost of freight at railroad rates	*$1,896,589.57*
Estimated cost at wagon rates	*$6,837,088.32*

Showing a total estimated cost for moving the troops and

termaster General can make," as W. T. Sherman, then General-in-Chief of the Armies reported, was to be found in the "opening up to settlement of regions now wild, which would give homes and employment to . . . industrious people."[60] It was to be found in the value added to land and its products. It was to be found in the transformation of nontaxable resources into property which furnishes the principal tax-base for the support of the state and local governments of half a continent.

More important even than these was the contribution of the land grant railroads to military security and national unity. Indeed, as General Sherman once wrote, at the time of its building the Pacific Railway was "looked upon as a military necessity and as the only thing positively essential to the binding together of the republic."[61]

Almost without exception, however, the history textbooks have failed to develop this major and essential fact that, whatever may have been its shortcomings, the land grant policy touched off national and individual energies which in a few short years accomplished the greatest engineering, construction, and colonization project ever undertaken up to that time, a project which transformed the West from a wilderness to a civilized community and welded the nation into one.

supplies by stage and wagon of	$9,850,134.67
Total actual cost by railroad	$3,342,851.82
Estimated difference . . .	
equivalent to about 66 per cent	$6,507,282.85

[60] Reports from General W. T. Sherman and the Quartermaster-General transmitted May 12, 1880, by Secretary of War Alexander Ramsey to Hon. R. M. McLane, Chairman, House of Representatives Committee on the Pacific Railroads. Original letters are on file in the Clerk's Office, House of Representatives. General Sherman's letter is reprinted in Railway World, May 22, 1880, pp. 492–3, as follows:

I have the honor to acknowledge the receipt, by reference, from you of the resolution of the House committee on Pacific railroads, calling for information as to the probable saving in money to the military authorities by the completion of the Northern Pacific Railroad from Bismarck westward, and its general effect on the military and Indian services in that quarter. . . . In a military sense, the immediate extension of this railroad from Bismarck to the Yellowstone, and up the valley of that river as high as the mouth of the Big Horn, will be beyond any estimate the Quartermaster-General can make, because this railroad will transport men and supplies for ten if not twelve months of the year, while the Missouri river and the Yellowstone are barely navigable by light draft boats for two or at most three months. . . . It is equally important to the military and civil interests of the whole country that Montana should fill up with hardy farmers, and this will be an immediate result of the extension westward of this northern railroad. . . . . I am unable to make even an approximate estimate of the saving in cost of transportation of men and military stores by the completion of this railroad, but this bears a small proportion to the great result of opening up to settlement regions now wild, which would give homes and employment to two or three millions of industrious people.

[61] Letter from General W. T. Sherman, dated January 16, 1867, to Major-General Grenville M. Dodge, in How We Built the Union Pacific Railway, Senate Doc. No. 447, 61 Cong., 2 Sess., 14.

APPENDIX

Federal land grants to railroads[1]

State	Total acreage[2]	Apparent area shown on Map No. 1		Actual area shown on Map No. 2	
		Acres	Per cent of state area	Acres[3]	Per cent of state area
Alabama	33,029,760	14,863,392	45	2,747,479	8.3
Arizona	72,901,760	34,263,827	47	7,695,203	10.6
Arkansas	33,985,280	12,574,554	37	2,586,970	7.6
California	101,563,520	40,625,408	40	11,585,393	11.4
Colorado	66,718,080	6,671,808	10	3,757,673	5.6
Florida	37,478,400	10,868,736	29	2,218,705	5.9
Idaho	53,476,480	8,021,472	15	1,320,591	2.5
Illinois	36,096,000	12,633,600	35	2,595,133	7.2
Indiana	23,226,240	2,322,624[4]	10	. . .	. . .
Iowa	36,019,200	32,417,280	90	4,711,328	13.1
Kansas	52,656,640	32,647,117	62	8,234,013	15.6
Louisiana	31,054,720	20,496,115	66	1,375,000	4.4
Michigan	37,258,240	27,943,680	75	3,134,058	8.4
Minnesota	53,803,520	37,662,464	70	9,953,008	18.5
Mississippi	30,538,240	6,718,413	22	1,075,345	3.5
Missouri	44,591,360	12,485,581	28	2,328,674	5.2
Montana	94,168,320	44,259,110	47	14,736,919	15.6
Nebraska	49,431,680	13,840,870	28	7,272,623	14.7
Nevada	70,745,600	8,489,472	12	5,086,283	7.2
New Mexico	77,866,240	26,474,522	34	3,355,179	4.3
North Dakota	45,225,600	22,612,800	50	10,697,490	23.7
Oregon	62,067,840	24,827,136	40	3,655,390	5.9
South Dakota	49,310,080	2,465,504[5]	5	. . .	. . .
Utah	54,346,240	4,347,699	8	2,230,085	4.1
Washington	43,642,880	29,240,730	67	9,582,878	22.0
Wisconson	35,938,560	24,438,221	68	3,666,062	10.2
Wyoming	62,664,960	13,786,291	22	5,749,051	9.2
Total	1,389,805,440	527,998,426	38	131,350,534	9.5

[1] As reported in U.S. General Land Office Information Bulletin, 1939 Series, No. 5, *Transportation. . . .*
[2] Table 1, *Report of Commissioner of General Land Office . . . June 30, 1943.*
[3] *Ibid.*, Tables 76 and 77.
[4] No Federal lands in Indiana were granted to railroads.
[5] 443,312 acres of the Winona & St. Peter R.R. extending into Dakota Territory (now part of South Dakota) are included with Minnesota by the General Land Office. No other railroad company received a land grant in South Dakota.

PERIODIC STOCK DIVIDENDS*

Periodic stock dividends have had a checkered history. Prior to 1929 their use was widespread, especially among public utility holding companies. Then financial abuses in the 1920's and the depressed conditions of the 1930's caused their disappearance. Now they are back again, stronger than ever. What are the reasons for this change? What are the underlying factors which seem to make this financial device useful to more and more corporations?

The revival of stock dividends is particularly remarkable considering the strong prejudice against them on the part of many executives, investors, and financial observers. Obviously there is also a growing group of executives who are enthusiastic about stock dividends because their companies have successfully used this device to solve many different financial problems arising from postwar economic conditions. Apparently, as stock dividends are better understood, we may expect to see an increasing number of companies utilizing them.

Unfortunately, few guideposts other than legal and accounting decisions are available. Nevertheless, from the experience of some companies which have used stock dividends much can be learned about such things as stockholder reaction and the effect of stock dividends on the market price of the stock. The evidence indicates, for example, that the type of reaction and the degree of severity will differ greatly depending upon current market conditions and the company's earning record.

Recently a company engaged the author to examine stock dividends in connection with its program of raising substantial equity funds for expansion, one of the major purposes for which these dividends have important implications. The study covered more than 50 textbooks, magazine articles, newspaper articles, and doctoral theses. Partially because the authorities in question failed to distinguish between extraordinary and periodic stock dividends, they differed widely in their final judgments. Even in specific cases like that of the North American Company (to be described later) they used the evidence to support opposite conclusions.

This divergence of opinion led the author to an independent study of the effect which periodic stock dividends had on the market prices of seven stocks listed on the New York Stock Exchange. Finding that some interesting conclusions could be drawn, the author then went on to interview officers of companies which at one time or another had made use of stock dividends. Their response, which was almost uniformly

* By Joseph C. Bothwell, Jr. Reprinted from Harvard Business Review, January, 1950, pp. 89–100. Used by permission.

enthusiastic, indicated the variety of problems which the use of stock dividends had solved.

GENERAL CONSIDERATIONS

Definite guidance from these case studies is, however, several steps away; it depends, for one thing, on an awareness of accumulated practice and thinking. For instance, with what purpose in mind have corporations used the stock dividend in the past? What have they thought to accomplish by means of it? To what extent have they used it? What groups have been affected and what responsibilities, therefore, are implicit in the act of paying such a dividend?

Definition

Stock dividends seem always to have been a controversial subject, one reason being an indiscriminate use of the term. There is a great difference between "extraordinary" stock dividends and "periodic" stock dividends. The former, often termed melon-cutting, generally represent a substantial percentage of the outstanding capitalization, are infrequently

Exhibit I. *Number of times various types of stock dividends or splits were used by companies listed on New York Stock Exchange—1945–1949*

	Periodic*	Extraordinary†	Common stock on preferred or preferred on common stock‡	Common stock split	Recapitalization	Divestment	Total
1945	18	18	1	19	5	5	66
1946	23	36	6	42	0	5	112
1947	27	31	1	20	3	8	90
1949 (1st half)	11	10	0	9	1	3	34
Total	79	95	8	90	9	21	302

* Dividends of less than 25% paid in addition to, or in place of, cash dividends, where the earnings which were capitalized were accumulated over a period of one year. Corresponding figures for 1940 to 1944 were: 1940, 6; 1941, 7; 1942, 2; 1943, 7; 1944, 12; total for the five years, 34.

† Dividends of less than 25% paid in addition to, or in place of cash dividends, where the earnings which were capitalized were accumulated over a period of more than one year.

‡ Stock of one class paid out as a dividend on stock of another class.

NOTE: Table gives no indication of the number of companies involved. Several companies paid only one stock dividend, while other companies had recapitalizations, paid stock dividends, and split their stock, each adding to the totals shown above.

SOURCE: *Barron's, Moody's, Wall Street Journal.*

declared, and are created from surplus accumulated over a period of years. In purpose and effect they are virtually identical with stock splits. Periodic stock dividends, on the other hand, are used in place of, or in addition to, the normal cash dividend; and they are far less well understood.

Extent of Use

During the 1920's, as noted, extensive use was made of this financial device. Two unpublished studies made in that period under the supervision of Professor Arthur Stone Dewing at the Harvard Business School, for example, revealed that 10% of the public utility holding companies used them regularly; another 10% occasionally.[1] A close correlation has been found to exist between the level of business activity and the number of stock dividends and splits,[2] and Exhibit I shows that, following the drop in the 1930's, the number is again rising. Taking only those companies listed on the New York Stock Exchange, 34 stock dividends of less than 25% were paid by 17 companies from 1940 through 1944; from 1945 through June 1948 the number of companies rose to 40 and the number of payments to 79. Of the 40 companies using this method of distributing profits, 10 paid them in place of cash dividends, the remainder using them to supplement regular dividends.

Purposes of Stock Dividends

Postwar economic conditions have made the use of stock dividends very attractive to many companies. High earnings figures, often misleading, have brought an insistent clamor from stockholders for more and more dividends. At the same time, reconversion costs, expansion, inflationary price levels, all have contributed to a situation where companies have high profits but low working capital. Although each of the companies which was studied faced a somewhat different problem, the need to retain earnings while placating stockholders was common to all.

It is no wonder, therefore, that stock dividends are once more coming into vogue. At a time when funds are most needed within the company, the stock type of dividend has provided a satisfactory solution for many companies. This is only one of the advantages and motives which have been discussed over the last quarter century. Frank Dame, President of the North American Company, which paid stock dividends from 1922 to 1934, has been an eloquent spokesman for their use as a means of obtaining low-cost capital (viz., using earnings for capital).[3] Others have emphasized that this financial device conserves cash for general

[1] See Arthur Stone Dewing, The Financial Policy of Corporations (New York, The Ronald Press Company, 4th Edition, 1941), Vol. II, p. 827, footnote 76.
[2] James C. Dolley, "Characteristics and Procedure of Common Stock Split-Ups," Harvard Business Review, Vol. XI, No. 3 (April 1933), p. 316.
[3] Frank L. Dame, Dividends Put to Work (New York, North American Company, 2nd Edition, 1929), a compilation of newspaper references to North American's stock dividend policy.

purposes, avoids underwriting fees, and may provide equity capital at times when, because of low stock prices or a situation making bond financing unwise, other means of fund raising are undesirable.

Stock dividends have been used, further, to conceal from investors a weak working capital position or unprofitable operations; and they may hide exorbitant profits from consumers and unions, since the larger sum can be distributed at the same dividend rate when the shares outstanding are increased. The procedure serves also to increase marketability by reducing the price per share and enables large stockholders to avoid taxation.

Stockholder Reaction

One of the first questions facing the board of directors contemplating a change in dividend policy is what the reaction of stockholders will be. Opinions seem equally divided between those who feel that stockholders will be satisfied with stock dividends and those who do not.

That income tax considerations make stock dividends welcome to large investors, however, seems less open to controversy. This is particularly true during the present period of high earnings and higher taxes, even though large stockholders are usually aware that stock dividends give them nothing more than they already own. Small investors, on the other hand, are frequently dependent upon the income from their investments and are likely to protest stock payment or to sell out. But even these may look with greater favor on a stock paying stock dividends than on one paying none at all, in the belief that the total value of their holdings has been augmented, or that their dividend has a readily realizable cash value. There are many small investors, consequently, who will hold equities paying stock dividends, though they would not hold the stock if no dividend at all were declared.

No generalizations apply equally to all stockholders of all companies, and the opinions of authorities on this subject are of little value. Companies obtain better information for their purposes by analyzing the stockholder list to determine the distribution of the stock. It has not been found difficult to learn the opinions of the larger holders.

Management should also take into account the buying motives of the various stockholder groups and what considerations influence their decisions. However wrong such concepts as "income stocks," "growth stocks," and the like may be, when a company's stock has been popularly placed in such a category, the directors have had to take that fact into consideration. Each company must resolve the question whether the wishes of the majority of stockholders or the stockholders owning the majority of stock should prevail.

Effect on Market Price

There are some executives who feel that sinister motives may be imputed to them if they consider dividend policy in the light of its probable effect upon market price; and, of course, stock dividends are no different from other financing methods in that they may influence market price. Yet, at the same time, the market price *is* of vital concern to stockholders, and management *does* have a responsibility to stockholders. Accordingly it seems only reasonable to consider their interests in this connection as one of the criteria in deciding whether to use stock dividends.

If, for example, stockholders do not approve of stock dividends and therefore dispose of their holdings, then the price will be lowered and those stockholders who would otherwise favor the stock dividend policy will also be displeased. Furthermore, the fact is important that periodic stock dividends are often employed in situations where the company needs more funds. If the policy is ill-conceived, it may have to be abandoned in favor of the sale of additional securities, by which time. the market price of the stock may have dropped to disastrous levels.

Opinions differ widely as to what effect, if any, the declaration of a stock dividend has upon the market price of a company's stock. Fifteen authorities on the question have split four ways, four thinking the declaration will have no effect; six, that it will cause the price to rise; four, that it will cause the price to fall; and one seeing it as a short-run stimulant but of little long-run importance.

In the most comprehensive study available, made in 1930, Professor Shaw Livermore concluded that the payment of a stock dividend makes no difference in market price. He examined the experience of 38 companies paying stock dividends of 10% or more in 1928 and 1929. In 19 cases the price rose after payment in comparison with the checking group of comparable stocks; in 17 it fell; and in 2 it stayed exactly in line.[4] Two years later, Seymour Siegel, author of a study in the *Harvard Business Review,* comparing the North American Company with the American Telephone and Telegraph Company,[5] similarly concluded that payment of stock dividends is not a price factor during major price movements. Other writers have felt that these dividends produce speculative price rises; and still others, that the increase in share numbers leads to price drops.

It should be kept in mind that despite certain common characteristics, periodic stock dividends, on the one hand, and common stock split-ups, extraordinary stock dividends, and the issuance of new common stock, on the other, do differ radically. Recent as well as older studies indicate that the latter cause the market price of the company's shares to decline, yet not in proportion to the increase in shares; thus the shareholder who maintains his proportionate equity will have the value of his holdings enhanced. It follows that the closer a periodic stock dividend approximates one of these less regular operations, or is so viewed by the investing public, the more likely the market price will be to follow the same pattern of a reduction in price per share but an increase in total value of the stock owned. This distinction, however, still leaves unanswered

[4] *Shaw Livermore, "Value of Stock Dividends,"* American Economic Review, *Vol. XX, No. 4 (December 1930), p. 688.*
[5] *Seymour Siegel, "Stock Dividends,"* Harvard Business Review, *Vol. XI, No. 1 (October 1932), p. 76.*

the question of the effect of the typical periodic stock dividend, particularly in recent years.

Responsibilities of the Company

The company which embarks on a stock dividend policy must be prepared to defend its decision and fulfill its responsibilities, especially since stock dividends have been used in the past to manipulate the market and obtain profits for insiders. Yet time has mellowed the attitude of many critics. In 1931 the *Magazine of Wall Street* took a hostile view toward stock dividends; less than ten years later it carried an article praising the Standard Oil Company of New Jersey for its decision to retain profits for expansion and issue stock dividends.

Nearly all critics agree that stock dividends should not be declared when a dilution in earning power or book value will result; the equities behind the capital must be increased more rapidly than the increase in capitalization. A responsible company should make sure that the stock dividend has been earned during the period, that the return from the reinvested earnings is as great as that obtainable elsewhere, that the funds are being used in the stockholders' interests. Above all, it must avoid any action which could be interpreted, or plausibly misinterpreted, as an attempt at manipulation.

Tax and Accounting Decisions

Great impetus to the use of stock dividends was given in 1920 by the *Eisner* v. *Macomber* decision.[6] In that case the Supreme Court ruled that when common stock was declared as a dividend on common stock, no income was received by the owner for tax purposes. The basis for the decision was that the recipient of a stock dividend receives nothing more than he already owns; there has been a bookkeeping transaction by which a position of surplus is transferred to the capital account, but proportionate ownership remains unchanged.

The rate of capitalization is strictly determined in accordance with New York Stock Exchange requirements that there be a relationship between the amount of earnings and the fair market value of the number of shares issued. The American Institute of Accountants stresses the importance of maintaining paid-in capital value, while relating the capitalization rate to the market price. These rulings prevent the type of manipulation which caused speculation in many stocks in the 1920's.

Evaluation

What conclusions can be drawn from this survey of opinion? Except for rulings on capitalization rates and income taxes, no over-all judgments can be substantiated. Some authorities believe that stockholders prefer stock dividends; others believe that they object. Many take a critical attitude toward the company and stress its many responsibilities;

[6] *252 U.S. 189 (1920).*

others believe that the company should be permitted the widest latitude. On the question of stock market reaction, the greatest difference of opinion exists. The available studies were made 20 years ago, were concerned with large stock dividends and stock splits more than with periodic stock dividends, and the results were highly inconclusive. Obviously, these sources provide little guidance for handling the present problem.

CASE STUDIES

In order to make head or tail of this legacy of unusually conflicting, often confused opinion, it seemed desirable to make independent case studies of current practice. The objective here was to determine why companies used periodic stock dividends, what the reaction had been among their stockholders and on the market, what problems had been encountered, and how the companies viewed the results.

Method of Study

The first step was to ascertain whether the stock dividend had affected the market price, and if so, how. Seven companies listed on the New York Stock Exchange had paid periodic stock dividends without cash during an 18-month period beginning in December 1946. These companies were selected because price information was readily available and there were no cash dividends to complicate the analysis.

The stock prices were observed for a period from about 90 days before the dividend to about 90 days afterward. They were then plotted on logarithmic graphs (as shown), along with Barron's Sixty-Five Composite Stock Group, the Thirty Industrial Stock Group, and the average price for a group of selected stocks in the same industry. A comparison was then made with the checking groups to determine whether the fluctuations in the price of the stock corresponded to the general market fluctuations and whether there was an influence exerted by the stock dividend.

For each company information on the type of business, size, earnings, and dividend record was obtained and taken into consideration in evaluating the price movements. A summary of this information is shown in Exhibit II.

Detailed statistical analysis shows that the prices of the stocks, although influenced by the earnings and cash dividend record, tended to follow the market trends. But, as may be seen on the accompanying graphs (Exhibits III and IV), there are strong indications that the stock dividend upset or modified that relationship.

Prior to Dividend Declaration

One of the most striking results of the study is the clear-cut evidence that the meeting of the board of directors is the signal for the stock price to rise, apparently in anticipation of the declaration of a dividend. The action of the stockholders will exert a stronger influence on the stock price than does the prevailing market trend, the degree of effect depending upon whether appraisal of the other stocks is similar or contrary to that of the dividend stock on the basis of past earnings and future prospects.

The seven companies declared nine periodic stock dividends, and in six cases the prices of the stocks rose during the week before the meeting of the board of directors. In four instances the price rise came when the prices of the checking group either remained the same or dropped. In these instances, Bush and Webster had rising earnings trends. Eversharp had suffered a loss during the last half of the year, and Publicker's earnings had fallen off considerably in 1947. Optimism was sufficiently high, however, to cause the prices of the stocks of these companies to rise when other similar stocks were declining.

Only in two cases, Columbia and Publicker (March 1947), did the price rise coincide with a general upward price movement. In both companies the earnings had shown a decline, but stockholder optimism appears to have been high, stimulated by favorable market conditions and the prospect of a dividend. During the week before the Thermoid directors met, Thermoid's price remained steady, as did that for the entire automobile equipment group.

There were only two cases in which the price fell just before the meeting of the boards. Publicker's earnings had been declining, and just prior to the declaration of its September 1947 dividend the price fell. Stock prices in the checking group dropped at the same time, but Publicker's decline was much greater, possibly accelerated by intimations that no favorable cash dividend action would be taken. Although Gair's earnings were rising, prospects of a dividend were not good enough to offset the general decline in stocks of that type.

Effect of Dividend Declaration

After the declaration of the stock dividend, a reaction generally occurs, with those who are displeased selling their holdings. In a falling market this action tends to accelerate the decline in the company's stock price; in a rising market, it appears to act as a brake upon the rise in price.

In six out of nine cases the price of the stock fell, in two it rose, and in one it remained the same. Five of the six cases coincided with a price decline of stocks of that type, but in all five cases the drop in the price of the company's stock was proportionately greater than for that of the group. Thermoid's price, which had remained steady prior to the declaration of the dividend, declined slightly, while the price of the checking group rose.

The price rise of both Columbia and Gair after declaration of the stock dividend was concurrent with a rise in the prices of all similar stocks, but the prices of the stocks of the two companies rose less than that of their respective groups. Webster's price, after the dividend declaration, remained at the same level it had attained just prior to the meet-

Exhibit II. Pertinent information on seven companies issuing stock dividends during 18–month period, December 1946 to April 1948

Name of company	Type of business	Stock outstanding	Capitalization
Bush Terminal Company	Operation of warehouses, piers, railroad facilities, etc.	Common: 544,370 shares	$ 19,000,000
Columbia Pictures Corporation	Production of motion pictures	Preferred: 71,765 shares 1,112 owners Common: 637,352 shares 2,535 owners	40,000,000
Eversharp, Inc.	Manufacture of pens, pencils, razors and blades	Preferred: 69,528 shares 870 owners Common: 941,689 shares 3,433 owners	18,000,000
Robert Gair, Inc.	Manufacture of paper and containers	Preferred: 298,873 shares 2,392 owners Common: 17,798,888 shares 7,906 owners	37,000,000
Publicker Industries, Inc. (3 separate occurrences)	Manufacture of industrial chemicals, alcoholic beverages	Preferred: 91,982 shares 1,919 owners Common: 2,150,594 shares 3,270 owners	136,000,000
Thermoid Company	Manufacture of auto, air, and oil products	Preferred: 53,984 shares 975 owners Common: 716,588 shares 5,600 owners	17,000,000
Webster Tobacco Company	Manufacture of cigar and pipe tobacco	Common: 450,079 shares 1,900 owners	13,000,000

SOURCE: *Moody's.*

ing of the board. During the same period the prices of the stocks in the checking group had also been relatively stable.

Movement after Ex-dividend

In all nine cases the price of the stock dropped off sharply after the stock went ex-dividend (i.e., when it was quoted at the closing price of the previous day less the amount of the dividend), continuing to de-

1946 Net income	1947 Net income	Past dividends	Stock dividend	Date of payment	Other information
$ 384,483	$ 652,768	1943–1947 Cash	5%	March 15, 1948	
3,450,490	3,707,000	1942–1947 Cash and stock	2½%	May 14, 1948	Earnings in early 1948 started to show a downward trend
4,214,000	−3,417,000 (deficit)	1942–1947 Cash and stock	2½%	January 15, 1948	
4,026,000	5,831,000	1941–1945 Cash	6%	December 20, 1946	1945 net income: $714,691
22,672,000	4,733,064	None	2½%	March 31, 1947 September 30, 1947 March 31, 1948	
853,197	963,468	1941–1947 Cash	5%	April 5, 1948	Additional shares reduced the earnings per share despite higher net income in 1947
825,010	252,227	1924–1946 None	10%	January 21, 1947	1945 net income: $357,659

cline for a period of two to four weeks. In all cases the drop was much more than the dilution caused by the additional shares. Conclusive evidence that the cause of this decline was the stock dividend is the fact that in five cases the prices of the stocks in the checking group rose, while in the four cases where the prices of the checking group fell, the decline in each company's stock price was proportionately greater than that for its checking group.

The sharp decline may have been due in part to continued selling by a number of displeased investors who were frightened because their shares were quoted at a lower price after going ex-dividend. At the same time, many investors would probably have avoided a stock which was not paying a cash dividend and appeared to be in a slump. Many may have had an imperfect understanding of the causes of the decline. With normal selling activity and buyer's hesitancy, the price would drop until sufficient upward pressure was created by more sophisticated traders who realized that the stock had become undervalued. The cases indicated that when the stock goes ex-dividend, it is likely to go into a short slump.

Payment of the Stock Dividend

The payment of the stock dividend is its last direct influence on market price. In all nine cases share movement after payment corresponded very closely to the movement of the checking group. In six cases the company's stock price began to rise after the payment, along with a rise in the market, but the rise was greater than that of the checking group. The receipt of the dividend in many instances may have stimulated further interest in the stock. Certainly the payment of the dividend in these cases did not serve to act as a depressant on the upward movement of the stock.

In the three cases where the price fell, the price of the checking group also declined, but not so severely. Eversharp's payment was made about January 15, which was the beginning of a long drop in its stock price. This downward trend probably resulted more from the fact that the year's operations had shown a deficit than from the stock dividend. The latter, however, may have accelerated the decline. Publicker's stock dividend payment in March 1947 seems also to have accelerated the decline in that company's stock, which continued to drop for several months as people realized that the price had initially been bid up too high. The slight drop in the market could have played no important part in Publicker's price drop. Gair's price drop was also more severe than that of the checking group. In these cases the payment of the dividend did nothing to halt a longer declining trend in the prices of the stocks.

The Entire Period

The stock dividend seems to have enhanced the value of the shareholder's stock in three cases and depressed it in six. Generally speaking, when business conditions for the company and in the stock market appear favorable, the stock dividend will tend to drive the price up. Under unfavorable conditions it will cause the price to fall.

Bush had shown a favorable earnings picture and paid its stock dividend at a time when comparable stock prices were rising. For the checking group the rise was 3.6% and for Bush only 2.6%, but the stock paid as a dividend had caused a dilution of 4.6%, so that Bush's price was actually 7.2% higher at the end than at the beginning of the period. In Webster's case the company's earnings were rising, but the price dropped 30% during the period. At the same time, prices for the checking group dropped 25%. The differential of 5% was more than adequately covered by Webster's 10% stock dividend. Gair is an exception. Although it had rising earnings, and the prices of the checking group were also climbing, Gair's price fell, indicating that many stockholders, viewing the large profits and anticipating a big cash dividend, were disappointed by the decision to pay a stock dividend.

With earnings dropping off and a bearish market, the stock dividend may drive the price lower than would be expected. Eversharp had suffered a severe drop in earnings. During the period under study its price fell 25.8% while that of the checking group fell only 1.4%. Publicker's stock dividend of September 1947 occurred when the checking group dropped only 8%, but the company's stock price fell 28.5%.

Even with favorable market action, the stock dividend does not seem to exert enough influence to offset declining earnings. In fact, it may help to force the price lower. The earnings for Columbia, Publicker at the time of its March 1947 payment, and Thermoid were slipping when stock dividends were paid. Despite an upward price movement in the checking groups, the prices of these stocks declined. One exception occurred at the time of Publicker's stock dividend payment of March 1948, the third stock dividend payment for the company during the period under study. While earnings were still low, a 12% rise in the checking group was accompanied by a 22% rise in Publicker's price. By that time the investors appear to have been well adjusted to Publicker's stock dividend policy.

Summary of Case Studies

This study indicates that stock exchange prices rose prior to the meeting of the board of directors and fell after the declaration of the stock dividend. The downward pressure was most severe when the stock went ex-dividend.

Thereafter the price of the stock tended to follow the prices of similar stocks with variations due to past earnings records and future prospects. In a period of rising earnings and a bullish market, payment acted as a stimulant to market price. When earnings were favorable and the market was bearish, the stock dividend prevented the price from falling as low as would be expected. In both cases the value of the stockholder's shares was enhanced.

When the company's prospects were unfavorable and the market declining, the stock dividend depressed price further. Even when general market action was favorable, if the company's prospects were poor, the stock dividend caused the stock to decline more than would be expected.

These findings cannot be taken as absolute rules, and even in this small sample there were exceptions. In general, however, there should

Exhibit III. Market prices of stock of companies using stock dividends compared with other stocks

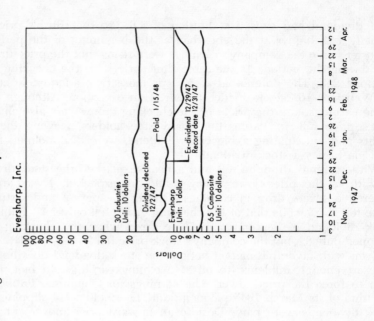

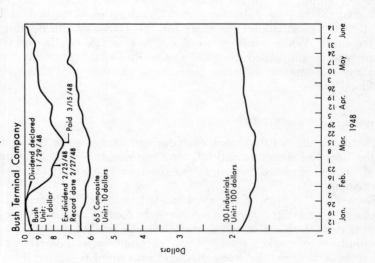

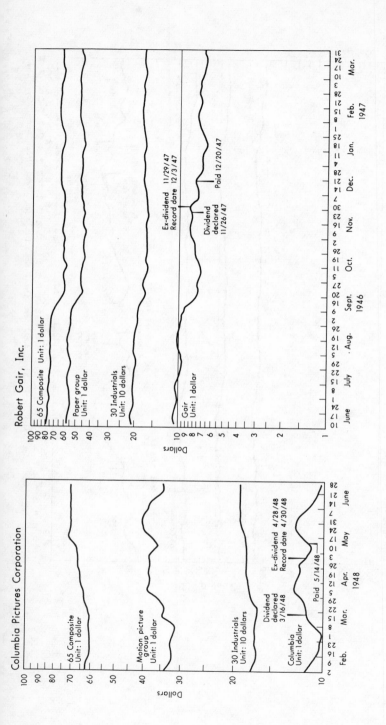

Columbia Pictures Corporation

65 Composite
Unit: 1 dollar

Motion picture group
Unit: 1 dollar

30 Industrials
Unit: 10 dollars

Columbia
Unit: 1 dollar

Dividend declared 3/16/48

Ex-dividend 4/28/48
Record date 4/30/48

Paid 5/14/48

Robert Gair, Inc.

65 Composite Unit: 1 dollar

Paper group
Unit: 1 dollar

30 Industrials
Unit: 10 dollars

Gair
Unit: 1 dollar

Ex-dividend 11/29/47
Record date 12/3/47

Dividend declared 11/26/47

Paid 12/20/47

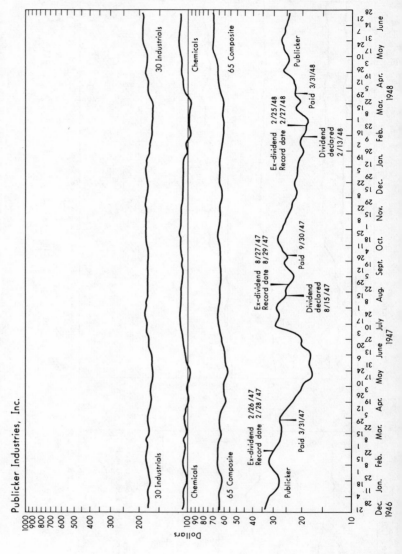

Exhibit IV. Market prices of stock of companies using stock dividends compared with other stocks

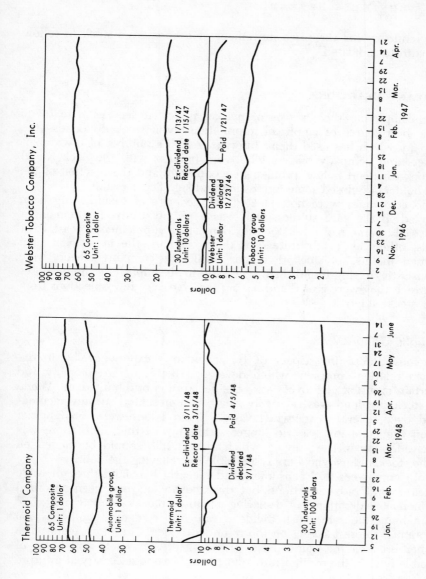

Thermoid Company

Dollars

100
90
80
70

60   65 Composite
      Unit: 1 dollar

50

40   Automobile group
      Unit: 1 dollar

30

20

      Thermoid
      Unit: 1 dollar   Ex-dividend 3/11/48
10   Record date 3/15/48
9   Paid 4/5/48
8
7   Dividend
6   declared
                                   3/1/48
5

4

3

      30 Industrials
2   Unit: 100 dollars

1

Jan.   Feb.   Mar.   Apr.   May   June
12 19 26 9 16 23 1 8 15 22 29 5 12 19 26 3 10 17 24 31 7 14
              1948

Webster Tobacco Company, Inc.

Dollars

100
90
80
70

60   65 Composite
      Unit: 1 dollar
50

40

30

20
      30 Industrials
      Unit: 10 dollars
10
9   Ex-dividend 1/13/47
8   Webster   Record date 1/15/47
7   Unit: 1 dollar   Paid 1/21/47
6   Dividend
      Tobacco group   declared
5   Unit: 10 dollars   12/23/46

4

3

2

1

Nov.   Dec.   Jan.   Feb.   Mar.   Apr.
 2 9 16 23 30 7 14 21 28 4 11 18 25 1 8 15 22 1 8 15 22 29 7 14 21
      1946   1947

281

be a tendency for the price movement of a company's stock to follow the patterns indicated.

COMPANY REACTIONS

After completing the analysis of market prices, it seemed wise to go to the best source of empirical information about stock dividends—the company which has used them. Interviews with a number of investment bankers and company officers who were familiar with the background of stock dividend policy, problems encountered, and the reaction of the stockholders disclosed some interesting and significant results.

The companies were not selected on the basis of their having been included in the case studies. One was a public utility, the remainder industrials. Some had used stock dividends as a supplement to cash dividends, others as a substitute. For the most part, the investment men opposed the use of stock dividends, while the company officers were enthusiastic, having found them successful in accomplishing the purposes for which they were issued and having received very few objections from their stockholders.

A Public Utility

The most interesting aspect of this company's experience lay in the human relations problem which developed between the company and a certain group of employees after the declaration of the dividend. While the stock dividend was relatively small, it represented surplus accumulated over several years when various bond issues were outstanding. When the company was no longer saddled with this debt, there was a considerable interest saving which, it was felt, should be passed on to the stockholders who were responsible for relieving the debt.

Both employees and consumers had recently benefited through wage increases and rate reductions, but the stockholders had been accorded no such consideration. By declaring a substantial stock dividend while maintaining the same cash dividend rate, the company could pass on the annual interest saving on the refunded bonds. The move would also further broaden the equity base, providing greater safety and being of possible help in the event a rate adjustment became necessary at a future time.

A satisfactory capitalization rate was determined in accordance with New York Stock Exchange requirements, and the dividend was declared. No objections were received from stockholders, but there was a sharp reaction from a certain group of lower echelon executives. The management realized that their protest had no rational basis and must have been a symptom of a more basic complaint. After a few months of investigation, it discovered what the problems of the employees were and reached a satisfactory solution. The company had an unusual purpose in declaring a stock dividend, and objections came from the most unexpected source.

Industrial Company I

More typical is the case of a company engaged in a large postwar expansion program. With earnings high and rising, the directors voted a stock dividend in place of the cash dividend. After the announcement more than 50% of the stockholders returned their proxies, with only a score protesting the dividend. The objections stemmed basically from a feeling of discrimination because they were receiving their dividend in stock while the officers, as a result of a profit-sharing plan, received a cash bonus. By selling his dividend stock, however, the stockholder received a greater cash return than had previously been obtained from the regular cash dividend. This, undoubtedly, served to soothe many feelings. The company was very well satisfied with the results of its action.

Industrial Company II

Originally started as a supplement to the cash dividend, the stock dividend became a substitute when earnings began to drop. With rising production costs and inadequate working capital, it was necessary to retain profits, as well as to procure additional funds through bank loans. Additional common stock would have been sold had the equity market been more favorable. Under the circumstances a stock dividend policy seemed to be the answer.

The reaction of the stockholders varied. Large stockholders seemed to favor the policy, but some registered objections. While the company's problems had not been entirely solved by the stock dividend, the move had permitted postponing sale of additional stock in a depressed market. The company officers consider it a good method for straddling, if not resolving, many current financial problems, particularly when used in conjunction with a small cash dividend.

Industrial Company III

Another medium-size corporation was also in a tight working capital position as a result of financing expansion and a higher volume of sales. The stock dividend replaced the cash dividend with only one or two objections from stockholders. Numerous inquiries, however, were received requesting further information on the handling of scrip, for which no market had been provided. By capitalizing at the current market price rather than at the average for the year, a 5% stock dividend brought the market value of the shares into a consistent relationship with the previous cash dividend. The company considered it a successful means of obtaining low-cost capital.

Industrial Company IV

This company's experience typifies the use of a stock dividend to pacify irate stockholders. According to company executives, it succeeded admirably.

High earnings during the war were plowed back to make up a deficit created during the depression. Stockholders, however, clamored for dividends. At each annual meeting a vocal minority would demand an explanation for the failure to receive them. While future prospects warranted considerable optimism, the management was inclined to adopt a conservative view. To quell the rising clamor, a stock dividend was declared, the first dividend in many years. The decision turned out to be a very successful one. There was no indication of dissatisfaction among any stockholders; many, in fact, wrote in to commend the board of directors for its action.

Family-owned Corporation

To ease estate settlement, some of the family holdings in this company were sold to the public. Unfortunately, the sale occurred shortly after the company had incurred heavy financial obligations due to expansion. Cash dividends were, therefore, a dim prospect, so a stock dividend policy was adopted. Although occasional letters of complaint have been received, the company is well pleased with this policy since it appears to satisfy the majority of stockholders while permitting the company to retain the full amount of its profits. The cash thus obtained has enabled the company to meet its other obligations with ease, and repayment of certain loans is being made at a faster rate than originally anticipated.

Wall Street Opinion

Certainly there can be no unanimity of opinion among financial men, but all the brokers and investment bankers interviewed strongly opposed the use of stock dividends. One investment banker explained his firm's attempts to discourage companies from declaring stock dividends on the ground that the stockholder is deluded into thinking he is receiving something more than what he already owns. Another firm expressed its relief when a company, rumored to be considering a stock dividend, announced that it was continuing its cash dividend and at a higher rate. This firm expressed the opinion that investors strongly prefer a payment in cash to one in stock.

Summary of Company Reaction

Officers of companies using stock dividends display enthusiasm for this method of obtaining funds. Even after discounting the natural inclination to support a company policy to an outsider, we must conclude that the policy appears to have been successful in the cases studied.

The general experience among these companies has been that the device is an excellent method for retaining funds while satisfying stockholder demands for dividends. On the other hand, investment people tend to look with disfavor on the use of stock dividends. One reason may be that they find it more difficult to interest the average investor in a stock which is not paying a cash dividend, particularly in a period of high earnings.

CONCLUSIONS

The increased use of periodic stock dividends in the postwar years is not surprising in view of inflationary price levels, unprecedented need for working capital, the depressed equity market, and persistent stock-holder demands for dividends. Under the circumstances it is rather surprising that many more companies have not turned to this device. Their reluctance may be explained, perhaps, as being due to a prejudice arising from past misuse and a lack of understanding of what stock dividends can do. The majority of writers who have considered the subject have harbored the same prejudices. Consequently, with the exception of legal and accounting decisions, little information is available to executives considering the policy as a part solution for financial difficulties.

Our study suggests the results to be expected from paying periodic stock dividends. Examining seven companies which after the war had paid dividends in stock of less than 10%, without cash, we found that the market price of the shares was in fact affected. In good times almost any action is likely to drive the stock price up, while in bad times it takes very little to drive it down. Stock dividends appear to cause such movements. With rising earnings and a bullish market, management may expect prices to rise higher than otherwise; in a period of declining earnings and a bearish market, or even declining earnings and a favorable market, prices will probably drop excessively.

Interviews with executives indicate that, at least from a company point of view, the results of periodic stock dividends are satisfactory. Furthermore, in no case has stockholder opposition been sizable; nor have other formidable obstacles appeared. Needless to say, there are undoubtedly companies which have considered and rejected such a policy because of intimations of stockholder objection or other practical considerations making the plan unfeasible, but that fact does not alter our judgment of the success of stock dividends where used.

As more companies feel the need to retain earnings while satisfying stockholder demands for a tangible return on their investment, we may expect to see greater use made of this financial device. With increased use will come further understanding, greater acceptance. Thus, properly used, periodic stock dividends appear to provide a satisfactory solution for many current financial problems.

EVALUATION OF
STOCK DIVIDENDS*

One of the most perplexing subjects today in corporation finance is the meaningfulness of stock dividends—this in spite of the fact that during 1955, 1956, and 1957 the number of stock dividends issued reached all-time highs:

> In 1955 stocks listed on the New York Stock Exchange paid 143 stock dividends in the 1% to 99% category.
>
> In 1956, a year that marked the leveling off of one of history's greatest bull markets, there was a new record of 197 stock dividends issued by NYSE-listed companies.
>
> In 1957, which saw a 100-point drop in the Dow-Jones industrial averages, stock dividends numbered 177—the second highest total in history.

Opinions of financial analysts differ widely and strongly. Some believe that small stock dividends lead to increases in market price by broadening the share ownership, while some feel they bring about real value enhancement for shareowners without any such rise. Others emphasize that stock dividends offer tax benefits to higher income bracket investors because they are not generally treated as income for tax purposes. Still others feel that although stock dividends may have no apparent effect on the market value of the investment, they are useful in conserving corporate cash and are therefore an inexpensive way to raise capital for expansion. A final school of thought claims that stock dividends, like stock splits, merely cut the same loaf of bread into a larger number of necessarily thinner slices.

A good deal of the confusion in this stock dividend controversy stems from the relatively simple fact that there are several kinds of stock dividends—a fact not always remembered by those concerned. One purpose of this article is to segregate stock dividends into three fundamentally different classes, thereby eliminating the confusion which results from treating all categories of stock dividends alike.

Throughout this analysis we should keep in mind the difference between a stock dividend and a stock split-up. Basically, it lies in the accounting treatment. A split involves no change in the total capital account or surplus account; the common stock account is merely apportioned among the increased shares outstanding after the split-up. The stock dividend, on the other hand, requires the transfer of a portion

* By C. Austin Barker. Reprinted from Harvard Business Review, *August, 1958, pp. 99–144. Used by permission.*

of earned surplus to the capital account, leaving unchanged the par or stated value of each share. A technical distinction also arises between the two because of the regulations of the New York Stock Exchange. Under a rather arbitrary "rule of thumb" regulation, the NYSE considers any distribution of stock totaling 24% or less to be a stock dividend, and any payment in stock of 25% or more to be a stock split-up.

EFFECT ON PRICE

The significant question is: What is the real effect of stock dividends on market price? A number of studies have been made in search of a factual answer.[1] Such studies are too numerous and diverse to be summarized here, except to point out that none of them uses separate measurements of stock dividends accompanied by cash dividend increases, as distinguished from those with no change or with a reduction in cash dividends. Such distinctions are all-important and must be made for purposes of more accurate analysis and comparison. Therefore, I shall classify stock dividends as:

1. Those which are accompanied by cash dividend increases.
2. Those with no increases or with actual declines in cash dividends.
3. Those omitting cash dividends altogether.

Procedures of Analysis

My study covers all NYSE-listed stock dividend issues of 5% or more paid in common stock during the years 1951 through 1954, as reported in the annual lists printed in the early January issues of *Outlook*, published by Standard & Poor's Corporation. The three years 1951–1953 cover a "sidewise" market, and 1954 is included to allow a separate analysis of stock dividends during a strong bull market year. As for the procedures followed:

The base date was established as six months prior to the ex-dividend date (i.e., when the stock was quoted at the closing price of the previous day less the amount of the dividend), the first comparison being made at the ex-dividend date and the final comparison six months after the ex-dividend date. This twelve-month period seems the ideal span for the purpose of reflecting the full effect of a stock dividend without introducing extraneous elements or encountering the chaotic effect of a second, overlapping stock dividend.

Omitted were 17 dividend issues because mergers or stock split-ups interfered with the comparisons during the one-year period studied. After elimi-

[1] See, for example, Joseph C. Bothwell, Jr., "Periodic Stock Dividends," HBR, January 1950, p. 89; Robert Sheehan, "The Big Pay-Out," Fortune, November 1956, p. 147; and John H. Myers and Loyd C. Heath, "The Periodic Stock Dividend—Boon or Sop!" The Commercial & Financial Chronicle, February 13, 1958, p. 3.

nation of these, 224 stock dividends of 5% or more remained to be analyzed.

In order to make possible significant price comparisons before and after the stock dividend, the price of the stock as of the base date (six months prior to the ex-dividend date) was converted to its equivalent dilution price. Each stock's diluted price at base date was then expressed in terms of its price relationship to the stock price index of that one of the 100 sub-industry groups published by Standard & Poor's to which it most logically belonged. To illustrate, American Bosch Corporation stock, the first company listed in Exhibit I, was adjusted by Standard & Poor's price index for "auto parts and accessories"; next, American Gas & Electric was adjusted by the price index for "utilities—electric power companies"; and so on.

Percentage changes in the adjusted market prices of all stocks in relation to the base date were calculated at the ex-dividend date and again six months later, and compared with *actual* market prices to determine the real gain or loss as compared to the general state of the market. For example, at the ex-dividend date and six months later the actual market price per share of American Bosch was 161% and 130%, respectively, over the general market of its subindustry.

In order to make meaningful cash-dividend-per-share comparisons before and after the stock dividend, each annual *cash dividend rate* at the base date likewise was converted to the equivalent dilution rate. For example, the $1.00 annual cash dividend rate of American Bosch was adjusted to $0.8333. The actual annual rate per share six months after the ex-dividend date was $1.20, representing an "effective" increase per share in the cash dividend rate of 44%.

My basic research method is based on the same reasoning and adjustment procedures for comparison explained in detail in my earlier HBR articles.[2]

With Cash Increases

Exhibit I indicates that the *real* price gain of the 190 companies which accompanied stock dividends with cash dividend increases averaged 9% over the six months preceding the ex-dividend date. It is significant to note that this proved to be a *lasting gain:* six months after the ex-dividend date it stood at 8%, virtually unchanged.

One incidental phenomenon not reflected in Exhibit I, but no surprise in any event, is the fact that there is often a strong but short-lived price run-up during the first few days after news of a stock dividend reaches the public, particularly when the dividend is a special, nonperiodic one, unexpected by the average investor.

Without Cash Increases

Exhibit II, in contrast, shows what happens when there are no cash dividend increases to accompany a stock dividend. These calculations are

[2] "*Effective Stock Splits,*" *January–February 1956, p. 101;* "*Stock Splits in a Bull Market,*" *May–June 1957, p. 72.*

also computed by excluding general market action, just as in Exhibit I. Although the prices of these stock-dividend stocks held approximately even with the general market through the ex-dividend date, they then dropped 12% below the general market in the following six months. This observation applies not only to the "sidewise" market years of 1951–1953 but with equal effect—a shade more, in fact—to the bull market of 1954; the four 1954 examples show average relative losses of 4% and 14% at the same respective dates.

Would the issues shown in Exhibit II have declined still further if they had not distributed stock dividends? There are some persuasive reasons for thinking not. On the basis of their average Standard & Poor's stock ratings, these stocks did not differ significantly in investment value from the Exhibit I group. Moreover, the Exhibit II stocks were not subjected to dramatically unfavorable dividend-action comparisons during three-fourths of the period in question, for there were no significant cash dividend increases in the general market in 1951–1953.

What can we learn from the experience of companies that have paid stock dividends both with and without cash dividend increases? Exhibit III, which includes all Exhibit II firms that in another year qualified for Exhibit I, is revealing. It shows that, with only one exception, all such companies achieved real price gains for the years in which their stock dividends *were* accompanied by cash dividend increases—and that without an exception these same companies suffered price declines relative to the market when they issued stock dividends *without* also increasing the cash dividend rate.

The fact that the price and dividend columns in Exhibit III are both adjusted to reflect the per-share dilution resulting from the stock dividends further supports the conclusion that stock dividends *per se* have no measurable market value.

In Exhibit III the relative price gains are not, of course, expected to be precisely proportionate to the cash dividend changes. Any such occurrence is pure happenstance, in view of the extraneous, yet often controlling, factors necessarily present in each instance; i.e., the different degrees of discounting of the event which have taken place prior to the period used in the study, the different degrees of contemporary cash dividend changes within each related industry, and so on. Nonetheless, the evidence presented reflects a strikingly uniform pattern in direction and trend.

CASH COMPETITION

How did the 190 stocks listed in Exhibit I make a real price gain of 8% over the general market? It can be seen from Exhibit IV that the Exhibit I group required an average increase of 17% in adjusted cash dividends per share in order to achieve an 8% average real gain in price. The dividend increase greatly exceeded the price gain in every year.

Exhibit I. Stock dividends accompanied by cash dividend increases bring lasting price gains

Company	Dividend size as percentage of shares outstanding	Ex-dividend date	Relationship of adjusted price to base date*	
			At ex-dividend date	Six months after "ex" date
Stock dividends paid in 1951				
American Bosch Corp.	20%	1–2–51	161%	130%
American Brake Shoe Co.	10	12–15–50	101	103
American Gas & Electric	5	8–20–51	109	109
American Seating Co.	5	11–15–51	106	105
Anderson, Clayton & Co.	100	9–10–51	137	151
Ashland Oil & Refining Co.	10	5–17–51	119	104
Byron Jackson	40	5–7–51	107	95
California Packing	100	7–23–51	109	101
Carpenter Steel Co.	5	7–25–51	131	125
Carrier Corp.	10	1–30–51	112	123
Cerro de Pasco Corp.	5	3–14–51	123	155
Clark Equipment Co.	25	2–21–51	104	101
Colgate-Palmolive Co.	5	12–11–50	100	111
Continental Copper & Steel Ind.	5	11–2–51	114	98
Cooper-Bessemer Corp.	10	12–14–51	118	117
Corn Products Refining Co.	5	1–3–51	102	103
Derby Oil Co.	10	12–6–51	123	106
Devoe & Reynolds Co.	10	1–25–51	110	90
Eagle-Picher Co.	10	11–9–51	193	188
Eastern Corporation	5	8–22–51	129	118
Eastman Kodak Co.	10	12–20–50	106	82
Elgin National Watch Co.	5	11–27–51	100	97
Federated Department Stores	20	6–14–51	103	99
General Time Corp.	10	12–15–50	125	123
Goodyear Tire & Rubber	100	9–11–51	98	91
Greenfield Tap & Die Corp.	25	9–5–51	130	123
Heinz (H. J.) Co.	20	9–20–51	116	113
Industrial Rayon Corp.	5	11–22–50	91	88
International Business Machines	5	1–2–51	82	69
International Tel. & Tel.	5	12–27–50	113	117
Lane Bryant, Inc.	5	3–13–51	106	114
Master Electric Co.	10	3–8–51	119	103
McKesson & Robbins, Inc.	10	6–28–51	87	94
Merritt-Chapman & Scott	5	12–13–51	127	112
Moore-McCormack Lines	25	10–30–51	117	119
Motorola, Inc.	10	12–26–50	107	104
Noma Electric	25	12–13–50	95	88
Panhandle Prod. & Ref. Co.	10	11–28–51	102	94
Philip Morris	5	3–29–51	107	106

* Six months prior to ex-dividend date.

Exhibit I. Continued

Company	Dividend size as percentage of shares outstanding	Ex-dividend date	Relationship of adjusted price to base date*	
			At ex-dividend date	Six months after "ex" date
Pittsburgh Forgings Co.	15	12–5–51	112	105
Remington Rand	5	12–7–50	122	157
Ruberoid Co.	5	12–5–51	101	101
Savage Arms Corp.	5	12–5–51	104	90
Standard Steel Spring	5	12–4–51	106	105
Stokely-Van Camp, Inc.	5	10–29–51	114	114
Sun Oil Company	10	11–13–51	108	100
United Aircraft Corp.	20	5–2–51	104	94
United Merchants & Mfrs.	10	7–5–51	109	119
U.S. Plywood Corp.	10	3–28–51	115	108
Visking Corp.	5	12–3–51	123	101
Wilson Jones Company	10	11–28–51	115	109
Average, 51 cases, 1951			113%	109%
Stock dividends paid in 1952				
American Car & Foundry	10%	9–2–52	113%	118%
Barber Oil Corp.	100	9–11–52	118	127
Beneficial Loan Corp.	5	12–31–51	106	107
Boeing Airplane	50	5–23–52	109	114
Cerro de Pasco Corp.	5	3–11–52	99	84
Cincinnati Gas & Electric	5	1–11–52	106	100
City Investing Co.	10	10–9–52	125	146
Clark Equipment Co.	50	11–21–52	106	106
Colgate-Palmolive Co.	5	12–13–51	97	92
Cooper-Bessemer Corp.	5	11–25–52	101	96
Cornell-Dubilier Electric	10	4–1–52	123	106
Eastman Kodak Co.	10	12–26–51	111	113
Elgin National Watch Co.	5	11–17–52	93	101
Evans Products Co.	5	1–15–52	92	81
Ex-Cell-O Corporation	10	3–5–52	126	125
Fansteel Metallurgical Corp.	5	11–25–52	96	103
Federal-Mogul Corp.	50	10–31–52	128	110
General Realty & Utilities	10	12–3–52	110	137
Goodyear Tire & Rubber	5	11–12–52	99	118
Grand Union Company	5	4–30–52	98	87
Houston Oil Co. of Texas	20	5–26–52	103	102
International Business Machines	5	1–2–52	95	105
Kaiser Aluminum & Chemical	5	8–6–52	102	87
Lane Bryant, Inc.	5	4–28–52	121	145
Lee Rubber & Tire Corp.	5	10–9–52	102	84

Exhibit I. Continued

Company	Dividend size as percentage of shares outstanding	Ex-dividend date	Relationship of adjusted price to base date*	
			At ex-dividend date	Six months after "ex" date
Marathon Corp.	100	1–28–52	123	107
Morotola, Inc.	100	7–31–52	115	114
Mullins Mfg.	5	12–12–51	160	148
Newmont Mining Corp.	100	5–26–52	78	71
Northrop Aircraft	10	10–2–52	106	103
Ohio Match Co.	5	9–10–52	110	96
Pittsburgh Forgings Co.	5	11–28–52	94	89
Rayonier Incorporated	100	3–6–52	113	118
Republic Aviation Corp.	10	11–25–52	118	131
Ruberoid Co.	5	11–25–52	101	112
St. Joseph Lead	10	5–20–52	103	108
Sheraton Corp. of America	5	7–2–52	118	130
Skelly Oil Co.	10	1–28–52	96	81
Standard Steel Spring	5	11–13–52	109	102
Sun Oil Company	8	11–10–52	112	105
Superior Steel Corp.	5	12–5–52	91	85
Tide Water Associated Oil Co.	100	6–4–52	95	96
Average, 42 cases, 1952			108%	107%
Stock dividends paid in 1953				
Admiral Corporation	20%	10–6–53	110%	90%
American Car & Foundry	10	7–27–53	115	112
American Metal Co. Ltd.	5	11–10–53	122	143
Babcock & Wilcox Co.	5	12–12–52	99	105
Bliss (E. W.) Co.	20	1–7–53	104	79
Carolina Power & Light	5	1–6–53	98	96
City Investing Co.	15	8–27–53	114	103
Colgate-Palmolive Co.	5	12–10–52	105	113
Continental Copper & Steel Ind.	5	2–6–53	107	106
Cornell-Dubilier Electric	10	5–22–53	124	101
Cosden Petroleum Corp.	20	8–5–53	121	108
Crown Zellerbach Corp.	100	4–15–53	107	102
Denver & Rio Grande Western RR.	50	12–31–53	119	133
Eastman Kodak Co.	5	4–28–53	96	98
Ekco Products Co.	5	10–9–53	118	126
Electric Auto-Lite Co.	5	4–30–53	94	90
Elgin National Watch Co.	5	11–16–53	100	93
Evans Products Co.	5	1–12–53	103	117
Ex-Cell-O Corporation	10	3–5–53	115	103
Fansteel Metallurgical Corp.	5	11–25–53	80	64

* Six months prior to ex-dividend date.

Exhibit I. Continued

Company	Dividend size as percentage of shares outstanding	Ex-dividend date	Relationship of adjusted price to base date*	
			At ex-dividend date	Six months after "ex" date
Food Fair Stores, Inc.	5	7–13–53	105	133
Franklin Stores Corp.	5	4–15–53	108	102
Garrett Corp.	10	9–4–53	98	69
Grand Union Company	5	4–29–53	94	98
Grayson-Robinson Stores, Inc.	5	12–15–52	117	96
Halliburton Oil Well Cementing	100	8–17–53	111	108
Hayes Industries, Inc.	10	11–10–53	118	99
Household Finance Corp.	10	2–25–53	108	99
Industrial Rayon Corp.	5	11–24–53	115	129
International Business Machines	5	12–30–52	115	128
International Paper	10	11–17–53	97	99
Kaiser Aluminum & Chemical	5	8–7–53	102	93
Kinney (G. R.) Co.	5	6–4–53	158	146
Lane Bryant, Inc.	5	4–8–53	115	119
Lee Rubber & Tire Corp.	5	10–9–53	102	88
Lockheed Aircraft	10	12–18–52	92	93
Master Electric Co.	10	11–27–53	87	83
National Cash Register	10	11–25–53	109	109
New York, Chi. & St. Louis RR.	10	7–14–53	98	101
Ohio Match Co.	5	11–9–53	89	111
Outboard, Marine & Mfg. Co.	20	2–19–53	135	187
Pennsylvania Glass Sand Corp.	10	2–18–53	115	112
Philco Corporation	5	11–23–53	105	101
Pittsburgh Forgings Co.	5	11–25–53	82	81
Reo Motors	10	12–22–52	94	122
Republic Aviation Corp.	10	11–25–53	94	88
Reynolds Metals Co.	5	6–11–53	100	85
Savage Arms Corp.	5	11–6–53	98	87
Shamrock Oil & Gas Corp.	10	12–11–52	126	149
Sheraton Corp. of America	5	6–30–53	112	108
Skelly Oil Co.	100	9–8–53	101	98
Sun Oil Company	8	11–9–53	103	89
Superior Steel Corp.	5	12–4–53	92	74
Sylvania Electric Products, Inc.	10	11–6–53	109	106
Talcott (James), Inc.	10	12–14–53	100	84
Tennessee Corporation	5	11–23–53	90	120
Texas Gulf Producing Co.	10	11–13–53	85	107
Thompson Products	10	8–26–53	98	118
Union Oil Co. of Cal.	10	11–9–53	111	107
Visking Corp.	10	12–10–53	141	149
Average, 60 cases, 1953			106%	106%

Exhibit I. Continued

Company	Dividend size as percentage of shares outstanding	Ex-dividend date	Relationship of adjusted price to base date*	
			At ex-dividend date	Six months after "ex" date
Stock dividends paid in 1954				
Aldens, Inc.	50%	5–7–54	119%	99%
American Metal Co., Ltd.	5	11–9–54	136	129.
American Stores Co.	5	11–24–53	107	110
Atlantic City Electric	5	2–2–54	109	114
Babcock & Wilcox Co.	5	12–4–53	105	105
Bendix Aviation Corp.	7	11–30–53	96	82
Borden Co.	10	9–7–54	109	108
Brunswick-Balke-Collender Co.	5	11–26–54	117	135
Bullard Co.	10	12–28–53	125	148
Cerro de Pasco Corp.	5	3–11–54	120	120
Colgate-Palmolive Co.	5	12–10–53	90	83
Combustion Engineering	5	12–23–53	100	98
Consolidated Cigar Corp.	5	12–7–54	103	95
Container Corp. of Amer.	25	5–27–54	109	111
Cosden Petroleum Corp.	25	8–25–54	122	124
Ex-Cell-O Corporation	10	3–5–54	119	129
General Telephone Corp.	50	5–17–54	109	109
Gould-National Batteries	100	7–1–54	96	112
Grand Union Company	5	4–28–54	100	130
Hussman Refrigerator Co.	50	10–11–54	119	105
International Paper	5	11–16–54	95	100
Kinney (G. R.) Co.	5	6–7–54	103	96
Lane Bryant, Inc.	5	4–7–54	110	107
Lily-Tulip Cup Corp.	50	1–27–54	131	135
Lockheed Aircraft	5	12–1–53	115	93
Merritt-Chapman & Scott	25	1–11–54	112	98
Minneapolis & St. Louis Ry.	33⅓	7–28–54	123	132
Northrop Aircraft	10	3–16–54	92	158
Ohio Match Co.	5	11–9–54	113	89
Republic Aviation Corp.	10	11–19–54	95	89
Reynolds Metals Co.	5	6–11–54	104	142
Solar Aircraft Co.	10	3–26–54	78	70
Standard Oil Co. of California	5	10–5–54	105	99
Standard Oil Co. (Indiana)	100	12–1–54	103	93
Twin Coach Company	5	10–27–54	138	118
Union Tank Car Co.	100	6–2–54	115	103
Visking Corp.	5	12–10–54	79	88
Average, 37 cases, 1954			109%	110%
Average, 190 cases, 1941–1954			109%	108%

* Six months prior to ex-dividend date.

Exhibit II. **Stock dividends unaccompanied by cash dividend increases are followed by real price declines**

			Relationship of adjusted price to base date*	
Company	Dividend size as percentage of shares outstanding	Ex-dividend date	At ex-dividend date	Six months after "ex" date
Stock dividends paid, 1951–1954				
American Cyanamid Co.	100%	7–16–52	90%	82%
Bohn Aluminum & Brass Corp.	50	6–23–52	95	68
Buffalo Forge Co.	100	2–3–54	92	62
Cerro de Pasco Corp.	5	3–10–53	89	69
Continental Oil	100	5–14–51	116	90
Davega Stores	10	12–12–50	95	93
Derby Oil Co.	5	6–25–52	86	85
Eastern Stainless Steel Corp.	5	6–5–53	104	79
Foster Wheeler Corp.	100	4–3–52	104	91
Gulf Oil Corp.	100	7–16–51	97	91
Hudson Motor Car	5	11–17–52	97	90
Johnson & Johnson	5	2–20–51	115	111
Lane-Wells Co.	100	5–2–51	103	89
Oliver Corp.	100	7–10–52	102	92
Remington Rand	5	12–10–51	109	98
Reynolds Metals Co.	10	7–18–52	96	94
Stokeley-Van Camp, Inc.	5	9–4–53	96	92
Sunbeam Corp.	10	1–6–54	113	91
Tide Water Associated Oil Co.	5	5–5–54	86	99
United Engineering & Foundry	200	5–20–52	109	94
U.S. Lines Co.	7½	2–24–54	94	93
Average, 21 cases, 1951–1954			99%	88%

* Six months prior to ex-dividend date.

Market Comparisons

It is obvious that some comparative measure of cash dividend competition is needed for proper appraisal; without it, the price gain seems disproportionately expensive.

Standard & Poor's reports provide quarterly cash dividend data only for the 50 industrials, 20 utilities, and 20 rails during the period I studied, and it was therefore necessary to calculate a "market" cash dividend comparison for Exhibit IV from the cash dividend statistics published in the New York Stock Exchange's magazine *The Exchange.* The NYSE statistics show in detail the dividend payments of listed cash-dividend-paying stocks for 27 industrial subgroups. Also, the aggregate disburse-

*Exhibit III. Companies paying stock dividends both with (°) and
without (†) cash dividend increases*

Company	Dividend size as percentage of shares outstanding	Year	Real price gain or loss from base date to end of period	Effective cash dividend change during period
Cerro de Pasco Corp.* (Average of 3 cases)	5%	1951 1952 1954	+20%	+40%
Cerro de Pasco Corp.†	5	1953	−31	−34
Derby Oil Co.*	10	1951	+ 6	+10
Derby Oil Co.†	5	1952	−15	−21
Remington Rand*	5	1951	+57	+ 5
Remington Rand†	5	1952	− 2	−21
Reynolds Metals Co.* (Average of 2 cases)	5	1953 1954	+14	+57
Reynolds Metals Co.†	10	1952	− 6	0
Stokely-Van Camp*	5	1951	+14	+ 5
Stokely-Van Camp†	5	1953	− 8	− 5
Tide Water Associated Oil Co.*	100	1952	− 4	+ 7
Tide Water Associated Oil Co.†	5	1953	− 1	−74

* As reported in Exhibit I.
† As reported in Exhibit II.

Exhibit IV. Real price gains vs. cash dividend increases

Year	Number of cases (Exhibit I)	Average real price gain over general market (6 months after)	Average effective cash dividend increase	Cash dividend increase of dividend-paying stocks in related NYSE groups
1951	51	9%	13%	2%
1952	42	7	13	1
1953	60	6	14	4
1954	37	10	28	15
Average, 190 cases, 1951–1954		8%	17%	5%

ments of each industry are compared with those for the preceding year, and the percentage change is noted. (The total number of cash-dividend–payment common stocks varied between 961 and 975 during the four years 1951–1954.)

To establish a more accurate relationship of cash dividend changes to price changes, I have assigned each of the 190 stock-dividend–paying companies to its appropriate NYSE industry subgroup and have derived from this a weighted, representative cash dividend behavior pattern for comparative purposes. This procedure produces a sounder reference base for our purposes in this article than such alternatives as simple comparison with, say, the dividends paid by the 50 Standard & Poor's or the 30 Dow-Jones industrials. The average derived cash dividend increases appearing in the last column of Exhibit IV have been calculated in this manner. With this data we see that:

> The stocks in Exhibit I increased their cash dividends 11 percentage points above competition in 1951, and made a real price gain of 9% over their competitors.
> In 1952 a 12-percentage-point differential in cash increase was accompanied by a 7% price gain over the general market.
> In 1953 a 10-percentage-point edge in cash dividends was followed by a 6% price gain.
> In 1954 a 13-point differential in effective cash increases was matched by a 10% price gain.

The 1954 record is particularly interesting. In that bull market year the 28% effective cash dividend increase of the 37 companies paying stock dividends was double that of the similar 60 companies of 1953—*against the very stiff competition* of the related cash-paying industry groups of the NYSE series, which paid out 15% more than the previous year for a 3½-fold increase over their percentage gain for 1953.

Earnings Protection

The 1954 performance is particularly noteworthy when it is recognized that the stock dividend issues faced another severe obstacle, this one of their own making. In 1954, as would be expected, there occurred the greatest proportionate number of larger stock dividends. Of the stock dividends issued in 1954, 30% were over 10%, and the larger ones were accompanied by greater cash dividend increases.

Although most analysts agree that an increased pay-out ratio of this nature tends to bring a relatively higher market price per share, the effect of thus diluting the earnings protection of the cash dividend has never been satisfactorily evaluated.

For example, assume that a share of stock earns $1.00 and pays out 50¢ in cash. The earnings cushion or dividend protection is 50%. After

Exhibit V. Real price gains classified by size of stock dividend group

Size of stock dividend	Number of cases (Exhibit I)	Average real price gain	Average effective cash dividend increase	Cash dividend increase of dividend-paying stocks in related NYSE groups
5 to 10%	144	8%	14%	5%
All other	46	8	25	4
Total	190	8	17	5

a 100% stock dividend the stock earns 50¢ per share and the dividend rate is 25¢. But if the cash dividend per share is increased by 25% to 31¼¢ per share, there is now only a 37½% earnings protection for the cash dividend. Such a change is more significant for a cyclical than a stable stock, but some of the lessened effect of the larger increases in cash dividends in 1954 undoubtedly may be attributed to the lesser degree of earnings protection.

This is illustrated in part in Exhibit V, where the 190 cases of Exhibit I are classified by *different-size* stock dividend groups. The 46 larger stock dividends included in the "all other" group break down as follows: 100%, 15 cases; 50%, 8 cases; 25%, 7 cases; 20%, 9 cases; and 7 odd-size stock dividends. Their average, real cash dividend increase per share (after adjustment for the stock split) is 25%, and that percentage is therefore used in the foregoing example illustrating dilution of earnings protection.

In the "all other" group the discrepancy between (a) the percentage cash dividend increases *net* of their "cash competition" and (b) the real price gain scored over the general market obviously is substantially greater than the over-all average for the year 1954 which appears in Exhibit IV. In other words, the relative improvement in dividends led to less relative improvement in market price—largely because of the lower earnings protection.

This discrepancy was substantiated by preparing a new representative all-industry group from the NYSE's 27 subindustry groups of cash-dividend–paying stocks solely for comparison with the 46 cases in the "all other" stock dividend group of Exhibit V. The "market" cash dividend increase represented by such a NYSE group, from 1951 through 1954, weighted by the type of industry participation of the "all other" group, is 5%—precisely the same as the average results for 1951–1954 weighted by *all* stock dividend cases.

Certainly it should be recognized that other, and perhaps conflicting, influences were present in the market in 1954. Nevertheless, the comparative evidence offered by Exhibits IV and V is compelling testimony that in the long run smaller cash dividend increases, paid more frequently and with an eye to sound earnings protection, have the greater relative impact, per dollar of increase, on market price.

SPECIAL SITUATIONS

The smallest class of stock dividends are those unaccompanied by any cash dividends. As shown in Exhibit VI, during the 1951–1954 period there were only 13 such cases, representing only 10 companies, among NYSE-listed firms paying stock dividends of 5% or more.

These are the "special situations" where each stock must be judged more than ever on an individual basis. In this group there occur the greatest extremes of price behavior, as would be expected, for companies withhold cash payments for different reasons and with different invest-ment results. The greatest real gain over the general market scored by any single stock in this category during any year of this study is 126%; the extreme decline in relation to the market during a single year is 30%. The average real gain for Exhibit VI cases is 21%.

At first glance this gain may seem inconsistent with the findings re-ported earlier in this article, i.e., that in the long run stock dividends in themselves have no effect on market price. Moreover, the capital gains tax offers no explanation; the effect is the same whether a stockholder sells his stock dividend or the proportionate amount of his original shares. Even if an Exhibit VI company paid no stock dividends, the shareholder could still benefit from the capital gains rate by selling some

Exhibit VI. Stock dividends of non-cash-dividend stocks

Stock dividends paid, 1951–1954	Size of stock dividend	Ex-dividend date	Relationship of adjusted price to base date*	
			At ex-dividend date	Six months after "ex" date
Capital Airlines	5%	12–2–54	122%	188%
Granite City Steel Co.	6	10–21–54	98	100
Mack Trucks, Inc.	5	12–15–53	107	104
Magma Copper Co.	10	10–26–53	100	131
Magma Copper Co.	7	10–25–54	120	160
Martin (Glenn L.) Co.	10	11–3–54	103	89
Ohio Match Co.	5	11–8–51	96	104
Pacific Western Oil	10	4–7–53	242	226
Pacific Western Oil	5	5–5–54	86	84
Publicker Industries, Inc.	5	8–26–53	92	70
Publicker Industries, Inc.	5	8–26–54	89	84
Raytheon Manufacturing Co.	10	7–7–54	91	145
Trans World Airlines, Inc.	10	12–10–52	90	93
Average, 13 cases, 1951–1954			110%	121%

* Six months prior to ex-dividend date.

of his shares, provided there was an unrealized appreciation in their market price.

Investment Worth

The explanation of the 21% average price gain in Exhibit VI is, I think, a very simple one: the prices reflect the stockholder's expectation that he will get something in the future. Some of the companies are earning and reinvesting all earnings at a very fast rate of growth—for example, the oil-producing companies. Progress in expansion of exploration and drilling may be greater than average. Their earnings, investment, and cash-dividend–paying potential thus will be compounded. The future cash dividends are distant and hard to estimate, but presumably they may be very large.

Some non-cash-dividend–paying companies do not show the expected real growth in earnings and future cash-dividend–paying ability after reinvestment of all earnings. The prices of their stocks then lose ground in relation to market competition. Both types of companies are found in Exhibit VI.

In either case it is the fundamental investment worth and not the stock dividend that influences market price behavior. For example, in each of the years covered by the survey, 50 to 80 NYSE-listed stocks paid *neither* cash *nor* stock dividends. In Exhibit VII 13 companies are listed from this category which nevertheless show a better-than-average price performance. These also are compared over a 12-month period, but calendar years have been used to simplify the calculations. Analysts

Exhibit VII. Stocks paying neither cash nor stock dividends

Company	Calendar year	Relationship of ad- justed price at year's end to base date*
Boston & Maine R.R.	1954	178%
Brewing Corp. of America	1951	155
Central of Ga. Ry. Co.	1952	153
Internat'l Hydro-Elec. System	1951	157
Missouri-Kansas-Texas R.R.	1954	161
N.Y. Shipbuilding	1953	218
Park & Tilford Distillers Corp.	1954	161
Reynolds Spring Co.	1954	330
RKO Pictures Corp.	1954	190
Speigel, Inc.	1954	154
Telautograph Corp.	1952	166
Virginia-Carolina Chem. Corp.	1954	157
Willys-Overland Motors, Inc.	1953	157
Average, 13 cases, 1951–1954		180%

* Beginning of calendar year.

familiar with "special situations" will recall the fundamental factors responsible for the superior price performance of these stocks. There are other instances as well; the list was arbitrarily limited to the same number of cases as in Exhibit VI.

The average real price gain in the Exhibit VII cases is substantially superior to that of the 13 companies in Exhibit VI: 80% as against 21%. This is additional proof that, in cases where no cash dividends are paid, the stock dividend is *not* "better than nothing."

MANAGEMENT STRATEGY

Let us turn now to the implications of this analysis for management. Here we will want to pay particular attention to stockholder relations and the need for retained earnings.

Finding a Market

Only a handful of companies pay stock dividends exclusively (in lieu of cash) over any length of time. For no single year during the period I studied do Exhibit VI–type companies make up more than one-third of 1% of all NYSE-listed common stock issues.

For companies paying stock dividends but no cash dividends, the most difficult problem is obtaining or maintaining an established market for the stock, so that holders who do try to sell their stock dividend shares will not force the market price down below the dilution value, or below a normal price earnings ratio. If management wants to maintain good relations with smaller and institutional stockholders, it may go to some lengths to solve this problem. Thus:

In 1956 an attempt was made by a small, but rapidly growing, unlisted company to finance to a greater extent from retained earnings by setting up two classes of stock. The Class A stock was to receive stock dividends and the Class B stock to receive dividends in cash. Presumably the company's expansion requirements would have justified retention of all earnings without tax penalties. In such cases stockholders normally obtain cash when they need it by selling part of their holdings at the capital gains tax rate.

However, to have paid out earnings in cash to some stockholders and not to others would have been inequitable. The stock dividend device was employed to maintain proportionate representation of the *growing* ownership of those stockholders (i.e., the Class A group) whose earnings were fully reinvested. Moreover, some of the institutional as well as the smaller stockholders strongly preferred cash dividends (subject to the ordinary income tax rate); the Class B series, representing about one-fourth of the total shares, was established to permit the continuance of cash dividends to them.

The company decided, as a final precautionary step, to assure maintenance of a market for the Class A (non-cash-paying) series. The Class A stock was therefore made convertible into Class B (cash-paying) stock at the holder's option.

Accordingly, the financial officers and analysts interested in a precise comparison of the effects of cash and stock dividends on market price were not able to get the answer they might otherwise have obtained, but it is significant that since 1956 the Class A stock has dropped to the approximate price level of the Class B stock as of the ex-dividend dates. In other words, the case illustrates that a stock-dividend stock is equal in value to a cash-dividend stock if it can be converted into the latter.

Cash Conservation?

Perhaps the most commonly expressed reason for companies to distribute stock dividends is to "conserve their cash resources for expansion," as two leading financial services explain annually in their reviews of stock dividends. They are "used in place of, or as a supplement to, cash dividends." What conclusions can we make about this practice?

For the relatively small number of 34 cases shown in Exhibits II and VI—where the stock dividend was used to supplement a partial reduction in cash dividends or used entirely in place of a cash dividend—cash conservation was actually accomplished. But these constitute only 15% of the 224 stock dividends in my study—a percentage which is scarcely large enough to indicate that cash saving is a major objective of stock dividends.

It is often stated as policy during a period of plant expansion and increasing earnings that a stock dividend is being given in lieu of an *increase* in the cash dividend, presumably to save cash that otherwise would have been paid out in higher cash dividends. That this is apparently true is seen in an analysis of the 190 cases in Exhibit I; in 72% of such cases the actual cash dividend rate *per share* remained unchanged during the twelve-month period for which the stock dividends were analyzed.

As previously explained, the cash rates have been adjusted in this study to reflect the same dilution as the price adjustment, in order to afford a more meaningful per-share comparison of price and dividends. For this purpose, a cash rate per share that remains unchanged after a 10% stock dividend, for example, represents an "effective" 10% increase in the per-share cash dividends and thus permits a proper comparison with price.

Such a comparison makes clear that the maintenance of the same actual cash dividend rate per share and distribution of a stock dividend in lieu of a cash increase—the practice followed in 72% of the cases studied—does *not* conserve the corporation's total cash. When new dividend shares were issued in these cases, the same per-share cash dividend rate also was paid on the additional shares, beginning in the following quarter. A $1.00 cash dividend rate per share on 1,000,000 shares, if maintained after a 10% stock dividend, must henceforth be paid on 1,100,000 shares at subsequent quarterly dividend dates. The result is an increase of 10% in the total corporate cash pay-out. If cash saving for expansion were necessary, the corporation could conserve three times as much cash by paying an amount equal to 10% of the quarterly cash dividend as a year-end or "extra" cash dividend once a year.

Protecting Investment

Exhibit VIII shows the number of cases in Exhibit I where the actual cash rate per share has remained the same *after* the distribution of stock dividends.

Exhibit VIII. Cases where management maintained same per-share cash dividend after stock dividend

Size of stock dividend	Total cases (Exhibit I)	Cash dividend rate per share unchanged	
		Number	*Per cent*
5%	90	79	87.8%
10%	54	37	68.5
All other	46	20	43.5
Total	190	136	71.6%

Understandably, none of the 100% stock dividend companies included in Exhibit I appear in Exhibit VIII. The companies in the "all other" category that maintained their cash dividend rate per share after the distribution of shares are in the 15%, 20%, 25%, and 50% (in two instances) stock dividend groups.

Thus, where stock dividends maintain the same actual cash rate per share before and after the stock distribution, the *total* corporate cash payment will increase by the same percentage as the stock dividend percentage when the next quarter's cash payments become due. Except for a three-month lag in total cash increase, there is no cash conservation in this practice.

The automatic three months' delay of a quarterly cash increase in such cases is usually too brief to have any significance in planning the availability of construction funds. In fact, a company operating on a cash budget so tight that the three months' lag in increased cash payment obtained from a stock dividend has a bearing on such planning cannot be considered financially sound enough to properly declare a stock dividend. Significantly, a few companies in Exhibit I especially timed the operation in order to declare cash dividends payable on stock dividend shares immediately on issuance.

What about the 54 cases in Exhibit I in which the per-share cash dividend rate did *not* remain unchanged? In about half of these instances the "effective" rate increased less than the percentage size of the dividend; in the other half, it increased more. It is easy to see, therefore, that in the great majority (85%) of all cases studied, the saving of corporate cash by means of a stock dividend was not an objective in the financial planning of management.

It should be noted that of the 21 companies which reduced the actual cash dividend rate by as much as or more than the dilution factor (the qualification for inclusion in Exhibit II), all but one suffered a real price decline as compared to the general market (although almost half showed some absolute price rise after adjustment for stock dilution but before adjustment to remove the general market's upward action).

Theoretically, if the general market's cash dividends remain the same, the stockholders' investment in such instances should remain even with the general market. For all practical purposes, this general condition prevailed in 1951 and 1952, when market cash dividends increased only 2% and 1%, respectively. Yet even in those years the Exhibit II companies lost ground pricewise relative to the general market.

We must conclude, then, that no corporate cash saving is achieved by means of a stock dividend unless the per-share cash dividend is reduced by at least the amount of the stock dilution factor—and if this is done, the company's stock tends to recede relative to the market.

Tax Benefits?

The "stock dividends in lieu of cash dividends" theory as actually practiced exposes a fallacious companion theory: that "stock dividends represent a special benefit because they are not taxable like cash dividends." The stockholder who needs more cash must sell a portion of his equity whether in the form of stock dividends or original holdings. In either event he pays a capital gains tax. He also pays the same regular income tax rate on cash dividends received from his stock dividend shares as on dividends from his original holdings. Since the tax effect is the same in either case, the stock dividend cannot be considered a device to avoid the so-called double taxation resulting from the corporation tax and the regular personal income tax on cash dividends.

FACTORS IN DISTRIBUTION

The size of a stock dividend, like that of a split-up, is related to obtaining or maintaining a popular price range, but the dividend must function within the accounting limitations imposed by the earned surplus account. In view of this, it would be expected that stock dividends would involve much smaller percentage distributions than stock splits. An analysis of *all* NYSE-listed stock dividends of *all* sizes in the years 1951 to 1954, including those below 5% and those on a "multiple" (i.e., quarterly, semi-annual, etc.) basis discloses this to be the fact.

Of the 338 stock dividend cases in the four-year survey, 83% were 10% in size or lower. However, only 22% of the 310 cases involving annual stock dividends (i.e., single dividends in one year) were below 5% in size.

Continuity of Payment

How much regularity and continuity should there be in stock dividend payments? In the case of multiple dividends especially—and to some extent in the case of the more common annual dividends—there is no consistent pattern of distribution. Much of the apparent lack of regularity is due not to poor planning by management but to accounting limitations which measure the requirements of a transfer from earned surplus on a fluctuating standard, i.e., the market price of the issuer's common stock.

A statement commonly heard on Wall Street is this: "If they aren't too large, stock dividends, issued with regularity, wash through without changing the per-share market price." If this is true, the stockholder's *total* investment value will increase relatively at the same percentage rate as the stock dividend. How does the observation stand up under examination?

Of the 241 companies paying any stock dividends 5% or greater in size between 1951 and 1954, only 10 paid the dividends in every year of the period. Of these 10 companies, 6 paid dividends in the 5% size class every year; 3 dropped from 5% to 3% or 2½% in 1954, and one paid 100% in 1954 and 4% each year thereafter. Taking the data on these 10 firms presented in Exhibits I, II and VI, we see that they do not differ on the whole from the pattern of price behavior shown for the other firms in those exhibits. For example:

The combined price behavior of the 6 *regular* issuers in Exhibit I that increased their cash dividends by 16% showed a real price gain after adjustment of approximately 5% over the general market, as compared with the 8% gain of the Exhibit I average. The real price gain, it should be noted, reflects the stockholder's *entire* investment.

The two regular issuers included in the Exhibit II category reduced their cash dividends by 17%. They had an average real net price decline of 20%, as compared to a 12% average decline for the whole group in Exhibit II.

The two comparable cases in Exhibit VI declined 9% in relation to their general market.

Exhibit III includes some of the so-called periodic stock dividends issued with some degree of regularity and, in that case, accompanied by cash dividends. There it can be seen that the *same* companies which effectively increased their cash dividend rates and accomplished real price gains suffered price declines in relation to their respective industry markets when they failed to increase their cash dividend rates.

Thus, there appears to be no special price benefit arising from a stock dividend even in those cases marked by complete regularity or continuity of dividend distribution. Indeed, all of the price comparisons indicate that the so-called periodic (or regular or continuing) stock dividends have no more effect on real market price gain or loss than other types of stock dividends; and that the competitive earnings and cash-dividend-paying ability is what determines the market price performance of stocks with similar risks.

GROWTH OF OWNERSHIP

In view of the importance of widespread stock ownership as a means of enhancing consumer-goods sales appeal, achieving better liquidity, and serving the national interest, let us turn now to the effect of stock dividends on stockholder growth.

In my 1956 article on stock splits[3] I compared gains in number of shareholders for split stocks and unsplit stocks. The increase in shareholders over the three-year period from year-end 1950 to year-end 1953 was 30% for split-ups and 6% for unsplit stocks. It seemed reasonable to assume that the difference in ownership growth between the two groups of well-known companies was due in some part to the interest created by stock splits. Do stock dividends lead to a similar result?

To get an answer, I took all the stock dividend cases in that earlier study and compared their shareholder growth with that of split stocks and that of unsplit, non-stock-dividend–paying stocks for the same period. The results for the entire period covered are shown in Exhibit IX. The data indicate that the average gain in number of common stock shareholders for the 224 stock dividend companies in this study was 20% during 1951–1953. This was 15 percentage points above the gain shown for companies having no splits or stock dividends in the 48 comparable Standard & Poor's subindustry groups—a striking difference. However, it was only two-thirds of the gain shown for the 90 companies having stock splits.

Stock dividends in the large classes of 25% and over led to results remarkably similar to those of stock split-ups. The increases were far superior to the gains from the smaller dividends under 25%. On the other hand, the smaller stock dividend is of more common occurrence and undoubtedly brings about a more continuous growth through its repetition. Thus, both types of distribution can be said to accomplish their goals—a healthy growth in number of shareholders.

Also of great significance in corporate financial planning is the fact that one-fourth of the stock dividend companies belonging in Exhibit II—those with no real cash increase or which reduced their cash dividend rate—showed no change or an actual decline in number of shareholders at the end of 1953. And in the Exhibit VI class—those paying no cash dividends—half of the companies had an actual decrease in number of shareholders over the three-year period.

Professional Investors

One of the most persistent arguments for stock dividends is that a wider market exists for stocks after stock dividends are issued, with a resultant greater demand that presumably enhances market price. The truth of the matter seems to be that although stockholders do indeed increase in number, changes in market price are more dependent on competitive

[3] Op. cit., p. 104.

cash dividends or on potential cash dividend ability, as illustrated in Exhibits I and II. In no aspect of this stock dividend study have I been able to find a single measurement approach that will show any proof that stock dividends, in and of themselves, enhance the market price of the stock.

This same puzzling finding appeared in my two previous studies on stock splits—i.e., a relative increase in *number* of shareholders, yet no ascertainable real price change attributable to the stock split itself.

My explanation in the case of stock dividends, as for stock splits, is simply this: so long as professional investors furnish the "marginal demand" for widely held, nationally listed stocks, the price will depend on the present value of estimated future earnings and, more fundamentally, on that of estimated future cash dividends in relation to inherent risk. Thus, both the broadening of ownership and the enhancement of market value in the long run are primarily dependent on fundamental investment *quality*.

Exhibit IX. Stock dividends and splits broaden the ownership base

	Number of common stock shareholders		Per cent increase
	12/31/50	*12/31/53*	
Stock dividends, 25% and over	248,942	324,665	30%
Stock dividends, 5% to 25%	861,494	1,007,064	17
Total, all stock dividends studied	1,110,436	1,331,729	20
Total, no split-ups or stock dividends in 48 Standard & Poor's industry groups	3,634,322	3,827,738	5
Total, all stock split-ups (2-for-1 to 3-for-1)	1,426,606	1,847,827	30
Total, no split-ups or stock dividends in 34 Standard & Poor's industry groups	2,430,892	2,582,639	6

To professional investors the question of whether or not there has been a stock split or a stock dividend is a matter of indifference. High dollar value does not deter them from purchasing, nor does cutting the stock into smaller pieces make it more attractive.

I should like to point out that the demand assumed to be generated by news of a stock dividend is only part of the story. Many investors customarily sell the shares resulting from stock dividends simply to avoid the nuisance or inconvenience of handling them, or for other reasons. The price impact of increasing supply must, therefore, also be considered.

Last year two important new studies dealing with this general problem appeared. One supports the approach to stock valuation through the "present value of future dividends" method. Written by John C. Clendenin, it is an excellent analysis, in tune with the needs of most institutional and long-term investors.[4] The second publication was a detailed study by William B. Nunan of institutional investment during the years 1951–1954, coinciding with the period covered by my analysis.[5] Nunan's evidence substantiates the point that the professional investors furnish the "marginal demand" that determines stock prices for nationally listed stocks.

Other supporting evidence is not hard to find. Following World War II, brokers' loans on margin accounts of individual speculators were at the lowest level in history for any bull market. Again, the dramatic ending in late October 1957 of the 100-point drop in the Dow-Jones industrial averages was brought about by the great volume of buy orders from institutional investors. This should bury any doubts that the objective long-term valuation of stocks by professional investors is the dominant price factor in our modern stock market.

The objective influence of the professional investors with their longer-term view has been a healthy influence on the market and should tend to reduce the wide range of market prices experienced in past market fluctuations. Moreover, this institutional growth, together with the broadened *direct* ownership base made up of increasing numbers of stockholders, has helped supply the vast amounts of new equity capital needed for postwar expansion. Both types of growth will be necessary to supply the equity capital required for the next wave of industrial expansion in the 1960's.

CONVENIENCE OR NUISANCE?

There are many factors other than market price to be weighed and considered by corporate financial managers contemplating the issuance of a stock dividend. For instance, some financial writers praise the convenience to the investor of stock dividends, while others classify them as a nuisance. "Convenience" generally means having some share dividends to sell if the cash dividend is cut or omitted and the investor needs cash. Actually, it is just as convenient for the investor to sell some of his original holdings if he needs cash, although many investors do not like to do that for other reasons.

To the smaller, less informed investor who sells stock dividends, the difficulty of determining the cost of stock held is a real nuisance factor, particularly when stock dividends are paid frequently in small amounts. To calculate capital gains for tax purposes, he must apply such dilution factors as 95.2381% for a 5% distribution and 90.9091% for a 10% distribution in assigning total average cost to old shares.

[4] *"Theory and Technique of Growth Stock Valuation," Occasional Paper No. 1, Bureau of Business and Economic Research (Los Angeles, University of California, 1957).*

[5] *"Review of Institutional Activity in the Equity Market, 1951–1954,"* Journal of Finance, *December 1957, p. 468.*

Fractional Interests

Another bothersome detail created by stock dividends is settling the fractional-share interests they produce. Some companies issue scrip certificates in settlement, the terms of which show considerable variation. Other companies settle the fractional-share interests by immediate cash payment instead of issuing scrip. Sometimes an agency is established to purchase and sell the fractional interests or to consolidate the fractions and convert them into full shares for recipients, in recognition of the fact that scrip is not dealt in on the NYSE.

A further complication involving certain stock dividends is that ex-dividend dealings must be deferred and due bills used. These, too, add to inconvenience and/or confusion for the stockholder.

When one considers the sheer volume of certificates in bank personal trust funds alone, comprising over $30 billion of common stock in 1954, it becomes apparent that any procedure which fills trust account boxes with numerous stock dividends is inconvenient for administrative reasons, too. The return of the certificates to the issuing companies for consolidation requires extra clerical and mailing expense for both issuer and recipient. Even if trustees sell the stock dividends, the proceeds usually must be reinvested and restored to the various funds to preserve the capital intact.

The brokerage fees involved in the sale of small stock dividends are usually at the so-called minimum, which is the highest commission rate percentagewise. In the case of a typical 5% stock dividend issued to a round-lot holder, the sale of the 5 shares at, say, $20 per share would require paying the broker 6% of the sale price. A large stock dividend of, say, 100% has the same effect on commissions paid by shareholders as a 2-for-1 split-up. As described in detail in my 1957 HBR article,[6] it would increase the brokerage fees for both round-lot and odd-lot holders who sell their entire investment, and would decrease such fees in the exceptional instance where the issuance moves an odd-lot holder into the round-lot category.

Costs of Certificates

How much does it cost the company to prepare and issue a dividend in common stock certificates? A careful study by a well-known Cleveland underwriting and brokerage firm estimates that the cost of distributing a 1% stock dividend is $1.00 per shareholder.[7] For larger stock dividends issued by widely held companies, the investigation of an issue's calendar-and-expense table would disclose the following more significant expenses: transfer agent's fees, paper and printing of certificates, coregistrar fees, state filing fee (in some states), federal original issue tax, New York Stock Exchange fees, and company labor.

The cost of a 100% stock dividend in the 25,000-to-35,000 shareholder

[6] Op. cit., *p.* 78.
[7] See *Fulton Reid & Co., Inc.,* The Bulletin, *March* 1957, *p.* 2.

class would range around $100,000, or about $3.00 per shareholder. The amount would vary somewhat in different states, and also reflect such variable factors as the size of the earned surplus transfer which is taxable at 11¢ per $100.

Small Dividends

Although the smaller, more continuous type of stock dividend can bring about shareholder growth, as Exhibit IX demonstrates, repeated issuance is required to keep pace with the increase which would result from an occasional stock split-up of, say, 2-for-1. In view of the foregoing disadvantages, it is difficult to justify the very small, more-or-less continuous stock dividend practice as sound management policy.

There are exceptions, of course, but these are confined almost entirely to instances of unusual and sustained growth of earnings and dividends in which management prefers to maintain a popular price level by small but continuous dilutions offset by the same, or increasing, rates per share in cash dividends. And even in such cases it is difficult for management to plan a consistent and effective policy when the earned surplus transfer is based on the fluctuating standard of market value.

Undoubtedly, many of the smaller stock dividends are distributed because they are "fashionable" or popular. In many such cases, careful measurements of the relative price trends of the stocks would suggest a change in policy. In any event, the possibility of utilizing a stock split-up at less frequent intervals as an alternative choice should not be overlooked. The split-up, undertaken only after special attention to its purpose and limitations, often might be more beneficial to corporation and shareholder alike.

PROBLEMS TO SOLVE

The magnitude of future financing needed to support American business expansion during the next two decades is almost unbelievable. The needs of a rising population, plus the increasing capital investment required per employee, have a double-barreled effect on capital requirements. Recently it was estimated that by 1970 the annual plant and equipment expenditure rate of American business will surpass $100 billion.[8]

The financial managers of corporations face ever-increasing competition for funds with industrial, trade, and utility corporations, with federal, state, and local governments, with individual investment in homes, and with growing foreign demands for capital.

There are many unresolved and contradictory problems in planning the issuance of securities and in developing broader markets for them—particularly in the case of common stocks, which involve cash dividend planning, pay-out ratios, and other problems. In a race for in-

[8] Andrew N. Overby, "Financing Your Company's Future," address before the Third Annual Industrial Economics Conference, sponsored by Stanford Research Institute, Los Angeles, January 13, 1958.

dustrial world leadership the needed funds must be obtained by private industry if we are to keep our free enterprise system. The financing problem of obtaining adequate common stock money is complicated by the double tax on corporate earnings paid out as cash dividends. When tax rates are high both on corporations and shareholders alike, the problem is compounded.

Our corporate financing problems cannot be resolved with prefabricated financial thinking, the anecdotal approach, or market platitudes. Capital markets cannot be soundly and permanently enlarged by financial "gimmicks" or stopgap devices. Moreover, such policies may ultimately lead to proxy battles. The problem of satisfying the relatively few shareholders who ask for gimmicks or "sweeteners" can better be solved by research and education.

Financial Research

Financial decisions in the future seem destined to be made more and more on a factual basis. Measurement, analysis, and the presentation of cold facts will be needed—in other words, financial research. There is no room for haphazard and costly "think pieces" in a business office, but progressive managements today incorporate comprehensive financial research in their planning of fiscal policies and programs. They realize that it is a basic requirement for success in competing for funds. The larger companies staff their own organizations for this purpose, while smaller companies frequently purchase the services of financial research organizations.

Unfortunately, qualified financial researchers and analysts are in critically short supply. Moreover, not enough financial research projects are being developed among foundations, colleges, and universities to meet the specific needs of business corporations. To be sure, progressive brokerage and underwriting firms with sufficient funds and the national exchanges are engaged in many sound securities research projects, but these are aimed primarily at widening the public knowledge of existing types of securities.

Under present circumstances, therefore, corporate management is obliged to supplement existing sources with basic, exploratory financial research of its own. Publication of advanced efforts and achievements on the part of recognized leaders in the field is particularly vital, for it helps to forestall wasteful duplicating activities. This in turn reduces the total cost of corporate financial research while at the same time producing a beneficial exchange of new knowledge that advances the mutual interests of the entire financial community. What we can learn about stock dividends or stock splits, for example, we can also learn—and *should* learn—about many other questions of financial policy. Leading authorities have made no secret of the unsolved issues they would like to see investigated.[9]

[9] See, for example, Sherwin C. Badger, "Thinking Ahead: Funds in the Stock Market," HBR, July–August 1956, p. 21.

CONCLUSION

To sum up, stock dividends, like split-ups, can produce a substantial increase in the number of shareholders. And do not forget that growing ranks of small shareholders are one of the bulwarks of our expanding free enterprise economy.

Despite strong opinion to the contrary, however, stock dividends alone, whether large or small, produce no lasting gains in market price for widely held stocks on national exchanges. They are not a means of avoiding double taxation of dividends, nor are they customarily employed to conserve cash. Moreover, plans for regularized issuance of stock dividends are extremely difficult to carry out, because of the fluctuating market-price limitation on earned surplus transfers imposed by accounting requirements. Stock dividends are also more expensive to issue than stock-split distributions and, all considered, an inconvenience to shareholders.

During an inflationary period in which substantial amounts of earned surplus may represent reinvestment to cover higher replacement costs of plants not recouped through depreciation accounting, the value of any earned surplus transfer accompanying a stock dividend should be carefully measured and investigated. In view of the findings reported in this article, a cost-conscious management will try to avoid the extremely small-size stock dividends and particularly the so-called multiple issue type of dividend involving two, three, or four issues annually. Where it is desirable to bring the common stock into a more popular price range, management may find it economically preferable to issue infrequent, larger-size stock dividends or, particularly if earned surplus is insufficient for that purpose, to undertake a stock split-up.

The final decision should be made in full recognition of the fact that the stock's competitive cash-dividend–paying power, as contrasted with general market dividend action, is the fundamental determining factor in achieving a real price gain. This is a basic economic fact of life, equally operative for a stock dividend or a stock split-up under whatever market conditions may prevail at the moment—bull, bear, or "normal."

STUDY OF
PETROLEUM PRICES*

When petroleum prices—first for crude oil, later for products—were increased recently, there was loud public protest. Many people were quick to charge that the oil industry was "gouging" the public.

Fortunately the presentation of the facts has done much to answer these charges in some circles. *Time* magazine in its issue of February 25 reported: "As the U.S. Senate stepped up its oil hearings last week, almost everyone had the industry pegged as the villain in the case. . . . But the hearings were hardly under way before the character of the villain underwent an amazing transformation: He began to look almost like a hero."

What testimony at those first hearings developed—and what later testimony clinched—was proof of two facts:

1. That the oil industry by a massive voluntary effort had more than adequately met free Europe's needs after the closing of the Suez canal.

2. That the increases in U.S. prices for both crude and products were entirely justified.

Unfortunately, however, much of the proof of the second point has stayed in the bulky transcript of the Washington hearings. It has not been given nearly the public notice that was given to earlier sensational accusations against the industry.

Standard Oil has been preparing to add the story of its own firsthand experiences with the necessities of pricing to the testimony before Congress. Although the additional testimony is not needed now in Washington, we believe the story as we know it should be brought to the public. So it is that we offer from our experience this documentation of the following facts:

As to Crude Oil Prices

1. The crude price increase in January of this year was the first such increase since June, 1953. The 1957 increase in price of 25¢ per barrel, or roughly 9%, must be compared with increases in costs of labor and materials since 1953 ranging from 15 to 40%.

* By Standard Oil Company (Indiana). Reproduced from original study of March 25, 1957. Used by permission.

2. Crude prices have been kept down, despite increased costs, due to the pressure of (a) domestic reserve producing capacity and (b) imports of low-cost foreign oil.

3. The impact of the Suez crisis on Europe shows how fortunate we are in not being overly dependent on foreign oil and having a self-sufficient petroleum industry in the United States, adequate to take care of our own needs, now and in the foreseeable future.

4. With oil hard to find in this country and costs continually increasing, crude prices must reflect the increasing costs. Otherwise, the incentive to search for oil in this country will disappear, threatening our assurance of future adequate supplies.

5. More than one-third of the crude oil produced in the United States is produced by some 12,000 independent producers. Testimony of independent producers has abundantly demonstrated to the Congressional committees that the last price increase was inadequate to take care of increased costs. The labor, material and other costs of the independent producer do not differ materially from those of an integrated producer; if the crude price is inadequate for the independent producer, the same is necessarily true with respect to the crude production operations of the integrated company.

6. The initial crude price increase announcement of January 3, 1957, was made by a competitor, and a number of other producers and purchasers had increased their prices before Standard Oil Company's purchasing subsidiary acted. We had to increase our prices if we were to continue to obtain sufficient supplies to meet our requirements. Our price increases, made on January 8, in most areas amounted to 25¢ a barrel, or 10¢ lower than increases previously announced for the same areas by other oil companies.

As to Petroleum Products Prices

1. Gasoline prices have been uniformly depressed for several years and still are.

2. Competition in the marketing of gasoline has been so intense that, more often than not, gasoline prices have resisted the upward trend in prices of most other commodities. In the face of annual wage increases, constantly increasing material costs, and also of costly quality improvements, gasoline prices were lower in 1956 than at the time of the last crude price increase in 1953. Since 1950, gasoline prices have risen somewhat but have lagged behind other commodity prices.

3. Taking into account the improved quality of gasoline, prices today are actually lower than in 1953. For example, our Company's RED CROWN, or regular, gasoline of today is superior in quality to our premium WHITE CROWN gasoline of 1953. Nevertheless, we sell our RED CROWN to dealers in Chicago today at ½¢ less than we sold our premium WHITE CROWN in 1953.

4. Even though stocks of gasoline are somewhat high, the crude oil price increase had to be reflected, in part at least, in product prices, in view of the low level of refining profits.

As to Oil Company Profits

1. Profits of companies engaged in the refining phase of the business were lower in 1955 (latest year for which published data are available) than they were in 1951. In 1955 their profits before taxes averaged only 33¢ per barrel of crude processed. If these refiners had to absorb a 25¢ per barrel increase, this would nearly wipe out their profits.
2. Profits in the petroleum industry are not high. They may seem high because of the millions of dollars involved. But oil company earnings are not high in relation to the enormous amounts of capital invested. Return on investment of oil companies from domestic operations has been constantly below the average for manufacturing industries generally and very substantially below other major industries in the United States. In 1955 the rate of return of major oil companies from domestic operations amounted to 9.8% compared to the average for all manufacturing industries of 12.55%. Returns of other key industries averaged from 13.5 to 21.7%.
3. Earnings of the oil industry have been inadequate in relation to the increasing sums required to be added to investment each year.

What follows will elaborate on and document the foregoing facts.

CRUDE OIL PRICE

Standard Oil Company (Indiana) is a net purchaser of crude oil. We buy more than half of the crude oil we process in our refineries. The price we pay for crude must be such as to assure an adequate supply to meet our requirements and those of other refiners who buy from us.

Our crude oil purchasing subsidiary increased the prices it pays for crude oil on January 8 of this year. We did not initiate the price increase. We took action five days after the first raise was announced, and after a number of other companies had announced increases. Our increases were, for the most part, less than those previously announced by many of our competitors. We had to increase our prices if we were to continue to obtain adequate supplies of crude oil.

Actually a crude oil price increase was long overdue. There had been no general price increase since 1953. Meanwhile, costs of exploration and production had been mounting and producers were complaining that crude prices were inadequate to overcome these cost increases. But economic conditions in the industry prevented any increase prior to this year.

Let us first develop the facts as to the cost increases affecting producers and then turn to the factors which prevented the cost increases from being reflected in prices: (1) reserve producing capacity in this country and (2) the pressure of low-cost foreign oil.

Rising costs since 1953 crude price increase. In 1953, the average cost of drilling a well of our company's principal producing subsidiary, Pan American Petroleum Corporation, was $76,888. In 1956, Pan American's average cost of a well was $100,957, or *$24,069 more for each well drilled* than in 1953. That is a 31.3% rise in cost in just three years.

In part, the higher per-well cost is attributable to greater drilling depths. We are drilling deeper wells these days, for the simple reason that most of the shallow, easy-to-find production has already been developed. During the period that we are considering, for example, the average depth of Pan American's wells has increased from 5,327 feet in 1953 to 6,877 in 1956, or 1,550 feet per well.

These data represent the experience of one company alone but they are unquestionably typical of experience in the industry generally. Frequent and substantial increases in costs of essential materials and wages also affected all producers alike.

Oil country tubular goods have increased in price on seven occasions since June 15, 1953. One kind of pipe, 9⅝-inch oil well casing, which sold for $370.36 per 100 feet in May, 1953, now sells for $516.26, an increase of $145.90, or 39%. Increases on other kinds of pipe have ranged from 25 to over 40%.

Christmas trees—wellhead production control equipment—that sold for $1,580 each in 1954 now cost $1,990, up 26%.

Pumping units that in 1953 cost $3,133.20, now cost $4,098.29, up 30.8%. Structural steel is up 27.6% since June, 1953.

Average hourly earnings of crude oil and gas production workers are up 14.7% since June of 1953.

These are only selected items. A more complete story is appended as Exhibits A, A–2, and A–3.

There is the further fact that oil is getting harder to find in the United States. We are not running out of oil by any means and we will not run out of oil in the foreseeable future. But it is requiring a more intensified effort to find oil these days. One illustration of the greater risks involved is the story of Pan American's efforts in the Williston Basin, located in the Dakotas and Montana, which many believe holds great promise as a major source of crude reserves.

From 1948 through 1956, Pan American had spent $47.4 million in the Williston Basin, searching for oil. Its revenue from production in the same period was only $1.1 million. Of the 113 wells it either drilled or was interested in, 12 were producers, 101 were dry holes.

It is obvious that oil producers have been subject to rising costs and substantially increased capital requirements just as has everyone else. With oil harder to find and costs and capital needs increased, crude prices must reflect these factors or the incentive to search for oil in this country will disappear.

The recent increase in crude oil prices amounted to a modest 8.9% compared with increasing costs of goods and services ranging from 14.7

to 40%. That prices have not increased heretofore is partly a tribute to increased efficiency in the industry but also the result of such external forces as reserve producing capacity and inventories and low-cost foreign oil.

Reserve domestic producing capacity. Our domestic reserve producing capacity, which affords protection to our country against an emergency, necessarily tends to depress crude prices.

That the domestic oil industry is carrying a very substantial reserve producing capacity over and above current demands for domestic oil is well known. It has done so for a number of years, to the great satisfaction of the military and other federal government officials. The Suez crisis dramatizes the security that we enjoy in this country from having an assured domestic supply which can be expanded in an emergency.

Of course, this reserve production is not such that it can be turned on and off overnight and brought instantly to the point of consumption. To accomplish the latter would require in addition a reserve capacity of pipe lines and tankers, particularly if we are to assume the responsibility of taking care of Europe's emergencies as well as our own. The industry cannot be expected to maintain that amount of standby tanker and pipe line capacity.

Fortunately transportation capacity can be added to in a reasonably short time—but productive capacity is something that takes time to develop. It takes many years to develop a producing area even after oil has been discovered and drilling has commenced. Reserves must be built up long in advance of any emergency.

If it is a wise policy for this country to have an adequate reserve producing capacity, then the cost must be reflected in crude prices. If the industry is to continue to raise sufficient capital to maintain an adequate reserve of production, it must charge enough for what it does produce to cover the cost of maintaining the reserve. Oil companies cannot continue to procure adequate funds to overcome the increasing difficulty and ever-increasing costs of providing oil reserves at a rate of return on investment which, as will appear later, has been going down year after year and consistently averages less than the average rate of return of manufacturing industries generally in the United States.

It is commonly overlooked that current profits are derived from production that was developed years ago at substantially lower costs. The oil industry could discontinue its exploration and drilling programs and just go ahead producing from existing oil fields. We would thereby improve our return on investment. Before long, however, our reserve of production would disappear, demand would outstrip productive capacity, and oil would be in short supply. Prices for petroleum products would swing upwards until such time as exploration and drilling programs were resumed and adequate supplies were again developed.

It should be noted that the petroleum industry is a growing, dynamic industry. Domestic demand for petroleum products has increased at an average rate of 5.8% per year since 1933. All projections indicate that demand will continue to increase in the future. The industry now must find about four billion barrels of oil each year simply to maintain the present relationship between reserves and projected demand.

The industry until now has supplied all the oil that has been needed, in spite of the hue and cry raised periodically that we are running out of oil. A policy on the part of Congressional committees or executive departments of discouraging price increases needed to offset increasing costs, or trying to roll back prices, would prevent the development of essential crude supplies.

During World War II, as a result of price and other governmental controls, there was a marked slowdown of exploration and drilling. When the war was over, reserve producing capacity was inadequate to take care of the sharply increased customers' needs. During the abnormally cold winter of 1947–1948, the inability of the industry to supply the nation's requirements was a matter of considerable concern in Washington. Despite a series of price increases during the year 1947, in the short time available it was not possible for the industry to overcome the shortage in productive capacity which resulted from the government controls of the war period.

Low-cost foreign oil. Foreign oil is the other factor previously mentioned as having acted as a depressing force on domestic crude prices.

The average production from a well in Kuwait, for example, is about 6,000 barrels daily. Average production from wells in the United States is 12 to 13 barrels per day. Apart from differences in labor rates, production costs in the Middle East are substantially below those in this country. But few people in this country today could be persuaded to risk the security of this country by relying to any undue extent on the foreign supply of oil, no matter how less costly. An oil shortage in war time would be even more serious than a peace time shortage caused by a blocked Suez canal.

It is nonetheless true that we have been importing increasing amounts of foreign oil since the end of World War II. From the end of the war to 1956, oil imports increased five-fold and reached 16% of total domestic demand.

With foreign oil increasingly supplanting domestic production, this exerted a downward pressure on domestic crude prices regardless of increasing costs of finding and developing oil in this country. The Suez developments eliminated this downward pressure, leaving the price of domestic oil free to seek a level more nearly consistent with the higher costs that the domestic industry had been facing since the last crude price increase in 1953.

Representatives of independent producers engaged exclusively in the production phase of the oil industry have convincingly demonstrated that the recent small increase in price was hardly adequate.

There are upwards of 12,000 independent crude producers in this country. As a group they account for more than one-third of our crude oil production.

The record before the Congressional committees leaves no doubt that this important segment of the industry had to have the last crude price increase as a very minimum. Crude prices cannot be increased for one segment of the industry only. It is erroneous to assume that the integrated oil companies can absorb increased production costs and make up the deficiency in other branches of their business. Crude production must stand on its own feet and crude prices of all producers must reflect costs that affect all producers alike.

Standard's part in last crude increase. The initial crude price increase announcement was made by a competitor of ours on January 3. Their increases generally ranged from 32 to 45¢ per barrel for most Gulf Coast fields and 35¢ in East Texas and 25¢ in East Central Texas, West Texas, West Central Texas and the Texas Panhandle.

Our crude purchasing subsidiary, Indiana Oil Purchasing Company (formerly Standolind Oil Purchasing Company), being in direct competition for supply with the first company to increase prices, had to give prompt consideration to raising its own prices. This was necessary if it was to continue to obtain sufficient supplies to meet its requirements.

By the time Indiana arrived at its decision, a number of other companies had announced increases. Indiana's increases, effective January 8, met the previous increases of 45¢ on the Gulf Coast and 35¢ in East Texas, but were limited to 25¢ in the principal areas serving the Middle West, namely, West Texas, West Central Texas, North Texas, New Mexico, Oklahoma, Kansas and Rocky Mountain areas. In each case the price we posted was designed to assure us of needed supply.

Indiana's price increase of 25¢ in West Texas, Mid-Continent and Rocky Mountain areas was generally 10¢ lower than increases previously announced by other oil companies. Increases of 35¢ per barrel initially posted by others in these areas were subsequently dropped back to the 25¢ basis announced by our purchasing subsidiary.

Exhibit B, appended, details chronologically the principal crude oil price changes announced from January 3 through January 16.

PRODUCT PRICES

So far as gasoline prices are concerned, without question they have been substantially depressed for several years.

In discussing gasoline prices the retail price should first be broken down into its component parts. A typical retail price today for regular grade gasoline in Chicago is 31.9¢. This price includes direct state, local and federal taxes of 8.8¢. What the motorist pays for the gasoline is only 23.1¢. Of this amount about 6¢ goes to pay the expenses of the service station operator and give him a fair profit. The typical jobber or wholesaler operates on a gross margin of about 3.25¢. There is a transportation cost of about one-half cent to move gasoline from the local refinery to the jobber's bulk plant. The refinery price of around 13¢ a gallon is considerably less than half of the price which the motorist pays at the pump.

Dealer tank wagon prices (ex. tax) of Standard Red Crown

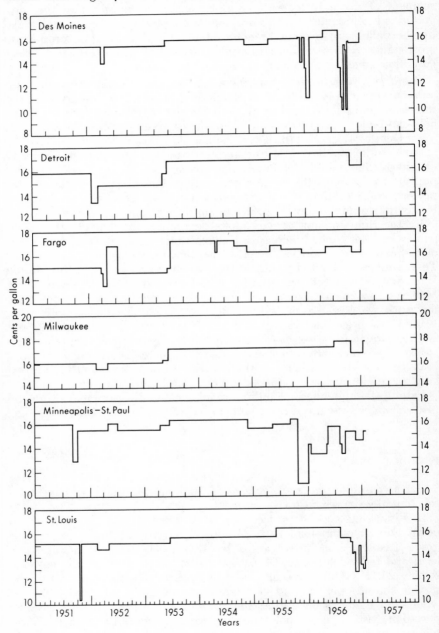

Intensity of competition. Gasoline prices are subject to most intense competition. Consequently, more often than not, gasoline prices have resisted the persistent upward trend of prices of most other commodities. Ironically enough, the widespread gasoline price cutting of the last several years attracted the attention of committees of the Congress on numerous occasions. Members of Congress were concerned that the severe price competition was hurting some sellers.

The intensity of competition in our industry is exemplified by the accompanying graphs of tank wagon prices, showing the movement of our prices to dealers in a number of typical cities in our parent company's marketing territory. It will be observed that the price movements vary materially among the cities on the basis of local competitive conditions, and the fluctuations are frequently somewhat violent.

Of exceptional significance is the fact that in all these cities, even after the recent increase, the price is no higher, and in some instances is lower, than it was at some time in the past.

Just last fall while prices of commodities in general were going up, our company was compelled by competition to reduce its wholesale prices throughout the Midwest in amounts up to 1¢ a gallon. Regrettably, these price cuts did not receive nearly the attention received by the subsequent price increases comparable in amount. These decreases just last fall were hardly noticed by the public or the press and we do not recall that they received any attention at all in Washington.

Over-all in the face of annual wage increases and constantly increasing material costs, and also of costly quality improvements, prior to 1956 gasoline prices had actually gone down, since the last crude price rise in 1953, to the levels of 1951 and 1952. The 1956 level was still below the level of 1953. This is shown by the United States Bureau of Labor Statistics Wholesale Price Index for gasoline (1947–49 = 100), as follows:

1951	114.9
1952	114.6
1953	120.4
1954	114.8
1955	114.6
1956 (11 months)	118.0

Going back to the pre-Korea year of 1950, and leaving aside quality improvements, gasoline prices have risen somewhat but have lagged behind other commodity prices, as shown in the accompanying chart. This chart shows that gasoline prices have increased only by 8% from 1950 to 1956 while the United States Bureau of Labor Statistics Wholesale Price Index for all commodities except farm and food products has increased 16.2%.

Taking improved quality into account, gasoline prices are actually lower today than they were in 1953. This is despite the two increases in crude prices, the one in 1953 and the recent one this year. Thus, our

Wholesale Price Index (ex. farm and foods) vs. Whole-
sale Gasoline Price Index   SOURCE: *Bureau of Labor
statistics.*

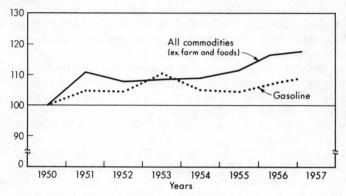

regular brand, RED CROWN, gasoline in Chicago today has a higher
octane (anti-knock) rating and is otherwise superior in quality to what
our WHITE CROWN, or premium gasoline, was in 1953. Yet our RED
CROWN price to dealers today is only 17.3¢, or 0.5¢ less than our
WHITE CROWN price was in 1953.

It is interesting to compare the level of gasoline prices with the level
of wages earned by the average working man. The following table shows
that in 1950, an hour's earnings of an average worker would purchase
about 7¼ gallons of gasoline. By 1955 an average hour's wages would
buy nearly 9 gallons of gasoline, and preliminary figures for 1956 indicate
that this latter figure is now in excess of 9 gallons. An average hour's
wage would buy more than twice as much gasoline in 1956 as in 1938.

*Gallons of gasoline purchas-
able with hour's earnings*

	Actual	*Index*
1938	4.456	100.0
1939	4.756	106.7
1940	5.184	116.3
1941	5.481	123.0
1950	7.271	163.2
1955	8.777	197.0
*1956**	9.135	205.0

* Preliminary figures.
SOURCE: 50 Cities Gasoline Price
Series; United States Bureau of
Labor Statistics.

It is worth repeating that the gasoline purchased in 1956 was a far better, greatly improved and much more costly product.

By way of contrast: The average hourly wage in 1938 would buy just a little less than a fifth of a pair of shoes—0.1997. In 1956 the average hourly wage would buy just a little more than a fifth of a pair—0.2275.

Wage and other cost increases. Since 1950, as shown in the following table, petroleum refining wages increased from an hourly average of $1.93 in 1950 to $2.69 in 1956, or 39.4%.

Wages in petroleum refining, 1950–56

Year	Average hourly wage	Index
1950	$1.93	100.0
1951	2.08	107.8
1952	2.20	114.0
1953	2.32	120.2
1954	2.37	122.8
1955	2.46	127.5
1956*	2.69	139.4

* As of September–October, 1956.
SOURCE: United States Bureau of Labor Statistics.

The statement below makes a comparison of petroleum product price changes from 1950 to 1956 with increases in costs of material and equipment during the same period. Whether the comparison is with iron and steel products, nonferrous metals, or electrical machinery and equipment, petroleum and its products have gone up the least:

Price indexes of important materials and products

Year	Iron & steel products	Nonferrous metals	Electrical machinery & eq.	Petroleum & products
1950	100.0	100.0	100.0	100.0
1951	108.9	119.3	114.6	106.6
1952	110.3	118.6	113.1	105.4
1953	116.1	120.2	116.3	108.7
1954	117.5	119.3	118.6	106.8
1955	124.3	137.1	120.5	108.8
1956*	143.6	143.8	135.1	113.3

* Data for November, 1956.
SOURCE: United States Bureau of Labor Statistics.

Quality improvements. Even more significant in the cost of producing gasoline than the increased costs of wages and materials is the factor of gasoline quality improvement. Constant increases in the compression ratios of automobiles in recent years have stimulated a competitive race among refiners to improve the anti-knock quality of their gasolines. There have also been many other costly quality improvements. We estimate that our company's capital expenditures for Ultraformer equipment alone, required to keep our product quality at top levels, will soon have amounted to more than $60 million. Operating costs for octane improvements in 1955 and 1956 cost us about $25 million each year.

Actually what has saved the refiners from disaster during the past several years of very intense competition has been the fortunate growth in demand, and resulting improvement in prices of some petroleum products other than gasoline. The demand for middle distillates (home heating fuels, diesel fuels, kerosene, etc.) has increased tremendously since World War II. A few examples illustrate this rise:

Increased demand—distillates, 1946–55

Railroads	up 382%
Heating oils	up 136%
Industrial use	up 105%
All distillates	up 140%

In order for the oil industry to meet this vast increase in demand, it was necessary that refining operations adapt to a sharp shift in yields. In other words, as distillates were increasing in demand, their prices rose to call forth the needed supply. Even so, the price in Chicago, for example, has increased less than 15% in the last eight years, from 14.9 to 17.1¢ per gallon.

The case for residual fuel oil or bunker fuel is somewhat different. At times in the past it has gone begging for a market and refiners reduced yields as much as possible. Prices fell off sharply in early 1952 and it was not until the close of the mild recession in 1954 and the upswing of industrial activity in 1955 that residual prices recovered to the 1951 level. Although the price of residual has continued upward as a result of the high level of industrial demand, there is as yet no evidence that refiners find its production sufficiently profitable to cause them to produce proportionately more residual than they have in the past.

Gasoline stocks. There has been a great deal of publicity about the quantities of gasoline currently in storage. The question has been raised—and we do not say that it is not a proper question—as to how a price increase can be reconciled with an excess of supply of petroleum products.

First, we should like to point out that the statistical picture has been somewhat overstated. It is not appreciated by many that a substantial part of the gasoline stocks that are reported represent stocks in transit from refinery to consumption point and that these are essential to steady supply. Our pipe lines have to be kept full at all times just as an operating matter. And we have to have a certain amount of stored products in all our terminals and bulk plants. Furthermore, it is the usual practice to build up stocks of gasoline during the winter months to meet the requirements of motorists and farmers for the succeeding spring and summer seasons. Also, as consumption increases year by year these winter stocks are bound to increase in quantity.

Currently there is only about a month's normal supply of gasoline available in inventory for motorists' use.

Nevertheless, it is a fact that current stocks are excessive, more so along the coast than inland. As indicated, these excessive stocks have tended to depress prices. But even in a situation of oversupply, where prices are substantially depressed to begin with and where refinery margins have been cut to the bone, it is too much to expect that a crude oil price increase would not have some effect on product prices.

The experience during 1953 to 1955, when gasoline prices actually went down following the crude price increase in 1953, demonstrates that in the final analysis the level of gasoline prices is determined by the forces of competition.

Oil industry profits. The question will be raised as to how the data that we have presented can be reconciled with the alleged high profits earned in the petroleum industry. But the truth is that profits from the *domestic* petroleum industry have not been high. They have been inadequate to supply the amounts of capital required to replace the crude oil that is being consumed and the facilities that are being worn out and to make provision for the increased requirements of the future.

A proper measure of profits is the return on capital invested and not the millions of dollars involved. The greater the capital requirements in an industry, the greater must be the dollar profits, or else the necessary capital will not be forthcoming. Basically, it is because of the enormous amounts of capital invested that the profits of the oil industry reach the dollar amounts that they do. Authoritative data, however, indicate that the average return on investment for the domestic petroleum industry has remained at or below the average for all manufacturing industries.

It will be noted that we refer to the domestic petroleum industry. We exclude the foreign operations of companies with large interests abroad. Returns from such foreign operations are necessarily substantially higher in view of the substantially greater risks involved.

What we are concerned with is the cost of maintaining a self-sufficient domestic oil industry in the United States. On this basis what is important is the return earned on domestic operations.

In 1954 the average net return on stockholder investment for all manufacturing in the United States, as reported by the Securities and Exchange Commission, was 9.8%. The average return for 35 leading oil companies from domestic operations was 9.34%. This, it should be noted, was after giving effect to percentage depletion on the income from production. Our own company's consolidated return on investment was only 7.44% in 1954. The SEC data indicate rates of return on invested capital in 1954 ranging from 10.5% for the rubber industry, to 11.4% for chemicals, 12.2% for electrical machinery, 13.9% for motor vehicles and parts, and 15.8% for transportation equipment.

Similarly for 1955, while the rate of return *from domestic operations* of the same leading oil companies increased only slightly to 9.85%, the average for all manufacturing jumped to 12.55%. Our own company came out somewhat closer to the average for other domestic oil companies than the year before, with a return of 9.23%.

The return from domestic oil operations in 1955 was substantially below the average of all manufacturing, and the petroleum industry's showing was particularly poor in comparison with the industries previously mentioned, whose returns ranged from 13.5 up to 21.7%. Comparable data for the year 1956 are not yet available. We are certain that the situation has not changed materially.

Not only have the returns from domestic operations in the petroleum industry been below average in relation to the capital invested, but they have been inadequate in relation to the amounts of additional capital required to be invested from year to year.

Each year capital expenditures in the domestic petroleum industry have substantially exceeded cash available, and the industry has had to resort to borrowings or sales of stock.

The statement which follows shows that cash income from all sources, including depreciation, depletion and retained income after dividends, fell short of capital expenditures during the period 1951–1955 by nearly $4 billion.

Estimated cash income and disposition of the United States petroleum industry, years 1951–55
(Millions of dollars)

Year	Cash income from operations	Dividends paid to owners	Retained cash income	Capital expenditures	Funds required externally
1951	$ 4,373	$ 875	$ 3,498	$ 3,625	$ 127
1952	4,536	907	3,629	4,400	771
1953	5,149	1,030	4,119	5,025	906
1954	5,335	1,067	4,268	5,350	1,082
1955	5,907	1,181	4,726	5,600	874
Total	$25,300	$5,060	$20,240	$24,000	$3,760

SOURCE: "Future Growth and Financial Requirements of the World Petroleum Industry" by Pogue & Hill, Chase Manhattan Bank, Petroleum Department, Feb. 21, 1956, p. 32. Also see below for estimated future capital requirements.

It is estimated that this need for outside capital will amount to another $5 billion during the next five years. According to the authoritative Petroleum Department of the Chase Manhattan Bank, ". . . the conclusion is indicated that the United States petroleum industry is operating at a cash deficit; that is to say, the amount of capital formation is inadequate and the prevailing price structure is subnormal in these terms."

The following analysis of the financial reports for the years 1950–1955 of companies engaged primarily in the refining phase of the industry indicates how narrow the margin of profit in refining is and why the recent crude price increase cannot be absorbed by the refiners. Their profits before taxes per barrel of crude processed were essentially the same in 1955 as in 1950 and substantially lower in 1955 than in 1951. Incidentally, the profits for 1955, the latest year for which published reports are available, averaged 33¢ per barrel, not nearly enough to enable these refiners to absorb a 25¢ per barrel crude price increase:

Average refiner margins,
based on profits before taxes
and annual crude runs to stills,
1950–55

Year	Margin/bbl
1950	32¢
1951	43¢
1952	30¢
1953	24¢
1954	29¢
1955	33¢
Average	32¢

SOURCE: *The Oil Record, Moody's Industrials,* National Scouts & Landsmen's Association Reports & Company Annual Reports. The following companies, essentially non-integrated refiners, are included: Ashland Oil & Refining Co., Delhi-Taylor Oil Co., Crown Central Petroleum Co., Cosden Petroleum Co., Frontier Refining Co., Leonard Refineries, Mid-West Refineries, Roosevelt Oil & Refining Co., Bareco Oil Co.

SUMMARY AND CONCLUSION

We in the industry object strenuously to statements that have been made about price gouging and about price rollbacks.

In the very best traditions of our free enterprise system our industry has discovered and developed, within our own borders, a supply of crude oil ample to meet our ever-increasing needs, with reserves sufficient to protect our country in any emergency. The state conservation laws and conservation commissions have contributed greatly. Crude prices and product prices are actually low.

The return on investment in the domestic oil industry has been below the average of manufacturing industries generally. If it were not for percentage depletion on the income from production, this return on investment would be a great deal lower.

Competition, always keen in our industry, has been exceptionally sharp in recent years. In fact, competition has caused intensive price-cutting and depressed prices even in the face of inflationary cost increases and increasing costs of improving the quality of our products. With this kind of competition, which has brought about reduced gasoline prices after raw material costs have gone up, as happened in 1954 and 1955 following the 1953 crude price increase, the consumers' interest is completely safeguarded.

*Exhibit A. Price changes per 100 feet—oil country tubular goods**

			Price list no. in effect				Increase since 5–16–53	
			35	37	39	42	Dollars per	Per
Size	Wt. per foot	Grade	5–16–53	5–20–54	7–6–55	2–9–57	100 feet	cent
5½″	14#	H–40	$106.74	$111.52	$122.85	$139.41	$ 32.67	30.6
7″	20#	H–40	148.26	155.08	171.27	192.47	44.21	29.8
8⅝″	32#	H–40	231.25	242.17	268.07	298.88	67.63	29.2
9⅝″	32.3#	H–40	239.57	250.59	276.74	307.85	68.28	28.5
10¾″	32.75#	H–40	244.81	256.02	282.52	314.06	69.22	28.3
13⅜″	48#	H–40	391.61	407.99	446.83	493.05	101.44	25.9
5½″	17#	N–80	146.67	157.76	174.91	208.42	61.75	42.1
7″	23#	N–80	196.79	211.80	234.94	276.85	80.06	40.7
9⅝″	43.5#	N–80	370.36	398.75	442.46	516.26	145.90	39.4

* Prices are f.o.b. McKeesport, Pennsylvania.

Exhibit A–2. Christmas trees: standard well head hook-up*

Date	Series 600†			Series 1500		
	Cost, $	Annual incremental increase, $	Annual incremental increase, %	Cost, $	Annual incremental increase, $	Annual incremental increase, %
June, 1953	1,580.00	...	...	4,576.00	...	...
June, 1954	1,580.00	0	0	4,576.00	0	0
June, 1955	1,606.00	26.00	1.6	4,626.00	50.00	1.1
June, 1956	1,753.00	147.00	9.2	4,869.00	243.00	5.2
January, 1957	1,990.00	237.00	13.5	5,599.00	730.00	15.0
Total increase from June, 1953, to present	$410.00 or 26%			$1,023.00 or 22.4%		

* Prices are f.o.b. Fort Worth, Texas.
† Estimate 50% of Christmas trees purchased are 600 Series.

Exhibit A–3. Pumping units: API Class 114,000 inch-pound torque rating pumping unit*

Data	Cost, $	Annual incremental increase, $	Annual incremental increase, %
June, 1953	3,133.20	...	...
June, 1954	3,176.72	43.52	1.4
June, 1955	3,289.94	113.22	3.6
June, 1956	3,753.16	463.22	14.1
January, 1957	4,098.29	345.13	9.2

* Total increase from June, 1953, to present: $965.09 or 30.8%.
Prices are f.o.b. Lufkin, Texas.

Exhibit B. Significant crude price changes—January 3–16, 1957; approximate changes in major producing areas

Date announced	Company	West Texas– New Mexico	West Central Texas	North Texas	Texas Gulf Coast	East Texas
January 3	Humble	25(a)	25		40–45	35
January 3	Continental	35(b)	35	35		
January 5	Continental					
January 7	D–X Sunray					
January 7	Phillips	35			35	
January 7	Texas Co.	35	35	35	37–45	35
January 7	Esso					
January 7	Carter					
January 8	Stanolind Oil Purch. Co. (d)	25	25	25	35–45	35
January 8	Sinclair	25	25	25	35–40	35
January 8	Cities Service	25	25			35
January 8	Sohio					35
January 8	Magnolia	25	25	25	40–45	35
January 8	Gulf	30		30	30–55	35
January 8	Sun	35			40–45	35
January 8	Ohio					35
January 9	Pure	25	25	25	35–45	
January 9	Phillips	−10				
January 9	D–X Sunray					
January 9	Atlantic	25			35–40	35
January 9	Ashland	25			35–45	35
January 10	Mobil					
January 10–13	Shell, Tidewater, and several others posted increases which generally were the same as those of Indiana, Sinclair, etc. Carter, Magnolia, Texas Company, and others made 10¢/B reductions similar to those of Phillips (January 9).					
January 16	Continental	−5(f)	−10			

(a) West Texas only.
(b) New Mexico only.
(c) Lesser increases for heavier crudes.
(d) Now Indiana Oil Purchasing Company.
(e) Still paying 15¢/B less than competitors for Kansas crude.
(f) New Mexico only. Net increase now 30¢/B.

Texas Panhandle	Oklahoma	Kansas	Louisiana Gulf Coast	North Louisiana–Arkansas	Rocky Mt. Sweet Crude	Rocky Mt. Sour Crude
25						
	35	35	40		35	35(c)
	35					
29	35	25			35	
25	35	35	40			
			40	30		
	35	35			35	35
	25	25	40	30	25	23(c)
	25	25			25	23(c)
	25	25	40			
	25	25(e)				
25						
	25		40			
			40			
				30	25	23(a)
	25	25	40		25	
−10	−10				−10	
	−10					
			40			
				35		
		25			25	23(c)
	−10	−10			−10	−12

OVERTIME HOURS
AS AN ECONOMIC
INDICATOR*

The availability of data on overtime hours, in a new series recently released by the U.S. Department of Labor's Bureau of Labor Statistics,
is of major significance for economic analysis. Much of the interest in
this new series[1] lies in its applications to the study of business cycles.
Monthly data on the volume of overtime hours and overtime as a proportion of average man-hours will contribute greatly to knowledge of
cyclical variations in earnings and income flows. For example, in the
spring of 1956 an estimated 10 per cent of factory production worker
pay was compensation, at premium rates, for overtime work. Further,
a drop of 1 hour in the average amount of overtime work each week
would have represented an estimated direct income loss of about $2 bil-
lion at annual rates.

These data on overtime will also provide valuable information on cyclical changes in labor costs in various industries which will help explain
divergent reactions among firms to changing labor market conditions.
For example, changes, or lack of change, in plant wage structures during
periods of expansion may be partially explained by the fact that one
firm offers overtime work at premium pay, while another increases wage
rates.

Possibly the greatest interest in the new series lies in its use as an
indicator of cyclical change. Examination of the behavior of the individual firm under varying conditions of market demand supports the
view that the overtime hours series should be one of the most sensitive
economic indicators. But firms react differently, and the series measures
the aggregate effect of the reactions of many firms in many industries.
The purpose of this article is to explore the effects of aggregation on
sensitivity of the series, as compared with that of other indicators.

For the new BLS overtime series, the basic concept of overtime man-
hours is hours worked by manufacturing production workers for which

* By Abraham Bluestone. Reprinted from the Monthly Labor Review, September,
1956, pp. 1024–1028.
NOTE: The author wishes to acknowledge his indebtedness to Gerson B. Kramer
for assistance in compiling many of the basic data and in making preliminary analysis.
[1] In January 1956, the BLS expanded its monthly survey of employment, hours,
and earnings of manufacturing production workers to include information on overtime
hours. The new series is comparable with the regularly published production-worker
employment, hours, and earnings series. For description of the scope and methodology of those series, see Techniques of Preparing Major BLS Statistical Series,
BLS Bull. 1168, 1954 (pp. 42–56).

premiums are paid. The premium concept applies to hours beyond the scheduled workday or workweek and therefore excludes such types of premium as shift differentials and incentive bonuses. The concept covers only hours worked at a rate higher than straight time and thus includes premium hours worked even when the weekly total is below 40. This may occur in industries where the normal workweek is under 40 hours (such as printing or apparel) or where employment falls under the provisions of the Walsh-Healey Public Contracts Act of 1936, which requires (on work done under Federal Government contract) the payment of premium rates when more than 8 hours are worked on any 1 day, regardless of the weekly total. On the other hand, hours paid for at double time for holidays actually worked when straight time is paid for holidays not worked is not within the concept. Also excluded are hours worked beyond the normal workweek which are not compensated at premium rates. This may occur in manufacturing under exemptions granted under the Fair Labor Standards Act.[2]

OVERTIME IN THE FIRM—A HYPOTHETICAL MODEL

When changes in demand, or anticipated demand, require changes in labor inputs, the firm may react in a number of ways. In the long run, it may substitute capital for labor, reorganize its production methods, break down its jobs, etc. In the short run, however, changing hours of work offers certain advantages to management, and such a line of action often is a firm's first response to changes in demand—actual or anticipated.[3] First, if the firm is not certain that the new conditions of demand will persist, increasing or decreasing hours of work offers a flexible method of adjusting labor inputs which—on the downswing—minimizes the disruption of a trained work force and the creation of morale problems, and—on the upswing—avoids the expense and difficulties of recruiting and training new workers. Secondly, changing hours of work is probably the fastest way of changing labor inputs. Another advantage of increasing hours of work rather than hiring additional workers is that it partially prevents the dilution of a scarce resource—trained supervisory and administrative personnel. Furthermore, in tight labor markets, overtime at premium pay may be an inducement in recruiting additional workers and preventing the loss of present staff. Or, in such circumstances, longer hours may be the only alternative to hiring less desirable, untrained workers.

On the other hand, overtime work typically involves the payment of premium wage rates and may in many instances create excessive pressures on manpower or, if maintenance schedules are affected, plant and

---

[2] See Annual Report of the Wage and Hour and Public Contracts Divisions, U.S. Department of Labor, 1954 (pp. 32–44).
[3] Changes of hours of work in this context obviously exclude those due to changes in the institutional framework, such as new legislation or union contracts.

equipment.[4] Either or both circumstances may result in higher unit costs and affect the firm's competitive position.

For these reasons, average hours of work have generally been regarded as a sensitive economic indicator—an evaluation which is substantially supported by analysis of cyclical changes in hours of work.[5] It is felt that the new series on overtime hours should be an even more valuable tool of analysis.

There are three main arguments in support of this contention. First, since overtime hours generally must be paid for at premium rates, increases in the volume of overtime may reflect significant changes in the firm's evaluation of its economic situation. Conversely, since overtime may result in high unit costs, any slackening of demand may cause firms with a large volume of overtime to cut overtime sharply in order to eliminate the most expensive units of labor input and avoid building up high-cost inventories. Thirdly, the series on overtime, being based on the most volatile component of the hours data, would show greater relative movement than would average weekly hours. For example, if average weekly hours in a plant fall from 42 to 41, the decline in average weekly hours is 2.5 per cent; the drop in overtime (assuming overtime begins at 40 hours) is 50 per cent.

EFFECTS OF AGGREGATION—IN THEORY

The foregoing assessment of the significance of overtime hours as an economic indicator is based on the probable reactions of the individual firm. As data are aggregated, however, the effects of differences in behavior of the individual components must be considered.

The examination of theoretical relationships between overtime hours and average weekly hours which follows is limited to what appear to be the major possibilities. Moreover, it does not consider the behavior of the two series under conditions of deep depression because, in such cycles, overtime would probably disappear as a significant factor at some point in the contraction phase and not reappear until the subsequent period of expansion was well under way. This analysis, then, is confined to those cyclical movements which are not extreme and during which some plants remain on overtime even at the trough, as occurred in 1949 and 1954, while others never reach the overtime level.

Business cycle indicators are of the greatest value if they can assist the analyst in determining when "turning points" will occur or are occurring. The following material emphasizes the behavior of overtime, relative to average weekly hours, at two critical points: the upper turning

[4] See Max D. Kossorls, The Facts About Hours of Work vs. Output (in Factory Management and Maintenance, New York, McGraw-Hill Publishing Co., February 1951).

[5] The National Bureau of Economic Research has classified the average workweek in manufacturing as a "leading" series—i.e., one that more quickly indicates the beginning of cyclical rises or declines than do other economic series. See Geoffrey H. Moore, Statistical Indicators of Cyclical Revivals and Recessions, New York, National Bureau of Economic Research, Inc. (Occasional Paper 31), 1950 (p. 64).

point, when the boom or period of full employment ends and economic activity begins to slide downward; and the lower turning point, when the rate of contraction dwindles and business conditions turn up.

The Lower Turning Point

At the lower turning point, overtime hours may move with average weekly hours, lead, or lag. A lag—where overtime starts moving up after average weekly hours—will occur if the upturn occurs first in those plants working below the standard workweek. To illustrate, assume a series based on two plants of equal size, where premium pay for overtime starts at 40 hours:

	Hours of work			Per cent change	
	May	June	July	May to June	June to July
Plant A	36.0	39.0	40.5		
Plant B	42.0	42.0	42.5		
Average weekly hours	39.0	40.5	41.5	+3.8	+2.5
Overtime hours, total	2.0	2.0	3.0		
Average overtime hours	1.0	1.0	1.5	0	+50.0

Obviously, in manufacturing as a whole, the comparative behavior of the two series depends upon a number of variables: the relative weights of the sectors working short and long hours,[6] the rate of change in average weekly hours, the level of hours when the movement begins, and the extent of overtime. The possibilities at the lower turning point are summarized below:

Lower turning point	Movement of average weekly hours	Comparative movements of overtime and average weekly hours	
		Timing	Per cent change
Hours of work level off	a. Level off in all plants.	Coincident.	Overtime greater.
	b. Rise in plants working long hours, fall or hold steady in plants on short hours.	Overtime leads.	?
	c. Rise in plants working short hours, fall or hold steady in plants on long hours.	Overtime lags.	?
Hours of work rise	a. Rise in all or most plants.	Coincident.	Overtime greater.
	b. Rise in plants working long hours, fall or hold steady in plants on short hours.	Coincident.	Overtime greater.
	c. Rise in plants working short hours, fall or hold steady in plants on long hours.	Overtime lags.	?

[6] Here and in the following tabulations, it is implicitly assumed that all sectors are of equal weight. However, the same reactions would probably occur regardless of the particular weighting system. For purposes of this discussion, "long hours" means hours of work above the established norm at which overtime premium payment begins; "short hours," the opposite.

The Upper Turning Point

As the economy reaches the top of a boom and "soft spots" appear, this development is ordinarily reflected in average weekly hours and overtime. Like the situation at the lower turning point, overtime may move with average weekly hours, lead, or lag.

Overtime may begin to drop in plants working long hours while the workweek is increasing—or holding steady—in plants well under the normal workweek. Such divergent movements may cause average weekly hours to rise for a brief period after overtime hours have already turned down, as in the following hypothetical case:

	Hours of work			Per cent change	
	May	*June*	*July*	*May to June*	*June to July*
Plant A	36.0	38.0	40.0		
Plant B	42.0	41.0	40.0		
Average weekly hours	39.0	39.5	40.0	+1.3	+1.3
Overtime hours, total	2.0	1.0	.0		
Average overtime hours	1.0	.5	.0	−50.0	−100.0

On the other hand, if weakness first appears in plants which have not reached the overtime level, average weekly hours may drop while overtime is still rising. Thus, one may encounter any of the following situations:

Upper turning point	Movement of average weekly hours	Comparative movements of overtime and average weekly hours	
		Timing	*Per cent change*
Hours of work level off	a. Level off in all plants.	Coincident.	Same.
	b. Drop in plants working long hours, continue up in plants on short hours.	Overtime leads.	?
	c. Drop in plants working short hours, continue up in plants on long hours.	Overtime lags.	Overtime greater.
Hours of work fall	a. Fall in all plants.	Coincident.	Overtime greater.
	b. Fall in plants working long hours, hold steady or rise in plants on short hours.	Coincident.	Overtime greater.
	c. Fall in plants working short hours, hold steady or rise in plants on long hours.	Overtime lags.	?

Expansion and Contraction

Finally, during the contraction and expansion phases of the business cycle, as well as at the turning points, it is possible for the two series to move together or in divergent directions. The various situations are summarized below:

*Comparative movements
of overtime and average
weekly hours*

Phase of cycle	Movement of average weekly hours	Timing	Per cent change
Expansion phase	Average weekly hours rise— a. in all or most plants.	Coincident.	Overtime greater.
	b. in plants on long hours, fall or hold steady in plants on short hours.	Coincident.	Overtime greater.
	c. in plants on short hours, fall or hold steady in plants on long hours.	Overtime lags.	?
Contraction phase	Average weekly hours fall— a. in all plants.	Coincident.	Overtime greater.
	b. in plants on long hours, rise or hold steady in plants on short hours.	Coincident.	Overtime greater.
	c. in plants on short hours, rise or hold steady in plants on long hours.	Overtime lags.	?

PROBABLE RELATIONSHIP OF THE TWO SERIES

Which of the two economic conditions assumed in the foregoing discussion—parallel or mixed movements in overtime and average weekly hours—is most likely to occur? As observed by Wesley C. Mitchell, "business cycles consist not only of roughly synchronous expansions in many activities, followed by roughly synchronous contractions in a slightly smaller number; they consist also of numerous contractions while expansion is dominant, and numerous expansions while contractions are dominant."[7]

Accordingly, one would expect to find, at any given turning point of the cycle, some industries in which average weekly hours were rising (and so, presumably, was overtime) and some in which average weekly hours were falling. The National Bureau of Economic Research staff found that this was the case—at least as far as average weekly hours are concerned. Their study showed that hours of work were rising in some industry groups at all times during the postwar period except for one brief period in mid-1953, although the average workweek declined rather sharply in both 1948–49 and 1953–54.[8] Therefore, it might seem that the situation most likely to be encountered in the analysis of overtime hours is one where changes in average weekly hours and in overtime hours are in different directions.

[7] What Happens During Business Cycles: A Progress Report, *New York, National Bureau of Economic Research, Inc., 1951 (p. 79).*
[8] *The analysis was based on the percentage of the 21 manufacturing industry groups for which the BLS average weekly hours series rose from one month to the next. The material appears on a National Bureau worksheet entitled "Current Diffusion Indexes," dated December 23, 1954.*

Other data also suggest that changes in average weekly hours and overtime in American factories are usually mixed. For example, Chart 1, based on the Bureau of Labor Statistics reports of average weekly hours by size of plant, shows the wide diffusion of hours of work under various economic conditions. The data are shown for May of 1953, 1954, and 1955, dates which can be taken as approximately the upper turning point, the trough, and the midpoint in the expansion phase of the 1953–55 cycle. In May 1953, when average weekly hours were at the relatively high level of 40.7, almost 30 per cent of manufacturing production workers were employed in plants where the workweek was under 40 hours. On the other hand, in May 1954, when average weekly hours had fallen to 39.3, almost 35 per cent of factory workers were employed in plants working 41 or more hours per week. In May 1955, when average weekly hours had risen to 40.8, slightly above their May 1953 level, about 28 per cent of the factory workers were in plants working 38 or fewer hours per, week.

Chart 1. Distribution of production workers in manufacturing, by length of workweek, May of 1953, 1954, and 1955 SOURCE: **U. S. Department of Labor, Bureau of Labor Statistics.**

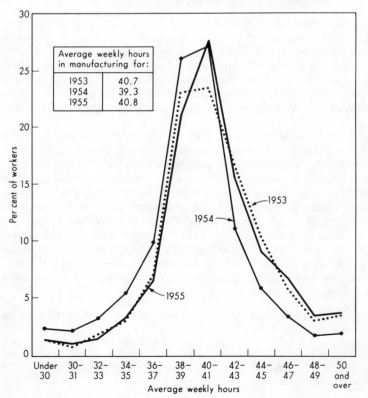

Chart 2. Percentage of wage and salary workers in manufacturing working more than 40 hours per week, July 1947–December 1955, seasonally adjusted SOURCE: *See text footnote 9.*

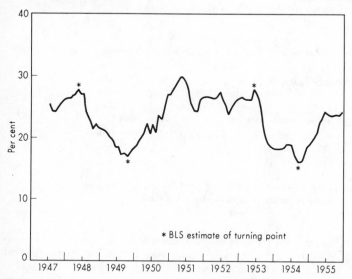

Chart 2 also supports the belief that mixed trends are likely to characterize the manufacturing economy. It shows the percentage of employees in manufacturing industries working more than 40 hours per week from mid-1947 to the end of 1955, as reported by the Census Bureau.[9] If it is considered that workweeks of such duration indicate overtime work, the series shows that, between 1947 and 1955, the proportion of persons working overtime ranged from 30 to 16 percent.[10]

On the basis of these data, it appears that Mitchell's observation about the mixed nature of cyclical movements is likely to be true for overtime hours. But whether the nature of these mixed trends will make overtime a "leading," "lagging," or "coinciding" indicator, relative to average

[9] *Data from table entitled, "Wage and Salary Workers, Classified by Full-Time or Part-Time Status, by Major Industry Group, for the United States," Current Population Reports—Labor Force, Series P–57; various numbers, U.S. Bureau of the Census, with seasonal adjustment, by BLS.*

[10] *This interpretation of the Census hours of work data is subject to several limitations. Most importantly, it is not known if all hours over 40 worked on one job were actually compensated at premium rates, as would be necessary for inclusion in the BLS series. Nor does this treatment of the Census figures allow for these premium hours paid for when the total workweek is lower than 40 hours. Another limitation of this use of the Census data is that hours of work of dual jobholders are included. This inclusion probably causes overstatement of the proportion working more than 40 hours per week on the principal job and of the amplitude of fluctuation in this proportion.*

weekly hours, is not known. The only information bearing on this point is the "overtime" series constructed from the Census data on hours of work, shown in Chart 2. The following tabulation compares the turning points of this series with those of average weekly hours and the overall cycle for the two most recent swings, those of 1948–49 and 1953–54.

| | | Date of turning point shown by— | |
Phase of cycle	Overall business cycle[1]	Census overtime data.[1]	BLS average hours[1]
Peak	November 1948	May 1948	November 1947.[3]
Trough	October 1949	October 1949	August 1949.
Peak	July 1953	June 1953	March 1953.
Trough	September 1954[4]	September 1954	June 1954.[2]

[1] See Geoffrey Moore, The Diffusion of Business Cycles, New York, National Bureau of Economic Research, Inc., May 1954 (mimeographed) except as otherwise noted.

[2] Tentative NBER data.

[3] The NBER staff has not designated a turning point in average weekly hours for this cycle. This estimate was made by BLS staff.

[4] BLS staff estimate.

It appears that when the Census overtime series leads the general business cycle, the margin of the lead is small and much less than that of the Bureau of Labor Statistics average weekly hours series. One factor accounting for the lag in Census overtime (as compared with BLS average weekly hours) is that housewives tend to give "usual" overtime rather than the amount actually worked.[11] Even if some allowance is made for these reporting errors by assuming that the peaks in overtime actually occurred earlier than reported by the Census Bureau, it still appears that the hypothesis that overtime hours coincide with, rather than lead, movements in average weekly hours is actually the most reasonable.

USEFULNESS OF THE OVERTIME HOURS SERIES

The preceding discussion has been based on the assumption that employers react in a uniform way to changing labor requirements—by changing hours of work. But employers may prefer to hire people, if workers with the requisite skills can be found, to permit more efficient utilization of plant capacity during most of an upswing or to lay off workers during a contraction period. For example, BLS hours and employment statistics have sometimes shown employment gains coincident with reductions in the factory workweek. Conversely, at other times,

[11] This limitation on the Census hours data is indicated by the tendency of the distribution to cluster around 40 hours. If housewives frequently report scheduled or usual hours of work of the employed workers in their families, rather than hours actually worked, this probably makes the series more stable than are actual hours of work and creates a lag in the movement of the series.

extra shifts were laid off, or the work force on one shift was reduced, while hours (and overtime) rose for those remaining on the rolls. A more significant possibility, particularly in making long-term comparisons, is a shift in the industrial composition of manufacturing. A large relative growth (or decline) of industries where overtime is usual, or where pay practices are such as to increase the volume of hours paid for at premium rates, can lead to incorrect conclusions about the economic significance of changes in overtime hours. The possibility of such occurrences, which would result in apparently contradictory movements of hours and employment, shows the necessity of detailed analysis of changes, and shows that the significance of the overtime hours series will be enhanced if studied in conjunction with other series such as employment, inventories, new orders, sales, and production.

PATTERNS OF PARTICIPATION IN LOCAL UNIONS*

Participation in union activities varies considerably from one local to another. In many cases it is low enough to cause considerable concern to union leaders.[1] Of course, this problem is not unique to labor unions.

It is perhaps less well known that an equal variation in participation exists among departments in a plant organized by a single union. Meetings have been observed in which 50 per cent of the attendance came from a single department. Some departments may have five or six candidates for steward, although in others not a single person is willing to make the race.

This study seeks to provide a tentative explanation of these departmental differences in participation. It is hoped that in doing so it may provide a useful first step in the analysis of participation.

The research upon which this article is based covered a total of fifteen locals, in basic and fabricated steel, automotive assembly, utilities, men's and women's clothing, chemical and food industries. In some cases, the field studies extended over a thirty-month period. One of the authors and his wife lived in a small community for eight months, spending full time in an intensive study of one union situation.

Throughout the research we attended formal and informal meetings of all kinds: membership, executive board, departmental, and grievance committee. We talked to leaders and rank and file at their homes, in

* By George Strauss and Leonard R. Sayles. Reprinted from Industrial and Labor Relations Review, October, 1952, pp. 31–43. Used by permission.

NOTE: What makes "good" union members, in the sense of active participants in the affairs of the local union? To obtain information on this and related questions, the authors of this article have "lived" with fifteen local unions over an extended period, in some cases up to thirty months, studying all aspects of their operations. The findings on forces influencing membership participation presented here constitute part of the authors' total study on human relations in local unions, supported by the Grant Foundation and under the general direction of Professor William F. Whyte of the New York State School of Industrial and Labor Relations, Cornell University. Part of the work was done while the authors were at the Massachusetts Institute of Technology. The general findings of this research are reported in a volume by the authors entitled, The Local Union: Its Place in Industrial Democracy (Harper).

[1] See Lloyd Reynolds, Labor Economics and Labor Relations (New York: Prentice-Hall, 1949), p. 139; Harry A. Millis and Royal Montgomery, Organized Labor (New York: McGraw-Hill, 1945), pp. 347–348; Maurice Neufeld, "State of the Union," The House of Labor, J. B. S. Hardman and Maurice Neufeld, eds. (New York: Prentice-Hall, 1951), pp. 22–23.

the union office, on the job, and at social affairs. Usually we had access to union voting and attendance records as well. In six instances, we engaged in intensive studies of single departments. This involved observation of the department at work as well as one- to three-hour interviews with the majority of workers.

Attendance averaged 5 per cent at meetings in these locals. In most instances, there was vigorous competition for top offices on the executive committee, but it was often difficult to draft men to accept minor positions such as steward. Naturally, the generalizations below apply only to the locals observed. Whether they apply to other situations is a matter requiring further research.

MEASURES OF PARTICIPATION

At the outset, it is important to make clear that by participation we mean expenditure of time on union affairs. Participation is more than emotional involvement in unionism: it is *doing*. There are many degrees of doing, ranging in scope from voting in elections to running for office. Attending union meetings, paying dues, reading union newspapers, filing grievances, going on strike, bringing the family to picnics—all these can be classified as forms of union activity.

Number of departments classified according to participation in union activity

	Per cent of Participation					
	0–10%	11–25%	26–50%	50–75%	76–100%	Total no. of departments
Union A						
Election: voting in union hall	8	4	3	4	3	22
Election: mail ballot	0	4	17	11	13	45
Union B						
Election: voting at plant gates	0	1	3	11	5	20
Attendance at one or more local meetings during year	7	9	2	2	0	20

Unfortunately, one cannot measure these types of participation just by counting those engaged in a particular activity. Different criteria must be used in different situations. Voting in elections, for instance, is a much more sensitive index when the members must make a special trip to the union office than when the voting booth is set up outside the plant gates. Attendance at union meetings is also significant, although at times it may reflect the distance members live from the meeting hall or the shifts on which they work. The number of candidates for stewardship from a given department is another indicator of union interest, but departments which are very much involved in the union may have a leader who is so strong, so generally accepted, that he is elected without opposition.

Some idea of the wide variation in department participation in union activities is given in the following summary of data from two locals on the number of persons from various departments voting in elections and attending local meetings.

GROUPS WHICH PARTICIPATE

First, let us look at the groups which do participate and then compare them with those which do not.

For many groups, turning to the union represents an act of expediency. These "practical" union members are primarily concerned with their own individual grievances or special interests. They see union activity as a means of protecting themselves, either from management or from competing groups within the union.[2] Their participation is for limited purposes and for a limited time.

Innumerable examples can be given of how economic dissatisfactions lead to greater union activity. The machinists, a strong and cohesive department, became active in organizing a new union when they learned that a similar group in another plant of the same company was receiving higher earnings.[3] They had hopes that the new union would eliminate this differential. The wheel-room men believed that technological change was restricting their job opportunities. They felt that the union could win for them a "wider promotional ladder." The binders protested to their supervisor that relatives of high company officials were obtaining more rapid promotions than the others. When his answer was unsatisfactory, they began to attend union meetings. The paint sprayers objected that management was not doing enough to reduce the dangers of the jobs.

In some of these cases, initial interest led to lasting participation. In others, it did not. An example of each is presented below. The frame fitters tired of union activity when their grievances were not attended to. On the other hand, the relayers found that union participation brought unexpected success and developed lasting interest.

The frame fitters were very active in organizing the union in a large service organization. They hoped that it would be successful in eliminating "contractors" (maintenance men from other companies doing work within the plant under contract). If these were removed, the fitters ex-

[2] See Leonard R. Sayles, "Seniority: An Internal Union Problem," Harvard Business Review, Vol. 30, No. 1 (Jan.–Feb. 1952), pp. 55–61.
[3] Job titles, personal names, and product descriptions have been changed to avoid identification.

pected there would be promotions for everyone. However, the officers negotiated with management for over a year without making significant progress. During this time, the members became increasingly dissatisfied with the way things were going.

Initially, there was no decline in their attendance at local meetings. The first indication of discontent was the "rough going over" members gave the local leadership at departmental meetings. They expressed their aggressions through increasingly skillful sniping at the officers. When this failed to speed up the negotiations, more drastic action was suggested. The following conversation took place between a frame fitter and a union officer:

FF   What we ought to do is get rid of the no-strike clause. I'm not sure whether you have the guts to do that—but that's what we have to do. If we could go out on strike, we could show the company what we meant.

OFFICER   I sympathize with you entirely. But that's not the way to approach the problem. You're going to wait till the contract expires—and then—if necessary, we will go on strike.

FF   Sure that's the way it always is. You guys always talk strike but you never do anything about it.

An increasingly common observation among this group was, "That's the way it always happens. Those boys sell out." Along with this loss of faith in the union, the frame fitters' attendance at departmental and local meetings began to decline. Members remarked, "What's the point of listening to them make excuses." Thus the frame fitters lost their interest in unionism when they couldn't get action.

The experience of the relayers with unionism was much more favorable. They were in a technologically declining department. In a company in which the over-all level of employment was generally expanding, the number of their jobs was contracting. Promotional opportunities were very poor.

In 1939 the relayers found an exceptionally able leader in the person of "Red" Newcomb. Newcomb built them into a tightly organized political bloc and won election to the local executive committee. Through a strategic manipulation of political forces, he was able to use his new position to win the relayers a special five-cents-an-hour wage increase—an increase which put them out of line with the rest of the men doing work requiring the same skill. Naturally the others reacted violently, but the wage differential was not eliminated until 1941. By this time, the relayers were convinced that political action within the union did "pay off."

As a consequence, a "tradition" of union activity was started among the relayers. Even after they lost their wage differential—and after Newcomb was expelled from the union (and lost his job under a union shop agreement)—the relayers remained active; several were elected to office, and, though they never again won anything so outstanding as their five-cents-an-hour differential, they secured many other benefits. For instance, they obtained the unusual privilege of being able to transfer into other departments without loss of pay.

As a result, they have remained highly active. Although they comprise but 5 per cent of the union membership, they often provide 25 per cent of the meeting attendance. Last year they elected two of their members to an eight-man executive board.

It should be noted that several other things happened in this case:

1. By the force of his own enthusiasm, Red Newcomb persuaded his fellow workers that they could protect their economic position through taking part in union activities. He accomplished this because he was liked and respected by the group.
2. After members of the group became active, they won political as well as economic success. Although their original motivation was economic, as they learned more about the union their interest deepened. Newcomb was no longer alone in his political ambitions. A number of other members aspired for office.
3. Finally, going to union meetings provided the relayers with the same kinds of social satisfactions as bowling or other forms of after-hours activity. Union politics provided the subject matter for conversation at work. The group made the union its "cause."

The relayers' story is far from unique. Many individuals or groups participate at first for limited, "practical" purposes only. And then as they go to more and more meetings, the "union fever" is catching; they become so intrigued with unionism that they continue their activity even after the immediate objectives are achieved.

All this emphasizes the circular nature of participation. Individuals or groups participate because they feel they will obtain benefits from the union, but, in most cases, they obtain benefits only when they participate. How this all starts may be a matter of accident. As we have seen, often it is a question of an individual who becomes active for reasons relevant to his individual personality and interests. However, once the group begins to participate, whether it will continue to do so depends upon the economic, political, and social rewards that are obtained.

NONPARTICIPATING GROUPS

The emphasis so far has been on groups which do participate. How about those who do not? How do they feel about the union?

First, it should be emphasized that no correlation has been found between union activity and expressed dissatisfaction with working conditions. It is true that highly active groups are frequently outspoken in their complaints. But so are those which are completely inactive!

Numerous examples can be given where differences in relative dissatisfaction seem to have little to do with the amount of participation. Take the example of two adjacent shops in a large mill, each putting out the same product and each being paid according to the same piecework system. In one shop, the equipment was very modern, while in the other it was forty years old. The workers in the second shop had to put forth twice as much effort as the first to obtain equivalent earnings. In spite of this, participation in both groups was almost identically low.

Some of these groups have "tried" participation without success; others, as far as can be discovered, have never made the attempt. Yet in both types of groups, there seems to be something that could be described as a feeling of "minority status"—the union is really for others, "our small bunch just doesn't have a chance."

In part, this attitude is an intensification of general rank-and-file lethargy, "Let the actives run the union." Too, there is a strong sentiment that the cards are stacked, that "there is no use in even trying to get the union to see our point of view." This, for example, is a common attitude among women in predominantly male locals; "There is no use asking for an increase (in pay); some of the fellows in the union think we're making too much money already doing this work and certainly shouldn't get more."

The barrel cleaners in a chemical plant were also resigned: "This is the dirtiest job in the plant and the union never gets back here."

Among high-skilled groups which have been unsuccessful in their attempts to dominate the union, this attitude can also be prevalent. The following are comments from one such low-participating group:

> We really ought to have a union of our own. We'd have done a lot better than we have now.
>
> It's my opinion that if it wasn't for the union, rather than $2.50 an hour, we'd be getting $3.50. You know this union has got one thing in mind—and that is to bring the lower-paid workers up to the higher-paid. They don't really recognize the craftsmen. They want to pay everyone almost the same.

Some groups lose their battles almost by default. They are convinced that participation is useless—and act accordingly. In a department which had been split by an internecine battle of serious proportion over scheduling, an informed observer said,

> The men on the second and third tricks could outvote us on this thing any time they wanted to. Obviously there are more men on the second and third shifts than on the first. The trouble is, they don't come to meetings. They figure that since they're the first ones to be booted out of a plant if there is a layoff, they shouldn't really have much interest in these things.

Such a defeatist attitude toward participation further reduces the group's bargaining position. The circular process continues: lower participation results in less attention being paid to their economic demands—this, in turn, intensifies their disinclination to take part in union activity.

All this, then, provides additional evidence that groups will participate only if they perceive that the union can provide economic or political or social satisfactions.

This still leaves unanswered the basic question: Why are some groups more likely to obtain success from union activity than others? Four factors seem to be involved: (1) the homogeneity of the group—its ability to unite to achieve its objectives; (2) its status or prestige in the plant community; and (3) the technological importance of its job to the company; (4) the nature of the job. These will be considered in turn.

HOMOGENEITY OF THE GROUP

The emphasis throughout has been on those factors which determine the level of participation within and among *groups*. Of course, the term "group" is only an abstraction. Each individual must make up his own mind whether he will give up an evening's rest to engage in union activity. The individuals with whom a person associates, however, play a large part in influencing his behaviour. Closely knit, unified groups exert greater influence over their members' actions than those which have little in common or are divided internally.

An attitude study in any given plant would probably show a vast majority of the departments favorably disposed toward the union. The members are glad to give it their verbal support. They will even engage in "token participation"—provided it doesn't take too much work. Thus they will vote in union shop elections or for union officers where the ballot boxes are in the plant or at the plant gates and sign petitions which are passed through the shop.

Substantial differences in departmental participation do not arise until the expenditure of time is required; for instance, in attending meetings or accepting union office. Under these circumstances, groups that have a cohesive social organization—in which individual attitudes are multiplied by group convictions—are more likely to show activity than those that are weak and divided.

In loosely knit departments, members may participate as "individuals." In fact, many of the most active local-wide officers come from such groups. However, the participation of these individuals can be explained much better on personal-psychological grounds than group-sociological grounds. For the rank-and-file member, individual motivation is not enough. What he needs is individual motivation *plus* group pressure. Thus only homogeneous groups are likely to have a high level of participation.

What makes a homogeneous group? In our experience, the more cohesive, more active groups are made up of men who (1) work closely together and under the same supervision, (2) who do approximately the same job and who are equal in pay, (3) who belong to the same ethnic group, and (4) who come from the same neighborhood.

Groups That Work Together

Unless members of a group work together, they are not likely to develop a "we" feeling. All the high-participating groups observed had ample opportunity to talk together during their working hours.

The following case indicates what happened to a group enjoying excellent communications opportunities after it was broken up into two distinct shifts.[4]

The newly formed union in a medium-sized fabricating plant had difficulty in finding people who were willing to risk management animosity by becoming candidates for office. Only the machine polishers showed much interest in union activity. This was generated by a rumor that men doing comparable work in another plant of the same corporation were receiving higher wages. Although the polishers comprised but 2 per cent of the work force, one of their group was elected union president and two others were elected to the ten-man executive board. The machine polishers were soon able to win generous rate concessions from management. For a number of years, they provided an exceptionally heavy proportion of union officers and attendance at meetings. Today, the polishers are rarely seen at meetings—and not one of them has attended a sufficient number of meetings to be eligible for office under the terms of the union constitution.

The explanation of this sudden change in participation seems to lie in a social split within the department. When the union was formed, almost all the machine polishers worked on the same shift. Since the polishing machines were located only two or three feet apart, high social solidarity resulted from the very nature of the work. Most of the machines were semiautomatic, so that once a man had properly "set" his machine he might have up to three quarters of an hour free for conversation.

About five years ago, management broke up the group by expanding the night shift. Many of the less senior men had to take this undesirable work. Immediately, a rash of disputes developed within the group over seniority and work assignments. Each shift complained that the other failed to clean the machines adequately and tried to monopolize the easier jobs. Being divided among themselves, they were unable to offer any candidate unified support.

In some cases, the chance to exchange information and gossip came while actually working; in others, the men "compared notes" while awaiting job assignments at the beginning of the shift or during lunch hours.

In a steel local, the burners provided the bulk of the leaders and interested members. Everyone knew that "they stick together like glue." The explanation given by observers in the local was that they all had the same foreman. While the men worked alone or with a small team in

[4] For a more complete discussion of this case see Leonard R. Sayles, "A Case Study of Union Participation and Technological Change," Human Organization, Vol. II, No. 1 (Spring 1952), pp. 5–15.

every part of the shop, their common supervision brought them together at least once a day.

In many plants, maintenance men show high participation, but at one mill they were political nonentities. Here, they worked under the direction of individual production foremen and rarely saw each other.

Cutters' locals are extremely active in almost every garment center. Although few of the plants studied had more than one or two cutters, there was considerable interchange of cutters from plant to plant. Over a period of time, each cutter got to know most of the others in his local, even though they were from other shops. In fact, they usually ate lunch together. This created a strong sense of comradeship and doubtless was an important factor in their political strength.

It should be emphasized, however, that communication is not the only requirement for high participation. Many departments were observed which had a high degree of interaction among their members, yet were never represented at union meetings.

Similar Pay

A number of different pay grades in a department may mar its social unity and serve to fragment the group. The most strongly united groups are those where each member performs approximately the same job and receives the same pay.

A comparison of tabulators and stockmen provides an excellent example of the effect of differences in pay. The two groups were very much alike in many ways: both were recruited from the "cream" of the company's applicants, they both had reasons to be dissatisfied because of poor promotional possibilities, and workers in each group had ample opportunity to talk with each other. However, all the tabulators earned the same amount, while pay differences within the stockmen were very great.

The tabulators were united and active—a powerful force in the union. In successive elections, a higher percentage of tabulators voted than any other group in the union. Although tabulators comprised less than 14 per cent of the membership, two members of the six-man executive board were currently tabulators and two had formerly held the job. Their esprit de corps was well known throughout the union. Men who had been promoted into higher paying jobs would say, "Of course, at heart, I'm a tabulator," or "I'm still one of the gang; there will never be another gang like ours."

The stockmen, on the other hand, were known for their internal quarrels and difficulties. Perhaps the very fact that most stockmen worked in close conjuction accentuated the importance of the pay differentials. A number of years ago, a seniority dispute between two leaders over who should get a promotion split the group. Even now they show little participation or interest in the union.

Commenting on the difference between these two groups, the local vice-president (who is a tabulator) said, "We just don't have the friction they do. That's the thing which determines whether a group can stick together. They are always fighting over seniority."

The forge crew in another local had fine leadership potentialities. The high skill, physical strength, and endurance required by the work earned them the respect of the rest of the shop. Over the years, however, their wage level had slipped, and management had neglected physical conditions to such an extent that men complained, "Fifty years ago, this shop was in better shape!" The department, moreover, was plagued with a complicated wage structure which most of the men considered inequitable. The men at the bottom complained that their own low wages were due to the men at the top "getting too damn much for what they do." On the other hand, those at the top of the pay ladder charged that they had already sustained an unnecessary reduction in their earnings. As a result, with the exception of one man, none of them attended a single local meeting for a year. They gained the reputation of being the last to go out on a strike. As one worker in the department admitted,

> Well, every so often we threaten the union officers that we're going to walk out or sit down, or somehow do something. They may get scared but then they know after a while that when nothing happens, that we're not going to do anything. So things go along like that for a time and then we start bothering them again and telling them that we've got to have something done. The whole trouble is that the men don't stick together.

Ethnic Similarities

In a study of one mill local, we compared departments composed of many nationality groups with those composed primarily of one ethnic group. Ethnically "united" departments provided higher attendance at meetings, brought forth a larger number of candidates for union office, and took the lead in many anti-management activities. In divided departments, the members expended their energies fighting each other and could rarely unite for common action through the union. On occasion, serious problems would cause one group or another within such a department to appeal to the union, but their support and interest in union affairs was so erratic that the officers often felt "they are more trouble than they are worth."

In such departments, it was frequently difficult to find individuals who would be willing to accept a steward's job. Members feared being placed in the "middle" and having to take responsibility for mediating disputes between ethnic groups. The contrast was so pronounced that officers often suspected that these ethnic differences were purposely fomented by management.

Neighborhood Influences

Even in larger communities, it is still possible for the workers in a department to live near each other. This greatly increases the "social unity" of the group involved. A recent study of a large shipyard showed that high participation on the part of the machinists was in part a result of their living close together and having built a tight social group which extended beyond the plant.[5] One small but extremely active local of brickmakers in another community consisted almost entirely of Italians. They live clustered together in one section of town. Many of them have grown up together, their families have intermarried, and the union is merely an extension of the numerous social and athletic activities engaged in through the year.

SOCIAL POSITION OR STATUS OF THE JOB

It appears that workers who are better paid or who have higher prestige in the plant are more likely to participate. If this at first seems startling, it should be recalled that men from lower-paid jobs are generally younger or considered less competent. As a consequence, when they participate they may be thought of as upstarts; their contributions are sometimes pointedly ignored. Consequently, these men soon lose their desire to take part. It is not difficult to discourage participation.

High pay is not the only factor determining the worker's prestige. Age, sex, ethnic factors, seniority, job skill, position on the production line, value of material handled, and a host of other influences enter into the evaluation of a worker's status. All of these affect the respect paid a worker by his fellows and consequently determine whether his participation is encouraged or discouraged.

It is not difficult to assess the relative status of various departments or groups in a plant. People will soon tell you, "They're the group that really counts around here." "Over in our department, it is pretty much up to the day shift; everyone looks to us to start things," or "Those young guys haven't been here long enough to know what they want."

The following cases may give some indication of the complexity of the "status" factors involved in specific situations.

Seven Needle Trades Locals

These provided a most illuminating example. Four of these locals had high participation; three had low.

Attendance in the high-participating locals ranged from 15 to 25 per cent at "routine" meetings to 70 to 90 per cent at important ones. Two of these locals were made up of cutters and pressers. These high-paid jobs were held almost entirely by men and were traditionally the keystones of the trade. The other two were small locals, representatives of declining trades (the community having shifted to cheaper products). They comprised almost entirely older workers, immigrant Jews, who could speak English only with difficulty.

[5] *Milton Vogel*, Fore River, A Study of Conflicting Loyalties (*M.S. thesis, Massachusetts Institute of Technology, 1948*).

The three low-participating locals were much larger and consisted primarily of semiskilled workers. They included two operators locals and an Italian local. Attendance at all meetings varied from 1 to 20 per cent.

Within these locals, only a small segment was active. In one operators local, this active group came largely from workers in "quality" shops. This group had a much higher proportion of male workers than the rest of the local. In the Italian local, participation came largely from the pressers, a highly paid job always filled by men. In the last of these three locals, however, union activity could be attributed more to outside political interest. A vocal leftist minority provided the bulk of the leadership and participation.

In all the locals, the least active were the "miscellaneous trades" or the "minority crafts"—low-paid, day-rated jobs requiring less skill than the machine operations. The members were agreed, "The minority crafts just don't attend meetings."

Summarizing, participation in these needle trades locals was a function of (1) the pay and prestige of the job, (2) sex, (3) ethnic differences, and (4) differences in political ideology.

The Machinists

This isolated department had few contacts with the rest of the plant and was sharply divided along job-class lines as follows:

	Average earnings	Number in group
Laborers	$52.00	75
Helpers	55.00	43
Machinists I & II	65–75	36

Prior to 1945, promotions within this department were extremely rare. A man hired as a laborer or as a helper would normally spend the rest of his life in that job. It took a wartime sit-down strike to establish the principle of promotion from within. More recently, a new man could start as a laborer and work his way up to Machinist I. The first members of this new postwar crew are now reaching the top of the helper group and will soon become machinists.

Before the war there were sharp class differences between the machinists, helpers, and laborers. Today the division between machinist and helper has somewhat lessened, but that between laborers and the others continues.

The prewar laborer had little education and could speak English only with difficulty. Of this group, thirty-three remain. Nine are broken-accented Irish, twenty-two are first generation Italians. None is considered eligible for promotion to helper or machinist. In spite of the fact that all forty-two "postwar" laborers have been picked for eventual promotion to machinist and are high school graduates, the laborer retains the reputation of being uneducated and "different." Particularly among the older service machinists, there is little recognition that the composition of the laborer group is changing. As a consequence, there is little communication between the two groups. Machinists will tell you, "The laborers stick to themselves—most of them don't speak English. . . . It's funny how you hang your hat and coat together, work together, yet hardly ever talk to the laborer."

Participation by laborers, particularly by the prewar group, has been low. This is true both at departmental and at union-wide meetings. To our knowledge, only one laborer has spoken at a union-wide meeting. Although laborers comprise half the department, their attendance is far smaller than that of machinists. Some of the older machinists say, "They just aren't interested in meetings—they wouldn't understand what goes on."

Prior to the war, the helper had almost no chance of promotion. As one "postwar" machinist said, "In those days, the helpers really got treated like dirt. The machinist was king and the helper was his valet. The machinist would never do any of the dirty work. Today things are different but some of the old feeling remains."

Two of the older machinists saw the situation this way,

Something had to be done for the helper, but I think things have gone too far. Management has had to talk to several machinists for letting their helpers get out of hand. The helper has got to learn. There are lots of things he doesn't know even yet.

Nowadays machinists and helpers sometimes exchange work. There's hardly a line between them. For my money that makes them learn faster, but that sure is a change.

Using attendance at union-sponsored department meetings as a measure of participation, we obtained these results:

	Number in group	Attendance at dept. meeting	
		Average	Maximum
Laborers	75	2	8
Helpers	43	6	22
Machinists	36	20	31

Thus participation is concentrated in the high-status machinists, even though the promotional ladder has now been clarified.

Soft-drink Plant

This plant was divided into two sharply separated departments: trucking and production. Both departments were represented by a city-wide teamsters local. The truckers earned almost twice as much as the production workers. Although one steward was nominally supposed to represent the entire department, the production workers never participated in his election. In fact, the steward said, "If they want a steward, let them elect one."

The informal leader of the production workers admitted, "We are a gang by ourselves. We take care of ourselves. The drivers have nothing to do with us. We aren't in the union. All we do is pay dues. If we were in the union, we'd have a shop steward. That union is for drivers."

When the time came for the plant to take part in a union shop election, none of the production workers took part—and the union lost the election by one vote. A production worker commented, "Why should I vote in the union's election? What have those so-and-so's ever done for me? They don't want me and I don't want them."

A broken-box carpenter said, "Sure, I know all about the union. My brother-in-law is in it. He's a driver. He said that election wasn't for the production workers. It was for the union (meaning the truckers). I figured that was right because we didn't vote in other elections. Nobody gives a damn for us. If you drive a truck, you're a big shot—but what would they do if they didn't have any boxes?"

Here there was no question of relative participation. The production workers totally ignored the union and assumed that the union ignored them. The truckers, on the other hand, were the union.

All of the above cases include examples of how status affects participation. In most of them, the status factor involved was one of pay. However, Sections A and B in the clerical department case both received the same pay. Here the difference was apparently seniority and job responsibility. In the needle trades, ethnic factors were important, although the left wing issue played its part. Helpers and laborers in the machinists case received almost the same average pay ($55 a week, as against $52), yet their meeting attendance was considerably different. Here status was as much determined by subjective evaluations as weekly pay. The laborers were considered to be "beneath" the machinists and the helpers.

STRATEGIC TECHNOLOGICAL POSITION

In many manufacturing plants, there are one or more key work groups whose production literally controls the output rate of the plant. If, for any reason, there is a slowdown at these particular points, the output of other groups almost automatically is reduced. Management, as might be expected, is anxious to do everything possible to encourage their productivity. These are the departments in which union pressures for wage and rate concessions are most effective.

For example, a new union in a metals-processing plant secured an improved incentive plan that almost doubled the earnings of a key group. Until that time, this shop's low output had been a major bottleneck in the plant. Management was persuaded rather easily to grant this "loose rate" in order to increase production. Since this department obtained economic success without excessive effort, union participation paid off rather handsomely. This group is now considered one of the most pro-union in the plant. For many years, it elected at least two members of the local's nine-man executive board and has always been "ready to walk out at the drop of a hat."

NATURE OF THE WORK

Some jobs leave a man so exhausted that he has no desire to take part in union activities when his work day is over. Others afford him plenty of opportunity to discuss union affairs, while on the job—and also leave him fresh to spend long hours after work.

Take, for instance, the engine overhaul crew in an antiquated plant. These men were extremely well paid, they had high status and social unity. They stuck together during sit-downs and slow-downs. In interviews most of them expressed great interest in their union. Yet their attendance at membership meetings was low—because they averaged a fifty-five hour work week and, as one man said, "When we get finished, we are too pooped to do much more than sit home, see the TV, and go to sleep."

Compare these to the route collectors in a service union. When these men had finished their assigned route, their day's work was over. A good man could easily finish in six hours, and many of them devoted their extra hours to union activity.

In almost every industry there are a few occupations whose main duty is to stand by for an emergency. Of one such group it was said, "Those guys are like firemen. They have nothing better to do than talk union."

The same holds true of groups of men who work in close proximity on semiautomatic equipment. People from both union and management have told us, "Those guys have so much time on their hands, they haven't got anything to do but gripe."

CONCLUSION

Groups with high participation are not necessarily those which are most dissatisfied with working conditions. Many departments with the lowest morale are also the least active. Before dissatisfaction can be translated into participation, certain other conditions must be met. One of these is the existence of respected *leaders* within the group who are interested in taking part in union activity. But this is not enough. For if other *group factors* are uniformly unfavorable, probably no leader, however dynamic, will be able to get the department to take an active part in the union. On the other hand, if the group factors are favorable, usually someone will be able to step forward and serve as a catalyst around whom union activity will develop.

The important thing is to distinguish between motivation for initial union activity and that for its continuance. Provided the group is fairly well united, accidental factors may encourage one of the leaders to "try out" union activity as a means of obtaining relief from unsatisfactory work conditions. By his personal drive, he may galvanize the group to action and set the stage for the growth of longer run interest.

Once groups participate, further activity is largely a function of the types of satisfactions gained. Most important is the feeling that members of the group are profiting economically from union activity or at least protecting themselves from being harmed. Also significant is the feeling of political success, when important members of the group are elected to union-wide office and have substantial influence on union decisions. Further, there are social satisfactions derived from political activity and attending meetings.

Not all departments with high initial participation are equally success-ful in their experience. Our evidence indicates that those which have free time, are socially united (either for technological or "human rela-tions" reasons), have high status within the plant community, or occupy a strategic position in the line of production usually obtain greater satis-faction from participation. These then are the ones which are more likely to participate.

CHANGES IN
RETAIL TRADE FLOW*

Few areas of exploration are more important or of more interest to marketing people than the flow of retail trade. The magnitude and direction of flow are determinants of the importance and location of retail markets; and these in turn influence the composition of wholesale networks and the location of manufacturing facilities to "feed" wholesale and retail markets.

This generalization may be carried even further by stating that the structure designed to feed retail markets has considerable influence on the character and location of manufacturers and distributors of industrial goods, and that, in a consumer-directed system such as ours, the whole economy tends to be oriented toward retail markets and their efficient exploitation.

Sometimes this orientation takes the form of product variation to fit the special needs of geographically dispersed retail concentrations; and sometimes suppliers' strategy involves the decentralization of production and distribution facilities in order to reduce transportation costs and to be more competitive in distant markets.

The importance of a retailing center depends on the size and income of its population, the power of its institutions of all kinds to attract people from the outside, and the relative drawing power of competing trading centers. Since all these factors are variable, shifts in population, changes in income and its distribution, and changes in the quality of institutions affect the relative importance of competing retailing centers over time.

William J. Reilly made a significant contribution to the understanding of retail trade flows in 1928 when he developed a formula for estimating the relative ability of cities of different sizes to draw trade from their hinterlands. This formula, which became known as "Reilly's Law of Retail Gravitation," was based on the assumption that, other things being equal, the ability of a city to attract trade from a distance was primarily a function of its size.

Marketing research has indicated that Reilly's Law tends to work. It has also stood up under the test of logic, as it is obvious that larger cities have a tendency to attract trade from greater distances than is possible for smaller ones. Not only does the retail structure of a major city offer the consumer a wider assortment of goods, but many nonretail-

* By Eli P. Cox. Reprinted from the Journal of Marketing, *national quarterly publication of the American Marketing Association, vol. 28, pp. 12–18, January, 1964. Used by permission.*

ing attractions bring him to the city and expose him to the shopping enticements which exist there in such abundance.

Reilly's Law captured the imagination of marketing men because it helped to explain tremendous changes in the nation's retail distribution pattern which had just taken place. The advent of the automobile, its almost universal acceptance, and the development of paved highways had given the consumer a mobility that brought distant trading centers closer in time than local centers used to be. Furthermore, going to larger and more distant centers opened his eyes to the limitations of local centers in satisfying his new-found wants.

Although there are no adequate comparable retail sales data available prior to 1929 to support such an assumption, it seems certain that retail activity concentrated in large population centers at a rapid rate during the second and third decades of this century. Increased consumer mobility was not the only factor at work to stimulate the flow of trade. Increasing cash incomes of nonmetropolitan residents made possible the purchase of greater quantities of shopping and luxury goods, and their increasing levels of education and sophistication seem to have directed the flow of trade toward the city.

CHANGES SINCE 1929

Although the forces which once caused trade to flow to larger centers are still present, the relative magnitude of the flow has dwindled and this process of diminution appears to be continuing.

During the past 30 years retail trade has not shifted to metropolitan areas at anything like the rate at which population has done so. In other words, while the share of the nation's population concentrated in metropolitan areas has increased dramatically, these same areas have not increased their share of retail sales at all.

Analysis of population and retail sales data for the 42 states which contained one or more Standard Metropolitan Statistical Areas in 1958 reveals the following: (1) the metropolitan areas increased their population share from 53.7% in 1929 to 61.5% in 1958; and (2) the metropolitan share of retail trade remained almost constant, amounting to 68% in 1929 and 67.6% in 1958.

To state the same facts in another way, metropolitan per capita retail sales were 83% above those of nonmetropolitan areas in 1929, and the difference had fallen to only 30% by 1958.

DESCRIPTION OF METHOD

These findings cannot be explained as being the natural result of the development of suburban rings around major cities, because Standard Metropolitan Statistical Areas, by definition, include their suburbs.

The Bureau of the Census defines a Standard Metropolitan Statistical Area as being made up of one or more highly urbanized counties containing at least one central city of 50,000 or more inhabitants. Standard Metropolitan Statistical Areas include both central cities and the urbanized rings that have formed around many of them. Consequently, the comparisons made in this article are not between central cities and suburbia, but between metropolitan areas (including suburbs) and nonmetropolitan sections.

Comparison of SMSAs over a period of time is complicated by the fact that their number increases from year to year, and that their geographical areas are sometimes enlarged by adding adjacent counties as they become more urban in character. Between 1950 and 1960 alone the number of SMSAs increased from 168 to 212. Consequently, any statistical analysis of the nation's SMSAs over time must be adjusted for the changes in their number and composition.

In the case of this study, the SMSAs were stabilized at the number and composition of those which existed in 1958, the year for which the last Census of Business was taken. Data for previous census years were then built up by reconstituting the SMSAs statistically from published county data. Once this was done, SMSA data were compared with those for the remainder of each state.

The basic results are summarized in Tables 1, 2, and 3, which contain data on the 42 states which had one or more population centers designated as SMSAs in 1958.

METROPOLITAN AREA POPULATION SHARES

The proportions of each state's population which lived in its metropolitan areas during each Census of Business year from 1929 through 1958 are shown in Table 1. Although for the 42 states as a whole the degree of population concentration increased steadily throughout the period, the degree in some states increased rapidly and in others little or not at all.

Those states in which metropolitan area population shares increased most are generally those which had low metropolitan area concentrations to begin with. In most cases they are states whose economies were largely oriented toward agriculture until World War II; and most of them are located west of the Mississippi River. In 11 states—Arizona, Arkansas, Georgia, Kansas, Mississippi, Nebraska, New Mexico, Oklahoma, South Dakota, Texas and Virginia—the population shares of metropolitan areas increased by at least one-third from 1939 to 1958. Of these 11, there are 8 west of the Mississippi River; and all were predominantly agricultural before World War II.

There are also 11 states in which metropolitan area population shares increased by one-twentieth or less during the same period: California, Connecticut, Delaware, Maine, Massachusetts, New Hampshire, New Jersey, New York, Oregon, Pennsylvania and Rhode Island. Of these 11, there are 9 east of the Mississippi River; and in general they are in a rather mature state of economic growth. (California and Oregon are "mavericks" which defy any generalization about the rest of the group.)

Table 1. Percentages of state populations concentrated in
standard metropolitan statistical areas[a]

SMSA	1929	1939	1948	1954	1958
Alabama	27.59	29.00	33.67	36.32	36.77
Arizona	46.64	51.49	61.49	67.53	70.34
Arkansas	10.82	11.15	13.17	15.03	16.49
California	83.39	83.96	84.37	85.50	86.27
Colorado	43.35	45.56	52.51	56.13	58.62
Connecticut	66.67	66.76	66.91	66.29	65.74
Delaware	67.45	67.39	68.56	68.84	68.86
Florida	47.27	52.95	56.98	58.25	58.66
Georgia	27.77	30.95	36.29	40.35	42.98
Illinois	69.92	70.50	72.81	74.58	75.71
Indiana	43.96	45.39	47.81	49.40	50.35
Iowa	25.49	26.82	29.10	31.44	32.29
Kansas	20.92	22.70	23.73	29.64	34.77
Kentucky	24.98	24.74	27.95	30.95	33.12
Louisiana	34.29	34.83	38.66	40.76	41.84
Maine	19.64	19.94	20.49	20.28	19.97
Maryland	69.90	71.73	71.54	76.59	77.63
Massachusetts	88.31	86.08	86.10	85.76	85.37
Michigan	67.95	68.80	71.00	72.19	72.83
Minnesota	35.02	41.36	45.47	47.57	49.43
Mississippi	4.14	4.85	6.20	7.36	8.20
Missouri	47.97	48.63	52.62	55.52	56.87
Nebraska	24.77	27.04	30.60	33.96	36.77
New Hampshire	17.51	16.82	17.66	17.69	17.53
New Jersey	84.69	84.21	82.75	80.73	79.29
New Mexico	10.68	12.86	20.02	24.36	26.63
New York	84.34	85.04	85.29	85.42	85.49
North Carolina	19.66	20.41	21.79	23.13	24.09
Ohio	65.70	65.83	68.04	68.92	69.25
Oklahoma	20.19	22.14	28.10	32.78	35.86
Oregon	43.47	41.61	40.83	40.82	40.90
Pennsylvania	74.89	75.23	76.21	76.95	77.44
Rhode Island	90.63	88.70	88.40	87.76	87.45
South Carolina	22.29	25.69	26.43	29.15	31.06
South Dakota	7.28	8.80	10.49	11.91	12.03
Tennessee	33.81	35.61	40.04	42.88	44.65
Texas	36.64	40.32	48.35	53.35	56.21
Utah	48.19	48.74	51.46	53.58	54.87
Virginia	35.62	34.23	42.40	46.79	49.16
Washington	57.36	57.07	58.65	61.37	62.57
West Virginia	25.53	26.19	27.45	28.89	30.13
Wisconsin	39.06	39.75	41.91	44.05	45.53
SMSAs of 42 states	53.75	54.83	57.89	60.19	61.55

[a] SOURCE: Developed from U.S. Census data.

SHARES OF RETAIL SALES

The metropolitan area shares of state retail sales for each of the Census of Business years are shown in Table 2.

Here, too, there is a great deal of variation between states. Generally, however, the changes in shares of retail trade have been much smaller than the corresponding changes in population shares. In some cases (Florida and Missouri, for example) the two changes have been in opposite directions, with relative population concentrations increasing and with corresponding retail concentrations diminishing.

RETAIL CONCENTRATION

The heart of this analysis is contained in Table 3, in which retail sales per capita in metropolitan areas are compared with those in nonmetropolitan areas of the same states.

The figures in the table may be used as indexes of retail concentration. It can be seen in Table 3 that the index for the 42 states has dropped consistently since 1929, falling from 183 in that year to 130 by 1958.

This means that metropolitan area per capita retail sales were 83% higher in 1929 than those in nonmetropolitan areas, and that the difference dropped to 30% by 1958.

The pattern of falling indexes was somewhat to the same degree in 38 of the 42 states, the exceptions being Connecticut, Massachusetts, New Jersey, and Virginia.

While there is a high degree of consistency in the direction of change in the various states, there is a wide "spread" in magnitudes of change. For instance, while the metropolitan areas of Alabama, Arkansas, Georgia, Kentucky, Louisiana, Mississippi, North Carolina, and Tennessee still had indexes of 150 or more in 1958, those of Arizona, California, Delaware, Maryland, New York, and Rhode Island were 110 or less.

As interesting as these variations are, however, the central fact is that population movement to metropolitan areas has not been accompanied in recent years by a proportionate increase in retail sales in those areas. In other words, nonmetropolitan retailing seems to be doing a progressively better job of preventing the flow of retail trade to metropolitan centers.[1]

ADDITIONAL FINDINGS

The fact that relative trade flow to metropolitan centers had diminished, despite the continuation of the forces which stimulated it in the first

[1] For additional discussion of these findings, see two previous articles by the author: "The Decline of Metropolitan Retailing," Business Topics, Vol. 9 (Spring, 1961), pp. 34–42; and "The Changing Pattern of Retail Concentration," in The Social Responsibilities of Marketing, Proceedings of the Winter Conference of the American Marketing Association, December 27–29, 1961 (Chicago: American Marketing Association, 1962), pp. 557–566.

Table 2. Percentages of state retail sales concentrated in standard metropolitan statistical areas[a]

SMSA	1929	1939	1948	1954	1958
Alabama	46.79	48.34	48.22	47.75	47.65
Arizona	52.83	58.82	67.98	69.52	72.39
Arkansas	18.03	22.75	22.28	22.95	24.48
California	86.06	85.76	85.42	86.45	87.22
Colorado	54.29	57.01	56.70	60.36	61.87
Connecticut	68.48	68.39	67.65	71.91	68.69
Delaware[b]	75.66	70.98	62.11	67.65	67.46
Florida	68.97	66.16	66.34	62.89	63.20
Georgia	51.21	52.35	52.70	53.93	54.50
Illinois	80.65	79.21	77.48	80.49	79.29
Indiana	55.52	54.58	53.96	54.25	54.94
Iowa	33.91	34.53	34.18	33.48	34.93
Kansas	23.73	28.39	27.57	34.10	36.11
Kentucky	45.92	45.17	44.47	46.38	45.63
Louisiana	51.17	53.21	50.51	52.15	52.31
Maine	29.31	27.89	26.75	26.19	25.89
Maryland	77.38	77.53	75.89	76.56	78.38
Massachusetts	89.00	85.39	86.78	87.38	87.75
Michigan	76.20	74.86	75.02	76.19	75.16
Minnesota	55.74	55.29	51.16	52.14	53.77
Mississippi	8.54	11.32	11.18	12.25	14.27
Missouri	68.31	67.52	65.11	65.16	64.98
Nebraska	31.36	37.94	33.99	35.81	37.97
New Hampshire	21.04	18.42	19.01	18.31	19.05
New Jersey	84.18	83.66	81.53	80.57	79.54
New Mexico	17.50	20.14	25.58	29.75	31.72
New York	87.52	87.02	86.29	85.81	86.15
North Carolina	33.22	33.98	33.11	32.35	33.75
Ohio	73.96	74.12	73.06	72.56	73.18
Oklahoma	31.93	36.25	37.85	41.50	43.69
Oregon	51.28	48.07	44.70	43.23	43.40
Pennsylvania	82.83	80.46	79.65	80.44	80.61
Rhode Island[b]	90.45	86.87	86.74	83.78	85.53
South Carolina	33.81	34.89	35.19	37.47	38.17
South Dakota	11.62	15.41	14.16	14.64	15.59
Tennessee	59.09	58.93	57.27	56.96	57.73
Texas	51.37	54.96	57.43	59.68	61.42
Utah	65.44	62.78	59.29	62.85	62.35
Virginia	39.94	42.21	52.76	55.64	60.37
Washington	64.03	62.84	60.68	63.52	65.17
West Virginia	36.18	35.99	34.93	38.54	38.69
Wisconsin	48.00	49.00	46.06	47.46	48.33
SMSAs of 42 states	68.02	67.81	66.08	67.10	67.56

[a] SOURCE: Developed from U.S. Census data.
[b] Data seem internally inconsistent.

364   BUSINESS RESEARCH

Table 3. Relative per capita retail sales in standard
          metropolitan statistical areas[a]

SMSA	1929	1939	1948	1954	1958
Alabama	230.80	229.10	183.46	160.23	156.53
Arizona	128.13	134.57	132.95	109.67	110.55
Arkansas	181.29	234.69	189.00	168.38	164.16
California	122.96	115.05	108.53	108.20	108.62
Colorado	155.21	158.45	118.43	119.01	114.53
Connecticut	108.61	107.72	103.43	130.18	114.33
Delaware[b]	150.00	118.36	75.17	94.65	93.75
Florida	247.94	173.73	148.81	121.46	121.03
Georgia	273.00	245.09	195.61	173.07	158.90
Illinois	179.31	159.43	128.48	140.61	122.84
Indiana	159.13	144.58	127.93	121.46	120.23
Iowa	149.98	143.92	126.53	109.42	112.53
Kansas	117.60	135.01	122.33	122.84	106.02
Kentucky	255.00	250.62	206.45	192.98	169.48
Louisiana	200.82	212.77	161.94	158.40	152.46
Maine	169.65	155.29	141.70	139.48	140.00
Maryland	147.31	136.00	125.21	99.83	104.47
Massachusetts	106.14	94.51	105.97	114.97	122.76
Michigan	151.01	135.03	122.66	123.27	112.89
Minnesota	233.70	175.34	125.61	118.93	118.99
Mississippi	216.20	250.43	190.43	175.72	186.34
Missouri	233.79	219.58	168.03	149.83	140.71
Nebraska	138.75	164.95	116.78	108.49	105.26
New Hampshire	125.53	111.65	109.43	104.28	110.71
New Jersey	96.20	96.01	92.02	98.98	101.55
New Mexico	177.41	170.88	137.31	131.51	127.99
New York	130.22	117.95	108.55	103.22	105.57
North Carolina	203.28	200.71	177.66	158.91	160.54
Ohio	148.27	148.65	127.39	119.24	121.16
Oklahoma	185.43	199.96	155.83	145.47	138.77
Oregon	136.89	129.90	117.14	110.39	110.80
Pennsylvania	161.74	135.57	122.18	123.19	121.11
Rhode Island[b]	97.92	84.29	85.84	62.75	84.82
South Carolina	178.07	155.00	151.14	145.64	137.02
South Dakota	167.46	188.80	140.76	126.85	135.06
Tennessee	282.75	259.47	200.72	176.30	169.29
Texas	182.67	180.61	144.12	129.43	124.03
Utah	203.57	177.40	137.38	146.57	136.20
Virginia	120.20	140.33	151.73	142.63	157.54
Washington	132.33	127.21	108.80	109.60	111.94
West Virginia	165.37	158.46	141.88	154.34	146.34
Wisconsin	144.02	145.62	118.35	114.73	111.90
SMSAs of 42 states	183.03	173.55	141.71	134.90	130.09

[a] SOURCE: Developed from U.S. Census data.
[b] Data seem internally inconsistent.

place, suggests that explanations lie in the changing contexts. Three additional findings may throw some light on these contexts.

1. The nation's largest cities do not "perform" particularly well. The indexes for all 8 cities shown in Table 4 are below the average of 130 (Table 3) for all the nation's SMSAs. Each of them, however, has a slightly higher index than that of the SMSA average for the state in which it is located.

Examination of the nation's smallest SMSAs reveals no pattern at all. Some of them have high retail concentration indexes, and some very low ones. If any generalization can be made about size and performance, it is that medium-sized metropolitan areas seem to "perform" fairly well.

Table 4. Relative per capita retail sales for eight major SMSAs (nonmetropolitan per capita retail sales in each state 100)

SMSA	1958 index
New York City	107
Los Angeles	113
Chicago	127
Detroit	114
Philadelphia	128
Cleveland	129
Baltimore	108
Houston	129

2. The growing relative importance of retailing in nonmetropolitan areas is not confined to a few merchandise types, but seems to apply to most types to greater or lesser degrees. Although no analysis for the whole nation has been made, figures for the states of California, Michigan, North Carolina, and Texas indicate that changes have been greatest in apparel, furniture and appliances, and eating and drinking establishments; and smallest in general merchandise (which includes department and variety stores), gasoline service stations, and food stores.

Despite losses which have taken place, SMSA concentrations still remain relatively high in general merchandise, apparel, furniture and appliances, and eating and drinking establishments.

Lowest SMSA concentrations appear to be in lumber, building materials and hardware, gasoline service stations, and food stores.

In other words, with the exception of the general merchandise category, the types which have the greatest SMSA concentrations appear to be suffering the greatest losses; and those with low concentrations seem to have neared something approximating equilibrium.

Further analysis of data for the four states provides as an interesting sidelight the information that changes in service sales appear to be in the opposite direction, with impressive increases in metropolitan concentration.

The opposite movement of the two indexes suggests interesting possibilities. First, it is taking place because of different propensities to consume—with that for service going up and that for merchandise going down as real income rises beyond some point.

Second, merchandise has become more standardized than many services and lends itself better to distribution in relatively small markets.

3. *The size and quality of a metropolitan area's "hinterland" seem to be important in determining the amount of trade which will flow in from the outside.* Table 5 has been developed on the assumption that the relationship between per capita retail sales and per capita income is an indication of the extent to which outside trade flows into a metropolitan area. Using per capita retail sales from the 1958 census and per capita "effective buying income" for the same year from *Sales Management's Survey of Buying Power,* approximate sales-income ratios were developed for all SMSAs. This information for 20 areas, the 10 high and the 10 low, is presented in Table 5.

Table 5. Per capita retail sales as a percentage of per capita effective buying power

High Cities	Percentage
Fort Smith, Ark.	101.5
Laredo, Tex.	100.1
West Palm Beach, Fla.	94.6
Lexington, Ky.	89.5
Jackson, Miss.	89.4
Asheville, N.C.	87.0
Chattanooga, Tenn.	85.8
Miami, Fla.	85.7
Atlantic City, N.J.	85.5
Portland, Me.	84.1
Low Cities	*Percentage*
Jersey City, N.J.	51.5
Lorain-Elyria, O.	51.5
Champaign-Urbana, Ill.	52.7
Paterson, Clifton, Passaic, N.J.	54.8
South Bend, Ind.	55.4
Columbus, Ga.	55.6
Steubenville-Weston, O.	55.9
Hamilton-Middleton, O.	56.4
Kenosha, Wis.	56.5
New York, N.Y.	56.9

Examination of the high sales-income ratio cities shows that some of them are resort areas. In these cases, the cause of trade flow from the outside is obvious.

Inspection of the others shows that they have similar "hinterlands" which are large in square miles and are rural in character. They also have low population densities, and are characterized by relatively low per capita incomes.

In other words, these cities have environments much like those of 50 years ago, with the added advantage of the wider trading area made possible by greater mobility and increased purchasing power of potential nonmetropolitan shoppers.

This can be illustrated by taking as examples the two metropolitan areas with the highest sales-income ratios: Fort Smith, Arkansas, and Laredo, Texas.

Fort Smith is without nearby competition. Its location on the western edge of the state places it 135 highway miles from its nearest competitor, Tulsa, Oklahoma, to the west. It is 160 miles from Little Rock to the east and 190 miles from Texarkana on the south. Springfield, Missouri, is approximately the same distance to the north. Within the area so bounded, Fort Smith has virtually no competition for shopping and specialty goods trade except from the four cities listed above. The area is large in square miles. The population is relatively small with few concentrations large enough to support adequate retail shopping facilities. Furthermore, the population is rural not only in residence but in occupation and outlook.

The situation is much the same for Laredo. It has competition on only three sides, with San Antonio 150 miles to the north, Corpus Christi 140 miles to the east, Monterrey, Mexico, 140 miles to the south, and nothing but the open spaces of northern Mexico to the west. The generalizations about Fort Smith's trading area are also applicable to Laredo.

Comparing two of the lowest sales-income ratio metropolitan areas with Fort Smith and Laredo provides an interesting contrast. It would be difficult to find a city with less in common with Fort Smith and Laredo than Jersey City, New Jersey. This city lies just across the harbor from New York City, and is "squeezed in" by Newark, Paterson, and Elizabeth, which surround it at distances of 6, 15, and 11 miles respectively. It is little wonder that Jersey City ranks at the bottom of the SMSAs in sales-income ratio.

The Lorain-Elyria, Ohio, SMSA seems to have a little more "breathing space" in surrounding land area; but examination of its geographical situation helps to explain its low sales-income ratio. Cleveland is 25 miles to the east, Akron 44 miles to the southeast, and Sandusky 31 miles to the west. Any retail trade from the north must come from residents of Lake Erie.

The contrasts between these two pairs of cities help to explain the changes in retail flows that have already taken place, and provide a basis for the prediction of changes which are likely to take place in the future.

The comparison indicates that for retail trade flow to be really significant there must be important differences between the metropolitan areas and the territory that surrounds them. In other words, the less urban the surrounding area and its population, the greater is the relative trade flow to the metropolitan center. On the other hand, nonmetropolitan areas of an urban character have sufficient population densities and purchasing power to make their own trading centers feasible and adequate.

Furthermore, going shopping in a distant metropolitan center is probably not very attractive when the main difference between the local shopping area and the metropolitan ones is that the latter are larger.

The growing efficiency of the distribution systems has brought this about, providing consumers with adequate and attractive choices wherever there are sufficient population densities and purchasing power to make viable retail systems possible. Any resident in or adjacent to a small city of 10,000 to 25,000 can satisfy most of his desires for goods without traveling far. The small city not only provides convenience goods, but offers every conceivable make and model of appliances, as well as increasingly wide selections of fashion goods, furniture, automobiles, and other merchandise.

Although nonmetropolitan sections have suffered relative population losses, their absolute populations have steadily increased in most states, and this increase has been accompanied by growing per capita income. The development of adequate trading centers in nonmetropolitan sections is likely to continue so long as nonmetropolitan population and income grow absolutely.

Consequently, it seems likely that the metropolitan areas retail systems will be faced with increasingly vigorous competition from nonmetropolitan trading centers.

RATE VARIATIONS AMONG SUPPLIERS OF AUTOMOBILE INSURANCE*

The cost of automobile insurance is a major component in the cost of car ownership. Insurance costs usually exceed maintenance costs, and for some drivers this expenditure is greater than their outlay for gasoline. However, little empirical evidence exists as to the variations in rates charged by the suppliers of this service.[1]

The major purposes of this study were to determine variations in prices charged for automobile insurance and to make some comparisons among the rates charged by insurance companies, brokers, and automobile dealers. Secondary purposes were to make price comparisons between companies dealing directly with the consumer and those using brokers, and between mutual and stock companies, as well as to ascertain the relationship between volume of business written and insurance charges.

The study found that there was considerable price variation for automobile insurance, but that the rates, on the average, charged by insurance companies, brokers, and automobile dealers did not vary substantially. There was not much variation in rates between direct selling companies and those that used brokers, or between mutual and stock companies. Volume of business showed no correlation with the rates charged. This study was conducted within a three week period in 1962.

METHODOLOGY AND SAMPLE

All charges were obtained by contacting firms that sell automobile insurance. These contacts were made by telephone and in some instances also in person. On all contacts the same standardized shopping procedure was followed. The interviewer was said to be in the process of purchasing a new automobile and was interested in obtaining insurance for it. All firms quoting charges for this study were contacted* both by the author and his assistant, David Thornton. In only three cases were different prices quoted. In these instances two additional contacts were made approximately two weeks later. The same price was quoted on three of the four contacts.[2]

* By Allen F. Jung. Reprinted from Journal of Risk and Insurance, December, 1963, pp. 573–576. Used by permission.
[1] Consumer Reports devoted considerable space recently in advising people how to shop for automobile insurance. See Automobile Insurance Series, Consumer Reports, March through September, 1962.
[2] Evidently a mistake in addition had been made on one of the original contacts.

With automobile dealers, it did not seem advisable to state that the shopper intended to purchase a new car. Therefore it was stated that a new automobile had been bought several months previously in the state of Ohio. The interviewer said he had been transferred to Chicago and was desirous of insuring his car in Illinois.

The sample was selected from insurance companies, brokers, and automobile dealers in Chicago, Illinois. A list of all companies selling automobile insurance in Illinois was provided by the Director of Insurance, State of Illinois. It was checked against the Chicago Telephone Directory, and only those firms listed there were considered. This list included 28 domestic and 115 foreign stock companies, 19 domestic and 18 foreign mutual companies, and 5 domestic and 4 foreign inter-insurance exchanges. This list was then stratified into three groups: large, firms that collected $1,000,000 or more in automobile insurance premiums in 1961; medium, firms that collected $500,000 but less than $1,000,000; and small, firms that received premiums of less than $500,000. A random sample of ten was selected from firms in the large, medium, and small categories.

A list of Chicago brokers mentioning automobile insurance in their ads or listings was compiled from the Chicago Classified Telephone Directory. Twenty brokers were selected at random from this list. Automobile zone offices provided a complete list of all dealers selling Ford and Plymouth automobiles in Chicago.[3] The study includes a random sample of 20 selected from Ford and Plymouth dealers.

Insurance rates were obtained on an eight cylinder 1962 Chevrolet Impala 4-door sedan. At Ford and Plymouth dealers, insurance rates were sought for a similar Ford Galaxie and Plymouth Fury, respectively. These three cars carry identical ratings in the State of Illinois for collision and comprehensive coverage.

The person interested in obtaining the insurance was 30 years old, married, and resided in Chicago, Illinois. He would not use his car for business, but would drive to and from work, a distance approximating 8 miles. The insured felt the car would aggregate 9,000 miles annually. The driver had not been involved in any accidents during the preceding 5 years. There would be no drivers other than he and his wife.

Identical insurance coverage was desired on all contacts. This included bodily injury protection of $50,000 for one person and $100,000 for one accident, and property damage coverage of $5,000. Physical damage insurance included $100 deductible for collision, and full comprehensive coverage. Several insurance companies offered package policies[4] on personal injury and/or physical damage. Any additional coverage included

[3] *The original idea of including only Chevrolet and Ford dealers had to be changed when six of the first seven Chevrolet dealers offered insurance only on the car and not on the driver. Evidently these General Motors dealers were influenced by the existence of Motors Insurance Company, a General Motors affiliate that does not write personal injury and property damage.*

[4] *Some package plans included $10,000 property damage, towing, medical payments, etc.*

in the price quotation, which was not desired in the original plan, has been adjusted by removing it from the price.

FINDINGS

The study found that there were considerable variations in charges for automobile insurance. Price ranged from $146.09 to $204.30 at insurance companies, from $145.80 to $204.30 at insurance brokers, and from $154.20 to $209.42 at automobile dealers (see Table 1). Insurance brokers did not, on average, quote prices very different from prices quoted by insurance companies, $176.11 vs. $175.01. The average price at automobile dealers was about 8 per cent higher, $189.83.

Table 1. *Annual charges for insurance on a new automobile in Chicago, Illinois, 1962*[a]

Type of organization	No. of sample ob- servations	Mean	Standard deviation	Median	Range
Automobile dealers	20	$189.83	$17.05	$191.95	$154.20–$209.42
Insurance brokers	20	176.11	19.17	177.70	145.80– 204.30
Insurance companies	30	175.01	15.15	177.70	146.09– 204.30
Large[b]	10	174.25	13.39	177.70	146.09– 191.00
Medium[c]	10	169.57	11.61	173.15	148.60– 185.00
Small[d]	10	181.19	18.69	177.70	148.56– 204.30
Mutual companies	9[e]	176.31	23.43	166.13	146.09– 204.30
Stock companies	20[e]	174.65	10.82	177.70	148.56– 191.00
Domestic (Illinois)	8	183.85	20.89	184.80	146.09– 204.30
Foreign (out of state)	22	171.79	11.44	177.70	148.56– 191.00
Direct sales	9	173.68	14.73	170.30	154.20– 204.30
Through brokers	21	175.58	15.30	177.70	146.09– 204.30

[a] Includes bodily injury insurance of $50,000/$100,000, $5,000 property damage, $100 deductible for collision, and full comprehensive coverage.
[b] Illinois sales $1 million or more.
[c] Illinois sales $500,000 but less than $1 million.
[d] Illinois sales less than $500,000.
[e] One insurance company contacted was an inter-insurance exchange.

A number of companies selling automobile insurance prefer to sell directly to the user, either through their own offices or through brokers who represent them exclusively.[5] Of the sample companies, nine sold automobile insurance directly to the consumer. They quoted average rates of $173.68, compared with an average of $175.58 for those that sold through brokers. It is interesting to note that all insurance companies contacted willingly quoted a price, even though all direct sales

[5] *This is similar to a franchise agreement. The broker agrees to engage in no other business activity except representing a particular company.*

were handled through a broker. In all instances, a broker was contacted when a company stated that it did not sell insurance directly. The broker, in all cases, quoted a price identical to the price obtained at the company. The company generally recommended two or more brokers, or referred the prospect to a list of its brokers in the "yellow pages" of the Chicago Classified Telephone Directory. In six cases[6] the broker quoted rates from a company other than the one that had recommended him. A specific mention of the company name was necessary to obtain its rates.

There was not very much variation when insurance companies were compared by size. Medium-size companies averaged the lowest rate, $169.57, and ranged from $148.60 to $185.00; large firms quoted prices of $174.25, on average, with a range from $146.09 to $191.00; average prices were highest at small firms, $181.19, ranging from $148.56 to $204.30.

Two other classifications of firms revealed some interesting comparisons. Mutual companies quoted rates that averaged $176.31 compared with average rates of $174.65 at stock companies. Domestic (Illinois) firms quoted average prices above those quoted by foreign (out of state) firms, $183.85 versus $171.79.

SALES BEHAVIOR

Most sales representatives readily quoted rates, with two notable exceptions. Several brokers with display advertisements in the Classified Telephone Directory attempted to qualify the buyers and it required some ingenuity on the part of the shopper to obtain rates. One broker confided that most of his calls were from people looking for the lowest price in town. Many representatives at automobile dealers preferred to quote approximate rates and a little urging was necessary to obtain exact rates. All personnel readily revealed the name of the company with which the insurance would be placed, with the exception of two brokers and four automobile dealers.

Most representatives did not take the name, address, or telephone number of the prospect. Brokers were more apt to ask for this information than were company representatives or automobile dealers. Follow-up letters and phone calls were received from five insurance brokers. One broker called in person at the prospect's home. Few representatives made a serious effort to sell the advantages of the broker they represented or the company from which the insurance would be purchased.

CONCLUSIONS

In Illinois, there are substantial variations in charges made by insurance companies for automobile insurance. Presumably similar variations exist

[6] *In three of these cases the insurance company had recommended only one broker.*

in many of the other states. It must be remembered that this study was concerned only with the cost of insurance. No attempt was made to measure differences in quality: some insurance companies undoubtedly offer better service, handle claims more readily, or are more liberal on adjustments than others are. From personal knowledge of some of these companies, it does not appear that firms that charge higher prices offer better service.

When insurance companies were classified by various means, smaller differences were found than might have been expected. There was no evidence that the amount of insurance the companies wrote in Illinois bore any direct relationship to the rates they charged. Companies that sold directly to the consumer, some of whom advertise or intimate that savings can be effected by eliminating the broker, did not offer substantially lower rates from those which sold through brokers. As it is often found in marketing, the middleman does not necessarily provide a higher cost of distribution.

A general belief held by many has been that mutual companies generally offer lower rates than stock companies do. The companies sampled in this study showed a slightly lower average price in favor of stock companies. If a price differential does indeed exist in favor of mutual companies, it is not so great as some may think.

Automobile dealers are generally believed to make unwarranted profits from the credit purchaser in the form of finance and insurance charges. The difference in insurance charges was less than 7 per cent lower at brokers than at automobile dealers.[7]

Sales personnel at automobile dealers, insurance brokers, and insurance companies could undoubtedly benefit from additional sales training, or an improved compensation plan. Their general attitude in cheerfully supplying requested information is commendable, but their lack of initiative in trying to convince the prospect of the desirability of dealing with the organization they represent is deplorable. Perhaps they feel that if they make enough quotations the law of averages will provide sales!

The consumer can benefit from contacting more than one source for insurance, be it an insurance company, broker, or automobile dealer. The broker who quoted the highest rate, quoted a rate 40.1 per cent above the rate quoted by the broker offering the lowest rate. Similar differences were found among automobile dealers and insurance companies. Unfortunately no pattern was found that could aid the consumer in determining a low cost supplier without extensive shopping. Price comparisons are rapidly becoming more complicated for the consumer with the introduction of "package" policies.

[7] *The average finance rate differential between automobile dealers and commercial banks was approximately 11 per cent in Chicago and 25 per cent in New York. For these and comparisons in other cities, see Allen F. Jung, "Charges for Appliance and Automobile Credit in Major Cities,"* Journal of Business, *October, 1962.*

SMALL BUSINESS
AND TIGHT MONEY*

By late 1957 a number of economists had apparently come to feel that the Federal Reserve's restraint on the growth of aggregate borrowing during the 1955–57 growth in aggregate expenditures had fallen especially hard on small businesses.[1] In general, two somewhat different explanations have been given to account for this differential impact. One is that the rising interest rates that resulted from credit restraint had a more inhibiting effect on the borrowing of small businesses than on the borrowing of large businesses.[2] The other is that many commercial banks did not try to reduce shortages by raising interest rates so much as by tightening other credit terms—that is, by "credit rationing"—and that the terms they chose to tighten—net worth, age, etc.—necessarily hurt small more than large businesses.[3]

The only systematic attempt to verify the hypothesis that small businesses have been hit harder by tight money—through the interest-rate effect or through "credit rationing"—than large businesses is that made by the Federal Reserve System for the Congressional Committees on Banking and Currency and on Small Business.[4] In general, the Federal Reserve found that borrowing by large businesses increased much more

* By Seymour Blank. Reprinted from the Journal of Finance, March, 1961, pp. 73–79. Used by permission.

NOTE: The author, formerly an instructor at Tulane University, wishes to acknowledge the assistance of Professors W. David Maxwell and Howard G. Schaller, of Tulane University, and of Charles F. Haywood, of the University of Mississippi.

[1] For example, Professor Galbraith (in "Market Structure and Stabilization Policy," Review of Economics and Statistics, May, 1957, p. 133) asserted that "there is a strong probability that in the past couple of years the effect of monetary policy has been to ration credit from all sources away from smaller firms in the competitive sector and to large firms in the oligopolistic sector." Allan Sproul (Commercial and Financial Chronicle, May 31, 1956, p. 35) commented along these lines: "I suspect that the impact of credit restraint is greater on 'small' business than on big business." Cf. also Arthur F. Burns, Prosperity without Inflation (New York: Fordham University Press, 1958).

[2] Cf., for example, John Galbraith, The Affluent Society (Boston: Houghton Mifflin, 1958), pp. 235–36.

[3] For a clear definition and discussion by Professor Samuelson of "credit rationing," cf. U.S. Congress, Joint Committee on the Economic Report, Subcommittee on General Credit Control and Debt Management, Hearings: Monetary Policy and Management of the Public Debt (82d Cong., 2d Sess. [1952]), pp. 697–98.

[4] U.S. Congress, Financing Small Business: Report to the Committees on Banking and Currency and the Select Committees on Small Business (85th Cong., 2d sess. [1958]); cf. also U.S. Congress, House, Select Committee on Small Business, Hearings: Problems of Small-Business Financing (85th Cong., 1st sess. [1957]).

during the 1955–57 period than did borrowing by small businesses but that this was due to a relatively greater increase in the demand for funds on the part of large businesses; that interest rates on loans to small businesses apparently rose relatively less than those to large businesses during this period; and that there was no significant volume of "credit rationing" against small businesses.[5] The issue is obviously not closed, though, especially the question of the extent to which "credit rationing" occurs and the extent to which its impact is heaviest on small businesses. Some of the evidence introduced in the Federal Reserve study on this "credit-rationing" hypothesis is, at best, ambiguous, and some offers rather strong support for it.[6]

As a contribution to the discussion of the "credit-rationing" question, I present in this paper the results of a survey which, I think, supports the position that commercial banks did not tend to ration funds during the 1955–57 upturn in such a way as to discriminate against small businesses or to cut small businesses off from an important source of funds to them. The survey also suggesets what perhaps should be fairly self-evident: that the opinions of small businessmen themselves can hardly be relied on as evidence of what, in fact, commercial banks in the aggregate do.

I

Questionnaires were submitted to 4,986 manufacturing businesses in the Sixth Federal Reserve District. These businesses had been selected by drawing every fourth name on the alphabetical list of the state directories of manufacturers.[7] Before drawing every fourth name from the state directories, subsidiaries of large national firms such as General Motors, DuPont, United States Steel, etc., and firms with headquarters out of the Sixth District were deleted because it seemed probable that these concerns would not seek bank credit in the Sixth District. Though exclusion of some large firms may bias this study to some degree, the bias might be less than that which would have been present if these firms had been included in the sample. Of the 4,986 questionnaires mailed, 4,763 reached the addressees. There were 577 responses, for a percentage response of approximately 12 per cent.[8]

[5] For a convenient summary of the Federal Reserve findings, cf. Edwin B. George and Robert J. Landry, "The Federal Reserve Board Report on Small-Business Financing," Journal of Business, XXXII (July, 1959), pp. 214–16.

[6] For example the fact that interest rates on loans to small businesses apparently rose less than those to large businesses can be used in support of the "credit-rationing" thesis. The Standard Factors, Inc., evidence (U.S. Congress, House, Select Committee on Small Business, op. cit., p. 44) that withdrawals of credit lines between March, 1955, and March, 1956, were confined to smaller firms obviously offers backing to the "credit-rationing" thesis.

[7] Mississippi does not appear in the analysis because there was no Mississippi directory available.

[8] The questionnaire was sent by first-class mail but was not directed to any particular

The respondents were asked to provide information about the size of their assets, net worth, and the number of their employees. However, too few firms supplied information about their assets and net worth to permit systematic classification on these bases. But 511 of the 577 respondents indicated the number of their employees. This information is shown in Table 1. Since only 20 of the respondents employed over

Table 1. Size of respondents by number of employees

No. of employees	No. of firms	No. of employees	No. of firms	No. of employees	No. of firms
1– 5	98	71–100	27	701–800	0
6–10	70	101–200	42	801–900	1
11–15	60	201–250	7	901–1,000	0
16–20	43	251–400	5	1,001–1,250	2
21–25	41	401–500	5	1,251–1,500	1
26–40	54	501–600	2	1,501–2,000	1
41–70	44	601–700	1	Over 5,000	2

250 employees, it would appear that nearly all the respondents could be classified as small business.[9]

The responses of these 577 firms are shown in Table 2. The first column lists the number of firms responding to the particular question, and the second column indicates the percentage of the 577 respondents who answered the particular question. The columns under "Affirmative Response," "Negative Response," and "Neutral Response"[10] indicate the percentage response in these three categories to the particular question. Every respondent fell into one of the three classes.

person or company officer. Addressed envelopes were inclosed for the return of answers and return postage was guaranteed. A letter stressing the importance of the project was sent with each questionnaire. This letter was signed personally. No directions for filling out the questionnaire, except those on the questionnaire, were supplied. The sample is probably biased in the direction of returns from (a) the larger firms answering the questionnaire and (b) firms with a special interest in replying, i.e., those affected by monetary stringency. To some extent, these factors are offsetting.

[9] The Small Business Administration defines a manufacturing firm as small if it employs 250 or fewer persons, and large if it employs more than 1,000 persons. A firm may be considered either small or large if it employs more than 250 persons but not more than 1,000 persons, depending on the employment size standard which the Small Business Administration has developed for its particular industry (Small Business Administration, SBA Business Loans [July, 1956], p. 1). The distribution by size of the firms classified in Table 1 is quite similar to this same distribution for the economy as a whole (see U.S. Department of Commerce, Survey of Current Business, May, 1954, p. 23).

[10] All respondents who did not specifically answer affirmatively or negatively to the particular question posed were listed under the "Neutral Response" category.

Table 2. Tabulation of 577 responses to questionnaire submitted to 4,986 manufacturing businesses in the Sixth Federal Reserve District in September, 1957

Question	Respondents answering this question No.	Per cent	Affirmative response (per cent)	Negative response (per cent)	Neutral response (per cent)
Part I					
1. Have you observed that small business firms have special difficulty in obtaining loans from banks?	526	91.1	53.2	46.7	...
2. Do you believe that small business firms are able to obtain:					
a) Adequate short-term credit (up to 1 year)?	503	87.1	65.2	34.7	...
b) Adequate long-term credit (over 1 year)?	474	82.1	27.8	72.1	...
3. Is short-term credit the greater problem?	514	89.0	5.6	58.1	36.1
4. Is the impact of tight money greater on small businesses than on large businesses, assuming that each has equal credit merit?	494	85.6	65.7	3.6	30.5
Part II					
1. Indicate if your firm has not attempted to borrow from any bank within the past 5 years	102	17.8	100.0	...	...
2. Was your firm refused a bank loan at any time within the past 5 years?	471	81.6	22.7	77.2	...
3. Indicate if your firm has had a request for a bank loan *reduced* but not denied at any time within the past 5 years	71	12.3	100.0	...	...
4. Indicate if your firm has tried to borrow from government or private sources *other* than banks at any time within the past 5 years	120	20.7	100.0	...	...
5. Was your firm refused by nonbank lenders at any time within the past 5 years?*	120	20.7	25.8	74.1	...

* The respondents to question 5 were the same as those to question 4.

Question 1 indicates that over half the respondents seem to feel that small business firms have special difficulty, or at least had special difficulty in 1957, in obtaining bank financing. And question 4 indicates that about two-thirds of the respondents held the opinion in 1957 that tight money falls harder on small rather than large businesses.

However, questions 2 and 3 show that a considerable majority of those answering felt that small business firms could find adequate short-term funds at the time and that the real financing problem involved long-term funds. Further, as questions 1 and 2 of Part II show, of the 471 firms that actually tried to borrow—short-term and/or long-term—from banks between 1953 and 1957, only 107 (23 per cent) were apparently refused. (Note question 3 of Part II, though, which shows that an additional 12 per cent were able to borrow but had their loan requests trimmed.)

Questions 4 and 5 of Part II indicate that 20 per cent of the 526 respondents also tried to borrow—again, short-term and/or long term—from non-bank sources during the five-year period.[11] (Unfortunately, it is not known which of these firms represented businesses that had been turned down by banks and which represented businesses that had not been refused.) About 22 per cent of these firms report that they had their requests refused by these non-bank sources. This is the same refusal percentage as in the case of bank-loan applicants.

II

The question now is whether the fact that 107 firms, of the 471 that applied to commercial banks for short- and/or long-term credit, were refused loans constitutes support for the hypothesis that banks rationed credit, using criteria that discriminated against small businesses.[12]

There is some evidence that is at least consistent with this hypothesis. Table 3 shows the number of firms granted credit and the number of firms refused credit, both in relation to number of employees. It suggests some correlation between size (by number of employees), but certainly not a striking amount. For example, of the firms granted bank credit, 55.2 per cent employed fewer than 26 persons, while, of the firms that were refused bank credit, 68.6 per cent employed fewer than 26 persons. Table 4 shows an age distribution of the firms, broken down into those granted and those refused credit. Here, again, the results do not contradict the discrimination thesis: older firms did fare somewhat better than younger firms. But, also as before, the correlation is modest.

[11] *The 120 firms that indicated that they approached non-bank sources during the 1953–57 period were asked to identify these sources. The replies were as follows:*

SBA	37	Savings and loan associations	3
RFC	9	Insurance companies	18
CCC	2	Stockholders	2
Private	33	Parent firm	1
Trust funds	1	Not indicated	14

[12] *Since the respondents were free to define "refused" as they saw fit, it is likely that some of these firms that reported they were refused credit simply meant that they found unacceptable the terms at which credit was actually offered.*

Table 3. Firms refused or granted commercial bank credit by number of employees

No. of employees	No. of firms		Percentage of total	
	Granted	Refused	Granted	Refused
1–5	48	24	14.3	24.2
6–10	44	13	13.1	13.1
11–25	93	31	27.8	31.3
26–50	37	12	11.0	12.1
51–100	58	10	17.3	10.1
101–200	30	4	8.9	4.0
201–400	14	0	4.1	...
401–500	3	2	0.9	2.0
501–600	2	0	0.6	...
601–1,000	...	2	...	2.0
1,001–1,500	3	0	0.8	...
1,501–2,500	...	1	...	1.0
Over 5,000	2	0	0.6	...
Not indicated	30	8	...	...
Total	364	107	99.4	99.8

Table 4. Firms refused or granted commercial bank credit by year of inception of firm

Year of inception	Number of firms		Year of inception	Number of firms	
	Refused	Granted		Refused	Granted
1830–40	0	2	1901–10	0	9
1841–50	0	1	1911–20	4	14
1851–60	0	2	1921–30	7	39
1861–70	0	3	1931–40	13	59
1871–80	0	4	1941–46	20	65
1881–90	1	7	1947–51	23	83
1891–1900	2	16	1952–57	30	37
			Not given	7	23

There is stronger evidence, however, that the experience of these 107 firms does not provide any significant degree of verification for the rationing hypothesis. First, 29 of the 102 firms refused loans were actually turned down during the 1953–54 period of easy money when banks were largely reducing surpluses rather than shortages. Second, and more important, Dun and Bradstreet, at my request, supplied on April 30, 1958, a credit analysis of 80 firms—those that had made their names available—of the 107 that reported loan refusals. The results are shown in

**Table 5. Dun and Bradstreet analysis of 80 firms that reported
commercial bank refusals of their loan requests**

No. of firms*	Credit status
43	Currently indebted to commercial banks or recently so indebted
2	Not currently indebted but did obtain commercial bank credit in past year or two
1	Currently owes the Production Credit Administration
1	Currently owes the Small Business Administration on a direct defense loan
1	Currently owes factor
2	Currently owe private individuals (perhaps by preference because probably could have obtained bank credit)
15	Have no commercial bank loans but probably could have obtained such loans by meeting reasonable bank requirements
11	Could hardly justify bank credit

* Four of the 80 firms submitted to D & B for analysis had gone out of the business between the time of the questionnaire and April 30, 1958.

Table 5. They suggest that few of the firms in question have actually been cut off from bank credit to the extent that their answers to the questionnaire would lead one to infer. About 63 per cent of the firms analyzed had, in fact, been bank debtors during 1957 or were debtors in April, 1958. Another 22 per cent could, in Dun and Bradstreet's opinion, have rather readily obtained bank credit.[13] The remaining 15 per cent "could hardly justify bank credit," which presumably means that these firms would be denied credit whether money was tight or easy.

III

As is the case with most surveys of the type this paper has reported, the results are not conclusive. However, of the two hypotheses—one that Sixth District banks have rationed their funds in such a way as to discriminate against small manufacturing businesses, and the other that Sixth District banks have not rationed their funds in this way—it does seem fair to say that the results fit the latter hypothesis better than the former. Since the survey also indicates that small businessmen themselves hold the former hypothesis, one is tempted to draw another conclusion: that the opinions of individual businessmen cannot be relied on as evidence of the way businessmen and banks behave in the aggregate.

[13] *There are two things to be noted about the Dun and Bradstreet analysis. First of all, some of the firms that D & B reported to be bank debtors may have become so after the onset of easy money in December, 1957. Second, what D & B regard as "reasonable bank requirements" may constitute "refusal" to some prospective borrowers.*

THE DIFFERENTIAL
EFFECTS OF
TIGHT MONEY*

Restrictive monetary policy is widely opposed because of its alleged undesirably discriminatory effects. Tight money, it is claimed, lets big borrowers go free while shutting off little ones. It restricts construction activity while letting investment in plant and equipment boom. Conversely, it restricts investment so sharply it induces recession. It runs up interest costs to those least able to pay. It penalizes new borrowers at the expense of old established customers. All these claims, and many more, have been urged upon Congress, by economists and by others, as powerful reasons against reliance on restricitive monetary policy to check moderate inflation.

Given substantially full employment, any restrictive policy is discriminatory in the sense that it changes the allocation of resources from what would have prevailed in the absence of the restriction. Assume full employment with excess demand (inflationary pressure) and some given allocation of resources. If monetary policy is now used to produce a smaller money supply than otherwise would have existed, a different allocation of resources may result. It is this shift in resources which is presumably meant when critics speak of the discriminatory (or differential) effects of tight money. We shall use the term in this sense.

The following pages describe an investigation of the "discriminatory" effects of tight money which isolates these effects by studying the differential lending-investing policies during the 1955–57 period of "tight" banks in contrast to those of "loose" banks which were otherwise substantially identical but where there was little or no pressure of tight money.

* By G. L. Bach and C. J. Huizenga. Reprinted from American Economic Review, March, 1961, pp. 52–80. Used by permission.

NOTE: The authors are, respectively, professor of economics at Carnegie Institute of Technology and acting assistant professor of business economics at the University of California, Los Angeles. We are indebted to the Ford Foundation for faculty research and doctoral fellowships which made this research possible, and to the Commission on Money and Credit for financial support. We are equally indebted to the Board of Governors of the Federal Reserve System for making available the basic data, for extensive statistical analytical problems. In the latter connection, James Eckert, Albert Koch, Roland Robinson and Edward Snyder were especially helpful, as were our colleagues Edwin Mansfield, Allan Meltzer and Franco Modigliani.

I. DESIGN OF STUDY

Identification of possible discriminatory effects of tight money during any period of credit restraint is difficult. In 1955–57, for example, we know that commercial bank lending to large borrowers rose much more than that to small borrowers. But this fact is not necessarily evidence that tight money led banks to discriminate against small borrowers. Instead, the observed results may have arisen largely from the demand side of markets rather than from the supply side, and indeed there is much evidence that such was the case in that particular period. The problem is to devise a method of isolating the supply effects (that is, the discriminatory effects of tight money in restricting lending) as distinct from the effects of differing demands for credit.

To isolate the effects of tight money on the behavior of lenders, the following basic design was used. First a period was chosen when money was generally agreed to be tight and growing tighter—October 1955 to October 1957. Then a large sample of banks (about 1700) was chosen, large enough to permit stratification so that substantial numbers of banks in all major cells were presumably substantially identical in all respects (including potential loan demand) except for the differential impact or tight money upon them. Then the banks were divided into three subgroups—"tight," "medium," and "loose," depending on the degree of tightness induced in them by the over-all tightness of money. The tightest quartile of banks was placed in the tight group, the next two quartiles in the medium group, and the loosest quartile in the loose group. The loose banks, as is explained below, were selected so that it would be agreed that they were loose by almost any reasonable test—for example, they were not tight by standard tests at the beginning of the period, and they gained more deposits over the period than they increased their loans and investments.[1]

Then the lending and investing behavior of these three groups of banks was compared over the period, with the presumption that the tight quartile could reflect the differential impact of tight money on the supply side, when compared with the loose quartile which apparently felt little if any pressure of tightness. This comparison between the tight and loose quartiles seems especially apt to isolate the differential effects of tight money, since loose banks were clearly quite loose and there is little evidence that they refused any borrowers because of shortage of lending power or for any reason other than failure of borrowers to meet general banking standards of credit-worthiness. In testing different hypotheses about possible discriminatory effects of tight money, banks were stratified by size and other major characteristics within each of the three tightness groupings, to assure comparability on factors other than tightness.

[1] *The terms tight, medium, and loose are intended as brief terms to indicate relative status. They are not intended to convey absolute status with any precision, except, as is noted below, that the loose banks were demonstrably loose by almost any reasonable standard.*

A. Nature of Sample and Information Obtained

The basic sample consisted of about 1700 Federal Reserve member banks, with identical banks reporting in October 1955 and October 1957. Reporting banks held nearly 90 per cent of all commercial and industrial loans at member banks. The sample provided almost complete coverage of all central reserve city and reserve city banks, with about one-fourth of all country member banks. The sample was drawn on a stratified basis by the Federal Reserve System for its two major studies of commercial and industrial loans in 1955 and 1957. All sample data were then "blown up" to cover all commercial member banks in the United States.[2]

Information in both years was collected on the following items: (1) complete call-report data for each reporting bank, including information on all major asset and liability items; (2) the following information on individual commercial and industrial loans on the books of each reporting bank as of October 5, 1955 and October 16, 1957: (a) business of borrower (13 categories); (b) total assets of borrower; (c) form of business organization—incorporated or unincorporated; (d) amount of loan outstanding; (e) original amount of loan; (f) whether loan was a term loan; (g) whether loan was secured or unsecured; (h) interest rate on loan.

B. Measures of Bank Tightness

For explaining banker (lender) behavior, how tight a bank is depends on how tight the banker (the decision-maker) feels it is. One bank may be extremely tight for lending purposes, even though it has a large volume of excess reserves and liquid securities, *if* the banker believes that these reserves and securities are essential to the sound operation of the bank. Another bank may be loose for lending purposes, even though it has very small excess reserves and only a modest supply of liquid securities, *if* the banker feels that he nevertheless has more reserves and more securities than he needs for normal operating purposes (assuming that he is within standard examination regulations). Thus, standard measures like excess reserves and free reserves are not reliable measures of bank tightness for lending purposes.

This point becomes clearer if one remembers that the individual banker can alter his volume of excess reserves (and hence his lending power) with relative freedom by restructuring his asset portfolio—say by selling off bills or bonds. Thus one must consider the whole asset portfolio—not just a simple measure of excess or free reserves—if he is to have a reasonable measure of how tight the individual bank is. And the banking system as a whole can similarly increase its excess reserves by selling securities to others, though to a lesser extent since it must find noncommercial-bank buyers, a limitation which the individual bank does not face.

[2] Details of the sampling procedure and the reporting forms were published in the Federal Reserve Bulletin [9, 10].

This poses difficult problems of measuring the tightness of individual banks and of the banking system. We cannot peer into the banker's mind to see what makes him feel tight or loose. Indeed, the banker's own word is possibly not to be accepted. So we need to search for surrogate measures.

Banking system as a whole. Over the period from October 1955 to October 1957, it is widely agreed that money was tight and becoming increasingly tighter for the banking system as a whole.[3] At least four types of evidence support this belief.

First, Federal Reserve authorities, bankers, and virtually all observers in the financial press spoke out on the increasing tightness of money. While such statements are of course not conclusive, their general uniformity was striking.[4]

Second, over the period commercial banks shifted heavily out of long-term bonds into short-term government securities and loans. Between October 1955 and October 1957, loans at all member banks increased from $67 billion to $80 billion while bonds of five years or longer maturity declined from $24 billion to $10 billion. This shift was a clear indication of increasing pressure on the banking system so far as the ability to make loans was concerned.

Third, interest rates had risen substantially by the beginning of the period, and continued to rise through it, as is indicated by Table 1.

Table 1. Interest rates, October 1955–October 1957

	Average for 1954	October 1955	October 1957
U.S. Treasury bills	.9	2.2	3.6
Prime commercial paper	1.6	2.7	4.1
Aaa corporate bonds	2.9	3.1	4.1

Fourth, there was virtually no growth in the money supply, although the volume of transactions to be financed and population rose substantially over the period. Currency and demand deposits outside banks totaled $132 billion in October 1955, and only $134 billion in October 1957. At the same time gross national product rose from $392 billion

---

[3] *The exact dates chosen (in October of each year) were dictated by the availability of data—both call-report data and, more important, data on the large-scale Federal Reserve commercial loan surveys which were available for only those two specific months. Actually, a period ending a few months earlier, in the summer of 1957, would have been better, since apparently the peak of tight money occurred some time in the late summer. However, there was no substantial easing of money over the few months before October.*

[4] *See, for example, the annual reports of the Board of Governors of the Federal Reserve System [7]; "Bank Credit and Money" [5] [6]; the New York Times financial pages [12]; and Business Week [8].*

(annual rate) for the third quarter of 1955 to $440 billion (annual rate) for the third quarter of 1957.[5]

Clearly, there have been other periods when money was tighter, and in part the increasing tightness was a return to more normal times from the very low interest rates of the preceding decades. For purposes of this study, however, it is important merely that money was tight enough to put the tighter banks under substantial pressure to refuse some otherwise acceptable borrowers, and that it was becoming tighter. These conditions were clearly present. Nor do the findings depend on the extent to which this tightness reflected conscious Federal Reserve policy. Since the money supply remained roughly constant, the increasing tightness obviously reflected mainly increasing demand for money.

Individual banks. To test tight-money hypotheses, we ranked all individual banks by degree of tightness as of October 1955, and by increase in tightness between October 1955 and October 1957. A more satisfactory measure than excess or free reserves appeared to be the ratio:

$$\frac{\text{excess reserves} - \text{borrowing} + \text{government bills and certificates}}{\text{deposits}}$$

We call this a looseness ratio, since an increase in the ratio means that the bank has become looser for lending purposes.

This ratio was used to rank individual banks as of October 1955. The ratio reflects the fact that banks consider short-term governments as secondary reserves, only slightly differentiated from actual reserves. Moreover, this ratio varies appreciably at individual banks with changes in economic conditions, at the same time that the ratio of excess reserves, or even free reserves, to deposits varies little for most banks. The ratio falls (indicates tightening) for the banking system as a whole and for most individual banks over the 1955–57 period, when we know that money was tightening for the system as a whole. On the other hand, the ratio has weaknesses. For example, it does not reflect the fact that

---

[5] *The traditional measures of excess reserves and "free" reserves provide little help in assessing the tightness of the banking system over the period in question. Excess reserves averaged about $500 million during October of each year. This reflected the fact that excess reserves were substantially at their operating minimum by 1955, given the mores of many bankers about excess reserves. Thus they could not practically be reduced further. Free reserves (excess reserves minus borrowing) averaged —$360 million in October 1955 and —$344 million in October 1957. Banks that were willing to borrow at the Federal Reserve were doing so substantially by October 1955, and again to about the same extent in October 1957. Both the free and the excess reserve figures emphasize that many banks nowadays manage their portfolios so as to hold excess and free reserves at what they consider reasonable minimum levels, especially when interest rates are high. Thus whether money is loose or tight, excess reserves for the system stay at about the same level. Free reserves are more volatile and are significant for many large banks. But they too provide a very imperfect measure of the tightness of the system, for the reasons noted above and because only a small fraction of banks view borrowing at the Federal Reserve as a significant device for adjusting their reserve positions.*

interbank deposits provide a special source of liquidity to some banks; thus, most small country banks were probably relatively looser than the ratio shows. Neither is vault cash included. Nor are near-maturity securities other than bills and certificates. Most important, it does not include longer-term government securities, but there are convincing reasons for this exclusion.[6]

We have no clean-cut objective basis for selecting the looseness ratio used. The case is that it is a reasonable measure a priori, and that all the likely alternatives have serious drawbacks. The ratio was tested against other measures, including excess and free reserves. For example, the ratio of loans to government securities was examined, on the theory that the higher the loan ratio becomes the tighter the bank will be since it has less opportunity left to shift from government securities to loans. This measure, like the looseness ratio including government bonds, proved of limited usefulness because it mainly reflected the lending-investment preferences of individual banks, rather than serving as a fundamental measure of tightness for the rank-ordering of banks.

To measure the *change* in tightness between October 1955 and October 1957 two tests were initially applied. First, all individual banks were ranked by the decrease in the looseness ratio between October 1955 and October 1957. Second, banks were ranked according to the percentage increase in their deposits over the period. For the individual bank, as distinguished from the banking system, it is primarily gain or loss of deposits which makes the bank looser or tighter for new lending and investing. Therefore, the simplest measure of whether an individual bank is growing looser or tighter is the extent to which it is gaining or losing deposits. Thus, all banks were ranked by percentage increase in deposits over the two-year period. Banks with the greatest loss of deposits showed the greatest increase in tightness, with others ranked in order of deposit gain.

Broadly, the rank-order results for individual banks were similar using these two methods over the 1955–57 period. However, the change-in-deposits method both seemed more significant in explaining individual bank lending-investment behavior and offered a more sharply discriminating measure as among individual banks. This is because changes in the tightness ratio were quite small for most banks, so that the individual bank ranking might be considerably influenced by small special circumstances, while differences in the rate of deposit growth were large. Thus, we decided to use the second measure alone—change in deposits be-

[6] *Government bonds, which are not included in the numerator, obviously help increase liquidity and hence decrease the tightness of a bank. While individual banks can obtain funds for loans by selling government securities, holdings of long-term governments at many banks are so large relative to bills, certificates, and free reserves, that their inclusion would swamp the ratio. Thus the ratio with long-term government securities included would tend to reflect primarily the investment preferences of individual banks and would lose most of its virtue as a measure of tightness for ranking individual banks.*

To avoid the danger that the deposits and reserve figures in the ratio would be thrown off by special temporary factors, monthly averages were used, rather than one-day figures.

tween October 1955 and October 1957—as the criterion of the extent to which banks became tighter or looser.[7]

To obtain the final tightness ranking of all individual banks, the ranking as of 1955 and the ranking by increase in tightness for the 1955–57 period were combined in the following way. First, banks were divided into the tightest and loosest halves on the basis of the looseness ratio as of October 1955. Then, all banks in the tightest half for 1955 were rank-ordered by the degree to which their tightness increased over the succeeding two years, as measured by relative deposit loss or gain. The tight group for the study (the tightest quartile) was then obtained by taking the 50 per cent of the tight half as of 1955 which showed the greatest further increase in tightness by 1957. Similarly, the loosest half as of 1955 was rank-ordered by change in tightness, and the 50 per cent showing the greatest increase in looseness was considered the loose group for the study. The remaining two inner quartiles were considered the medium group.[8]

This test combines tightness as of the beginning of the period with change in tightness. In principle, there need be no relationship between these two measures. On the other hand, the purpose was to segregate at the two extremes banks which both were tight in absolute level and became tighter, from those that were clearly loose in absolute level and became looser. The procedure followed achieved this result. Thus, banks in the loose quartile had looseness ratios of 3 per cent and higher in October 1955, as compared to only 1+ per cent for all banks. Moreover, their gain in deposits ranged from 8 per cent to over 100 per cent for the two-year period, compared to only a 4.5 per cent increase for the banking system as a whole—while about half the banks in the tight group actually lost deposits over the two-year period.[9] Most important, the loose banks as a group gained more deposits over the period than they expanded their loans and investments. Thus, they obtained more new funds for loans and investments than they used. Under this circumstance it is hard to see how these banks can have felt themselves seriously restrained by tight money.[10]

[7] *A further study was made to test the significance of using both measures. Limitation of the tight group to banks that were in the tightest quartile by* both *the change-in-looseness ratio and the change-in-deposits tests eliminated only a small fraction of the banks. This further refinement was therefore dropped.*

[8] *Since large city banks were heavily concentrated in the tight group, about 40 per cent of total commercial bank assets were included in that group. About 45 per cent were in the medium group, and about 15 per cent in the loose group in which smaller country banks predominated.*

[9] *Studies were made of the differences in groupings obtained by using either the as-of-1955 or the 1955–57 change measure alone. Surprisingly, not very great changes were obtained in the tight and loose groups by limiting the test to the situation as of October 1955 or by taking the change-in-deposit ranking alone. Thus, it appears that, in a broad sense, the banks that were already tight in late 1955 were the ones that tended to become even tighter over the following two years.*

[10] *This same excess of new deposits over new loans and investments was shown by all small (country) banks as a group. There was a massive shift of deposits (and lending power) from very large to small banks. See [11, p. 424].*

C. Hypotheses Investigated

Using this analytical approach, five general hypotheses were considered: (1) That tight money induced banks to shift from government securities to loans. (2) That tight money led banks to discriminate against small borrowers in lending to businesses. (3) That tight money led banks to differentiate in favor of particular industry groups among business borrowers. (4) That tight money was effective in checking loans especially to those firms which were primarily responsible for the 1955–57 investment and inventory boom. (5) That tight money led banks to raise interest charges especially to small borrowers and to particular industry groups against which they wished to discriminate. The succeeding sections examine these hypotheses in turn.

II. EFFECTS ON BANK LENDING AND INVESTING

Table 2 compares the behavior of tight, medium, and loose banks in extending loans and investment over the 1955–57 period as money grew tighter. The left-hand portion of the table shows the percentage increases of total loans and investments and all major subclasses at loose, medium, and tight banks. Percentage increase figures are used because absolute figures would overweight the large banks in whatever groups they fell (largely the tight and medium groups). The right-hand portion of the table shows the relative increases (or decreases) in loans and investments at loose, medium, and tight banks. Though only relative changes are shown, the absolute amounts in all cells are large.

As the left-hand portion shows, all banks increased their total loans and investments, but the loose banks did so the most. All banks sold off long-term government securities, presumably to obtain funds to increase other assets. All banks increased their holdings of short-term government securities and of commercial and industrial loans, loans to individuals, and real estate loans. The large percentage increase in short-term government securities of all banks, however, is caused in substantial part merely by long-term bonds moving down into the under-five years category, rather than by actual bank sales of long-term bonds and purchase of short-term issues. If adjustment is made for the moving down in issues held, it is still true for all banks combined that there was some shift from long- to short-term government securities, but not much. This qualification does not, so far as we can tell, throw doubt on the *differential* behavior shown by loose and tight banks.[11]

But there were appreciable differences in the behavior of tight and loose banks, as indicated by both halves of the table. Tight banks substantially reduced their holdings of other securities and of agricultural

[11] *This result seems surprising, since bankers are generally thought to draw first on short-term government securities to obtain loan funds when reserves become tight. Once adjustment is made for the downshifting of maturities, the actual dollar increase in bills and certificates at tight banks in Table 2 is small, but not insignificant. In any case, it is clear that tight banks drew most heavily on longer-term securities to obtain loan funds.*

Table 2. Increase in asset classes, October 1955–October 1957

Asset groups	Per cent increase at:			Relative increase, with per cent increase at loose banks = 100		
	Loose banks	Medium banks	Tight banks	Loose banks	Medium banks	Tight banks
Total loans and investments	*23*	*9*	*1*	*100*	*39*	*4*
Bills and certificates	87	85	242	100	98	278
Other government securities under five years	36	26	12	100	72	33
Government securities over five years	−49	−52	−52	(a)	(a)	(a)
Other securities	34	5	−10	100	15	−129
Commercial and industrial loans	47	33	25	100	70	53
Real estate loans	32	16	6	100	50	19
Security loans	154	22	−20	100	14	−13
Agricultural loans	4	3	−10	100	75	−250
Loans to individuals	30	24	11	100	80	37

ª Decrease in all groups.

and security loans, while building up their short-term government securities more heavily than other banks. Their increase in loans was smaller than at other banks, and the differences in lending-investing behavior at tight and loose banks were greatest within the loan categories. Tight banks increased real estate loans much less than did loose banks. But still more, they squeezed security and agricultural loans heavily to obtain funds for modest expansions in other loan categories. On the other hand, security and agricultural loans have never been dominant parts of the loan portfolio of the banking system, and the actual dollar shift of loans was more modest than might appear from the relative increases.[12]

[12] *It might appear that this differential behavior of tight and loose banks is explained not by differing tightness, but merely by the fact that the expected mean value of the lending-investing behavior of the two groups is similar so that they will both tend to move toward it—the so-called "regression fallacy." In Table 2, the greater shift from government securities to loans at loose banks might simply represent a movement of the loose and tight banks back toward a common portfolio balance after the tight group had by chance increased their loans more rapidly. But examination of the nine asset categories in Table 2 shows disparate behavior that is not explained by the regression fallacy. While we cannot be sure that the observed lending-investing differences between tight and loose banks are explained by differing tightness, the behavior is generally consistent with what we would a priori expect to observe from the tight-money hypothesis; and we find no other reasonable hypothesis to which the observed behavior can be attributed.*

It may be surprising that the tight banks did not shift *more* heavily from low- to high-yield assets under the pressure of tight money. The explanation is probably found largely in the force of traditional standards of banking practice. Most bankers, even when very tight, are reluctant to go beyond certain widespread notions of portfolio balance, which vary substantially by class and location of bank. For example, loans amounting to much more than 50 per cent of total assets apparently seem excessive, or at least of dubious propriety, to many bankers. Moreover, bankers understand their needs for liquidity and do not consider loans very liquid, in spite of the technical availability of the Federal Reserve rediscount window. Federal Reserve informal and formal actions reinforce this reluctance to rely extensively on rediscounting except in special temporary circumstances. Thus, many bankers continue to be the generally careful, cautious people they are commonly reputed to be in determining their portfolio balance, even when profits beckon in, say, higher automobile or real estate loans.[13]

If we assume that loose banks felt little or no restraint from tight money (as is strongly suggested by the evidence presented above), then the comparative data for tight banks provide a direct measure of the differential impact of tight money. Even if the loose banks felt some restraint, since the tight banks clearly were much tighter the comparative data still provide direct evidence on the "discriminatory" effects of tight money on bank lending and investing behavior.

Attributing the differences in Table 2 to tight money implies that banks of comparable size in the three groups were substantially identical on other grounds, particularly in the loan demands they felt. We believe this was substantially true.[14] The 1700 banks in the sample, as indicated above, provide substantially complete coverage of large- and medium-sized banks; and the sample of small banks was carefully stratified geographically and in terms of other significant bank characteristics. Lend-

[13] *For a summary of banker interviews on the extent to which tight money changed lending policies, see [11; p. 431ff.].*

Apparently bank examination standards per se did not significantly limit bank loan expansion during the period. In an unpublished doctoral dissertation at Carnegie Institute of Technology, David Chambers found that even tight banks (using our groupings) generally stayed well within the formal examiners' limits. Other tests confirmed this general conclusion. But widespread knowledge of examiners' expectations, of course, may have helped mold bankers' mores as to how far they can reasonably go in shifting to loans, and to higher-yield risky loans within the loan category, when money becomes tight.

[14] *This is, of course, a crucial assumption. Otherwise, observed differences between the behavior of tight and loose banks cannot necessarily be attributed primarily to differences in tightness. We can only report that, in addition to the careful sampling procedure followed, we have examined the bank groups in detail for other characteristics that might explain a significant part of the observed differences, and have been unable to find any—for example, geographical or urban vs. country location. It is important to remember, however, that separate analysis of banks of different sizes is important at several points because of the relative concentration of large, city banks in the tight group and small, country banks in the loose group.*

Table 3. Increase in assets at banks of different sizes,
      October 1955–October 1957

Assets at banks of different sizes[a]	Per cent increase at:			Relative increase, with per cent increase at loose banks = 100		
	Loose banks	Medium banks	Tight banks	Loose banks	Medium banks	Tight banks
Total loans and investments						
All banks	23	9	1	100	39	4
Under $10 million	31	10	1	100	32	3
$10–100 million	19	4	4	100	21	21
$100–1,000 million	23	13	0	100	54	0
Over $1 billion	(b)	8	1		100	15
Bills and certificates						
All banks	87	85	242	100	98	278
Under $10 million	127	91	938	100	72	739
$10–100 million	78	86	211	100	110	271
$100–1,000 million	43	91	338	100	212	790
Over $1 billion	(b)	66	85		100	129
Other government securities under five years						
All banks	36	26	12	100	72	46
Under $10 million	41	19	9	100	46	22
$10–100 million	32	25	27	100	78	85
$100–1,000 million	38	26	11	100	68	29
Over $1 billion	(b)	35	7		100	19
Government securities over five years						
All banks	−49	−52	−52			
Under $10 million	−48	−48	−45			
$10–100 million	−51	−52	−55	(c)	(c)	(c)
$100–1,000 million	−47	−51	−50			
Over $1 billion	(b)	−56	−52			
Other securities						
All banks	34	5	−10	100	15	−29
Under $10 million	55	17	3	100	31	1
$10–100 million	27	12	7	100	44	26
$100–1,000 million	23	5	−18	100	21	−76
Over $1 billion	(b)	− 8	−17		(c)	(c)

[Continued]

[a] All categories by bank size are based on deposits as of October 1955.
[b] No banks over $1 billion deposits in the loose category.
[c] Decrease in all groups.

Table 3. (*Continued*)

Assets at banks of different sizes[a]	Per cent increase at:			Relative increase, with per cent increase at loose banks = 100		
	Loose banks	Medium banks	Tight banks	Loose banks	Medium banks	Tight banks
Commercial and industrial loans						
All banks	*47*	*33*	*25*	*100*	*70*	*53*
Under $10 million	68	18	4	100	26	6
$10–100 million	36	24	16	100	67	44
$100–1,000 million	51	31	19	100	60	37
Over $1 billion	(b)	47	30		100	64
Real estate loans						
All banks	*32*	*16*	*6*	*100*	*50*	*19*
Under $10 million	35	19	13	100	54	37
$10–100 million	31	13	8	100	42	26
$100–1,000 million	23	20	6	100	84	25
Over $1 billion	(b)	14	3		100	22
Security loans						
All banks	*154*	*22*	*−20*	*100*	*14*	*−113*
Under $10 million	1248	542	948	100	43	76
$10–100 million	13	68	16	100	523	123
$100–1,000 million	54	− 1	− 1	100	− 3	− 2
Over $1 billion	(b)	1	−32		100	−467
Agricultural loans						
All banks	*4*	*3*	*−10*	*100*	*75*	*−250*
Under $10 million	2	8	− 5	100	400	−250
$10–100 million	8	−27	9	100	−338	113
$100–1,000 million	13	22	−25	100	175	−202
Over $1 billion	(b)	1	−77		100	−1316
Loans to individuals						
All banks	*30*	*24*	*11*	*100*	*80*	*37*
Under $10 million	28	22	14	100	79	50
$10–100 million	25	21	14	100	84	56
$100–1,000 million	42	31	11	100	75	27
Over $1 billion	(b)	18	7		100	39

ing-investing behavior varied at banks of different sizes. Table 3 provides complete data, comparable to Table 2 above, for banks of different sizes.

Another possible objection to this interpretive pattern is that tight money may have driven some borrowers away from tight banks, but that these borrowers readily obtained the desired loans at loose banks (which were under little restraint), so the apparent differential effects at tight banks were just offset at loose banks. This hypothesis depends on the assumption of high mobility of borrowers between tight and loose banks. While some such mobility certainly existed, it was far from perfect. For large borrowers, loose banks of adequate size to make large loans were very scarce; there were no banks of over $500 million deposits in the loose category. For smaller borrowers geographical mobility is limited, and even within given areas small firms find it harder to move readily from one bank to another for credit. It seems unlikely that the apparent impact of tight money at tight banks was completely, or even substantially, offset by shifts to loose banks.[15]

III. DISCRIMINATION BY SIZE OF BUSINESS BORROWER

One of the commonest objections to the use of tight money to check moderate inflation is that this policy discriminates against small businesses. During the 1955–57 period as shown in Table 4, loans to big

Table 4. Bank loans to businesses[a]

Asset size of borrower[b] (000's omitted)	Per cent increase in loans, October 1955–October 1957
All borrowers	31.9
Under 50	− 3.0
$50–250	16.7
$250–1,000	24.8
$1,000–5,000	21.3
$5,000–25,000	24.7
$25,000–100,000	51.1
$100,000 and over	66.4

[a] Reproduced from [11, p. 37]. Data cover commercial and industrial loans at all member banks, plus real estate loans to businesses.
[b] As of October 1955.

businesses did indeed expand much more than those to small businesses. This does not, however, necessarily mean that tight money led to discrimination against small borrowers. Instead, the pattern of loans may have reflected differing demands from large and small borrowers, where the loan demands of credit-worthy large borrowers (as judged by commercial banking credit standards) rose more rapidly than those from credit-worthy small borrowers.

In fact, the recent major Federal Reserve study of lending to small business arrives at this conclusion. This study found that most bankers

[15] *For an analysis of the effect of monetary restraint on different sectors of the economy, which includes noncommercial-bank lenders, see W. L. Smith [4, pp. 362–94].*

were ready and willing to lend to small businesses whenever small businesses met normal standards of credit-worthiness. The demand for bank credit rose much less rapidly at small businesses between 1955 and 1957 than at large businesses, and the study reports that this was the main apparent reason for the differential growth in lending. Little evidence was found of discrimination against small borrowers, except in so far as refusal of loans because of inability to meet traditional banking credit standards is considered discrimination. But even here, there was little evidence of a substantial increase in potential small borrowers turned away over the period of tight money.[16]

While the evidence generally fails to support the hypothesis that tight money leads banks to discriminate against small business borrowers, the argument has not been unmistakably refuted. We therefore conducted the following test of the hypothesis. The same groupings of banks into tight, medium, and loose were continued. To improve comparability banks were further divided into five different size-groups (based on volume of deposits). For this and all succeeding analyses of business loans, data include all commercial and industrial loans plus real estate loans to businesses at all member banks. The increase in loans to borrowers of different sizes was compared at tight, loose, and medium banks, both for all banks combined and for banks in each of the five size-groups. If tight banks increased loans relatively more to large (compared to small) borrowers than did comparable loose banks, this test says that tight banks discriminated against small borrowers. Since the demand for loans was presumably substantially identical at tight and loose banks within bank size-groups and since loose banks were not restrained significantly by tight money, the analysis presumes that any such discrimination by tight banks would be attributable to tight money.

Table 5, for example, shows that at medium-sized banks loans to borrowers of all sizes rose more at loose than at tight banks, with the behavior of medium banks intermediate. We might say that tight banks discriminated against borrowers of all sizes, but they surely did not discriminate especially against small borrowers. On the contrary, compared to loose banks, they discriminated especially against most *large* borrowers. That is, loose banks increased their loans to large borrowers by percentages far in excess of the increases of loans to small borrowers, while tight banks increased their loans to large borrowers only somewhat more than to small borrowers. Since borrower loan-demand was presumably substantially identical at loose, medium, and tight banks this evidence appears, at least for these medium-sized banks, clearly to reject the hy-

---

[16] *For summaries of the evidence on a variety of tests, see especially [11, pp. 368–69, 374–81, 427–31, and 436–39]. The entire Part 2 of this volume, prepared by the Federal Reserve staff, provides a well-rounded analysis of the total problem of possible discrimination against small borrowers; it concludes that most evidence fails to support this criticism of tight money. A strong statement of the counterview is presented by J. K. Galbraith [1], but without extensive empirical data to support his argument. Data contradicting the Galbraith argument are presented by Allen Meltzer [2].*

Table 5. Increase in loans to business borrowers at medium-sized banks, October 1955–October 1957.

Assets of borrower (000's omitted)	Per cent increase in loans at:		
	Loose banks	Medium banks	Tight banks
Under $50	21	−11	−13
$50–250	76	10	5
$250–1,000	72	25	25
$1,000–5,000	72	50	30
$5,000–25,000	90	49	30
$25,000–100,000	266	104	14
$100,000 and over	25	30	22

ᵃ Commercial and industrial loans plus real estate loans to businesses at all member banks with total deposits of $100–500 million as of October 1955.

pothesis that tight money led banks to discriminate especially against small borrowers.[17]

Figures 1 through 6 are intended to facilitate examination of comparative increases in loans to different-sized borrowers at loose, medium, and tight banks. Figure 1 shows the data for the entire banking system; the others show the data for banks in five different size-groups. When the curves slope upward, large borrowers received larger percentage increases in loans than did small borrowers over the two-year period. When the curves slope downward, the reverse was true. Least-squares lines have been fitted to facilitate these visual comparisons. For example, Figure 4 shows the same data as are presented in Table 5 above.[18]

In Figure 1, for all banks combined, the upward slopes of the curves for tight, medium, and loose banks are very similar, indicating similar treatment of small and large borrowers by all three groups of banks. The tight-bank least-squares line slopes upward slightly more than the other two, reflecting primarily, as is explained below, the behavior of banks in the $500–1,000 million deposits size-class. But we interpret the data as substantially rejecting the hypothesis that tight money led banks to discriminate especially against small business borrowers. Special allowance must be made for a crucial point on the loose-bank curve which

[17] In Table 5, as in Table 4, the fact that loans rose more to large than to small borrowers does not necessarily indicate discrimination against small borrowers, because the observed differences may reflect primarily differences in loan demand from different-sized borrowers. Only a test like that in the text to eliminate possible demand differences can isolate possible lender discrimination.

[18] In Figure 1, total business loans in 1957 to all borrowers were $40.8 billion. Loans to borrowers with assets under $50,000 were $1.5 billion; those to each other size-group of borrower shown in Figure 1 ranged from about $5 billion to $8.8 billion.

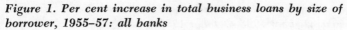

Figure 1. Per cent increase in total business loans by size of borrower, 1955–57: all banks

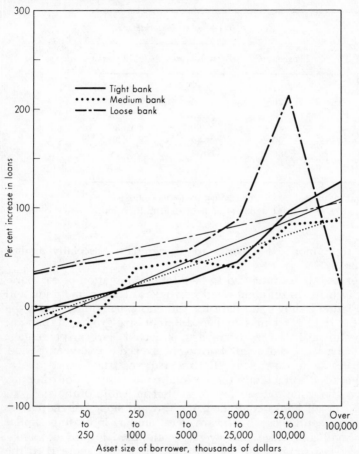

is based on inadequate data,[19] and the charts for the different bank size-groups strengthen this interpretation.

Figures 2 and 3 show the behavior of very large and large banks (over $500 million deposits), which included no loose banks. In this comparison between tight and medium banks, tight banks in the $500–$1,000

---

[19] *The final point on the loose-bank curve (loans to borrowers with over $100 million assets) pulls the loose-bank least-squares line down substantially. Since nearly all banks big enough to have such large borrowers were in the tight and medium groups, this particular point is based on a small number of relatively small loans, and has very limited significance. A least-squares fit omitting this one point would give a loose-bank line rising more sharply than the tight-bank line, and would thus remove the small amount of all-bank evidence appearing to support the hypothesis of discrimination against small borrowers.*

Figure 2. Per cent increase in total business loans by size of borrower, 1955–57: banks with more than $1 billion deposits

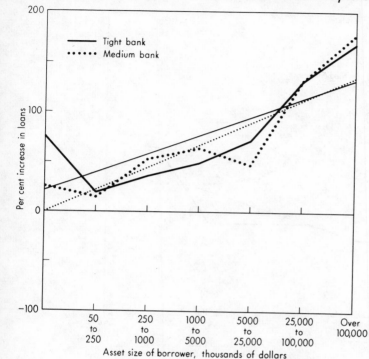

million deposits class did discriminate more against small borrowers than did medium banks of the same size. But Figures 4, 5 and 6 show no such discrimination at other banks where tight and loose banks could be compared directly. On the contrary, at these banks, tight money led to discrimination especially in favor of smaller borrowers.

Similar comparisons of loans by tight, medium, and loose banks to different-sized borrowers were made, breaking businesses into 13 different industry groups—five groups in manufacturing and mining, plus wholesale trade, retail trade, commodity dealers, sales finance companies, public utilities, construction, real estate, and services. The comparisons indicate a wide diversity of lending behavior to borrowers in different industries and at banks of different sizes. No clear patterns emerge as between different industries at all banks combined or at banks of different sizes separately. This is not surprising, since there is no a priori reason to expect such size-of-borrower differences as between different industries.[20]

In summary, the size-of-borrower data reject the hypothesis that tight

[20] *Basic data showing separately each industry's borrowing from each bank size-group are available for inspection in our files.*

Figure 3. *Per cent increase in total business loans by size of borrower, 1955–57: banks with $500–1,000 million deposits*

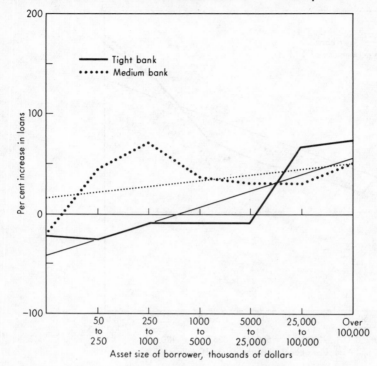

money led banks to discriminate substantially against small borrowers in favor of large. Only at banks in the $500–1,000 million deposit size-group are the data consistent with this hypothesis of substantial discrimination; for the banking system as a whole and for all other size-groups of banks, either the differential behavior at tight and loose banks was slight or it was in favor of small borrowers. Crudely, the data suggest that bankers tended under tight money, as would have been expected, to meet their strongest credit-worthy loan demands while in the main adhering to their regular criteria of credit-worthiness; and that in so far as limited discrimination occurred on other bases, bankers may well have tended to care especially for their best customers—at large banks especially larger businesses and at small banks especially smaller businesses.[21] But this last sentence is based more on the "feel" of the

[21] *Nearly all bankers, however, deny that they discriminate against small borrowers per se but instead base credit extension on the credit-worthiness and general "goodness" of the applicant, regardless of size. [See 11, pp. 401–02]. Bankers we have interviewed are surprisingly consistent in holding that the most important criterion of a "good" customer is the size of deposit balance he will maintain over the long run, assuming, of course, that he meets the traditional standards of credit-worthiness on individual loans, as most reasonably good customers do.*

Some large branch bankers emphasize that lending procedures clearly lead to dis-

Figure 4. Per cent increase in total business loans by size of borrower, 1955–57: banks with $100–500 million deposits

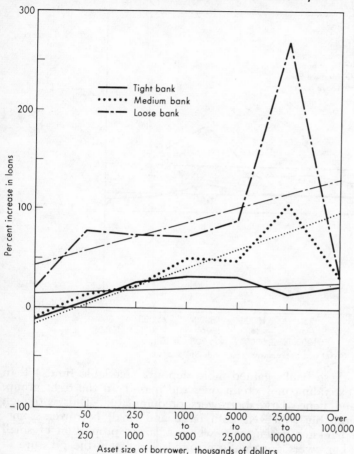

data and on interviews with bankers than on rigorous analysis of the data; and the central fact of lack of substantial lender discrimination by size of borrower is the one that emerges from the data.

It is useful to ask directly: Who were the marginal borrowers turned away under tight money—large or small businesses? At loose banks, and at small banks as a class, apparently neither large nor small credit-worthy borrowers were turned away to any substantial extent. Remember the

crimination in favor of small business. Under tight money all large loans must be reviewed by the central loan committee, which is highly sensitive to the scarcity of funds for lending. But branch managers are often left substantially free, under decentralization policies, to make all loans that seem good without central loan committee review as long as the loan is below some prescribed size, for example $25,000.

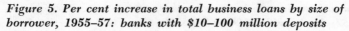

Figure 5. Per cent increase in total business loans by size of borrower, 1955–57: banks with $10–100 million deposits

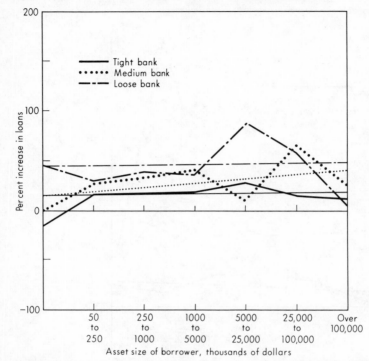

evidence that these banks gained more deposits (lendable funds) than they used in extending new credit over the period. In the tight group, large banks and hence large borrowers predominated. Thus, although tight banks probably squeezed both large and small borrowers somewhat, for the banking system as a whole a larger proportion of small than of large borrowers apparently escaped completely the pressure of tight money on their bank borrowing.

A more complete picture of tight money's effects on borrowers of different sizes would need to take into account lenders other than commercial banks. During the 1955–57 period, small business borrowing in total rose much more rapidly than is indicated by the commercial bank data, since big firms extended a large amount of additional trade credit to smaller firms. These credits arose mainly through the extension of open-book accounts, but also through other forms of credit from vendors to buyers. Two major studies agree that the rapid rise in trade credit to small from large businesses accounted for a very large sum. This fact, although outside the immediate purview of the present study, adds further weight to the refutation of the claim that tight money discriminated especially against small business borrowers.[22]

[22] *See especially Allan H. Meltzer [3] and [11, pp. 363 and 482].*

Figure 6. Per cent increase in total business loans by size of borrower, 1955–57: banks with under $10 million deposits

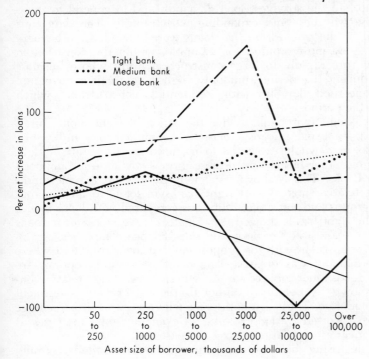

IV. BUSINESS OF BORROWER AND THE INVESTMENT BOOM

Table 6 shows, for all banks combined and for tight, medium, and loose banks separately, the percentage increase in loans to borrowers in different industry groups. The first column indicates that for all banks combined loans to metal and metal products, petroleum-coal-chemicals, and transportation-public utilities companies showed the largest increases. Indeed, nearly half the total increase in loans to all business borrowers over the two years was accounted for by these three groups. At the other extreme sales finance, construction, real estate, and textiles companies showed the smallest increases. In general, loans to manufacturing firms increased more than to other types of business borrowers.[23]

It is striking that the rapid growth of loans in the metals, petroleum-rubber-chemicals, and public utilities industry groups was in precisely

[23] *The data in Table 6 for all business loans do not agree precisely with those in Table 2 for commercial and industrial loans as to relative increases at tight, medium, and loose banks. Part of the difference is due to the inclusion of real estate loans to businesses in the "business loan" figures but not in the "commercial and industrial loan" figures. There may be other factors involved, but if so we do not know what they are.*

those areas where the 1955–57 investment boom was strongest. In a tight-money period, banks generally increased their loans most to those borrowers who had the strongest loan demands, and in general to those whose business was best and expanding most rapidly. The data thus generally support the proposition that loans were expanded most where loan demand grew most rapidly. For example, within the construction industry loans rose rapidly to large construction firms, whose business rose rapidly during the period, but only slightly to small construction borrowers concerned largely with residential construction, which declined over the period.

Broadly speaking, tight banks under the pinch of tight money used available funds to expand loans where—in manufacturing and public utilities—banks as a whole expanded loans most. But the shift of tight banks away from other businesses to these groups was more pronounced than at loose banks. This is shown especially by column 7, which indicates the big relative increases at tight banks in loans to most manufacturing subgroups and to public utilities as compared with loose banks. Conversely, the tight banks showed very small relative increases in loans to construction, real estate, services, and sales finance companies. Again, the evidence is consistent with the proposition that loans rose most where the borrower demand was greatest. The main apparent exceptions are textiles, and food-liquor-tobacco firms, where very large relative increases are shown by column 7 although their aggregate investment growth was moderate. These are both cases where very small percentage increases were reported by loose banks, so even moderate increases at tight banks appear as very large relative increases.

It may be surprising that tight banks increased their commercial and industrial loans more than loose banks over the period, in total, for most of the manufacturing groups, for wholesale trade and commodity dealers, and for public utilities. This was accounted for by the very large banks—those with deposits over $1 billion—none of which fell in the loose group. At all other tight banks, business loans increased substantially less than at loose banks. Data comparing the lending patterns of tight, medium, and loose banks separately for banks in five size-classes are presented in Table 7, which is comparable to Table 6.

The Table 7 breakdown by size of bank shows substantial diversity, but no pattern of differences in lending behavior at banks of different sizes. This may not be surprising, since there is no a priori reason to suppose that banks of different sizes would react differently in a systematic way to loan demands from different industries. In each of the industry groups, small as well as large firms are represented, although in different proportions at different size-groups of banks.

In summary, these data suggest that increasingly tight money during the 1955–57 period was reflected in significantly different increases of loans for different industry groups; and that especially at tight banks, as well as for the banking system as a whole, the loan expansion was greatest to those industries which were expanding most rapidly in terms of plant and equipment expenditure, inventory accumulation, and general level of activity. Thus, broadly speaking, banks increased their loans

Table 6. Per cent increase in business loans, October 1955–October 1957

Business of borrower	Per cent increase at:				Relative increase, with per cent increase at loose banks = 100		
	All banks (1)	Loose banks (2)	Medium banks (3)	Tight banks (4)	Loose banks (5)	Medium banks (6)	Tight banks (7)
All borrowers	52	52	46	56	100	88	108
All manufacturing and mining	66	71	56	76	100	79	107
Food, liquor and tobacco	48	8	62	46	100	775	575
Textiles, apparel, etc.	31	1	4	53	100	400	5300
Metal and metal products	98	132	71	118	100	54	89
Petroleum, chemicals, etc.	67	42	49	82	100	117	195
Other manufacturing and mining	59	35	71	53	100	203	151
Trade							
Wholesale	43	65	19	75	100	29	115
Commodity dealers	36	37	12	51	100	32	138
Retail	48	62	45	45	100	73	73
Sales finance companies	27	41	20	28	100	49	68
Public utilities, transportation, etc.	89	23	56	126	100	243	548
Construction	29	33	40	14	100	121	42
Real estate	33	81	41	15	100	51	19
Services	40	56	52	16	100	93	29

most where the credit-worthy loan demand was greatest. This does not, of course, say that the rapidly expanding industries necessarily received the most credit *relative to* their loan demands.[24]

But it was not true that bank loans uniformly expanded most rapidly to those industries whose business was growing most rapidly. For example, sales finance companies, whose business expanded rapidly over the period, obtained only a modest increase in bank loans. This was probably in part because they had fairly ready access to the money market through other channels. But it also apparently was because banks generally do not consider sales finance companies highly preferred customers, since finance companies generally do not promise large long-run deposit bal-

[24] The Federal Reserve interview study of bankers in 1957 found "almost complete absence" of any indication of bank policy changes as to the type of industry most desirable to accommodate. Decisions continued to be made on prevailing criteria, though the actual loan distribution shifted with the shifting positions of potential borrowers. See [11, p. 436].

Table 7. Per cent increase in business loans at different-sized banks, October 1955–October 1957[a]

| | | Business of borrower | | | | | |
| | | Manufacturing & mining | | | | | |
Size of bank (deposits)[b]	All borrowers	All	Food, etc.	Textiles, etc.	Metals	Petroleum, etc.	Other
Over $1 billion:[c]							
% Increase in loans at:							
Medium banks	79	93	119	−25	77	88	210
Tight banks	105	121	81	76	200	118	83
Relative increase at:							
Medium banks	100	100	100	100	100	100	100
Tight banks	133	130	68	504	260	134	40
$500–1,000 million:[c]							
% Increase in loans at:							
Medium banks	41	54	51	8	81	36	59
Tight banks	14	12	27	−18	15	−30	50
Relative increase at:							
Medium banks	100	100	100	100	100	100	100
Tight banks	34	22	53	−225	19	−83	85
$100–500 million:							
% Increase in loans at:							
Loose banks	75	89	20	−23	312	56	23
Medium banks	39	45	52	17	78	32	27
Tight banks	27	27	2	32	39	40	26
Relative increase at:							
Loose banks	100	100	100	100	100	100	100
Medium banks	52	51	260	274	25	57	117
Tight banks	29	30	10	339	13	71	113
$10–100 million:							
% Increase in loans at:							
Loose banks	37	24	−2	24	19	32	48
Medium banks	29	22	8	16	33	21	22
Tight banks	16	22	17	21	37	26	6
Relative increase at:							
Loose banks	100	100	100	100	100	100	100
Medium banks	78	92	600	67	174	66	46
Tight banks	43	92	1050	88	195	88	13
Under $10 million:							
% Increase in loans at:							
Loose banks	47	19	−14	8	10	41	35
Medium banks	24	11	−8	6	19	55	5
Tight banks	15	1	24	−43	−17	40	17
Relative increase at:							
Loose banks	100	100	100	100	100	100	100
Medium banks	51	58	143	75	190	134	14
Tight banks	32	5	371	−537	−170	98	49

[a] For corresponding all-bank data, see text Table 5.
[b] Deposits as of October 1955.
[c] No banks in the over $1 billion and the $500–1,000 million deposit classes fell in the loose group.

			Business of borrower				
Wholesale trade	Commodity dealers	Retail trade	Sales finance cos.	Public utilities, etc.	Construc-tion	Real estate	Services
−13	−2	46	138	131	38	141	90
101	74	91	76	193	30	35	37
100	100	100	100	100	100	100	100
977	3900	198	55	147	79	25	41
34	93	71	−21	25	92	−6	57
18	380	11	−25	91	−19	−6	18
100	100	100	100	100	100	100	100
53	409	15	81	364	−21	100	32
126	21	132	−3	−10	65	169	48
37	−19	45	16	22	58	39	50
65	12	35	20	14	2	8	−2
100	100	100	100	100	100	100	100
29	−90	34	733	420	89	23	104
52	57	27	867	340	3	5	−4
29	52	37	121	48	22	55	54
31	19	42	6	39	11	30	38
27	−10	40	−24	26	25	11	8
100	100	100	100	100	100	100	100
107	37	114	5	81	50	55	70
93	−19	108	−20	54	114	20	15
54	30	42	41	116	31	63	64
31	54	29	7	49	15	22	27
21	35	15	−7	108	45	2	11
100	100	100	100	100	100	100	100
57	180	69	17	42	48	35	42
39	117	36	17	93	145	3	17

ances to the extent that many manufacturing and commercial borrowers do.

V. INTEREST RATES

Small businesses generally pay higher interest rates at banks than do large businesses, primarily reflecting differences in size of loan. Small businesses usually borrow small amounts, and investigation charges, servicing charges, and related expenses bulk relatively much larger than on the large loans customarily obtained by large businesses. Large businesses often pay lower interest rates on comparable-sized loans than do small businesses, but the differences are small and probably reflect mainly differences in risk and in loan-administration costs.

Table 8 shows interest rates paid by borrowers of different sizes in 1955, in 1957, and the net increase over the two-year period. In both 1955 and 1957, the average interest rate paid varied inversely with the

Table 8. Interest rates on business loans, by size of borrower[a]

| Asset size of borrower (000's omitted) | Average interest rate (per cent per annum) | | |
	1955	1957	Absolute increase
All borrowers	4.2	5.0	.8
Under $50	5.8	6.5	.7
$50–250	5.1	5.7	.6
$250–1,000	4.6	5.4	.8
$1,000–5,000	4.1	5.1	1.0
$5,000–25,000	3.7	4.8	1.1
$25,000–100,000	3.4	4.5	1.1
$100,000 and over	3.3	4.4	1.1

[a] Size of borrower as of October 1955. Rates are average rates charged by reporting banks over the July–October period for 1955 and 1957. More detailed data, for loans at different-sized banks, are presented by the Federal Reserve in [11, pp. 388–89].

size of borrower. But as interest rates rose with tight money over the two-year period, rates to large borrowers were increased considerably more than rates to small borrowers. Over the two years, the spread between average rates to the largest and smallest borrowers declined from 2.5 to 2.1 per cent. While the average rate on all new loans rose from 4.2 to 5 per cent, that on loans to large borrowers rose nearly twice as much absolutely, and even more relatively, as that on loans to small borrowers. During the period, moreover, bank requirements that borrowers maintain compensating balances also became more widespread. Since these requirements apply primarily to large borrowers[25] it is prob-

[25] See [11, p. 433].

able that differences in effective interest rates narrowed even more than the data in Table 8 indicate.

This greater increase in rates to large borrowers probably reflected, at least in part, the fact that small borrowers by 1955 were already paying rates near the customary or legal upper limits for nonconsumer loans at many banks. These legal limits are as low as 6 per cent in eleven states, including New York, New Jersey and Pennsylvania, and range up to 15 per cent in others. Thus as interest rates rose, rates to large borrowers could be increased without violating the customary or legal upper limit, while rates to small borrowers could be raised little or not at all. In any case, for the banking system as a whole, it is clear that interest rates to small borrowers rose less than those to large borrowers. In the aggregate tight money did not lead to discrimination in interest costs against small borrowers.

To what extent did tight banks, under the pinch of tight money, use higher interest rates as a device for discouraging especially particular classes of borrowers? Figure 7 shows the change in the distribution of business loans made at different interest rates by tight, medium, and loose banks over the 1955–57 period.

The average interest rate charged rose at all three classes of banks. Loans made at less than 4 per cent declined at all classes, as the rate structure moved up. The largest percentage increase at both tight and medium banks was in the 4.5–4.9 per cent range, while that for loose banks was in the 5–5.9 per cent range. The apparent differences between tight and loose banks reflect primarily the larger proportion of large banks (and large loans) in the tight group, where rates in the 4.5–5

Figure 7. Per cent increase in business loans made at different interest rates, 1955–57

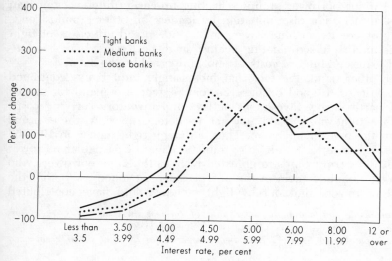

per cent range represented a large increase for large borrowers. At tight banks, nearly half the total loan volume was in loans of $1 million or more, as compared to less than 5 per cent at loose banks. By 1957, two-thirds of these larger loans at tight banks were made at 4 or 4.5 per cent, while in 1955 nearly two-thirds were made at rates below 3.5 per cent.[26]

Data showing separately changes in loans made at different interest rates on loans of different sizes at tight, medium, and loose banks indicate that tight, medium, and loose banks raised interest rates over the period by similar amounts for loans of the same size—though with some wide differences that appear to be random.[27]

In summary, therefore, there is little evidence of much differential interest rate behavior at tight and loose banks during the period of increasingly tight money. This finding is consistent with the hypothesis that the pattern of interest rates at banks is set by general market forces, and that banks generally follow a policy of price leadership in establishing interest rates, rather than using them as a device to discriminate among borrowers. The hypothesis that tight money raised interest costs especially to small borrowers is clearly rejected by the data.

VI. CONCLUSION

What is the significance of these findings for the use of restrictive monetary policy in the future? Tight money in 1955–57 apparently led those commercial banks which felt its impact to alter their asset portfolios significantly; they shifted to obtain funds to increase loans to profitable borrowers, especially business firms, even at the cost of liquidating government securities on a declining market. Discrimination amongst borrowers was apparently largely on traditional banking standards of credit-worthiness and goodness of borrowers, with differing changes in loans to various borrower groups reflecting primarily differences in loan demands, rather than discrimination by lenders on other grounds, once standards of credit-worthiness were met. Widespread criticisms of tight money as unfairly discriminating against small borrowers, both in availability of loans and interest costs, are not supported by the data.

On the other hand, the fact that increasingly tight banks continued to increase loans to good business customers, whose demand for money reflected partly heavy investment outlays and inventory carrying costs, meant that tight money did not act to deter especially these prime movers in the investment boom. Thus, although tight money in 1955–57 may have led to little "unfair" discrimination against particular borrower groups, it did permit funds to go extensively to the same borrowers who would have obtained them in the absence of tight money. Whether the marginal borrowers shut out by tight money would have contributed

---

[26] *Most borrowers pay about the same rate of interest on their loans, regardless of the size of the bank from which they borrow. See [11, p. 389].*

[27] *Charts comparable to Figure 7 have been prepared for loans in six different-sized groups.*

significantly to either undesirable investment or inflation cannot be told from these data. Probably at least as much (more, on the objective evidence) of the marginal credit shut off was to large as to small firms, but no comparable generalization as to industry is possible from these data.[28]

Over all, tight money in 1955–57 appears not to have changed greatly the allocation of bank credit among major classes of business borrowers from what it would have been with looser money, certainly not by size of firm and only moderately by industry—partly because money was not tight enough to limit seriously loans to credit-worthy customers at a substantial proportion of all banks. Tight money's main effect was apparently to hold down the total volume of credit while inducing credit rationing at tight banks mainly in response to relative strength of demand among "good" bank customers. Whether one evaluates this conclusion as strengthening or weakening the case for restrictive monetary policy may depend largely on his taste for direct controls as against market forces. Tight money helped to restrict total spending and keep the price level down while doing relatively little directly to reallocate resources— the traditional objective of general monetary policy. It apparently did not especially check the industries at the core of the investment boom.

REFERENCES

1. J. K. Galbraith, "Market Structure and Stabilization Policy," *Rev. Econ. Stat.*, May 1957, *39*, 124–33.
2. A. H. Meltzer, "A Comment on Market Structure and Stabilization Policy," *Rev. Econ. Stat.*, Nov. 1958, *40*, 413–15.
3. ———, "Mercantile Credit, Monetary Policy, and Size of Firms," *Rev. Econ. Stat.*, Nov. 1960, *42*, 429–37.
4. W. L. Smith, "Monetary Policy and Debt Management," in *Employment Growth, and Price Levels,* Staff report prepared for the Joint Economic Committee, 86th Cong., 1st sess., Dec. 24, 1959. Washington 1959.
5. "Bank Credit and Money," *Fed. Res. Bull.*, Feb. 1956, *42*, 97–105.
6. ———, *Fed. Res. Bull.*, July 1957, *43*, 753–58.
7. Board of Governors of the Federal Reserve System, *Annual Report,* 1955, 1956 and 1957.
8. *Business Week,* Oct. 15, 1955, p. 200 and Sept. 21, 1957, p. 26.
9. *Federal Reserve Bulletin,* Apr. 1956, *42*, 338–39.
10. ———, Apr. 1958, *44*, 410–11.
11. *Financing Small Business.* Report to the Committees on Banking and Currency and the Select Committees on Banking and Currency, 85th Cong., 2nd sess., by the Federal Reserve System. Parts 1 and 2. Washington 1958.
12. *New York Times,* Nov. 11, 1955 and May 17, 1957.

[28] *Unfortunately, the Federal Reserve obtained separate information on loans to new businesses only in the 1957 survey. Thus it was impossible to test the hypothesis that tight money leads banks to discriminate against new businesses. For some evidence on the point, see [11, pp. 390 ff.].*

THE IMPACT OF THE BUSINESS CYCLE ON NEW LIFE INSURANCE PURCHASES*

Business cycle analysis is receiving increased attention by many econo-mists in order to isolate those elements which contribute to economic upswings and downswings. Little attention, however, is devoted to the influence of the business cycle on the life insurance industry. It is the purpose of this paper to analyze empirically the impact of cyclical fluc-tuations on new purchases of ordinary, group, and industrial life insur-ance during the postwar recessions experienced in the economy between October 1945 and February 1961. The study does not consider the influ-ence of the business cycle on existing life insurance in force; this is a separate problem and is beyond the scope of this paper.[1]

Table 1. Periods of cyclical upswings and downswings in the United States, 1945–1961

Cycle	Trough	Peak	Trough	Months of expansion	Months of contraction
I	Oct. 1945	Nov. 1948	Oct. 1949	37	11
II	Oct. 1949	July 1953	Aug. 1954	45	13
III	Aug. 1954	July 1957	Apr. 1958	35	9
IV	Apr. 1958	May 1960	Feb. 1961	25	9

SOURCE: National Bureau of Economic Research.

The postwar business cycles are illustrated by Table 1. The periods are delineated into four specific cycles, with the number of months of expansion and contraction during each cycle.

The data for this paper were derived from the monthly totals of new

*By George E. Rejda. Reprinted from The Journal of Risk and Insurance, December, 1963, pp. 525–534. Used by permission.
NOTE: The author wishes to thank Dr. Richard Porter, Chairman, Department of Economics, Marquette University, and Dr. Thomas Nitsch, Economics Department, Creighton University, for their valuable and constructive criticisms in reviewing this manuscript.
[1] The data are not available in satisfactory form.

410

purchases of ordinary, industrial, and group life insurance as reported by the *Survey of Current Business*. Because of the extreme seasonality present in the raw data, it was necessary to deseasonalize such data in order to remove this influence.[2]

Ordinary Life Insurance

Based on a priori reasoning, it would appear that new purchases of life insurance should decline as the economy turns downward. Many consumers regard life insurance as an optional purchase, which implies that other needs must be satisfied before new insurance purchases are undertaken. In recessions unemployment increases, and incomes decline; consequently, one might expect consumers to be reluctant to purchase new life insurance during such periods of declining economic activity.

When one examines the empirical evidence, however, the opposite appears to be true; that is, new life insurance purchases tend to remain stable or increase relatively during periods of business downturns. This

[2] *The seasonal indexes for ordinary, industrial, and group life insurance computed by the author are as follows:*

Month	Ordinary	Industrial	Group
Jan.	91.4%	89.9%	74.9%
Feb.	92.3	99.3	92.7
Mar.	110.1	110.6	99.2
Apr.	105.0	104.8	92.6
May	104.0	112.3	88.0
June	103.4	102.4	98.7
July	98.7	94.0	87.4
Aug.	96.3	97.2	82.9
Sept.	90.2	98.0	84.3
Oct.	100.2	104.1	84.8
Nov.	99.4	98.6	106.4
Dec.	109.1	88.8	208.2

Ordinary and industrial life insurance purchases are below normal during the winter months of January and February. This may be partially explained by inclement weather during these months which prevents agents from contacting as many prospects as they would like, by the impact of Christmas purchases and debts which may be coming due during this period, and by the increased unemployment in those industries where seasonality is present. The slump of the summer months can be explained by the fact that prospects, as well as agents, are on vacation which results in below normal purchases during these months. It should also be noted that new purchases of group life insurance exhibit extreme seasonality during the months of November and December, rising above normal with seasonal rates of 106.4 per cent and 208.2 per cent, respectively. This above normal pattern can be partially explained by the fact that many new group life insurance benefits are the result of collective bargaining contracts. Many of these agreements require that the new group life insurance benefits go into effect January 1 of the subsequent calendar year. This would require the purchase of group insurance benefits before January 1, thus contributing to the extreme seasonal, above normal pattern of November and December.

may be illustrated by Table 2 which indicates the total volume and average monthly volume of new ordinary life insurance purchases during four recessions.

Table 2. *New purchases of ordinary life insurance in the United States during periods of economic expansion and contraction, 1945–1961*

($000,000 omitted)

Cycle	Months of expansion	Months of contraction	Total purchases during expansion	Total purchases during contraction	Average monthly purchase during expansion	Average monthly purchase during contraction
I	37	11	$ 44,863	$13,206	$1,213	$1,201
II	45	13	70,363	26,217	1,564	2,017
III	35	9	100,126	34,149	2,861	3,794
IV	25	9	102,065	38,518	4,083	4,280

NOTE: The data are seasonally adjusted.
SOURCE: Computed from *Survey of Current Business*, 1945–1961 editions, *passim.*

Based on absolute volume alone, new purchases of ordinary life insurance have declined during recessions. This has been attributable to the length of the periods of expansion which have been longer than the periods of contraction. Consequently, absolute purchases of new ordinary life insurance have been larger during periods of economic expansion than during economic contraction; but it would be erroneous to conclude that the demand for new ordinary life insurance has declined during business downturns. The empirical evidence suggests a different conclusion when average monthly purchases of ordinary life insurance during expansion periods are compared with average monthly purchases during contraction periods.

During the complete cycle of October 1945–October 1949 (Cycle I), average monthly purchases during expansion were $1,213 million, and during the contraction period, they declined slightly to $1,201 million. However, when the other three recessionary periods are examined, average monthly purchases of ordinary life insurance are shown to have increased relatively during cyclical downturns. During the cycle of October 1949–August 1954 (Cycle II), monthly purchases averaged $1,564 million on the upswing and $2,017 on the downswing. During the expansion phase of the August 1954–April 1958 cycle (Cycle III), average monthly purchases were $2,861 million, and during the downswing of this cycle, they were $3,794 million. Finally, during the cycle of April 1958–February 1961 (Cycle IV), monthly purchases averaged $4,083 million on the upswing and $4,280 million on the downswing. Thus, while one might expect the demand for new ordinary life insurance to decline during economic downswings, the empirical evidence indicates that, with the exception of the October 1945–October 1949 cycle (Cycle I), new average monthly purchases have increased relatively during business declines.

Table 3. Comparison of family income with new ordinary life insurance purchases in the United States 1959
(Per cent)

Family personal income (before income taxes)	Per cent of total income received	Per cent of total amount of new ordinary life insurance purchases
Under $3,000	3.8%	4.0%
$3,000–$4,999	11.6	26.0
$5,000–$7,499	23.3	32.0
$7,500 or over	61.3	38.0
Total	100.0	100.0

SOURCE: Data for family personal income received were computed from *The Economic Almanac*, National Industrial Conference Board, 1962 edition, p. 384. Data for per cent of new ordinary life insurance purchased were computed from the *Life Insurance Fact Book*, Institute of Life Insurance, 1960 edition, p. 20.

How can this anomaly be explained? A partial explanation can be obtained by comparing the distribution of family income received with new ordinary life insurance purchases, since previous empirical studies have indicated that income is the major determinant in the purchase of life insurance.[3] This may be illustrated by Table 3 which indicates that a large percentage of new ordinary life insurance purchases is attributable to family units in the upper income groups (i.e. $7,500 and over). This group purchased 38 per cent of the total amount of new ordinary life insurance in 1959, while consumer units with annual incomes under $3,000 accounted only for 4 per cent of the total new purchases.

Consumers in the lower income groups are typically unskilled workers who would be the first to be laid off during economic recession; while individuals in the upper income groups are primarily professional men, managerial personnel, or highly skilled workers who would not be affected as severely by the business cycle as the lower income groups.[4]

[3] *For an excellent empirical analysis of a consumption function for life insurance premiums, see Mordechai E. Kreinin, John B. Lansing, and James N. Morgan, "Analysis of Life Insurance Premiums,"* Review of Economics and Statistics, Vol. 39 (*February, 1957), pp. 46–54.*

[4] *In 1960, 43 per cent of the new ordinary life insurance purchases were purchased by professionals, semi-professionals, and other executives. See* Life Insurance Buying, Analysis of Ordinary Life Insurance Purchases in the United States (*New York: Division of Statistics and Research, Institute of Life Insurance, 1960), p. 10.*

Consequently, the upper income groups may be receptive to new life insurance purchases during economic declines since layoffs with reduction of income may not be imminent for individuals in these groups. Since these groups may be relatively immune to the business cycle, it follows that purchases of new insurance during economic declines could take place in large amounts.[5] The available empirical evidence suggests that this may be true.

Table 4. *Comparison of the lead or lag of personal income with the general business cycle peaks and troughs, 1948–1961*

Cycle	Peak	Trough	Number of months where personal income led(+) or lagged(−) at business cycle peak or trough	
			Peak	*Trough*
I	Nov. 1948	Oct. 1949	+2	0
II	July 1953	Aug. 1954	−3	+5
III	July 1957	Apr. 1958	−1	+2
IV	May 1960	Feb. 1961	−4	+2

SOURCE: National Bureau of Economic Research.

Another reason why new life insurance purchases do not coincide precisely with the business cycle is that personal income, as an indicator of economic activity, may not decline at the same time that the economy turns downward. The National Bureau of Economic Research classifies personal income as a series which tends to lag behind the general business cycle.[6] This may be illustrated by Table 4 which indicates the number of months that personal income led or lagged at the turning points of the general business cycle. Personal income tended to lag at the peak turning point in three out of the four postwar recessions, and because of this lag, personal income was still increasing even though general business activity turned downward. Since new life insurance purchases are usually made out of personal income,[7] it is possible that new sales could actually increase during a recession because of this lag in personal income behind the general cycle. As one marketing expert stated:

[5] *For purposes of this study, the ideal solution would be to compare the relative amounts of new life insurance purchased by the various income groups with the unemployment rate for each income group during different phases of the business cycle. To the author's knowledge, however, no such data exist.*

[6] *Robert Aaron Gordon*, Business Fluctuations (*New York: Harper & Brothers, 1961*), p. 517.

[7] *Technically speaking, new consumption expenditures are made out of disposable income, rather than personal income. Personal income is not the amount of spendable income available for consumption. Income taxes must be deducted in order to arrive at disposable income. Disposable income series, however, coincide closely with personal income series, and it would appear that no great inaccuracy results by assuming that new insurance purchases are made out of personal income.*

. . . it is obvious that our cycle of "boom and bust," as it is popularly called, does not coincide time-wise or event-wise with the normal cycle for other business. Just as the building industry appears usually to be among the first to signal a coming depression and again the last to spark a recovery, we appear to be among the last to fall and last to rise.[8]

It should also be noted in Table 4 that personal income has demonstrated a tendency to lead the general business cycle at the trough, which implies that personal income has tended to turn upward some months before the general cycle reversed itself. This has occurred in three out of the four postwar recessions; consequently, personal income would be increasing, and new life insurance purchases could materialize even though the economy is still declining.

Finally, it is important to examine consumption expenditures and the level of income during economic downswings. If these series fluctuate violently during economic declines, one might also expect the purchases of new life insurance to exhibit some marked degree of cyclical fluctuation. This, however, is not the case. Consumption expenditures, as well as personal disposable income, have not exhibited any tendency to fluctuate violently according to the business cycle.[9] This may be illustrated by Table 5 which indicates the level of consumption expenditures and disposable personal income at the peaks and troughs of the general business cycle.

Table 5. Comparison of consumption expenditures and disposable personal income during four business cycle downturns, 1948–1961

(Billions of dollars)

Peak	Trough	Consumption expenditures*			Personal disposable income*		
		Peak	Trough	Per cent	Peak	Trough	Per cent
Nov. 1948	Oct. 1949	$180.9	$179.8	−0.61%	$196.2	$190.7	−2.80%
July 1953	Aug. 1954	231.2	237.9	2.90	251.2	254.5	1.31
July 1957	Apr. 1958	288.3	290.9	0.90	308.7	312.9	1.36
May 1960	Feb. 1961	329.9	330.7	0.24	352.7	354.3	0.45

* Seasonally adjusted annual rates.
NOTE: Consumption expenditures and personal disposable income data are on a quarterly basis and represent the quarter in which the business cycle peak or trough month occurred.

With the exception of the November 1948–October 1949 downswing (Cycle I), consumption expenditures and personal disposable income have demonstrated relative stability during economic declines. As stated

[8] W. R. Jenkins, "Marketing Planning," Life Insurance Sales Management (Homewood, Ill.: Richard D. Irwin, Inc., 1957), p. 90.
[9] This is not true of the durable goods component of total consumption expenditures since this series will fluctuate according to changes in general economic activity.

earlier, new life insurance purchases are a function of income, and since personal disposable income has demonstrated marked stability during periods of contraction, it follows that new life insurance purchases have remained relatively immune to cyclical downturns because of this stability.

Group Life Insurance

The empirical data also indicate that new purchases of group life insurance do not appear to be affected severely by business recessions. This is illustrated by Table 6 which shows total new sales and average monthly sales for group insurance during four complete cycles.

Table 6. *New purchases of group life insurance in the United States during periods of economic expansion and contraction, 1945–1961*

($000,000 omitted)

Cycle	Months of expansion	Months of contraction	Total purchases during expansion	Total purchases during contraction	Average monthly purchase during expansion	Average monthly purchase during contraction
I	37	11	$ 7,741*	$ 3,525	$ 235*	$ 320
II	45	13	20,514	7,050	456	542
III	35	9	42,122	10,942	1,203	1,216
IV	25	9	24,855	11,950	994	1,328

* Total and average purchases during the expansion period represent data for only thirty-three months. Data prior to March 1946 were not comparable to data subsequent to March 1946 and could not be used.

NOTE: The data are seasonally adjusted.

SOURCE: Computed from *Survey of Current Business*, 1945–1961 editions, *passim*.

In all four recessionary periods since 1945, average monthly purchases of group life insurance have increased relatively during periods of economic contraction. During the October 1945–October 1949 cycle (Cycle I), average monthly purchases during the upswing were $235 million, contrasted with $320 million on the downswing. For the October 1949–August 1954 cycle (Cycle II), monthly purchases averaged $456 million on the upswing and $542 million on the downswing. Average monthly purchases during the August 1954–April 1958 cycle (Cycle III) were $1,203 million during the upswing and $1,216 million on the downswing. Finally, during the April 1958–February 1961 cycle (Cycle IV), new average monthly purchases were $994 million during expansion and $1,328 million during contraction.

Thus, the data suggest that new purchases of group insurance have not been affected severely by postwar cyclical forces operating in the economy. This may be explained, in part, by the strong upward trend in group insurance purchases since 1940. Factors underlying this upward trend are: the beliefs of employers that worker productivity is improved and labor turnover reduced because group insurance is initiated; the influence of collective bargaining in improving group insurance benefits; and the impact of inflation which increases the amount of group insurance in force when benefit schedules are related to earnings.[10] These factors may have counteracted any tendencies towards a relative reduction in new group insurance purchases during business downturns because of cyclical forces.

Finally, it should be noted that the influence of collective bargaining in improving group insurance benefits[11] affords a partial explanation why new purchases of group insurance can increase relatively during periods of contraction. Many of these contracts extend for several years into the future and may require increased group life insurance benefits at some later date. It is quite possible that the economy may be declining during the period in which these increased group life benefits have to be provided for under the collective bargaining contract. This would be reflected in the empirical data which would indicate a relative increase in new group life benefits during a period of economic contraction.

Industrial Life Insurance

Although not conclusive, the empirical data present some fragmentary evidence that new purchases of industrial life insurance may be influenced by the business cycle. This may be illustrated by Table 7 which indicates that new purchases of industrial life insurance increased relatively during the downswing of the October 1945–October 1949 cycle (Cycle I) and also during the contraction stage of the October 1949–August 1954 cycle (Cycle II). However, during the downswing of the August 1954–April 1958 cycle (Cycle III), new purchases of industrial insurance declined relatively; they also declined slightly during the downswing of the recent April 1958–February 1961 cycle (Cycle IV).

Industrial insurance is usually purchased by individuals in the lower income groups who would be susceptible to changes in employment because of cyclical forces. During the downswings of Cycle III and IV when new industrial purchases declined relatively, the severity of unemployment was more pronounced than it was during the downswings of Cycle I and II when new industrial purchases increased relatively. This may be illustrated by Table 8 which indicates the unemployment rate, average duration of unemployment in weeks, and the percentage of workers who were unemployed over twenty-six weeks during four recession years.

[10] *Davis W. Gregg*, Group Life Insurance (*Homewood, Ill.: Richard D. Irwin, Inc., 1962*), p. 16.
[11] *For example, three-fifths of the new group life insurance purchases in 1961 represented additions to existing group insurance contracts, and two-fifths of the new purchases represented new plans. See Life Insurance Fact Book, 1962 edition, p. 27.*

Table 7. *New purchases of industrial life insurance in the United States during periods of economic expansion and contraction, 1945–1961*
($000,000 omitted)

Cycle	Months of expansion	Months of contraction	Total purchases during expansion	Total purchases during contraction	Average monthly purchase during expansion	Average monthly purchase during contraction
I	37	11	$11,492*	$4,256	$348*	$387
II	45	13	20,621	6,786	458	522
III	35	9	18,705	4,562	534	507
IV	25	9	14,110	5,074	564	563

* Total and average purchases during the expansion period represent data for only thirty-three months. Data prior to March 1946 were not comparable to data subsequent to March 1946 and could not be used.
NOTE: The data are seasonally adjusted.
SOURCE: Computed from *Survey of Current Business*, 1945–1961 editions, *passim*.

The unemployment rate during the recession years of 1949 and 1954 was slightly under 6 per cent of the labor force, with an average duration of unemployment of approximately ten to twelve weeks. During the recession year of 1958 (Cycle III), however, the rate of unemployment increased to almost 7 per cent, and the average duration of unemployment increased to approximately fourteen weeks. There was also a sharp increase in the percentage of workers who were unemployed over twenty-six weeks (14.3 per cent). Thus, the increased severity of unemployment may have been partially responsible for causing new industrial

Table 8. *Comparison of average rate of unemployment, average duration of unemployment, and percentage of workers unemployed over twenty-six weeks during four recession years, 1949–1961*

Recession year	Unemployment rate*	Average duration of unemployment (weeks)	Percentage of workers unemployed over 26 weeks
1949 (Cycle I)	5.9%	10.0	7.5%
1954 (Cycle II)	5.6	11.7	9.8
1958 (Cycle III)	6.8	13.8	14.3
1960 (Cycle IV)	5.6	12.8	11.5

* Data are seasonally adjusted and refer to the rate of unemployment for the total labor force.
SOURCE: *Economic Report of the President* (Washington, D.C.: United States Government Printing Office, 1962), pp. 230–234.

life insurance purchases to decline relatively during the downswing of this cycle.

Finally, during the downswing of Cycle IV, new industrial purchases declined slightly to $563 million per month, in contrast to new purchases of $564 million per month during the upswing of the same cycle. Thus, the relative decline in industrial purchases was very small, which may be partially explained by the fact that unemployment was not as severe during this cycle as it was during the prior recession year of 1958.

It should be noted that the relative decline of new industrial purchases during the downswings of Cycle III and IV can also be partially explained by the continuing structural shift away from industrial insurance towards ordinary and group life insurance. This structural change is attributed to the redistribution of income upward which permitted individuals to own larger amounts of insurance, to the increased growth and scope of group sales which reduced the market for industrial insurance, and to the advent of the family policy which encroached upon the sales of industrial insurance.

One manifestation of this structural change is to be found in the number of new industrial insurance policies sold during the recession years of Cycle III and IV. During the contraction period of 1957–1958 (Cycle III), the number of new industrial policies sold declined from 13,842 thousand in 1957 to 13,186 thousand in 1958.[12]

The number of new industrial policies sold also declined during the recession year of 1960 (Cycle IV). During 1959, 12,336 thousand new industrial policies were sold, while during 1960, a recession year, the number sold declined to 12,287 thousand.[13] Consequently, the structural shift away from industrial insurance, as well as the impact of the business cycle itself, may have been partially responsible for causing the relative decline of new purchases during the downswings of Cycle III and IV.

ECONOMIC INFERENCES

Since the empirical data indicate that new life insurance purchases tend to increase, relatively speaking, during business downturns, certain economic conclusions result. The position could be taken that business recessions are aggravated by the relatively increased purchases during such periods. Expenditures on new life insurance, in the form of premium outlays, may be looked upon as a form of savings; consequently, it could be argued that consumption expenditures are reduced by the amount of premium outlays for new life insurance.[14] According to Keynesian eco-

---

[12] Life Insurance Fact Book, 1962 edition, p. 20.

[13] Ibid.

[14] The question of whether consumption is increased or decreased because of life insurance is presently in dispute. Strain argues that the insured has a higher average propensity to consume than an uninsured person since the uninsured individual would have to provide a reserve fund to meet unexpected contingencies. The reserve fund would have to be larger than the smaller insurance premiums, thus reducing consumption. On the other hand, Williams rejects this view and argues that the impact

nomics, premium outlays would be a leakage from the income stream since they are looked upon as a form of savings.

When one examines the operations of the life insurance industry, the above analysis is questionable. The sale of new life insurance results in heavy first-year acquisition expenses, and from the viewpoint of an individual company, more money is paid out than is received in the form of premium income during the first year that a policy is on the books. One estimate is that first-year acquisition expenses are at least 115 per cent of the first-year premium.[15] Thus, one might argue that the relatively increased new life insurance purchases during business recessions tend to mitigate the cycle since more money is injected into the income stream than is withdrawn in the form of premium payments. This would assume, of course, that the recipients of the money representing these heavy acquisition expenses actually spend the money and do not hoard it. If new income is generated by the spending of these funds, then the relatively increased life insurance purchases during business declines may actually mitigate the cycle.[16]

Another element which must be considered in assessing the impact of increased life insurance purchases on the business cycle is the concept of savings and investment. As stated earlier, premium funds may be looked upon as a form of savings or leakage from the income stream. Insurance companies, in their role as financial intermediaries, will invest much of the increased premium income which is received during the downswing of a cycle. If the funds are invested in securities which represent *new investment* in the economic sense (i.e. purchase of a bond issue, the proceeds of which are used to build new plants or equipment), then *savings*, as represented by the increased premium funds, would be offset by a corresponding increase in investment. Consequently, the destabilizing impact of increased savings during the downswing of the cycle would be neutralized by the new investment, and the cycle would not be aggravated by the increased withdrawal of savings from the income stream. On the other hand, if the premium funds are invested in secondary investments (i.e. an existing bond issue), no new investment in the economic sense is forthcoming. Savings, therefore, would

---

of insurance upon consumption is a moot question until more empirical evidence on spending units is collected. See Robert W. Strain, "The Impact of Increased Life Insurance Purchases on the Consumption Function," Journal of Insurance, Vol. XXV, No. 4 (February 1959), pp. 28–31 and Walter Williams, "A Comment on Insurance and the Consumption Function," Journal of Insurance, Vol. XXVII, No. 2 (June 1960), p. 109–112.

[15] *Dan M. McGill, Life Insurance (Homewood, Ill.: Richard D. Irwin, Inc., 1959), p. 245.*

[16] *This is an area for further research and study. One would have to trace the increased money flows from the insurance companies to the recipients of the flows. If the recipients of the money resulting from the heavy first-year expenses actually hoard the money instead of spending it, the tendency for relative purchases of new life insurance to increase during recessions would probably aggravate the cycle.*

not be offset by investment, and this would exert some destabilizing or aggravating influence upon the cycle.

SUMMARY

The empirical evidence indicates that new purchases of ordinary life insurance have not been affected severely by the business cycle. This can be partially explained by the fact that a large amount of new ordinary purchases is attributable to the upper income groups who are relatively immune to the cycle. Personal income and general consumption expenditures have also tended to remain relatively stable during the downswing of a cycle which would permit the continuance of new purchases during the contraction phase of a cycle.

The empirical data suggest that the business cycle has had little influence on new purchases of group insurance. New purchases of group insurance have exhibited a strong upward trend which has tended to counteract the dampening impact of the cycle. Finally, many group benefits are a result of collective bargaining, which may require increased benefits at some future period. It is possible that the economy may be experiencing a cyclical downturn, yet the increased group benefits may still be purchased because of the collective bargaining contract.

Finally, the data indicate that new purchases of industrial insurance declined relatively during the downswings of Cycle III and IV. This may be explained, in part, by the fact that unemployment during these two cycles was more severe than the earlier cycles and by the fact that there was a structural shift away from industrial insurance which was still continuing during the contraction phases of Cycle III and IV.

THE IMPACT OF
THE BUSINESS
CYCLE ON NEW
LIFE INSURANCE
PURCHASES: COMMENT*

The purpose of this communication is to point out the need for adjustment of the data in the Rejda study in order to pursue the announced objective of the research.

Professor Rejda is testing the hypothesis that new ordinary life insurance purchases are (or are not) affected by the business cycle. What classification and adjustments will assist in isolating the effects of the cycle on life insurance purchases?

Professor Rejda's classification of new life insurance purchases into classes of ordinary, group, and industrial is indicated by the hypothesis that lower income people may be more severely affected by business cycles. Hence he is correct in not examining the aggregate of all types of life insurance since doing so masks the supposed relation.

Likewise, since he proposes to use the cyclical analysis of the National Bureau of Economic Research to establish the months of expansion and contraction and to compare disposable personal income during such months with new life insurance purchases in such months, he has developed a seasonal index for each of the three types of insurance (footnote 2) so that seasonally adjusted life insurance purchases may be compared to seasonally adjusted disposable personal income. Professor Rejda is assuming that there is no lead or lag between personal income and life insurance purchases. Seasonal adjustment and classification of types of life insurance are his only adjustments of the data on life insurance purchases.

The hypothesis proposed in this communication is that ordinary life insurance purchases are correlated with real disposable personal income and with the number of dependents. Accordingly two additional adjustments are suggested, namely, the use of per capita figures for ordinary life insurance purchases and disposable personal income and also placing all dollar figures in constant dollar terms.

Professor Rejda is examining ordinary life insurance purchases from October, 1945 through February, 1961. This is a period of 15 years and 5 months. During this period, the population increased from 140.5 million at July 1, 1945 to 183.7 million at July 1, 1961. Perhaps this population

*By Erwin Esser Nemmers. Reprinted from The Journal of Risk and Insurance, December, 1964, pp. 631–640. Used by permission.

increase is associated with the increase in life insurance purchases. If we rearrange the researcher's Table 2 showing average monthly purchase of life insurance, the results are as shown in Table 1 below:

Table 1. *Seasonally adjusted average monthly purchases of ordinary life insurance during expansion and contraction of economy, 1945–1961*

Period	Monthly life insurance purchases in millions
Oct. 1945 to Nov. 1948	$1,213
Nov. 1948 to Oct. 1949	1,201
Oct. 1949 to July 1953	1,564
July 1953 to Aug. 1954	2,017
Aug. 1954 to July 1957	2,861
July 1957 to Apr. 1958	3,794
Apr. 1958 to May 1960	4,083
May 1960 to Feb. 1961	4,280

SOURCE: Table 2 of Rejda study.

To complicate matters, the growth of life insurance holdings per family has been faster than the growth in disposable personal income per family, as appears in the following Table 2. From 1945 to 1961, per family life insurance holdings have increased 238 per cent while per family disposable income has increased only 97 per cent.

Our hypothesis is that purchases of life insurance are dependent on both the income of the buyer and the number of dependents. Table 3 shows that the relative number of dependents increased during the period from 1945 to 1961.

The insurance-buying age group is concentrated in ages 15 to 44, as Table 4 shows, and this group has not grown at the same rate as the total population, as Table 3 shows. Specifically, from 1945 to 1959, the insurance-buying group increased only 7.7 per cent, but the total population increased 26.5 per cent and the population other than ages 15 to 44 increased 45.8 per cent.

Hence it is clear that the vast increase in the number of dependents must be included in any analysis of the effect of the business cycle on the purchases of ordinary life insurance or we would be attributing all of the changes in the purchases of ordinary life insurance to changes in the business cycle. The latter is what Professor Rejda does.

The second broad adjustment we propose involves the matter of inflation. From October, 1945 to February, 1961, the consumer price index increased as shown in Table 5.

Although life insurance is a "dollar" asset whose face does not change with the price level, the income of life insurance buyers changes in pur-

*Table 2. Per family life
insurance holdings
and per family
disposable personal
income, 1945–1961*

Year	Insurance	Disposable personal income
1945	$ 3,200	$3,200
1946	3,600	3,400
1947	3,800	3,500
1948	4,200	3,900
1949	4,300	3,800
1950	4,600	4,100
1951	4,900	4,400
1952	5,300	4,600
1953	5,800	4,800
1954	6,300	4,800
1955	6,900	5,100
1956	7,600	5,400
1957	8,300	5,600
1958	8,800	5,700
1959	9,500	5,900
1960	10,200	6,100
1961	10,800	6,300

SOURCE: *Life Insurance Fact
Book,* 1962, p. 15.

chasing power and the "value" of competing items changes with the price
level. Accordingly, we propose the hypothesis that ordinary life insurance
purchases in constant dollars on a per capita basis are sensitive to disposable personal income in constant dollars. Hence we suggest converting Rejda's Table 2 to this basis as shown in Table 6 in this communication. We might also make an adjustment for the question of the number
of dependents in order to obtain a result that is more refined than the
per capita basis used in Table 6.

If the percentage decline in disposable personal income from the peak
to the trough of each of the four cycles is contrasted with the percentage
change in per capita life insurance purchases in constant dollars between
expansion and contraction, the results would be as shown in Table 7.

The inference to be drawn from Table 7 is that disposable personal
income and ordinary life insurance purchases appear to correlate well
in times of economic contraction as well as in the previous expansion.
In order to maintain comparability with the Rejda study we have paired
peak to trough annual rate changes in income with average monthly
life insurance purchases from expansion to contraction (rather than peak

Table 3. U.S. Population and for ages 14 to 44, 1945–1961

Year	(1) Total U.S. population in millions—includes Alaska, Hawaii and overseas Armed Forces	(2) Insurance-buying age group in millions—ages 14 to 44, inclusive
1945	140.5	68.4
1946	141.9	68.6
1947	144.7	68.9
1948	147.2	69.3
1949	149.8	69.6
1950	152.3	69.9
1951	154.9	70.3
1952	157.6	70.6
1953	160.2	70.8
1954	163.0	71.0
1955	165.9	71.3
1956	168.9	71.8
1957	172.0	72.6
1958	174.9	73.1
1959	177.8	73.7
1960	180.7	Not available on same basis
1961	183.7	NA

SOURCES: (1) *Statistical Abstract of U.S.*, 1963, p. 5, Table 2.
(2) *Historical Statistics of the United States, Colonial Times to 1957*, Series A 22–23, and *Current Population Reports*, Series P–25, No. 212.

Table 4. Purchases of life insurance, 1956 and 1961

Age of insured	Per cent of policies 1956	1961	Per cent of amount 1956	1961
Under 15	30	21	9	5
15–24	21	27	7	23
25–34	24	23	35	34
35–44	16	17	27	26
45 and over	9	12	12	12
	100	100	100	100

SOURCE: *Life Insurance Fact Book*, 1962, p. 21.

Table 5. Annual average consumer price index,
1945–1961 with base 1957–1959 = 100

Year	Index
1945	62.7
1946	68.0
1947	77.8
1948	83.8
1949	83.0
1950	83.8
1951	90.5
1952	92.5
1953	93.2
1954	93.6
1955	93.3
1956	94.7
1957	98.0
1958	100.7
1959	101.5
1960	103.1
1961	104.2

SOURCE: *Statistical Abstract of U.S.*, 1963, p. 356, Table 473.

Table 6. Seasonally adjusted monthly purchases of ordinary life insurance
per capita and in constant dollars during expansion (E) and
contraction (C), 1945–1961

	(1) Monthly life ins. purchases in millions	(2) Consumer Price Index 1957–1959 = 100	(3) Purchases in constant dollars	(4) Population in millions	(5) Per capita constant dollar purchases
E Oct. 1945 to Nov. 1948	$1,213	75.1	$1,615	143.9	$11.2
C Nov. 1948 to Oct. 1949	1,201	83.2	1,444	149.5	9.7
E Oct. 1949 to July 1953	1,564	89.1	1,755	155.2	11.3
C July 1953 to Aug. 1954	2,017	93.5	2,157	162.0	13.3
E Aug. 1954 to July 1957	2,861	94.9	3,015	168.0	18.0
C July 1957 to Apr. 1958	3,794	98.9	3,836	173.1	22.2
E Apr. 1958 to May 1960	4,083	101.5	4,023	177.3	22.7
C May 1960 to Feb. 1961	4,280	103.2	4,147	181.3	22.9

SOURCES: (1) Table 2 of Rejda study.
    (2) CPI from Table 5, supra, weighted by number of months of expansion and contraction.
    (3) Column (1) divided by column (2).
    (4) Population from Table 3, supra, centered at midpoint of expansion or contraction.
    (5) Column (3) divided by column (4).

to trough). This is to be contrasted with Professor Rejda's conclusion that

> it would be erroneous to conclude that the demand for new ordinary life insurance has declined during business downturns. The empirical evidence suggests a different conclusion . . . .

Thus there is no need that "this anomaly be explained" as Professor Rejda attempts to do by falling back upon the proposition that high income groups who are not hit by a recession buy a substantial proportion of the ordinary life insurance. The correlation between disposable personal income and ordinary life insurance purchases demonstrated in Table 7 below, plus the fact that disposable personal income may rise in a recession, appears in fact to be the explanation.

The preceding serves our purpose of illustrating the adjustment of data in order to pursue any hypothesis being explored in research. This is not to imply that other parts of the Rejda study (such as group and

Table 7. Correlation of percentage changes in per capita disposable personal income and per capita ordinary life insurance purchases during contraction of economy*

	(1)	(2)	(3)	(4)	(5)
		Disposable personal income			Insurance purchases
	Change from peak to trough in billions of constant dollars, 1957– 1959 = 100 annual rate	Percentage change from peak to trough	Per capita change in annual constant dollars	Percentage change from peak to trough	Percentage change in average monthly per capita purchases of ordinary life insurance in constant dollars
Nov. 1948 to Oct. 1949	−$32.1	−12.3%	−$83.8	−4.6%	−13.4%
July 1953 to Aug. 1954	−9.7	−3.4	−21.4	−1.2	17.7
July 1957 to Apr. 1958	−8.9	−2.8	−16.4	−0.8	23.3
May 1960 to Feb. 1961	−4.2	−1.2	−6.7	−0.3	0.9

* This table has been corrected for error in the table as originally published. The error does not affect the argument.

SOURCES: (1) and (2) Computed from Table 5 of Rejda study using Table 6, column (2) above.
  (3) Computed from column (1) above and Table 6, column (4).
  (4) Computed from column (3) above, Table 5 of Rejda study, and Table 6, columns (2) and (4).
  (5) Computed from Table 6, column (5).

industrial insurance) are beyond criticism. Thus the assertion "According to Keynesian economics, premium outlays would be a leakage from the income stream since they are looked upon as a form of savings" is open to question. Whether a premium payment constitutes a leakage depends on what the insurance company does with the premium. If the premium is committed to new construction by the insurance company there is no leakage. Quite the reverse is true if the policyholder takes the premium from a hoard and the insurance company applies it to new construction. There is no need to fall back on Professor Redja's special argument that expenses of a policy's first year exceed the premium.

AUTHOR'S REPLY*

Professor Nemmers' hypothesis that ordinary life insurance purchases are correlated with real personal disposable income and with the number of dependents contributes nothing new to the problem under discussion. The hypothesis that he propounds was tested essentially in the 1957 Kreinin, Lansing, and Morgan study.[1] The results of this study indicated that personal disposable income and the number of dependents were highly significant variables in the purchase of life insurance. Professor Nemmers, however, attempts to link real personal disposable income with constant life insurance purchases, whereas the Kreinin, Lansing, and Morgan study related personal disposable income to life insurance purchases by using empirical data expressed in current dollars rather than constant dollars.

The methodology utilized by Professor Nemmers is questionable, since serious conceptual and statistical difficulties arise when he attempts to relate constant life insurance purchases to real personal disposable income and the number of dependents. First, he argues that the number of dependents is a highly significant variable in the purchase of new ordinary life insurance. He attempts to indicate the importance of dependents by the employment of population data for the United States between 1945 and 1961 in Table 3 of his comment. In this table he proceeds to delineate the insurance-buying group from the total population by segregating the age group of 14 to 44 from the total population, and concludes that the insurance-buying group is concentrated in this age category.

Professor Nemmers also argues that any increase in the number of dependents must be included in the analysis of the effect of the business cycle on purchases of ordinary life insurance. However, in Table 6 he

* By George E. Rejda, Assistant Professor of Economics, University of Nebraska. The author wishes to thank Dr. Wallace Peterson, Professor of Economics, University of Nebraska, Dr. Richard Porter, Professor of Economics, Marquette University, and Dr. Thomas Nitsch, Associate Professor of Economics, St. Mary's University, for their helpful comments in the drafting of this reply.
[1] Mordechai E. Kreinin, John B. Lansing, and James N. Morgan, "Analysis of Life Insurance Premiums," Review of Economics and Statistics, Vol. 39 (February, 1957), pp. 46–54.

divides ordinary life insurance purchases in constant dollars by the mean population (average of the total population at the center of expansion or contraction) in order to compute the per capita purchases of ordinary life insurance in constant dollars.' Professor Nemmers is inconsistent because in Table 3 he argues that it is necessary to isolate the insurance-buying group from the total population, whereas in Table 6 he computes the per capita purchases of ordinary life insurance for the entire population.

By the computation of per capita purchases of ordinary life insurance, Professor Nemmers is essentially implying that ordinary life insurance purchases are made uniformly by the entire population. This is erroneous because certain segments of the population do not purchase ordinary life insurance. Furthermore, the incidence of purchases is highly uneven in the population, with purchases of ordinary life insurance concentrated more in some income groups than in others.[2]

In computing the per capita purchases of ordinary life insurance, Professor Nemmers is also implying that the business cycle affects the entire population uniformly insofar as their purchases of ordinary life insurance are concerned. This is also erroneous because all individuals in the economy are not equally affected by the business cycle. Therefore, his attempts to adjust the data for dependents are completely obscured and defeated when the per capita purchases of ordinary life insurance are computed. To be consistent he should have linked the total purchases of ordinary life insurance to the insurance-buying group (14–44) which he delineates in his Table 3.[3]

Another conceptual difficulty arises in Professor Nemmers' methodology when ordinary life insurance purchases and personal disposable income data are adjusted to constant dollars. While this may be interesting, it does not conform to reality. He is, in effect, arguing by this adjustment that ordinary life insurance purchases (in constant dollars) are a function of real personal disposable income. I would argue that ordinary life insurance purchases are a function of the money incomes[4] (personal disposable income in current dollars) that individuals receive and not of their real incomes. When the impact of the business cycle on ordinary life insurance purchases is analyzed, the results may be misleading if constant-dollar data are employed. For example, during the business downturn of November, 1948 to October, 1949, Professor Nemmers indi-

[2] I would again argue that a substantial share of new ordinary life insurance purchases is accounted for by individuals with above-average incomes.
[3] If this adjustment were made, the results would still be misleading. To adjust properly the data for dependents, the insurance-buying age group of 14–44 would have to be broken down by age, marital status, and geographic location. From a conceptual viewpoint, the amounts of ordinary life insurance would then have to be related to these different classifications in order to determine the impact of dependents on new ordinary life insurance purchases.
[4] The 1957 study of Kreinin, Lansing, and Morgan indicated that the most significant variable in the ownership of life insurance was the amount of personal disposable income that an individual receives. Personal disposable income data in this study were current dollars and not constant dollars.

cates that real per capita disposable income declined 4.6 per cent and that per capita purchases of ordinary life insurance in constant dollars declined 13.4 per cent (Table 7).[5] However, when current dollars of ordinary life insurance purchases are linked to personal disposable income in current dollars, the results are markedly different. During the contraction period of November, 1948 to October, 1949, personal disposable income in current dollars declined 2.8 per cent, while average monthly purchases of ordinary life in current dollars declined only 1 per cent.[6] Thus, using constant dollars may be misleading since the decline in average monthly purchases of ordinary life insurance (in current dollars) was very slight during this period of time.

In addition, the use of constant dollars is justified only if the researcher is able to achieve a greater correlation between consumption and income. In regard to the general relationship between consumption and income, economists have not found empirically any important differences between constant dollars and current dollars, at least in the type of postwar inflation that we have experienced in the United States. Indeed, Professor Gardner Ackley argues that for the postwar period in the United States the correlation between consumption expenditures and income is improved when the data are expressed in money terms rather than real terms. Professor Ackley states the following:

> What may be more surprising is the fact that in the early postwar years . . . the *correlation between money values of consumption and money income is on the whole closer than between the real values.*[7] [Emphasis added.]

Therefore, I would argue that, for the postwar recessions, a more logical approach would be to observe the relationship between current ordi-

[5] *Professor Nemmers would attribute this decline to the fact that real disposable income was reduced during this period. (See his Table 7.) However, the decline in per capita purchases of ordinary life insurance in constant dollars during the November, 1948 to October, 1949 downturn may also be explained by the population data that he employs. After World War II, the population increased rapidly because of a "baby boom." Between 1945 and 1949, the total United States population increased from 140.5 million to 149.8 million, or an increase of 6.6 per cent (see Professor Nemmers' Table 3). Therefore, when he adjusts the data to arrive at per capita constant dollar purchases of ordinary life insurance, he is dividing through by a population base that is inflated because of the "baby boom." Consequently, this results in a reduction in per capita constant-dollar purchases of ordinary life insurance for the contraction period of November, 1948 to October, 1949. Professor Nemmers attributes this reduction to a decline in real disposable income; however, the data that he provides suggest that this reduction could be attributable to an inflated population base because of the "baby boom," with a subsequent reduction of per capita constant-dollar purchases as a result.*

[6] George E. Rejda, "The Impact of the Business Cycle on New Life Insurance Purchases," The Journal of Risk and Insurance, Vol. XXX, No. 4 (December, 1963), Table 2, p. 526, and Table 5, p. 529.

[7] *Gardner Ackley,* Macroeconomic Theory (New York: The Macmillan Co., 1961), p. 230.

nary life insurance purchases and money income rather than constant dollars of life insurance purchases and real income. As stated earlier, the use of constant dollars may distort the influence of the business cycle on ordinary life insurance purchases and disposable income. It would not be correct to assume that Professor Nemmers' adjustments for constant dollars give a better correlation between ordinary life insurance purchases and disposable income. A more precise relationship between ordinary life insurance purchases and disposable income during different stages of the business cycle may be obtained by using current dollars instead of constant dollars.

Professor Nemmers rejects my conclusion that one of the reasons why the demand for ordinary life insurance purchases has held up well during recessions is the fact that a large percentage of the new purchases is attributable to the upper income groups, which may be relatively immune to the business cycle. Nowhere in my paper have I argued that this is the sole reason why the purchases of ordinary life insurance are somewhat insensitive to the business cycle. I did argue, however, that another reason why purchases of ordinary life insurance have held up well during recessions is the fact that personal income tended to lag behind the peak turning point of the general business cycle in three out of the four postwar recessions; therefore, because of this lag, personal income was still increasing even though general business activity had turned downward.[8]

I also stated in my paper that new insurance purchases are usually made out of personal income,[9] and thus it is possible that new sales could actually increase during a recession because of the lag in personal income behind the general business cycle. Therefore, Professor Nemmers' conclusions that ordinary life insurance purchases are correlated with disposable personal income ". . . plus the fact that disposable personal income may rise in a recession appear in fact to be the explanation" contribute nothing new to the analysis. The fact that personal disposable income is a significant variable in the purchase of life insurance was previously established in the 1957 Kreinin, Lansing, and Morgan study. Professor Nemmers adds nothing significant when he concludes that disposable income may increase during a recession since I established the same point in my paper when I demonstrated that personal income lagged behind the general business cycle and could increase during a recession—with a subsequent increase in life insurance purchases as a result.[10]

[8] Redja, op. cit., p. 528.
[9] As indicated in the original paper, from a technical viewpoint new insurance purchases are made out of disposable income rather than personal income since income taxes must be deducted in order to arrive at disposable income. Disposable income data, however, coincide closely with personal income, and it would appear that no conceptual error arises by assuming that new insurance purchases are made out of personal income.
[10] Of course, Professor Nemmers utilizes disposable income data whereas I employ personal income data. Since both series move together very closely, no inaccuracy results from the employment of personal income data.

Furthermore, as indicated earlier, Professor Nemmers questions the idea that ordinary life insurance purchases have held up well during recessions because of the relative insensitivity of the upper income groups to the business cycle. If there is a positive correlation between real disposable income and the amount of new ordinary life insurance purchases in constant dollars, as he suggests, then certainly the upper income groups who purchase a large percentage of new ordinary life insurance cannot be brushed aside so easily. After all, the upper income groups account for a rather large share of the total disposable income. Since disposable income is a significant factor in new purchases of ordinary life insurance, the upper income groups are extremely important because they receive a large portion of the total disposable income in the economy. Again I would argue that the upper income groups are relatively immune to the business cycle, and new purchases of ordinary life insurance could increase during a business recession because of the purchases made by this group.

Professor Nemmers also stated that I attribute all of the changes in purchases of ordinary life insurance to changes in the business cycle. This statement is erroneous. In my paper I have analyzed the behavior of ordinary life insurance purchases during the business cycle and attempted to account for such behavior, but nowhere in the paper have I stated that all of the changes in the purchases of ordinary life insurance are attributed to the business cycle. I have maintained, however, that new purchases of ordinary life insurance have held up well during the cycle downswings because of the following reasons: (1) a large percentage of new ordinary life insurance purchases is attributed to the upper income groups who are somewhat immune to the cycle; (2) personal income tended to lag behind the general business cycle in three out of the four postwar recessions, and since personal income was increasing while the economy was declining, new purchases of ordinary life insurance could be made because of the increase in personal income during these three recessions; and (3) personal disposable income has demonstrated marked stability during business cycle downswings, and since ordinary life insurance purchases are closely linked to disposable income, new purchases of ordinary life insurance have remained relatively immune to the cycle downturns because of the stability of personal disposable income.

Professor Nemmers also takes exception to my statement that it would be erroneous to conclude that the demand for new ordinary life insurance has declined during cyclical downturns. The empirical data that I present in my paper suggest that, with the exception of the November, 1948 to October, 1949 downturn, new purchases of ordinary life insurance have tended to increase relatively during the business recessions. The same conclusion will be reached after analyzing the data in Professor Nemmers' Table 6, which indicate that the per capita purchases of ordinary life insurance have also increased in three out of the four postwar downswings. Therefore, Professor Nemmers again is inconsistent when he questions my conclusion that the demand for new ordinary life insurance has not declined relatively during cycle downturns. My conclusion will be corroborated when the data in column 5 of Professor Nemmers' Table 6 are analyzed.

Professor Nemmers also questions some of the economic inferences that were made in the paper. He challenges the statement that premium outlays are a leakage from the income stream since they can be looked upon as a form of savings, with a possible reduction in consumption expenditures because of the insurance premiums that are paid. However, an eminent Keynesian economist, Professor Dudley Dillard, made the following statement regarding life insurance premiums:

> The desirability of life insurance and the various forms of social insurance is not to be questioned from the standpoint of the individual or family unit. Nevertheless, it must be recognized that *such insurance involves large withdrawals from the income stream which might otherwise be spent for current consumption.*[11] [Emphasis added.]

Professor Nemmers maintains that whether an insurance premium is a leakage from the income stream will depend on what the insurance company does with the premium. He states that "If the premium is committed to new construction by the insurance company there is no leakage." I am assuming that by "new construction" he is referring to investment in the economic sense and not merely to a financial investment. Again he contributes nothing original to the analysis by this statement since I have argued in my paper that premium outlays for new insurance may be looked upon as a form of leakage from the income stream and that insurance companies, in their role as financial intermediaries, will invest much of the premium income that is received. If the premium funds are invested in securities that represent new investment in the economic sense (such as the purchase of a bond issue, the proceeds of which are used by a firm to build a new plant or purchase new equipment), then the savings or leakage factor of premium funds would be offset by a corresponding increase in new investment. Thus the destabilizing impact of the leakage factor of premium funds during the downswing of the cycle would be neutralized by the new investment.

Finally, Professor Nemmers rejects my argument that consumption could be increased during a business cycle downturn because of the fact that first-year acquisition expenses exceed the first-year premium, with the result that more funds are injected into the income stream than are withdrawn in the form of premium payments. He conveniently brushes aside the problem by stating that "There is no need to fall back on Professor Rejda's special argument that expenses of a policy's first year exceed the premium." However, he merely expresses an opinion and offers no analytical argument or presents any empirical data refuting my position. It can be demonstrated that, as a result of the excess of

[11] *Dudley Dillard,* The Economics of John Maynard Keynes (*London: Crosby Lockwood & Sons Ltd., 1956*), *p. 84.*

acquisition expenses over premiums collected, a multiplier effect can take place, thereby expanding the level of income and consumption.[12] The empirical evidence with respect to the macroeconomic impact of ordinary life insurance purchases on the economy is not yet in, and research in this area is needed. Professor Nemmers' opinion does nothing to advance the frontiers of knowledge regarding the macroeconomic impact of ordinary life insurance purchases on the economy.

[12] *The author is currently doing research on a multiplier/accelerater interaction model which is designed to measure the impact of new ordinary life insurance purchases on consumption, income, and saving.*

BACKGROUND FOR THE FOLLOWING ARTICLE "THE USE OF AVERAGE MATURITY IN THE ANALYSIS OF COMMERCIAL BANK INVESTMENTS"

Ever since the Federal government was embarrassed by its difficulties in floating bond issues during the Civil War, the practice of the United States in wartime has been to carry tremendous cash balances and to borrow far in advance for this purpose. Thus in the 1930s the balance in the General Fund of the United States Treasury was $2 to $3 billion, but at the end of fiscal 1945 it was $25 billion.

It can be argued that this practice was no longer required under the monetary structure existing during World War II (and now). The monetary and banking structure permitted the United States Treasury to sell bonds to the Federal Reserve System and to accept deposit credit at the Federal Reserve banks in payment. The only limit to the amount of bonds that could be so bought by the System was the requirement as to the ratio of gold certificates to the total of deposits at Federal Reserve banks and Federal Reserve notes outstanding.

This ratio of gold certificates to such deposits and notes was at 25 per cent in World War II and has so continued. Since this ratio can be lowered at the discretion of the Congress, there is no technical limit to the ability of the United States Treasury to sell bond issues if Congress will reduce the gold certificate requirement.

Immediately after World War II, the United States Treasury drastically reduced the balance in the General Fund, as indicated in the following table:

Date	General fund balance (in millions)
December 31, 1945	$26,003
May 30, 1946	18,536
September 30, 1946	10,171
November 30, 1946	6,665
June 30, 1947	3,308

SOURCE: United States Treasury Department, *Treasury Bulletin.*

This decline was accompanied by a reduction in outstanding Federal debt, particularly marketable securities:

Date	Federal public debt (In billions)	Federal marketable public debt (In billions)
February 28, 1946*	$277.9	$199.8
November 30, 1946	262.3	180.3
November 30, 1947	258.2	166.4
November 30, 1948	250.4	157.7

* Peak of war period.
SOURCE: United States Treasury Department, *Treasury Bulletin.*

This drastic reduction was accompanied by the reduction of commercial bank investment in marketable issues of the Federal government from $84.7 billion on February 28, 1946, to $55.1 billion on December 31, 1948. Such a reduction might have had serious consequences in terms of the banking system as a whole; namely, the liquidity of the system might have been jeopardized. This would depend upon what was done by banks with the funds generated by any reduction in their holdings of marketable Federal issues. Since the big city banks serve to an extent as a fulcrum of liquidity for their correspondent banks, it is a matter of acute importance to them to know of any reduction in bank liquidity for the banking system as a whole. Knowledge of such a reduction in liquidity would enable the big city banks to counsel correspondents and even to compensate in their own liquidity position.

Not only is the Federal debt split between marketable and nonmarketable issues, but many differing maturities, ranging from 91 days to 38 years at present, are offered for marketable issues. Some of these securities are redeemable at the option of the holder, beginning at a stated period after issuance. Others are callable at the option of the government after a stated period. Upon maturity (by the lapse of time or call), the government may offer cash or new securities. When new securities are offered, the debt is said to be "rolled over." Thus, if a security holder acts passively, he accepts cash or the roll-over offering.

Hence, the following study by Rivel had immediate importance to the then Chase National Bank and other big city banks. Rivel was employed by the then Chase National Bank at the time of writing this article.

THE USE OF AVERAGE MATURITY IN THE ANALYSIS OF COMMERCIAL BANK INVESTMENTS*

Commercial bank investments in marketable issues of the federal government were reduced from $84.7 to $55.0 billion, or by 35.1 per cent, between February 28, 1946, when the peak in holdings was reached, and December 31, 1948.[1] This reduction in investment holdings has evoked numerous analytical treatments of concomitant changes in portfolio structure. In such analyses, changes in the term structure of the portfolios have usually been given greatest emphasis.

Portfolio term structure is customarily portrayed by the use of call-date or maturity classes. However, this form of statistical description is difficult to employ in measuring portfolio changes from one date to another. The reason is that the passage of time causes blocks of securities to shift from one maturity class to another, thereby obscuring changes caused by the policy actions of investors. Furthermore, both the employment of extremely narrow maturity class intervals and the actual study of specific security issues (particularly when the number of such issues is large) are cumbersome analytical methods.

A weighted average maturity, however, offers certain advantages which these other methods lack. Although obscuring the detailed composition of the underlying data, a series of weighted average maturities provides a simple and useful device for measuring changes in portfolio structure through time as well as for comparing differences in the security holdings of specific investors and investor groups. Furthermore, as will be shown, weighted average maturities may be employed to isolate the positive or voluntary actions of investors from other factors of change.

Three factors are constantly at work tending to change the average maturities of the government securities portfolios of commercial banks. These are: (1) the passage of time, (2) the redemption and refunding by the Treasury of maturing issues, and (3) active trading in securities by the investing banks. The passage of time obviously is a factor tending

* By Robert B. Rivel. Reprinted from The Journal of Finance, December, 1949, pp. 343–347. Used by permission.
[1] Treasury Bulletin. Data quoted for banks included in the Treasury's Survey of Ownership, which comprises institutions owning approximately 95 per cent of all commercial bank-held government obligations.

Average maturity of commercial bank investments in marketable
*United States government issues**

End of month	Actual		Hypothesis No. 1		Hypothesis No. 2		Deviation of actual from Hypothesis No. 1 (in days)	Hypothesis No. 2 (in days)
	Years	Days	Years	Days	Years	Days		
1945								
December	3	353	3	353	3	353	0	0
1946								
January	3	331	4	12	3	363	− 46	− 32
February	3	316	4	49	4	18	− 98	− 67
March	3	362	4	115	4	34	−118	− 37
April	3	358	4	147	4	37	−154	− 44
May	4	1	4	141	4	29	−140	− 28
June	4	43	4	166	4	34	−123	+ 9
July	4	62	4	217	4	47	−155	+ 15
August	4	63	4	226	4	39	−163	+ 24
September	4	86	4	257	4	43	−171	+ 43
October	4	85	4	287	4	46	−202	+ 39
November	4	110	4	322	4	49	−212	+ 61
December	4	146	5	18	4	70	−237	+ 76
1947								
January	4	145	4	352	4	9	−207	+136
February	4	151	4	325	3	325	−174	+191
March	4	152	4	327	3	342	−175	+175
April	4	126	4	297	3	338	−171	+153
May	4	126	4	266	3	308	−140	+183
June	4	123	4	236	3	288	−113	+200
July	4	105	4	205	3	273	−100	+197
August	4	100	4	174	3	246	− 74	+219
September	4	109	4	246	3	251	−137	+223
October	4	88	4	226	3	233	−138	+220
November	4	71	4	196	3	211	−125	+225
December	4	4	4	185	3	187	−181	+182
1948								
January	3	307	4	175	3	190	−233	+117
February	3	300	4	125	3	157	−190	+143
March	3	320	4	152	3	146	−197	+174
April	3	272	4	122	3	119	−215	+153
May	3	260	4	91	3	89	−196	+171
June	3	264	4	145	3	83	−246	+181
July	3	241	4	113	3	76	−237	+165
August	3	207	4	82	3	46	−240	+161
September	3	228	4	179	3	61	−316	+167
October	3	178	4	148	3	73	−335	+105
November	3	161	4	118	3	44	−322	+117
December	3	135	4	106	3	18	−336	+117

* *Treasury Bulletin.* Calculated on basis of actual days to earliest call or maturity dates.

Average maturity of commercial bank investments in marketable United States government issues, monthly, December, 1945 to December, 1948. SOURCE: Treasury Bulletin. *Averages calculated to earliest call or maturity classes (as shown in preceding table).*

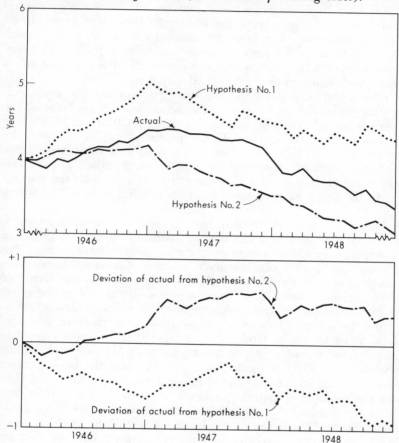

to shorten average maturity, since, unless offset by other factors, it results in a greater concentration of investment funds in near-dated issues. Debt redemption, on the other hand, reduces the volume of funds invested at near-date and causes average maturity to lengthen.[2] This tendency, however, is dampened by the extent to which maturing issues are refunded into new obligations and the latter are acquired by the banks.[3]

[2] *Under existing practice, the Treasury redeems securities only at their earliest call or maturity dates.*
[3] *Since the end of the war, it has been the Treasury's policy, with minor exceptions, to refund maturing issues not redeemed for cash into new obligations having maturities not exceeding one year.*

In contrast with transactions of these types, which yield definite and predictable results, trading in securities may lengthen, shorten, or not affect average maturity, depending upon the ways in which the portfolio term structure is altered.

The investing banks exercise some measure of discretionary control over each of these factors except the passage of time. Market purchases and sales of securities obviously are initiated by the investing banks. On the other hand, when new securities are offered by the Treasury in exchange for maturing obligations, the banks have the option of either exchanging their holdings or of taking cash payment.

The influence of bank-initiated transactions upon portfolio term structure may be measured by comparing the actual average maturity of the banks' investments with a hypothetical average maturity calculated on the assumption that the content of the portfolio is affected solely by the passage of time. In order to do this a base date must be selected and average maturities calculated for a series of hypothetical portfolios established on the assumption that the portfolio ages with the passage of time. In the accompanying table this case is referred to as Hypothesis No. 1.

The discretion exercised by bank management in acquiring securities offered by the Treasury in exchange for maturing obligations differs in certain respects from that expressed through market transactions. This is so because, in the case of Treasury refundings, the banks do not have complete freedom of choice, since the Treasury decides the terms on which the exchanges are made. Therefore, in order to isolate the effect of their market transactions, in which *complete* freedom of choice is exercised, from the other factors affecting portfolio term structure, a second hypothesis must be made. Under this, the portfolio on some base date may be projected through time on the assumptions (1) that the portfolio ages with time, as in Hypothesis No. 1, and (2) that the banks replace maturing securities with those offered in exchange by the Treasury. Estimates of the amounts of maturing issues held by the banks on refunding dates can be obtained by allocating to the banks the amounts equal to their holdings of the issues on the latest Ownership Survey dates preceding the refunding transactions.[4] A comparison of the average maturity of the hypothetical portfolio thus computed with that of the actual portfolio will reflect the influence of the purely voluntary investment activities of the banks, i.e., their market transactions.

In the accompanying table are given, for the December, 1945–December, 1948 period, the writer's calculations of the average maturities of commercial bank-held marketable United States government issues.[5] In

[4] *The banks are assumed to hold a constant amount of Treasury bills. This assumption is necessary because of the lack of information concerning the disposition of particular issues of maturing Treasury bills. Data reported do not permit estimates to be made of the volume of Treasury bills redeemed for cash.*

[5] *Averages were obtained by weighting investments in specific issues by the actual number of days to their earliest call or maturity dates. Treasury bills, published as a single datum, were treated as maturing in one and one-half months.*

the first column are listed averages calculated on the basis of actual holdings of the banks on successive month-end dates. The second and third columns, on the other hand, list the results of averages computed under the assumptions of Hypotheses No. 1 and No. 2 described above. In the final two columns are tabulated the difference between actual and theoretical average maturities, thus indicating the extent to which shortening or lengthening of investment portfolios was attributable to policy actions. In turn, these data are shown in the accompanying chart.

Changes in the actual average maturities of bank-held issues reflected the varying influence upon portfolio term structure of each of the factors of change described above. From February, 1946, until March, 1947, the Treasury's debt-redemption program was the primary force affecting the actual average maturity. This factor, which reduced the amount of near-dated issues held by the banks, more than offset forces tending to shorten average maturity, e.g., the passage of time and the refunding of maturing obligations into issues of one year's maturity, and caused average maturity to lengthen. In contrast, from April, 1947, to December, 1948, the actual average maturity of bank investment portfolios shortened considerably. In this period, the Treasury's program of debt redemption was to a large extent curtailed, with the result that market purchases and sales of securities by the banks together with the passage of time were the primary forces affecting the actual average maturity.

Throughout the major portion of the period reviewed, the actual average maturity of the banks' investments was shorter than would have been the case had portfolio term structure been affected solely by the passage of time and longer than would have evolved from the joint influence of time and the acquisition of exchange issues. This is illustrated by the deviations of the actual average maturity from those obtained under the assumptions of Hypotheses No. 1 and No. 2.

Had the banks' investments on December 31, 1945, been affected thereafter only by the passage of time, average life would have increased in 1946 by nearly thirteen months as a result of the maturing of near-dated issues and their consequent withdrawal from the portfolio. Thereafter, the passage of time would have shortened the average life of the securities held, except on those occasions when large blocks of short-term issues matured and this trend was temporarily reversed. As it was, however, bank absorption of exchange issues combined with purchases and sales of outstanding issues in the securities market permitted the actual average maturity of the banks' investments to lengthen by only 82 days in 1946 and caused it to shorten thereafter.

Projection of the year-end 1945 portfolio on the additional assumption that the banks acquired those securities offered by the Treasury in exchange for maturing issues (Hypothesis No. 2) yielded results somewhat different from those of the first hypothesis. On this basis, the average maturity of the bank's security holdings would have lengthened only slightly in 1946 and shortened steadily thereafter. Comparison, therefore, of these results with the average maturity actually obtained indicates that after the first five months of 1946, the banks "reached out" in the sense that their investment holdings were of longer average maturity than would have been the case had portfolio term structure been affected only by the combined influences of time and Treasury refundings. The extent to which the actual average maturity differed from that calculated on the assumptions of Hypothesis No. 2 was attributable, therefore, to bank policy expressed through investment operations in the securities market.

The use of theoretical average maturities, predicated upon the hypotheses given, has obvious shortcomings. Most important is that, since the theoretical portfolios are functions of the actual portfolio on the base date, the more remote in time is the base date the less significant are the results. For this reason, the method described for isolating bank investment decisions possesses greater merit as a tool for short-run rather than for long-run analysis. However, the deviation of actual from theoretical average maturities, calculated so as to isolate market operations over a period as long as that used herein, certainly suggests the *direction* of commercial bank investment policy.

THE "PER DIEM"
RATE*

I. THE "PER DIEM" RATE

A large percentage of freight cars owned by a railroad is located at any point of time on "foreign" roads. The location of cars owned by one road on another's line is due mainly to the fact that a large part of the traffic in the United States originates on a line of one railroad and terminates on a line of a different railroad. However, quite frequently "foreign" cars are used by a road for local hauls. The existing arrangement between railroads concerning these "foreign" cars is that a certain fixed per day (per diem) charge is paid to the owning railroad by the railroad on which a "foreign" car is located. The per diem rate is identical for all regions in the United States and *does not vary* seasonally or by type of car.

The per diem rate is supposed to be a payment for the hire of freight-car services paid by the using road to the owning road. The magnitude and structure of the per diem rate has been a topic of controversy in the railroad industry for a long time. The conceptual basis for determining the appropriate per diem rate was established fifty years ago and has not undergone any fundamental change. The conceptual basis requires that the owner of a freight car should obtain a "fair yield" on his investment. Any change in the magnitude of the per diem rate has to be agreed upon by a large majority of the railroads, the procedure being that the American Association of Railroads has to recommend such a change and the railroads have to confirm it by ballot.

The main reason for the permanent controversies on the proper way to calculate the per diem rate is that "fair yield," which has been taken as the conceptual basis for these rates, is unsatisfactory. In the first place, it is a very vague concept. How do we determine the fairness of a yield? What, for example, is a fair yield on the risk that the owning road is taking on itself?

Furthermore, it may well be asked whether a per diem rate should primarily assure a fair yield on investment in freight cars or whether there are some specific economic functions it should perform, with a fair yield to the owner of a car being only a kind of "by-product" to these specific economic functions. The McCrea Committee relates "fair yield" to the incentive to purchase new cars. Would it not be better to make clear that we wish the per diem rate structure to induce an optimal purchase of new cars, in terms of both number purchased and

* By Yale Brozen. Reprinted from The University of Chicago School of Business Newsletter, Spring, 1958, pp. 14–17.

444   BUSINESS RESEARCH

type, and then ask what yield that will imply for the owners of the existing car fleet?

In addition, we find that in many of the arguments used in the controversies on the proper per diem rate some economic functions other than providing an optimal supply of cars are introduced explicitly or implicitly. For example, it has been pointed out that one of the functions of the per diem rate is to move cars from location to location. It thus seems necessary to analyze carefully all the economic functions that a per diem rate structure can fulfill and then determine what implications these different economic functions have on the desired per diem rate structure.

II. THE ECONOMIC FUNCTIONS OF FREIGHT-CAR RENTAL PRICES

The approach adopted in the present study is to consider the per diem rate as a price charge for freight-car services.[1] It differs in its basic conceptual framework from the "fair-yield" approach, in that it sets out to specify the economic functions that a per diem rate can and should perform in determining the utilization of resources in the railroad industry.

The per diem rate is not the only way by which car owners are compensated for the use of their cars by "foreign" railroads. Quite often special agreements between railroads regarding the division of revenue from a common haul take account of car-ownership costs in addition to regular per diem rates. But it is quite clear that an optimal structure of per diem charges for car-hire payments will be superior to these private agreements.

Many of the economic functions that an optimal per diem rate structure can perform are presently produced by direct controls of the AAR or the ICC. It is the function of a good car-rental structure to dispose of such direct control as much as possible. One measure of the success or failure of such a system is the amount of direct control that is necessary to supplement it.

The main direct effects of the per diem charge on the operations of the railroad industry can be summarized as follows:

A. The per diem rate has a great effect on the number of cars purchased by railroads. A railroad that purchases a new car has to take into account the fact that the cars will be located a considerable fraction of their lives on "foreign" lines, where they will "earn" only per diem charges. If the per diem rate is too "low," railroads will be reluctant to purchase new cars. Instead, they will try to use cars owned by other railways as much as possible, thus creating a general shortage of cars.

[1] It should be noted at the outset that this statement is true only generally speaking and not in every case. One has to remember that under the present arrangement of "car service rules" a road does not have the discretion to reject cars brought to its line. Hence, for a particular road, the per diem rate may not be at all a price for freight-car services, for a true price is a payment for a commodity or a service that is voluntarily obtained. But for the industry as a whole, the per diem rate is a price for the use of a car, and the above difficulty arises only because we must specify who should pay this price.

If the per diem rate is too "high," railroads will purchase new cars to keep them on foreign lines as much as possible and to avoid using foreign cars. That situation will give rise to a general surplus of cars. An optimal per diem rate would be such that railroads would be indifferent on the margin as to whether they purchased a car to be used solely on their own lines, solely on foreign lines, or any combination of the two.

B. The structure of car rentals has a direct impact on the type of car that will be bought by railroads. Different structures of car-rental settlements will induce purchase of different types of cars. To demonstrate this point, suppose that a railroad is confronted with two alternative situations: (1) a certain shipper offers a contract to the road to ship a certain commodity, both the origin and destination being on the railroad lines; (2) a shipper offers a contract to a road to ship the same commodity; the origin is on the railroad's own line, the destination is on another railroad's line.

The railroad considers the first offer and finds that the commodity would be shipped at minimum cost if a heavy, specialized type of car were used. Consider now the second offer. Since the same commodity has to be shipped, it is clear that, from the point of view of efficiency, the same car has to be used as was used in the first situation. But in the second situation the railroad will not necessarily use the more expensive car but may rather use a less expensive one that is actually less efficient. The reason for this different choice will be due to the fact that both cars earn the same rental as long as they are on a foreign line.

To make the argument above more concrete, consider the following example. Suppose that in the first situation the more expensive car will earn 10 per cent and the less expensive car 8 per cent. In the second situation, suppose that only one-third of the haul is on the originating line and that the per diem rate is such that in the event that a car earns only per diem, the more expensive car would yield 4 per cent on its cost, and the less expensive car 8 per cent on its cost.

In the first situation the more expensive car will be used because it yields 10 per cent, while the inexpensive one yields only 8 per cent. In the second situation the expensive car will yield

$$r_1 = \tfrac{1}{3} \times 10\% + \tfrac{2}{3} \times 4\% = 6\%$$

and the less expensive car will yield

$$r_2 = \tfrac{1}{3} \times 8\% + \tfrac{2}{3} \times 8\% = 8\%$$

Thus the less expensive car will be chosen. It is for this reason that special features, such as roller bearings and DF attachments, are purchased in less than optimal amounts. *It will be noted that a higher per diem rate would not necessarily change the above conclusion.* It is thus evident that the problem of finding the right *rate structure* for different cars is a different problem from finding the appropriate *average rate.* Any average rate, whatever its magnitude, will induce the type of inefficiency in the structure of the car fleet that has been discussed in this paragraph.

C. The considerations analyzed in the preceding two paragraphs pertain to the factors that affect the decisions made by the railroads as to whether to purchase new cars, and what type to purchase; and that is essentially a long-run problem. For a given number of cars in the industry, there also exists the problem of allocating the existing stock of cars among the different lines.

A per diem scheme that will assure an optimal number of cars purchased by the industry will not necessarily assure an optimal allocation of cars among roads at each point in time. The requirements of cars undergo seasonal and cyclical fluctuations. At least the seasonal fluctuations can be fairly well predicted in advance. At a period of peak demand for cars, the costs of car services are not determined by the price of new cars. New cars are not bought for peak periods only. *The real cost of car service at any given time is the revenue that can be earned by them on the margin in other uses.* Thus, to be an efficient instrument in allocating cars among lines, the car-rental or per diem charge should be different in different seasons. Abstracting from cyclical fluctuations, *the average car rental over a year* should be equated to depreciation plus maintenance and repair plus the relevant interest charge; but, given the monthly fluctuation in car demand, the rates should differ from season to season. The per diem rate should be such that at any given time, be it a peak or a trough in the demand for cars, each railroad should be indifferent on the margin whether its cars are located on its own line or on a foreign line.

The present study concerns itself only with the two long-run functions of the per diem rate. We analyze the components of the long-run optimal per diem rate.

D. The per diem rate has indirect effects on other railroad investments which affect car utilization, as well as direct effects on the number and type of cars purchased. If the rate is too low, a railroad handling a large number of cars from foreign lines will find it uneconomic to invest in automatic classification yards or additional locomotives, although it would be economic to do so if it were using its own cars. In effect, the losses resulting from low car utilization are borne by foreign roads through the underpayment for the use of their cars.

This point can be made clear by the following example. Suppose a railroad could invest $34,000,000 in an automatic yard to replace non-automatic facilities. By making the investment, 7,000 cars could be delivered one day sooner to consignees every day. This would make it possible to provide the same amount of transportation with 7,000 fewer cars. An investment of $56,000,000 in rolling stock would be saved (since the average car costs $8,000) with an investment of $34,000,000. If all the cars are from foreign lines, however, the road installing the new yard will not save the $56,000,000. It will save per diem of $2.75 a day. At $2.75 a day on an $8,000 car, the return on capital invested is 3 per cent. The road installing the yard, in effect, saves 3 per cent on $56,000,000 or $1,680,000 annually.

If it installs a new yard, the capital will cost it 7 per cent[2] on $34,000,000, or $2,180,000 annually. By not installing the yard, then, the road saves $500,000. Other roads, however, are saddled with annual costs of 7 per cent on $56,000,000 less the return through per diem on the car fleet. The net cost after per diem amounts to $2,240,000 annually for other roads to save this road $500,000. Costs for the railroad industry as a whole are increased by $1,740,000 because of the low per diem rate. Also, service is poorer, since cars will not be delivered as rapidly without the installation of the automatic yard.

III. THE COST OF FREIGHT-CAR SERVICES

Several elements enter into the determination of a proper long-run per diem rate. To induce optimal purchase of new cars, the rate should be sufficient to cover maintenance, depreciation, cost of capital, and taxes.

In the study it was found that maintenance, repairs, and taxes come to $1.49 per active car day (323 active car days per year). In determining the rates given in Table 1, this was reduced to $1.32 on the basis that

Table 1. Long-run optimal per diem rate (in cents) by price of car and rate of return on capital

Price of car	Rate of return (per cent)					
	3	4	5	6	7	8
$ 6,000	237	249	260	272	286	300
6,500	246	258	271	284	299	314
7,000	254	268	281	296	312	329
7,500	262	277	292	307	325	343
8,000	271	286	302	319	338	357
8,500	279	296	313	331	351	371
9,000	287	305	323	343	363	385
9,500	296	315	334	354	376	400
10,000	304	324	345	366	389	415
10,500	312	334	355	378	402	428
11,000	321	343	366	389	415	442
11,500	329	352	376	401	428	456
12,000	338	362	387	413	441	470
12,500	346	371	397	424	454	485
13,000	354	381	408	436	467	499

repairs and maintenance were heavier in the later years of a car's life than in the earlier years. Since $1.32 per day early in a car's life would not all be expended, the remainder could be, so to speak, invested in other railroad activities and save a road from the necessity of raising

[2] *This capital cost figure was determined as the* minimum *cost of capital to railroads in 1956 in the financial section of the study.*

capital at a cost of 7 per cent. This remainder, plus interest, compounded at 7 per cent, plus $1.32 per day would pay for repairs, maintenance, and taxes, amounting to more than $1.49 per day late in a car's life. (If 6 per cent had been used as the cost of capital, this item would be $1.35.)

Actually, the evidence was not clear that repairs and maintenance would be concentrated late in a car's life, and property taxes are usually higher on a car when new. (Since the average tax per active car day was measured as 18¢, this was a small element in the total, and the time pattern was, therefore, not measured.) However, the sketchy evidence available indicated that this (the concentration of repair costs late in car life) might be the case. Since conservative assumptions were chosen, wherever possible, which would produce the *minimum* per diem rate, the sketchy evidence available was accepted.

Similarly, a minimum estimate of taxes was used. The tax figure used in computing the $1.49 total for repairs, maintenance, and taxes was 18¢. If taxes on new cars are assessed at the average rate for various jurisdictions in the United States, the tax per day on the average *new* car installed in 1956 would amount to 49¢. However, actual taxes paid on *all* cars in the present fleet and on repair materials and facilities in the twelve months ending July, 1956, was 18¢.

The figure for depreciation and interest depends on the original cost of cars (which varied between $6,000 and $22,000 in the sample examined). The daily return required to cover depreciation and interest on an $8,000 car at 6 per cent is $1.81 (assuming a fixed life of 30 years). This, plus $1.32 for repairs and taxes, yields a per diem rate of $3.13.

This rate has to be adjusted, however, for the fact that each car does not necessarily last exactly 30 years, although the average car does so. (Actual average car life is slightly more than 29 years. Thirty years was used in determining the per diem rate in order to produce a conservative figure, that is, one which was on the low side.) There is a mortality experience for freight equipment just as there is for human life. Some cars may last only 5 years; some may last as long as 50. Since the offset against the losses on cars which do not produce earnings beyond 5 years are the earnings on cars which last beyond 30 years, the per diem figure must be adjusted upward. The earnings beyond 30 years are not available until after 30 years to offset earnings lost earlier. In the meantime, the railroad has lost the use of the capital which would have been returned earlier if cars had not "died" at the ages of 5, 10, or 15 years. To cover the loss of use of capital, a further adjustment in per diem rate must be made. In the case of an $8,000 car with interest at 6 per cent, this amounts to 5¢, making the total per diem rate $3.18.

The table shows appropriate rates for various classes of cars. Lower-cost cars do not need as high a rate to recover capital and cover interest as do high-cost cars. The table shows per diem figures also for various interest rates, although the financial section of the study indicates that the minimum cost of capital used should be at least 7 per cent.

HOW MANY
SERVICE STATIONS
ARE "TOO MANY"?*

I. TOO MANY FOR WHAT?

As of June, 1948, some 3,881,500 business firms were operating in the United States. Of these, 1,771,000, or 45.6 per cent, were retailers. Both figures represented new highs. Recovering sharply after a setback suffered during the war, the business population grew rapidly from 1944 to 1947 and then leveled off. By the end of 1947, the number of firms in operation virtually equaled the number calculated by the United States Department of Commerce as "normal" or "expected" on the basis of the prewar relationship between the business population and the general level of business activity.[1]

Statistics of this sort have long evoked two contradictory responses from observers of business. One is based upon a faith in the social desirability of having the business of this country in the hands of numerous free and independent businessmen. It leads to programs for the encouragement and protection of small business. The other response depends upon an emphasis on technical efficiency, especially in marketing institutions. It believes that goods and services would be produced and distributed more cheaply if society could rid itself of large numbers of small, weak, and badly managed firms. Observers who take this point of view are the ones who ask, in particular: "Are there too many retailers?" Usually they mean this as a rhetorical question, to which the answer is a self-evident affirmative.

If the question is considered seriously as a question, however, the answer ceases to seem obvious. One soon discovers that "too many" is a term not easily or precisely defined. Its meaning depends upon the objectives one thinks retailing should achieve, and one soon must ask: "Too many for what?"

The present essay summarizes the results of an attempt to determine whether, even with this addition, the question lends itself to a single meaningful answer. Attention has been centered upon the service station as a type case of retailer. The author has first set up certain assumptions as to the objectives service stations are supposed to achieve. Where possible, he has then estimated the number of stations required to achieve

* By *Richard D. Lundy.* Reprinted from *Reaves Cox* and *Wroe Alderson,* Theory in Marketing (*Homewood, Ill.: Richard D. Irwin, Inc., 1950*), pp. 321–333. *Used by permission.*
[1] Survey of Current Business, *XXVIII* (*November, 1948*), 12–13.

these objectives, as of 1946. The results have some interest for their own sake and may be helpful in suggesting how one may go about measuring the extent to which the number of retailers is too large, too small, or about right to accomplish the purposes for which they are established and maintained.

II. BASES OF MEASUREMENT

The service station may be considered to have three basic functions in the community:

1. Like any other retail enterprise, the service station supplies certain needs of the consumer. It has the function of providing service for the motorist in keeping with what he can and will pay.
2. To the operator, the service station is a way of making a living. In return for rendering to the consumers the services they want, he expects personal benefits. To him, the function of the service station is to yield a satisfactory money profit.
3. In addition to performing these functions for specific individuals, the service station operates in a social setting toward which it has responsibilities. To justify its existence in the social picture, it must do more good than harm; it must in some sense add value to the community.

Provision of direct service to the consumer, of profit to the operator, and of general benefit to the community are, then, the functions of the service station. In relation to each of these functions, the term "optimum number" is a problem of services performed at convenient locations for reasonable prices without a serious threat of monopoly. To the dealer, it is a problem of earning profits and maintaining a market position. To the community, it means a source of employment and taxes, an effective choice among alternative uses of land, and an interest in community appearance.

Measured against each of these functions, the optimum will come out differently. The degree of overcapacity or undercapacity present in the actual market will vary as the basis of measurement varies.

In the actual community, judgments will be based upon a combination of these various viewpoints. Only by integrating them in some workable fashion can the observer achieve the results more desirable to all. However, the difficulties inherent in integration are great, and all that will be attempted here is to study each phase of the problem independently for whatever light it may throw upon the over-all question.

Thus limited, the problem to be solved is either to measure separately the contribution a given number of service stations makes toward fulfilling each of the three functions described or, alternatively, to determine how many stations would be required to perform these functions at any specified level of adequacy. For present purposes, the second alternative is accepted, and measurement is attempted against four tests of adequacy:[2]

1. The minimum number of stations needed to provide the physical supply of gasoline that consumers must have in their tanks, with no consideration of convenience or amenities.
2. The number of stations needed to provide maximum convenience for consumers.
3. The number of stations needed to maximize net profit for the individual stations.
4. The number of stations needed to produce the optimum positive effect on the welfare of the communities in which they are located.

III. MINIMUM NUMBER OF STATIONS REQUIRED FOR PHYSICAL SUPPLY

The absolute minimum number of service stations is set by the bare physical job of putting gasoline into the tanks of the motor vehicles in the United States. If the amount of gasoline consumed is taken as given, then the number of stations required will be fixed by the capacity of a service-station pump and the number of pumps per station. For any given number of pumps per station, the number of stations will be a minimum under the following conditions, which represent no inconsiderable degree of austerity for consumers and operators:

1. All stations operate twenty-four hours during every day in the year.
2. All supply tanks in the stations are refilled as needed without interruption of service to consumers.
3. The customers' automobiles are lined up one behind the other, so that no time is lost between cars.
4. Each customer arrives at the station with his tank empty and has it filled to capacity.
5. Only one brand is offered for sale, and that in a single grade.
6. Consumers will move their residences, if necessary, to be near a station that can serve them. Presumably, the extreme limit of the distance from a station at which any consumer will locate is something less than the mileage he can travel from station to home and back on one tankful of gasoline.
7. Population so distributes itself that the amount of gasoline sold by the various stations is equalized.
8. Once the population is thus distributed, there are no further shifts, although individuals may replace or be replaced by others in the groups assigned to particular stations.
9. Consumption of gasoline is steady throughout the year, with no seasonal or other fluctuations.

[2] *The present analysis has also been restricted to the work of the service station as a distributor of gasoline alone.*

Under these rigorous conditions, the minimum number of service stations that could have met the 1946 consumption of 30,039,823,000 gallons of gasoline is set by making two more assumptions: that each station has three pumps, and that each pump dispenses gasoline at the rate of ten gallons per minute.[3] On this basis, the United States in 1946 "needed" only 1,906 three-pump service stations, or a total of 5,718 pumps. For purposes of comparison, it may be noted that in 1946 there actually were approximately 215,000 service stations and approximately 180,000 retailers of other types who sold gasoline. There were approximately 1,500,000 gasoline pumps in the country.[4]

The figure of 1,906 stations represents the extreme minimum number possible in 1946 only on the further supposition that the conditions imposed would not themselves act to reduce consumption. Because consumption almost certainly would be reduced in these circumstances, 1,906 stations cannot be taken as a "workable minimum" for the distribution of 30,039,823,000 gallons of gasoline. For such a figure, it is clear, some of the conditions must be relaxed. It is interesting to note how rapidly the numbers rise as conditions are relaxed.

Operation for twenty-four hours each day in the year presumably is physically feasible for filling stations; but allowances must be made for unavoidable interruptions. There will be some nonpumping time between the moment when one car's tank has been filled and the moment when the next has been pulled into place. This nonpumping time includes time for taking the nozzle out of the tank, replacing the cap, making change, resetting the pump's gauge, waiting for the change of cars, removing the cap of the new car, and inserting the nozzle. If one allows only thirty seconds for these operations and ninety seconds to fill a fifteen-gallon tank, there will be a 25 per cent time loss per car, or a loss of six hours per day. As a result, the number of stations must be increased by one-third to 2,542.

A system of refilling underground tanks that avoids interfering with service to consumers is quite feasible. Therefore, this assumption requires no modification. However, a steady stream of cars, each arriving with an empty fifteen-gallon tank to be filled to capacity, is not likely to make even a remote approach to workability, and thirty seconds between cars is obviously too little. If we assume that the average buyer takes five gallons and if we allow for a two-minute interval between cars throughout the twenty-four hours, the number of stations needed rises to 19,060.

[3] The figures for the 1946 consumption of gasoline include all gasoline-consuming equipment (American Petroleum Institute, Petroleum Facts and Figures, New York: 1947, pp. 18–19). The rate of operation of the average pump was established at ten gallons per minute on the advice of the American Petroleum Institute.

[4] These estimates were made for the writer by the research staff of a large oil company. The retailers other than service stations proper include vehicle dealers, garages, repair shops, parts and accessories dealers, and country general stores. Approximately 120,000 pumps were operated by fleet owners and others to provide gasoline for their own vehicles rather than for resale. The remaining 1,380,000 average 3.5 pumps per gasoline retailer.

How far will a consumer really drive to obtain gasoline? If the station is so far from his home that he would use his entire tankful in one round trip, then the gasoline would have no utility to him. Assuming that he insists upon having at least two-thirds of this gasoline for uses other than that of getting the gasoline itself, we put a limit of approximately fifty miles (or one hundred miles per round trip) upon the distances drivers who have their tanks filled will go for gasoline.[5] Although consumers would suffer considerably less hardship with the 19,060 stations permitted under the loosening of assumptions thus far than with the 1,906 stations set as the absolute minimum, a good deal of movement of consumers would still be necessary to make sure that each station had its full quota of customers within the fifty-mile radius.

If consumers are not to move at all, the number of stations required presumably will rise still further. It is now necessary to assume that a service station exists within fifty miles of every consumer, no matter where he may be. Furthermore, we can no longer assume that every station is used to capacity before another is installed. This would be true even if the three-pump station were taken as an average rather than as a uniform standard for every station, so that, in sparsely settled areas, stations could have a single pump and elsewhere more than three.

An approach to estimating the number of stations required under this standard could be made by using data on the physical areas of the various counties and the number and basic location of the automobiles in each. Since such a computation lies beyond the resources of the author of this essay, he must rest content with the guess that consumers could be thus served only by a further substantial rise in the number of stations.

Admission of seasonal variation in the use and purchase of gasoline would add still more to the number of stations required to give minimal service to consumers. Day-to-day and hour-to-hour variations would also increase the number, especially if these vary sharply from one location to another. This is true because a peaking of service at some times, with appropriate expansion of facilities, means idle equipment and staff at other times. Hence, in areas where previous computations have assumed that there are enough consumers to keep all the stations completely busy twenty-four hours a day, additional facilities would be needed to carry the peak loads. Here, again, the precise number of stations required could be determined only by laborious computations that lie beyond the writer's resources.

Since there has been no effort to compute the number of stations made necessary by reintroduction of a population scattered without regard to the convenience of service stations and wide fluctuations in consumption, it is not possible to say how close the relaxation of conditions thus far has carried the minimal number of stations to the number actually operating. The author's guess is that minimal and actual would still be rather far apart, since the number last computed (19,060 stations) could

[5] This assumes that the consumer gets twenty miles to the gallon in his trips to and from the station.

be doubled to take care of the scattered population, doubled again to allow for fluctuations in consumption, and still fall well under 100,000 as compared with the actual number—395,000.

Before we can assume that the difference of 285,000 represents "waste," we must remember at least one other fact. In practice, gasoline is only one of many products and services sold by most distributors. A station as a whole is not idle because no one is pumping gasoline, and it is by no means certain that the lowest cost for gasoline itself would be achieved if gasoline were singled out for separate handling in order to keep the pumps fully occupied within the limits prescribed.

IV. NUMBER OF STATIONS REQUIRED TO GIVE MAXIMUM CONVENIENCE TO CONSUMERS

At the opposite extreme from the austere economy assumed at the beginning of Section III is a situation that makes very little demand upon the consumer for foresight or exertion in buying. The consumer unquestionably attaches considerable value to what is vaguely called "convenience." The larger this element of service is in his purchase from the service station, the less meaningful become criteria for numbers of service stations worked out by reference solely to the physical task of getting gasoline into automobile tanks. Since the desire for additional sorts and amounts of service is extensible virtually without limit, a maximum can be set only by arbitrary definition. Accordingly, for purposes of the present analysis, maximum convenience will be assumed to exist when the following conditions are met:

1. Service stations are located at intervals of one mile along all streets and roads, so that no consumer is ever more than half a mile from a station.
2. Along sections of streets or highways where crossing over would involve hazard for the motorist, service stations are located at intervals of one mile on both sides.
3. There are enough stations to serve all cars in the country within any one consecutive hour, allowing six minutes per car. This service is to be provided without any motorist's having to travel more than half a mile to the nearest station, no matter where he may be, or to cross over anywhere along busy highways.
4. All stations operate twenty-four hours every day in the year.
5. Every consumer has a choice among three brands of gasoline at each station.

Presumably, the first test of convenience for a consumer is that a station be always close at hand, so that he need never go a great distance if he runs out of gasoline. He wants a station within a few minutes' driving range of any point to which he may go, preferably in the direction he is already traveling; and he wants to use as little as possible of his gasoline in driving to and from the station itself. If stations are placed at one-mile intervals on all roads, streets, and highways, we shall assume that this test of convenience is met satisfactorily. On this basis, approximately 3,450,000 stations will be needed.[6]

It has been observed that, in fast-moving traffic along busy highways and on congested streets, motorists very seldom cross traffic to reach a service station. Often they cannot do so with reasonable safety or without violating traffic regulations. The remedy for this inconvenience is to construct stations on both sides of the busier thoroughfares. Some 950,000 miles of streets and highways that carry 86 per cent of the traffic[7] can be counted as the "busy" ones for present purposes. Construction of stations on both sides of these sections at intervals of one mile would add 950,000 stations and raise the total required to 4,400,000.

To provide maximum convenience, all stations must be open all the time, so that any consumer can buy gasoline whenever and wherever the need (or the whim) seizes him. Furthermore, there must be sufficient stations to take care of all consumers at the same time if they simultaneously get the impulse to buy. For present purposes, "the same time" will not be interpreted literally but will be taken to mean within any one continuous hour during the twenty-four. Since a three-pump station can serve three vehicles at a time, it can provide service in the one peak hour, at six minutes per vehicle, for thirty vehicles. The absolute minimum number of stations required under this standard in 1946 to serve 34,000,000[8] motor vehicles would have been 1,133,333. This total is substantially smaller than the totals already required to meet the preceding two conditions of geographic distribution.

In practice, even 4,400,000 stations would probably be too small a number. It has been assumed that stations would be located at uniform intervals along all highways and streets, but it cannot be assumed that customers would be so distributed at all times as to have each station accessible to its quota of thirty peak-hour vehicles. At particular hours, some stations would have few customers, or none, whereas others would have many more than thirty. In order to meet the requirement that all cars can be served within any one-hour period, wherever they may be, additional stations would be needed at any location if the stations already provided for find themselves with more than thirty customers to serve in any hour. How many more stations would be needed could be determined only by traffic counts throughout the country. These, again, call for resources far beyond those of the present writer.

If recognition is to be given by every station to brand preferences of consumers, still more stations would be needed. With three pumps available, each station could offer three brands. Additional brands could be provided for only by increasing the number of pumps or the number

[6] Figures on road mileage are from D. G. Kennedy, The Role of the Federal Government in Highway Development, printed for the use of the U.S. Senate Special Committee on Post-war Economic Policy and Planning, 78th Congress, 2d Session (Washington: Government Printing Office, 1944).

[7] Ibid.

[8] American Petroleum Institute, op. cit.

of stations at locations already specified. If the stations set up under the preceding assumptions differed among themselves as to brands carried, some individual customers would find that they were not at all times within half a mile of the particular brand they wanted or that they could not be served within the one-hour peak specified. Thus would arise the phenomenon of "four stations on every corner" to which critics of marketing often refer.

Furthermore, even if customers were satisfied with three brands, since each station is limited to one brand per pump, additional pumps or stations would be required at particular locations unless each station's customers divided their trade precisely in thirds among the various brands. Exactly how many additional stations would be made necessary by enlarging the number of brands could be determined only if the distribution of customer preferences among brands were known.

Except for enlarging the number of brands, the conditions here set up make no allowance for establishing a vigorous competition among retailers. If the strict definition of "competition" used by economists of the monopolistic-competition school were adhered to, there would have to be so many stations at each location that no one of them could exert any influence upon its particular local market. This would raise the total number of stations to levels considerably more fantastic than those already reached in the present analysis. For practical purposes, the number already provided could be expected to produce a reasonably good approximation to the results of pure and perfect competition.

The present analysis has paid no attention to costs and their effects, through prices, upon consumption. It has simply been assumed that consumption would remain as it is. In fact, of course, if 4,400,000 service stations operating twenty-four hours a day were to divide the total sales among themselves, many would do so little business that their unit costs would rise enormously. Consumers would have to compromise between their desires for convenience and limitations on their purchasing power.

We may conclude that, large though it is in absolute terms, the number of service stations operating in this country is considerably smaller than would be necessary to meet what we have called the standard of maximum convenience to consumers. Not less than 4,400,000 stations would have been required by this standard in 1946, and the number might well have run above 5,000,000. Although many consumers might welcome this degree of service, they obviously cannot afford the cost. The strength of their desires and of their pocketbooks is such, however, as to pull the number of stations operated far away from the minimum required by physical supply and well over into the area of convenience.

V. NUMBER OF STATIONS REQUIRED TO MAXIMIZE PROFITS

The third test of adequacy looks to the service station as a device by means of which the operator makes an income rather than as a device by which consumers are served. Here, effectiveness is measured by the closeness of the actual situation to that in which returns to the individual stations would be maximized. If those who manage to get into the business maximize their individual profits, it makes no difference, under this standard, whether the aggregate profit of all the stations operating is maximized or not.

A full analysis of what would be required to meet this standard is impossible in the absence of much information about demand and supply factors in thousands of localities. It will throw light on the problem under analysis, however, if an effort is made to determine the number of stations required to achieve the following conditions:

1. The maximum gallonage per station operating
2. The maximum price for each gallon
3. The minimum expenditure for costs and expenses

If continuous operation every minute of every day is maintained by a station, it will achieve its maximum output of 10,939,050 gallons per year, allowing only for minimum necessary time losses, as in Section III. Naturally, each station operating, to achieve this maximum gallonage, must have enough customers to consume the amount pumped.

Seasonal, weekly, daily, and hourly fluctuations would have to be eliminated. If the station's output were geared to either average or peak consumption during the year, it would be idle part of the time, thereby preventing the attainment of maximum output. In other words, if all stations operating are to operate at capacity all year, their total output cannot exceed the annual total computed by extending throughout the year the rate of consumption reached in the poorest period. This low point in consumption is ordinarily in February.[9] The largest number of stations that could have been kept fully occupied during 1946, then, was the February consumption multiplied by twelve and divided by the individual station's capacity. This gives a total of 2,127 stations. Such a number would give each station operation at 100 per cent of its capacity but would, of course, leave a good deal of consumer demand unsatisfied.

Further analysis indicates that even 2,127 stations is too high a number for the purpose sought. In order to satisfy the conditions laid down, each station must be guaranteed enough customers to maintain continuous operation at full capacity. This would require that there be no change in the motorist population in any area once stations had been located, and probably would mean leaving some consumers out entirely. The stations would operate only in territories having a sufficient number of customers to take their full output. Areas without such populations would have to do without gasoline. Here, again, only detailed and laborious computations would tell how many stations could operate; but the number must be smaller than 2,127. Each station would be designed to achieve minimum costs at its location. Since customers would not transfer from one station to another, costly competition would not exist.

Each operator, having a complete monopoly in dealing with his particular segment of consumers, could charge each individual customer a

[9] *American Petroleum Institute,* op. cit., *pp. 18–19.*

price just below that which would drive him away from the use of gasoline. It might be, of course, that revenue per station operating would increase if the volume of gasoline sold were reduced below the amount that would keep each of 2,127 stations operating at capacity. In that event, the number of stations operating might have to be reduced still further. In no event would more than 2,127 stations be called for, since the 1946 consumption was achieved at much less than monopoly prices.

As to expenses of operation, it can be assumed that the conditions set forth would reduce them to a minimum. Costs of competitive selling would be eliminated by the absence of competition. As to other costs, with each station operating at full capacity, its unit costs should be as low as they could go. This assumes, of course that the three-pump station specified is just large enough but not too large to keep expenditures at their minimum when operations are at capacity. If this assumption is modified in practice, the number of stations required could go either up or down, according to the facts as regards the relationship between size and cost.

VI. NUMBER OF STATIONS REQUIRED TO MAXIMIZE WELFARE

As to the effects of the number of stations upon the social values they add to their communities, there seems to be no workable way to measure them quantitatively, even though it is possible to set up lists of ways in which the stations ought to contribute to community welfare. Thus, one could say that service stations:

1. Should carry their fair share of the group costs of community life through payment of taxes.
2. Should provide a fair share of the employment needed by the community's labor force.
3. Should contribute to the most effective use of the community's land.
4. Should enhance the physical beauty of the community.
5. Should contribute to protecting the safety of the people in the community, especially from fire and traffic hazards.

There is no convenient index by which to determine what a particular station is contributing in each of these particulars. Furthermore, even if the contributions made could really be measured, one would still find it difficult, perhaps impossible, to correlate the contributions made with the number of stations operated. One cannot even assume that there is a consistent relationship between number of stations operated and contributions to welfare.

Case studies, community by community, could perhaps determine the number of stations that would be of most benefit in some ways at given times and under given circumstances. They might, for example, be able to decide whether additional stations would absorb the unemployed or merely shift workers from other and possibly more useful jobs; whether closing down stations would release workers to more useful tasks or merely throw them out of work. They could make decisions as to the probable effects of increasing or decreasing the number of stations upon land utilization, community appearance, and safety.

In the absence of case studies of this sort, there is no readily apparent answer to the question as to whether service stations are too numerous or not numerous enough to maximize their contribution to community welfare. All one can say with conviction is that no evidence bears very heavily in either direction.

VII. CONCLUSION

The answer to the question, "How many service stations are too many?" turns out to be, then, a very wide range of numbers in so far as a quantitative solution is possible. If the criterion of adequacy is to maximize the profits of individual station operators, anything more than approximately 2,000 stations would have been too many in 1946. Correspondingly, if the criterion of adequacy is to pump a given quantity of gasoline over a given period of time, through as few pumps as possible, without regard to what the consumer wants from the retailer other than the physical product gasoline, then anything more than 1,000 or 2,000 stations in 1946 would have been hard to justify. On the other hand, 4,000,000 or even 5,000,000 stations might have been necessary to provide gasoline plus maximum convenience for consumers.

The 395,000 retailers of gasoline and the 1,500,000 pumps in operation in 1946, it is thus evident, may have been either far too many or far too few. In a society organized to give the consumer as little as possible for the station from which he buys, the number operating in 1946 was excessively large. The number of stations fell very far short indeed, however, of what would be required for a consumer's paradise where everything possible was done to reduce the energy and foresight he must himself exercise if he is always to have gasoline for his automobile tank exactly where and when he wants it with no more than a few moments' delay.

OFFSHORE DRILLING IN THE GULF OF MEXICO:* A FORECAST OF FUTURE STEEL REQUIREMENTS

This study is included for methodological purposes only. Changes in the basic assumptions which may have occurred since the date (1957) when it was released would affect the forecasts indicated and conclusions made.

FOREWORD

A race for future oil and gas reserves that will consume thousands of tons of steel is taking place in the Gulf of Mexico. The estimated twelve billion barrels of oil and seventy trillion cubic feet of gas that lie beneath these shallow waters represent the last sizable untapped source of petroleum in the United States. Nearly every major oil company is risking millions of dollars to explore and develop leases that have been bid to fantastic prices.

United States Steel Corporation has undertaken a study of steel requirements necessary for offshore drilling, in order to meet adequately the expanding needs of its customers. To develop the forecasts shown on the following pages, the Commercial Research Division of United States Steel Corporation has combined its analysis with the opinions of major oil companies, drilling contractors, and equipment designers, fabricators and producers. Since methods used to drill the leases and market the oil and gas vary widely with conditions at particular well locations, detailed attention is given to the relationship between the leases held and the preferences for equipment which have been expressed.

The forecast of offshore drilling activity is shown year-by-year to demonstrate the growing magnitude of operations in open water. However, equipment requirements are shown as a normal year to average out wide fluctuations which might occur over a period of time.

DRILLING ACTIVITY

Drilling activity in the Gulf of Mexico has shown wide fluctuations since the war. After the first sizable discovery in 1947, lack of offshore experience, equipment and geological knowledge slowed progress. Then, when it appeared that operations would expand rapidly, a decision by the Supreme Court in March, 1950, placed the extent of state ownership in doubt.

* Prepared by Commercial Research Division, United States Steel Corporation. Used by permission.

Drawing of oil rig

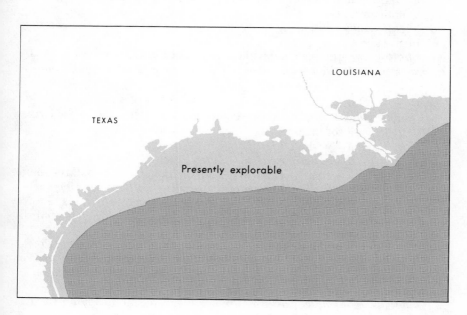

LOUISIANA

TEXAS

Presently explorable

Limited activity followed, principally on leases which were not likely to be disputed. Not until May, 1953, did the Submerged Lands and Continental Shelf Act temporarily clarify the boundary limits| of the State and Federal Government. A rush to secure leases and equipment followed. Adequate facilities became available gradually, and drilling programs were accelerated to prove up leases and save rentals and unnecessary bonuses.

In recent months, the future has again been in doubt. The State of Louisiana claims its boundary as 10½ miles from shore, the same as Texas and Florida, contrasting with the 3-mile limit for all other states. Further, the method of setting the boundary, no matter what the distance, will present serious problems before settlement. To prevent another setback such as that between 1950 and 1953, and the possible loss of millions of dollars by oil companies, a plan to hold the disputed funds in escrow has been negotiated.

Below is a summary of the factors which will influence tideland activity:

1. *Decelerating Factors*

  a. The *litigation* mentioned above.
  b. *Reduction in offshore allowables* resulting from general refining volume and imports.
  c. *Material shortages.* Shortages of steel structurals and plates as well as fabricating facilities for certain equipment have retarded the overall program.
  d. *Tight money.* Financing costs have risen steadily with the shortage of money.
  e. *Shortage of qualified personnel.* Some localities have had difficulty in attracting skilled personnel. This is not a general problem.

2. *Accelerating Factors*

  a. *Rental clauses in the leasing contracts.* The following annual rates are incurred for inactivity on a particular lease:
      Louisiana—½ the bonus payment per acre,
      Texas—$2 per acre, Federal—$3 per acre.
  b. *Dollar return on investment.* Tremendous capital outlays have placed increasing importance on developing an offsetting income.
  c. *Committed investment.* The money already spent on leases, equipment and other facilities precludes any lengthy deferment of drilling programs.
  d. *Sufficient development of gas fields to obtain Federal Power Commission approval for pipelines.* Since the only way to market gas is by pipeline, it is necessary under government regulation to prove sufficient volume to warrant construction of a line.
  e. *Threats to Middle Eastern supplies.* This recent development has heightened interest in Western Hemisphere drilling.

Figure 1 shows the differences of opinion on future activity. The forecast selected is based on a weighted average of these opinions with nec-

Figure 1. Well completions

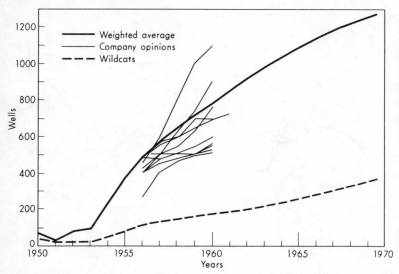

essary refinements for extensions into the future. No serious curtailment of offshore activity is considered in these future projections.

Because of a very high success ratio, ranging between 50 and 70%, the percentage of wildcats offshore has been below the national average of 25% of total completions. This is likely to continue through 1962 with increasing geological knowledge and a great number of untapped fields. After that time, maturity of operations will force the number of exploratory wells upward as the frequency of strikes decreases.

Greater penetrations are expected as depletion forces companies to produce from deeper strata. In addition, the total cost of the leases makes it imperative to find out what the commercial value is before the payment of excessive rentals and the expiration of contracts. Therefore, exploratory wells will commonly reach great depths.

Development of commercially valuable sands at comparatively moderate depths is expected to balance deeper wildcats through 1957, but a gradual increase in the years following is anticipated. Figure 2 shows the gradual increase of the average depth.

A forecast of activity in future years

	1957	*1958*	*1959*	*1960*	*Normal year 1961–1965*	*Normal year 1966–1970*
Well completions	570	650	720	780	960	1,200
Average depth (in feet)	9,700	10,050	10,300	10,600	11,350	12,400
Footage (in thousands)	5,530	6,530	7,410	8,270	10,900	14,880
Exploratory wells	125	145	160	170	200	305

Figure 2. Average depth per well offshore

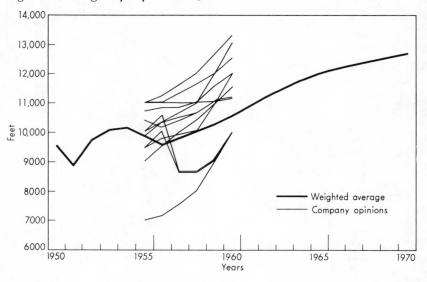

Left to right, mobile type, minimum platform with tender, and self-contained platform

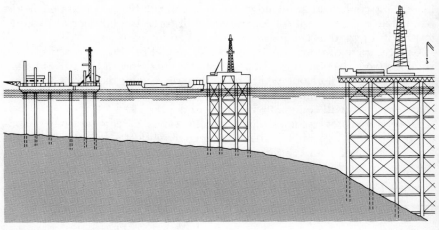

DRILLING PLATFORMS

There are three general types of platforms used to drill in open water. Wide variations in design are possible within these classifications.

1. *The mobile type* can be moved in its entirety from one well site to another. All equipment is on the structure so that it can be self-sufficient for short periods of time.

Photograph showing mobile platform

2. *The minimum platform* is only large enough for the drilling equipment and is stabilized on piles. It depends on a tender for supplementary
equipment, supplies, quarters, etc.

3. *Self-contained platforms* are permanently located with complete
facilities on the structure.

Each kind has advantages and there is no standard solution, even considering a given set of conditions. Company policies have dictated the
type of platform to be used on a particular lease, and these preferences

are considered in compiling the following summary and forecast:

Mobile Platforms

1. Statistics. Thirty-five mobile platforms are in operation or under construction. The rate paid to the owner of the platform while drilling on a site ranges between $4,500 and $8,500 per day, depending on actual costs. Because of the risk and high initial cost of the platform, a high rate of return is necessary to obtain financing for the venture. Eleven are owned and operated by oil companies. Water depth limitation now extends to approximately 125 feet.

2. Facilities. The mobile unit includes space for drilling equipment, a helicopter port, mud tanks, pipe racks, a crane, quarters, communication, cooking and recreational facilities, auxiliary power and other miscellaneous equipment.

3. Advantages. (*a*) Its mobility allows a quick and comparatively inexpensive move from a well site. (*b*) This flexibility also enables a company to drill vertical holes which are as much as 50% cheaper than directional. (*c*) Being able to move to another location diminishes the danger of a blowout destroying a cluster of wells as is the case on more permanent platforms. (*d*) With all equipment located on the platform there is less downtime resulting from wave action.

4. Disadvantages. (*a*) High cost of daily operations narrows an already thin profit margin. (*b*) Since they are not permanently located, their vulnerability to unfavorable weather is increased. (*c*) The limitation in the depth of water in which they can now drill is a restriction to future use. (*d*) Maintenance of dispersed wells is higher in cost.

5. Summary. The high success ratio will preclude the use of the mobile platforms in most areas until day rates become competitive. Greater availability should reduce their cost to oil companies, and policy decisions will have to be based on the remaining disadvantages as opposed to the above-mentioned advantages.

Minimum Platform with Tender

1. Statistics. Forty-seven tenders are in operation or under construction. Conversions include 19 LST's, 11 YF's and 1 tanker; 16 were built specifically for offshore drilling. Day rates are reduced 15 to 40% by the cheaper financing involved in a boatlike tender, self-propelled or not. Also, savings in daily operational expenses are possible by owning instead of contracting. All but 13 are owned by major oil companies or combinations of companies. The cost of minimum platforms is small enough to be covered by the working capital of major oil firms. Water depth now extends to 103 feet.

2. Facilities. The platform is usually designed for drilling equipment alone. Mud tanks and pipe racks are often included. Some have auxiliary power that could prevent stoppages for short periods when the tender is withdrawn in heavy weather. A tender generally supplies the power,

Photograph showing minimum platform with tender

quarters, communication, cooking and recreational facilities, a helicopter port, a crane, additional supplies and miscellaneous items. Elaborate anchorage equipment is required.

3. *Advantages.* (*a*) Most important is the fact that it can be expanded to a self-contained platform by the addition of other sections when the location is proven. (*b*) Reduction in total well costs is significant on high chance locations. (*c*) In the event of a dry hole, current designs allow for recovery of the structure in sections with the exception of pil-

ing. (d) Quick withdrawal of the tender to safe waters decreases the possibility of storm loss. The permanent platform, under improving inclement weather techniques, would be expected also to ride out a storm better than a mobile type.

4. *Disadvantages.* (a) The cost of recovering the platform on a dry hole and moving to a new site is almost as expensive as a whole new structure. (b) The deeper the water the more difficult it is to anchor the tender securely, and the size of platform has to be increased to give proper stability. After 125 feet many designers feel it is more advisable to build the larger self-contained type. (c) A cluster of directional wells is necessary from the permanent location, which increases vulnerability to losses from blowout. (d) The extra expense of marine equipment and a ship's crew must be absorbed.

5. *Summary.* The 70% success ratio achieved thus far has strongly influenced the use of this method of exploration by diminishing its disadvantages on a dry hole. Development is possible by skidding the rig a few feet and drilling 3 to 5 additional wells. The flexibility of adding another section, if warranted by the size of the strike, is extremely desirable.

Self-contained Platforms

1. *Statistics.* Thirty-seven are located in the Gulf; all are owned by oil companies or combinations of companies. Water depth limitation is 112 feet, but engineers feel that this could now be extended to at least 200 feet. Daily operational expenses are less with this method than any other. Maximum existing dimensions for a self-contained platform are 220 by 706 feet.

2. *Facilities.* All equipment necessary to drill a well, quarter and feed the crew, store and transfer supplies is located on the platform. In addition, there are recreational facilities, standby equipment, a helicopter port and a complete communication system throughout the platform and to shore.

3. *Advantages.* (a) The lower cost of drilling a producing well has prompted adoption of this method for the development phase. As many as 12 wells per rig can be drilled, and 2 of these platforms have two rigs on them, thus averaging out the expense of each well. (b) Its size and permanent location on piles serve to strongly resist severe weather and thereby avoid excessive downtime. (c) In the opinion of many observers, the economies of drilling and servicing a cluster of wells more than compensate for the dangers involved. (d) Large storage tanks, auxiliary equipment and supplementary pipe racks are possible because designers may disregard mobility limitations. (e) The restriction of water depth appears to be overcome for the present.

4. *Disadvantages.* (a) The permanent nature of the platform increases the average cost per well with each dry hole. The ultimate investment in a self-contained structure is such that only in isolated cases will ex-

Photograph showing self-contained platform

ploratory tests be made. (*b*) Although about 60 to 80% can be salvaged and moved to another well site, the expense of these transfers can reach $500,000.

5. *Summary*. A self-contained platform is best suited to development of a proven area. The initial cost, plus the expense of relocating, restricts use for wildcats to specific conditions. Coast Guard regulations demand removal of the structure after permanent abandonment, but this normally follows the production period and return on investment.

FORECAST SUMMARY

The use of a particular type platform will certainly depend upon the conditions at a given location. More important, however, will be the preferences influenced by previous purchases of equipment and company policies that vary widely in their approach to the same problem. In a few cases, firms were forced to contract and buy platforms which were available at the time. They have since purchased equipment accordingly and now make many of their decisions on the basis of what they already own.

Generally, the mobile platforms are preferred by drilling contractors. They can move quickly and inexpensively to another well site and begin operations without delay. On the other hand, oil companies have leaned strongly toward the minimum platform–tender type for exploration and development. Considering the high success ratio and the use of only a small permanent platform, most of the equipment can be moved to another site in the case of a dry hole. The minimum platform can be expanded into the self-contained type if production warrants. The figures shown below indicate a reasonable forecast of platform use.

Percentage breakdown of platform use

	1957	1958	1959	1960	Normal year 1961–1965	Normal year 1966–1970
Exploratory						
Mobile	85	85	80	75	70	65
Tender	15	15	20	25	30	35
Development						
Mobile	5	5	3	2	1	1
Tender	55	50	50	49	44	39
Self-contained	40	45	47	49	55	60

Exploratory Factors

1. Although opinion varies on the effect of drilling in deeper water, it is generally agreed that anchorage difficulties on the tender are about equal to the engineering problems of the mobile platform. Designs for both types are being altered to allow for greater water depth.
2. Mobile platforms will be used for lower chance locations because they are the cheapest type for drilling a dry hole.
3. Oil companies regard the fact that minimum platforms can be converted to the self-contained type for additional wells as an important solution to exploration.
4. Expansion plans of most companies show a preference for the use of tenders.

Development Factors

1. A cluster of wells about a single platform provides greater economies while drilling, and later in maintaining the producing equipment.
2. Conversion to a self-contained platform after use of the tender method eventually means a greater number of wells originating from the enlarged platform. Self-contained platforms should average a total of 10 wells instead of 4 for the minimum type.
3. Deeper water locations, which are expected in the years ahead, definitely favor the large, permanent platform. Anchorage problems on the tender prevent extensive development usage.
4. Mobile platforms will become less a factor in development because of: (*a*) maintenance and marketing problems on dispersed wells, and (*b*) higher operational costs.

Forecast of well completions by platform

	1957	1958	1959	1960	Normal year 1961–1965	Normal year 1966–1970
Exploratory						
Mobile	105	120	130	130	140	200
Tender	20	25	30	40	60	105
	125	145	160	170	200	305
Development						
Mobile	20	25	20	10	5	10
Tender	245	250	280	300	335	350
Self-contained	180	230	260	300	420	535
	445	505	560	610	760	895
Total	570	650	720	780	960	1,200

Future requirements

Mobile platform

	Normal Year 1957–1960	Normal Year 1961–1965	Normal Year 1966–1970
Platforms			
Required[1]	35	36	50
Available—35	. . .	. . .	. . .
New mobile platforms required annually	0	1	3
Steel usage: Total	0	3,650	11,250

Based on an average of 4 wells. This would include the move to a new site, downtime, withdrawal for repairs and a deeper average depth per well for wildcats. An upward swing in the 1966–1970 period reflects an increased percentage on wildcats.

Minimum platform–tender

	Normal year 1957–1960	Normal year 1961–1965	Normal year 1966–1970
Tenders			
Required[1]	50	66	76
Available—46	...	...	...
New tenders			
required annually	1	3	2
Steel usage (1,500 tons per tender)			
Total tonnage	1,500	4,500	3,000
Platforms[2]			
Well sites	75	100	115
Platforms required	45	60	70
Steel usage (600 tons per platform)			
Total tonnage	27,000	36,000	42,000

[1] Based on an average of 6 wells per year. Allowance is made for moving to a new well site, directional holes, downtime resulting from bad weather and annual repairs.

[2] Based on an average of 4 wells per platform; 60% are expected to be converted to the self-contained type or remain at the well site for production. Consideration was given to dry holes, activity of platforms built late in 1956, a greater number of wells on some larger platforms and the fact the platform can usually be placed while the tender is on another site.

Self-contained platform

	Normal year 1957–1960	Normal year 1961–1965	Normal year 1966–1970
Platforms			
Original type[1]	6	10	15
Conversion of			
Minimum platform[2]	22	40	49
Steel usage Total[3]	28,800	51,000	66,600

[1] On self-contained platforms developing a location tested by the mobile type, 10 wells would be the average capacity of a platform, all factors considered. It is expected that an average of 5 wells could be completed in a year's time.

[2] Based on the assumption that an average of 4 wells were drilled with a tender present, 6 additional holes could be completed on the enlarged platform. In 1957, 21 platforms built previously will drill 60 of the forecasted wells.

[3] Tonnages averaged from 8 sources: converted, 900; original, 1,500.

Well protector jackets are protective structures used for producing wells after drilling has been completed. When the platform is moved to another site the jacket is substituted to elevate equipment and break water action. This practice is especially common in isolated wells.

	Normal year 1957–1960	Normal year 1961–1965	Normal year 1966–1970
Required	140	145	210
Steel usage (50 tons each)			
Total	7,000	7,250	10,500

OIL COUNTRY TUBULAR GOODS

Requirements for casing, tubing and drill pipe will increase significantly with the deeper wells expected in the Gulf of Mexico during the years ahead. These tubular products comprise the largest single category in the consumption of steel offshore.

Because all strings of casing come to the surface, tonnage increases at geometric rates rather than by simple arithmetic progression. The average well depth offshore (9,600 feet) is roughly 2½ times the onshore depth (4,070 feet).

In addition, the use of longer strings of large diameter casing has become common practice to maintain maximum inside diameter clearance. Due to operational expense and the cost of financing, oil companies now prefer to disregard possible collapse of the larger diameter casing, rather than tie up their rig for any unusual length of time on bottom hole problems. This also makes allowance for multiple completions. The results of these developments will mean increasing tonnage per well.

Oil country tubular goods[1]

	1955	Normal year 1957–1960	Normal year 1961–1965	Normal year 1966–1970
Casing	71,200	130,800	206,000	311,700
Tubing	13,000	30,700	48,500	50,900
Drill pipe	1,800	3,500	5,500	7,400
Total	86,000	165,000	260,000	370,000
% of U.S. oil country tubular goods	3%	6%	8%	10%
Average tonnage per well	239	240	270	310

[1] The forecast takes into consideration conditions peculiar to the Gulf Coast area including the geology, drilling practices and depth of well.

These tonnages become increasingly significant, and they magnify storage and transportation problems. More than normal quantities of casing,

Figure 3. Tubular goods composite of the preferences expressed by the operating companies contacted

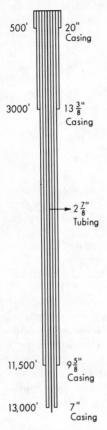

tubing and drill pipe must be stocked on racks as a reserve against severance of supply lines. Barges must carry the tubular products, mobile mud tanks for dumping into permanent tanks on the platform, and many other miscellaneous items.

Although the actual drilling of an offshore well is similar to methods used onshore, assembling such quantities of equipment and materials makes even this phase a pioneering venture.

NON-TUBULAR EQUIPMENT

Drilling a well in open water requires no more non-tubular equipment than is necessary for a comparable well onshore. Three important factors, however, increase the usage of steel.

1. *Standby equipment* is required to reduce downtime. Time lost to obtain parts or machinery from operational bases may be far more

expensive than the pro-rated cost of equipment that can later be used at another well site.

2. *Additional safety measures* are being employed to protect the huge investment at each location. Extra blowout preventors and auxiliary engines, elaborate lighting systems, communication equipment and other machinery are used which are not necessary onshore. Also, heavier equipment with more than adequate capacity has been purchased to meet emergencies.

3. *Marine equipment* for tender operations is significant. Anchors, mooring winches, pumps and innumerable small items contribute to the total market.

The consensus of opinion among major producers is that nearly a third more non-tubular steel will be used than for the same number of wells onshore. This means the following tonnages:

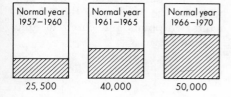

Normal year 1957–1960	Normal year 1961–1965	Normal year 1966–1970
25,500	40,000	50,000

The trend toward using diesel-electric power for this equipment is expected to continue. Although such equipment is initially more expensive, advantages in lining up and general flexibility, as well as lower operational costs, compensate the purchaser in the long run. The problems of corrosion, and investment already incurred for mechanical power equipment, will serve to restrain any sudden movement toward diesel-electric power.

MARKETING PROBLEMS

The volume provided by pipelines, and consequent savings in transportation costs, has been one of the major stimulants to the growth of the petroleum industry. A consideration of the offshore situation, however, must include more than the usual pattern of hauling by vehicle or barge until sufficient reserves warrant the construction of a line. The expense involved is approximately 3 to 4½ times a comparable pipeline onshore. The potential of a producing location must be carefully evaluated to determine what is the most profitable method to begin the marketing process. Below are possible solutions to the problems involved:

1. A cluster of wells in a reasonably prolific sand would offer the most favorable opportunity for a pipeline. For marketing gas, it is the only solution. Small diameter lines would connect the well sites to a central gathering system, which might be entirely submerged or have a compressor station located on an island. This would depend on its location in

the Gulf. It then ties into an existing onshore pipeline. The advantages of such a system would be:

a. Volume production.
b. Consistent flow despite weather conditions.
c. Accelerated dollar return on investment.
d. Lower operational expense.

The capital outlay is the only disadvantage, and it is important because of other tremendous expenses incurred in drilling offshore. Costs can reach $60 per foot of line in the Gulf of Mexico, and the greater the water depth, the higher the cost.

2. To circumvent a sizable portion of the cost, man-made islands with tanker loading and storage facilities are being seriously considered for marketing crude. Smaller tankers could load from these centralized platforms and deliver the crude directly to the refining area. Only small diameter lines would be required between the well and the island. Barges could possibly shuttle between the two points and eliminate line pipe completely. Advantages of such a system are:

a. Lower capital expenditures, the main gathering line being eliminated.
b. Moderate production volume.

Disadvantages are significant and may limit this solution to isolated locations:

a. Higher operating expenses increase the cost per barrel.
b. Inclement weather could shut in a group of wells by keeping the tankers from loading for a period of time.
c. Vulnerability to storm damage is greater.

3. The use of barges to deliver crude to the nearest refinery or pipeline is the most common method while testing a particular location. They can service a number of wells, the total depending on the daily production rate. The principal advantage is the lower capital expenditure required, but the drawbacks, as listed below, are too serious for permanent usage.

a. Lower volume.
b. Higher operational costs.
c. Loss of production from unfavorable weather restricting the loading process.
d. Reduced return on investment.

Barge use on dispersed well sites can be an economical practice.

A forecast of the number and size of pipelines to be laid and barges required is purely speculation. It depends on assumptions regarding dis-

Figure 4. Line pipe projection

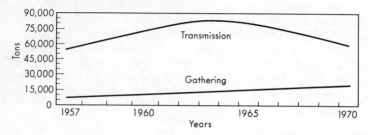

coveries and their location, company policies, government regulations, and innovations that might facilitate the marketing of oil and gas.

With these variables in mind, estimates of the future market have been made to give a complete picture of steel requirements. The tonnages below are a result of carefully evaluating the leases held, the maturity

	Normal year 1957–1960	Normal year 1961–1965	Normal year 1966–1970
Line pipe			
Total	75,000	100,000	90,000
Barges (offshore design)			
Required	10	15	20
Tonnage	5,000	7,500	10,000

of operations and their distance from existing shore installations. Emphasis is placed on the use of pipelines as the consistent, reliable method of transporting crude and gas.

The tonnages shown consider availability of steel pipe through 1960. The projection to 1970 weighs the possibilities of additional tonnages resulting from looping of present lines, new discoveries, locations in greater water depths and added emphasis on development and recovery by latecomers.

The peak for offshore transmission lines should be reached before 1965, but smaller diameter pipe is expected to continue in demand. Figure 4 illustrates the anticipated future trend. The large number of leases maturing in 1958 will accelerate marketing action. This is combined with the fact that more companies are reaching the development phase in their offshore operations.

MISCELLANEOUS VESSELS

The requirements for drilling a well from an island in unprotected water frequently necessitate quick, emergency transportation as well as a steady flow of supplies. In addition, mobile crane units are used to move a platform to another location, along with specialized barges designed to haul the individual sections. Several types of crew boats have been purchased, depending on the location of the leases.

Below is an estimate of possible future requirements for the various kinds of vessels used offshore. Consideration is given to the distance from lease to lease, and from lease to shore of major buyers. Also, the factors of replacement, obsolescence and maturity of operations are considered.

	Normal year 1957–1960	Normal year 1961–1965	Normal year 1966–1970
Crew boats			
Required	25	15	10
Tonnage	500	300	200
Supply boats			
Required	5	3	2
Tonnage	750	450	300
Cargo barges			
Required	35	20	15
Tonnage	7,000	4,000	3,000
Mobile crane units			
Required	1	1	2
Tonnage	2,100	2,100	4,200
Special barges			
Required	3	3	6
Tonnage	1,050	1,050	2,100
Total tonnage	11,400	7,900	9,800

CONCLUSIONS

The normal annual market for steel attributable to offshore drilling will be about 350,000 tons between 1957 and 1960. The tempo of activity will become greater with increased availability of equipment, facilities, and personnel, as well as growing geological knowledge of the deeper strata. However, two factors will initially retard the rise in consumption of steel.

1. A significant number of platforms and tenders are presently under contract and will be completed throughout the remainder of 1957.

The addition of this equipment to that now in operation will relieve many of the existing shortages. Its lifetime, as illustrated by the good condition of platforms that have been in open water for nearly ten years, is quite extensive.

2. The preferences expressed for the use of a tender in open water drilling have served to reduce future requirements for the mobile platform. The latter type is a much larger consumer of steel.

Summary of future steel requirements

By use	Normal year 1957–1960	Normal year 1961–1965	Normal year 1966–1970
Drilling platforms			
Mobile type	0	3,650	11,300
Minimum	27,500	36,000	42,000
Self-contained	28,800	51,300	66,600
Well protector jackets	7,000	7,250	10,500
Tenders	1,500	4,500	3,000
Oil country			
tubular goods	165,000	260,000	370,000
Non-tubular equipment	25,500	40,000	50,000
Marketing			
Line pipe	75,000	100,000	90,000
Barges	5,000	7,500	10,000
Miscellaneous vessels	11,400	7,900	9,800
Total Tonnage	346,700	518,100	663,200

These developments will be counter-balanced in part by the need for line pipe to begin the marketing process. The high cost of offshore operations places continuing emphasis on obtaining profits from a consistent flow of crude and gas. Production from these fields should grow as indicated below:

Annual liquid hydrocarbon production: Gulf of Mexico

	1955	Normal year 1957–1960	Normal year 1961–1965	Normal year 1966–1970
Crude				
(million barrels)	30	95	165	280
% U.S. total production	1	3	5	8

Although allowables per well will undoubtedly decrease through the years, these estimates may prove conservative. Wells that have been capped and sizable discoveries will assist in accelerating the rate of gain in production of crude beyond that of drilling activity.

Gas sales will be given periodic upward lifts from large scale negotiated contracts, and will grow at a faster pace than the national average. Approximately seventy billion cubic feet were produced in 1955.

The recovery of sulphur from offshore leases promises to be another factor in the use of steel. Although in the embryo stages of operation, development will require platforms, pipe, thermos barges, and other products for production and marketing.

The intensive activity in the Gulf of Mexico has had a tremendous effect on the economy of coastal areas proximate to the operations. Populations have doubled in many localities, and a great number of buildings and shore installations have been constructed to better facilitate offshore drilling. Although indirect and difficult to determine, it will be a significant stimulant to steel consumption in the South.

The future outlook is extremely favorable despite high costs, the constant risk of severe storms, and the dispute between Louisiana and the Federal Government. The area off the coasts of Louisiana and Texas is the greatest single source of crude and gas remaining in this country, and it is essential for the future of the domestic petroleum industry to explore and develop the 17-million-acre reserve on the continental shelf.

STUDENT RESEARCH PROJECT

INTRODUCTION

This preliminary study of the demand aspect of the American toy industry is intended to serve several purposes. The first purpose is to aid a beginner in research by presenting a chronological statement of the activities undertaken by the student-author of the study. There is a danger that this statement may be taken as a model appropriate to many other studies, and we must emphasize that no mold will serve all research activity. We cannot even say that one mold is most appropriate for even a narrow segment of research study such as a demand analysis of an industry.

What this chronological report is intended to do is to serve as an illustration of the step-by-step method of proceeding and the need for planning so that parts of a research activity may be fitted together to form a whole. This step-by-step method is only partially revealed in a final research report. For every positive or affirmative result achieved there are many negative results and many a cul-de-sac. Although good research reporting requires presentation of negative results, there are many times when a process has to be abandoned and cannot profitably be carried through to a conclusion.

Another purpose in including this student work is to give an introduction to the use of the computer in research. In this connection, the multiple regression program has been chosen as the illustration because it is widely used in business and economic research and is readily available for any type of computer, including small units.

It may seem that this report is burdened with the reproduction of too many of the runs or print-outs which were made. But these serve to bring out the fact that numerous runs are involved in research and that for every run which survives to appear in the final report there are many which are ineffective and will never be reported.

In addition, we are concerned in this study with illustrating the *use* of a computer program as a research tool while using the results of one computer run to establish succeeding hypotheses rather than with the mere statement of the final result or of the *theory* behind the various statistics. Reference to the discussion of multiple regression in Part 3 of this book and to the Appendix at the end of the toy study should assist anyone who feels inadequate in the use of the multiple regression technique.

The reader should note the large volume of supporting data and graphs as well as the many computer runs which were necessary to develop the relatively short text of this report. Recasting the chronological report of research activity set out here into final form would substantially shorten even this brief report.

HOW I STARTED MY RESEARCH PAPER ON THE AMERICAN TOY INDUSTRY*

INTRODUCTION

It is the purpose of the following narrative to describe the steps taken in developing a research study of the American toy industry. Although the complete study will not be presented here, the narrative of the development will contain virtually all of the data and descriptive information up to the completion of the demand section. In order to impart a reasonable structure to this narrative, it will be developed on the basis of the steps taken in collecting and analyzing data for the study. The procedure in this study is illustrative of the techniques and means of developing research studies for other industries.

INITIAL DESIGN AND RESEARCH

At the beginning of the study it is possible to designate only a very general goal, namely, whether long-term funds should be invested in the industry. Alternatively, the goal can be stated as whether a young man should associate his career with this industry. The route to this goal is to develop the demand determinants in the present part and then later to expand into profitability, supply-costs, ease of entry, and competitive structure. Because of the general nature of this statement, only broad and descriptive information is needed at the outset. This information will be useful in further refining the goal and thus the limits of the study and in suggesting feasible areas for further research.

A number of reference sources can be used in this first step, including the *Reader's Guide to Periodical Literature* [8],[1] the *Monthly Catalog of U.S. Government Publications* [24], *The Wall Street Journal Index* [4], and *The Business Periodicals Index* [2]. These sources yield a long list of readings on the industry in such magazines and newspapers as *Sales Management* [39], *Printer's Ink* [36–38], *Financial World* [30–31], *Management Review* [35], *Barron's* [26], *Chemical Week* [29], *Business Week* [27–28], *Advertising Age* [25], *Iron Age* [33–34], *Fortune* [32], and the *Wall Street Journal* [40]. These sources lead to several books

---

* By Don Cooke, M.B.A. (*Northwestern*), 1964.
[1] *Numbers in brackets refer to the numbered entries in the Bibliography at the end of this paper.*

about the industry, including *Toys in America* by Marshall and Inez McClintock [5], *Toy Manufacturing and Toy Marketing* by Homer Sinclair [9], and the *Merchandise Manual for Toys and Playthings* [11] by Toy Manufacturers of the U.S.A., Inc., and to the Toy Wholesalers Association of America, which furnished a copy of *The 1963 Toy Industry Manual* [12], a distribution guide for manufacturers and wholesalers. The readings also lead to two toy industry trade journals, *Playthings* [41] and *Toys and Novelties* [42].

These readings present much of the general descriptive information on structure, size of the industry, and channels of distribution and in addition suggest ideas for further investigation. These ideas include the relationship between toy sales, the number of children in the country, and the standard of living. On the supply side, the impact of imported toys, the use of plastics, and the increasing number of publicly owned toy companies are suggested as important.

DEFINITION OF INDUSTRY

The first problem is to define the toy industry, that is, what products are included and what excluded. The industry might be neatly defined if this study were to involve original data collection. But since we are working with library materials, the definition of the industry will involve a choice based on available data categories.

SOURCES OF DATA

On the basis of the descriptive information, the industry and some of its problems can be described in a general way. However, in order to proceed with demand analysis, data are needed on toy sales, plastic toys, toy imports and exports, disposable personal income, population under 14, and publicly owned toy companies.

The first source is the federal government in the *U.S. Census of Manufactures: 1958* [15, page 39B–4, Table 1]. This table yields total toy sales at manufacturers' prices for 1939, 1947, and 1953 through 1958, sales by category of plastic, wooden, and rubber toys at manufacturers' prices for 1954 and 1958, and the specialization ratio (the percentage of goods produced by toy companies that are in fact toys) for the industry. These are set out in Tables 5–1, 5–2, and 5–3. As the data are accumulated in this source only through 1958, it is necessary to find another source which provides more recent data. The *U.S. Industrial Outlook* [18] and the *Annual Survey of Manufactures* [14], both published yearly by the U.S. Department of Commerce, were found to furnish such data. The sales data provided by these sources are compatible with the census data in definition except for the earlier years of the *U.S. Industrial Outlook*.

At this point a problem presents itself. The census figures are for the value of toy shipments by American manufacturers and do not include imported toys and do not exclude exported toys. Since this is a study of the American market and the demand determinants in that market, the ideal figure would include imports and exclude exports. However, much of the dollar value of imported toys includes toy parts for assembly in American plants, and we cannot separate the two categories of toys and toy parts. Thus, there would be an element of double counting if the available import figures were added to shipments by American manufacturers. Further, the adjustment to American manufacturers' shipments which is of interest is the *net* of imports and exports. Except for recent years, the *net* adjustment is less than 2 per cent (Table 5–7). Under these circumstances, no adjustment has been made for imports and exports.

Use of the census data requires that a consistent definition of toys and toy companies be used for comparison between government and private data. As a result, it was decided to use the Standard Industrial Classification definition used in the census and other government data. This definition limits toy companies to those manufacturing:

1. Toys and games, except dolls and children's vehicles—Standard Industrial Classification 3941 [10, page 415].
2. Dolls—Standard Industrial Classification 3942 [10, page 331].
3. Children's vehicles, except bicycles—Standard Industrial Classification 3943 [10, page 419].

If all data obtained from non-government sources are consistent with this definition, data compatibility is assured.

The data on disposable personal income were obtained from the *Survey of Current Business, Supplement, 1961* [23] and from the *Survey of Current Business* of November, 1963 [22]. Population data were secured from the *Statistical Abstract of the United States: 1963* [13] and from *Current Population Reports* [19]. Data on imports and exports of toys at wholesale prices were taken from the *Quarterly Summary of Foreign Commerce of the United States* [21] from 1953 through 1960, from FT110, *United States Imports of Merchandise for Consumption* [20] for 1961 and 1962, and from the *U.S. Industrial Outlook* [18] for exports of 1961 and 1962. These data appear in Tables 5–7, 5–8, and 5–9.

In order to obtain data on publicly owned toy companies, several visits were made to the Securities and Exchange Commission Library in Chicago, where stock prospectuses[2] are filed for those corporations whose stocks or bonds are publicly held. A review of those prospectuses provides data on sales, gross profit, and net income for publicly owned toy companies from 1957 through 1962 (using Moody's *Industrials* for late years, but this source does not have as great detail as a prospectus).

A letter to the Monsanto Company in an attempt to obtain additional data on plastics in the toy industry yielded three studies made

[2] *Prospectuses are also available in most brokers' offices.*

by that company and the retail dollar volume of plastic toy sales in 1958, 1959, and 1960. The three studies are:

1. "Facts about the Toy Market and a Plastic Toy Survey," June, 1954 [43].
2. "Consumer Study of Plastic Model Kits," 1959 [44].
3. "Thermoplastic Molding Compound Purchases for Toys—Year 1960 and First Six Months of 1961," November, 1961 [45].

ADJUSTMENT OF DATA TO CONSTANT DOLLARS

Before beginning analysis of the data, all current dollar figures are converted to constant dollars. This step is necessary to remove from the series the effects of a changing price level and is particularly useful in regression analysis of time series in order to avoid artificially overstating the degree of association between those variables which are in dollar units. Such an overstatement would result from the parallel impact of price level changes on two or more time series stated in current money units.

The disposable personal income series is adjusted by the Consumer Price Index [16]. Toy imports and exports, plastic toy sales, total toy sales, and the toy sales of publicly owned toy companies are adjusted by the use of a Wholesale Toy Price Index [17]. Both of the indices used for adjusting the time series have the same base period: 1957–1959 = 100. The disposable personal income series is adjusted by the Consumer Price Index in order to place income in constant purchasing power terms. The Wholesale Toy Price Index is used to adjust toy sales to a constant physical unit basis. Using the Consumer Price Index to adjust toy sales figures would cause distortion to the extent that the prices of toys were affected differently by price level changes than in the case of the average of all consumer goods.

In the case of the Wholesale Toy Price Index, the exact index desired is not available. There is an index of the prices of toys, sporting goods, and small arms [17, code 15–1]. There is also an index of toys and children's vehicles [17, code 15–11]. The latter index includes only 1 doll item but 3 children's vehicle items in the 11 items used. However, as Table 5–2 makes clear, the dollar sales volume of dolls is more than three times that of children's vehicles.[3] On the other hand, the former index covers 18 items in addition to the 11 included in the latter index but is distorted by 9 items of small arms. The former index includes the price of a bicycle, roller skates, a football, and a baseball glove, which are not included in the latter index. Although these items are not included within the definition of toys used in this study, the former

---

[3] The doll carries a weight of 20 per cent, and a plastic toy carries a weight of 21 per cent, with a coaster wagon carrying a weight of 1 per cent in this index. Private communication of Arnold E. Chase, Assistant Commissioner, Price and Living Conditions, Bureau of Labor Statistics.

index appears more representative for our purposes. These two indices vary as follows with both indices having a base of 1957–1959 = 100:

Wholesale price indices

	Toys, sporting goods, and small arms	Toys and children's vehicles
1947	82.2	89.9
1953	96.3	100.9
1954	95.8	98.7
1955	96.2	98.6
1956	98.4	99.0
1957	99.7	99.1
1958	100.8	101.1
1959	99.5	99.8
1960	100.2	100.5
1961	100.5	101.3
1962	100.4	100.6

If our sole purpose were to determine the degree of association between toy sales as an independent variable and such dependent variables as disposable personal income and population under 14, we would not need to put the series into constant dollars but could use "first differences" (a technique to be explained later).

FIRMS PRODUCING TOYS

After converting all time series to constant dollars, the first step in detailed analysis is to investigate the structure of the industry, utilizing the specialization ratio (the percentage of goods produced by toy companies that are toys), the number and size of the firms, and total toy sales at manufacturers' prices.

The relative size of toy manufacturers is presented through the use of a Lorenz curve [3, page 210] applied to census data [15, page 39B–9, Table 4] in Table 5–1. This curve is presented in Figure 5–1 and shows the distribution of sales by size of the firms in the industry. Most of the total of 1,397 toy establishments are small, with 61 per cent of the firms having fewer than 20 employees. There are only a few large firms in the industry, as shown by the fact that only 12 per cent of the firms employ more than 100 people.

The specialization ratio, as a measure of the extent to which toy manufacturers produce only toys, gives an indication of possible changes in the structure of the industry. The high specialization ratio of the firms within the toy industry (Table 5–3) indicates that toy manufacturers are very specialized in toys and that since 1947 there is no indication of diversification by the industry into goods other than toys.

The data on the number of firms in the industry (Table 5–4) indicate a leveling off in the number of firms in the industry since 1954. This cannot be further substantiated since an accurate count of the number of firms in the industry has not been made since 1958.

For use in describing the industry and for use again in the demand analysis, the volume of toy sales in constant dollars at manufacturers' prices is plotted, both in the aggregate and by category. The aggregate plotting in Figure 5–2 indicates a saturation has not yet been reached. The conclusion as to saturation is drawn from the fact that the time series shows no indication of leveling off. In this sense, the industry has not reached absolute saturation. Relative saturation would be reached when per capita sales per child (or possibly toy sales per family) level off.

The plot by category in Figure 5–3 shows that the production of children's vehicles is actually declining while the rest of the industry continues to grow in constant dollar sales. The erratic growth of the dolls category should also be noted. A further charting of sales by category, on semi-logarithmic paper, indicates that the toys and games category is growing at a roughly constant rate, as appears in Figure 5–3A.

All but a very few of the many firms in the industry are privately owned and are thus not required to publish financial data. It is not possible to obtain financial data for the industry as a whole in the *Census of Manufactures* beyond a few figures such as value added and payroll. It is possible to obtain financial data on 15 firms[4] which have sold stock or bonds to the public. From these data, at least rough approximations of the financial conditions of the industry can be made. The information thus collected shows a growth in sales of 174 per cent (in constant dollars) for the 15 publicly owned toy firms in the six years between 1957 and 1962, as compared with a 31 per cent growth for the toy industry in the United States as a whole for those years (Table 5–5). This difference in the rates of growth casts doubt on the comparability of privately and publicly owned toy companies. Because of the explosive growth in sales of the Mattel Toy Company a separate computation removing this company's sales from the series of the publicly owned companies was made, and the growth rate for the 14 remaining is 131 per cent in the six-year period. This faster growth of publicly owned companies might be associated with the advertising effect of TV programs used by the publicly owned companies. Total TV expenditures on toys grew from $1.8 million in 1956 to $51.6 million in 1962.[5]

[4] *The 15 companies are shown in Table 5–6. Other publicly held firms which produce sizable quantities of toys are so diversified as to make their data useless since they do not release data by divisions. A good example is Lionel.*

[5] *TV expenditures by toy companies were (in millions):*

| 1956 | $1.8 | 1957 | $ 2.2 | 1958 | $ 3.4 | 1959 | $6.2 |
| 1960 | 7.3 | 1961 | 15.3 | 1962 | 51.6 | | |

SOURCES: *1956–1957*—Printers' Ink, *December 18, 1959; 1958–1959*—Broadcasting, *April 18, 1960, p. 40; 1960–1961*—ibid., *May 21, 1962, p. 34; 1962*—ibid., *November 25, 1963, p. 62.*

The financial data may indicate typical cost conditions within the industry. For publicly held companies, gross profit (defined as sales less cost of goods sold) is typically between 20 and 30 per cent of sales (Table 5–6). This suggests that a large portion of the costs is in materials and labor, and much less in administrative and selling expenses. (Sales of publicly owned companies are plotted in Figure 5–4.)

The value of imports has risen very rapidly since 1953, when imports were 1.9 per cent (Figure 5–5 and Table 5–7), until in 1962 imports represented 6.2 per cent of total toy sales. Because imports still represent a low percentage of the total sales, this is not a serious problem for toy manufacturers at the present time. However, if the percentage increase from 1.9 per cent in 1953 continues, imported toys could become of considerable importance to the industry. It is not possible to ascertain what percentage of imported toys become parts of toys manufactured in the United States. It is not possible, therefore, to ascertain the extent of double counting of imported toys.

As was noted earlier, data on plastic toys are available in the census for two years, 1954 and 1958, and from the Monsanto Company for 1959 and 1960. These data are collected in Table 5–8, giving the time series of plastic toy sales at manufacturers' prices in constant dollars. Although plastic toy manufacturers realized a 56 per cent increase in sales from 1954 to 1960, the trend has tapered off since 1958.

DEMAND AND DEMAND DETERMINANTS

Demand analysis begins with a review of the industry sales series discussed earlier (Figure 5–2 and Table 5–2). This review, coupled with the ideas suggested by the descriptive information that toy sales are related to the number of children and to the standard of living, leads to an effort to measure the relationship, if any. The first step in developing this measure is to draw scatter diagrams. The first scatter diagram shows aggregate toy sales in constant dollars and population under 14 (Figure 5–6). The second shows aggregate toy sales in constant dollars and disposable personal income in constant dollars (Figure 5–7). Data for disposable personal income, population under 14, and the Consumer Price Index, all for 1939, 1947, and 1953 to 1962, appear in Table 5–9. Both of these diagrams show the possibility of a relationship between toy sales and each of disposable personal income and population under 14.

To refine the analysis of the relationship of toy sales to population under 14, the average dollar amount (in constant dollars) of toys purchased per child under 14 in 1939, 1947, and 1953 is multiplied by the number of children under 14 in each succeeding year (Figure 5–8 and Table 5–10). This results in three extrapolations of toy purchases and, by comparison with the actual level of toy sales in the latest year of the series, gives a measure of the impact of population change on toy sales.

The same technique is used to refine the relationship of toy sales to disposable personal income. These extrapolations are based on the toy sales per dollar of disposable personal income in 1939, 1947, and 1953 multiplied by the growth in disposable personal income (Figure 5–9 and Table 5–11).

In the case of both disposable personal income and population under 14, the extension of the 1953 rates provides the greatest percentage explanation of changes in toy sales. These approximations are imprecise, at best, since in each of the two-variable relationships investigated the third variable is present but assumed constant, thus distorting the attempted measurement of the effect of the second variable. It should be noted that the extrapolation of the toy sales rate per child under 14 times population under 14 does not anticipate the 1957 drop in toy sales, while the extrapolation of the toy sales rate per dollar of disposable personal income times disposable personal income at least indicates a decreased gain in toy sales in that year. It would thus appear that disposable personal income is a more important factor in toy sales than is the child population.[6] It would appear, also, that a decrease in the rate of growth of disposable personal income has an aggravated effect on toy sales.

USE OF THE COMPUTER FOR MULTIPLE REGRESSION ANALYSIS: TIME SERIES USING AGGREGATES RATHER THAN FIRST DIFFERENCES

In order to refine the measurement of these possibilities, it was decided to use the data from Tables 5–2 and 5–9 for input to an available computer program (UCLA BIMED 29 on the IBM-709 computer)[7] which gives a multiple regression analysis of the series. This program provides a measurement of the individual relationships between the variables of the time series and a test of the significance of the measurement.

The first problem processed through the computer program (Table 5–12, problem 1) indicates by the partial determination coefficients (square of partial correlation coefficient) that disposable personal income explains 54.8 per cent of the variation in toy sales,[8] while population under 14 explains only 0.8 per cent. Furthermore, the reliability of the relationship of population is subject to considerable error since the standard error of the regression coefficient of population under 14 is large with respect to the regression coefficient (computed t value ad-

[6] The conclusion that the number of children under 14 is not a significant factor in toy sales is uniformly confirmed in all the succeeding tests in this study. This conclusion flatly contradicts the position taken by Beatrice Judelle, "Child Population: A Study in Statistics," Toys and Novelties (New York: Haire Publishing Company, 1962), a four-page publication. Judelle attempts a projection of potential toy sales for areas of the country on the basis of child population.

[7] Appendix A gives a detailed explanation of each statistic in the computer print-out.

[8] Instead of proceeding in terms of percentage of explained variation (R^2) we could translate this into terms of percentage of association, a statistic explained above, p. 151.

justed for degrees of freedom is only 0.28).[9] The reliability of the relationship of disposable personal income to toy sales seems good because
the t value of the regression coefficient adjusted for degrees of freedom
is 3.3. The program yields the following equation for toy sales in relation
to disposable personal income and population under 14:[10]

$$\text{Toy sales} = -47.183 + 0.367X_1 + 0.024X_2 \tag{1}$$
$$(0.112) \qquad (0.091)$$

where toy sales are in units of tens of millions of constant dollars
X_1 = disposable personal income in billions of constant dollars
X_2 = population under 14 in hundreds of thousands
with the figures in parentheses indicating the standard error of the coefficient immediately above. This equation is considered reliable for forecasting and accepted as an hypothesis that describes relationships not
due to chance, because the multiple determination coefficient (R^2),
when adjusted for degrees of freedom,[11] is 0.98 and the computed t value
of X_1 is 3.3. The standard error of estimate is an important measure of
fit of the computed equation to the actual data and indicates the range
above and below the computed equation line within which there is a
68.27 per cent probability that any item in the sample will fall. The
multiple and simple determination and correlation coefficients are the
only terms which need to be corrected for degrees of freedom, as the
computer program performs the adjustment of all of the other measures
for degrees of freedom.

Figure 5–10 shows toy sales as computed by this equation compared
with actual toy sales.

The von Neumann ratio indicates there is autocorrelation in the residuals at the 1 per cent level of confidence, but in later computer runs
autocorrelation is frequently absent.

We can say multicollinearity is present in the data. This is established
by the matrix of simple correlation coefficients where there is a high
simple correlation between the independent variables. Multicollinearity
makes it difficult to state separately the effect of each independent variable, but the results are still usable for forecasting from the two independent variables.

The rerunning of problem 1 (Table 5–12), deleting[12] alternately each

---

[9] *Throughout this study, the position is taken that tests of significance are applicable
to a universe containing a small number of items. This has been generally accepted
in modern research work. Another view is that tests of significance are applicable
only to a sample rather than a universe containing a small number of items.*
[10] *All statements of the estimating equation are given as the calculated form of
equation and not as the hypothesized estimating equation including an error term.*
[11] *See Erwin E. Nemmers,* Managerial Economics: Text and Cases, *rev. printing
(New York: John Wiley & Sons, Inc., 1964), p. 26, for the computational procedure
involved.*
[12] *In the BIMED 29 program, it is necessary to use a replacement and deletion
card in order to get the first print-out. This is a misnomer because there is no*

independent variable, also indicates there is high multicollinearity. This is evidenced by the fact that when disposable income is deleted, population under 14 picks up a high t value (14.8) and r^2 is high, namely, 96 per cent. Conversely, when population under 14 is deleted, disposable personal income has a t value of 22.1 and r^2 is 0.98.

Because of the previously noted possibility of an accelerated effect of disposable personal income on toy sales beginning with 1957, another computer run of the time series was prepared to measure this effect.[13] The computer program used in problem 1 contains the alternative of processing data in logarithmic form. By using this option, the data from Tables 5–2 and 5–9 are transformed to logarithms by the computer and processed, thus arriving at an output (problem 2, Table 5–13) which yields the following type of equation:

$$Y = aX_1^b X_2^c$$

which, when changed to logarithms, becomes

$$\log Y = \log a + b \log X_1 + c \log X_2$$

where Y, X_1 and X_2 are the same variables but with different units than in problem 1.

Table 5–13 (problem 2) shows the results to be

$$\log Y = -4.573 + 2.474 \log X_1 - 0.726 \log X_2; R^2 = 0.99 \qquad (2)$$
$$ (0.215) (0.304)$$

where Y = toy sales in tens of thousands of constant dollars
       X_1 = disposable personal income in millions of constant dollars
       X_2 = population under 14 in units of hundreds

The t value of X_1 is 11.5, and of X_2 is -2.4. The standard error of estimate is 4.1 per cent. This result may seem disturbing in that it states toy sales move directly with income but *inversely with the population* under 14. However, the relatively low t value of -2.4 indicates that population under 14 may not have a significant relation to the dependent variable. The t table shows a probability of 0.984 for a t of 2.4 and N of 13. The autocorrelation of the residuals is positive and significant at the 5 per cent level of confidence but not at the 1 per cent.

Again as in the case of the arithmetic straight line, the high simple correlation coefficients between the independent variables in the opening matrix indicate multicollinearity.

The logarithmic option permits the rerunning of the data after deleting one of the independent variables. In this way we can measure the elas-

replacement or deletion. Hence, the first actual replacement or deletion will be identified as the second.
[13] *In this procedure, we are assuming that the demand function is stable over time
(shifts along one demand curve) rather than that there are structural changes in
demand (shifts in the demand curve).*

ticity of demand of toy sales with respect to disposable personal income.[14] The resulting equation (problem 2–1, Table 5–14) is:

$$\log Y = (4.051 - 10) + 1.973 \log X_1 \qquad (2a)$$
$$(0.058)$$

which can be restated in untransformed form as $Y = 0.000001125\, X_1^{1.973}$

The result of the rerun shows 1.973 as the elasticity of demand for toys with respect to disposable personal income. This means that demand is income elastic since each additional 1 per cent of disposable personal income results in an increase of 1.973 per cent in toy sales. The t value of 34 associated with the exponent would indicate significance from a sampling point of view if we had no strong trend in each of the variables. The correlation coefficient is 0.99, and the standard error of the estimate is 4.98 per cent. The toy sales computed by this equation are charted in Figure 5–11 together with actual toy sales.

It should be noted that in the present process we have ignored the identification problem.[15] We have assumed that the demand curve for toys has not shifted but that all movements have been along the demand curve.

The logarithmic option was then used with population under 14 replacing disposable income as the independent variable (problem 2–2, Table 5–15) with the resulting equation:

$$\log Y = (9.620 - 20) + 2.684 \log X_2 \qquad (2b)$$
$$(0.253)$$

The t value of X_2 is 10, r is 0.96, and the standard error of estimate is 16.2 per cent.

We are again in a position to conclude that there is serious multicollinearity because the regression coefficient of population under 14 when disposable personal income is included in the analysis (problem 2, Table 5–13) is −0.726 and without X_1 present has become 2.684. In short, there are three parallel upward trends: toy sales, disposable income, and population under 14. Whichever of the two independent variables is present picks up the high t value when one independent variable is present.

Because of the possibility of a major change in the demand relationship between 1939 and 1953 (as already indicated in our reference to the identification problem), the multiple correlations were rerun, using

[14] As appears in any standard advanced economics text, the exponent of the independent variable is the elasticity of that variable with respect to the dependent variable when the equation is in multiplicative form. See Erwin E. Nemmers, Managerial Economics: Text and Cases, rev. printing (New York: John Wiley & Sons, Inc., 1964), p. 27.

[15] For a discussion of the identification problem, see Erwin E. Nemmers, Managerial Economics: Text and Cases, rev. printing (New York: John Wiley & Sons, Inc., 1964), pp. 123–129.

the arithmetic straight line without the data for 1939 and 1947. The print-out appears in Table 5–16 (problem 3). This results in the following equation:

$$\text{Toy sales} = -40.431 + 0.693X_1 - 0.198X_2 \tag{3}$$
$$(0.226) \qquad (0.179)$$

with toy sales in units of tens of millions of constant dollars, disposable personal income (X_1) in billions of constant dollars, and population under 14 (X_2) in hundreds of thousands. The computed t value of disposable personal income is 3.06, and of population under 14 is −1.1. Toy sales computed by this equation are plotted together with actual toy sales in Figure 5–12. There is no great difference in results compared with the inclusion of the years 1939 and 1947 above.

The data of Tables 5–2 and 5–9 are then used for the years 1953 through 1962 in logarithmic form with the results shown in Table 5–17 (problem 4):

$$\log Y = (6.367 - 10) + 2.278X_1 - 0.701X_2$$
$$(0.845) \qquad (1.045)$$

The variables have the same units as in equation 2. The low t value of −0.67 of the regression coefficient of population under 14 indicates a lack of reliability for this variable.

The same data were rerun, deleting population under 14 as a variable. These results appear in Table 5–18 (problem 4–1):

$$\log Y = (5.451 - 10) - 1.719X_1$$
$$(0.129)$$

The t value of disposable income, which is 2.7 in Table 5–17 (problem 4), has now increased to 13.2 with the elimination of the unreliable variable, population under 14.

All of the results in the 12-item correlation (problem 2–1, Table 5–14) in logarithmic form are better than for the 10-item period (problem 4–1, Table 5–18). The income elasticity in the 10-item case is 1.719 with standard error of 0.129, and in the 12-item case it is 1.973 with standard error of 0.058.

TIME SERIES ANALYSIS USING FIRST DIFFERENCES

Further to refine the measure of the relationship, it was decided to pursue the matter of multicollinearity which is present when a linear relationship exists between the independent variables. The technique of first differences may remove multicollinearity. The first difference technique involves subtracting each of the figures for each year in Tables 5–2 and 5–9 from the preceding year and using the results as input. The purpose of this technique is to ascertain the extent to which the period-to-period changes of each of the variables in the original times series move together. This procedure tends to cancel out the secular trend effects.

The print-out from this computer run of first differences (problem 5, Table 5-19) reinforces our conclusions about the other computer problems run with the original data. The multiple determination coefficient is 0.9, and the computed t value is 5.8 for the disposable personal income variable but only 0.18 for population under 14. Problem 5 (Table 5-19) uses the years 1939, 1947, and 1953 to 1962, and the variables are in the following units: toy sales in hundreds of thousands of constant dollars, population under 14 in tens of thousands, and disposable personal income in hundreds of millions of constant dollars. The absence of autocorrelation in the residuals is some indication that multicollinearity has been eliminated by the first difference technique.

In working with first differences, the changes between 1939 and 1947 and between 1947 and 1953 are large relative to the changes between succeeding years and would unduly weight the results. Hence, the program was rerun without the differences between 1939 and 1947 and between 1947 and 1953. This result (problem 5-1, Table 5-20) is in the same units as problem 5 (Table 5-19) and shows that disposable personal income is a major factor with a t value of 3.17 and a multiple correlation coefficient of 0.81 when both independent variables are used, and a partial determination coefficient of 0.79 for disposable income alone. The partial determination coefficient for disposable personal income was 0.76 when the original data were run in problem 3 (Table 5-16). This increase in the measure of partial correlation occurs only infrequently when original data are rerun as first differences. Usually, the partial correlation drops as trend is removed.

CROSS-SECTIONAL ANALYSIS ON A STATE-BY-STATE BASIS

To establish the reliability of the analysis so far, a cross-sectional test on a state-by-state basis was undertaken. Toy sales *at retail* by states for 1960 are obtained from *Playthings* [41, pages 14 and 15], personal income by states is obtained from the *Statistical Abstract* [13], and population under 15[16] by states from *U.S. Census of Population: 1960*. The data of toy sales and personal income (Table 5-21) are first plotted as a scatter diagram (Figure 5-13) to assess the feasibility of continuing the investigation. The pattern on this plot raises the possibility of success by more sophisticated techniques. These data are then prepared for com-

[16] *It was at this point that it was discovered that the previous selection of under 14 years might have been a poor choice since apparently all the Bureau of Census projections of population (to be used later in forecasting toy sales) use a population classification of 0 to 4 years, 5 to 9 years, and 10 to 14 years (inclusive). Accordingly, a shift has been made to the use of population under 15 years for the cross-sectional analysis. However, a Bureau of the Census projection of population with the under 14 group broken out was finally located, as appears in the footnotes to Table 5-27.*

puter processing as problem 6 (Table 5–22) and for the logarithmic option as problem 7 (Table 5–23).

In problems 6 and 7, the units are as follows: toy sales are in hundreds of thousands of current dollars, personal income (X_1) is in tens of millions of current dollars, and population under 15 (X_2) is in tens of thousands.

Problem 6 yields a multiple correlation coefficient of 0.987,[17] a standard error of the estimate of $7,045,600, or 22 per cent of the mean of toy sales, and a t value of 9.7 for personal income but only 0.4 for population under 15. Problem 6 yields the following equation for retail toy sales:

$$\text{Retail toy sales} = -3.389 + 0.408X_1 + 0.165X_2 \qquad (4)$$
$$(0.042) \qquad (0.375)$$

It is interesting to note that population under 15 adds nothing to the explanation and R on a cumulative basis does not increase when population under 15 is added. When the program is run deleting personal income as an independent variable, population under 15 shows an r of 0.96 and a t value of 24. This seems to confirm the multicollinearity of personal income and population under 14 previously established.

The estimated values of toy sales for six states are negative when substitution is made in the two-variable regression equation of toy sales on population under 15 only (the last rerun of Table 5–22). This indicates the arbitrary character of either population under 15 as an explanatory variable or the use of an arithmetic straight line as the regression hypothesis.

The logarithmic option results in an output (problem 7, Table 5–23), with multiple correlation coefficient of 0.99, standard error of estimate of 11.7 per cent of the mean of toy sales, and a computed t value of 11.4 for personal income and of 1.2 for population under 15. The cross-sectional elasticity of personal income from this print-out is 0.956 with standard error of 0.084, which differs from the elasticity of disposable personal income found in the time series as 1.973 with standard error of 0.058 (problem 2–1, Table 5–14) and 1.719 with standard error of 0.129 (problem 4–1, Table 5–18), but this elasticity rises to 1.053 with standard error of 0.021 when population under 15 is dropped and the t value for personal income rises to 51 (problem 7–1, Table 5–23). Because of this sharp rise in the t value, the exponent from the simple correlation of toy sales and personal income, rather than the exponent from the multiple correlation of toy sales with population under 15 and personal income, will later be used for predicting.

Income elasticity of demand established from a time series is not the same thing as income elasticity of demand established from a cross section of states. For example, if low-income states are participating to a lesser degree in economic growth, the income elasticity derived from a time series analysis would be of more interest to a toy manufacturer.

[17] *This high coefficient raised the question whether toy sales at retail might have been computed in the original data as a percentage of income for each state. Communication with the publisher of the statistics [40] showed this not to be the case.*

The lower cross-sectional income elasticity would indicate in the present case that the toy manufacturer should concentrate his efforts in higher-income states—not only to benefit from the higher per capita expenditure on toys in such states but also to benefit from the higher growth rate in toy sales of such states from *each* added dollar of income.

CROSS-SECTIONAL ANALYSIS ON A REGIONAL BASIS

As a further test of these data, personal income and retail toy sales are summarized by region (Table 5–24) and plotted on a scatter diagram (Figure 5–14). The data are then used for input to computer problem 8 (Table 5–25) and with the logarithmic option as problem 9 (Table 5–26). Problem 8 results in a print-out of the equation:

$$\text{Retail toy sales} = -6.378 + 4.409X \tag{5}$$
$$(0.167)$$

where X = personal income in billions of current dollars and retail toy sales are in millions of current dollars. In this print-out the multiple correlation coefficient is 0.99, the standard error of the estimate is $13,061,890, or 7 per cent, and the computed t value of personal income is 26.

With the logarithmic option, an elasticity value of 1.00 with a standard error of 0.032 and with a t value of 32 is obtained for personal income with respect to retail toy sales in problem 9 (Table 5–26). The standard error of estimate is 10.6 per cent. In the logarithmic option, retail toy sales are in thousands of current dollars, and personal income is in millions of current dollars.

USE OF ANALYSIS FOR PREDICTION

On the basis of the foregoing analysis, several predictions[18] of future toy sales at manufacturers' prices and at retail prices may be made. To make these predictions, it is necessary to obtain forecasts of future levels of disposable personal income, personal income, and population under 14. The population data are obtained from the *Statistical Abstract* [13, page 6]. A forecast of spendable income[19] was obtained from *Income Trends in the United States through 1975*, published by the Stanford Research Institute [1, page 21]. The Stanford income data, which are forecast on the basis of a price level of 1947–1949 = 100, are changed to the 1957–1959 = 100 base. This is accomplished by multiplying the data by 1.285 (the ratio of the 1957–1959 base to the 1947–1949 base).

[18] *Analysis so far has indicated that population under 14 is not a significant factor and does not seriously affect the result.*
[19] *The Stanford series for spendable income is used to approximate disposable personal income. The net difference between the two series is state and local personal taxes which make spendable income about 2.5 per cent larger than disposable personal income.*

Examination of the Stanford prediction shows that this forecast made in 1957 is an underestimate for 1960. Thus disposable personal income in 1960 was $339.0 billion, but the Stanford forecast of spendable income for that year was $320.5 billion, both figures being in 1957–1959 dollars. The $320.5 billion is further reduceable by $7 billion for personal state and local taxes to equate spendable income with disposable personal income. Hence, the Stanford forecast is an underestimate of $25.5 billion, or 8 per cent, for 1960. Accordingly, the Stanford estimates for 1960 and succeeding years were increased by 8 per cent to adjust spendable income to disposable personal income and also to correct for the known underestimate.

The first prediction of toy sales is based on the equation developed in problem 1 (Table 5–12). The predicted sales levels in 1965, 1970, and 1975 are shown in tabular form in Table 5–27 and in chart form, as an extension of the current sales series, in Figure 5–15.[20]

Prediction on the basis of the calculated elasticity of demand with respect to disposable personal income results in the data tabulated in Table 5–28 and Figure 5–16 for an elasticity of 1.973 (from problem 2–1, Table 5–14) and again in Table 5–29 and Figure 5–17 for an elasticity of 1.719 (from problem 4–1, Table 5–18).

The prediction based on the income elasticity of 1.053 for personal income derived in problem 7–1 (Table 5–23) is tabulated in Table 5–30 and plotted in Figure 5–18. To be useful to the toy industry, however, this prediction of toy sales at retail prices must be translated into toy sales at manufacturers' prices. Such a prediction of sales at the manufacturers' level may be derived by assuming that the same relationship will hold in the future as was true of the ratio between manufacturers' prices and retail prices in 1960. In that year, manufacturers' prices equaled 54 per cent of retail.[21] This sales prediction results in manufacturers' sales of $1,068 million[22] in constant dollars (1957–1959 = 100) in 1965, which is close to the 1962 level of actual manufacturers' sales of $1,060 million in constant dollars.

SUMMARY

The foregoing narrative has covered the primary steps involved in developing an industry demand study. Certainly, it is not the finished study. A significant amount of purely descriptive information would be added to form the finished study. The descriptive information would present those areas of the study for which numerical data are not available, such as the importance of imagination and creativity in toy design.[23]

[20] *In making these predictions, we must be aware of the distinction between the standard error of estimate and the standard error of forecast. See above, pp. 154–159.*
[21] *1960 retail sales in constant dollars $1,648 million [6]; 1960 manufacturers' sales in constant dollars $887 million (Table 5–2).*
[22] *Predicted 1965 sales of $1,978 million at retail from Table 5–30 times factor of 0.54.*
[23] *Mattel Toy Company is reputed to have made an extensive study of decision processes in toy creation by employing operations research techniques. Whether this is causally related to the sales growth of Mattel is an interesting item.*

*Table 5–1. Cumulative percentage of toy manufacturers and toy sales in 1958 vs. cumulative percentage of Standard Industrial Classification Group 39 manufacturers and sales in 1958**

Number of employees†	Number of establishments		Sales (in thousands of dollars)		Cumulative percentage of total			
					Toy manufacturers		SIC 39	
	Toy manufacturers	SIC 39	Toy manufacturers	SIC 39	Establishments	Sales	Establishments	Sales
1–4	402	5,022	$ 11,225	$ 184,429	28.8%	1.45%	44.5%	4.37%
4–9	210	1,995	16,145	205,580	44.0	3.52	61.9	9.22
10–19	223	1,666	36,216	330,845	61.2	8.06	76.7	17.04
20–49	266	1,491	107,760	699,945	79.9	23.18	90.0	33.61
50–99	148	582	128,765	578,111	88.0	39.28	96.1	47.31
100–249	100	353	198,056	851,596	96.1	54.72	98.7	67.49
250–499	37	98	165,934	587,755	98.8	76.41	99.2	81.29
500–999	8	41	97,521	583,806	99.5	90.13	99.8	95.31
1,000–2,499	2	16	44,836	200,630	100.0	100.00	100.0	100.00
	1397	11,264	$706,458	$4,222,698	100.0	100.00	100.0	100.00

* Standard Industrial Classification Group 39 consists of miscellaneous manufactures, including toys, dolls, and children's vehicles. In this table, toys, dolls, and children's vehicles are excluded from the SIC Group 39 figures.

† Total number of employees by toy manufacturers in 1958 was 61,540 with a payroll of $213,334,000 for an average of $3,467 per employee per year. Some 55 per cent of the toy establishments are located in the states of New York, New Jersey, and Pennsylvania.

SOURCE: U.S. Bureau of the Census, *U.S. Census of Manufacturers: 1958*, Vol. I, *Summary Statistics* (Washington, D.C.: Government Printing Office), pp. 2–60 to 2–63, Table 3.

499

In addition, the finished study would be presented in a far different format than used above and would extend into examination of the reasons for the relationships indicated by the quantitative analysis undertaken. Final design of the format would be such as to present the study logically and forcefully, rather than on the basis of chronology and procedural steps, as is done here.

Figure 5–1. Cumulative percentage of toy manufacturers' establishments and cumulative percentage of toy sales (total of SIC 3941, 3942, and 3943) compared with other SIC 39   SOURCE: *Table 5–1.*

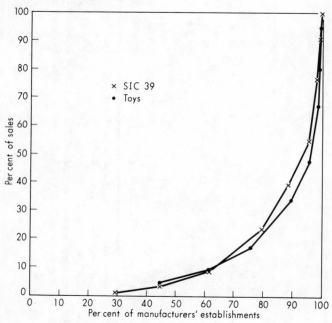

Table 5–2. Toy sales* at manufacturers' prices, total and by category, 1939, 1947, and 1953–1962 in both current and constant dollars (1957–1959 = 100)

(In thousands)

Number in computer program	Year	Wholesale price index of toys, sporting goods, and small arms	Toys and games‡		Dolls‡		Children's vehicles‡		Total toy sales‡	
			Unadjusted	Adjusted	Unadjusted	Adjusted	Unadjusted	Adjusted	Unadjusted	Adjusted
1	1962	100.4	$715,015	$712,165	$273,577	$272,487	$75,550	$ 75,249	$1,064,142	$1,059,901
2	1961	100.5	736,507	732,843	194,685	193,716	67,354	67,019	998,546	993,578
3	1960	100.2	635,322	634,053	178,302	177,946	75,191	75,041	888,815	887,041
4	1959	99.5	595,306	598,297	168,225	169,070	78,742	79,138	842,273	846,505
5	1958	100.8	544,056	539,738	161,924	160,638	70,438	69,879	776,418	770,256
6	1957	99.7	448,940	450,291	203,141	204,000	81,449	81,650	733,530	735,000
7	1956	98.4	469,131	476,759	201,799	203,752	85,266	86,652	756,619	768,922
8	1955	96.2	456,064	474,079	158,820	165,094	81,652	84,877	696,536	724,050
9	1954	95.8	397,323	414,742	145,210	151,576	77,213	80,598	619,746§	646,916
10	1953	96.3	359,108	372,906	171,839	178,441	59,193	61,467	590,140	612,814
11	1947	82.2	181,939	221,337	67,786	84,898	85,831	104,417	337,556	410,652
12	1939	53.0	49,108	92,657	18,482	34,872	19,117	36,070	86,707	163,598

* The United States Census uses the term "value of shipments" rather than "sales." However, "value of shipments" appears to have the same definition as "sales." U.S. Bureau of the Census, *U.S. Census of Manufactures: 1958*, Vol. II, *Industry Statistics*, Part 2 (Washington, D.C.: Government Printing Office), p. 11.

† SOURCE: U.S. Bureau of Labor Statistics, *Wholesale Price Index—Historical Index Series*, code 15–1, base 1957–1959 = 100 (Washington, D.C.: U.S. Department of Labor). The same index appears in U.S. Department of Commerce, *Survey of Current Business, Supplement, 1963* (Washington, D.C.: Government Printing Office), p. 45.

‡ SOURCE: 1939–1958—U.S. Bureau of the Census: *Census of Manufactures: 1958*, Vol. II, *Industry Statistics*, Part 2, Washington, D.C.: Government Printing Office), p. 39B–4, Table 1, "General Statistics for the United States, 1958 and Earlier", 1959–1960—U.S. Department of Commerce, *Annual Survey of Manufactures, 1959, 1960* (Washington, D.C.: Government Printing Office, 1962), pp. 44ff; 1961–1962—U.S. Department of Commerce, *Annual Survey of Manufactures, 1962* (Washington, D.C.: Government Printing Office, 1964), pp. 46ff.

§ U.S. Department of Commerce, *Annual Survey of Manufactures, 1955* (Washington, D.C.: Government Printing Office); shows $602 million for 1954.

Figure 5–2. Toy sales at manufacturers' prices in constant dollars (1957–1959 = 100) for 1939, 1947, and 1953–1962
SOURCE: *Table 5–2.*

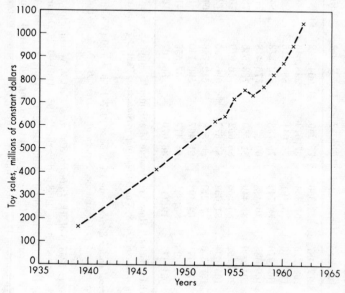

Figure 5–3. Toy sales (toys and games, excluding dolls and children's vehicles) at manufacturers' price in constant dollars (1957–1959 = 100) by category for 1939, 1947, and 1953–1962   SOURCE: *Table 5–2.*

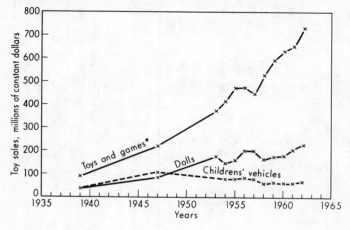

Figure 5–3A. Toy sales (toys and games, excluding dolls and children's vehicles) at manufacturers' prices in constant dollars (1957–1959 = 100) by category—ratio scale 1939, 1947, and 1953–1962 SOURCE: *Table 5–2.*

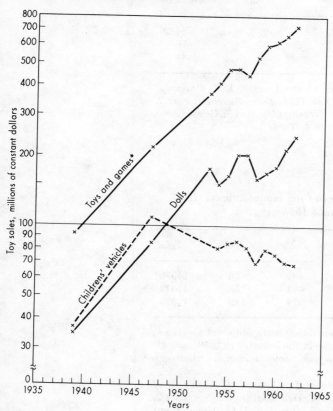

504   BUSINESS RESEARCH

Table 5–3. Specialization ratio of toy
manufacturers, 1947, 1954, and 1958

	Toys	Dolls	Vehicles
1958	93%	98%	84%
1954	95	92	76
1947	92	89	81

SOURCE: U.S. Bureau of the Census, *U.S. Census of Manufactures: 1958*, Vol. II, *Industry Statistics*, Part 2, Major Groups 29–39 (Washington, D.C.: Government Printing Office), p. 39B–4, Table 1.

Table 5–4. Number of toy manufacturers, 1947,
1954, and 1958

	Toys	Dolls	Vehicles	Total
1958	832	482	56	1,370*
1954	872	484	58	1,414
1947	830	374	119	1,323

* There were 1,397 establishments (different locations) for the 1,370 companies in the industry in 1958, indicating that only a few companies had more than one location.
SOURCE: U.S. Bureau of the Census, *U.S. Census of Manufactures: 1958*, Vol. II, *Industry Statistics*, Part 2, Major Groups 29–39 (Washington, D.C.: Government Printing Office), p. 39B–4, Table 1.

Table 5–5. Industry total of toy sales at manufacturers' prices in constant dollars (1957–1959 = 100) and share of publicly owned toy manufacturers and comparative growth rates, 1957–1962

	Toy sales in constant dollars			Growth rates	
	Industry* total (In thousands)	15 publicly held toy companies† (In thousands)	Share of market by 15 publicly held companies (per cent)‡	Industry total (per cent)§	15 publicly held companies (per cent)§
1957	$ 735,000	$ 72,277	9.8	. . .	. . .
1958	771,256	76,064	9.8	4.9	5.3
1959	846,505	98,014	11.6	10.0	28.9
1960	887,041	120,399	13.5	4.8	22.6
1961	993,578	141,603	14.3	12.0	17.9
1962	1,059,901	197,666	18.7	6.7	38.1
1957–1962				30.7	173.5

* SOURCE: Table 5–2.
† SOURCE: Table 5–6.
‡ Column 2 divided by column 1 for each year. In this computation, we are assuming that all of the sales of the publicly held toy companies are of toys. This is an over-statement because of the fact that some of the sales of these companies are of products outside of the toy category. In addition, publicly held companies have grown by merger, such as that of Playskool in 1961.
§ Difference between each succeeding two years divided by the first of the two years.

Table 5–6. Financial data for publicly owned toy companies, 1957–1962

Year		AMT.	Aurora Plastics	Milton Bradley	Creative Playthings	Eldon Industries	Emenee Corporation	Gabriel Industries	A. C. Gilbert	Mattel Toy Company	Pal Playwell, Inc.	Playskool Manufacturing Company	Remco Industries	Tonka Toy Company	Transogram	Visual Art Industries
Sales in thousands of current dollars*																
1957	Net sales	$ 2,571	$ 5,255	$ 7,696	$1,152	$ 4,383		$1,269	$15,973	$ 9,064	$265	$ 6,260	$ 5,426	$3,965	$ 8,529	$ 307
	Gross profit	551	N.A.	2,630	N.A.	1,942		264	764	2,848	81	1,251	292	592	2,565	129
	Net income	143	303	251	59	260		(34)	215	104	1	203	141	16	504	27
1958	Net sales	2,962	4,682	8,800	1,282	7,324		1,634	11,993	9,155	347	5,748	7,651	4,055	10,036	531
	Gross profit	696	530	3,217	N.A.	2,337		365	1,075	3,178	110	1,319	1,328	902	3,067	225
	Net income	92	305	339	84	344	42	41	409	215	1	133	642	123	603	51
1959	Net sales	5,810	4,949	12,336	1,454	10,593		2,256	13,138	13,912	378	6,713	10,919	3,925	9,663	729
	Gross profit	1,489	581	4,970	N.A.	3,256		512	1,594	4,940	118	1,581	1,667	951	2,517	321
	Net income	221	312	746	99	374		97	670	695	3	203	805	146	224	61
1960	Net sales	9,685	6,177	14,472	1,915	13,743	4,320	4,166	12,598	18,368	391	8,141	10,293	5,554	10,015	903
	Gross profit	2,745	1,385	5,863	365	3,943	N.A.	993	1,002	6,737	129	1,701	1,659	1,189	2,369	382
	Net income	609	181	877	161	520	42	160	378	1,036	2	58	821	159	123	62
1961	Net sales	10,874	8,639	17,790	2,166	18,514	4,958	4,369	11,563	25,724	521	16,205	18,427	6,935	12,531	1,039
	Gross profit	3,231	1,965	7,827	441	5,090	N.A.	1,053	310	8,727	227	3,562	2,987	1,843	4,282	454
	Net income	670	383	1,483	202	128	(94)	186	20	1,260	13	556	1,446	398	724	67
1962	Net sales	13,586	13,658	19,140	2,490	17,975	5,779	4,245	10,907	49,355		18,541	21,802	8,264	12,509	1,066
	Gross profit	3,329	3,185	8,385	362	861	N.A.	988	(404)	18,430		4,162	3,233	2,293	3,156	400
	Net income	407	827	1,351	179	(3,401)	108	179	(281)	4,006		684	653	506	(267)	(12)

Table 5-6. Continued

Year	AMT.	Aurora Plastics	Milton Bradley	Creative Playthings	Eldon Industries	Emenee Corporation	Gabriel Industries	A. C. Gilbert	Mattel Toy Company	Pal Playwell, Inc.	Playskool Manufacturing Company	Remco Industries	Tonka Toy Company	Transogram	Visual Art Industries
Sales in thousands of constant dollars (1957–1959 = 100)*															
1957	$ 2,579	$ 5,270	$ 7,719	$1,156	$ 4,441		$1,270	$16,000	$ 9,080	$265	$ 6,279	$ 5,430	$3,979	$ 8,505	$ 304
1958	2,938	4,645	8,730	1,272	7,266		1,622	11,900	9,100	345	5,702	7,598	4,040	10,280	526
1959	5,839	4,965	12,397	1,461	10,646		2,261	13,200	14,000	380	6,747	10,970	3,945	9,724	732
1960	9,667	6,150	14,443	1,911	13,716	$4,311	4,150	12,550	18,300	390	8,125	10,240	5,545	10,001	900
1961	10,820	8,580	17,701	2,155	18,422	4,933	4,342	11,585	25,600	518	16,286	18,350	6,899	12,480	1,032
1962	13,532	13,600	19,064	2,480	17,903	5,756	4,228	10,880	49,158	N.A.	18,615	21,760	8,231	12,459	1,002

Percentage gross profit and net income of publicly owned toy companies as percentage of sales

Year		AMT.	Aurora Plastics	Milton Bradley	Creative Playthings	Eldon Industries	Emenee Corporation	Gabriel Industries	A. C. Gilbert	Mattel Toy Company	Pal Playwell, Inc.	Playskool Manufacturing Company	Remco Industries	Tonka Toy Company	Transogram	Visual Art Industries
1957	Gross profit	21.5%	N.A.	34.2%		N.A.		20.9%	4.8%	31.4%	30.5%	20.0%	5.4%	14.9%	30.1%	41.9%
	Net income	5.6	5.7	3.3	5.1	5.9		(2.7)	1.3	1.2	0.3	3.2	2.6	0.4	5.9	9.3
1958	Gross profit	23.5	11.3	36.6		N.A.		22.3	8.9	34.6	31.8	22.9	17.3	22.2	30.5	41.4
	Net income	3.1	6.4	3.9	6.6	4.7		2.5	3.4	2.3	0.4	2.3	8.4	3.0	6.0	9.6
1959	Gross profit	25.6	11.7	40.3		30.8		22.7	12.1	35.4	31.2	23.6	15.2	24.2	26.0	44.1
	Net income	3.8	6.3	6.0	6.8	3.5		4.2	5.1	5.0	0.9	3.0	7.4	3.7	2.3	8.4
1960	Gross profit	28.4	22.4	40.5	19.1	28.7	N.A.	23.9	8.0	36.7	32.8	20.9	16.1	21.4	23.6	42.3
	Net income	6.9	2.9	6.1	8.4	3.7	1.0	3.9	3.0	5.6	0.6	0.7	8.0	2.9	1.2	6.9
1961	Gross profit	29.7	22.8	44.0	20.4	27.5	N.A.	24.1	2.7	33.9	43.5	21.7	16.2	25.6	28.0	43.6
	Net income	6.2	4.4	8.3	9.3	0.7	(1.9)	4.3	0.2	4.9	2.4	3.4	7.8	5.8	5.8	6.5
1962	Gross profit	24.5	23.3	43.8	14.5	4.8	N.A.	23.3	(3.8)	37.4	N.A.	22.5	14.8	27.7	25.2	N.A.
	Net income	3.0	6.1	7.1	7.2	(18.9)	1.9	4.2	(2.6)	8.1	N.A.	3.7	3.0	6.1	(2.1)	N.A.

* All sales adjusted by Wholesale Toy Price Index, Table 5–2.

SOURCE: Stock prospectuses on file with the Securities and Exchange Commission and *Moody's Industrial Manual*. This table does not include several large toy manufacturers whose figures for toys are not published separately since these companies operate many divisions.

Figure 5–4. Annual sales of publicly owned toy companies in constant dollars from 1957 to 1962   SOURCE: *Table 5–6.*

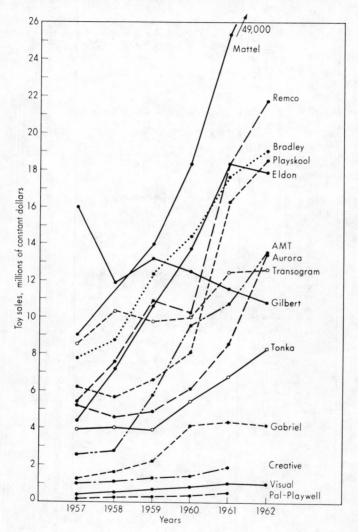

Table 5–7. *Total imports and exports of toys in constant dollars (1957–1959 = 100) for 1953–1962**

	Imports	Exports
1953	$12,202,000	$13,820,000
1954	14,630,000	13,710,000
1955	20,320,000	14,050,000
1956	28,550,000	16,400,000
1957	30,720,000	17,300,000
1958	27,820,000	17,730,000
1959	37,405,000	17,350,000
1960	42,743,000	17,395,000
1961	47,800,000	19,532,000
1962	59,080,000	18,227,000

* Values deflated by Wholesale Toy Price Index (Table 5–2).

SOURCE: 1953–1960—U.S. Department of Commerce, *Quarterly Summary of Foreign Commerce of the United States* (Cumulative Year to Date), December issues, 1953–1960 (Washington, D.C.: Government Printing Office); imports for 1961–1962—U.S. Department of Commerce, FT110, *United States Imports of Merchandise for Consumption, 1961, 1962* (Washington, D.C.: Government Printing Office), 1961, pp. 181–182; 1962, pp. 219–220; exports for 1961–1962—U.S. Department of Commerce, *U.S. Industrial Outlook,* (Washington, D.C.: Government Printing Office), 1963, ER–27; 1964, ER–23. Data on imports and exports of toys in the *U.S. Industrial Outlook* differ slightly from those in the *Quarterly Summary of Foreign Commerce of the United States,* being lower for exports but higher for imports. FT420, *United States Exports, Country by SITC Commodity Group,* is not useful here because Standard International Trade Classification Group 894 includes perambulators, toys, games, and sporting goods, whereas imports are presented on a four-digit basis in FT125, namely SITC 8942, toys, indoor games, etc.

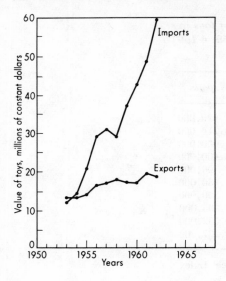

Figure 5–5. Value of toy imports and exports in constant dollars (1957–1959 = 100) from 1953 to 1962 SOURCE: *Table 5–7.*

Table 5–8. Total toy sales and plastic toy sales, both at manufacturers' prices and in constant dollars (1957–1959 = 100) for 1954, 1958, 1959, and 1960

	Total toy sales (in millions)*	Plastic toy sales (in millions)†	Plastics as percentage of total toy sales
1954	$646.9	$ 86.5	13.3%
1958	770.3	113.6	14.7
1959	846.5	127.3	15.0
1960	887.0	132.2	15.0

* SOURCE: Table 5–2.
† SOURCE: Monsanto Company, in a private letter quoting a federal government survey of end uses of plastics.

Table 5–9. Consumer Price Index, disposable personal income, and population under 14 years for 1939, 1947, and 1953–1962

Number in computer program	Year	Consumer price index (1957–1959 = 100)*	Disposable personal income (in billions)†		Population under 14 (in millions)‡
			Unadjusted	Adjusted to 1957–1959 = 100	
1	1962	105.4	$384.4	$365.0	54.634
2	1961	104.2	364.4	349.0	53.936
3	1960	103.1	349.9	339.0	53.062
4	1959	101.5	337.3	332.0	51.714
5	1958	100.7	317.9	315.8	50.304
6	1957	98.0	308.8	311.2	49.206
7	1956	94.7	292.9	309.1	47.915
8	1955	94.3	274.4	291.0	46.406
9	1954	93.6	256.9	274.0	44.778
10	1953	93.2	252.5	271.0	43.148
11	1947	77.8	170.1	219.0	34.499
12	1939	48.4	70.4	145.2	30.671

* U.S. Bureau of Labor Statistics, *Consumer Price Index—Historical Index Series (1957–1959 = 100)* (Washington, D.C.: U.S. Department of Labor).

† SOURCE: 1939–1959—U.S. Department of Commerce, *Survey of Current Business, Supplement, 1961 (Business Statistics)*, p. 5, "General Business Indicators"; 1960–1962—*Survey of Current Business*, November, 1963, p. 4, Table 3, "Personal Income and Its Use."

‡ SOURCE: 1939–1957—U.S. Bureau of the Census, *Historical Statistics of the United States from Colonial Times to 1957* (Washington D.C.: Government Printing Office, 1958), Series A22–33, "Estimated Population by Sex, Color and Age: 1900–1957"; 1958–1962—U.S. Department of Commerce, *Current Population Reports*, May 21, 1963, Series P–25, No. 265, p. 17, Table 5, "Population Change by Age, Each Year 1950–1962."

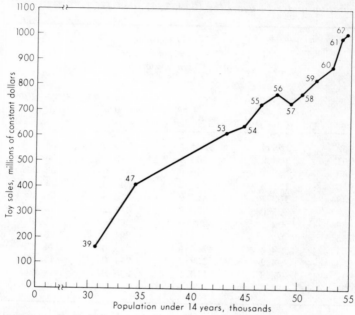

Figure 5–6. Toy sales at manufacturers' prices in constant
dollars (1957–1959 = 100) and population under 14 for
1939, 1947, and 1953–1962   SOURCE: Tables 5–2 and 5–9.

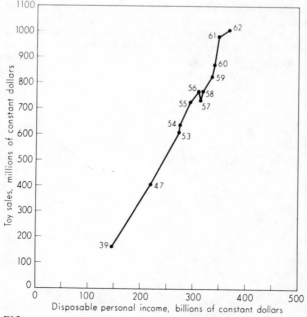

Figure 5–7. Toy sales at manufacturers' prices and
disposable personal income, both in constant dollars
(1957–1959 = 100) for 1939, 1947, and 1953–1962
SOURCE: Tables 5–2 and 5–9.

Table 5–10. Population under 14 related to sales per child under 14 in constant dollars (1957–1959 = 100)

	1939 ratio of $5.36 per child × population under 14 (in millions)	1947 ratio of $11.79 per child × population under 14 (in millions)	1953 ratio of $14.21 per child × population under 14 (in millions)
1939	$163.6	...	...
1947	185.0	$410.6	...
1953	231.5	509.0	$612.8
1954	240.3	528.0	636.0
1955	248.5	546.2	659.9
1956	256.7	565.0	680.9
1957	264.0	580.1	699.8
1958	269.9	595.0	715.0
1959	277.5	610.0	735.0
1960	284.8	626.0	755.0
1961	289.0	635.9	765.1
1962	293.7	644.1	776.2

Percentage of change explained:

$$\frac{293.7 - 163.6}{1060.0 - 163.6} =$$

14.5% explained

Percentage of change explained:

$$\frac{644.1 - 410.6}{1060.0 - 410.6} =$$

36.5% explained

Percentage of change explained:

$$\frac{776.2 - 612.8}{1060.0 - 612.8} =$$

34.3% explained

SOURCE: Tables 5–2 and 5–9.

*Figure 5–8. Toy sales, actual and extrapolation based on
under 14 population growth, 1939, 1947, and 1953–1962*
SOURCE: *Table 5–10. 1. Actual toy sales adjusted by Wholesale
Toy Price Index, 1957–1959 = 100 (Table 5–2), at manufacturers' prices. 2. Population under 14 × spending per child
under 14 in 1953 on toys. 3. Population under 14 × spending
per child under 14 in 1947 on toys. 4. Population under
× spending per child under 14 in 1939 on toys.*

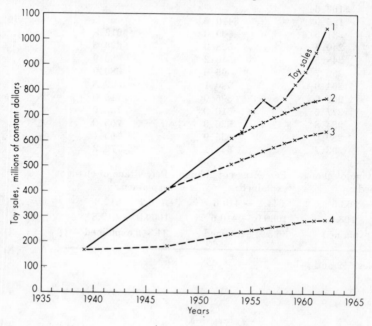

Table 5–11. **Disposable personal income related to toy sales per dollar of disposable personal income, both in constant dollars (1957–1959 = 100)**

	1939 rate: $.001105 per dollar of disposable income × disposable income (in millions)	*1947 rate:* $.001858 per dollar of disposable income × disposable income (in millions)	*1953 rate:* $.002262 per dollar of disposable income × disposable income (in millions)
1939	$163.6	. . .	. . .
1947	243.8	$410.6	. . .
1953	301.3	504.0	$612.8
1954	304.4	508.3	620.0
1955	323.8	540.3	659.0
1956	343.9	574.8	699.8
1957	346.0	577.8	704.8
1958	351.0	585.5	714.7
1959	369.0	616.0	751.0
1960	377.0	630.0	767.0
1961	388.0	648.0	790.0
1962	406.0	677.5	825.3

Percentage of change explained

$$\frac{406.0 - 163.6}{1060 - 163.6} =$$

27.0% explained

Percentage of change explained

$$\frac{677.5 - 410.6}{1060 - 410.6} =$$

41.1% explained

Percentage of change explained:

$$\frac{825.3 - 612.8}{1060.0 - 612.8} =$$

47.6% explained

SOURCE: Tables 5–2 and 5–9.

Figure 5–9. Toy sales, actual and extrapolation based on disposable personal income, 1939, 1947, and 1953–1962
SOURCE: *Table 5–11. 1. Disposable personal income adjusted by Consumer Price Index (Table 5–9), 1957–1959 = 100. 2. Actual toy sales adjusted by wholesale Toy Price Index, 1957–1959 = 100 (Table 5–2). Sales at manufacturers' prices. 3. Disposable personal income × percentage of income spent on toys in 1953. 4. Disposable personal income × percentage of income spent on toys in 1947. 5. Disposable personal income × percentage of income on toys in 1939.*

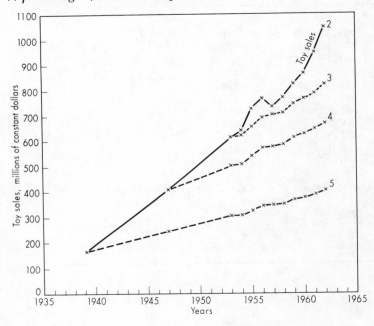

Table 5–12. Computer output, multiple regression
of toy sales (variable 3) as a function
of disposable personal income
(variable 1) and of population under
14 years (variable 2) for 1939,
1947, and 1953–1962*

(Units: toy sales in tens of millions of constant dollars, disposable personal income in billions of constant dollars, and population under 14 in hundreds of thousands.)

PROBLEM NUMBER		1	
NUMBER OF VARIABLES		3	
SAMPLE SIZE		12	
SUMS			
	3521	5603.	862
SUMS OF SQUARES			
	1074531	2678267	68525
CROSS PRODUCT SUMS			
ROW 1	1074531	1694067	269274
ROW 2	1694067	2678267	422291
ROW 3	269274	422291	68525
CROSS PRODUCTS OF DEVIATIONS			
ROW 1	41235	49993	16349
ROW 2	49993	62386	19864
ROW 3	16349	19864	6615
SIMPLE CORRELATION COEFFICIENTS			
ROW 1	1.000	0.986	0.990
ROW 2	0.986	1.000	0.978
ROW 3	0.990	0.978	1.000

* For a definition of each statistic Appearing in the computer output, see Appendix A on pages 579–583.

Table 5–12. *Continued*

ANALYSIS OF VARIANCE FOR REGRESSION

SOURCE OF VARIATION	D.F.	SUM OF SQUARES	MEAN SQUARES	F VALUE
DUE TO REGRESSION	2	6482.	3242.	221.
DEVIATION ABOUT REGRESSION	9	132.	15.	
TOTAL	11	6614.		

INTERCEPT (A VALUE) IS −47.183

NO.	VARIABLE NAME	MEAN	STANDARD DEVIATION	REG. COEF.	STD. ERROR OF REG. COEF.	COMPUTED T VALUE	PARTIAL CORR. COEF.
1	DPICON	293.	61.	0.367	0.112	3.289	0.739
2	POP14A	467.	75.	0.024	0.091	0.264	0.088

DEPENDENT

NO.	VARIABLE NAME	MEAN	STANDARD DEVIATION
3	TOYCON	72.	25.

INCREMENTS FOR INDEPENDENT VARIABLES / CUMULATIVE REGRESSIONS

NO.	VARIABLE NAME	SUMS OF SQUARES	PROP. VAR.	F VALUE EACH TERM	STD. ERROR OF ESTIMATE	SUMS OF SQUARES	PROP. VAR. = R SQ.	F VALUE	MULTIPLE R
1	DPICON	6482.	0.980	488.	3.644	6482.	0.980	488.	0.990
2	POP14A	1.	0.000	0.	3.827	6483.	0.980	221.	0.990

PROPORTION OF VARIANCE SPECIFIED TO LIMIT VARIABLES   0.

Table 5-12. Continued

TABLE OF RESIDUALS

OBSERVATION		Y VALUE	Y ESTIMATE	RESIDUAL
1	1962	105.990	100.024	5.966
2	1961	99.358	93.978	5.380
3	1960	88.704	90.094	-1.390
4	1959	84.650	87.199	-2.548
5	1958	77.026	80.908	-3.882
6	1957	73.500	78.955	-5.455
7	1956	76.892	77.874	-0.982
8	1955	72.405	70.862	1.543
9	1954	64.692	64.225	0.467
10	1953	61.281	62.732	-1.451
11	1947	41.065	41.553	-0.488
12	1937	16.360	13.518	2.842

VON NEUMANN RATIO IS 0.787   POSITIVE AUTOCORRELATION AT 1% LEVEL
DURBIN-WATSON COEFFICIENT   0.721
RATIO OF RANGES FOR THE SMALLEST RESIDUAL   0.268
RATIO OF RANGES FOR THE LARGEST RESIDUAL   0.317
CRITICAL VALUE OF THE RATIO AT ALPHA = 0.10   0.490

Table 5–12. Continued

PROBLEM NUMBER	1
REPLACEMENT AND DELETION	2
DEPENDENT VARIABLE IS NOW	3
NUMBER OF VARIABLES DELETED	1
VARIABLE DELETED	1

ANALYSIS OF VARIANCE FOR REGRESSION

SOURCE OF VARIATION	D.F.	SUM OF SQUARES	MEAN SQUARES	F VALUE
DUE TO REGRESSION	1	6325.	6325.	218.
DEVIATION ABOUT REGRESSION	10	290.	29.	
TOTAL	11	6615.		

INTERCEPT (A VALUE) IS −76.837

VARIABLE NO.	NAME	MEAN	STANDARD DEVIATION	REG. COEF.	STD. ERROR OF REG. COEF.	COMPUTED T VALUE	PARTIAL CORR. COEF.
2	POP14A	467.	75.	0.318	0.022	14.764	0.978
DEPENDENT							
3	TOYCON	72.	25.				

INCREMENTS FOR INDEPENDENT VARIABLES

VARIABLE NO.	NAME	SUMS OF SQUARES	PROP. VAR.	F VALUE EACH TERM	STD. ERROR OF ESTIMATE	CUMULATIVE REGRESSIONS SUMS OF SQUARES	PROP. VAR. = R SQ.	F VALUE	MULTIPLE R
2	POP14A	6325.	0.956	218.	5.387	6325	0.956	218	0.978

PROPORTION OF VARIANCE SPECIFIED TO LIMIT VARIABLES	0.

Table 5–12. Continued

TABLE OF RESIDUALS

OBSERVATION		Y VALUE	Y ESTIMATE	RESIDUAL
1	1962	105.990	97.123	8.867
2	1961	99.358	94.900	4.457
3	1960	88.704	92.118	−3.414
4	1959	84.650	87.826	−3.175
5	1958	77.026	83.336	−6.310
6	1957	73.500	79.840	−6.340
7	1956	76.892	75.729	1.163
8	1955	72.405	70.925	1.480
9	1954	64.692	65.741	−1.049
10	1953	61.281	60.551	0.730
11	1947	41.065	33.011	8.054
12	1939	16.360	20.823	−4.463

VON NEUMANN RATIO IS 1.382   NO AUTOCORRELATION AT 1% OR 5% LEVEL
DURBIN-WATSON COEFFICIENT   1.267
RATIO OF RANGES FOR THE SMALLEST RESIDUAL   0.130
RATIO OF RANGES FOR THE LARGEST RESIDUAL   0.291
CRITICAL VALUE OF THE RATIO AT ALPHA = 0.10   0.490

Table 5–12. Continued

PROBLEM NUMBER   1
REPLACEMENT AND DELETION   3
DEPENDENT VARIABLE IS NOW   3
NUMBER OF VARIABLES DELETED   1
VARIABLE DELETED   2

ANALYSIS OF VARIANCE FOR REGRESSION

SOURCE OF VARIATION	D.F.	SUM OF SQUARES	MEAN SQUARES	F VALUE
DUE TO REGRESSION	1	6482.	6482.	488.
DEVIATION ABOUT REGRESSION	10	132.	13.	
TOTAL	11	6614.		

INTERCEPT (A VALUE) IS −44.521

VARIABLE NO. NAME	MEAN	STANDARD DEVIATION	REG. COEF.	STD. ERROR OF REG. COEF.	COMPUTED T VALUE	PARTIAL CORR. COEF.
1 DPICON	293.	61.	0.396	0.018	22.094	0.990
DEPENDENT						
2 TOYCON	72.	25.				

INCREMENTS FOR INDEPENDENT VARIABLES

VARIABLE NO. NAME	SUMS OF SQUARES	PROP. VAR.	F VALUE EACH TERM	STD. ERROR OF ESTIMATE	CUMULATIVE SUMS OF SQUARES	PROP. VAR. = R SQ.	F VALUE	MULTIPLE R
1 DPICON	6482.	0.980	488.	3.644	6482.	0.980	488.	0.990

PROPORTION OF VARIANCE
SPECIFIED TO LIMIT
VARIABLES   0.

Table 5–12. Continued

TABLE OF RESIDUALS

OBSERVATION		Y VALUE	Y ESTIMATE	RESIDUAL
1	1962	105.990	100.199	5.791
2	1961	99.358	93.855	5.503
3	1960	88.704	89.891	-1.187
4	1959	84.650	87.115	-2.464
5	1958	77.026	80.692	-3.666
6	1957	73.500	78.868	-5.368
7	1956	76.892	78.035	-1.143
8	1955	72.405	70.859	1.546
9	1954	64.692	64.119	0.573
10	1953	61.281	62.929	-1.648
11	1947	41.065	42.311	-1.246
12	1939	16.360	13.050	3.310

VON NEUMANN RATIO IS 0.844   POSITIVE AUTOCORRELATION AT 1% LEVEL

DURBIN-WATSON COEFFICIENT   0.773

RATIO OF RANGES FOR THE SMALLEST RESIDUAL   0.267

RATIO OF RANGES FOR THE LARGEST RESIDUAL   0.262

CRITICAL VALUE OF THE RATIO AT ALPHA = 0.10   0.490

SOURCE: Tables 5–2 and 5–9.

Figure 5–10. Actual toy sales in constant dollars and toys sales computed for 1939, 1947, and 1953–1962 from regression equation $Y = -47.183 + 0.367\ X_1 + 0.024X_2$, *where* Y = *Toy sales in tens of millions of dollars,* X_1 = *disposable personal income in billions, and* X_2 = *population under 14 in hundreds of thousands*   SOURCE: *Table 5–12.*

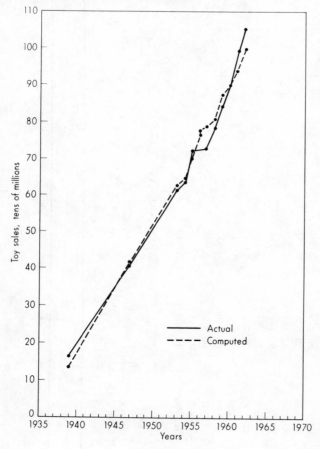

*Table 5–13. Computer output, multiple regression of toy
sales (variable 3) as a function of disposable
personal income (variable 1) and of population
under 14 years (variable 2) in logarithmic
form for 1939, 1947, and 1953–1962*

Units: toy sales in tens of thousands of constant dollars, disposable
personal income in millions of constant dollars, and population
under 14 in hundreds.*

PROBLEM NUMBER	2		
NUMBER OF VARIABLES	3		
SAMPLE SIZE	12		

SUMS

65.47603	67.95896	57.82205

SUMS OF SQUARES

357.39294	384.93533	279.14104

CROSS PRODUCT SUMS

ROW 1	357.39294	370.89921	315.76043
ROW 2	370.89921	384.93533	327.64031
ROW 3	315.76043	327.64031	279.14104

CROSS PRODUCTS OF DEVIATIONS

ROW 1	0.13374	0.09232	0.26392
ROW 2	0.09232	0.06700	0.17980
ROW 3	0.26392	0.17980	0.52527

SIMPLE CORRELATION COEFFICIENTS

ROW 1	1.000	0.975	0.996
ROW 2	0.975	1.000	0.958
ROW 3	0.996	0.958	1.000

* The units for the variables are different in several computer runs
to avoid overloading the computer.

Table 5-13. Continued

ANALYSIS OF VARIANCE FOR REGRESSION

SOURCE OF VARIATION	D.F.	SUM OF SQUARES	MEAN SQUARES	F VALUE
DUE TO REGRESSION	2	0.52254	0.26127	862.
DEVIATION ABOUT REGRESSION	9	0.00273	0.00030	
TOTAL	11	0.52527		

INTERCEPT (A VALUE) IS −4.57257*

VARIABLE NO.	NAME	MEAN	STANDARD DEVIATION	REG. COEF.	STD. ERROR OF REG. COEF.	COMPUTED T VALUE	PARTIAL CORR. COEF.
1	DPICON	5.45634	0.11026	2.47424	0.21532	11.491	0.968
2	POP14A	5.66325	0.07804	−0.72559	0.30422	−2.385	−0.622

DEPENDENT			
3	TOYCON	4.81850	0.21852

INCREMENTS FOR INDEPENDENT VARIABLES

VARIABLE NO.	NAME	SUMS OF SQUARES	PROP. VAR.	F VALUE EACH TERM
1	DPICON	0.52082	0.992	1170.
2	POP14A	0.00172	0.003	6.

CUMULATIVE REGRESSIONS

STD. ERROR OF ESTIMATE	CUMULATIVE SUMS OF SQUARES	PROP. VAR. = R.SQ.	F VALUE	MULTIPLE R
0.02110	0.52082	0.991	1170.	0.996
0.01741	0.52254	0.995	862.	0.997
ANTILOG = 4%				

PROPORTION OF VARIANCE
SPECIFIED TO LIMIT
VARIABLES   0.

* The number −4.57257 must be put in the form 5.42743 − 10 to get the antilog.

Table 5-13. Continued

TABLE OF RESIDUALS

OBSERVATION		Y VALUE		Y ESTIMATE		LOG RESIDUAL*	RESIDUAL OF ANTILOGS†
		LOG	ANTILOG	LOG	ANTILOG		
1	1962	5.02526	105990	5.02682	106370	-0.00155	-380
2	1961	4.99720	99358	4.98270	96095	0.01450	3263
3	1960	4.94794	88704	4.95661	90492	-0.00867	-1788
4	1959	4.92763	84650	4.94230	87559	-0.01467	-2909
5	1958	4.88664	77026	4.89725	78932	-0.01062	-1906
6	1957	4.86629	73500	4.88844	77347	-0.02215	-3847
7	1956	4.88588	76892	4.88954	77543	-0.00366	-651
8	1955	4.85977	72405	4.83479	68359	0.02498	4046
9	1954	4.81085	64692	4.78136	60445	0.02949	4247
10	1953	4.78733	61281	4.78121	60425	0.00611	856
11	1947	4.61347	41065	4.62278	41955	-0.00931	-890
12	1939	4.21378	16360	4.21824	16529	-0.00446	-169

VON NEUMANN RATIO IS 1.175   POSITIVE AUTOCORRELATION AT 5% BUT NOT AT 1% LEVEL
DURBIN-WATSON COEFFICIENT   1.077
RATIO OF RANGES FOR THE SMALLEST RESIDUAL   0.245
RATIO OF RANGES FOR THE LARGEST RESIDUAL   0.339
CRITICAL VALUE OF THE RATIO AT ALPHA = 0.10   0.490

SOURCE: Tables 5-2 and 5-9.

* This residual column is Y value in logarithms $-$ Y estimate in logarithms and hence is the logarithm of (Y value/Y estimate). Thus for the year 1962, the residual -0.00155 is put into the form $9.99845 - 10$ to get the antilog 0.99644. Hence Y estimate is 0.356% greater than Y value.

† The last column is the antilog of Y value $-$ the antilog of Y estimate.

Table 5–14. Computer output, simple correlation of toy sales (variable 3) as a function of disposable personal income (variable 1) in logarithmic form for 1939, 1947, and 1953–1962

Units: toy sales in tens of thousands of constant dollars and disposable personal income in millions of constant dollars. Sums, sums of squares, cross-product sums, and cross products of deviations are deleted.

PROBLEM NUMBER	2–1
REPLACEMENT AND DELETION	3
DEPENDENT VARIABLE IS NOW	3
NUMBER OF VARIABLES DELETED	1
VARIABLE DELETED	2

ANALYSIS OF VARIANCE FOR REGRESSION

SOURCE OF VARIATION	D.F.	SUM OF SQUARES	MEAN SQUARES	F VALUE
DUE TO REGRESSION	1	0.52082	0.52082	1170.
DEVIATION ABOUT REGRESSION	10	0.00445	0.00045	
TOTAL	11	0.52527		

INTERCEPT (A VALUE) IS -5.94896

VARIABLE NO. NAME	MEAN	STANDARD DEVIATION	REG. COEF.	STD. ERROR OF REG. COEF.	COMPUTED T VALUE	PARTIAL CORR. COEF.
1 DPICON	5.45634	0.11026	1.97339	0.05770	34.	0.996

DEPENDENT NO. NAME	MEAN	STANDARD DEVIATION	STD. ERROR OF ESTIMATE	F VALUE	MULTIPLE R
3 TOYCON	4.81850	0.21852	0.02110	1170.	0.996

ANTILOG = 4.98%

INCREMENTS FOR INDEPENDENT VARIABLES

VARIABLE NO. NAME	SUMS OF SQUARES	PROP. VAR.	F VALUE EACH TERM	CUMULATIVE REGRESSIONS SUMS OF SQUARES	PROP. VAR. = R SQ.	F VALUE	MULTIPLE R
1 DPICON	0.52082	0.992	1170.	0.52082	0.992	1170.	0.996

PROPORTION OF VARIANCE
SPECIFIED TO LIMIT
VARIABLES 0.

Table 5-14. Continued

TABLE OF RESIDUALS

OBSERVATION		Y VALUE		Y ESTIMATE		LOG	RESIDUAL OF
		LOG	ANTILOG	LOG	ANTILOG	RESIDUAL	ANTILOGS
1	1962	5.02526	105990	5.02760	106560	−0.00233	−570
2	1961	4.99720	99358	4.98918	97540	0.00802	1818
3	1960	4.94794	88704	4.96427	92103	−0.01632	−3399
4	1959	4.92763	84650	4.94638	88386	−0.01875	−3736
5	1958	4.88664	77026	4.90351	80078	−0.01687	−3052
6	1957	4.86629	73500	4.89094	77793	−0.02465	−4293
7	1956	4.88588	76892	4.88513	76760	0.00075	132
8	1955	4.85977	72405	4.83342	68143	0.02635	4262
9	1954	4.81085	64692	4.78183	60511	0.02902	4181
10	1953	4.78733	61281	4.77239	59210	0.01493	2071
11	1947	4.61347	41065	4.58980	38887	0.02367	2178
12	1939	4.21378	16360	4.23760	17283	−0.02382	−923

VON NEUMANN RATIO IS 1.125   POSITIVE AUTOCORRELATION AT 5% BUT NOT AT 1% LEVEL

DURBIN-WATSON COEFFICIENT 1.0311

RATIO OF RANGES FOR THE SMALLEST RESIDUAL 0.116

RATIO OF RANGES FOR THE LARGEST RESIDUAL 0.101

CRITICAL VALUE OF THE RATIO AT ALPHA = 0.10 0.490

SOURCE: Tables 5-2 and 5-9.

Table 5–15. Computer output, simple correlation of toy sales (variable 3) as a function of population under 14 years (variable 2) in logarithmic form for 1939, 1947, and 1953–1962

Units: toy sales in tens of thousands of constant dollars and population under 14 in hundreds. Sums, sums of squares, cross-product sums, and cross products of deviations are deleted.

PROBLEM NUMBER 2–2
REPLACEMENT AND DELETION 2
DEPENDENT VARIABLE IS NOW 3
NUMBER OF VARIABLES DELETED 1
VARIABLE DELETED 1

ANALYSIS OF VARIANCE FOR REGRESSION

SOURCE OF VARIATION	D.F.	SUM OF SQUARES	MEAN SQUARES	F VALUE
DUE TO REGRESSION	1	0.48252	0.48252	112
DEVIATION ABOUT REGRESSION	10	0.04275	0.00428	
TOTAL	11	0.52527		

INTERCEPT (A VALUE) IS -10.37968

VARIABLE NO.	NAME	MEAN	STANDARD DEVIATION	REG. COEF.	STD. ERROR OF REG. COEF.	COMPUTED T VALUE	PARTIAL CORR. COEF.
2	POP14A	5.66325	0.07804	2.68365	0.25261	10.6	0.958

DEPENDENT

VARIABLE NO.	NAME	MEAN	STANDARD DEVIATION
3	TOYCON	4.81850	0.21852

STD. ERROR OF ESTIMATE 0.06539

ANTILOG = 16.2%

INCREMENTS FOR INDEPENDENT VARIABLES   CUMULATIVE REGRESSIONS

VARIABLE NO.	NAME	SUMS OF SQUARES	PROP. VAR.	F VALUE EACH TERM	SUMS OF SQUARES	PROP. VAR. = R SQ.	F VALUE	MULTIPLE R
2	POP14A	0.48252	0.91861	113.	0.48252	0.919	113	0.958

PROPORTION OF VARIANCE SPECIFIED TO LIMIT VARIABLES 0.

Table 5–15. Continued

TABLE OF RESIDUALS

OBSERVATION		Y VALUE LOG	Y VALUE ANTILOG	Y ESTIMATE LOG	Y ESTIMATE ANTILOG	LOG RESIDUAL	RESIDUAL OF ANTILOGS
1	1962	5.02526	105990	5.01768	104158	0.00759	1832
2	1961	4.99720	99358	5.00269	100622	−0.00549	−1264
3	1960	4.94794	88704	4.98365	96306	−0.03571	−7602
4	1959	4.92763	84650	4.95366	89880	−0.02603	−5230
5	1958	4.88664	77026	4.92144	83453	−0.03480	−6427
6	1957	4.86629	73500	4.89572	78654	−0.02943	−5154
7	1956	4.88588	76892	4.86473	73237	0.02115	3655
8	1955	4.85977	72405	4.82743	67210	0.03233	5195
9	1954	4.81085	64692	4.78581	61068	0.02504	3624
10	1953	4.78733	61281	4.74259	55283	0.04473	5998
11	1947	4.61347	41065	4.48187	30330	0.13161	10735
12	1939	4.21378	16360	4.34479	22120	−0.13101	−5760

VON NEUMANN RATIO IS 2.066   NO AUTOCORRELATION AT 5% OR 1% LEVEL

DURBIN-WATSON COEFFICIENT	1.894
RATIO OF RANGES FOR THE SMALLEST RESIDUAL	0.547
RATIO OF RANGES FOR THE LARGEST RESIDUAL	0.594
CRITICAL VALUE OF THE RATIO AT ALPHA = 0.10	0.490

SOURCE: Tables 5–2 and 5–9.

Figure 5–11. Actual toy sales in constant dollars (1957–1959 = 100) and toy sales computed for 1939, 1947, and 1953–1962, computed from regression equation log Y = (4.05104 − 10) + 1.97339 log X, where Y = toy sales in tens of thousands of constant dollars and X = disposable personal income in millions of constant dollars SOURCE: Table 5–14.

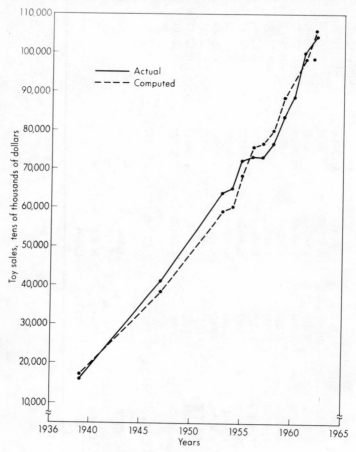

Table 5–16. Computer output, multiple regression of toy sales (variable 3) as a function of disposable personal income (variable 1) and of population under 14 years (variable 2) for 1953–1962

Units: toy sales in tens of millions of constant dollars, disposable personal income in billions of constant dollars, and population under 14 in hundreds of thousands.

PROBLEM NUMBER	3		
NUMBER OF VARIABLES	3		
SAMPLE SIZE	10		
SUMS			
	3157	4951	804
SUMS OF SQUARES			
	1005487	2465178	66571
CROSS-PRODUCT SUMS			
ROW 1	1005487	1573980	257905
ROW 2	1573980	2465178	403107
ROW 3	257905	403107	66571
CROSS PRODUCTS OF DEVIATIONS			
ROW 1	8759	10890	3917
ROW 2	10890	13909	4797
ROW 3	3917	4797	1849
SIMPLE CORRELATION COEFFICIENTS			
ROW 1	1.000	0.987	0.973
ROW 2	0.987	1.000	0.946
ROW 3	0.973	0.946	1.000

Table 5–16. Continued

ANALYSIS OF VARIANCE FOR REGRESSION

SOURCE OF VARIATION	D.F.	SUM OF SQUARES	MEAN SQUARES	F VALUE
DUE TO REGRESSION	2	1766.	883.	75.
DEVIATION ABOUT REGRESSION	7	83.	12.	
TOTAL	9	1849.		

INTERCEPT (A VALUE) IS −40.431

VARIABLE NO.	NAME	MEAN	STANDARD DEVIATION	PROP. VAR.	F VALUE EACH TERM	REG. COEF.	STD. ERROR OF REG. COEF.	COMPUTED T VALUE	PARTIAL CORR. COEF.
1	DPICON	316.	31.	0.947	144.	0.693	0.226	3.06	0.757
2	POPU14	495.	39.	0.008	1.	−0.198	0.179	−1.10	−0.385

DEPENDENT NO.	NAME	MEAN	STANDARD DEVIATION
3	TOYCON	80.	14.

		INCREMENTS FOR INDEPENDENT VARIABLES				CUMULATIVE REGRESSIONS	
VARIABLE NO.	NAME	SUMS OF SQUARES	PROP. VAR. = R SQ.	F VALUE	STD. ERROR OF ESTIMATE	SUMS OF SQUARES	MULTIPLE R
1	DPICON	1751	0.947	144	3.489	1751	0.973
2	POPU14	14	0.955	75	3.443	1766	0.977

PROPORTION OF VARIANCE
SPECIFIED TO LIMIT
VARIABLES   0

Table 5–16. Continued

TABLE OF RESIDUALS

OBSERVATION		Y VALUE	Y ESTIMATE	RESIDUAL
1	1962	105.990	104.479	1.511
2	1961	99.358	94.769	4.589
3	1960	88.704	89.567	-0.863
4	1959	84.650	87.381	-2.730
5	1958	77.026	78.942	-1.916
6	1957	73.500	77.926	-4.426
7	1956	76.892	79.024	-2.132
8	1955	72.405	69.464	2.941
9	1954	64.692	60.901	3.791
10	1953	61.281	62.046	-0.766

VON NEUMANN RATIO IS 1.368   NO AUTOCORRELATION AT 5% OR 1% LEVEL

DURBIN-WATSON COEFFICIENT   1.231
RATIO OF RANGES FOR THE SMALLEST RESIDUAL   0.206
RATIO OF RANGES FOR THE LARGEST RESIDUAL   0.109
CRITICAL VALUE OF THE RATIO AT ALPHA = 0.10   0.409

SOURCE: Tables 5–2 and 5–9.

Figure 5–12. Actual toy sales in constant dollars (1957–1959 = 100) and toy sales computed from regression equation for 1953–1960, $Y = -40.431 + 0.693X_1 - 0.198X_2$ where Y = toys sales at manufacturers' prices in tens of millions of constant dollars, X_1 = disposable personal income in billions of constant dollars, and X_2 = population under 14 in hundreds of thousands   SOURCE: Table 5–16.

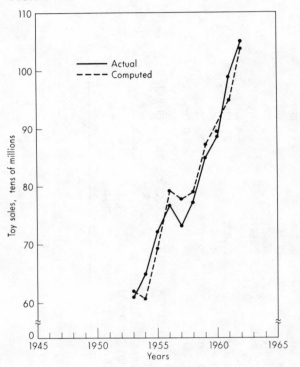

*Table 5–17. Computer output, multiple regression of toy
          sales (variable 3) as a function of disposable
          personal income (variable 1) and of population
          under 14 years (variable 2) in logarithmic
          form for 1953–1962*

Units: toy sales in tens of thousands of constant dollars, disposable
personal income in millions of constant dollars, and population
under 14 in hundreds.

PROBLEM NUMBER	4		
NUMBER OF VARIABLES	3		
SAMPLE SIZE	10		
SUMS			
	54.97362	56.93442	48.99479
SUMS OF SQUARES			
	302.22670	324.16385	240.10095
CROSS PRODUCT SUMS			
ROW 1	302.22670	313.00256	269.37104
ROW 2	313.00256	324.16385	278.97192
ROW 3	269.37104	278.97192	240.10095
CROSS PRODUCTS OF DEVIATIONS			
ROW 1	0.01683	0.01343	0.02893
ROW 2	0.01343	0.01099	0.02288
ROW 3	0.02893	0.02288	0.05197
SIMPLE CORRELATION COEFFICIENTS			
ROW 1	1.00000	0.98731	0.97805
ROW 2	0.98731	1.00000	0.95752
ROW 3	0.97805	0.95752	1.00000

Table 5–17. Continued

ANALYSIS OF VARIANCE FOR REGRESSION

SOURCE OF VARIATION	D.F.	SUM OF SQUARES	MEAN SQUARES	F VALUE
DUE TO REGRESSION	2	0.04985	0.02493	82
DEVIATION ABOUT REGRESSION	7	0.00212	0.00030	
TOTAL	9	0.05197		

INTERCEPT (A VALUE) IS −3.63300

VARIABLE NO.	NAME	MEAN	STANDARD DEVIATION	REG. COEF.	STD. ERROR OF REG. COEF.	COMPUTED T VALUE	PARTIAL CORR. COEF.
1	DPICON	5.49736	0.04324	2.27763	0.84471	2.70	0.714
2	POPU14	5.69344	0.03494	−0.70053	1.04534	−0.67	−0.246

DEPENDENT

	NAME	MEAN	STANDARD DEVIATION
3	TOYCON	4.89948	0.07599

INCREMENTS FOR INDEPENDENT VARIABLES / CUMULATIVE REGRESSIONS

VARIABLE NO.	NAME	SUMS OF SQUARES	PROP. VAR.	F VALUE EACH TERM	STD. ERROR OF ESTIMATE	SUMS OF SQUARES	PROP. VAR. = R SQ.	F VALUE	MULTIPLE R
1	DPICON	0.04972	0.957	176.3	0.01679	0.04972	0.957	176	0.978
2	POPU14	0.00014	0.002	0.4	0.01740	0.04985	0.959	82	0.979

ANTILOG = 4.09%

PROPORTION OF VARIANCE
SPECIFIED TO LIMIT
VARIABLES   0.

Table 5–17. Continued

TABLE OF RESIDUALS

OBSERVATION		Y VALUE LOG	Y VALUE ANTILOG	Y ESTIMATE LOG	Y ESTIMATE ANTILOG	LOG RESIDUAL	RESIDUAL OF ANTILOG
1	1962	5.02526	105990	5.01653	103880	0.00873	2110
2	1961	4.99720	99358	4.97610	94646	0.02110	4712
3	1960	4.94794	88704	4.95232	89603	−0.00437	−899
4	1959	4.92763	84650	4.93951	86999	−0.01187	−2349
5	1958	4.88664	77026	4.89843	79147	−0.01180	−2121
6	1957	4.86629	73500	4.89063	77738	−0.02435	−4238
7	1956	4.88558	76892	4.89202	77987	−0.00614	−1095
8	1955	4.85977	72405	4.84207	69514	0.01770	2891
9	1954	4.81085	64692	4.79339	62143	0.01746	2549
10	1953	4.78733	61281	4.79379	62200	−0.00646	−919

VON NEUMANN RATIO IS 1.309   NO AUTOCORRELATION AT 1% OR 5% LEVEL

DURBIN-WATSON COEFFICIENT   1.178

RATIO OF RANGES FOR THE SMALLEST RESIDUAL   0.297

RATIO OF RANGES FOR THE LARGEST RESIDUAL   0.103

CRITICAL VALUE OF THE RATIO AT ALPHA = 0.10   0.409

SOURCE: Tables 5–2 and 5–9.

Table 5–18. Computer output, simple correlations of toy sales (variable 3) as a function of disposable personal income (variable 1) in logarithmic form for 1953–1962

Units: toy sales in tens of thousands of constant dollars and disposable personal income in millions of constant dollars. Sums, sums of squares, cross-product sums, and cross products of deviations are deleted.

PROBLEM NUMBER 4–1
REPLACEMENT AND DELETION 3
DEPENDENT VARIABLE IS NOW 3
NUMBER OF VARIABLES DELETED 1
VARIABLE DELETED 2

ANALYSIS OF VARIANCE FOR REGRESSION

SOURCE OF VARIATION	D.F.	SUM OF SQUARES	MEAN SQUARES	F VALUE
DUE TO REGRESSION	1	0.04972	0.04972	176.
DEVIATION ABOUT REGRESSION	8	0.00226	0.00028	
TOTAL	9	0.05197		

INTERCEPT (A VALUE) IS –4.54896

VARIABLE NO. NAME	MEAN	STANDARD DEVIATION	PROP. VAR.	F VALUE EACH TERM	REG. COEF.	STD. ERROR OF REG. COEF.	COMPUTED T VALUE	PARTIAL CORR. COEF.
1 DPICON	5.49736	0.04324	0.957	176.	1.71872	0.12945	13.2	0.978
DEPENDENT								
3 TOYCON	4.89948	0.07599						

STD. ERROR OF ESTIMATE 0.01679 ANTILOG = 3.95%

INCREMENTS FOR INDEPENDENT VARIABLES | CUMULATIVE REGRESSIONS

VARIABLE NO. NAME	SUMS OF SQUARES	PROP. VAR. = R SQ.	F VALUE	SUMS OF SQUARES	PROP. VAR. = R SQ.	F VALUE	MULTIPLE R
1 DPICON	0.04972	0.957	176.	0.04972	0.957	176	0.978

PROPORTION OF VARIANCE
SPECIFIED TO LIMIT
VARIABLES   0.

Table 5-18. Continued

TABLE OF RESIDUALS

OBSERVATION		Y VALUE		Y ESTIMATE		LOG RESIDUAL	RESIDUAL OF ANTILOG
		LOG	ANTILOG	LOG	ANTILOG		
1	1962	5.02526	105990	5.01108	102590	0.01419	3440
2	1961	4.99720	99358	4.97762	94978	0.01958	4380
3	1960	4.94794	88704	4.95592	90349	-0.00798	-1645
4	1959	4.92763	84650	4.94034	87165	-0.01271	-2515
5	1958	4.88664	77026	4.90300	79984	-0.01637	-2958
6	1957	4.86629	73500	4.89205	77992	-0.02576	-4492
7	1956	4.88588	76892	4.88700	77091	-0.00112	-199
8	1955	4.85977	72405	4.84196	69497	0.01781	2908
9	1954	4.81085	64692	4.79702	62665	0.01383	4027
10	1953	4.78733	61281	4.78881	61492	-0.00148	-211

VON NEUMANN RATIO IS 1.050   POSITIVE AUTOCORRELATION AT 5% BUT NOT AT 1% LEVEL
DURBIN-WATSON COEFFICIENT   0.945
RATIO OF RANGES FOR THE SMALLEST RESIDUAL   0.216
RATIO OF RANGES FOR THE LARGEST RESIDUAL   0.049
CRITICAL VALUE OF THE RATIO AT ALPHA = 0.10   0.409

source: Tables 5-2 and 5-9.

*Table 5–19. Computer output, multiple regression
of first differences of toy sales (variable
3) as a function of disposable personal
income (variable 2) and of population
under 14 years (variable 1) for 1939,
1947, and 1953–1962*

Units: toy sales in hundreds of thousands of constant dollars,
disposable personal income in hundreds of millions of constant
dollars, and population under 14 in tens of thousands.

PROBLEM NUMBER		5	
NUMBER OF VARIABLES		3	
SAMPLE SIZE		11	
SUMS			
	2396	2198	8943
SUMS OF SQUARES			
	1049717	946906	13649847
CROSS PRODUCT SUMS			
ROW 1	1049717	852081	3229234
ROW 2	852081	946906	3494252
ROW 3	3229234	3494252	13649847
CROSS PRODUCTS OF DEVIATIONS			
ROW 1	527694	373257	1281036
ROW 2	373257	507706	1707272
ROW 3	1281036	1707272	6379140
SIMPLE CORRELATION COEFFICIENTS			
ROW 1	1.000	0.721	0.698
ROW 2	0.721	1.000	0.949
ROW 3	0.698	0.949	1.000

Table 5–19. Continued

ANALYSIS OF VARIANCE FOR REGRESSION

SOURCE OF VARIATION	D.F.	SUM OF SQUARES	MEAN SQUARES	F VALUE
DUE TO REGRESSION	2	5743725.	2871863.	36.
DEVIATION ABOUT REGRESSION	8	635415.	79427.	
TOTAL	10	6379140.		

INTERCEPT (A VALUE) IS 133.8

VARIABLE NO.	NAME	MEAN	STANDARD DEVIATION	REG. COEF.	STD. ERROR OF REG. COEF.	COMPUTED T VALUE	PARTIAL CORR. COEF.
2	DPICON	200.	225.	3.288	0.571	5.76	0.898
1	POPU14	218.	230.	0.102	0.560	0.18	0.064

DEPENDENT			
3	TOYSAL	813.	799.

INCREMENTS FOR INDEPENDENT VARIABLES / CUMULATIVE REGRESSIONS

VARIABLE NO.	NAME	SUMS OF SQUARES	PROP. VAR.	F VALUE EACH TERM	STD. ERROR OF ESTIMATE	CUMULATIVE SUMS OF SQUARES	PROP. VAR. = R SQ.	F VALUE	MULTIPLE R
2	DPICON	5741082.	0.900	81.	266.26	5741082.	0.900	81.	0.949
1	POPU14	2644.	0.000	0	281.83	5743725.	0.900	36.	0.949

PROPORTION OF VARIANCE
SPECIFIED TO LIMIT
VARIABLES 0.

Table 5–19. Continued

TABLE OF RESIDUALS

OBSERVATION		Y VALUE	Y ESTIMATE	RESIDUAL
1	1961–1962	663.23	471.51	191.72
2	1960–1961	1065.37	666.97	398.40
3	1959–1960	405.36	377.73	27.63
4	1958–1959	762.49	680.82	81.67
5	1957–1958	352.56	296.27	56.29
6	1956–1957	−339.22	216.05	−555.27
7	1955–1956	448.72	744.30	−295.58
8	1954–1955	771.34	709.35	61.99
9	1953–1954	321.02	249.10	71.92
10	1947–1953	2021.62	1931.74	89.88
11	1939–1947	2470.54	2599.19	−128.65

VON NEUMANN RATIO IS 1.387   NO AUTOCORRELATION AT 1% OR 5% LEVEL
DURBIN-WATSON COEFFICIENT   1.261
RATIO OF RANGES FOR THE SMALLEST RESIDUAL   0.571
RATIO OF RANGES FOR THE LARGEST RESIDUAL   0.445
CRITICAL VALUE OF THE RATIO AT ALPHA = 0.10   0.517

source: Tables 5–2 and 5–9.

Table 5–20. Computer output, multiple regression of first differences of toy sales (variable 3) as a function of disposable personal income (variable 2) and of population under 14 years (variable 1) for 1953–1962

Units: toy sales in hundreds of thousands of constant dollars, disposable personal income in hundreds of millions of constant dollars, and population under 14 in tens of thousands.

PROBLEM NUMBER	5–1		
NUMBER OF VARIABLES	3		
SAMPLE SIZE	9		

SUMS

1149	940	4451

SUMS OF SQUARES

155129	131862	3459332

CROSS PRODUCT SUMS

ROW 1	155129	119827	535013
ROW 2	119827	131862	619752
ROW 3	535013	619752	3459332

CROSS PRODUCTS OF DEVIATIONS

ROW 1	8542	−138	−33017
ROW 2	−138	33684	154883
ROW 3	−33017	154883	1258194

SIMPLE CORRELATION COEFFICIENTS

ROW 1	1.000	−0.008	−0.318
ROW 2	−0.008	1.000	0.752
ROW 3	−0.318	0.752	1.000

Table 5–20. Continued

ANALYSIS OF VARIANCE FOR REGRESSION

SOURCE OF VARIATION	D.F.	SUM OF SQUARES	MEAN SQUARES	F VALUE
DUE TO REGRESSION	2	834926.	417463.	5.9
DEVIATION ABOUT REGRESSION	6	423268.	70545.	
TOTAL	8	1258194.		

INTERCEPT (A VALUE) IS 499.7

VARIABLE NO.	NAME	MEAN	STANDARD DEVIATION	REG. COEF.	STD. ERROR OF REG. COEF.	COMPUTED T VALUE	PARTIAL CORR. COEF.
2	DPICON	104.	65.	4.583	1.447	3.17	0.791
1	POPU14	128.	33.	-3.791	2.874	-1.32	-0.474

DEPENDENT			
3	TOYSAL	495.	397.

INCREMENTS FOR INDEPENDENT VARIABLES

VARIABLE NO.	NAME	SUMS OF SQUARES	PROP. VAR.	F VALUE EACH TERM	STD. ERROR OF ESTIMATE	CUMULATIVE REGRESSIONS SUMS OF SQUARES	PROP. VAR. = R SQ.	F VALUE	MULTIPLE R
2	DPICON	712166.	0.566	9.1	279.	712166.	0.566	9.13	0.752
1	POPU14	122760.	0.098	1.7	266.	834926.	0.664	5.91	0.815

PROPORTION OF VARIANCE
SPECIFIED TO LIMIT
VARIABLES   0.

Table 5-20. Continued

TABLE OF RESIDUALS

OBSERVATION		Y VALUE	Y ESTIMATE	RESIDUAL
1	1961–1962	663.23	626.65	36.57
2	1960–1961	1065.37	968.33	97.04
3	1959–1960	405.36	309.49	95.87
4	1958–1959	762.49	707.58	54.91
5	1957–1958	352.56	294.28	58.28
6	1956–1957	−339.22	106.55	−445.77
7	1955–1956	448.72	757.11	−308.39
8	1954–1955	771.34	661.59	109.75
9	1953–1954	321.02	19.28	301.74

VON NEUMANN RATIO IS 1.302   NO AUTOCORRELATION AT 5% OR 1% LEVEL
DURBIN-WATSON COEFFICIENT   1.157
RATIO OF RANGES FOR THE SMALLEST RESIDUAL   0.247
RATIO OF RANGES FOR THE LARGEST RESIDUAL   0.315
CRITICAL VALUE OF THE RATIO AT ALPHA = 0.10   0.441

source: Tables 5–2 and 5–9.

547

Table 5-21. 1960 toy sales at retail, personal income, and number of children under 15, all by states

Number in program	State	Population under 15 (in thousands)	Personal income (in millions)	Toy sales (in tens of thousands)
1	Alabama	1,109	$ 4,782	$ 2,055
2	Alaska	80	631	187
3	Arizona	453	2,668	1,031
4	Arkansas	571	2,390	954
5	California	4,765	43,122	15,934
6	Colorado	570	4,037	1,973
7	Connecticut	748	7,250	2,505
8	Delaware	144	1,345	400
9	District of Columbia	194	2,292	1,164
10	Florida	1,468	9,830	3,833
11	Georgia	1,323	6,357	3,120
12	Hawaii	218	1,445	504
13	Idaho	232	1,182	554
14	Illinois	3,002	26,535	12,804
15	Indiana	1,482	10,199	4,041
16	Iowa	858	5,568	1,987
17	Kansas	673	4,480	1,367
18	Kentucky	1,000	4,668	1,707
19	Louisiana	1,149	5,240	2,241
20	Maine	301	1,820	900
21	Maryland	993	7,444	2,688
22	Massachusetts	1,482	12,936	6,586
23	Michigan	2,593	18,151	6,979
24	Minnesota	1,121	7,079	3,599
25	Mississippi	781	2,548	1,037
26	Missouri	1,266	9,510	5,124
27	Montana	207	1,362	466
28	Nebraska	436	3,022	1,093
29	Nevada	87	814	256
30	New Hampshire	183	1,266	468
31	New Mexico	361	1,731	645
32	New Jersey	1,748	16,171	6,154
33	New York	4,628	46,784	20,199
34	North Carolina	1,520	7,130	3,322
35	North Dakota	218	1,106	386
36	Ohio	3,078	22,697	9,607
37	Oklahoma	698	4,296	1,501
38	Oregon	546	3,692	1,731
39	Pennsylvania	3,297	25,506	13,962
40	Rhode Island	244	1,873	895
41	South Carolina	850	3,297	1,243
42	South Dakota	229	1,264	422
43	Tennessee	1,128	5,488	2,740
44	Texas	3,174	18,461	7,384
45	Utah	334	1,721	838
46	Vermont	123	732	354
47	Virginia	1,265	7,371	2,859
48	Washington	892	6,593	3,219
49	West Virginia	598	3,095	1,346
50	Wisconsin	1,269	8,548	3,421
51	Wyoming	111	762	221

SOURCE: Population under 15—U.S. Bureau of the Census, *U.S. Census of Population: 1960*, Table 96 of state volumes; personal income—*Statistical Abstract of the United States: 1963*, p. 329; toy sales at retail—McCready Publishing Company, *Playthings*, Directory issue, February 28, 1962, pp. 14, 15.

Figure 5–13. Scatter diagram of 1960 toy sales at retail and personal income by states as numbered in Table 5–21, using 15 largest states SOURCE: Table 5–21.

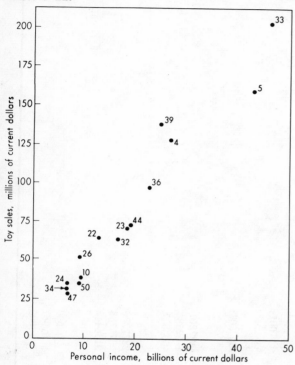

Table 5–22. Computer output, multiple regression of toy sales (variable 3) as a function of personal income (variable 2) and of population under 15 years (variable 1) for the 50 states and the District of Columbia in 1960

Units: toy sales in hundreds of thousands of current dollars, personal income in tens of millions of current dollars, and population under 15 in tens of thousands.

PROBLEM NUMBER	6
NUMBER OF VARIABLES	3
SAMPLE SIZE	51

SUMS			
	5580.	39829.	17001.

SUMS OF SQUARES			
	1226556.	80108417.	14803507.

CROSS PRODUCT SUMS

ROW 1	1226555	9689368	4137301
ROW 2	9689368	80108417	34152586
ROW 3	4137301	34152586	14803507

CROSS PRODUCTS OF DEVIATIONS

ROW 1	616038	5331597	2277236
ROW 2	5331597	49003387	20875756
ROW 3	2277236	20875756	9136442

SIMPLE CORRELATION COEFFICIENTS

ROW 1	1.000	0.970	0.960
ROW 2	0.970	1.000	0.987
ROW 3	0.960	0.987	1.000

Table 5–22. Continued

ANALYSIS OF VARIANCE FOR REGRESSION

SOURCE OF VARIATION	D.F.	SUM OF SQUARES	MEAN SQUARES	F VALUE
DUE TO REGRESSION	2	8894187.	4447094	881.
DEVIATION ABOUT REGRESSION	48	242255.	5047.	
TOTAL	50	9136442.		

INTERCEPT (A VALUE) IS −3.38903

VARIABLE NO.	NAME	MEAN	STANDARD DEVIATION	REG. COEF.	STD. ERROR OF REG. COEF.	COMPUTED T VALUE	PARTIAL CORR. COEF.
2	PERINC	781.	990.	0.408	0.042	9.7	0.814
1	POPU15	109.	111	0.165	0.375	0.4	0.064

DEPENDENT			
3	TOYSAL	333.	427.

		INCREMENTS FOR INDEPENDENT VARIABLES			CUMULATIVE REGRESSIONS			
VARIABLE NO.	NAME	SUMS OF SQUARES	PROP. VAR.	F VALUE EACH TERM	STD. ERROR OF ESTIMATE	SUMS OF SQUARES	PROP. VAR. = R SQ.	F VALUE	MULTIPLE R
2	PERINC	8893205.	0.973	1792.	70.45	8893205.	0.973	1792.	0.987
1	POPU15	982.	0.000	0.	71.04	8894187.	0.973	881.	0.987

PROPORTION OF VARIANCE
SPECIFIED TO LIMIT
VARIABLES   0.

Table 5–22. Continued

TABLE OF RESIDUALS

	OBSERVATION	Y VALUE	Y ESTIMATE	RESIDUAL
1	ALABAMA	205.5	210.1	−4.6
2	ALASKA	18.7	23.7	−5.0
3	ARIZONA	103.1	113.0	−9.9
4	ARKANSAS	95.4	103.6	−8.2
5	CALIFORNIA	1593.4	1834.8	−241.4
6	COLORADO	197.3	170.8	26.5
7	CONNECTICUT	250.5	304.8	−54.3
8	DELAWARE	40.0	53.9	−13.9
9	DISTRICT OF COLUMBIA	116.4	93.3	23.1
10	FLORIDA	383.3	422.0	−38.7
11	GEORGIA	312.0	277.9	34.1
12	HAWAII	50.4	59.2	−8.8
13	IDAHO	55.4	48.7	6.7
14	ILLINOIS	1280.4	1128.9	151.5
15	INDIANA	404.1	437.2	−33.1
16	IOWA	198.7	238.0	−39.3
17	KANSAS	136.7	190.6	−53.8
18	KENTUCKY	170.7	203.6	−32.9
19	LOUISIANA	224.1	229.4	−5.3
20	MAINE	90.0	75.8	14.2
21	MARYLAND	268.8	316.8	−48.0
22	MASSACHUSETTS	658.6	549.0	109.7
23	MICHIGAN	697.9	780.0	−82.2
24	MINNESOTA	359.9	304.0	55.9
25	MISSISSIPPI	103.7	113.5	−9.8
26	MISSOURI	512.4	405.6	106.8
27	MONTANA	46.6	55.7	−9.0
28	NEBRASKA	109.3	127.1	−17.8
29	NEVADA	25.6	31.3	−5.7
30	NEW HAMPSHIRE	46.8	51.3	−4.5
31	NEW MEXICO	64.5	73.2	−8.7
32	NEW JERSEY	615.4	685.3	−69.9
33	NEW YORK	2019.9	1982.0	37.9
34	NORTH CAROLINA	332.2	312.7	19.5
35	NORTH DAKOTA	38.6	45.3	−6.7
36	OHIO	960.7	973.6	−12.9
37	OKLAHOMA	150.1	183.4	−33.3
38	OREGON	173.1	156.3	16.8
39	PENNSYLVANIA	1396.2	1091.8	304.4
40	RHODE ISLAND	89.5	77.1	12.4
41	SOUTH CAROLINA	124.3	145.2	−20.9
42	SOUTH DAKOTA	42.2	52.0	−9.8
43	TENNESSEE	274.0	239.2	34.8
44	TEXAS	738.4	802.3	−63.9
45	UTAH	83.8	72.4	11.4
46	VERMONT	35.4	28.5	6.9
47	VIRGINIA	285.9	318.3	−32.4
48	WASHINGTON	321.9	280.4	41.5
49	WEST VIRGINIA	134.6	132.8	1.8
50	WISCONSIN	342.1	366.4	−24.3
51	WYOMING	22.1	29.5	−7.4

VON NEUMANN RATIO IS 2.255
    NO AUTOCORRELATION AT EITHER 5% OR 1% LEVEL
DURBIN-WATSON COEFFICIENT   2.210
RANGE OF RESIDUALS   545.840
RANGE/STD. ERROR OF ESTIMATE   7.683

SOURCE: Table 5–21.

Table 5–22. Continued

PROBLEM NUMBER	6-1
REPLACEMENT AND DELETION	2
DEPENDENT VARIABLE IS NOW	3
NUMBER OF VARIABLES DELETED	1
VARIABLE DELETED	1

ANALYSIS OF VARIANCE FOR REGRESSION

SOURCE OF VARIATION	D.F.	SUM OF SQUARES	MEAN SQUARES	F VALUE
DUE TO REGRESSION	1	8893205	8893205	1792
DEVIATION ABOUT REGRESSION	49	243237	4964	
TOTAL	50	9136442		

INTERCEPT (A VALUE) IS 0.65

VARIABLE NO. NAME	MEAN	STANDARD DEVIATION	REG. COEF.	STD. ERROR OF REG. COEF.	COMPUTED T VALUE	PARTIAL CORR. COEF.
2 PERINC	781	990	0.426	0.01	42	0.987
DEPENDENT						
3 TOYSAL	333	427				

INCREMENTS FOR INDEPENDENT VARIABLES / CUMULATIVE REGRESSIONS

VARIABLE NO. NAME	SUMS OF SQUARES	PROP. VAR.	F VALUE EACH TERM	STD. ERROR OF ESTIMATE	SUMS OF SQUARES	PROP. VAR. = R SQ.	F VALUE	MULTIPLE R
2 PERINC	8893205	0.973	1792	70.46	8893205	0.973	1792	0.987

PROPORTION OF VARIANCE
SPECIFIED TO LIMIT
VARIABLES 0.

Table 5–22. Continued

TABLE OF RESIDUALS

	OBSERVATION	Y VALUE	Y ESTIMATE	RESIDUAL
1	ALABAMA	205.5	204.4	1.2
2	ALASKA	18.7	27.5	−8.8
3	ARIZONA	103.1	114.3	−11.2
4	ARKANSAS	95.4	102.5	−7.1
5	CALIFORNIA	1593.4	1837.7	−244.3
6	COLORADO	197.3	172.6	24.7
7	CONNECTICUT	250.5	309.5	−59.0
8	DELAWARE	40.0	57.9	−17.9
9	DISTRICT OF COLUMBIA	116.4	98.3	18.1
10	FLORIDA	383.3	419.4	−36.1
11	GEORGIA	312.0	271.5	40.5
12	HAWAII	50.4	62.2	−11.8
13	IDAHO	55.4	51.0	4.4
14	ILLINOIS	1280.4	1131.0	149.3
15	INDIANA	404.1	435.1	−31.0
16	IOWA	198.7	237.9	−39.2
17	KANSAS	136.7	191.5	−54.8
18	KENTUCKY	170.7	199.5	−28.8
19	LOUISIANA	224.1	223.9	0.2
20	MAINE	90.0	78.2	11.8
21	MARYLAND	268.8	317.8	−49.0
22	MASSACHUSETTS	658.6	551.7	106.9
23	MICHIGAN	697.9	773.9	−76.0
24	MINNESOTA	359.9	302.2	57.7
25	MISSISSIPPI	103.7	109.2	−5.5
26	MISSOURI	512.4	405.8	106.6
27	MONTANA	46.6	58.7	−12.1
28	NEBRASKA	109.3	129.4	−20.1
29	NEVADA	25.6	35.3	−9.7
30	NEW HAMPSHIRE	46.8	54.6	−7.8
31	NEW MEXICO	64.5	74.4	−9.9
32	NEW JERSEY	615.4	689.5	−74.1
33	NEW YORK	2019.9	1993.7	26.2
34	NORTH CAROLINA	332.2	304.4	27.8
35	NORTH DAKOTA	38.6	47.8	−9.2
36	OHIO	960.7	967.6	−6.9
37	OKLAHOMA	150.1	183.7	−33.6
38	OREGON	173.1	157.9	15.2
39	PENNSYLVANIA	1396.2	1087.2	309.0
40	RHODE ISLAND	89.5	80.4	9.0
41	SOUTH CAROLINA	124.3	141.1	−16.8
42	SOUTH DAKOTA	42.2	54.5	−12.3
43	TENNESSEE	274.0	234.4	39.6
44	TEXAS	738.4	787.1	−48.7
45	UTAH	83.8	74.0	9.8
46	VERMONT	35.4	31.8	3.6
47	VIRGINIA	285.9	314.7	−28.8
48	WASHINGTON	321.9	281.5	40.4
49	WEST VIRGINIA	134.6	132.5	2.1
50	WISCONSIN	342.1	364.8	−22.7
51	WYOMING	22.1	33.1	−11.0

VON NEUMANN RATIO IS 2.23832
    NO AUTOCORRELATION AT 1% OR 5% LEVEL
DURBIN-WATSON COEFFICIENT   2.1944
RANGE OF RESIDUALS   553.253
RANGE/STD. ERROR OF ESTIMATE   7.842

Table 5–22. Continued

PROBLEM NUMBER	6–2
REPLACEMENT AND DELETION	3
DEPENDENT VARIABLE IS NOW	3
NUMBER OF VARIABLES DELETED	1
VARIABLE DELETED	2

ANALYSIS OF VARIANCE FOR REGRESSION

SOURCE OF VARIATION	D.F.	SUM OF SQUARES	MEAN SQUARES	F VALUE
DUE TO REGRESSION	1	8417993.	8417993.	574.
DEVIATION ABOUT REGRESSION	49	718449.	14662.	
TOTAL	50	9136442.		

INTERCEPT (A VALUE) IS −71.1

VARIABLE NO. NAME	MEAN	STANDARD DEVIATION	REG. COEF.	STD. ERROR OF REG. COEF.	COMPUTED T VALUE	PARTIAL CORR. COEF.
1 POPU15	109.	111.	3.697	0.154	24.	0.96

DEPENDENT		
3 TOYSAL	333.	427.

STD. ERROR OF ESTIMATE	MULTIPLE R
121.088	0.96

INCREMENTS FOR INDEPENDENT VARIABLES

VARIABLE NO. NAME	PROP. VAR.	F VALUE EACH TERM	SUMS OF SQUARES
1 POPU15	0.921	574.	8417993.

CUMULATIVE REGRESSIONS

SUMS OF SQUARES	PROP. VAR. = R SQ.	F VALUE	MULTIPLE R
8417993.	0.921	574.	0.96

PROPORTION OF VARIANCE SPECIFIED TO LIMIT VARIABLES	0.

Table 5–22. Continued

TABLE OF RESIDUALS

	OBSERVATION	Y VALUE	Y ESTIMATE	RESIDUAL
1	ALABAMA	205.5	338.8	−133.3
2	ALASKA	18.7	−41.5	60.2
3	ARIZONA	103.1	96.4	6.7
4	ARKANSAS	95.4	140.0	−44.6
5	CALIFORNIA	1593.4	1690.3	−96.9
6	COLORADO	197.3	139.6	57.7
7	CONNECTICUT	250.5	205.4	45.1
8	DELAWARE	40.0	−17.9	57.9
9	DISTRICT OF COLUMBIA	116.4	0.6	115.8
10	FLORIDA	383.3	471.6	−88.3
11	GEORGIA	312.0	418.0	−106.0
12	HAWAII	50.4	9.5	40.9
13	IDAHO	55.4	14.7	40.7
14	ILLINOIS	1280.4	1038.6	241.8
15	INDIANA	404.1	476.7	−72.6
16	IOWA	198.7	246.1	−47.4
17	KANSAS	136.7	177.7	−41.0
18	KENTUCKY	170.7	298.6	−127.9
19	LOUISIANA	224.1	353.6	−129.5
20	MAINE	90.0	40.2	49.8
21	MARYLAND	268.8	296.0	−27.2
22	MASSACHUSETTS	658.6	476.7	181.9
23	MICHIGAN	697.9	887.4	−189.5
24	MINNESOTA	359.9	343.3	16.6
25	MISSISSIPPI	103.7	217.6	−113.9
26	MISSOURI	512.4	396.9	115.5
27	MONTANA	46.6	5.4	41.2
28	NEBRASKA	109.3	90.1	19.2
29	NEVADA	25.6	−38.9	64.5
30	NEW HAMPSHIRE	46.8	−3.5	50.3
31	NEW MEXICO	64.5	62.3	2.1
32	NEW JERSEY	615.4	575.1	40.3
33	NEW YORK	2019.9	1639.7	380.2
34	NORTH CAROLINA	332.2	490.8	−158.6
35	NORTH DAKOTA	38.6	9.5	29.1
36	OHIO	960.7	1066.7	−106.0
37	OKLAHOMA	150.1	186.9	−36.8
38	OREGON	173.1	130.7	42.4
39	PENNSYLVANIA	1396.2	1147.7	248.5
40	RHODE ISLAND	89.5	19.1	70.4
41	SOUTH CAROLINA	124.3	243.1	−118.8
42	SOUTH DAKOTA	42.2	13.5	28.7
43	TENNESSEE	274.0	345.9	−71.9
44	TEXAS	738.4	1102.2	−363.8
45	UTAH	83.8	52.4	31.4
46	VERMONT	35.4	−25.6	61.0
47	VIRGINIA	285.9	396.5	−110.6
48	WASHINGTON	321.9	258.6	63.3
49	WEST VIRGINIA	134.6	150.0	−15.4
50	WISCONSIN	342.1	398.0	−55.9
51	WYOMING	22.1	−30.1	52.2

VON NEUMANN RATIO IS 2.218
    NO AUTOCORRELATION AT 5% OR 1% LEVEL
DURBIN-WATSON COEFFICIENT   2.174
RANGE OF RESIDUALS   744.017
RANGE/STD. ERROR OF ESTIMATE   6.144

Table 5–23. Computer output, multiple regression of toy sales (variable 3) as a function of personal income (variable 2) and of population under 15 years (variable 1) in logarithmic form for 50 states and the District of Columbia in 1960

Units: toy sales in hundreds of thousands of current dollars, personal income in tens of millions of current dollars, and population under 15 in tens of thousands.

PROBLEM NUMBER	7		
NUMBER OF VARIABLES	3		
SAMPLE SIZE	51		
SUMS			
	93.23467	134.45117	114.48465
SUMS OF SQUARES			
	180.86589	365.66886	269.66518
CROSS PRODUCT SUMS			
ROW 1	180.86589	256.27263	220.39097
ROW 2	256.27263	365.66886	313.62450
ROW 3	220.39097	313.62450	269.66518
CROSS PRODUCTS OF DEVIATIONS			
ROW 1	10.42071	10.47830	11.09806
ROW 2	10.47830	11.21557	11.80891
ROW 3	11.09806	11.80891	12.67040
SIMPLE CORRELATION COEFFICIENTS			
ROW 1	1.000	0.969	0.966
ROW 2	0.969	1.000	0.991
ROW 3	0.966	0.991	1.000

Table 5–23. Continued

ANALYSIS OF VARIANCE FOR REGRESSION

SOURCE OF VARIATION	D.F.	SUM OF SQUARES	MEAN SQUARES	F VALUE
DUE TO REGRESSION	2	12.44042	6.22021	1298
DEVIATION ABOUT REGRESSION	48	0.22998	0.00479	
TOTAL	50	12.67040		

INTERCEPT (A VALUE) IS −0.45616

VARIABLE NO.	NAME	MEAN	STANDARD DEVIATION	REG. COEF.	STD. ERROR OF REG. COEF.	COMPUTED T VALUE	PARTIAL CORR. COEF.
2	PERINC	2.63630	0.47362	0.956	0.084	11.	0.854
1	POPU15	1.82813	0.45652	0.104	0.087	1.	0.169

DEPENDENT

3	TOYSAL	2.24480	0.50340

INCREMENTS FOR INDEPENDENT VARIABLES

CUMULATIVE REGRESSIONS

VARIABLE NO.	NAME	SUMS OF SQUARES	PROP. VAR.	F VALUE EACH TERM	STD. ERROR OF ESTIMATE	CUMULATIVE SUMS OF SQUARES	PROP. VAR. = R SQ.	F VALUE	MULTIPLE R
2	PERINC	12.43364	0.981	2573.	0.070	12.43364	0.981	2573.	0.991
1	POPU15	0.00678	0.001	1.	0.069	12.44042	0.982	1298.	0.991

ANTILOG = 11.7%

SOURCE: Table 5–21.

Table 5–23. Continued

TABLE OF RESIDUALS

	OBSERVATION	Y VALUES LOG	ANTI-LOG	Y ESTIMATE LOG	ANTI-LOG	RESIDUAL OF ANTILOGS
1	ALABAMA	2.31281	205.5	2.30868	203.6	1.9
2	ALASKA	1.27184	18.7	1.34939	22.4	−3.7
3	ARIZONA	2.01326	103.1	2.02608	106.2	−3.1
4	ARKANSAS	1.97955	95.4	1.99082	97.9	−2.5
5	CALIFORNIA	3.20232	1593.4	3.28743	1938.3	−144.9
6	COLORADO	2.29513	197.3	2.20840	161.6	35.7
7	CONNECTICUT	2.39881	250.5	2.46374	290.9	−40.4
8	DELAWARE	1.60206	40.0	1.69010	49.0	−9.0
9	DISTRICT OF COLUMBIA	2.06595	116.4	1.92484	84.1	32.3
10	FLORIDA	2.58354	383.3	2.62050	417.3	−34.0
11	GEORGIA	2.49415	312.0	2.43483	272.2	39.8
12	HAWAII	1.70243	50.4	1.73854	54.8	−4.4
13	IDAHO	1.74351	55.4	1.65793	45.5	9.9
14	ILLINOIS	3.10735	1280.4	3.06502	1161.5	118.9
15	INDIANA	2.60649	404.1	2.63623	432.8	−28.7
16	IOWA	2.29820	198.7	2.36031	229.3	−30.6
17	KANSAS	2.13577	136.7	2.25911	181.6	−44.9
18	KENTUCKY	2.23223	170.7	2.29400	196.8	−26.1
19	LOUISIANA	2.35044	224.1	2.34825	223.0	1.1
20	MAINE	1.95424	90.0	1.84887	70.6	19.4
21	MARYLAND	2.42943	268.8	2.48746	307.2	−38.4
22	MASSACHUSETTS	2.81862	658.6	2.73493	543.2	115.4
23	MICHIGAN	2.84379	697.9	2.90075	795.7	−97.8
24	MINNESOTA	2.55618	359.9	2.47204	296.5	63.4
25	MISSISSIPPI	2.01578	103.7	2.03150	107.5	−3.8
26	MISSOURI	2.70961	512.4	2.60009	398.2	114.2
27	MONTANA	1.66839	46.6	1.71165	51.5	−4.9
28	NEBRASKA	2.03862	109.3	2.07609	119.2	−9.9
29	NEVADA	1.40824	25.6	1.45890	28.8	−3.2
30	NEW HAMPSHIRE	1.67025	46.8	1.67575	47.4	−0.6
31	NEW MEXICO	1.80956	64.5	1.83623	68.6	−4.1
32	NEW JERSEY	2.78916	615.4	2.83504	684.0	−68.6
33	NEW YORK	3.30533	2019.9	3.31996	2089.2	−69.3
34	NORTH CAROLINA	2.52140	332.2	2.48873	308.1	24.1
35	NORTH DAKOTA	1.58659	38.6	1.62753	42.4	−3.8
36	OHIO	2.98259	960.7	3.00127	1006.3	−45.6
37	OKLAHOMA	2.17638	150.1	2.24334	175.1	−25.0
38	OREGON	2.23830	173.1	2.16937	147.7	25.4
39	PENNSYLVANIA	3.14495	1396.2	3.05282	1129.3	266.9
40	RHODE ISLAND	1.95182	89.5	1.85134	71.0	18.5
41	SOUTH CAROLINA	2.09447	124.3	2.14231	138.7	−14.4
42	SOUTH DAKOTA	1.62531	42.2	1.68519	48.4	−6.2
43	TENNESSEE	2.43775	274.0	2.36662	232.6	41.4
44	TEXAS	2.86829	738.4	2.91688	825.8	−87.4
45	UTAH	1.92324	83.8	1.83033	67.7	16.1
46	VERMONT	1.54900	35.4	1.43040	26.9	8.5
47	VIRGINIA	2.45621	285.9	2.49426	312.1	−26.2
48	WASHINGTON	2.50772	321.9	2.43222	270.6	51.3
49	WEST VIRGINIA	2.12905	134.6	2.10023	126.0	8.6
50	WISCONSIN	2.53415	342.1	2.55592	359.7	−17.6
51	WYOMING	1.34439	22.1	1.44246	27.7	−5.8

VON NEUMANN RATIO IS 2.256
  NO CORRELATION AT 5% AND 1% LEVELS
DURBIN-WATSON COEFFICIENT   2.212
RANGE OF RESIDUALS   0.264
RANGE/STD. ERROR OF ESTIMATE   3.821

Table 5–23. Continued

PROBLEM NUMBER	7–1
REPLACEMENT AND DELETION	2
DEPENDENT VARIABLE IS NOW	3
NUMBER OF VARIABLES DELETED	1
VARIABLE DELETED	1

ANALYSIS OF VARIANCE FOR REGRESSION

SOURCE OF VARIATION	D.F.	SUM OF SQUARES	MEAN SQUARES	F VALUE
DUE TO REGRESSION	1	12.43364	12.43364	2573
DEVIATION ABOUT REGRESSION	49	0.23676	0.00483	
TOTAL	50	12.67040		

INTERCEPT (A VALUE) IS −0.53097

VARIABLE NO. NAME	MEAN	STANDARD DEVIATION	PROP. VAR.	REG. COEF.	F VALUE EACH TERM	STD. ERROR OF REG. COEF.	COMPUTED T VALUE	PARTIAL CORR. COEF.
2 PERINC	2.63630	0.474	0.981	1.053	2573	0.021	51	0.991
DEPENDENT								
3 TOYSAL	2.24480	0.503						

INCREMENTS FOR INDEPENDENT VARIABLES

VARIABLE NO. NAME	SUMS OF SQUARES	STD. ERROR OF ESTIMATE	CUMULATIVE REGRESSIONS			
			SUMS OF SQUARES	PROP. VAR. = R SQ.	F VALUE	MULTIPLE R
2 PERINC	12.43364	0.06951	12.43364	0.981	2573	0.991
		ANTILOG = 11.7%				

PROPORTION OF VARIANCE SPECIFIED TO LIMIT VARIABLES 0.

560

Table 5–23. Continued

TABLE OF RESIDUALS

	OBSERVATION	Y VALUE LOG	ANTI-LOG	Y ESTIMATE LOG	ANTI-LOG	RESIDUAL OF ANTI-LOGS
1	ALABAMA	2.31281	205.5	2.29040	195.2	10.3
2	ALASKA	1.27184	18.7	1.36429	23.1	−4.4
3	ARIZONA	2.01326	103.1	2.02357	105.6	−2.5
4	ARKANSAS	1.97955	95.4	1.97325	94.0	1.4
5	CALIFORNIA	3.20232	1593.4	3.29602	1977.1	−383.7
6	COLORADO	2.29513	197.3	2.21296	163.3	34.0
7	CONNECTICUT	2.39881	250.5	2.48069	302.4	−51.9
8	DELAWARE	1.60206	40.0	1.71037	51.3	−11.3
9	DISTRICT OF COLUMBIA	2.06595	116.4	1.95411	90.0	26.4
10	FLORIDA	2.58354	383.3	2.61990	416.8	−33.5
11	GEORGIA	2.49415	312.0	2.42058	263.4	48.6
12	HAWAII	1.70243	50.4	1.74316	55.4	−5.0
13	IDAHO	1.74351	55.4	1.65130	44.8	10.6
14	ILLINOIS	3.10735	1280.4	3.07398	1185.8	94.6
15	INDIANA	2.60649	404.1	2.63675	433.3	−29.2
16	IOWA	2.29820	198.7	2.35999	229.1	−30.4
17	KANSAS	2.13577	136.7	2.26057	182.2	−45.5
18	KENTUCKY	2.23223	170.7	2.27937	190.3	−19.6
19	LOUISIANA	2.35044	224.1	2.33222	214.9	9.2
20	MAINE	1.95424	90.0	1.84867	70.6	19.4
21	MARYLAND	2.42943	268.8	2.49276	311.0	−42.2
22	MASSACHUSETTS	2.81862	658.6	2.74546	556.5	102.1
23	MICHIGAN	2.84379	697.9	2.90034	795.0	−97.1
24	MINNESOTA	2.55618	359.9	2.46978	294.9	65.0
25	MISSISSIPPI	2.01578	103.7	2.00253	100.6	3.1
26	MISSOURI	2.70961	512.4	2.60477	402.5	109.9
27	MONTANA	1.66839	46.6	1.71611	52.0	−5.4
28	NEBRASKA	2.03862	109.3	2.08054	120.4	−11.1
29	NEVADA	1.40824	25.6	1.48073	30.3	−4.7
30	NEW HAMPSHIRE	1.67025	46.8	1.68269	48.2	−1.4
31	NEW MEXICO	1.80956	64.5	1.82574	67.0	−2.5
32	NEW JERSEY	2.78916	615.4	2.84752	703.9	−88.5
33	NEW YORK	3.30533	2019.9	3.33329	2154.2	−134.3
34	NORTH CAROLINA	2.52140	332.2	2.47306	297.2	35.0
35	NORTH DAKOTA	1.58659	38.6	1.62091	41.8	−3.2
36	OHIO	2.98259	960.7	3.00254	1005.9	−45.2
37	OKLAHOMA	2.17638	150.1	2.24139	174.3	−24.2
38	OREGON	2.23830	173.1	2.17211	148.6	24.5
39	PENNSYLVANIA	3.14495	1396.2	3.05590	1137.4	258.8
40	RHODE ISLAND	1.95182	89.5	1.86179	72.7	16.8
41	SOUTH CAROLINA	2.09447	124.3	2.12037	131.9	−7.6
42	SOUTH DAKOTA	1.62531	42.2	1.68197	48.1	−5.9
43	TENNESSEE	2.43775	274.0	2.35337	225.6	48.4
44	TEXAS	2.86829	738.4	2.90808	809.2	−70.8
45	UTAH	1.92324	83.8	1.82309	66.5	17.3
46	VERMONT	1.54900	35.4	1.43218	27.1	8.3
47	VIRGINIA	2.45621	285.9	2.48826	307.8	−21.9
48	WASHINGTON	2.50772	321.9	2.43725	273.7	48.2
49	WEST VIRGINIA	2.12905	134.6	2.09146	123.4	11.2
50	WISCONSIN	2.53415	342.1	2.55600	359.8	−17.7
51	WYOMING	1.34439	22.1	1.45055	28.2	−6.1

VON NEUMANN RATIO IS 2.187
    NO AUTOCORRELATION AT EITHER 5% OR 1% LEVEL
DURBIN-WATSON COEFFICIENT   2.144
RANGE OF RESIDUALS   0.242
RANGE/STD. ERROR OF ESTIMATE   3.476

Table 5–23. Continued

PROBLEM NUMBER	7-2
REPLACEMENT AND DELETION	3
DEPENDENT VARIABLE IS NOW	3
NUMBER OF VARIABLES DELETED	1
VARIABLE DELETED	2

ANALYSIS OF VARIANCE FOR REGRESSION

SOURCE OF VARIATION	D.F.	SUM OF SQUARES	MEAN SQUARES	F VALUE
DUE TO REGRESSION	1	11.81944	11.81944	681.
DEVIATION ABOUT REGRESSION	49	0.85096	0.01737	
TOTAL	50	12.67040		

INTERCEPT (A VALUE) IS 0.29784

VARIABLE NO. NAME	MEAN	STANDARD DEVIATION	REG. COEF.	STD. ERROR OF REG. COEF.	COMPUTED T VALUE	PARTIAL CORR. COEF.
1 POPU15	1.82813	0.45652	1.065	0.041	26.	0.966

DEPENDENT

	MEAN	STANDARD DEVIATION
3 TOYSAL	2.24480	0.50340

INCREMENTS FOR INDEPENDENT VARIABLES					CUMULATIVE REGRESSIONS			
VARIABLE NO. NAME	SUMS OF SQUARES	PROP. VAR.	F VALUE EACH TERM	STD. ERROR OF ESTIMATE	SUMS OF SQUARES	PROP. VAR. = R SQ.	F VALUE	MULTIPLE R
1 POPU15	11.81944	0.933	681.	0.13178	11.81944	0.933	681.	0.966

ANTILOG = 13.5%

PROPORTION OF VARIANCE SPECIFIED TO LIMIT VARIABLES	0.

Table 5–23. Continued

TABLE OF RESIDUALS

	OBSERVATION	Y VALUE		Y ESTIMATE		RESIDUAL
		LOG	ANTI-LOG	LOG	ANTI-LOG	OF ANTILOG
1	ALABAMA	2.31281	205.5	2.47569	299.1	−93.6
2	ALASKA	1.27184	18.7	1.25963	18.2	0.5
3	ARIZONA	2.01326	103.1	2.06158	115.2	−12.1
4	ARKANSAS	1.97955	95.4	2.16866	147.5	−52.1
5	CALIFORNIA	3.20232	1593.4	3.14997	1412.5	180.9
6	COLORADO	2.29513	197.3	2.16784	147.2	50.1
7	CONNECTICUT	2.39881	250.5	2.29354	196.6	53.9
8	DELAWARE	1.60206	40.0	1.53149	34.0	6.0
9	DISTRICT OF COLUMBIA	2.06595	116.4	1.66935	46.7	69.7
10	FLORIDA	2.58354	383.3	2.60540	403.1	−19.8
11	GEORGIA	2.49415	312.0	2.55730	360.8	−48.8
12	HAWAII	1.70243	50.4	1.72329	52.9	−2.5
13	IDAHO	1.74351	55.4	1.75208	56.6	−1.2
14	ILLINOIS	3.10735	1280.4	2.93628	863.5	416.9
15	INDIANA	2.60649	404.1	2.60979	407.2	−3.1
16	IOWA	2.29820	198.7	2.35700	227.5	−28.8
17	KANSAS	2.13577	136.7	2.24467	175.6	−38.9
18	KENTUCKY	2.23223	170.7	2.42784	267.8	−97.1
19	LOUISIANA	2.35044	224.1	2.49208	309.1	−85.0
20	MAINE	1.95424	90.0	1.87251	74.6	15.4
21	MARYLAND	2.42943	268.8	2.42459	265.8	3.0
22	MASSACHUSETTS	2.81862	658.6	2.60979	407.2	251.4
23	MICHIGAN	2.84379	697.9	2.86854	738.8	−40.9
24	MINNESOTA	2.55618	359.9	2.48067	302.5	57.4
25	MISSISSIPPI	2.01578	103.7	2.31351	205.8	−102.1
26	MISSOURI	2.70961	512.4	2.53693	344.3	168.1
27	MONTANA	1.66839	46.6	1.69935	50.0	−3.4
28	NEBRASKA	2.03862	109.3	2.04389	110.6	−1.3
29	NEVADA	1.40824	25.6	1.29843	19.9	5.7
30	NEW HAMPSHIRE	1.67025	46.8	1.64235	43.9	2.9
31	NEW MEXICO	1.80956	64.5	1.95658	90.5	−26.0
32	NEW JERSEY	2.78916	615.4	2.68614	485.4	130.0
33	NEW YORK	3.30533	2019.9	3.13648	1369.2	650.7
34	NORTH CAROLINA	2.52140	332.2	2.62150	418.3	−86.1
35	NORTH DAKOTA	1.58659	38.6	1.72329	52.9	−14.3
36	OHIO	2.98259	960.7	2.94784	886.8	73.9
37	OKLAHOMA	2.17638	150.1	2.26154	182.6	−32.5
38	OREGON	2.23830	173.1	2.14795	140.6	32.5
39	PENNSYLVANIA	3.14495	1396.2	2.97963	954.2	442.0
40	RHODE ISLAND	1.95182	89.5	1.77541	59.6	29.9
41	SOUTH CAROLINA	2.09447	124.3	2.35267	225.3	−101.0
42	SOUTH DAKOTA	1.62531	42.2	1.74606	55.7	−15.5
43	TENNESSEE	2.43775	274.0	2.48355	304.5	−30.5
44	TEXAS	2.86829	738.4	2.96205	916.3	177.9
45	UTAH	1.92324	83.8	1.92063	83.3	0.5
46	VERMONT	1.54900	35.4	1.45859	28.8	6.6
47	VIRGINIA	2.45621	285.9	2.53656	344.0	−58.1
48	WASHINGTON	2.50772	321.9	2.37498	237.1	84.8
49	WEST VIRGINIA	2.12905	134.6	2.19002	154.9	−20.3
50	WISCONSIN	2.53415	342.1	2.53802	345.2	−3.1
51	WYOMING	1.34439	22.1	1.41111	25.8	−3.7

VON NEUMANN RATIO IS 2.004
 NO AUTOCORRELATION AT EITHER 5% OR 1% LEVEL
DURBIN-WATSON COEFFICIENT   1.964
RANGE OF RESIDUALS   0.694
RANGE/STD. ERROR OF ESTIMATE   5.269

Table 5–24. 1960 toy sales by region at retail related to personal income, both in current dollars

	Personal income (in millions)	Retail toy sales (in thousands)	Number in computer program
New England	$25,877	$117,045	1
Middle Atlantic	88,461	403,155	2
East North Central	86,130	368,517	3
West North Central	32,029	139,782	4
South Atlantic	48,161	199,747	5
East South Central	17,486	75,385	6
West South Central	30,387	120,798	7
Mountain	14,277	59,826	8
Pacific	55,753	215,744	9

Regions	States	Regions	States
New England	Maine	South Atlantic	Delaware
	New Hampshire		Maryland
	Vermont		Dist. of Columbia
	Massachusetts		Virginia
	Rhode Island		West Virginia
	Connecticut		North Carolina
Middle Atlantic	New York		South Carolina
	New Jersey		Georgia
	Pennsylvania		Florida
East North Central	Ohio	East South Central	Kentucky
	Indiana		Tennessee
	Illinois		Alabama
	Michigan		Mississippi
	Wisconsin	West South Central	Arkansas
West North Central	Minnesota		Louisiana
	North Dakota		Oklahoma
	South Dakota		Texas
	Nebraska	Mountain	Montana
	Kansas		Idaho
	Iowa		Wyoming
	Missouri		Colorado
			New Mexico
			Arizona
			Utah
			Nevada
		Pacific	Washington
			Oregon
			Alaska
			Hawaii
			California

SOURCE: Table 5–21.

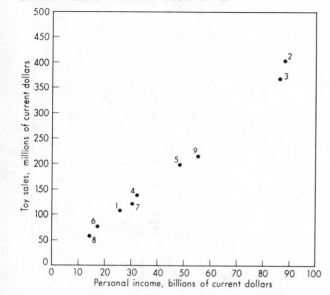

Figure 5–14. Scatter diagram of 1960 toy sales at retail and personal income, both by regions and in current dollars SOURCE: *Table 5–24.*

Table 5–25. Computer output, simple correlation of toy sales at retail (variable 2) as a function of personal income (variable 1) by regions 1960

Units: toy sales in millions of current dollars and personal income in billions of current dollars.

PROBLEM NUMBER	8	
NUMBER OF VARIABLES	2	
SAMPLE SIZE	9	
SUMS		
	399.	1700.
SUMS OF SQUARES		
	23800.	441876.
CROSS PRODUCT SUMS		
ROW 1	23800.	102401.
ROW 2	102401.	441876.
CROSS PRODUCTS OF DEVIATIONS		
ROW 1	6150.	27117.
ROW 2	27117.	120765.
SIMPLE CORRELATION COEFFICIENTS		
ROW 1	1.000	0.995
ROW 2	0.995	1.000

Table 5-25. Continued

ANALYSIS OF VARIANCE FOR REGRESSION

SOURCE OF VARIATION	D.F.	SUM OF SQUARES	MEAN SQUARES	F VALUE
DUE TO REGRESSION	1	119571.	119571.	701.
DEVIATION ABOUT REGRESSION	7	1194.	171.	
TOTAL	8	120765.		

INTERCEPT (A VALUE) IS −6.378

VARIABLE NO. NAME	MEAN	STANDARD DEVIATION	REG. COEF.	STD. ERROR OF REG. COEF.	COMPUTED T VALUE	PARTIAL CORR. COEF.
1 PERINC	44.	28.	4.41	0.167	26.	0.995
DEPENDENT						
2 TOYSAL	189.	123.				

INCREMENTS FOR INDEPENDENT VARIABLES / CUMULATIVE REGRESSIONS

VARIABLE NO. NAME	SUMS OF SQUARES	PROP. VAR.	F VALUE EACH TERM	STD. ERROR OF ESTIMATE	SUMS OF SQUARES	PROP. VAR. = R SQ.	F VALUE	MULTIPLE R
1 PERINC	119571.	0.990	701.	13.062	119571.	0.990	701.	0.995

PROPORTION OF VARIANCE SPECIFIED TO LIMIT VARIABLES 0.

Table 5–25. Continued

TABLE OF RESIDUALS

OBSERVATION		Y VALUE	Y ESTIMATE	RESIDUAL
1	NEW ENGLAND	117.05	107.72	9.32
2	MIDDLE ATLANTIC	403.15	383.68	19.47
3	EAST NORTH CENTRAL	368.52	373.40	-4.88
4	WEST NORTH CENTRAL	139.78	134.85	4.93
5	SOUTH ATLANTIC	199.75	205.98	-6.23
6	EAST SOUTH CENTRAL	75.38	70.72	4.66
7	WEST SOUTH CENTRAL	120.80	127.61	-6.81
8	MOUNTAIN	59.83	56.57	3.26
9	PACIFIC	215.74	239.46	-23.72

VON NEUMANN RATIO IS 1.880   NO AUTOCORRELATION AT 5% AND 1% LEVELS
DURBIN-WATSON COEFFICIENT   1.672
RATIO OF RANGES FOR THE SMALLEST RESIDUAL   0.512
RATIO OF RANGES FOR THE LARGEST RESIDUAL   0.386
CRITICAL VALUE OF THE RATIO AT ALPHA = 0.10   0.441

SOURCE: Table 5–24.

Table 5–26. Computer output, simple correlation of toys sales at retail (variable 2) as a function of personal income (variable 1) in logarithmic form by regions in 1960

Units: toy sales in thousands of current dollars and personal income in millions of current dollars.

PROBLEM NUMBER	9	
NUMBER OF VARIABLES	2	
SAMPLE SIZE	9	
SUMS		
	41.10934	46.75639
SUMS OF SQUARES		
	188.41045	243.55055
CROSS PRODUCT SUMS		
ROW 1	188.41045	214.20664
ROW 2	214.20664	243.55055
CROSS PRODUCTS OF DEVIATIONS		
ROW 1	0.63512	0.63728
ROW 2	0.63728	0.64392
SIMPLE CORRELATION COEFFICIENTS		
ROW 1	1.000	0.997
ROW 2	0.997	1.000

Table 5–26. Continued

ANALYSIS OF VARIANCE FOR REGRESSION

SOURCE OF VARIATION	D.F.	SUM OF SQUARES	MEAN SQUARES	F VALUE
DUE TO REGRESSION	1	0.63944	0.63944	1000.
DEVIATION ABOUT REGRESSION	7	0.00448	0.00064	
TOTAL	8	0.64392		

INTERCEPT (A VALUE) IS 0.61195

VARIABLE NO. NAME	MEAN	STANDARD DEVIATION	REG. COEF.	STD. ERROR OF REG. COEF.	COMPUTED T VALUE	PARTIAL CORR. COEF.
1 PERINC	4.56770	0.28176	1.003	0.032	32.	0.997

DEPENDENT

	MEAN	STANDARD DEVIATION
2 TOYSAL	5.19515	0.28371

	INCREMENTS FOR INDEPENDENT VARIABLES				CUMULATIVE REGRESSIONS			
VARIABLE NO. NAME	SUMS OF SQUARES	PROP. VAR.	F VALUE EACH TERM	STD. ERROR OF ESTIMATE	SUMS OF SQUARES	PROP. VAR. = R SQ.	F VALUE	MULTIPLE R
1 PERINC	0.63944	0.99305	1000.	0.02529	0.63944	0.99305	1000.	0.997

ANTILOG = 10.6%

PROPORTION OF VARIANCE
SPECIFIED TO LIMIT
VARIABLES   0.

Table 5–26. Continued

TABLE OF RESIDUALS

OBSERVATION	Y VALUE LOG	Y VALUE ANTILOG	Y ESTIMATE LOG	Y ESTIMATE ANTILOG	RESIDUAL OF ANTILOGS
1 NEW ENGLAND	5.06835	117045	5.03984	109610	7435
2 MIDDLE ATLANTIC	5.60547	403155	5.57549	376270	26885
3 EAST NORTH CENTRAL	5.56646	368517	5.56385	366310	2207
4 WEST NORTH CENTRAL	5.14545	139782	5.13278	135760	4022
5 SOUTH ATLANTIC	5.30048	199747	5.31054	204430	−4683
6 EAST SOUTH CENTRAL	4.87729	75385	4.86904	73968	1417
7 WEST SOUTH CENTRAL	5.08206	120798	5.10985	128780	−7982
8 MOUNTAIN	4.77689	59826	4.78068	60351	525
9 PACIFIC	5.33394	215744	5.37432	236770	−21026

VON NEUMANN RATIO IS 1.239   NO AUTOCORRELATION AT EITHER 5% OR 1% LEVEL
DURBIN-WATSON COEFFICIENT   1.101
RATIO OF RANGES FOR THE SMALLEST RESIDUAL   0.183
RATIO OF RANGES FOR THE LARGEST RESIDUAL   0.025
CRITICAL VALUE OF THE RATIO AT ALPHA = 0.10   0.441

SOURCE: Table 5-24.

Table 5–27. Prediction of toy sales at manufacturers' prices in constant dollars (1957–1959 = 100), based on projected disposable personal income and population under 14, using equation $Y = -47.183 + 0.367X_1 + 0.024X_2$

Year	Predicted spendable income in billions of 1957–1959 dollars* (1)	Adjusting column 1 to disposable personal income in constant dollars† X_1 (2)	Population under 14 (in hundreds of thousands)‡ X_2 (3)	Predicted toy sales in tens of millions of constant dollars (1957–1959 = 100)§ Y_c (4)	Range of toy sales in tens of millions of constant dollars (1957–1959 = 100)¶ (5)
1960	$335.4				
1965	393.3	$424.8	578.55	$122.60	$126.28 High
			560.92	122.18	118.51 Low
1970	466.1	503.4	637.72	152.87	157.46
			584.81	151.60	130.63
1975	551.9	596.1	717.23	189.00	194.67
			627.62	186.65	161.32

* Brown, Bonnar, and Janet Hansen Tate, *Income Trends in the United States through 1975* (Menlo Park, Calif.: Stanford Research Institute, 1957), p. 21, Table III, "United States: Tax and Spendable Income Data 1929–1975." This forecast was based on 1947–1949 = 100. Therefore it was recomputed to the base of 1957–1959 for use here by multiplying by 1.285, the ratio of the 1957–1959 base to the 1947–1949 base, using the Consumer Price Index.

† Column 1 increased by 8 per cent as explained in text.

‡ U.S. Bureau of the Census, *Statistical Abstract of the United States: 1963*, p. 6. The Bureau of the Census prepares four population projections, each on different assumptions. The above are the two middle estimates computed by deducting estimated population 14 and over from total population.

§ Computation based on the regression equation developed in Table 5–12: $Y = -47.183 + 0.367X_1 + 0.024X_2$.

¶ Range established on the basis of plus or minus 3 per cent from the computed toy sales. The 3 per cent is derived from the ratio of standard error of the estimate to the mean of the dependent variable.

Figure 5–15. Predicted toy sales at manufacturers'
prices in constant dollars (1957–1959 = 100), based on
regression equation $Y = -47.183 + 0.367X_1 + 0.024X_2$,
where Y = *toy sales in tens of millions of dollars,*
X_1 = *disposable personal income in billions, and*
X_2 = *population under 14 in hundreds of thousands*
SOURCE: *Tables 5–2 and 5–27.*

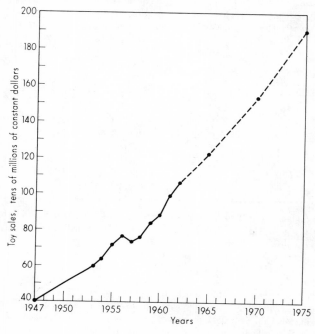

Table 5–28. *Prediction of toy sales at manufacturers' prices in constant dollars (1957–1959 = 100), based on income elasticity of 1.973**

	Percentage change in spendable income (from 1960)† (1)	Predicted percentage change in toy sales (from 1960)‡ (2)	Predicted toy sales in billions of constant dollars (1957–1959 = 100)§ (3)
1965	18.0%	35.5%	$1.202
1970	39.8	78.5	1.583
1975	65.5	129.2	2.033

* SOURCE: Table 5–14.
† Percentage change based on difference between spendable income from Stanford forecast (Table 5–27) and predicted 1960 spendable income.
‡ Percentage change in toy sales based on 1.973 times percentage change in spendable income.
§ 1960 toy sales of $887 million in constant dollars (1957–1959 = 100) from Table 5–2 times column 2 as 100 per cent plus percentage change stated in column 2.

Figure 5–16. *Predicted toy sales at manufacturers' prices in constant dollars (1957–1959 = 100) on the basis of income elasticity of 1.973* SOURCE: *Tables 5–14 and 5–28.*

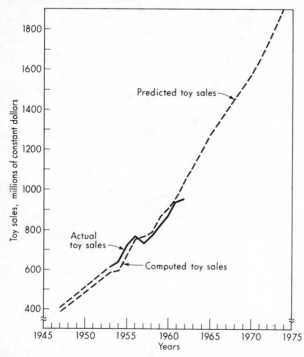

Table 5–29. Prediction of toy sales at manufacturers' prices in constant dollars (1957–1959 = 100), based on income elasticity of 1.719°

	Percentage change in spendable income (from 1960)† (1)	Computed percentage change in toy sales (from 1960)‡ (2)	Predicted toy sales in billions of constant dollars (1957–1959 = 100)§ (3)
1965	18.0%	30.9%	$1.161
1970	39.8	68.4	1.494
1975	65.5	112.6	1.886

* SOURCE: Table 5–18.

† Percentage change based on difference between spendable income from Stanford forecast (Table 5–27) and predicted 1960 spendable income.

‡ Percentage change in toy sales as 1.719 times percentage change in spendable income in column 1.

§ 1960 toy sales of $887 million in constant dollars (1957–1959 = 100) from Table 5–2 times column 2 as 100 per cent plus percentage change stated in column 2.

Figure 5–17. Predicted toy sales at manufacturers' prices in constant dollars (1957–1959 = 100), based on income elasticity of 1.719 SOURCE: **Tables 5–18 and 5–29.**

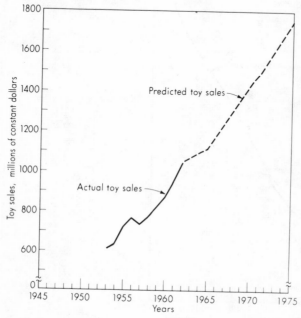

Table 5–30. Prediction of toy sales at retail in constant dollars (1957–1959 = 100), based on income elasticity with respect to retail toy sales of 1.053*

	Spendable income in billions of constant dollars (1957–1959 = 100)† (1)	Percentage change in spendable income‡ (2)	Percentage change in retail toy sales§ (3)	Predicted retail toy sales in billions of constant dollars (1957–1959 = 100)¶ (4)
1960	$318.5			
1965	375.9	18.0%	19.0%	$1.961
1970	445.4	39.8	41.9	2.339
1975	527.2	65.5	69.0	2.785

* SOURCE: Elasticity developed in problem 7–1, Table 5–23 (which is based on pretax personal income).

† Brown, Bonnar, and Janet Hansen Tate, *Income Trends in the United States through 1975* (Menlo Park, Calif.: Stanford Research Institute, 1957), p. 21. This forecast is based on 1947–1949 = 100 and has been corrected to the 1957–1959 base by multiplying by 1.285, the ratio of the 1957–1959 base to the 1947–1949 base.

‡ Percentage change from spendable income in 1960.

§ 1.053 times percentage change in spendable income (column 2).

¶ Toy sales in 1960 ($1.648 billion in constant dollars, 1957–1959 = 100) from McCready Publishing Company, *Playthings*, Directory issue, February 28, 1962, p. 15, times column 3 as 100 per cent plus percentage change stated in column 2.

Figures 5–18. Predicted retail toy sales at retail in constant dollars (1957–1959 = 100), based on income elasticity of 1.053   SOURCE: Tables 5–23 and 5–30.

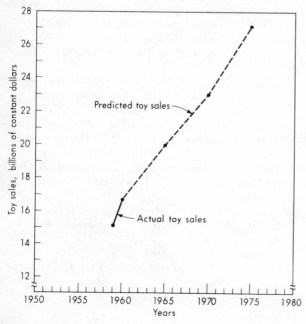

BIBLIOGRAPHY

BOOKS

1. Brown, Bonnar, and Janet Hansen Tate, *Income Trends in the United States through 1975* (Menlo Park, Calif.: Stanford Research Institute, 1957).
2. Craumer, Lucille V., Editor, *The Business Periodicals Index, July, 1960* (New York: The H. W. Wilson Company, 1963).
3. Croxton, Frederick E., and Dudley J. Crowden, *Practical Business Statistics*, 3d edition (Englewood Cliffs, N.J.: Prentice-Hall, Inc., 1960).
4. Dow Jones and Co., *The Wall Street Journal Index, 1955–1963* (New York).
5. McClintock, Marshall, and Inez McClintock, *Toys in America* (Washington, D.C.: Public Affairs Press, 1963).
6. McCready Publishing Company, *Playthings,* Annual Directory Issue (New York: 1961).
7. Nemmers, Erwin E., *Managerial Economics: Text and Cases,* rev. printing (New York: John Wiley & Sons, Inc., 1964).
8. Robinson, Sarita, and Zada Limerick, Editors, *Reader's Guide to Periodical Literature,* Vols. XX–XXIII (New York: The H. W. Wilson Company).
9. Sinclair, Homer, *Toy Manufacturing and Toy Marketing* (Springfield, Ill.: Phillips Bros., 1931).
10. Technical Committee on Industrial Classification, *Standard Industrial Classification Manual* (Washington, D.C.: Government Printing Office, 1957).
11. Toy Manufacturers of the U.S.A., Inc., *Merchandise Manual for Toys and Playthings* (New York: 1963).
12. Toy Wholesalers Association of America, *The 1963 Toy Industrial Manual* (Evanston, Ill.).
13. U.S. Bureau of Census, *Annual Survey of Manufactures* (Washington, D.C.: Government Printing Office, annually).
14. U.S. Bureau of the Census, *Statistical Abstract of the United States: 1963,* 84th edition (Washington, D.C.: Government Printing Office, 1963).
15. U.S. Bureau of the Census, *U.S. Census of Manufactures: 1958,* Vol. II, *Industry Statistics,* Part 2, Major Groups 29–39 (Washington, D.C.: Government Printing Office).
16. U.S. Bureau of Labor Statistics, *Consumer Price Index—Historical Index Series (1957–1959 = 100)* (Washington, D.C.: U.S. Department of Labor).
17. U.S. Bureau of Labor Statistics, *Wholesale Price Index—Historical Index Series,* base 1957–1959 = 100 (Washington, D.C.: U.S. Department of Labor).
18. U.S. Business and Defense Services Administration, *U.S. Industrial Outlook, 1963 and 1964,* ER–27 for 1961 and ER–23 for 1962 (Washington, D.C.: Government Printing Office).
19. U.S. Department of Commerce, *Current Population Reports,* Series P–25, No. 187, No. 251, and No. 265 (Washington, D.C.: Government Printing Office).
20. U.S. Department of Commerce, FT110, *United States Imports of Merchandise for Consumption, 1961, 1962* (Washington, D.C.: Government Printing Office).

21. U.S. Department of Commerce, *Quarterly Summary of Foreign Commerce of the United States* (Cumulative Year to Date), January–December, 1953, 1954, 1955, 1956, 1957, 1958, 1959, 1960 (Washington, D.C.: Government Printing Office).

22. U.S. Department of Commerce, *Survey of Current Business*, November, 1963 (Washington, D.C.: Government Printing Office).

23. U.S. Department of Commerce, *Survey of Current Business, Supplement, 1961 (Business Statistics)* (Washington, D.C.: Government Printing Office).

24. U.S. Superintendent of Documents, *Monthly Catalog of U.S. Government Publications, 1955–1963* (Washington, D.C.: Government Printing Office).

PERIODICALS

25. ———, "California National Adds 40 to List of TV Inspired Toys," *Advertising Age*, Vol. 29, June 2, 1958, p. 70.

26. ———, "Troubles in Toyland," *Barron's*, Vol. XLII, No. 10, March 5, 1962, pp. 5, 19.

27. ———, "Fun and Games Has Its Troubles," *Business Week*, No. 1698, March 17, 1962, pp. 32–33.

28. ———, "It's Not the Doll," *Business Week*, No. 1685, December 16, 1961, pp. 48–52.

29. ———, "Plastics Ring Up Toy Gains," *Chemical Week*, Vol. 89, No. 25, December 23, 1961, p. 16.

30. ———, "Profits in Playthings, with Data on Leaders," *Financial World*, Vol. 116, No. 4, July 26, 1961, p. 20.

31. ———, "Toy Makers: Growth Group with Data," *Financial World*, Vol. 117, No. 16, April 18, 1962, pp. 22, 30.

32. ———. "Fun and Games in St. Paul," *Fortune*, Vol. LXI, No. 1, January, 1960, p. 190.

33. Carr, G. C., "Why Toyland Leans to Plastics," *Iron Age*, Vol. 180, No. 25, December 19, 1957, pp. 98–99.

34. ———, "Toymakers Up Tooling Outlays," *Iron Age*, Vol. 187, No. 9, March 2, 1961, p. 64.

35. ———, "Toys: There's a Profit in Fun," *Management Review*, Vol. 52, No. 6, June, 1963, pp. 53–55.

36. ———, "Growing Battle for Toy Market Billions," *Printers' Ink*, Vol. 275, No. 1, April 7, 1961, pp. 11–12.

37. ———, "March of the Toy Makers Swells on T.V.," *Printers' Ink*, Vol. 269, No. 12, December 18, 1959, pp. 40–41.

38. ———, "Revell Expands Its Market to All Ages," *Printers' Ink*, Vol. 266, No. 10, March 6, 1959, pp. 69–71.

39. ———, "Let Kids Build Your Corporate Image," *Sales Management*, Vol. 84, No. 10, May 20, 1960, pp. 36–37.

40. Dow Jones and Co., *Wall Street Journal*, Daily issues.

41. McCready Publishing Company, *Playthings*, Monthly trade journal of the toy industry (New York).

42. Toy Manufacturers of America, Inc., *Toys and Novelties*, Monthly trade journal (New York).

SPECIAL STUDIES

43. Market Research Group, Monsanto Chemical Company, 800 North Lindbergh Boulevard, St. Louis, Mo., "Consumer Study of Plastic Model Kits," 1959, a privately circulated study.

44. Market Research Group, Monsanto Chemical Company, 800 North Lindbergh Boulevard, St. Louis, Mo., "Facts about the Toy Market and a Plastic Toy Survey," June, 1954, a privately circulated study.

45. Market Research Group, Monsanto Chemical Company, 800 North Lindbergh Boulevard, St. Louis, Mo., "Thermoplastic Molding Compound Purchases for Toys—Year 1960 and First Six Months of 1961," November, 1961, a privately circulated study.

APPENDIX A. EXPLANATION OF ABBREVIATIONS AND TERMS IN COMPUTER OUTPUT OF BIMED 29

1. *Sums.*

   The algebraic sums of each of the variables in the problem. The order of the sums follows the numbering of the variables.

2. *Sum of squares.*

   The sum of the squares of each item for each variable.

3. *Cross-product sums.*

   The sums of the products of all the possible pairs of the variables. These appear in matrix form so that over and below the diagonal (from top left to bottom right) the sums are repeated. Row 1, column 1, is the sum of the squares of the items of variable 1. Row 1, column 2 (and likewise row 2, column 1), shows the sum of the products of each item of variable 1 times each item of variable 2, etc.

4. *Cross products of deviations.*

   This is presented in the same format as the "cross-product sums." Each item of each variable is here measured as a deviation from the mean of that variable. These sums can be positive or negative, with negative sums indicating an inverse relationship of the two variables.

5. *Simple correlation coefficients.*

   These are the simple correlation coefficients between each possible pair of variables computed linearly and by least squares. These coefficients are presented in the same format as the "cross-product sums." Thus down the diagonal of each the coefficient is always 1, namely, the correlation of each variable with itself. These correlation coefficients are not adjusted for degrees of freedom lost in computation. To adjust these simple correlation coefficients for degrees of freedom, multiply the coefficient by $(N-1)/N$, where N is the number of items in the sample. This matrix enables us to judge multicollinearity between the independent variables. If the simple correlation coefficient between the independent variables is high, there is multicollinearity.

6. *Analysis of Variance for Regression.*

   This section gives the data for a probability calculation as to whether the observed degree of relationship can be attributed to chance. This involves two assumptions about the data: (1) that the same is a fair (random) representation of the universe from which it comes and (2) that the universe consists of normally distributed items.

7. *Source of variation.*

   Total variation is composed of explained (by the regression line) variation plus unexplained variation (deviations from the regression line). "Due to regression" identifies the explained variation (the sum of the squares of the difference between the arithmetic mean of the dependent variable and the value of the dependent value established by the estimating equation). "Deviation about regression" identifies the unexplained variation (the sum of the squares of the difference between the actual value of the dependent variable and the value of the dependent variable from the estimating equation).

8. *D.F. (Degrees of freedom).*
The total degrees of freedom for the standard deviation is 1 less than the sample size because 1 degree of freedom is used up in the computation of the arithmetic mean before computation of the standard deviation (on which the total variation is based). The remaining $(N-1)$ degrees of freedom are allocated between the explained variation and the unexplained. The explained variation requires the prior calculation of the regression line. For the case of two independent variables there will be three constants in the estimating equation: the intercept and the coefficient (slope) of each independent variable. Hence, the explained variation uses up 2 degrees of freedom (3 less the 1 already used up in the computation of the arithmetic mean). This leaves $N-1-2$ degrees of freedom for the unexplained variation.

9. *Sum of squares.*
This column shows in the first row the sum of the squares of the deviations of the values of the dependent variable computed by the regression equation from the mean of the values of the dependent variable. In row 2 appears the sum of the squares of the deviations of the actual values of the dependent variable from the computed values of the dependent variable. The third row in this column gives the sum of the squares of deviations of the actual values of the dependent variable from the mean of the dependent variable.

10. *Mean [of] squares.*
This is the result of dividing the "sum of squares" by its associated "degrees of freedom." Note: the BIMED 29 program does not calculate the total variance, but this can be done by dividing the total sum of squares by $N-1$ degrees of freedom.

11. *F value.*
This is the ratio of the "between variation" divided by the "within variation" where both have been adjusted for degrees of freedom. Hence the ratio of the "mean squares" column is used. The interpretation of this ratio requires the use of an F table to establish the probability that the result is attributable to chance. A high F value does *not* mean that there is significant correlation in the universe but that *such correlation as there is shown* is significantly better than what would arise by chance.

12. *Intercept (A value) is.*
This is the value of the first constant in the regression equation. This is the value of the dependent variable in the equation when the values of independent variables are 0. Since this value of the dependent variable is outside the range of data used to establish the equation, its practical meaning is usually useless. However, it is a necessary component of the equation.

13. *Variable.*
This column identifies by number and by brief name the independent variables.

14. *Mean.*
This column gives the mean of each variable.

15. *Standard deviation.*
This column gives the standard deviation of each variable calculated for $N-1$ degrees of freedom.

16. *Reg. coef. (regression coefficient).*
This column gives the coefficient of each independent variable in the regression equation. Together with the A value in item 12, above, these values are all the constants needed to determine the regression equation.

17. *Std. error of reg. coef. (standard error of regression coefficient).*
This measures the sampling error of each regression coefficient. The standard error here computed takes account of the degrees of freedom involved, as is usual with a standard error form. The standard error of the regression coefficient carries a level of probability. If the number of items in the sample is under 30, the "t" distribution will give the probability for the appropriate degree of freedom. Over 30 in the sample the normal curve is used, and the standard error of the regression coefficient carries a 2 out of 3 probability that the regression coefficient of the universe would fall within 1 standard error either side of the regression coefficient.

18. *Computed t value.*
This value is the result of dividing the regression coefficient of each variable by its standard error. The unit of the t value is a standard unit, and it is applied to testing the hypothesis that the correlation in the universe is 0. Hence, the larger the t value, the farther out on the tail of the probability distribution (from a mean of 0) is the probability that 0 correlation exists in the universe and the present value of the regression coefficient has occurred by chance. The conventional rule is that if the t value is 3 (either plus or minus t) or more, the regression coefficient is significant.

19. *Partial corr. coef. (partial correlation coefficient).*
This measures the relationship between the independent variables when the effect of the other independent variables in the analysis is held statistically constant (that is, the dependent variable is adjusted for the effect of the other independent variables as indicated by their relationship as developed in the analysis). This is a better indication of the effect of the independent variable on the dependent variable than is obtained from the simple correlation coefficient of the same independent variable.

20. *Increments for independent variables.*
This section gives further indication of the relative importance of the several independent variables. In this section, the independent

variables are ranked in the order of their apparent importance on the basis of the F value for each variable.

21. *Sum of squares.*

This column gives the sum of the squares of the deviations of (*a*) the values of the dependent variable computed by the use of each independent variable from (*b*) the mean of the dependent variable but giving cognizance to the number of independent variables actually used (usually more than 1).

22. *Prop. var. (proportion of variation).*

This figure states the proportion of the variation in the dependent variable explained as each successive independent variable is added to the equation. In this way, we can evaluate when the addition to "explanation" does not justify the risk that chance is at work as shown by the t value of each regression coefficient.

23. *Cumulative regressions.*

This section cumulates the increments shown in the section "increments for independent variables."

24. *Std. error of estimate (standard error of estimate).*

This is the square root of the mean of the unexplained variation. Hence it is the average amount by which (2 times out of 3) the estimate of the dependent variable computed from the equation will differ from the actual value of the dependent variable. This value will usually decrease as successive independent variables are added (that is, if the added independent variables are statistically significant).

25. *Prop. var. = R. sq. (Proportion of variation = R squared).*

This is the ratio of explained variation to total variation, which is *R squared*.

26. *F value.*

This is the ratio of "between variation" divided by the "within variation."

27. *Multiple R.*

This is the square root of item 25.

28. *Proportion of variance specified to limit variables.*

This sets the percentage contribution to the explanation that an independent variable must be before being included in the output. If this is set at 0, the results of all the independent variables will be reported regardless of how insignificant the results of a particular variable may be. Setting this value at a figure above 0 will facilitate a "fishing expedition" with many independent variables and will not clutter up the output with insignificant independent variables.

29. *Table of residuals.*

This lists the actual values of the dependent variable in the first column, the values of the dependent variable computed from the regression equation in the second column, and the difference between these values in the third column.

30. *Von Neumann ratio.*

This ratio tests for autocorrelation in the residuals in item 29 and is explained at page 171 of this book. The table to interpret this ratio is set forth at p. 601.

31. *Durbin-Watson coefficient.*

This is $(N-1)/N$ times the von Neumann ratio in item 30. A separate table is used to interpret this ratio, but the interpretation is the same as for the von Neumann ratio. J. Durbin and G. S. Watson, "Testing for Serial Correlation in Least Squares Regression I," *Biometrika*, vol. 37, pp. 409–421, 1950, and Part II in *ibid.*, vol. 38, pp. 159–178, 1951.

32a. *Ratio of ranges for the smallest residual; ratio of ranges for the largest residual; critical value of the ratio at alpha = 0.10.* These

three statistics appear in the print-out when the sample size is less than 30. When the sample size exceeds 30, the computation at item 32b below appears. These three statistics are explained in W. J. Dixon and F. J. Massey, Jr.. *Introduction to Statistical Analysis*, 2d edition (New York: McGraw-Hill Book Company, 1957), pages 275–278, and employ the table of critical values appearing there at page 412. Briefly this is a test to determine the probability that the extreme residuals come from the same or a different population than that of the other values. The authors of this reference were professors at University of California at Los Angeles, and the particular program here involved (BIMED 29, UCLA) was developed there, which may explain the incorporation of unusual statistics into the program.

32b. *Range of residuals; range/std. error of estimate.*

These two statistics appear in the print-out when the sample size is over 30. The range of the residuals is the numerical difference between the largest positive and largest negative residuals. This range divided by the standard error of estimate is a quick but crude test of the normality of the distribution of the residuals. If this ratio is close to 6, there is some evidence of a normal distribution if we remember that ± 3 includes 99.75 per cent of all cases in a normal curve. This statistic is explained and a table of critical values for various sizes of sample is given in E. S. Pearson, "The Percentage Limits for the Distribution of the Range of Samples from a Normal Population," *Biometrika*, vol. 24, pp. 404–417, 1932 and E. S. Pearson, "The Probability Integral of the Range in Samples of n Observations from a Normal Population," *Biometrika*, vol. 32, pp. 301–308, 1941–1942.

Table A. Areas under the normal curve* (proportion of total area under the curve from $-\infty$ to designated Z value)

Z	0.00	0.01	0.02	0.03	0.04	0.05	0.06	0.07	0.08	0.09
-3.5	0.00023	0.00022	0.00022	0.00021	0.00020	0.00019	0.00019	0.00018	0.00017	0.00017
-3.4	0.00034	0.00033	0.00031	0.00030	0.00029	0.00028	0.00027	0.00026	0.00025	0.00024
-3.3	0.00048	0.00047	0.00045	0.00043	0.00042	0.00040	0.00039	0.00038	0.00036	0.00035
-3.2	0.00069	0.00066	0.00064	0.00062	0.00060	0.00058	0.00056	0.00054	0.00052	0.00050
-3.1	0.00097	0.00094	0.00090	0.00087	0.00085	0.00082	0.00079	0.00076	0.00074	0.00071
-3.0	0.00135	0.00131	0.00126	0.00122	0.00118	0.00114	0.00111	0.00107	0.00104	0.00100
-2.9	0.0019	0.0018	0.0017	0.0017	0.0016	0.0016	0.0015	0.0015	0.0014	0.0014
-2.8	0.0026	0.0025	0.0024	0.0023	0.0023	0.0022	0.0021	0.0021	0.0020	0.0019
-2.7	0.0035	0.0034	0.0033	0.0032	0.0031	0.0030	0.0029	0.0028	0.0027	0.0026
-2.6	0.0047	0.0045	0.0044	0.0043	0.0041	0.0040	0.0039	0.0038	0.0037	0.0036
-2.5	0.0062	0.0060	0.0059	0.0057	0.0055	0.0054	0.0052	0.0051	0.0049	0.0048
-2.4	0.0082	0.0080	0.0078	0.0075	0.0073	0.0071	0.0069	0.0068	0.0066	0.0064
-2.3	0.0107	0.0104	0.0102	0.0099	0.0096	0.0094	0.0091	0.0089	0.0087	0.0084
-2.2	0.0139	0.0136	0.0132	0.0129	0.0125	0.0122	0.0119	0.0116	0.0113	0.0110
-2.1	0.0179	0.0174	0.0170	0.0166	0.0162	0.0158	0.0154	0.0150	0.0146	0.0143
-2.0	0.0228	0.0222	0.0217	0.0212	0.0207	0.0202	0.0197	0.0192	0.0188	0.0183
-1.9	0.0287	0.0281	0.0274	0.0268	0.0262	0.0256	0.0250	0.0244	0.0239	0.0233
-1.8	0.0359	0.0351	0.0344	0.0336	0.0329	0.0322	0.0314	0.0307	0.0301	0.0294
-1.7	0.0446	0.0436	0.0427	0.0418	0.0409	0.0401	0.0392	0.0384	0.0375	0.0367
-1.6	0.0548	0.0537	0.0526	0.0516	0.0505	0.0495	0.0485	0.0475	0.0465	0.0455

z	0.00	0.01	0.02	0.03	0.04	0.05	0.06	0.07	0.08	0.09
−1.5	0.0668	0.0655	0.0643	0.0630	0.0618	0.0606	0.0594	0.0582	0.0571	0.0559
−1.4	0.0808	0.0793	0.0778	0.0764	0.0749	0.0735	0.0721	0.0708	0.0694	0.0681
−1.3	0.0968	0.0951	0.0934	0.0918	0.0901	0.0885	0.0869	0.0853	0.0838	0.0823
−1.2	0.1151	0.1131	0.1112	0.1093	0.1075	0.1057	0.1038	0.1020	0.1003	0.0985
−1.1	0.1357	0.1335	0.1314	0.1292	0.1271	0.1251	0.1230	0.1210	0.1190	0.1170
−1.0	0.1587	0.1562	0.1539	0.1515	0.1492	0.1469	0.1446	0.1423	0.1401	0.1379
−0.9	0.1841	0.1814	0.1788	0.1762	0.1736	0.1711	0.1685	0.1660	0.1635	0.1611
−0.8	0.2119	0.2090	0.2061	0.2033	0.2005	0.1977	0.1949	0.1922	0.1894	0.1867
−0.7	0.2420	0.2389	0.2358	0.2327	0.2297	0.2266	0.2236	0.2207	0.2177	0.2148
−0.6	0.2743	0.2709	0.2676	0.2643	0.2611	0.2578	0.2546	0.2514	0.2483	0.2451
−0.5	0.3085	0.3050	0.3015	0.2981	0.2946	0.2912	0.2877	0.2843	0.2810	0.2776
−0.4	0.3446	0.3409	0.3372	0.3336	0.3300	0.3264	0.3228	0.3192	0.3156	0.3121
−0.3	0.3821	0.3783	0.3745	0.3707	0.3669	0.3632	0.3594	0.3557	0.3520	0.3483
−0.2	0.4207	0.4168	0.4129	0.4090	0.4052	0.4013	0.3974	0.3936	0.3897	0.3859
−0.1	0.4602	0.4562	0.4522	0.4483	0.4443	0.4404	0.4364	0.4325	0.4286	0.4247
−0.0	0.5000	0.4960	0.4920	0.4880	0.4840	0.4801	0.4761	0.4721	0.4681	0.4641

* Adapted from E. L. Grant, *Statistical Quality Control*, 2d ed. (New York: McGraw-Hill Book Company, 1952) Table A, pp. 510–511. By permission from the publisher and of the adapter, Charles R. Hicks, *Fundamental Concepts in the Design of Experiments* (New York: Holt, Rinehart and Winston, Inc., 1964), pp. 266ff.

Table A. Continued

Z	0.00	0.01	0.02	0.03	0.04	0.05	0.06	0.07	0.08	0.09
+0.0	0.5000	0.5040	0.5080	0.5120	0.5160	0.5199	0.5239	0.5279	0.5319	0.5359
+0.1	0.5398	0.5438	0.5478	0.5517	0.5557	0.5596	0.5636	0.5675	0.5714	0.5753
+0.2	0.5793	0.5832	0.5871	0.5910	0.5948	0.5987	0.6026	0.6064	0.6103	0.6141
+0.3	0.6179	0.6217	0.6255	0.6293	0.6331	0.6368	0.6406	0.6443	0.6480	0.6517
+0.4	0.6554	0.6591	0.6628	0.6664	0.6700	0.6736	0.6772	0.6808	0.6844	0.6879
+0.5	0.6915	0.6950	0.6985	0.7019	0.7054	0.7088	0.7123	0.7157	0.7190	0.7224
+0.6	0.7257	0.7291	0.7324	0.7357	0.7389	0.7422	0.7454	0.7486	0.7517	0.7549
+0.7	0.7580	0.7611	0.7642	0.7673	0.7704	0.7734	0.7764	0.7794	0.7823	0.7852
+0.8	0.7881	0.7910	0.7939	0.7967	0.7995	0.8023	0.8051	0.8079	0.8106	0.8133
+0.9	0.8159	0.8186	0.8212	0.8238	0.8264	0.8289	0.8315	0.8340	0.8365	0.8389
+1.0	0.8413	0.8438	0.8461	0.8485	0.8508	0.8531	0.8554	0.8577	0.8599	0.8621
+1.1	0.8643	0.8665	0.8686	0.8708	0.8729	0.8749	0.8770	0.8790	0.8810	0.8830
+1.2	0.8849	0.8869	0.8888	0.8907	0.8925	0.8944	0.8962	0.8980	0.8997	0.9015
+1.3	0.9032	0.9049	0.9066	0.9082	0.9099	0.9115	0.9131	0.9147	0.9162	0.9177
+1.4	0.9192	0.9207	0.9222	0.9236	0.9251	0.9265	0.9279	0.9292	0.9306	0.9319
+1.5	0.9332	0.9345	0.9357	0.9370	0.9382	0.9394	0.9406	0.9418	0.9429	0.9441
+1.6	0.9452	0.9463	0.9474	0.9484	0.9495	0.9505	0.9515	0.9525	0.9535	0.9545
+1.7	0.9554	0.9564	0.9573	0.9582	0.9591	0.9599	0.9608	0.9616	0.9625	0.9633
+1.8	0.9641	0.9649	0.9656	0.9664	0.9671	0.9678	0.9686	0.9693	0.9699	0.9706
+1.9	0.9713	0.9719	0.9726	0.9732	0.9738	0.9744	0.9750	0.9756	0.9761	0.9767
+2.0	0.9773	0.9778	0.9783	0.9788	0.9793	0.9798	0.9803	0.9808	0.9812	0.9817

	.00	.01	.02	.03	.04	.05	.06	.07	.08	.09
+2.1	0.9821	0.9826	0.9830	0.9834	0.9838	0.9842	0.9846	0.9850	0.9854	0.9857
+2.2	0.9861	0.9864	0.9868	0.9871	0.9875	0.9878	0.9881	0.9884	0.9887	0.9890
+2.3	0.9893	0.9896	0.9898	0.9901	0.9904	0.9906	0.9909	0.9911	0.9913	0.9916
+2.4	0.9918	0.9920	0.9922	0.9925	0.9927	0.9929	0.9931	0.9932	0.9934	0.9936
+2.5	0.9938	0.9940	0.9941	0.9943	0.9945	0.9946	0.9948	0.9949	0.9951	0.9952
+2.6	0.9953	0.9955	0.9956	0.9957	0.9959	0.9960	0.9961	0.9962	0.9963	0.9964
+2.7	0.9965	0.9966	0.9967	0.9968	0.9969	0.9970	0.9971	0.9972	0.9973	0.9974
+2.8	0.9974	0.9975	0.9976	0.9977	0.9977	0.9978	0.9979	0.9979	0.9980	0.9981
+2.9	0.9981	0.9982	0.9983	0.9983	0.9984	0.9984	0.9985	0.9985	0.9986	0.9986
+3.0	0.99865	0.99869	0.99874	0.99878	0.99882	0.99886	0.99889	0.99893	0.99896	0.99900
+3.1	0.99903	0.99906	0.99910	0.99913	0.99915	0.99918	0.99921	0.99924	0.99926	0.99929
+3.2	0.99931	0.99934	0.99936	0.99938	0.99940	0.99942	0.99944	0.99946	0.99948	0.99950
+3.3	0.99952	0.99953	0.99955	0.99957	0.99958	0.99960	0.99961	0.99962	0.99964	0.99965
+3.4	0.99966	0.99967	0.99969	0.99970	0.99971	0.99972	0.99973	0.99974	0.99975	0.99976
+3.5	0.99977	0.99978	0.99978	0.99979	0.99980	0.99981	0.99981	0.99982	0.99983	0.99983

Table B. Table of chi square*

(For larger values of ν, the expression $\sqrt{2\chi^2} - \sqrt{2\nu - 1}$ may be used as a normal deviate with unit variance, remembering that the probability for χ^2 corresponds with that of a single tail of a normal curve)

ν	Probability										
	0.99	0.98	0.95	0.90	0.80	0.20	0.10	0.05	0.02	0.01	0.001
1	$0.0^{3}157$	$0.0^{3}628$	0.00393	0.0158	0.0642	1.642	2.706	3.841	5.412	6.635	10.827
2	0.0201	0.0404	0.103	0.211	0.446	3.219	4.605	5.991	7.824	9.210	13.815
3	0.115	0.185	0.352	0.584	1.005	4.642	6.251	7.815	9.837	11.341	16.268
4	0.297	0.429	0.711	1.064	1.649	5.989	7.779	9.488	11.668	13.277	18.465
5	0.554	0.752	1.145	1.610	2.343	7.289	9.236	11.070	13.388	15.086	20.517
6	0.872	1.134	1.635	2.204	3.070	8.558	10.645	12.592	15.033	16.812	22.457
7	1.239	1.564	2.167	2.833	3.822	9.803	12.017	14.067	16.622	18.475	24.322
8	1.646	2.032	2.733	3.490	4.594	11.030	13.362	15.507	18.168	20.090	26.125
9	2.088	2.532	3.325	4.168	5.380	12.242	14.684	16.919	19.679	21.666	27.877
10	2.558	3.059	3.940	4.865	6.179	13.442	15.987	18.307	21.161	23.209	29.588
11	3.053	3.609	4.575	5.578	6.989	14.631	17.275	19.675	22.618	24.725	31.264
12	3.571	4.178	5.226	6.304	7.807	15.812	18.549	21.026	24.054	26.217	32.909
13	4.107	4.765	5.892	7.042	8.634	16.985	19.812	22.362	25.472	27.688	34.528
14	4.660	5.368	6.571	7.790	9.467	18.151	21.064	23.685	26.873	29.141	36.123
15	5.229	5.985	7.261	8.547	10.307	19.311	22.307	24.996	28.259	30.578	37.697
16	5.812	6.614	7.962	9.312	11.152	20.465	23.542	26.296	29.633	32.000	39.252
17	6.408	7.255	8.672	10.085	12.002	21.615	24.769	27.587	30.995	33.409	40.790
18	7.015	7.906	9.390	10.865	12.857	22.760	25.989	28.869	32.346	34.805	42.312
19	7.633	8.567	10.117	11.651	13.716	23.900	27.204	30.144	33.687	36.191	43.820
20	8.260	9.237	10.851	12.443	14.578	25.038	28.412	31.410	35.020	37.566	45.315

21	8.897	9.915	11.591	13.240	15.445	26.171	29.615	32.671	36.343	38.932	46.797
22	9.542	10.600	12.338	14.041	16.314	27.301	30.813	33.924	37.659	40.289	48.268
23	10.196	11.293	13.091	14.848	17.187	28.429	32.007	35.172	38.968	41.638	49.728
24	10.856	11.992	13.848	15.659	18.062	29.553	33.196	36.415	40.270	42.980	51.179
25	11.524	12.697	14.611	16.473	18.940	30.675	34.382	37.652	41.566	44.314	52.620
26	12.198	13.409	15.379	17.292	19.820	31.795	35.563	38.885	42.856	45.642	54.052
27	12.879	14.125	16.151	18.114	20.703	32.912	36.741	40.113	44.140	46.963	55.476
28	13.565	14.847	16.928	18.939	21.588	34.027	37.916	41.337	45.419	48.278	56.893
29	14.256	15.574	17.708	19.768	22.475	35.139	39.087	42.557	46.693	49.588	58.302
30	14.953	16.306	18.493	20.599	23.364	36.250	40.256	43.773	47.962	50.892	59.703

* This table is reproduced in abridged form from Table IV of Fisher and Yates, "Statistical Tables for Biological, Agricultural, and Medical Research," published by Oliver & Boyd, Ltd., Edinburgh, by permission of the authors and publishers and of the abridger, Charles R. Hicks, *Fundamental Concepts in the Design of Experiments* (New York: Holt, Rinehart and Winston, Inc., 1964), p. 269.

Table C. F distribution[a]

df for denom.	1 − α	df for numerator											
		1	2	3	4	5	6	7	8	9	10	11	12
1	.75	5.83	7.50	8.20	8.58	8.82	8.98	9.10	9.19	9.26	9.32	9.36	9.41
	.90	39.9	49.5	53.6	55.8	57.2	58.2	58.9	59.4	59.9	60.2	60.5	60.7
	.95	161	200	216	225	230	234	237	239	241	242	243	244
2	.75	2.57	3.00	3.15	3.23	3.28	3.31	3.34	3.35	3.37	3.38	3.39	3.39
	.90	8.53	9.00	9.16	9.24	9.29	9.33	9.35	9.37	9.38	9.39	9.40	9.41
	.95	18.5	19.0	19.2	19.2	19.3	19.3	19.4	19.4	19.4	19.4	19.4	19.4
	.99	98.5	99.0	99.2	99.2	99.3	99.3	99.4	99.4	99.4	99.4	99.4	99.4
3	.75	2.02	2.28	2.36	2.39	2.41	2.42	2.43	2.44	2.44	2.44	2.45	2.45
	.90	5.54	5.46	5.39	5.34	5.31	5.28	5.27	5.25	5.24	5.23	5.22	5.22
	.95	10.1	9.55	9.28	9.12	9.10	8.94	8.89	8.85	8.81	8.79	8.76	8.74
	.99	34.1	30.8	29.5	28.7	28.2	27.9	27.7	27.5	27.3	27.2	27.1	27.1
4	.75	1.81	2.00	2.05	2.06	2.07	2.08	2.08	2.08	2.08	2.08	2.08	2.08
	.90	4.54	4.32	4.19	4.11	4.05	4.01	3.98	3.95	3.94	3.92	3.91	3.90
	.95	7.71	6.94	6.59	6.39	6.26	6.16	6.09	6.04	6.00	5.96	5.94	5.91
	.99	21.2	18.0	16.7	16.0	15.5	15.2	15.0	14.8	14.7	14.5	14.4	14.4
5	.75	1.69	1.85	1.88	1.89	1.89	1.89	1.89	1.89	1.89	1.89	1.89	1.89
	.90	4.06	3.78	3.62	3.52	3.45	3.40	3.37	3.34	3.32	3.30	3.28	3.27
	.95	6.61	5.79	5.41	5.19	5.05	4.95	4.88	4.82	4.77	4.74	4.71	4.68
	.99	16.3	13.3	12.1	11.4	11.0	10.7	10.5	10.3	10.2	10.1	9.96	9.89
6	.75	1.62	1.76	1.78	1.79	1.79	1.78	1.78	1.77	1.77	1.77	1.77	1.77
	.90	3.78	3.46	3.29	3.18	3.11	3.05	3.01	2.98	2.96	2.94	2.92	2.90
	.95	5.99	5.14	4.76	4.53	4.39	4.28	4.21	4.15	4.10	4.06	4.03	4.00
	.99	13.7	10.9	9.78	9.15	8.75	8.47	8.26	8.10	7.98	7.87	7.79	7.72

df	P												
7	.75	1.57	1.70	1.72	1.72	1.71	1.71	1.70	1.70	1.69	1.69	1.69	1.68
	.90	3.59	3.26	3.07	2.96	2.88	2.83	2.78	2.75	2.72	2.70	2.68	2.67
	.95	5.59	4.74	4.35	4.12	3.97	3.87	3.79	3.73	3.68	3.64	3.60	3.57
	.99	12.2	9.55	8.45	7.85	7.46	7.19	6.99	6.84	6.72	6.62	6.54	6.47
8	.75	1.54	1.66	1.67	1.66	1.66	1.65	1.64	1.64	1.64	1.63	1.63	1.62
	.90	3.46	3.11	2.92	2.81	2.73	2.67	2.62	2.59	2.56	2.54	2.52	2.50
	.95	5.32	4.46	4.07	3.84	3.69	3.58	3.50	3.44	3.39	3.35	3.31	3.28
	.99	11.3	8.65	7.59	7.01	6.63	6.37	6.18	6.03	5.91	5.81	5.73	5.67
9	.75	1.51	1.62	1.63	1.63	1.62	1.61	1.60	1.60	1.59	1.59	1.58	1.58
	.90	3.36	3.01	2.81	2.69	2.61	2.55	2.51	2.47	2.44	2.42	2.40	2.38
	.95	5.12	4.26	3.86	3.63	3.48	3.37	3.29	3.23	3.18	3.14	3.10	3.07
	.99	10.6	8.02	6.99	6.42	6.06	5.80	5.61	5.47	5.35	5.26	5.18	5.11
10	.75	1.49	1.60	1.60	1.59	1.59	1.58	1.57	1.56	1.56	1.55	1.55	1.54
	.90	3.28	2.92	2.73	2.61	2.52	2.46	2.41	2.38	2.35	2.32	2.30	2.28
	.95	4.96	4.10	3.71	3.48	3.33	3.22	3.14	3.07	3.02	2.98	2.94	2.91
	.99	10.0	7.56	6.55	5.99	5.64	5.39	5.20	5.06	4.94	4.85	4.77	4.71
11	.75	1.47	1.58	1.58	1.57	1.56	1.55	1.54	1.53	1.53	1.52	1.52	1.51
	.90	3.23	2.86	2.66	2.54	2.45	2.39	2.34	2.30	2.27	2.25	2.23	2.21
	.85	4.84	3.98	3.59	3.36	3.20	3.09	3.01	2.95	2.90	2.85	2.82	2.79
	.99	9.65	7.21	6.22	5.67	5.32	5.07	4.89	4.74	4.63	4.54	4.46	4.40
12	.75	1.46	1.56	1.56	1.55	1.54	1.53	1.52	1.51	1.51	1.50	1.50	1.49
	.90	3.18	2.81	2.61	2.48	2.39	2.33	2.28	2.24	2.21	2.19	2.17	2.15
	.95	4.75	3.89	3.49	3.26	3.11	3.00	2.91	2.85	2.80	2.75	2.72	2.69
	.99	9.33	6.93	5.95	5.41	5.06	4.82	4.64	4.50	4.39	4.30	4.22	4.16

* This table is abridged from Table 18 in *Biometrika Tables for Statisticians*, vol. 1, (2d ed.) New York: Cambridge, 1958. Edited by E. S. Pearson and H. O. Hartley. Reproduced with the kind permission of E. S. Pearson and the trustees of *Biometrika* and of the abridger, Charles R. Hicks, *Fundamental Concepts in the Design of Experiments* (New York: Holt, Rinehart and Winston, Inc. 1964), p. 270.

Table C. Continued

df for denom.	1 − α	df for numerator											
		15	20	24	30	40	50	60	100	120	200	500	∞
1	.75	9.49	9.58	9.63	9.67	9.71	9.74	9.76	9.78	9.80	9.82	9.84	9.85
	.90	61.2	61.7	62.0	62.3	62.5	62.7	62.8	63.0	63.1	63.2	63.3	63.3
	.99	246	248	249	250	251	252	252	253	253	254	254	254
2	.75	3.41	3.43	3.43	3.44	3.45	3.45	3.46	3.47	3.47	3.48	3.48	3.48
	.90	9.42	9.44	9.45	9.46	9.47	9.47	9.47	9.48	9.48	9.49	9.49	9.49
	.95	19.4	19.4	19.5	19.5	19.5	19.5	19.5	19.5	19.5	19.5	19.5	19.5
	.99	99.4	99.4	99.5	99.5	99.5	99.5	99.5	99.5	99.5	99.5	99.5	99.5
3	.75	2.46	2.46	2.46	2.47	2.47	2.47	2.47	2.47	2.47	2.47	2.47	2.47
	.90	5.20	5.18	5.18	5.17	5.16	5.15	5.15	5.14	5.14	5.14	5.14	5.13
	.95	8.70	8.66	8.64	8.62	8.59	8.58	8.57	8.55	8.55	8.54	8.53	8.53
	.99	26.9	26.7	26.6	26.5	26.4	26.4	26.3	26.2	26.2	26.2	26.1	26.1
4	.75	2.08	2.08	2.08	2.08	2.08	2.08	2.08	2.08	2.08	2.08	2.08	2.08
	.90	3.87	3.84	3.83	3.82	3.80	3.80	3.79	3.78	3.78	3.77	3.76	3.76
	.95	5.86	5.80	5.77	5.75	5.72	5.70	5.69	5.66	5.66	5.65	5.64	5.63
	.99	14.2	14.0	13.9	13.8	13.7	13.7	13.7	13.6	13.6	13.5	13.5	13.5
5	.75	1.89	1.88	1.88	1.88	1.88	1.88	1.87	1.87	1.87	1.87	1.87	1.87
	.90	3.24	3.21	3.19	3.17	3.16	3.15	3.14	3.13	3.12	3.12	3.11	3.10
	.95	4.62	4.56	4.53	4.50	4.46	4.44	4.43	4.41	4.40	4.39	4.37	4.36
	.99	9.72	9.55	9.47	9.38	9.29	9.24	9.20	9.13	9.11	9.08	9.04	9.02
6	.75	1.76	1.76	1.75	1.75	1.75	1.75	1.74	1.74	1.74	1.74	1.74	1.74
	.90	2.87	2.84	2.82	2.80	2.78	2.77	2.76	2.75	2.74	2.73	2.73	2.72
	.95	3.94	3.87	3.84	3.81	3.77	3.75	3.74	3.71	3.70	3.69	3.68	3.67
	.99	7.56	7.40	7.31	7.23	7.14	7.09	7.06	6.99	6.97	6.93	6.90	6.88

df	P												
7	.75	1.65	1.65	1.65	1.65	1.65	1.65	1.66	1.66	1.66	1.67	1.67	1.68
	.90	2.47	2.48	2.48	2.49	2.50	2.51	2.52	2.54	2.56	2.58	2.59	2.63
	.95	3.23	3.24	3.25	3.27	3.27	3.30	3.32	3.34	3.38	3.41	3.44	3.51
	.99	5.65	5.67	5.70	5.74	5.75	5.82	5.86	5.91	5.99	6.07	6.16	6.31
8	.75	1.58	1.58	1.58	1.58	1.58	1.59	1.59	1.59	1.60	1.60	1.61	1.62
	.90	2.29	2.30	2.31	2.32	2.32	2.34	2.35	2.36	2.38	2.40	2.42	2.46
	.95	2.93	2.94	2.95	2.97	2.97	3.01	3.02	3.04	3.08	3.12	3.15	3.22
	.99	4.86	4.88	4.91	4.95	4.96	5.03	5.07	5.12	5.20	5.28	5.36	5.52
9	.75	1.53	1.53	1.53	1.53	1.53	1.54	1.54	1.55	1.55	1.56	1.56	1.57
	.90	2.16	2.17	2.17	2.18	2.19	2.21	2.22	2.23	2.25	2.28	2.30	2.34
	.95	2.71	2.72	2.73	2.75	2.76	2.79	2.80	2.83	2.86	2.90	2.94	3.01
	.99	4.31	4.33	4.36	4.40	4.42	4.48	4.52	4.57	4.65	4.73	4.81	4.96
10	.75	1.48	1.48	1.49	1.49	1.49	1.50	1.50	1.51	1.51	1.52	1.52	1.53
	.90	2.06	2.06	2.07	2.08	2.09	2.11	2.12	2.13	2.16	2.18	2.20	2.24
	.95	2.54	2.55	2.56	2.58	2.59	2.62	2.64	2.66	2.70	2.74	2.77	2.85
	.99	3.91	3.93	3.96	4.00	4.01	4.08	4.12	4.17	4.25	4.33	4.41	4.56
11	.75	1.45	1.45	1.46	1.46	1.46	1.47	1.47	1.47	1.48	1.49	1.49	1.50
	.90	1.97	1.98	1.99	2.00	2.00	2.03	2.04	2.05	2.08	2.10	2.12	2.17
	.95	2.40	2.42	2.43	2.45	2.46	2.49	2.51	2.53	2.57	2.61	2.65	2.72
	.99	3.60	3.62	3.66	3.69	3.71	3.78	3.81	3.86	3.94	4.02	4.10	4.25
12	.75	1.42	1.42	1.43	1.43	1.43	1.44	1.44	1.45	1.45	1.46	1.47	1.48
	.90	1.90	1.91	1.92	1.93	1.94	1.96	1.97	1.99	2.01	2.04	2.06	2.10
	.95	2.30	2.31	2.32	2.34	2.35	2.38	2.40	2.43	2.47	2.51	2.54	2.62
	.99	3.36	3.38	3.41	3.45	3.47	3.54	3.57	3.62	3.70	3.78	3.86	4.01

Table C. Continued

df for denom.	1 − α	\multicolumn{12}{c}{df for numerator}											
		1	2	3	4	5	6	7	8	9	10	11	12
13	.75	1.45	1.54	1.54	1.53	1.52	1.51	1.50	1.49	1.49	1.48	1.47	1.47
	.90	3.14	2.76	2.56	2.43	2.35	2.28	2.23	2.20	2.16	2.14	2.12	2.10
	.95	4.67	3.81	3.41	3.18	3.03	2.92	2.83	2.77	2.71	2.67	2.63	2.60
	.99	9.07	6.70	5.74	5.21	4.86	4.62	4.44	4.30	4.19	4.10	4.02	3.96
14	.75	1.44	1.53	1.53	1.52	1.51	1.50	1.48	1.48	1.47	1.46	1.46	1.45
	.90	3.10	2.73	2.52	2.39	2.31	2.24	2.19	2.15	2.12	2.10	2.08	2.05
	.95	4.60	3.74	3.34	3.11	2.96	2.85	2.76	2.70	2.65	2.60	2.57	2.53
	.99	8.86	6.51	5.56	5.04	4.69	4.46	4.28	4.14	4.03	3.94	3.86	3.80
15	.75	1.43	1.52	1.52	1.51	1.49	1.48	1.47	1.46	1.46	1.45	1.44	1.44
	.90	3.07	2.70	2.49	2.36	2.27	2.21	2.16	2.12	2.09	2.06	2.04	2.02
	.95	4.54	3.68	3.29	3.06	2.90	2.79	2.71	2.64	2.59	2.54	2.51	2.48
	.99	8.68	6.36	5.42	4.89	4.56	4.32	4.14	4.00	3.89	3.80	3.73	3.67
16	.75	1.42	1.51	1.51	1.50	1.48	1.48	1.47	1.46	1.45	1.45	1.44	1.44
	.90	3.05	2.67	2.46	2.33	2.24	2.18	2.13	2.09	2.06	2.03	2.01	1.99
	.95	4.49	3.63	3.24	3.01	2.85	2.74	2.66	2.59	2.54	2.49	2.46	2.42
	.99	8.53	6.23	5.29	4.77	4.44	4.20	4.03	3.89	3.78	3.69	3.62	3.55
17	.75	1.42	1.51	1.50	1.49	1.47	1.46	1.45	1.44	1.43	1.43	1.42	1.41
	.90	3.03	2.64	2.44	2.31	2.22	2.15	2.10	2.06	2.03	2.00	1.98	1.96
	.95	4.45	3.59	3.20	2.96	2.81	2.70	2.61	2.55	2.49	2.45	2.41	2.38
	.99	8.40	6.11	5.18	4.67	4.34	4.10	3.93	3.79	3.68	3.59	3.52	3.46
18	.75	1.41	1.50	1.49	1.48	1.46	1.45	1.44	1.43	1.42	1.42	1.41	1.40
	.90	3.01	2.62	2.42	2.29	2.20	2.13	2.08	2.04	2.00	1.98	1.96	1.93
	.95	4.41	3.55	3.16	2.93	2.77	2.66	2.58	2.51	2.46	2.41	2.37	2.34
	.99		6.01										

19	.75	1.40	1.40	1.41	1.41	1.42	1.43	1.44	1.46	1.47	1.49	1.49	1.41
	.90	1.91	1.94	1.96	1.98	2.02	2.06	2.11	2.18	2.27	2.40	2.61	2.99
	.95	2.31	2.34	2.38	2.42	2.48	2.54	2.63	2.74	2.90	3.13	3.52	4.38
	.99	3.30	3.36	3.43	3.52	3.63	3.77	3.94	4.17	4.50	5.01	5.93	8.18
20	.75	1.39	1.39	1.40	1.41	1.42	1.42	1.44	1.45	1.46	1.48	1.49	1.40
	.90	1.89	1.92	1.94	1.96	2.00	2.04	2.09	2.16	2.25	2.38	2.59	2.97
	.95	2.28	2.31	2.35	2.39	2.45	2.51	2.60	2.71	2.87	3.10	3.49	4.35
	.99	3.23	3.29	3.37	3.46	3.56	3.70	3.87	4.10	4.43	4.94	5.85	8.10
22	.75	1.37	1.38	1.39	1.39	1.40	1.41	1.42	1.44	1.45	1.47	1.48	1.40
	.90	1.86	1.88	1.90	1.93	1.97	2.01	2.06	2.13	2.22	2.35	2.56	2.95
	.95	2.23	2.26	2.30	2.34	2.40	2.46	2.55	2.66	2.82	3.05	3.44	4.30
	.99	3.12	3.18	3.26	3.35	3.45	3.59	3.76	3.99	4.31	4.82	5.72	7.95
24	.75	1.36	1.37	1.38	1.38	1.39	1.40	1.41	1.43	1.44	1.46	1.47	1.39
	.90	1.83	1.85	1.88	1.91	1.94	1.98	2.04	2.10	2.19	2.33	2.54	2.93
	.95	2.18	2.21	2.25	2.30	2.36	2.42	2.51	2.62	2.78	3.01	3.40	4.26
	.99	3.03	3.09	3.17	3.26	3.36	3.50	3.67	3.90	4.22	4.72	5.61	7.82
26	.75	1.35	1.36	1.37	1.37	1.39	1.40	1.41	1.42	1.44	1.45	1.46	1.38
	.90	1.81	1.84	1.86	1.88	1.92	1.96	2.01	2.08	2.17	2.31	2.52	2.91
	.95	2.15	2.18	2.22	2.27	2.32	2.39	2.47	2.59	2.74	2.98	3.37	4.23
	.99	2.96	3.02	3.09	3.18	3.29	3.42	3.59	3.82	4.14	4.64	5.53	7.72
28	.75	1.34	1.35	1.36	1.37	1.38	1.39	1.40	1.41	1.43	1.45	1.46	1.38
	.90	1.79	1.81	1.84	1.87	1.90	1.94	2.00	2.06	2.16	2.29	2.50	2.89
	.95	2.12	2.15	2.19	2.24	2.29	2.36	2.45	2.56	2.71	2.95	3.34	4.20
	.99	2.90	2.96	3.03	3.12	3.23	3.36	3.53	3.75	4.07	4.57	5.45	7.64

Table C. Continued

df for denom.	$1-\alpha$	15	20	24	30	40	50	60	100	120	200	500	∞
								df for numerator					
13	.75	1.46	1.45	1.44	1.43	1.42	1.42	1.42	1.41	1.41	1.40	1.40	1.40
	.90	2.05	2.01	1.98	1.96	1.93	1.92	1.90	1.88	1.88	1.86	1.85	1.85
	.95	2.53	2.46	2.42	2.38	2.34	2.31	2.30	2.26	2.25	2.23	2.22	2.21
	.99	3.82	3.66	3.59	3.51	3.43	3.38	3.34	3.27	3.25	3.22	3.19	3.17
14	.75	1.44	1.43	1.42	1.41	1.41	1.40	1.40	1.39	1.39	1.39	1.38	1.38
	.90	2.01	1.96	1.94	1.91	1.89	1.87	1.86	1.83	1.83	1.82	1.80	1.80
	.95	2.46	2.39	2.35	2.31	2.27	2.24	2.22	2.19	2.18	2.16	2.14	2.13
	.99	3.66	3.51	3.43	3.35	3.27	3.22	3.18	3.11	3.09	3.06	3.03	3.00
15	.75	1.32	1.41	1.41	1.40	1.39	1.39	1.38	1.38	1.37	1.37	1.36	1.36
	.90	1.97	1.92	1.90	1.87	1.85	1.83	1.82	1.79	1.79	1.77	1.76	1.76
	.95	2.40	2.33	2.29	2.25	2.20	2.18	2.16	2.12	2.11	2.10	2.08	2.07
	.99	3.52	3.37	3.29	3.21	3.13	3.08	3.05	2.98	2.96	2.92	2.89	2.87
16	.75	1.41	1.40	1.39	1.38	1.37	1.37	1.36	1.36	1.35	1.35	1.34	1.34
	.90	1.94	1.89	1.87	1.84	1.81	1.79	1.78	1.76	1.75	1.74	1.73	1.72
	.95	2.35	2.28	2.24	2.19	2.15	2.12	2.11	2.07	2.06	2.04	2.02	2.01
	.99	3.41	3.26	3.18	3.10	3.02	2.97	2.93	2.86	2.84	2.81	2.78	2.75
17	.75	1.40	1.39	1.38	1.37	1.36	1.35	1.35	1.34	1.34	1.34	1.33	1.33
	.90	1.91	1.86	1.84	1.81	1.78	1.76	1.75	1.73	1.72	1.71	1.69	1.69
	.95	2.31	2.23	2.19	2.15	2.10	2.08	2.06	2.02	2.01	1.99	1.97	1.96
	.99	3.31	3.16	3.08	3.00	2.92	2.87	2.83	2.76	2.75	2.71	2.68	2.65
18	.75	1.39	1.38	1.37	1.36	1.35	1.34	1.34	1.33	1.33	1.32	1.32	1.32
	.90	1.89	1.84	1.81	1.78	1.75	1.74	1.72	1.70	1.69	1.68	1.67	1.66
	.95	2.27	2.19	2.15	2.11	2.06	2.04	2.02	1.98	1.97	1.95		

df	p												
19	.75	1.30	1.31	1.31	1.32	1.32	1.33	1.33	1.34	1.35	1.36	1.37	1.38
	.90	1.63	1.64	1.65	1.67	1.67	1.70	1.71	1.73	1.76	1.79	1.81	1.86
	.95	1.88	1.89	1.91	1.93	1.94	1.98	2.00	2.03	2.07	2.11	2.16	2.23
	.99	2.49	2.51	2.55	2.58	2.60	2.67	2.71	2.76	2.84	2.92	3.00	3.15
20	.75	1.29	1.30	1.30	1.31	1.31	1.32	1.33	1.33	1.34	1.35	1.36	1.37
	.90	1.61	1.62	1.63	1.64	1.65	1.68	1.69	1.71	1.74	1.77	1.79	1.84
	.95	1.84	1.86	1.88	1.90	1.91	1.95	1.97	1.99	2.04	2.08	2.12	2.20
	.99	2.42	2.44	2.48	2.52	2.54	2.61	2.64	2.69	2.78	2.86	2.94	3.09
22	.75	1.28	1.29	1.29	1.30	1.30	1.30	1.31	1.31	1.32	1.33	1.34	1.36
	.90	1.57	1.58	1.59	1.60	1.61	1.64	1.65	1.67	1.70	1.73	1.76	1.81
	.95	1.78	1.80	1.82	1.84	1.85	1.89	1.91	1.94	1.98	2.03	2.07	2.15
	.99	2.31	2.33	2.36	2.40	2.42	2.50	2.53	2.58	2.67	2.75	2.83	2.98
23	.75	1.26	1.27	1.27	1.28	1.28	1.29	1.29	1.29	1.30	1.32	1.33	1.35
	.90	1.53	1.54	1.56	1.57	1.58	1.61	1.62	1.64	1.67	1.70	1.73	1.78
	.95	1.73	1.75	1.77	1.79	1.80	1.84	1.86	1.89	1.94	1.98	2.03	2.11
	.99	2.21	2.24	2.27	2.31	2.33	2.40	2.44	2.49	2.58	2.66	2.74	2.89
24	.75	1.25	1.25	1.26	1.26	1.26	1.28	1.28	1.29	1.30	1.31	1.32	1.34
	.90	1.50	1.51	1.53	1.54	1.55	1.58	1.59	1.61	1.65	1.68	1.71	1.76
	.95	1.69	1.71	1.73	1.75	1.76	1.80	1.82	1.85	1.90	1.95	1.99	2.07
	.99	2.13	2.16	2.19	2.23	2.25	2.33	2.36	2.42	2.50	2.58	2.66	2.81
25	.75	1.24	1.24	1.25	1.25	1.26	1.27	1.27	1.28	1.29	1.30	1.31	1.33
	.90	1.48	1.49	1.50	1.52	1.53	1.56	1.57	1.59	1.63	1.66	1.69	1.74
	.95	1.65	1.67	1.69	1.71	1.73	1.77	1.79	1.82	1.87	1.91	1.96	2.04
	.99	2.06	2.09	2.13	2.17	2.19	2.26	2.30	2.35	2.44	2.52	2.60	2.75

Table C. Continued

df for denom.	1 − α	df for numerator											
		1	2	3	4	5	6	7	8	9	10	11	12
30	.75	1.38	1.45	1.44	1.42	1.41	1.39	1.38	1.37	1.36	1.35	1.35	1.34
	.90	2.88	2.49	2.28	2.14	2.05	1.98	1.93	1.88	1.85	1.82	1.79	1.77
	.95	4.17	3.32	2.92	2.69	2.53	2.42	2.33	2.27	2.21	2.16	2.13	2.09
	.99	7.56	5.39	4.51	4.02	3.70	3.47	3.30	3.17	3.07	2.98	2.91	2.84
40	.75	1.36	1.44	1.42	1.40	1.39	1.37	1.36	1.35	1.34	1.33	1.32	1.31
	.90	2.84	2.44	2.23	2.09	2.00	1.93	1.87	1.83	1.79	1.76	1.73	1.71
	.95	4.08	3.23	2.84	2.61	2.45	2.34	2.25	2.18	2.12	2.08	2.04	2.00
	.99	7.31	5.18	4.31	3.83	3.51	3.29	3.12	2.99	2.89	2.80	2.73	2.66
60	.75	1.35	1.42	1.41	1.38	1.37	1.35	1.33	1.32	1.31	1.30	1.29	1.29
	.90	2.79	2.39	2.18	2.04	1.95	1.87	1.82	1.77	1.74	1.71	1.68	1.66
	.95	4.00	3.15	2.76	2.53	2.37	2.25	2.17	2.10	2.04	1.99	1.95	1.92
	.99	7.08	4.98	4.13	3.65	3.34	3.12	2.95	2.82	2.72	2.63	2.56	2.50
120	.75	1.34	1.40	1.39	1.37	1.35	1.33	1.31	1.30	1.29	1.28	1.27	1.26
	.90	2.75	2.35	2.13	1.99	1.90	1.82	1.77	1.72	1.68	1.65	1.62	1.60
	.95	3.92	3.07	2.68	2.45	2.29	2.17	2.09	2.02	1.96	1.91	1.87	1.83
	.99	6.85	4.79	3.95	3.48	3.17	2.96	2.79	2.66	2.56	2.47	2.40	2.34
200	.75	1.33	1.39	1.38	1.36	1.34	1.32	1.31	1.29	1.28	1.27	1.26	1.25
	.90	2.73	2.33	2.11	1.97	1.88	1.80	1.75	1.70	1.66	1.63	1.60	1.57
	.95	3.89	3.04	2.65	2.42	2.26	2.14	2.06	1.98	1.93	1.88	1.84	1.80
	.99	6.76	4.71	3.88	3.41	3.11	2.89	2.73	2.60	2.50	2.41	2.34	2.27
∞	.75	1.32	1.39	1.37	1.35	1.33	1.31	1.29	1.28	1.27	1.25	1.24	1.24

30	.75	1.32	1.30	1.29	1.28	1.27	1.26	1.26	1.25	1.24	1.24	1.23	1.23
	.90	1.72	1.67	1.64	1.61	1.57	1.55	1.54	1.51	1.50	1.48	1.47	1.46
	.95	2.01	1.93	1.89	1.84	1.79	1.76	1.74	1.70	1.68	1.66	1.64	1.62
	.99	2.70	2.55	2.47	2.39	2.30	2.25	2.21	2.13	2.11	2.07	2.03	2.01
40	.75	1.30	1.28	1.26	1.25	1.24	1.23	1.22	1.21	1.21	1.20	1.19	1.19
	.90	1.66	1.61	1.57	1.54	1.51	1.48	1.47	1.43	1.42	1.41	1.39	1.38
	.95	1.92	1.84	1.79	1.74	1.69	1.66	1.64	1.59	1.58	1.55	1.53	1.51
	.99	2.52	2.37	2.29	2.20	2.11	2.06	2.02	1.94	1.92	1.87	1.83	1.80
50	.75	1.27	1.25	1.24	1.22	1.21	1.20	1.19	1.17	1.17	1.16	1.15	1.15
	.90	1.60	1.54	1.51	1.48	1.44	1.41	1.40	1.36	1.35	1.33	1.31	1.29
	.95	1.84	1.75	1.70	1.65	1.59	1.56	1.53	1.48	1.47	1.44	1.41	1.39
	.99	2.35	2.20	2.12	2.03	1.94	1.88	1.84	1.75	1.73	1.68	1.63	1.60
120	.75	1.24	1.22	1.21	1.19	1.18	1.17	1.16	1.14	1.13	1.12	1.11	1.10
	.90	1.55	1.48	1.45	1.41	1.37	1.34	1.32	1.27	1.26	1.24	1.21	1.19
	.95	1.75	1.66	1.61	1.55	1.50	1.46	1.43	1.37	1.35	1.32	1.28	1.25
	.99	2.19	2.03	1.95	1.86	1.76	1.70	1.66	1.56	1.53	1.48	1.42	1.38
200	.75	1.23	1.21	1.20	1.18	1.16	1.14	1.12	1.11	1.10	1.09	1.08	1.06
	.90	1.52	1.46	1.42	1.38	1.34	1.31	1.28	1.24	1.22	1.20	1.17	1.14
	.95	1.72	1.62	1.57	1.52	1.46	1.41	1.39	1.32	1.29	1.26	1.22	1.19
	.99	2.13	1.97	1.89	1.79	1.69	1.63	1.58	1.48	1.44	1.39	1.33	1.28
8	.75	1.22	1.19	1.18	1.16	1.14	1.13	1.12	1.09	1.08	1.07	1.04	1.00
	.90	1.49	1.42	1.38	1.34	1.30	1.26	1.24	1.18	1.17	1.13	1.08	1.00
	.95	1.67	1.57	1.52	1.46	1.39	1.35	1.32	1.24	1.22	1.17	1.11	1.00
	.99	2.04	1.88	1.79	1.70	1.59	1.52	1.47	1.36	1.32	1.25	1.15	1.00

Table D. Student's t distribution°

df	\multicolumn{7}{c}{Percentile point}
	70	80	90	95	97.5	99	99.5
1	.73	1.38	3.08	6.31	12.71	31.82	63.66
2	.62	1.06	1.89	2.92	4.30	6.96	9.92
3	.58	.98	1.64	2.35	3.18	4.54	5.84
4	.57	.94	1.53	2.13	2.78	3.75	4.60
5	.56	.92	1.48	2.01	2.57	3.36	4.03
6	.55	.91	1.44	1.94	2.45	3.14	3.71
7	.55	.90	1.42	1.90	2.36	3.00	3.50
8	.55	.89	1.40	1.86	2.31	2.90	3.36
9	.54	.88	1.38	1.83	2.26	2.82	3.25
10	.54	.88	1.37	1.81	2.23	2.76	3.17
11	.54	.88	1.36	1.80	2.20	2.72	3.11
12	.54	.87	1.36	1.78	2.18	2.68	3.06
13	.54	.87	1.35	1.77	2.16	2.65	3.01
14	.54	.87	1.34	1.76	2.14	2.62	2.98
15	.54	.87	1.34	1.75	2.13	2.60	2.95
16	.54	.86	1.34	1.75	2.12	2.58	2.92
17	.53	.86	1.33	1.74	2.11	2.57	2.90
18	.53	.86	1.33	1.73	2.10	2.55	2.88
19	.53	.86	1.33	1.73	2.09	2.54	2.86
20	.53	.86	1.32	1.72	2.09	2.53	2.84
21	.53	.86	1.32	1.72	2.08	2.52	2.83
22	.53	.86	1.32	1.72	2.07	2.51	2.82
23	.53	.86	1.32	1.71	2.07	2.50	2.81
24	.53	.86	1.32	1.71	2.06	2.49	2.80
25	.53	.86	1.32	1.71	2.06	2.48	2.79
26	.53	.86	1.32	1.71	2.06	2.48	2.78
27	.53	.86	1.31	1.70	2.05	2.47	2.77
28	.53	.86	1.31	1.70	2.05	2.47	2.76
29	.53	.85	1.31	1.70	2.04	2.46	2.76
30	.53	.85	1.31	1.70	2.04	2.46	2.75
40	.53	.85	1.30	1.68	2.02	2.42	2.70
50	.53	.85	1.30	1.67	2.01	2.40	2.68
60	.53	.85	1.30	1.67	2.00	2.39	2.66
80	.53	.85	1.29	1.66	1.99	2.37	2.64
100	.53	.84	1.29	1.66	1.98	2.36	2.63
200	.52	.84	1.29	1.65	1.97	2.34	2.60
500	.52	.84	1.28	1.65	1.96	2.33	2.59
∞	.52	.84	1.28	1.64	1.96	2.33	2.58

* This table is reproduced from Charles R. Hicks, *Fundamental Concepts in the Design of Experiments* (New York: Holt, Rinehart and Winston, Inc., 1964), p. 268. By permission.

Table E. Von Neumann ratio; 5 and 1 per cent significance points for the ratio of the mean-square successive-difference to the variance

N	Values of K P = 0.01	Values of K P = 0.05	Values of K' P = 0.05	Values of K' P = 0.01		Values of K P = 0.01	Values of K P = 0.05	Values of K' P = 0.05	Values of K' P = 0.01
4	0.8341	1.0406	4.2927	4.4992	33	1.2667	1.4885	2.6365	2.8583
5	0.6724	1.0255	3.9745	4.3276	34	1.2761	1.4951	2.6262	2.8451
6	0.6738	1.0682	3.7318	4.1262	35	1.2852	1.5014	2.6163	2.8324
7	0.7163	1.0919	3.5748	3.9504	36	1.2940	1.5075	2.6068	2.8202
8	0.7575	1.1228	3.4486	3.8139	37	1.3025	1.5135	2.5977	2.8085
9	0.7974	1.1524	3.3476	3.7025	38	1.3108	1.5193	2.5889	2.7973
10	0.8353	1.1803	3.2642	3.6091	39	1.3188	1.5249	2.5804	2.7865
11	0.8706	1.2062	3.1938	3.5294	40	1.3266	1.5304	2.5722	2.7760
12	0.9033	1.2301	3.1335	3.4603	41	1.3342	1.5357	2.5643	2.7658
13	0.9336	1.2521	3.0812	3.3996	42	1.3415	1.5408	2.5567	2.7560
14	0.9618	1.2725	3.0352	3.3458	43	1.3486	1.5458	2.5494	2.7466
15	0.9880	1.2914	2.9943	3.2977	44	1.3554	1.5506	2.5424	2.7376
16	1.1024	1.3090	2.9577	3.2543	45	1.3620	1.5552	2.5357	2.7289
17	1.0352	1.3253	2.9247	3.2148	46	1.3684	1.5596	2.5293	2.7205
18	1.0566	1.3405	2.8948	3.1787	47	1.3745	1.5638	2.5232	2.7125
19	1.0766	1.3547	2.8675	3.1456	48	1.3802	1.5678	2.5173	2.7049
20	1.0954	1.3680	2.8425	3.1151	49	1.3856	1.5716	2.5117	2.6977
21	1.1131	1.3805	2.8195	3.0869	50	1.3907	1.5752	2.5064	2.6908
22	1.1298	1.3923	2.7982	3.0607	51	1.3957	1.5787	2.5013	2.6842
23	1.1456	1.4035	2.7784	2.9362	52	1.4007	1.5822	2.4963	2.6777
24	1.1606	1.4141	2.7599	3.0133	53	1.4057	1.5856	2.4914	2.6712
25	1.1748	1.4241	2.7426	2.9919	54	1.4107	1.5890	2.4866	2.6648

* Adapted, with the kind permission of the editor, from B. I. Hart, Significance levels for the ratio of the mean square successive difference to the variance, *Annals of Mathematical Statistics*, Vol. 13, No. 4, p. 446, 1942. Values of K are for positive autocorrelation and K[1] for negative autocorrelation. For explanation, see text, p. 171.

NAME INDEX

SUBJECT INDEX

DATE DUE

GAYLORD   PRINTED IN U.S.A.